# HEALTH CARE

# FRAUD *and* ABUSE:

## Practical Perspectives

## Publications From BNA Books on Related Topics

*E-Health Business & Transactional Law*

*Prosecuting and Defending Health Care Fraud Cases*

*Medical Ethics: Codes, Opinions, and Statements*

*Medical Ethics: Analysis of the Issues Raised by the Codes, Opinions, and Statements*

*Codes of Professional Responsibility: Ethics Standards in Business, Health, and Law*

*Occupational Safety and Health Law*

For details on these and other titles, visit BNA Books' home page on the Internet at ***http://www.bnabooks.com*** or call **800-960-1220** to request a catalog. All BNA books are available on a 30-day free-examination basis.

# HEALTH CARE

# FRAUD *and* ABUSE:

# Practical Perspectives

*Editor-in-Chief*

Linda A. Baumann
*Reed Smith LLP*
*Washington, D.C.*

The American Bar Association
Health Law Section

The Bureau of National Affairs, Inc., Washington, D.C.

The materials contained in this work represent the opinions of the individual authors and should not be construed to be those of either the American Bar Association (ABA) or the ABA Health Law Section, or any other person or entity. The authors expressly reserve the right to freely advocate other positions on behalf of clients. Nothing contained herein is to be considered the rendering of legal advice for specific cases, and readers are responsible for obtaining such advice from their own legal counsel. These materials are intended for educational and informational purposes only.

Published by BNA Books
1231 25th St., N.W., Washington, D.C. 20037
http://www.bnabooks.com

International Standard Book Number: 1-57018-124-1
Printed in the United States of America

# Contributing Authors

Linda A. Baumann
*Reed Smith LLP*
*Washington, D.C.*

Thomas S. Crane
*Mintz, Levin, Cohn, Ferris,*
*Glovsky, and Popeo, P.C.*
*Boston, Massachusetts*

Robert Salcido
*Akin, Gump, Strauss, Hauer*
*& Feld L.L.P.*
*Washington, D.C.*

Patric Hooper
*Hooper, Lundy & Bookman, Inc.*
*Los Angeles, California*

Dennis M. Barry
*Vinson & Elkins, L.L.P.*
*Washington, D.C.*

Robert L. Roth
*Crowell & Moring, LLP*
*Washington, D.C.*

Alicia J. Palmer
*Crowell & Moring, LLP*
*Washington, D.C.*

Nancy S. Jones
*Waller Lansden Dortch*
*& Davis*
*Nashville, Tennessee*

Nora L. Liggett
*Waller Lansden Dortch*
*& Davis*
*Nashville, Tennessee*

Michelle B. Marsh
*Waller Lansden Dortch*
*& Davis*
*Nashville, Tennessee*

George E. McDavid
*Reed Smith LLP*
*Princeton, New Jersey*

# Foreword

The publication of HEALTH CARE FRAUD AND ABUSE: PRACTICAL PERSPECTIVES marks a significant milestone in the development of the American Bar Association (ABA) Health Law Section. With over 10,000 members, the Section is now one of the largest organizations of health lawyers in the United States. As we celebrate our Fifth Anniversary of the elevation of the Health Law Forum to ABA Section status, we join our more than 10,000 members in looking back with pride on our successful educational programs and important government submissions. We also are proud of our substantive publications, THE HEALTH LAWYER and our Monograph series, which further the Section's goal to provide pragmatic information on complex legal issues facing the health law bar.

HEALTH CARE FRAUD AND ABUSE: PRACTICAL PERSPECTIVES, our first full-length book, continues the tradition of our other publications. As Editor-in-Chief Linda Baumann explains in greater length in her *Preface*, this book is designed to provide practical guidance on fraud and abuse issues both for those who are new to health law and for those who have expertise in this area. The eight chapters contain valuable insights from our experienced health care practitioner authors.

Our primary objective in participating in this project was to create a fraud and abuse desk reference book that shares the expertise of our Section. To that end, the eight substantive chapters are followed by numerous appendix documents, including materials on the anti-kickback statute, the Stark law, the civil False Claims Act, the civil monetary penalty and exclusion provisions, and selected statutes relating to private payer fraud. We also have included many other documents whose existence and availability may not be widely known. After using this book in your day-to-day practice, we hope that you will agree with us that we have achieved our main objective. Annual updates will be available to ensure that this remains an essential part of your health law library.

This is the Section's initial collaborative legal reference published with BNA Books, a Division of The Bureau of National Affairs, Inc. We are starting with fraud and abuse because, after many years of emerging legal theories, there is now a significant body of established law. Accordingly, the time is right for a single volume that covers past developments, current trends, and future prospects. We expect to join with BNA to publish our second book, E-HEALTH BUSINESS AND TRANSACTIONAL LAW, in mid 2002.

The Health Law Section wishes to express its appreciation to editor Linda Baumann, whose countless hours of dedication were essential to the realization of this project. We also recognize the contribution of past Section chairs Howard Wall and Patricia Meador, who helped shepherd this project; to James F. Fattibene at BNA Books; and, particularly, to the chapter authors, for their valuable insights. Finally, we thank each of the Section's 10,000 members for making it so vibrant and successful.

On behalf of the ABA and its Health Law Section, we are pleased that we have an opportunity to share our members' collective experience on fraud and abuse strategies. We are confident that you will find it to be useful and welcome your thoughts about how the Section can further use its book series to address your practice needs.

ROBERT L. ROTH
SECTION CHAIR

SARA A. KELLER
CHAIR-ELECT

BRUCE SHIH
CHAIR
PUBLICATIONS COMMITTEE

HEALTH LAW SECTION
AMERICAN BAR ASSOCIATION

December 2001

# The American Bar Association
# Health Law Section
## 2001–2002 Officers

# Preface

It is change, continuing change, inevitable change, that is the dominant factor in society today. No sensible decision can be made any longer without taking into account not only the world as it is, but the world as it will be . . . . This, in turn, means that our statesmen, our businessmen, our everyman must take on a science fictional way of thinking.

—Isaac Asimov, *Asimov on Science Fiction*.

Change often makes accepted customs into crimes.

—Mason Cooley, *City Aphorisms*.

It goes without saying that lawyers, too, must take on Asimov's "science fictional" way of thinking. The law is constantly evolving and, in recent times, the field of health care law seems to change more than most. Even the names of various divisions and other entities affiliated with the U.S. Department of Health and Human Services (HHS) are being changed. The Health Care Financing Administration (HCFA), which plays a primary role in government health care reimbursement (and thus is integrally involved in initiatives related to health care fraud and abuse), has been renamed the Centers for Medicare and Medicaid Services (CMS).[1] Similarly, the concept of health care "fraud and abuse" continues to evolve. For example, initially enforcement efforts focused on government overpayments due to improper conduct such as upcoding or billing for services that were never provided. More recently, the fraud and abuse laws are also being used in connection with claims that involve care of inadequate quality or quantity.

Some of these changes have created a situation where practices and customs, long accepted as legitimate in many industries, may now be characterized as "crimes" in the health care context. To give just one example, paying billing companies or salesmen a percentage of the revenues they generate has long been a standard business practice. This method of compensation helps align the interest of both parties in maximizing business revenues. However, under certain circumstances in the health care field, the government may interpret this type of payment as an attempt to induce improper behavior and a violation of the anti-kickback statute, which can lead to criminal penalties including fines and up to 5 years' imprisonment.

---

[1] Because HHS plans to convert references from "HCFA" to "CMS," for purposes of consistency, this book will do likewise.

What explains this disparate treatment of the health care industry? In large part, the sheer amount of money involved and the perceived abuses of the past likely account for this situation. Other contributing factors include the huge and growing market for health care services as scientific advances create more and better treatments to prevent and cure disease and the percentage of the population over the age of 50 steadily increases. In fact, more than $1 trillion is spent on health care in the United States each year; approximately 15 percent of the gross national product. Moreover, many of these health care products and services will be paid for, at least in part, by federally funded health care programs such as Medicare and Medicaid. However, the HHS Office of Inspector General (OIG) has estimated that over 10 percent of these expenditures, or over $100 billion annually, are lost to fraud and abuse.

As a result, it is not surprising that the government and private industry are continually devoting additional resources to identifying, redressing, and preventing such perceived fraud and abuse.[2] These efforts have led to an explosion in the volume of laws, regulations, and other materials regulating the health care industry and its business partners. The information technology revolution has further contributed to the rapid pace at which these changes occur. The consequences of failure to fully comply with all applicable laws and regulations can be frightening. The penalties range from imprisonment to treble damages to exclusion from participation in federal health care programs, which has been characterized as a "financial death sentence" for a health care provider. Under these circumstances, it is critically important for individuals and organizations involved in the health care industry to be thoroughly familiar with the applicable law. Typically, a health care provider or other business entity will turn to legal counsel for the requisite in-depth knowledge of the laws and regulations, and how they are being enforced.

Interpretive guidance is particularly critical here where the applicable laws are often ambiguous, leaving large "gray" areas and few "bright lines." However, although many documents are available online, knowing how to access and interpret them can be a challenge, particularly since the traditional tools of legal research may not be sufficient in this area. There is relatively little case law relating to many of these issues although certain types of guidance materials are sometimes available from other sources. Where there is such a scarcity of precedent and other interpretive materials, practical experience with the issues can be an invaluable asset. In other areas, such as the civil False Claims Act, the volume of relevant case law can be overwhelming. Here too, advice from experienced practitioners can be extremely helpful.

---

[2]While certain government resources have been shifted in light of the events of September 11, 2001, it is still to early to tell whether there will be a significant decrease in health care fraud enforcement efforts. On the contrary, there are numerous indications that health care fraud and abuse remains a major government priority.

This book is designed to help address these problems by providing practical guidance for those who are new to the field as well as for those who have expertise in this area. The authors of each of the chapters are leading health care practitioners who offer their professional perspectives on a wide range of issues. While these eight chapters do not purport to be a comprehensive analysis of all aspects of health care fraud and abuse, they can provide valuable insights into many of the issues an attorney is likely to face when representing a client involved in the health care industry. There is some overlap among the chapters. However, because various issues arise in different contexts, the unique perspective each author brings to his or her analysis should be valuable.

The first chapter, which I have written, "An Introduction to Health Care Fraud and Abuse" (Chapter 1), is designed for those who are starting with more limited experience in this area. It provides a brief summary and overview of some of the more important topics in health care fraud and abuse, focusing on the statutory and regulatory framework; particularly, those laws not covered extensively in other chapters of the book. This chapter also describes other guidance documents and resources that may assist an attorney in advising his or her clients on how to reduce exposure under the fraud and abuse laws. This introductory chapter may facilitate review of the subsequent chapters in the book, each of which address a specific aspect of health care fraud and abuse.

Tom Crane's chapter on "Federal Physician Self-Referral Restrictions" (Chapter 2) provides a comprehensive analysis of the federal Stark law and its complex regulations, as well as a detailed examination of the exceptions available to help protect transactions that otherwise implicate the statute.

Robert Salcido's chapter on "The False Claims Act in Health Care Prosecutions: Application of the Substantive, *Qui Tam*, and Voluntary Disclosure Provisions" (Chapter 3) contains an extensive discussion of the False Claims Act and interpretive cases focusing on the substantive elements of the statute as well as the *qui tam* (whistleblower) provisions. The discussion of the public disclosure jurisdictional bar to *qui tam* actions may help attorneys defend their clients from such lawsuits. The chapter also contains insights into the use of the OIG's Voluntary Disclosure Program.

Patric Hooper's chapter on "Practical Considerations for Defending Health Care Fraud and Abuse Cases" (Chapter 4) provides background on the development of the fraud and abuse laws; an overview of the enforcement agencies, their weapons and strategies; as well as specific, practical approaches to consider when developing a defense strategy.

Dennis Barry's chapter on "Legal Issues Surrounding Hospital and Physician Relationships" (Chapter 5) examines the myriad of issues that must be considered in the context of physicians' varied relationships with hospitals, including implications of tax, anti-trust,

and corporate practice of medicine requirements as well as the prohibitions against kickbacks, self-referrals, and gainsharing. The chapter will be particularly helpful to practitioners because it addresses
these issues in the context of many common arrangements between
hospitals and physicians.

Robert Roth and Alicia Palmer's chapter on "Managed Care
Fraud and Abuse: Risk Areas for Government Program Participants"
(Chapter 6) explains how fraud and abuse issues differ when they
arise in the managed care (as opposed to the fee-for-service) setting,
and provides an in-depth discussion of the role of compliance programs in the managed care context; emphasizing prompt payment
and denial of care compliance issues as well as marketing practices.

The chapter by Nancy Jones, Nora Liggett, and Michelle Marsh
on "Corporate Compliance Programs" (Chapter 7) describes the advantages of implementing a corporate compliance program, particularly under the U.S. Sentencing Guidelines, and what elements and
practical issues should be addressed. The chapter also summarizes
the more important aspects of the various compliance program guidance documents that the OIG has published for different types of
health care providers.

Finally, the chapter I co-authored with George McDavid on
"Potential Liabilities for Directors and Officers of Health Care Organizations" (Chapter 8) examines the various types of civil and criminal liability that directors and officers may face, with particular
emphasis on the evolving *Caremark* doctrine, and measures that may
help reduce exposure.

The Appendices contain a ready source for many of the more
important documents in the field of health care fraud and abuse.
Appendices A through J include not only the texts of relevant statutes
and regulations but also contain various guidance documents necessary for analysis of these issues (but whose existence and availability
are not uniformly well-known). The Appendices include materials concerning the

- Anti-kickback statute and safe harbor regulations
- Stark law and regulations
- False Claims Act
- Civil monetary penalties and exclusions laws and regulations
- Selected statutes relating to private payer fraud
- Special Fraud Alerts and Special Advisory Bulletins
- Advisory opinions relating to the anti-kickback statute and the
  Stark law
- OIG Provider Self-Disclosure Protocol
- OIG Compliance Program Guidance for hospitals and for indi-
  vidual and small group physician practices, and the corporate
  integrity agreement with Vencor, Inc.
- Contract for Participation in Medicare+Choice Program.

Appendices A through E are reprinted and located at the end of this volume. Appendices F through J are provided on the CD-ROM that accompanies this volume.

This book was designed in order to provide a desk reference for members of the health law bar and other attorneys who counsel clients involved in the health care industry. The materials contained in the eight substantive chapters are current through June 2001.

Due to the constant changes in this subject, as discussed above, this book will be updated annually. The supplemental volumes will not only update the material in the "core" chapters but may also add new chapters as various "hot" topics arise. Finally, the reader should remember that the content of this book is designed for general informational purposes only, and should not be construed as legal advice or opinion on any specific facts or circumstances. The views expressed in the chapters are those of the individual authors, and do not reflect the views of their firm or its clients, myself, or the other authors of this volume.

It has been a privilege to work with the many people who have helped bring this book to fruition, and I would like to extend my personal thanks to all of them. The chapter authors have devoted a tremendous amount of their time and shared a great deal of their invaluable professional knowledge. Many members of the leadership in the American Bar Association (ABA) Health Law Section have also made a substantial contribution of their time and energy, as described in more detail in the Foreword. In addition, BNA Books has provided very helpful guidance and assistance throughout the process. Their continuing support and dedication to this project has been essential to its completion.

On behalf of all those who have contributed to this volume, we hope these materials will help the reader counsel his or her clients on this ever-changing area of the law.

LINDA A. BAUMANN
EDITOR-IN-CHIEF
Reed Smith LLP
Washington, D.C.

December 2001

# About the Authors

### Linda A. Baumann (Chapter 1: An Introduction to Health Care Fraud and Abuse)

Linda Baumann serves as editor-in-chief of this volume, in addition to authoring two of the chapters. Ms. Baumann is counsel at Reed Smith LLP, where she concentrates her practice on health care regulatory matters, particularly those relating to fraud and abuse. She has worked with clients throughout the industry ranging from national chains to community providers, including hospitals, skilled nursing facilities, independent diagnostic testing facilities, clinical laboratories, DME suppliers, ESRD facilities, management companies, and many other organizations involved in the health care industry. She has designed corporate compliance programs, handled government investigations (from the initial audit through negotiation and settlement), served as outside regulatory counsel, and helped clients develop strategies to promote business objectives while ensuring compliance with applicable laws and regulations. She has extensive experience in the government, in private practice, and in academia, having lectured at Princeton University. She frequently speaks before health care providers as well as attorneys, and has published numerous articles on various health care topics. Ms. Baumann also serves on the Advisory Board of THE HEALTH LAWYER. She received her J.D. from Columbia University, where she was an editor of the COLUMBIA UNIVERSITY LAW REVIEW, and an International Fellow. She received her undergraduate degree, magna cum laude, from Brown University.

### Thomas S. Crane (Chapter 2: Federal Physician Self-Referral Restrictions)

Tom Crane is a member at Mintz, Levin, Cohn, Ferris, Glovsky, and Popeo, P.C., where he co-coordinates the firm's Health Care Fraud and Abuse and Corporate Compliance practice group. Mr. Crane is nationally recognized as an authority on fraud and abuse, and provides comprehensive fraud and abuse services to clients, from defense to compliance advice to compliance programs. His work in defending clients against false claims, whistleblower, and anti-kickback allegations includes internal investigations, voluntary disclosures, and negotiating settlements and corporate integrity agreements (CIAs). He also provides compliance advice to clients in structuring complex transactions to comply with fraud and abuse laws and the variety of regulatory requirements that must be met. He received his undergraduate degree from Harvard College (1972), a Masters degree in health administration from the University of Michigan (1976), and his law degree from Antioch School of Law in Washington, D.C. (1983).

### Robert Salcido (Chapter 3: The False Claims Act in Health Care Prosecutions: Application of the Substantive, *Qui Tam*, and Voluntary Disclosure Provisions)

Robert Salcido is a partner at Akin, Gump, Strauss, Hauer & Feld, L.L.P., in its Washington, D.C. office. Mr. Salcido has practiced extensively in the area of the False Claims Act (FCA), having previously been a trial attorney with the Civil Fraud Unit of the Civil Division of the U.S. Department of Justice (DOJ), which has nationwide jurisdiction over FCA actions. At the DOJ, he prosecuted actions under the FCA, handled actions under the FCA's voluntary disclosure provisions, and specialized in whistleblower actions brought under the *qui tam* provisions of the FCA. Mr. Salcido is the author of the books FALSE CLAIMS ACT & THE HEALTHCARE INDUSTRY: COUNSELING & LITIGATION (Amer. Health Lawyers 1999), and FALSE CLAIMS ACT & THE HEALTHCARE INDUSTRY: COUNSELING & LITIGATION: NOVEMBER 2000 SUPPLEMENT (Am. Health Lawyers 2000). He is a graduate of Harvard Law School and received his Bachelor of Arts degree summa cum laude from Claremont McKenna College.

### Patric Hooper (Chapter 4: Practical Considerations for Defending Health Care Fraud and Abuse Cases)

Patric Hooper is a founding principal of Hooper, Lundy & Bookman, Inc., a health law specialty firm with a national practice. Mr. Hooper has practiced in the health law field for nearly 30 years, and has been involved in many high profile health law cases. In addition to his involvement in resolving disputes, Mr. Hooper regularly advises nonprofit and for-profit health care organizations regarding reimbursement, certification, and licensure issues associated with business transactions and combinations. He continuously advises health care providers on Medicare, Medicaid, and Tricare fraud and abuse issues and on state anti-kickback and referral issues. Mr. Hooper is a frequent writer and lecturer on fraud and abuse issues and was the first chairman of the Fraud and Self-Referral interest group of the American Bar Association (ABA) Health Law Section. He received his J.D. from the University of San Diego in 1973 and his A.B. from the University of California, Los Angeles in 1970.

### Dennis M. Barry (Chapter 5: Legal Issues Surrounding Hospital and Physician Relationships)

Dennis Barry is a partner in the Washington, D.C., office of Vinson & Elkins, L.L.P. He leads his firm's health care practice in that office, and is co-chair of the firm's Health Section. His practice deals exclusively with health care clients whom he represents on a broad range of issues, and he spends the majority of his time on Medicare payment and compliance issues. Since 1989, Mr. Barry has served as the editor and principal author of *Dennis Barry's Reimbursement Advisor*, a monthly newsletter published by Aspen Publishing. Mr. Barry serves as co-chair of the Medicare & Medicaid Institute, an annual 3-day program sponsored by the American Health Lawyers Association (AHLA). Mr. Barry is listed in BEST LAWYERS IN AMERICA. He has been active in a number of professional associations including the Healthcare Financial Management Association, and he has received the Follmer, Reeves, and Muncie awards from that organization. He received his J.D. from the University of Virginia in 1975.

### Robert L. Roth (Chapter 6: Managed Care Fraud and Abuse: Risk Areas for Government Program Participants)

Robert Roth is a partner in the Health Care Group at Crowell & Moring, LLP, in Washington, D.C., and has been in private practice since 1993. Previously, Mr. Roth represented the Health Care Financing Administration (now the Centers for Medicare & Medicaid Services) as a member of the Office of the General Counsel of the U.S. Department of Health and Human Services, served as an Assistant Attorney General assigned to Maryland's Department of Health and Mental Hygiene, and counseled the Maryland General Assembly. Mr. Roth is an adjunct professor of law at the University of Baltimore School of Law and has been active in the leadership of the ABA's Health Law Section, serving as Section Chair for 2001–2002. He also serves on the Advisory Board of *BNA's Health Law Reporter* and *BNA's Health Care Fraud Report*. He received his undergraduate degree from Lehigh University and his Juris Doctor degree from Syracuse University College of Law.

### Alicia J. Palmer (Chapter 6: Managed Care Fraud and Abuse: Risk Areas for Government Program Participants)

Alicia Palmer is an associate in the Health Care Group of Crowell & Moring, LLP, in Washington, D.C. Prior to joining Crowell & Moring, Ms. Palmer was an associate with Michaels & Bonner, and worked in various operational and legal positions with Blue Cross and Blue Shield of the National Capital Area. Ms. Palmer's practice focuses primarily on federal and state regulatory issues affecting managed care plans and health insurers, particularly issues related to the federal Medicare+Choice program and state licensure and operating requirements for managed care plans. Ms. Palmer has written on topics such as the D.C. Health Maintenance Organization (HMO) Act and telemedicine and confidentiality. Ms. Palmer is a 1995 graduate of the American University, Washington College of Law; she obtained her undergraduate degree in Human Resources at the Indiana University of Pennsylvania in 1988.

### Nancy Jones (Chapter 7: Corporate Compliance Programs)

Nancy Jones is a member of Waller Lansden Dortch & Davis, in Nashville, Tennessee. Ms. Jones has extensive experience in general commercial litigation (both plaintiff and defendant), health care law, securities class action litigation, and corporate criminal defense. Ms. Jones received her Bachelor of Arts degree, with Honors, from the University of Missouri in 1971. In 1978, she received her Juris Doctor degree from Syracuse University. Prior to joining Waller Lansden, Ms. Jones was an Assistant U.S. Attorney for the Middle District of Tennessee, from 1991 to 1993. From 1987 to 1991, she was an Assistant U.S. Attorney for the Western District of Oklahoma; from 1980 to 1987, she served as Assistant U.S. Attorney for the Northern District of New York. Ms. Jones has participated in many seminars and has written for the *Journal of the Tennessee Society of Certified Public Accountants*. She is a member of the New York and Nashville, Tennessee Bar Associations and the ABA.

### Nora L. Liggett (Chapter 7: Corporate Compliance Programs)

Nora Liggett is a member of Waller Lansden Dortch & Davis, in Nashville, Tennessee. Ms. Liggett has extensive experience in the area of health care operations and regulatory issues. She advises health care providers and hospital and physician practice-management companies on a variety of health care related issues, including Medicare fraud and abuse, physician self-referral prohibitions, third-party reimbursement, managed care contracting and development, and related health care operations issues. Ms. Liggett received her Bachelor of Arts degree, cum laude, from the University of the South in 1986, and her Juris Doctor degree from Washington and Lee University in 1989. She is a frequent contributor to health law publications, speaks regularly at health law seminars, and is the co-editor of Waller Lansden's *Health Law Newsletter*. Ms. Liggett is active in the Health Law Sections of the Nashville and Tennessee Bar Associations and is a member of the AHLA, and the Antitrust and Health Law Sections of the ABA.

### Michelle Bellamy Marsh (Chapter 7: Corporate Compliance Programs)

Michelle Marsh is an associate with the firm Waller Lansden Dortch & Davis, in Nashville, Tennessee. Ms. Marsh practices in the area of health care operations, including Stark compliance, fraud and abuse issues, facility and practice acquisitions, and other regulatory issues. Ms. Marsh received her Bachelor of Arts degree, cum laude, from Vanderbilt University in 1990. In 1996, she received her Juris Doctor degree from the College of William and Mary, Marshall-Wythe

School of Law. She is a member of the Nashville and the Tennessee Bar Associations and the Health Law Section of ABA. Ms. Marsh is also a member of the AHLA.

## Linda A. Baumann (Chapter 8: Potential Liabilities for Directors and Officers of Health Care Organizations)

See entry for Linda A. Baumann at Chapter 1, above.

## George E. McDavid (Chapter 8: Potential Liabilities for Directors and Officers of Health Care Organizations)

George McDavid is a partner with Reed Smith LLP in the firm's Princeton, New Jersey office. His national practice focuses on complex commercial litigation, including representation of pharmaceutical manufacturers and distributors, hospitals, and other health care providers. His experience also includes products liability and toxic tort defense work. Mr. McDavid has extensive experience defending and counseling health care companies in respect of their decisions concerning the marketing of drugs and medical devices. Since his admission to the bar in 1982, he has maintained an extremely active trial practice and tried to verdict over 30 cases before juries. He has tried cases before administrative law tribunals, arbitration panels, and state and federal courts. Mr. McDavid earned his J.D. from Case Western Reserve University in 1982 and his A.B. from Dartmouth College in 1978.

# Summary Table of Contents

# Detailed Table of Contents

**Chapter 3.  The False Claims Act in Health Care Prosecutions: Application of the Substantive, *Qui Tam*, and Voluntary Disclosure Provisions**............................ 111

# 1

# An Introduction to Health Care Fraud and Abuse*

---

*Linda A. Baumann, Reed Smith LLP, Washington, D.C.

## I. Introduction

Health care fraud and abuse has become a growth industry. For the past several years, numerous state and federal government agencies have increased the amount of staff, time, and resources they dedicate to investigating and prosecuting it. All types of health care providers, practitioners, and suppliers have been affected including hospitals, nursing homes, home health agencies, renal dialysis facilities, hospices, rehabilitation facilities, clinics, physician practices, and durable medical equipment (DME) suppliers. Other types of organizations that happen to do business with individuals or entities in the health care industry also have felt the effects of the explosion of laws and regulations in this area. Individuals at all levels may face potential liability, from employees and independent contractors up through management to the board of directors. Almost every health care attorney already has or will have to address the fraud and abuse laws in the context of what used to be considered a routine corporate transaction. Litigators representing health care clients are finding that reimbursement cases often contain additional allegations of health care fraud that can lead to far more serious consequences than the original overpayment in question. Other attorneys who do not frequently represent health care clients will begin to structure a commercial arrangement along terms and conditions that are standard in other industries only to find that the proposed transaction could create exposure under one or more of the health care fraud and abuse laws. As a result, attorneys who represent clients involved in the health care industry are well advised to develop some degree of familiarity with the fraud and abuse laws in order to protect their clients, and themselves, from exposure.

There has been a tremendous increase in the number and complexity of laws, regulations, and other guidance materials relating to this area over the past decade. The range of topics being addressed and the level of detail with which they are regulated are similarly expanding. Even experts in health care fraud and abuse frequently comment on how difficult it is to keep up with so many diverse developments. The intricacy of the laws and regulations can be daunting, particularly for those who do not have to deal with these issues on a regular basis. The situation is exacerbated by the fact that there are so few bright lines, thus many issues fall within a "gray area." Despite having spent years in the field, health care attorneys sometimes have difficulty providing clients with definitive guidance because the laws and regulations are often ambiguous.

### A. The Potential Risks

Nevertheless, it is essential to be fully informed about any potential issues because the liabilities can be enormous. Health care fraud and abuse likely will be a high-priority issue for the federal government for the foreseeable future because millions of dollars have been recovered as a result of numerous investigations, prosecutions, and settlements with various individuals, health care providers, and other entities. The Department of Health and Human Services (HHS) and the Department of Justice (DOJ) announced that in fiscal year (FY) 1999 alone, the federal government won or negotiated more than $524 million in judgments, settlements, and administrative impositions in health care fraud cases. In addition, federal prosecutors filed 371 criminal indictments (a 16 percent increase over the previous year), and 396 defendants were convicted for health care fraud–related crimes. There also were 91 civil cases filed in addition to the 2,278 civil matters pending in FY 1999. During this same year, HHS excluded 2,976 individuals and entities from participating in federal health programs and continued to monitor over 400 corporate integrity agreements (CIAs).[1]

These figures do not reflect various settlement agreements reached in 2000 that are reported by the HHS Office of Inspector General (the OIG) to include $1.2 billion in investigative receivables.[2] In late 2000, $840 million in criminal fines, civil penalties and damages was assessed against the largest for-profit hospital chain in the United States, HCA—The Healthcare Company, formerly known as Columbia/HCA (HCA), for alleged unlawful billing practices. The HCA agreement, announced in December 2000,[3] was headlined as the largest government fraud settlement in U.S. history, and also involved HCA subsidiaries pleading guilty to certain criminal conduct. The range of sanctions facing HCA is extensive. Under the agreement, HCA will pay a total of $745 million to resolve five allegations regarding the manner in which it billed the federal government and the states for health care costs.[4] Of the $745 million, the settlement requires HCA to pay the following:

- more than $95 million to resolve civil claims arising from HCA's outpatient laboratory billing practices, which included billing to Medicare, Medicaid, the Defense Department's Tricare program, and the Federal Employees Health Benefits Program, for labo-

---

[1] U.S. DEP'T OF HEALTH & HUMAN SERVS. & DEP'T OF JUSTICE, HEALTH CARE FRAUD AND ABUSE CONTROL PROGRAM ANNUAL REPORT FOR FY 1999, at i, 8–9 (Jan. 2000), *available at* http://oig.hhs.gov/press/hipaa2.htm [hereinafter 1999 HHS/DOJ REPORT].

[2] U.S. DEP'T OF HEALTH & HUMAN SERVS., OFFICE OF INSPECTOR GEN., SEMIANNUAL REPORT APRIL 1, 2000–SEPTEMBER 30, 2000, *available at* http://oig.hhs.gov/semann/00fsemi.pdf [hereinafter SEMIANNUAL REPORT APR.–SEPT. 2000].

[3] Press Release, U.S. Dep't of Justice, HCA—The Health Care Company & Subsidiaries to Pay $840 Million in Criminal Fines and Civil Damages and Penalties (Dec. 14, 2000), *available at* http://www.usdoj.gov/opa/pr/2000/December/696civcrm.htm [hereinafter DOJ Press Release—HCA—The Health Care Company & Subsidiaries to Pay $840 Million].

[4] This agreement does not resolve other allegations that HCA used unlawful cost-reporting practices and that it paid kickbacks to physicians to get Medicare and Medicaid patients referred to its facilities. Thus, further settlement agreements and payments may follow.

ratory tests that were not medically necessary, and not ordered by physicians, as well as other billing violations;

- more than $403 million to resolve civil claims arising from "upcoding," where false diagnosis codes were assigned to patient records in order to increase hospital reimbursement;
- $50 million to resolve civil claims that the company illegally claimed nonreimbursable marketing and advertising costs it disguised as community education;
- $90 million to resolve civil claims that HCA illegally charged Medicare for nonreimbursable costs incurred in the purchase of certain home health agencies owned by the Olsten Corporation, as well as other agencies in Florida, Georgia, and Alabama. According to the government, HCA devised an elaborate scheme to hide these costs in reimbursable "management fees" paid to third parties;[5] and
- $106 million to resolve civil claims for billing Medicare, Medicaid, and Tricare for home health visits for patients who did not qualify to receive them, or that were not performed, and for committing other billing violations.[6]

In addition to the civil settlement, two subsidiaries of Tennessee-based HCA, Columbia Homecare Group, Inc. and Columbia Management Companies, Inc., entered into an agreement in which they agreed to pay more than $95 million in criminal fines and plead guilty to charges involving a wide range of criminal conduct that occurred at HCA's hospitals nationwide. According to the terms of the plea agreement, which have yet to be approved by the courts, the companies will plead guilty to charges involving cost report fraud, fraudulently billing Medicare for personnel who worked at home health agencies and at wound care centers, fraudulently billing Medicare for patients diagnosed with pneumonia, paying kickbacks and other remuneration to doctors to induce referrals, paying kickbacks in connection with the purchase and sale of home health agencies, and fraudulently billing Medicare for fees paid to manage the home health agencies. Sentencing is to follow.

In addition to the financial penalties and criminal sentences, HCA is entering into an 8-year CIA[7] that reportedly contains audit and com-

---

[5] In 1999, a subsidiary of Olsten Corporation, Kimberly Quality Care, entered into criminal plea agreements and paid more than $10 million in criminal fines. Olsten itself paid nearly $41 million as part of a civil settlement arising from its collusion with HCA for this same conduct.

[6] DOJ Press Release—HCA—The Health Care Company & Subsidiaries to Pay $840 Million.

[7] CIAs, which are frequently imposed by the government as part of a health care fraud settlement agreement, generally resemble a corporate compliance program. However, CIAs usually are much more extensive and expensive than compliance programs voluntarily adopted by private companies. They usually have a 5-year duration. For further information, see http://oig.hhs.gov/cia/.

pliance requirements that are "unprecedented"[8] in scope and detail. HCA also has agreed to exclude two subsidiaries from participating in Medicare and other federal health care programs and to divest one hospital, subject to numerous requirements as to the conditions and timing of the divestiture. Moreover, the settlement only resolves corporate criminal liability. The government reserves the right to investigate and prosecute individuals, and expressly notes HCA's obligation to cooperate with the government in such ongoing investigations.[9] Since the settlement, the DOJ has intervened in several additional False Claims Act (FCA) lawsuits, brought by whistleblowers, alleging fraud by HCA.[10]

Other recent major Medicare fraud settlements include a government agreement with Fresenius Medical Care Holdings, Inc. (Fresenius), the nation's largest provider of kidney dialysis products and services, under which three subsidiaries pled guilty, and Fresenius agreed to pay $486 million to resolve the criminal and civil aspects of the case. The alleged misconduct involved kickbacks, submission of false claims for dialysis-related nutrition therapy services, improper billing for laboratory services, and false reporting of credit balances by National Medical Care, a nationwide dialysis company and various of its subsidiaries, prior to a 1996 merger with Fresenius. Fresenius was also required to enter an extensive, 8-year CIA.

With regard to nursing homes, Beverly Enterprises, Inc. (Beverly), the nation's largest nursing home chain, and a subsidiary corporation agreed to pay the government a total of $175 million to resolve criminal and civil issues, and enter a CIA. This multimillion-dollar settlement resolved allegations that Beverly engaged in a scheme to defraud Medicare of approximately $400 million by inflating nursing costs charged to the program. Beverly will pay $170 million under the terms of the civil settlement. A Beverly subsidiary, which also pled guilty to criminal charges, will pay $5 million in criminal fines and divest itself of 10 nursing homes.[11]

In addition to government investigations, there is a tremendous incentive for private citizens to look for health care fraud, become whistleblowers/relators, and file suit under the *qui tam* provisions of the FCA. Even if the case never goes to trial, whistleblowers can receive millions of dollars as part of an FCA settlement.[12] Some state

---

[8] DOJ Press Release—HCA—The Health Care Company & Subsidiaries to Pay $840 Million.

[9] *Id.*

[10] Press Release, U.S. Dep't of Justice, Justice Department Sues HCA—The Health Care Company and Its Hospital for Fraud (Mar. 16, 2001), *available at* http://www.usdoj.gov/opa/pr/2001/March/111civ.htm.

[11] U.S. Dep't of Health & Human Servs., Office of Inspector Gen., Semiannual Report October 1, 1999–March 30, 2000, at ii (June 19, 2000), *available at* http://oig.hhs.gov/semann/ 00fsemi.pdf.

[12] The Civil False Claims Act is described more fully in Chapter 3 (Salcido, The False Claims Act in Health Care Prosecutions: Application of the Substantive, *Qui Tam*, and Voluntary Disclosure Provisions).

statutes have similar incentives as described later in this chapter. The federal government has implemented several additional programs to encourage beneficiaries to report potential fraud; however, any subsequent prosecutions would likely be undertaken by the government.[13] Moreover, there is always the risk that shareholders, disgruntled by falling stock prices or other corporate problems, will try to use the fraud and abuse laws in connection with a derivative or class action lawsuit filed against the directors and officers of a company.[14]

As indicated above, the financial implications of a fraud and abuse case can be staggering. In addition to sizable criminal penalties, depending on the applicable law, the government can invoke statutory provisions that allow it to collect several thousand dollars per improper claim as well as treble damages. In the health care industry, where hundreds and even thousands of claims may be filed by a single provider on a single day, it is easy to see how the volume of monetary damages can escalate dramatically. Even if the case never goes to court, the settlement amounts are usually very high because the government is generally unwilling to discuss settlement for less than double damages in an alleged fraud case. The settlement can be significantly reduced if the provider is able to show that there was no fraud involved. In such cases, return of any overpayment may suffice. However, despite frequent government statements that inadvertence or negligence will not result in civil or criminal claims for penalties,[15] it can be extremely difficult to convince the government that there was no fraudulent behavior.

## B. Exposure for Attorneys

Lawyers themselves also are at risk as demonstrated by the indictment of two experienced health care counsel in connection with the *LaHue* case.[16] In the *LaHue* case and its related proceedings doctors and hospital executives were indicted under allegations that they engaged in a criminal scheme to receive remuneration from various hospitals in return for the referral of Medicare patients.[17] Attorneys for the hospital were charged with conspiracy in connection with the indictment.[18] Although the attorneys' motion for acquittal was later

---

[13] One such program involves the creation of the Medicare Fraud Hotline. According to the SEMIANNUAL REPORT, *supra* note 11, the hotline has received 1.5 million calls since its inception leading to recoveries of over $38 million.

[14] Issues of director and officer liability are discussed in Chapter 8 (Baumann & McDavid, Potential Liabilities for Directors and Officers of Health Care Organizations).

[15] *See, e.g.,* OIG Compliance Program Guidance for Individual and Small Group Physician Practices, 65 Fed. Reg. 59,434, 59,436 (Oct. 5, 2000); for text of guidance, see Appendix I-2 on the disk accompanying this volume.

[16] United States v. LaHue, 998 F. Supp. 1182 (D. Kan. 1998), *aff'd*, 170 F.3d 1026 (10th Cir. 1999).

[17] United States v. Anderson, 85 F. Supp. 2d 1047, 1052 (D. Kan. 1999).

[18] *Id.*

granted,[19] the charges were a sobering reminder to all attorneys that representing clients in the health care industry can be a high-risk endeavor.

In addition, in June 2001 the OIG issued a new Special Advisory Bulletin on Practices of Business Consultants. While acknowledging the integral role that consultants can play in improving the integrity of the health care system, the OIG warned that certain "questionable practices" could expose both providers and their consultants to legal liability. The practices identified as suspect include (1) making illegal or misleading representations; (2) offering promises or guarantees that are unreasonable or improbable; (3) encouraging abusive practices such as advising "a client to adopt a patently unreasonable interpretation of a reimbursement law, regulation, or rule to justify substantially greater reimbursement"; and (4) discouraging compliance efforts including making "blanket statements that a client should not undertake certain compliance efforts (such as retrospective billing reviews) or cooperate with payor audits, regardless of the client's circumstances."[20] Because attorneys were specifically identified as one of the types of consultants the OIG was addressing in this Special Advisory Bulletin, attorneys can expect the OIG to scrutinize their actions as well as those of their clients.

## C. Likelihood of Increased Enforcement Efforts in the Future

In addition to the multimillion-dollar recoveries discussed above, the government also points to the role of the OIG and the Centers for Medicare and Medicaid Services (CMS)[21] in correcting systemic vulnerabilities. These "corrections" led to $11.8 billion in savings for Medicare and Medicaid in 1999 because funds were not spent for improper or unnecessary care. Such policy and procedural changes, along with aggressive enforcement are credited with preserving the solvency of the Medicare Trust Fund until 2025.[22]

In light of these many "successes," government support for health care fraud and abuse enforcement is likely to continue and the federal mechanism for funding such efforts makes it likely that the amount of money available for enforcement will increase. The Health Insurance Portability and Accountability Act of 1996 (HIPAA),[23] set up a

---

[19]*See* United States v. McClatchey, 217 F.3d 823, 828 (10th Cir.), *cert. denied*, 531 U.S. 1015, 121 S. Ct. 574 (2000).

[20]OIG Special Advisory Bulletin, Practices of Business Consultants, 66 Fed. Reg. 36,583 (July 12, 2001); for text of the Special Advisory Bulletin, see Appendix F-12 on the disk accompanying this volume.

[21]On June 14, 2001, the former Health Care Financing Administration (HCFA) was renamed the Centers for Medicare and Medicaid Services (CMS). For purposes of this chapter, references will be to CMS.

[22]"A Message From the Secretary," in SEMIANNUAL REPORT APR.–SEPT. 2000, *supra* note 2.

[23]Pub. L. No. 104–191, 110 Stat. 1936 (1996).

Health Care Fraud and Abuse Control Account (Health Care Fraud Account) within the Federal Hospital Insurance Trust Fund. Proceeds from enforcement of federal health care cases are generally deposited in the Health Care Fraud Account and made available to finance additional fraud investigations and prosecutions. In 1999, $98.2 million was allotted to the OIG from this account, a $12 million increase over 1998. The OIG used these funds to hire over 100 new staff members and to open two new investigative offices. These expanded resources helped the OIG conduct or participate in 942 prosecutions or settlements in 1999 alone. HIPAA also provided funding to the Federal Bureau of Investigation (FBI) for health care fraud enforcement. In 1999, the FBI received $66 million that it used in large part to fund 40 additional agents and 42 support positions and to create several new health care fraud squads. As a result, by the end of 1999, the FBI had 493 agents focusing on health care fraud compared with 192 in 1992. Moreover, the HHS/DOJ Report described health care fraud investigations as being among those having the "highest priority" within the FBI.[24]

Various ongoing efforts to collaborate among federal and state agencies and private payers also increase the likelihood that the number, type, and scope of health care fraud investigations will continue to escalate.[25] Under these circumstances, expanded focus on health care fraud and abuse seems probable for the foreseeable future.

## II. THE FEDERAL FRAUD AND ABUSE LAWS

There are many federal laws specifically designed to address health care fraud and abuse including the anti-kickback statute,[26] the Stark law prohibiting physician self-referrals,[27] the FCA,[28] various civil monetary penalty (CMP) provisions,[29] and mandatory and permissive exclusion authorities.[30] Many of these laws focus on fraud and abuse affecting various federally funded health care programs such as Medicare, Medicaid, and veterans health care programs, although other statutes address fraudulent practices affecting nongovernmental payers as well.[31]

---

[24] 1999 HHS/DOJ REPORT, *supra* note 1.

[25] The 1999 HHS/DOJ REPORT, *supra* note 1, states that collaboration increased through 1999 with the creation of the National Health Care Fraud Task Force chaired by the deputy Attorney General, joint training, and heightened data sharing.

[26] 42 U.S.C. §1320a-7b(b); see Appendix A-1.

[27] 42 U.S.C. §1395nn; see Appendix B-1.

[28] 31 U.S.C. §3729; see Appendix C-1.

[29] 42 U.S.C. §1320a-7a; see Appendix D-1.

[30] 42 U.S.C. §1320a-7; see Appendix D-3.

[31] See discussion *infra* Section II.F. The historical development of the federal health care fraud and abuse laws is discussed in more detail in Chapter 4 (Hooper, Practical Considerations for Defending Health Care Fraud and Abuse Cases).

There are also numerous other federal statutes that do not specifically address any type of health care program but may be used to prosecute fraud and abuse in the health care industry, including the Racketeer Influenced and Corrupt Organizations Act (RICO)[32] and money-laundering prohibitions.[33] In addition, various other laws including certain provisions of the tax code, such as those relating to private inurement, may also be implicated by some of the same transactions that potentially implicate the fraud and abuse laws. However, it is critical to remember that the factors (e.g., community benefit) that may protect an arrangement from violating certain Internal Revenue Code provisions will not necessarily protect an arrangement under the fraud and abuse statutes.

## A. The Anti-Kickback Statute

### 1. The Prohibitions

The federal anti-kickback statute establishes criminal penalties with respect to any person who knowingly and willfully offers, pays, solicits, or receives any remuneration to induce or in return for: (1) referring an individual to a person for the furnishing or arranging for the furnishing of any item or service payable in whole or in part under a federal health care program; or (2) purchasing, leasing, ordering, or arranging for, or recommending purchasing, leasing, or ordering any good, facility, service, or item payable under a federal health care program. Remuneration is defined broadly to include the transfer of anything of value, in cash or in kind, directly or indirectly, overtly or covertly.[34]

Violation of the anti-kickback statute constitutes a felony punishable by a maximum fine of $25,000, imprisonment up to 5 years, or both. Conviction will also lead to automatic exclusion from Medicare, Medicaid, and other federally funded health care programs. Exclusion from these programs may also be sought by HHS through an administrative proceeding, irrespective of any criminal charges. In addition, under the Balanced Budget Act of 1997,[35] violations of the anti-kickback statute are also subject to CMPs of up to $50,000 and damages of up to three times the amount of the illegal kickback.

The anti-kickback statute is expansive in scope and clearly prohibits payments for patient referrals. The applicability of the statute becomes less clear, however, as applied to arrangements that do not simply involve a payment per patient referral, but instead contemplate investment or business relationships between two or more individuals or organizations. The courts have interpreted this prohibition

---

[32] 18 U.S.C. §§1961 *et seq.*

[33] 18 U.S.C. §1956. *See also, e.g.,* 18 U.S.C. §§286 (conspiracy to defraud the government), 287 (submission of fraudulent claims), 371 (conspiracy to defraud), and 1001 (false statements).

[34] 42 U.S.C. §§1320a-7b(b)(1), (2).

[35] Pub. L. No. 105-93, 111 Stat. 251 (1997).

broadly. In 1985, in *United States v. Greber*,[36] the Third Circuit established the "one purpose" test, holding that the anti-kickback statute was violated where one purpose of the payment in question was to induce referrals, irrespective of the existence of other legitimate purposes. Over the years, this approach has been adopted by three other circuits.[37] Further, in *United States v. Bay State Ambulance & Hospital Rental Service*,[38] the court held that simply giving a person an opportunity to earn money may be an inducement to that person to channel Medicare payments toward a particular recipient in violation of the anti-kickback statute. However, in a recent Tenth Circuit case, *United States v. McClatchey*,[39] the court stated that the mere hope or expectation that referrals may result from remuneration designed for entirely different purposes is not a violation, and that there must be an actual offer or payment of remuneration to induce referrals. Moreover, "the intent to gain such influence must, at least in part, have been the reason the remuneration was offered or paid."[40]

In addition, while cases have interpreted the concept of inducement quite broadly, judicial guidance with respect to the criminal intent that must be shown in order to prove a violation of the anti-kickback statute has been inconsistent. For example, the Ninth Circuit and some other courts have suggested that a defendant must violate a known legal duty.[41] However, the federal district court in *United States v. Neufeld*[42] refused to adopt the Ninth Circuit's definition of "willful," but at the same time hesitated from "embarking on an exact definition of the scienter requirement. . . ."[43] In 1998 the Eleventh Circuit found, in *United States v. Starks*,[44] that "willfully" meant an act "committed voluntarily and purposely, with the specific intent to do something the law forbids, that is, with a bad purpose, either to disobey or disregard the law."[45] Further, the court noted that the anti-kickback statute was not analogous to other highly technical laws, and thus knowledge of the specific law was unnecessary.[46]

---

[36] 760 F.2d 68 (3d Cir. 1985).

[37] *See, e.g.*, United States v. McClatchey, 217 F.3d 823 (10th Cir.), *cert. denied*, 531 U.S. 1015, 121 S. Ct. 574 (2000); United States v. Bay State Ambulance & Hosp. Rental Serv., 874 F.2d 20 (1st Cir. 1989); United States v. Kats, 871 F.2d 105 (9th Cir. 1989).

[38] 874 F.2d 20, 29 (1st Cir. 1989).

[39] 217 F.3d 823 (10th Cir.), *cert. denied*, 531 U.S. 1015, 121 S. Ct. 574 (2000).

[40] *Id.* at 834.

[41] *See, e.g.*, Hanlester Network v. Shalala, 51 F.3d 1390 (9th Cir. 1995). The *Hanlester* case was also the first judicial decision to specially address the application of the anti-kickback statute to joint venture arrangements.

[42] 908 F. Supp. 491 (S.D. Ohio 1995).

[43] *Id.* at 497.

[44] 157 F.3d 833 (11 Cir. 1998).

[45] *Id.* at 837.

[46] *Id.*

Most recently, in *United States v. McClatchey*,[47] the Tenth Circuit used the same language as the *Starks* court to define "willfully." A jury had convicted McClatchey, a hospital executive, of violating the anti-kickback statute but the district court had granted a motion for acquittal, concluding that no reasonable jury could find that McClatchey deliberately intended to violate the statute. On appeal, the Tenth Circuit held that a jury might reasonably have found that McClatchey specifically intended to violate the anti-kickback statute because he renegotiated, rather than terminated, a contract with physicians (1) who had not performed substantial services required under prior contracts, (2) whom staff did not want to perform certain services at the hospital, and (3) who made referrals that were important to the hospital's financial health. The court stated that under these circumstances, a jury could have determined that McClatchey's very reason for negotiating a new contract was to induce continuing referrals.

The Tenth Circuit dismissed McClatchey's claims that he did not have improper intent because he directed legal counsel to remedy the physicians' prior failure to provide services. The appellate court closely examined the underlying facts in the case, noting that hospital staff did not want or need some of the services the physicians were to provide, and stating that a jury might have found McClatchey's directions to counsel were a subterfuge to ensure the contract appeared on its face to constitute a legal arrangement. Further, the court pointed out that McClatchey was directing counsel on certain matters, and not vice versa; and did not always follow the advice of counsel when he received it.

In sum, given the undetermined state of the law, judicial inquiry into intent may frequently involve an objective and detailed examination of the facts, circumstances, and structure of each transaction, especially the financial effects of the relationships and arrangements.

## 2. *Exceptions and Safe Harbors*

Because of the broad sweep of the anti-kickback prohibitions, Congress created a number of statutory exceptions to protect legitimate business arrangements including the following:

- properly disclosed discounts or other reductions in price;
- payments to bona fide employees;
- certain payments to group purchasing organizations;
- waivers of coinsurance for Medicare services for individuals who qualify for certain Public Health Service programs; and
- certain risk-sharing and other arrangements with managed care organizations.[48]

In addition, Congress authorized HHS to establish further "safe harbors" by regulation.[49] The OIG has created a number of regulatory

---

[47] 217 F.3d 823, 829 (10th Cir.), *cert. denied*, 531 U.S. 1015, 121 S. Ct. 574 (2000).

[48] 42 U.S.C. §1320a-7b(b)(3).

[49] 42 U.S.C. §1320a-7b(b)(3)(E).

safe harbors over the years, and in November 1999 the OIG clarified a number of the existing safe harbors and added several new ones. Note, however, that safe harbor protection is only available if the arrangement fulfills *all* the regulatory criteria. Currently there are safe harbors covering the following types of arrangements:[50]

- investments in certain large or small[51] entities;
- investments in entities in underserved areas;[52]
- space rentals;[53]
- equipment rentals;[54]
- personal services and management contracts;[55]
- sales of physician practices in health professional shortage areas to hospitals or other entities;[56]
- sales of practices by one practitioner to another;[57]
- referral services;[58]
- warranties;[59]
- discounts;[60]
- bona fide employment arrangements;[61]
- group purchasing organizations;[62]
- coinsurance and deductible waivers;[63]
- increased coverage, reduced cost-sharing amounts, or reduced premium amounts offered by health plans;[64]
- price reductions offered to health plans;[65]
- practitioner recruitment activities in underserved areas;[66]
- subsidies for obstetrical malpractice insurance in underserved areas;[67]
- investments in group practices;[68]

---

[50] See Appendix A-2 for full text of the anti-kickback safe harbor regulations.

[51] 42 C.F.R. §§1001.952(a)(1), (a)(2).

[52] 42 C.F.R. §1001.952(a)(3).

[53] 42 C.F.R. §1001.952(b).

[54] 42 C.F.R. §1001.952(c).

[55] 42 C.F.R. §1001.952(d).

[56] 42 C.F.R. §1001.952(e)(2).

[57] 42 C.F.R. §1001.952(e)(1).

[58] 42 C.F.R. §1001.952(f).

[59] 42 C.F.R. §1001.952(g).

[60] 42 C.F.R. §1001.952(h). This safe harbor contains various differing requirements for buyers, sellers, and offerors depending on the types of parties involved.

[61] 42 C.F.R. §1001.952(i).

[62] 42 C.F.R. §1001.952(j).

[63] 42 C.F.R. §1001.952(k).

[64] 42 C.F.R. §1001.952(l).

[65] 42 C.F.R. §1001.952(m).

[66] 42 C.F.R. §1001.952(n).

[67] 42 C.F.R. §1001.952(o).

[68] 42 C.F.R. §1001.952(p).

- cooperative hospital service organizations;[69]
- investments in ambulatory surgical centers (ASCs);[70]
- referral arrangements for specialty services;[71]
- price reductions for eligible managed care organizations;[72] and
- price reductions offered to managed care organizations by contractors with substantial financial risk.[73]

A common theme that runs through these safe harbors is the intent to protect certain arrangements in which commercially reasonable items or services are exchanged for fair market value compensation. While the statute does not contain a general definition of the term, "fair market value" is defined in the space and equipment rental safe harbors. For example, under the space rental safe harbor, fair market value means the value of rental property for general commercial purposes, but should not be adjusted to reflect the additional value that one party would attribute to the property as a result of its proximity or convenience to sources of Medicare or Medicaid business or referrals.[74] The term "commercially reasonable business purpose" is discussed in the preamble to the 1999 safe harbor regulations, which indicates that in the space and equipment rental, and personal services and management contracts safe harbors, the term means that the space, equipment, or services involved must have "intrinsic commercial value" to the lessee or purchaser.[75]

In addition, several of the frequently used safe harbors, including those for space or equipment rentals, and personal services or management contracts, require that *aggregate* compensation be set in advance.[76] Many of the safe harbors require a 1-year written agreement, signed by the parties. A number of the safe harbors added or clarified in 1999 focus on medically underserved areas and populations, although the criteria for determining whether an area is underserved vary depending on the particular safe harbor involved.[77]

---

[69] 42 C.F.R. §1001.952(q).

[70] 42 C.F.R. §1001.952(r). This safe harbor has different criteria for four types of ASCs.

[71] 42 C.F.R. §1001.952(s).

[72] 42 C.F.R. §1001.952(t).

[73] 42 C.F.R. §1001.952(u). The OIG also has proposed new safe harbors relating to ambulance restocking arrangements. *See* Ambulance Restocking Safe Harbor Under the Anti-Kickback Statute, 65 Fed. Reg. 32,060 (proposed May 22, 2000).

[74] 42 C.F.R. §1001.952(b). The term is also defined in the Stark law and regulations as discussed *infra*. However, the requirements of the two statutes differ in various respects, and thus such definitions may not be used interchangeably.

[75] *See* Clarification of the Initial OIG Safe Harbor Provisions and Establishment of Additional Safe Harbor Provisions Under the Anti-Kickback Statute, 64 Fed. Reg. 63,518, 63,525 (Nov. 19, 1999).

[76] 42 C.F.R. §§1001.952(b)(5), (c)(5), (d)(5).

[77] Some safe harbors involve health professional shortage areas (HPSAs), while others involve medically underserved areas and populations. The definition of these

While each of the safe harbors have numerous criteria, the regulations confirm that the safe harbors do not broaden the scope of the statute.[78] Further, in Advisory Opinion No. 98-4, the OIG emphasized that compliance with a safe harbor is not mandatory. Rather, the safe harbors set forth specific threshold requirements that, if fully met, will assure the entities involved that they will not be prosecuted for the arrangement. In other words, while the safe harbors provide protection from liability under the statute, failure to comply with these regulations does not mean that the activity is illegal. Moreover, in the 1999 safe harbor regulations, the OIG went further and stated that failure to comply with a safe harbor does not necessarily mean that an arrangement is "suspect."[79]

The OIG defined the safe harbors very narrowly, using numerous criteria, in order to prevent any risk of fraud or abuse. Therefore, many common arrangements in the health care industry will at least potentially implicate the anti-kickback statute, and will not fully qualify for protection under the safe harbors. Nevertheless, even when an arrangement cannot satisfy all the criteria of a safe harbor, it is generally advisable to meet as many of the requirements as possible. However, under these circumstances, it becomes necessary to examine the arrangement under the terms of the statute with particular reference to the intent of the parties. As noted above, the anti-kickback statute may be violated if only one purpose of the arrangement is to induce referrals. Therefore, when the anti-kickback statute is implicated, and a safe harbor is not fully applicable, the arrangement should be analyzed in light of the Special Fraud Alerts and other relevant materials described below that may help assess a transaction's legality.

*3. Special Fraud Alerts*

Special Fraud Alerts, which the OIG issues periodically, provide further insight into the OIG's views on the application of the anti-kickback statute to various types of arrangements. These documents cannot create new law but may influence judicial decisions.[80] They often contain descriptions of specific features that the OIG considers "suspect" or "questionable," and arrangements that contain such features are more likely to be subject to further government review. Nevertheless, it is important to remember that even "suspect" arrangements are not necessarily illegal.

---

various concepts is somewhat uncertain at this time pending the issuance of final regulations. For further discussion of this subject, see Linda Baumann, *Navigating the New Safe Harbors to the Anti-Kickback Statute*, THE HEALTH LAW., Feb. 2000, at 8–9.

[78] *E.g.*, Clarification of the Initial OIG Safe Harbor Provisions and Establishment of Additional Safe Harbor Provisions Under the Anti-Kickback Statute, 64 Fed. Reg. 63,518, 63,521 (Nov. 19, 1999); OIG Anti-Kickback Provisions, 56 Fed. Reg. 35,952, 35,954 (July 29, 1991).

[79] 64 Fed. Reg. 63,518, 63,521 (Nov. 19, 1999).

[80] *See* Polk County, Tex. v. Peters, 800 F. Supp. 1451, 1455 (E.D. Tex. 1992).

The OIG has issued Special Fraud Alerts on the following topics:

- Rental of Space in Physician Offices by Persons or Entities to Which Physicians Refer;[81]
- Physician Liability for Certifications in the Provision of Medical Equipment and Supplies and Home Health Services;[82]
- Fraud and Abuse in Nursing Home Arrangements With Hospices;[83]
- Fraud and Abuse in the Provision of Services in Nursing Facilities;[84]
- Home Health Fraud;[85]
- Fraud and Abuse in the Provisions of Medical Supplies to Nursing Facilities;[86]
- Joint Venture Arrangements;[87]
- Routine Waiver of Medicare Part B Copayments and Deductibles;[88]
- Hospital Incentives to Referring Physicians;[89]
- Prescription Drug Marketing Practices;[90] and
- Arrangements for the Provision of Clinical Laboratory Services.[91]

### 4. *Office of Inspector General Advisory Opinions*

In 1996 Congress directed the OIG to establish a process to enable members of the public to request advisory opinions on whether individual transactions might violate the anti-kickback and certain other statutes. Under the OIG's implementing regulations, advisory opinions may address the following issues:

- what constitutes prohibited remuneration;
- whether an arrangement fits an exception or safe harbor;
- what constitutes inducement to reduce or limit services; and

---

[81]*See* 65 Fed. Reg. 9274 (Feb. 24, 2000).

[82]*See* 64 Fed. Reg. 1813 (Jan. 12, 1999).

[83]*See* 63 Fed. Reg. 20,415 (Apr. 24, 1998).

[84]*See* 61 Fed. Reg. 30,623 (June 17, 1996).

[85]*See* 60 Fed. Reg. 40,847 (Aug. 10, 1995).

[86]*Id.*

[87]*See* 59 Fed. Reg. 65,372 (Dec. 19, 1994). Because there are many joint ventures in the health care industry and little available guidance, this Special Fraud Alert is often consulted, and recommends analyzing a joint venture in terms of three key areas:
- the manner in which investors are selected and retained;
- the nature of the business structure (i.e., is it a "shell" or "sham" arrangement); and
- financing and profit distributions.

These Special Fraud Alerts are available at http://oig.hhs.gov/frdalrt/index.htm and in the Appendix materials in F on the disk accompanying this volume.

[88]*Id.*

[89]*Id.*

[90]*Id.*

[91]*Id.*

- whether the activity described would constitute grounds for the imposition of sanctions.[92]

However, the OIG will not address in an advisory opinion what constitutes fair market value or whether a person is a bona fide "employee."[93]

The OIG does not accept requests for advisory opinions on abstract questions. The request must involve an actual, or intended, business arrangement. If the request involves a proposed business arrangement, the requestor must certify that it intends, in good faith, to undertake the arrangement or that it will undertake the arrangement if a favorable advisory opinion is issued.[94] Moreover, advisory opinions are only legally binding with regard to the parties that requested the opinion, although the reasoning of the opinion provides guidance on the OIG's likely approach to similar arrangements in the future. Detailed requirements for the submission of an advisory opinion request are set forth in regulations[95] and in other OIG guidance documents.[96]

Issues that the OIG has addressed in its past advisory opinions include the following:

- ambulance restocking arrangements;[97]
- waivers of deductibles and copayments;[98]
- discounts;[99]
- percentage compensation arrangements;[100]
- joint ventures;[101] and
- beneficiary inducement.[102]

It should be noted that while there is no "de minimis" exception to the anti-kickback statute, several advisory opinions indicate that the OIG may use its discretion not to impose sanctions on certain arrangements for this reason.[103]

---

[92] 42 C.F.R. §1008.5(a).

[93] 42 C.F.R. §1008.5(b).

[94] 42 C.F.R. §1008.38(b).

[95] *See* 42 C.F.R. §§1008.1–1008.40; see Appendix G-1 on the disk accompanying this volume.

[96] *See, e.g.*, Preliminary Checklist for Advisory Opinion Requests, *available at* http://oig.hhs.gov/ advopn/precheck.htm, and in Appendix G-3.

[97] *E.g.*, Advisory Opinion Nos. 97-6, 98-7, 98-13, 98-14, and 00-9. The OIG advisory opinions are available at http://www.org.hhs.gov/advopn/index.htm.

[98] *E.g.*, Advisory Opinion Nos. 98-5, 99-1, 99-6, 99-7, and 00-5.

[99] *E.g.*, Advisory Opinion Nos. 98-2, 98-5, 98-15, 99-2, 99-12, and 99-13.

[100] *E.g.*, Advisory Opinion Nos. 98-1, 98-4, and 98-10.

[101] *E.g.*, Advisory Opinion Nos. 97-5, 98-12, and 98-19.

[102] *E.g.*, Advisory Opinion Nos. 97-4, 98-9, 99-9, 99-11, 00-3, 00-5, 00-7, and 00-10.

[103] *See, e.g.*, Advisory Opinion No. 98-12. The OIG specifically found that there was minimal risk that the return on investment would be a disguised payment for referrals in part because the estimated revenues from Medicare beneficiaries were only 5 percent of the total anticipated revenues of the venture. *See also* Advisory Opinion Nos. 00-5 and 00-11.

The statutory authority for the OIG to issue advisory opinions expired on August 22, 2000. However, its authority has been indefinitely extended under the Medicare, Medicaid, and SCHIP Benefits Improvement and Protection Act of 2000.[104]

### 5. *Other Guidance*

Other available guidance documents from the OIG relating to the anti-kickback statute (and other fraud and abuse laws) include Special Advisory Bulletins, Medicare Advisory Bulletins, Medicare Fraud Alerts, informal advisory letters, and management advisories. Special Advisory Bulletins have been issued on "The Patient Anti-Dumping Statute,"[105] "The Effect of Exclusion From Participation in Federal Health Care Programs,"[106] "Gainsharing Arrangements and CMPs for Hospital Payments to Physicians to Reduce or Limit Services to Beneficiaries,"[107] and "Practices of Business Consultants."[108] Other guidance documents include a Medicare Advisory Bulletin on "Questionable Practices Affecting the Hospice Benefit,"[109] a "National Medicare Fraud Alert on Billing for Services Not Rendered; Upcoding on Billings for Powered Wheelchairs and Delivering Scooters and/or (POVs),"[110] and an OIG Management Advisory Report on "Financial Arrangements Between Hospitals and Hospital-Based Physicians."[111] There also have been numerous informal letters issued by the OIG relating to subjects such as the provision of free items or services, and discounts. Most of these and other federal government documents related to health care fraud and abuse can be located at or through the OIG's Web site: http://www.dhhs.gov/progorg/oig/. For the reader's convenience, many of these documents are contained in Appendix F to this book (on disk).

---

[104] This statute was enacted by the Omnibus Consolidated and Emergency Supplemental Appropriations Act for Fiscal Year 2001, Pub. L. No. 106-554, 114 Stat. 2763.

[105] OIG/HCFA Special Advisory Bulletin on the Patient Anti-Dumping Statute, 64 Fed. Reg. 61,353 (Nov. 10, 1999).

[106] Publication from the OIG Special Advisory Bulletin on the Effect of Exclusion From Participation in Federal Health Care Programs, 64 Fed. Reg. 52,791 (Sept. 30, 1999); see discussion *infra*.

[107] Publication of the OIG Special Advisory Bulletin on Gainsharing Arrangements and CMPs for Hospital Payments to Physicians to Reduce or Limit Services to Beneficiaries, 64 Fed. Reg. 37,985 (July 14, 1999). The subject of gainsharing is addressed in more detail in Chapter 5 (Barry, Legal Issues Surrounding Hospital and Physician Relationships).

[108] OIG Special Advisory Bulletin, Practices of Business Consultants, 66 Fed. Reg. 36,583 (July 12, 2001).

[109] Publication of the Medicare Advisory Bulletin on Hospice Benefits, 60 Fed. Reg. 55,721 (Nov. 2, 1995).

[110] HCFA Medicare Fraud Alert 98-02 (June 9, 1998).

[111] OEI-09-89-00330 (Jan. 1991).

## B. The Stark Law

### 1. The Prohibitions

The Stark law, as amended, prohibits physicians from referring Medicare and Medicaid patients to an entity for the furnishing of certain designated health services (DHS) if the physician (or an immediate family member) has a financial relationship with the entity.[112] In addition, the entity generally may not present, or cause to be presented, a claim for payment for services furnished pursuant to a prohibited referral.[113] While the original law, Stark I, pertained solely to clinical laboratory services, Stark II added 10 other categories of DHS, including inpatient and outpatient hospital services, as well as radiology services; radiation therapy services and supplies; physical therapy services; occupational therapy services; DME and supplies; parenteral and enteral nutrients, equipment, and supplies; prosthetics, orthotics, and prosthetic devices and supplies; home health services; and outpatient prescription drugs.[114]

Violation of the Stark self-referral prohibitions may subject the offending individual or entity to a range of civil sanctions including nonpayment for the relevant services, CMPs, and exclusion from the Medicare and Medicaid programs. There is also a penalty of not more than $100,000 for circumvention schemes.[115]

Final regulations relating to Stark I were issued in 1995.[116] Phase I of the Stark II regulations was finalized in early 2001, to become effective in 2002.[117] There are numerous issues remaining to be addressed when Phase II of the Stark II regulations is published. Due to the importance of the Stark law, and the length and complexity of the Stark II regulations, a subsequent chapter has been devoted to these issues.[118] This chapter presents only a brief overview of this subject.

The Stark law defines a "financial relationship" as an ownership or investment interest in, or a compensation arrangement between the physician (or an immediate family member) and an entity. In turn, an "ownership or investment interest" is defined to encompass "equity, debt, or other means and includes an interest in an entity that holds an ownership or investment interest in any entity providing the designated health service."[119] A "compensation arrangement" is broadly defined as "any arrangement involving any remuneration between a

---

[112] 42 U.S.C. §1395nn(a)(1)(A).

[113] 42 U.S.C. §1395nn(a)(1)(B). The term "referral" has a specific meaning in this context and the definition in both the statute and the regulations should be reviewed.

[114] 42 U.S.C. §1395nn(h)(6).

[115] 42 U.S.C. §1395nn(g).

[116] 42 C.F.R. §§411.350 *et seq.*

[117] 66 Fed. Reg. 856 (Jan. 4, 2001).

[118] See Chapter 2 (Crane, Federal Physician Self-Referral Restrictions).

[119] 42 U.S.C. §1395nn(a).

physician (or an immediate family member of such physician) and an entity . . . other than certain specifically noted kinds of remuneration."[120] Both types of financial relationships can trigger the Stark law whether they are direct or indirect, although the Stark II final regulations have defined indirect ownership and indirect compensation arrangements rather narrowly.[121]

## 2. *The Exceptions*

Unlike the anti-kickback statute, the Stark law is a strict liability statute, and referrals for DHS cannot be made once the statute is implicated, unless the arrangement qualifies for an exception. Some of the statutory exceptions are applicable to ownership arrangements, others are applicable to compensation arrangements, and some apply to both types of financial relationships. Exceptions applicable to ownership arrangements include the following:

- rural providers;
- hospitals in Puerto Rico;
- hospital ownership;[122] and
- ownership or investment in publicly traded securities and mutual funds.[123]

Exceptions applicable to compensation arrangements include the following:

- office space or equipment rentals;
- bona fide employment relationships;
- personal service arrangements;
- remuneration unrelated to the provisions of DHS;
- physician recruitment;
- isolated transactions;
- certain group practice arrangements with a hospital; and
- payments by physicians.[124]

The exceptions for both ownership and compensation arrangements include the following:

- physicians' services;
- in-office ancillary services; and
- prepaid plans.[125]

---

[120] 42 U.S.C. §1395nn(h)(1)(A).

[121] 66 Fed. Reg. 856, 958 (Jan. 4, 2001) (to be codified at 42 C.F.R. §411.354).

[122] 42 U.S.C. §1395nn(d).

[123] 42 U.S.C. §1395nn(c).

[124] 42 U.S.C. §1395nn(e).

[125] 42 U.S.C. §1395nn(b). The exception for in-office ancillary services is very commonly used but has numerous complex requirements. See Chapter 2, Section VIII.C. (Crane, Federal Physician Self-Referral Restrictions) for additional information.

In addition, several new exceptions were published in 2001 as part of Phase I of the Stark II final regulations (the Phase I regulations). These regulations, which do not become effective until 2002, include exceptions applicable to both ownership and compensation relationships for the following:

- clinical laboratory services furnished in an ASC, end-stage renal disease (ESRD) facility, or by a hospice;
- academic medical centers;
- implants in an ASC;
- Erythropoietin and other dialysis-related outpatient prescription drugs furnished in or by an ESRD facility;
- preventive screening tests, immunizations, and vaccines; and
- eyeglasses and contact lenses following cataract surgery.[126]

The Phase I regulations also add several new compensation exceptions:
- nonmonetary compensation up to $300;[127]
- fair market value compensation;[128]
- medical staff incidental benefits;[129]
- risk-sharing arrangements;[130]
- compliance training;[131] and
- indirect compensation arrangements.[132]

Other existing exceptions are substantially revised in these new regulations. A new exception to the statutory prohibition allows payment to certain entities for DHS referrals that would otherwise implicate the Stark law, if the entity did not have actual knowledge of, and did not act in reckless disregard or deliberate ignorance of, the identity of the physician who made the DHS referral, and the claim otherwise complies with all applicable federal laws, rules, and regulations.[133]

Each exception has a number of very specific criteria that must be met, including the requirement in numerous exceptions that compensation be set in advance, be consistent with fair market value,[134] and not be determined in a manner that takes into account the volume or value of any referrals or other business generated between the parties. However, unlike the requirement in several anti-kickback safe harbors, *aggregate* compensation need not be set in advance.

---

[126] 66 Fed. Reg. 856, 959 (Jan. 4, 2001) (to be codified at 42 C.F.R. §411.355).

[127] *Id.* at 961 (to be codified at 42 C.F.R. §411.357).

[128] *Id.*

[129] *Id.* at 962 (to be codified at 42 C.F.R. §411.357).

[130] *Id.*

[131] *Id.*

[132] *Id.*

[133] *Id.* at 958 (to be codified at 42 C.F.R. §411.353).

[134] "Fair market value" is defined in the Stark law, 42 U.S.C. §1395nn(h)(3), and in the Phase I regulations, 42 C.F.R. §411.351.

The preambles to both the Stark II regulations and the anti-kickback safe harbors emphasize that the two statutes overlap in areas but do not necessarily have the same requirements. At the present time, several of the criteria for protection under one statute seem inconsistent with the requirements under the other (e.g., the physician recruitment safe harbor and Stark exception). On the other hand, there are a number of areas of convergence (e.g., where a Stark exception requires compliance with the anti-kickback statute[135] or where the anti-kickback safe harbor incorporates requirements from the Stark law).[136] Many of the other laws and regulations impacting physicians are discussed in a later chapter.[137]

### 3. Advisory Opinions

The Stark law and its implementing regulations are extremely complex. Theoretically, some additional guidance is available from CMS.[138] Advisory opinions regarding whether a business arrangement constitutes a "financial relationship" as defined in the Stark law and whether an exception applies may be submitted to CMS pursuant to 42 C.F.R. §411.370 *et seq*. Thus far, CMS has issued only two advisory opinions although more are expected to be published once the Stark II regulations are finalized.[139]

## C. False Claims Statutes

### 1. The False Claims Act

There are several federal statutes that impose criminal or civil penalties for the submission of false claims to the government or others. These statutes can create substantial exposure for health care providers, suppliers, and others involved in the industry. Perhaps the most well-known of these federal laws is the civil FCA.[140] In recent years, particularly after the 1986 amendments to the statute, government enforcement actions have increased dramatically. Similarly, lawsuits brought by private plaintiffs, known as "relators" or "whistle-

---

[135]*E.g.*, 66 Fed. Reg. 856, 959 (Jan. 4, 2001) (to be codified at 42 C.F.R. §§411.355(e), (g)); *id*. at 961–962 (to be codified at 42 C.F.R. §§411.357(k), (l), (m), (n), and (p)).

[136]*E.g.*, 42 C.F.R. §1001.952(p).

[137]See Chapter 5 (Barry, Legal Issues Surrounding Hospital and Physician Relationships).

[138]*See, e.g.*, advisory opinions relating to physician referrals, 42 C.F.R. §411.370; procedure for submitting a request, 42 C.F.R. §411.372; certification, 42 C.F.R. §411.373; fees for the cost of advisory opinions, 42 C.F.R. §411.375; expert opinions from outside sources, 42 C.F.R. §411.377. See Appendix G-4 for these and other regulations applicable to advisory opinions under the Stark law.

[139]It is not clear whether the advisory opinions will be issued now that Phase I of the Stark II regulations has been finalized or whether CMS will wait until Phase II of the Stark II regulations is published before issuing additional advisory opinions.

[140]31 U.S.C. §§ 3729–3733.

blowers," under the *qui tam* provisions of the FCA have proliferated steadily. For example, in 1987, 33 *qui tam* cases were brought resulting in $355,000 in recoveries. By 1999, 483 *qui tam* suits led to $458 million in recoveries.[141] The reason for this increase is readily apparent because those who bring a successful case under the FCA are entitled to a percentage of the recovery, and thus may themselves be awarded millions of dollars. As a result, the number of FCA cases is likely to continue to increase in the future.

Due to the frequency with which the FCA is invoked and the magnitude of the recoveries that often result, an entire chapter of this book is devoted to it.[142] Consequently, this chapter will provide a brief summary of this statute, as well as some of the other laws prohibiting false claims.

The FCA is a Civil War–era statute originally aimed at corrupt military contractors. Among other acts, the FCA prohibits knowingly submitting, or causing to be submitted, false or fraudulent claims for payment, or knowingly making, using, or causing to be made or used, false records or statements to conceal, avoid, or decrease an obligation to pay or transmit money or property to the government.[143]

Because the FCA is not a criminal statute, it offers the government a more favorable burden of proof (i.e., the civil standard of "preponderance of the evidence" rather than the criminal standard of "beyond a reasonable doubt"). The statute requires specific intent, that is, the defendant must have acted knowingly, or in deliberate ignorance, or with "reckless disregard" for the truth or falsity of the submission. However, the government is not required to prove a specific intent to defraud.[144]

The penalties under the FCA are potentially quite large. The law provides for treble damages, plus an additional penalty of $5,500 to $11,000 for each "false claim" filed.[145] The statute of limitations allows false claims actions to be brought within 6 years after the date of the violation, or within 3 years after the date when material facts are or should have been known by the government, but in no event later than 10 years after the date the violation was committed.[146]

The FCA has been used by the OIG, working with the DOJ, to launch several nationwide projects to recover alleged overpayments

---

[141]Marc S. Raspanti, *Qui Tam* Practice and Procedure 6–7 (2000), presented at American Health Lawyers Association Annual Meeting, *available at* http://www.ahla.org/gsms/gsm_00_ann.pdf.

[142]See Chapter 3 (Salcido, The False Claims Act in Health Care Fraud Prosecutions: Application of the Substantive, *Qui Tam*, and Voluntary Disclosure Provisions).

[143]*See* 31 U.S.C. §3729(a).

[144]31 U.S.C. §3729(b).

[145]The penalties under the FCA were originally $5,000 to $10,000 per claim but were increased pursuant to the 1996 Debt Collection Improvement Act, Pub. L. No. 104-134, 110 Stat. 1321 (1996). *See* 64 Fed. Reg. 47,099 (Aug. 30, 1999). These increased penalties apply to violations occurring after September 29, 1999.

[146]31 U.S.C. §3731(b).

(plus penalties and interest) incurred in connection with specific types of improper claims. As of 2001, there have been five nationwide projects initiated. The Physicians at Teaching Hospitals (PATH) initiative involves reimbursement to physicians at teaching hospitals and focuses on compliance with Medicare rules concerning payment for physician services provided by residents and teaching physicians. This initiative is premised on the requirement under Medicare Part B that a teaching physician can receive a separate payment for a service rendered to a patient only if he or she personally provided the service or was present when the resident furnished the care. If the resident alone performed the service, the government pays through Medicare Part A's graduate medical education and indirect medical education programs. According to the government, if the teaching physician submits a claim for reimbursement for the same service, the physician is submitting a duplicate claim that may lead to liability under the FCA. Under the PATH initiative, as of September 2000, seven institutions had settled with the government for $76 million, and two other institutions were allowed to simply return overpayments to the appropriate carrier. No problems were found after review at four other institutions.[147] The OIG has stated that the PATH initiative is ongoing but will be limited to those institutions that received clear guidance before December 30, 1992, from their Part B carrier as to the applicable Medicare reimbursement requirements.

The "72-Hour Rule" Project involves payments made to hospitals for certain non-physician services provided to patients within 72 hours of their admission to the hospital.[148] Reimbursement for these services is included in Medicare's Prospective Payment System (PPS) payment to the hospital, and billing separately for them can result in a duplicate payment. This project is being coordinated by the U.S. Attorney's Office for the Middle District of Pennsylvania and has resulted in 2,799 settlements as of March 31, 2001.[149]

The Hospital Outpatient Laboratory Project began in Ohio and relates to claims submitted for hematology and automated blood chemistry tests by hospital outpatient labs. Under Medicare guidelines, such labs are required to bill certain groups of tests together using a bundled code. (The payment for the panel is substantially less than payment for each test individually.) The project also involves lab billing for certain tests that were not medically necessary.

---

[147] Six investigations that involved reimbursement for teaching physicians that were not part of the PATH national initiative have also resulted in FCA settlements and CIAs. *See* SEMIANNUAL REPORT APR.–SEPT. 2000, *supra* note 2, at 9.

[148] The Medicare statute stipulates that certain outpatient services performed by a hospital or an entity wholly owned or operated by the hospital, within 72 hours of an inpatient admission, are reimbursed as part of the diagnosis related groups (DRGs) and may not be separately billed. 42 U.S.C. §1385ww(a)(4).

[149] U.S. DEP'T OF HEALTH & HUMAN SERVS., OFFICE OF INSPECTOR GEN., SEMIANNUAL REPORT OCTOBER 1, 2000–MARCH 31, 2001, *available at* http://www.dhhs.gov/progorg/ oig/semann/ index.htm.

The PPS Patient Transfer Project involves payments to hospitals when patients are transferred between two PPS hospitals. Medicare regulations provide that the receiving hospital may receive payment based on the diagnosis related groups (DRGs) while the transferring hospital is to receive a per diem amount based on the patient's length of stay as well as the DRG. Since the OIG has reportedly identified several hundred million dollars in overpayments to transferring hospitals, and had settled with only three hospitals as of September 2000 as reported in the *Semiannual Report*, further enforcement efforts nationwide in connection with this project should be expected.

The fifth national project involves pneumonia upcoding. Under Medicare regulations, hospital stays are reimbursed on the basis of the DRGs assigned, which in turn result from the diagnosis and procedure codes assigned by the hospital. Most pneumonia cases are grouped into one of four DRGs, and one of these DRGs pays substantially more than the others. The OIG believes that a number of hospitals have improperly assigned the higher paying DRG to a number of pneumonia cases and thus is currently investigating pneumonia coding at over 100 hospitals.

The manner in which these national initiatives have been conducted has caused considerable concern in the health care industry as well as in Congress, and there have been allegations that providers are being penalized unfairly and threatened with liability under the FCA for making inadvertent mistakes or billing errors. Various lawsuits have been brought challenging these national projects, but have generally been dismissed on procedural grounds (e.g., as not ripe for review).[150] Efforts to amend the FCA in 1997–1998 did not succeed, but the OIG[151] and the DOJ[152] issued guidelines on the use of the FCA in civil health care matters to help defuse the situation.

The DOJ implemented new procedures with regard to national health care fraud initiatives in the "Holder memorandum," which directs DOJ attorneys not to allege violations of the FCA in connection with a national initiative or otherwise unless there was sufficient legal and factual predicate for alleging that the provider submitted false claims to the government *and* such false claims (or false statements) were submitted with "knowledge" of their falsity as defined in the

---

[150]*See, e.g.*, Greater N.Y. Hosp. Ass'n v. United States, 1999 WL 1021561 (S.D.N.Y. 1999); Association of Am. Med. Colls. v. United States, 34 F. Supp. 2d 1187 (C.D. Cal. 1998); New Jersey Hosp. Ass'n v. United States, 23 F. Supp. 2d 497 (D.N.J. 1998). *But see* Ohio Hosp. Ass'n v. Shalala, 978 F. Supp. 735 (N.D. Ohio 1997), *aff'd in part, rev'd in part*, 201 F.3d 418 (6th Cir. 1999), *cert. denied*, 121 S. Ct. 762 (2001). This case was ultimately settled.

[151]Memorandum From June Gibbs Brown, to Deputy Inspector General for Investigations *et al.*, re National Project Protocols–Best Practice Guidelines, (June 3, 1998).

[152]Memorandum From Eric H. Holder, Jr., to All United States Attorneys *et al.*, re Guidance on the Use of the False Claims Act in Civil Health Care Matters (June 3, 1998) [hereinafter Holder memorandum]; for text of the Holder Memorandum, see Appendix C-2.

FCA.[153] When determining whether false claims exist, DOJ attorneys are to do the following:

- examine relevant statutory and regulatory provisions and interpretive guidance;
- verify the data and other evidence; and
- conduct necessary investigative steps.[154]

In order to determine whether the provider "knowingly" submitted false claims, DOJ attorneys are directed to consider numerous factors, including:

- whether the provider had actual or constructive notice of the rule or policy on which the case is based;
- whether it is reasonable to conclude, under the circumstances, that the provider understood the rule or policy;[155]
- the pervasiveness and magnitude of the false claims (e.g., do they support an inference that they resulted from deliberate ignorance or intentional or reckless conduct?);
- compliance measures implemented by the provider including the existence of and adherence to a compliance program and steps taken to comply with the particular billing rules at issue;
- past remedial efforts;
- prior guidance requested from or provided by the program agency (e.g., did the provider furnish all material information when requesting guidance and did it reasonably rely on the guidance provided?); and
- whether the provider had prior notice of similar billing concerns.[156]

The Holder memorandum also directs DOJ attorneys to use "contact letters" to initiate a discussion of the issues before making a demand for payment. Moreover, in determining how to respond to a particular situation, they are to consider issues such as the provider's ability to pay, the impact of an enforcement action on the community (i.e., access to adequate health care), minimizing burdens imposed on providers during the investigation (which might entail accepting results from a sample audit rather than insisting on a complete audit), and provider cooperation.[157]

The OIG subsequently has issued numerous letters offering assurances that health care providers, practitioners, and suppliers will not be subject to the FCA (or the CMP prohibitions) for billing

---

[153] Holder memorandum, at 2.

[154] *Id.*

[155] This is a particularly important consideration in light of the well-known ambiguity of numerous Medicare regulations.

[156] Holder memorandum, at 3–4.

[157] *Id.* at 5–6.

errors, honest mistakes, or negligence. According to these letters, law enforcement efforts are to focus on improper claims made intentionally, with reckless disregard for the truth or with deliberate ignorance of the truth. Moreover, "in almost all cases, reckless disregard or intentional filing of false claims is proved by establishing a pattern of conduct."[158] Nevertheless, despite the complexity of Medicare laws and regulations, the lack of written guidance on many issues, and the frequent inability to obtain oral guidance from the government, it can be very difficult, as a practical matter, to convince the government that certain practices did result from inadvertence or honest mistake. Toward this end, if a provider is able to obtain oral guidance from the government or one of its agents, it is essential that such advice be documented. While some government employees or agents may be reluctant to provide "official" advice, a provider may be able to obtain a written response if a written inquiry is submitted. While such a response does not have the force of law, it can help document the provider's (or other entity's) intention to comply with the law, thus undercutting any claim of improper intent in violation of the FCA or other statutes with similar scienter requirements.

In addition to the national projects described above, there have been a very wide range of false claims prosecuted under the FCA, ranging from cases involving billing for items or services not rendered to quality of care to the waiver of coinsurance or deductibles. There also continue to be ongoing efforts to use the FCA in connection with violations of other laws such as the anti-kickback statute or the Stark law.[159]

### 2. Other Statutes Prohibiting False Claims

Various other statutes may also be invoked by the government in connection with false claims, including several provisions imposing criminal liability. Under Section 1128B of the Social Security Act, various types of false statements, made knowingly and willfully, are criminal offenses. For example, it is a felony to knowingly and willfully make, or cause to be made, a false statement of material fact in any application for payment or for use in determining the right to such payment under a federal health care program.[160] Presenting, or causing to be presented, a claim for a physician's services for payment under a federal health care program knowing that the individual furnishing the services was not licensed as a physician is also a felony

---

[158] Letters From June Gibbs Brown, Inspector General, to Marilou King, Executive Vice President, American Health Lawyers Ass'n, and to William Coughlan, President and Chief Executive Officer, National Ass'n for Medical Equipment Services (Aug. 5, 1998).

[159] *See, e.g.,* United States v. McLaren Reg'l Med. Ctr., No. 97-CV-72992 (E.D. Mich. filed Sept. 26, 2000); United States *ex rel.* Pogue v. American Healthcorp., 914 F. Supp. 1507 (M.D. Tenn. 1996); United States *ex rel.* James M. Thompson v. Columbia/HCA Healthcare Corp., 938 F. Supp. 399 (S.D.Tex. 1996), *aff'd in part, vacated in part,* 125 F.3d 899 (5th Cir. 1997).

[160] 42 U.S.C. §§1320a-7b(a)(1), (2).

under this statute.[161] There is also criminal liability for concealing or failing to disclose an event affecting an individual's initial or continued right to a benefit or payment if done with intent to fraudulently secure the benefit or payment, when no such benefit or payment is authorized or in a greater amount than is due.[162] Making, inducing, or seeking to induce the making of any false statement of a material fact regarding the conditions or operation of certain institutions, facilities, or entities in order that they may qualify for certification or recertification, including a hospital, skilled nursing facility, nursing facility, or home health agency, or with respect to information required under 42 U.S.C. Section 1320a-3a, also is a felony.[163]

The HIPAA added several additional criminal penalties for the use of false statements or false pretenses in connection with any health care benefit program, thus making these prohibitions applicable to statements made to private payers as well as to federal health care programs.[164]

A criminal false claims statute provides for fines and imprisonment of up to 5 years for filing fraudulent claims with the government, and up to 10 years for conspiring to file fraudulent claims.[165] Various other general criminal prohibitions also may be used in connection with false or fraudulent representations made in the health care context, including provisions relating to mail or wire fraud,[166] RICO,[167] money laundering,[168] conspiracy to defraud,[169] and submission of fictitious or fraudulent claims.[170] Common law causes of action and state statutes may also be used in connection with a false claims case.

## D. Civil Monetary Penalties

### 1. *The Prohibitions*

The OIG has the authority to impose CMPs on any person (including an organization or other entity, but excluding a beneficiary) who knowingly presents, or causes to be presented, to a state or federal government employee or agent certain false or improper claims.[171] Section 1128A of the Social Security Act authorizes imposition of CMPs up to

---

[161] 42 U.S.C. §1320a-7b(a)(5).

[162] 42 U.S.C. §1320a-7b(a)(3).

[163] 42 U.S.C. §1320a-7b(c).

[164] *See* 18 U.S.C. §§1347 and 1035, and discussion *infra* Section II.3.F.

[165] *See* 18 U.S.C. §286.

[166] 18 U.S.C. §§1341, 1343.

[167] 18 U.S.C. §§1961 *et seq.*

[168] 18 U.S.C. §§1956–57.

[169] 18 U.S.C. §§286, 371.

[170] 18 U.S.C. §287.

[171] *See* 42 U.S.C. §1320a-7a(a). A "beneficiary" is defined as an individual eligible to receive items or services for which payment may be made under a federal health care program, but excludes a provider, supplier, or practitioner. 42 U.S.C. §1320a-7a(i)(5).

$10,000 per item or service in most cases, and in certain cases up to $50,000 per act, as well as treble damages.[172]

The basic prohibitions to which the CMPs apply include knowingly filing claims for:

- services that were not provided as claimed (e.g., upcoding);
- medical or other items or services that are fraudulent;
- services of a physician or services provided "incident to" a physician's service if the physician:
  —was not licensed as a physician;
  —obtained his or her license through misrepresentation; or
  —falsely represented to the patient at the time the service was furnished that he or she was certified by a medical specialty board;
- medical or other items or services furnished during a time in which the person was excluded from participation in the program under which the claim was made; or
- a pattern of medical or other items or services that a person knows or should know are not medically necessary.[173]

Additional grounds for imposition of CMPs include the following:
- knowingly presenting or causing to be presented claims in violation of certain assignment agreements or participating provider agreements;[174]
- knowingly giving or causing to be given false or misleading information about Medicare coverage of inpatient hospital services that could reasonably be expected to influence the decision when to discharge a patient from the hospital;[175]
- individuals excluded from Medicare or Medicaid and who
  —retain a direct or indirect ownership or control interest in an entity participating in these programs and know or should know of the action constituting the basis for exclusion; or
  —are officers or managing employees of such an entity;[176]
- offering to transfer or transferring remuneration to a beneficiary to influence such beneficiary to order or receive from a particular provider, or supplier, items or services that may be reimbursed, in whole or in part, under Medicare or Medicaid;[177]

---

[172] 42 U.S.C. §1320a-7a(a). The OIG considers various factors when determining the CMP amount to impose. *See* 42 C.F.R. §1003.106. Persons who violate certain CMPs may also be subject to exclusion from federal health care programs. See discussion, *infra*.

[173] 42 U.S.C. §1320a-7a(a)(1).

[174] 42 U.S.C. §1320a-7a(a)(2).

[175] 42 U.S.C. §1320a-7a(a)(3). The OIG's regulations provide for CMPs of up to $15,000 for each person with respect to whom false information was provided. 42 C.F.R. §1003.103(b).

[176] 42 U.S.C. §1320a-7a(a)(4).

[177] 42 U.S.C. §1320a-7a(a)(5).

- arranging or contracting with an individual or entity that the person knows, or should know, is excluded from participating in federal health care programs[178] for the provision of items or services that may be reimbursed under such programs;[179]
- direct or indirect payment as an inducement by certain hospitals to physicians to limit or reduce services to Medicare or Medicaid beneficiaries who are under the direct care of the physician;[180]
- false certifications by physicians of a patient's eligibility for home health services;[181]
- violations of the anti-kickback statute;[182] or
- violations of the Stark self-referral prohibitions.[183]

Intent is an important element in CMP cases. The statute creates liability for actions taken "knowingly" and/or where the individual "knows or should know" of the falsity of the claim. "Should know" is defined to mean that the individual acts in deliberate ignorance, or reckless disregard, of the truth or falsity of the information. No proof of specific intent to defraud is required.[184] Moreover, principals may incur CMP liability or exclusion as a result of the actions of their agents.[185]

The OIG's implementing regulations (contained in Appendix D-4) largely reiterate the above cited statutory bases for CMPs, and list a number of additional conditions under which CMPs may be imposed. They include the following:

- failure to report
  —payments made under insurance policies, self-insurance, or otherwise, for the benefit of a health care practitioner in settlement or satisfaction of a medical malpractice claim, and as required by law or regulation; or

---

[178]"Federal health care programs" are defined as "any plan or program that provides health benefits, whether directly, though insurance, or otherwise, which is funded directly, in whole or in part, by the United States Government" (excluding the Federal Employees Health Benefits Program). 42 U.S.C. §1320a-7b(f). Medicare, Medicaid, Tricare, and veterans' programs are the most significant federal health care programs.

[179]42 U.S.C. §1320a-7a(a)(6).

[180]42 U.S.C. §1320a-7a(b)(1). The statute initially prescribed a CMP of $2,000 per occurrence. This penalty was increased to $10,000 for acts occurring on or after January 1, 1997, by Pub. L. No. 104-191. 42 C.F.R. §1003.103(a).

[181]42 U.S.C. §1320a-7a(b)(3).

[182]42 U.S.C. §1320a-7a(a)(7).

[183]42 C.F.R. §1003.102(a)(5).

[184]42 U.S.C. §1320a-7a(i)(7). This is the same intent requirement applicable under the FCA. *See* 31 U.S.C. §3729.

[185]42 U.S.C. §1320a-7a(*l*).

—other adverse actions required to be reported to the Healthcare Integrity and Protection Data Bank;[186]
- improper use or disclosure of, or access to, information reported
  in accordance with the requirements for the National Practitioner Data Bank;[187]
- use of letters, symbols, or emblems that falsely imply that an
  advertisement, solicitation, or other item was authorized,
  approved or endorsed by HHS or CMS;[188]
- contracting organizations that fail to comply with certain
  requirements;[189]
- failure to refund, on a timely basis, amounts collected for DHS
  provided as the result of a referral prohibited under the Stark
  law or other attempts to circumvent the Stark law;[190] and
- certain Emergency Medical Treatment and Active Labor Act
  (EMTALA) violations.[191]

## 2. Beneficiary Inducement

Many arrangements could potentially implicate this CMP; however, the law and recent regulations have clarified the scope of the
restriction, to a certain extent. Remuneration under this CMP includes
the transfer of items or services for free or other than fair market value
and the waiver of coinsurance and deductible amounts except under
certain, narrowly defined circumstances. Such copayment waivers are
not included in the definition of remuneration if

- they are not offered as part of any advertisement or solicitation;
- the person does not routinely waive coinsurance and deductible
  amounts; and
- the person
  —waives the coinsurance and deductible amounts after deter-
    mining in good faith that an individual is in financial need; or
  —fails to collect the coinsurance and deductible after making
    reasonable collection efforts.[192]

---

[186] 42 C.F.R. §1003.102(b)(5). The CMP for this violation has been increased to
$11,000, pursuant to the Federal Civil Monetary Penalty Inflation Adjustment Act of
1990. 42 C.F.R. §1003.103(c), n.1.

[187] 42 C.F.R. §1003.102(b)(6).

[188] 42 C.F.R. §1002.103(b)(7). Under certain circumstances, a CMP may be
imposed despite the use of a disclaimer of affiliation with the federal government or
HHS or its programs. *See* 42 C.F.R. §1003.102(b)(7)(i).

[189] 42 C.F.R. §1003.102(b)(8).

[190] *See* 42 C.F.R. §1003.102(b)(9)–(10).

[191] *See* 42 C.F.R. §1003.102(c). The penalties for these types of violations are set
forth at 42 C.F.R. §1003.103(e). Also note that under the Program Fraud Civil Remedies Act, 31 U.S.C. §3802, CMPs may be imposed for making, presenting, or submitting a claim that the person knows, or has reason to know is false, fictitious, or
fraudulent.

[192] 42 U.S.C. §1320a-7a(i)(6)(A).

In addition, remuneration generally does not include (1) practices protected by the exceptions or safe harbors to the anti-kickback statute, (2) certain differentials in coinsurance and deductible amounts as part of a benefits plan design, (3) incentives given to individuals to promote the delivery of preventive care, and (4) reductions in the copayment amount for certain outpatient services for the aged and disabled (OPD services).[193]

"Preventive" care is defined in regulations as a prenatal service or post-natal well-baby visit or a specific clinical service described in the current U.S. Preventive Services Task Force's Guide to Clinical Preventive Services that is reimbursable in whole or in part by Medicare or Medicaid.[194] Moreover, the regulations clarify that permissible preventive care incentives cannot be tied (directly or indirectly) to the provision of other services reimbursed, even in part, by Medicare or Medicaid. Permissible incentives may include the provision of preventive care itself but may not include (1) cash or instruments convertible to cash; or (2) an incentive whose value is disproportionately large in relation to the preventive care service (e.g., the value of the service itself or the future health care costs reasonably expected to be avoided as a result of the preventive care).[195]

The preamble to the regulations specifically states that preventive care involves services provided to *asymptomatic* individuals and does not apply to tertiary preventive care (i.e., preventive care that is part of the treatment and management of persons with existing clinical illnesses).[196] The regulations decline to expand this exception to cover disease management programs or other services designed to prevent the deterioration of or complications from an acute or chronic illness. Moreover, there cannot be any tie between the provision of an exempt, covered preventive care service and a nonpreventive covered service.[197] The regulations do provide considerable flexibility with regard to the type and value of permissible preventive care exceptions, noting that blood sugar screening, cholesterol tests, as well as gift certificates to encourage beneficiaries to obtain preventive care may be permissible. Moreover, despite their continuing concern with routine copayment waivers, the OIG specifically allows providers to waive copayments as an incentive to promote the delivery of preventive care.[198] In addition, preventive care incentives do not have to be of nominal value or offered to all similarly situated individuals in a given community.[199]

---

[193] 42 U.S.C. §§1320a-7a(i)(6)(B)–(D). "Covered OPD services" are defined at 42 U.S.C. §1395*l*(t)(1)(B).

[194] 42 C.F.R. §1003.101.

[195] *Id.*

[196] 65 Fed. Reg. 24,400, 24,408 (Apr. 26, 2000).

[197] *Id.*

[198] *Id.* at 24,409.

[199] *Id.* at 24,410.

Items of nominal value are not prohibited under this CMP because their value is minimal and unlikely to influence a beneficiary's choice of provider. The OIG interprets "nominal" to be no more than $10 per item or $50 in the aggregate per year.[200] Finally, the OIG notes that incentives that are not advertised or otherwise disclosed to a beneficiary before he or she selects a provider do not come within the statutory proscription because the beneficiary is not being influenced in his or her choice of provider.[201]

There are some areas of similarity between the CMPs and the anti-kickback statute. For example, the OIG will use the advisory opinion process to respond to inquiries as to what constitutes prohibited remuneration under the anti-kickback statute as well as to whether an arrangement constitutes grounds for sanctions under the CMP (or exclusion) provisions.[202] Numerous advisory opinions have specifically addressed the CMP prohibiting beneficiary inducement. Moreover, in addition to the safe harbors for the anti-kickback statute, the OIG recently proposed a new safe harbor from the beneficiary-inducement CMP to provide protection for independent dialysis facilities that pay premiums for Supplementary Medical Insurance (Medicare Part B) or Medicare Supplemental Health Insurance policies (Medigap) for financially needy Medicare beneficiaries with ESRD.[203]

## E. Exclusion Authorities

One of the most severe sanctions results from the OIG's ability to exclude individuals and entities from participation in federal health care programs, including Medicare and Medicaid.[204] Exclusion is mandatory in some cases, and permissive in others, left to the OIG's discretion. The potential impact of exclusion, which can be a financial death sentence for a provider, provides significant leverage to the OIG in settlement negotiations.

### 1. Mandatory Exclusion

The law mandates exclusion from federal health care programs of individuals or entities convicted of the following offenses:

- a criminal offense related to the delivery of an item or service under Medicare or Medicaid;
- a criminal offense related to the neglect or abuse of a patient in connection with the delivery of a health care item or service;

---

[200] *Id.* at 24,411.

[201] *Id.* at 24,409.

[202] *See* 42 C.F.R. §1008.5(a).

[203] *See generally* 65 Fed. Reg. 25,460 (May 2, 2000).

[204] There are various other sanctions available to the government, including asset freezes and payment suspensions. For text of the exclusion statute and regulations, as well as a table of exclusion authorities, see Appendix D-3, Appendix D-5, and Appendix D-2.

- any felony relating to fraud, theft, embezzlement, breach of fiduciary responsibility, or other financial misconduct under federal or state law relating to health care fraud for an offense that occurred after August 21, 1996; and
- any felony conviction under federal or state law occurring after August 21, 1996, relating to the unlawful manufacture, distribution, prescription, or dispensing of a controlled substance.[205]

Mandatory exclusion is for a minimum 5-year term,[206] which increases to 10 years for repeat convictions that occur after August 5, 1997.[207] Exclusion can become permanent for multiple convictions.[208] There are limited exceptions to mandatory exclusions for sole community health care providers where a state program requests an exception.[209]

"Conviction" includes (1) judgments entered by state, federal, or local courts (regardless of whether an appeal is pending or the records have been expunged); (2) findings of guilt by state, federal, or local courts; (3) pleas of guilty or nolo contendere accepted by the courts; or (4) when the individual or entity is participating in a first offender or similar program where judgment of convictions has been withheld.[210]

## 2. Permissive Exclusion

The OIG has discretionary or "permissive" authority to exclude individuals and entities on the basis of the following:

- convictions for offenses under federal or state law occurring after HIPAA's enactment (August 21, 1996) for:
  —criminal misdemeanors related to health care program fraud, theft, embezzlement, breach of fiduciary responsibility, other financial misconduct, or related to other programs operated or financed in whole or in part by a state, federal, or local government agency;
  —obstruction of justice in health care investigations; and
  —certain misdemeanors related to the unlawful manufacture, distribution, prescription, or dispensing of controlled substances;
- revocation or suspension of an individual or entity's license to provide health care, including surrender of a license pending a disciplinary hearing for reasons relating to the individual's professional competence, performance, or financial integrity;
- suspension or exclusion under any federal program involving the provision of health care, or state health care program, for

---

[205] 42 U.S.C. §1320a-7(a). For text of the exclusion statute, see Appendix D-3.

[206] 42 U.S.C. §1320a-7(c)(3)(B).

[207] 42 U.S.C. §1320a-7(c)(3)(G)(i).

[208] 42 U.S.C. §1320a-7(c)(3)(G)(ii).

[209] 42 U.S.C. §1320a-7(c)(3)(B).

[210] 42 U.S.C. §1320a-7(i).

reasons related to the individual or entity's competence, performance, or financial integrity;

- submission of claims for items or services furnished substantially in excess of the individual or entity's usual charges, without good cause; provision of unnecessary or substandard services; failure of a medical plan to offer necessary services required by law or contract that adversely affects Medicare or Medicaid beneficiaries; or failure of an entity to provide medically necessary items and services required for individuals covered under a risk-sharing contract, if the failure adversely affected those individuals;
- activities involving fraud or kickbacks;[211]
- any entity controlled by a person convicted of various program-related abuses, or who has been excluded from Medicare or Medicaid or had a CMP imposed against him or her;[212]
- individuals controlling a sanctioned entity (i.e., having a direct or indirect ownership or control interest in a sanctioned entity) in which the person knew or should have known of the action constituting the basis for the conviction or exclusion, or being an officer or managing employee of such an entity;[213]
- any entity's failure to disclose certain required information;
- a disclosing entity's failure to supply requested information on ownership of certain subcontractors or failure to supply information as to significant business transactions between the entity and any wholly owned supplier, or between the entity and any subcontractor, for the 5-year period ending on the date of the request;
- failure to supply certain payment information;
- failure to grant immediate access to a facility, records, or documents on reasonable request by the HHS, OIG, a state agency, or a state Medicaid Fraud Control Unit;
- failure by a hospital to take corrective action required by HHS with regard to improper hospital admission practices; and
- default on education loans or scholarship obligations in connection with health professions education made or secured, in whole or in part, by HHS.[214]

---

[211] 42 U.S.C. §1320a-7(b).

[212] 42 U.S.C. §1320a-7(b)(8). A sanctioned individual is deemed to "control" an entity where the individual has a direct or indirect ownership or control interest of 5 percent or more in the entity, or is an officer, director, agent, or managing employee. The prohibition also applies if such a person held an ownership interest, but transferred it to an immediate family member or household member in anticipation of, or following, a conviction, assessment, or exclusion. *Id.*

[213] 42 U.S.C. §1320a-7(b)(15)(A). A "sanctioned entity" is one that has been convicted of various program-related abuses or has been excluded from Medicare or Medicaid participation. 42 U.S.C. §1320a-7(b)(15)(B).

[214] 42 U.S.C. §1320a-7(b).

Initially, the OIG took the position that it would only apply the exclusion authority to so-called "direct providers" of medical items and services (e.g., physicians and pharmacists). However, on September 2, 1998, the OIG published a final rule that reversed this policy, extending exclusion authority to "indirect providers" of services, such as manufacturers of drugs, medical devices, and other medical supplies.[215] The exclusion would apply to all of a manufacturer's items and services, even those unrelated to the item or practice that formed the basis for the exclusion.[216] However, OIG stated in the preamble to these regulations that it intended to exercise its sanction authority "prudently" and would entertain requests for waivers in certain cases.[217]

### 3. Special Advisory Bulletin

The OIG interpreted its exclusion authority even more expansively in the Special Advisory Bulletin on The Effect of Exclusion From Participation in Federal Health Care Programs (Exclusion Special Advisory Bulletin), particularly with regard to the CMP that prohibits arranging or contracting with an individual or entity that the person knows or should know is excluded from participation in federal health care programs.[218] The Exclusion Special Advisory Bulletin asserts that no federal program funds can be used to cover an excluded individual's salary, expenses, or fringe benefits, regardless of whether they provide direct patient care. Moreover, the prohibition can extend to payment for administrative and management services not directly related to patient care if they are a necessary component of providing items and services to federal health care program beneficiaries. Therefore, although an excluded individual can provide items and services to non-federal health care program beneficiaries, such excluded individuals can only be paid with private funds or other nonfederal sources. As a result, according to the OIG, an excluded individual or entity is effectively precluded from being employed by, or under contract with, *any* practitioner, provider, or supplier to furnish *any* items or services reimbursed by a federal health care program.

The OIG provides several examples of the types of items and services that can subject an employer or contractor to possible CMP liability if they are furnished by excluded parties, including the following:

- services performed for program beneficiaries by excluded individuals who sell, deliver, or refill orders for medical devices or equipment reimbursed by a federal health care program;

---

[215] 63 Fed. Reg. 46,676, 46,677 (Sept. 2, 1998) (to be codified at 42 C.F.R. pts. 1000, 1001, 1002, 1005). The final rule became effective October 2, 1998. Note that the HHS appropriations bill for fiscal 1999 directs the OIG to reexamine this issue. Omnibus Consolidated and Emergency Appropriations Act, 1999, Pub. L. No. 105-277, 112 Stat. 2681 (1998).

[216] See definition of "exclusion" at 42 C.F.R. §1001.2.

[217] 63 Fed. Reg. 46,676, 46,679 (Sept. 2, 1998).

[218] 42 U.S.C. §1320a-7a(a)(6). The Exclusion Special Advisory Bulletin is contained in Appendix F-14, on the disk accompanying this volume.

- services performed by an excluded administrator, billing agent, accountant, or claims processor that are related to and reimbursed, directly or indirectly, by a federal health care program; and
- items or equipment sold by an excluded manufacturer or supplier, used in the care of beneficiaries and reimbursed, directly or indirectly, by a federal health care program.

The prohibition applies regardless of whether federal reimbursement is based on itemized claims, cost reports, fee schedules, or PPS; and the prohibition applies even when payment is made to an individual or entity that is not excluded. Moreover, items and services furnished at the medical direction or prescription of an excluded physician are not reimbursable when the individual or entity furnishing the services knew or should have known of the exclusion. Toward this end, the OIG asserts that providers and contracting entities have an affirmative duty to check program exclusion status before entering into arrangements with individuals or entities.[219] As a practical matter, the OIG claims that these sanctions will likely prevent any entity receiving federal health care program funds, directly or indirectly, from hiring an excluded individual in any capacity.

Individuals sanctioned under the CMP and exclusion authorities may request a hearing before an administrative law judge (ALJ)[220] and may appeal to the Departmental Appeals Board.[221] The ALJ may hold a hearing, issue subpoenas, review evidence, and examine witnesses. The parties have the right to counsel, to conduct discovery as permitted, and to submit written briefs.[222] The ALJ may modify the sanction,[223] but may not review the OIG's exercise of discretion to impose permissive exclusion, or a CMP.[224]

## F. Federal All-Payer Statutes

There are several statutory provisions that apply broadly to all payers, not just federal health care programs. These include, by way of example, prohibitions on knowingly and willfully falsifying or concealing material facts or making materially false statements in matters involving a health care benefit program.[225] There is also a federal statute

---

[219] The OIG recommends periodically checking its Web site for the list of excluded individuals/entities with regard to both prospective and current employees and contractors (http://oig.hhs.gov). However, there may be numerous practical difficulties inherent in using the list to identify all excluded individuals and organizations.

[220] *See* 42 C.F.R. §§1005.2–1005.19. The regulations contain detailed rules concerning these proceedings.

[221] The Departmental Appeals Board may decline to review the case. 42 C.F.R. §1005.21(g).

[222] 42 C.F.R. §1005.3.

[223] 42 C.F.R. §10005.20.

[224] 42 C.F.R. §1005.4.

[225] 18 U.S.C. §1035. For text of §1035, see Appendix E-1.

making it a crime to knowingly and willfully execute, or attempt to execute, a scheme or artifice to defraud any health care benefit program, or obtain through false representations or pretenses any money or property owned or under the custody or control of any health care benefit program.[226] "Health care benefit program" is defined as any public or private plan or contract, affecting commerce, under which any medical benefit, item, or service is provided to any individual, and includes any individual or entity who is providing a medical benefit, item, or service for which payment may be made under the plan or contract.[227] Violation of the statute can lead to a fine or imprisonment for up to 10 years. However, if the violation results in serious bodily injury, the violator may be fined and/or imprisoned up to 20 years. If the violation results in death, the violator may be imprisoned for any number of years, or for life.[228]

It is particularly important to note that although various federal statutes specifically apply to federal health care programs, attempts to "carve out" Medicare or Medicaid beneficiaries from an arrangement may be viewed with suspicion by the OIG[229] and result in increased scrutiny.

## III. State Laws

Most states have fraud and abuse prohibitions, some of which are quite similar to their federal counterparts. However, there can be diverse variations, so any applicable state laws should be closely examined. Generally, states are likely to have an anti-kickback statute(s) and a law restricting physician self-referrals. Many states also have fee-splitting prohibitions, commercial bribery statutes, deceptive trade practice laws, and/or consumer protection statutes that may apply in the health care context. Some states have legislation prohibiting providers from waiving coinsurance or deductible amounts while case law in other states indicates that such practices would constitute fraud under state law. A number of states have recently enacted laws similar to the federal FCA, although some of the state versions are more stringent than their federal counterpart.[230] Finally, there are state insurance fraud statutes that may also be used to prosecute certain types of health care fraud.

Some state laws may be limited to fraud and abuse affecting the Medicaid program, however, many state fraud and abuse laws apply to all payers. Thus, transactions that may be acceptable under federal law because Medicare and Medicaid beneficiaries are not affected by the arrangements might still violate state law. Even state laws that

---

[226] 18 U.S.C. §1347. For text of §1347, see Appendix E-2.

[227] 18 U.S.C. §24. For text of §24, see Appendix E-3.

[228] 18 U.S.C. §1347.

[229] *See, e.g.,* Advisory Opinion Nos. 98-15 and 00-1, *available at* http://oig.hhs.gov/advopn/index.htm.

[230] *E.g.,* 2000 Mass. Legis. Service 159, §18 (West).

are generally based on their federal counterparts can vary in subtle, but significant ways. Unlike the federal Stark law, which applies only to physicians, state self-referral prohibitions may apply to other types of health care practitioners.[231] Similarly, state self-referral laws may apply to different types of services, not the 11 DHS listed under federal law.[232] Some state self-referral prohibitions apply only to ownership, but not to compensation relationships. Self-referral prohibitions are often extended to family members of physicians, but the type of "family member" implicated by the statute can vary. Violations can be subject to a variety of penalties, including professional discipline and/or CMPs. In other cases, there is no violation of the self-referral prohibition as long as the affected physician discloses his or her financial relationship as required by the applicable law.[233]

Another major difference between federal and state law may involve the anti-kickback prohibitions. The federal anti-kickback statute is an intent-based statute, and there can be no violation absent knowing and willful action. In contrast, numerous state laws do not contain such a qualification within the language of the statute. Many state anti-kickback laws also contain far fewer exceptions or safe harbors. There may be case law, attorney general opinions, or regulatory board decisions providing further guidance on the interpretation of these seemingly inflexible laws, but many times no further guidance is available and it becomes necessary to analyze the particular facts at issue very carefully within the context of the statutory language.

Fee-splitting statutes often prohibit kickbacks or similar remuneration arrangements. Some states are interpreting these laws broadly to prohibit physicians from paying a percentage of their revenues to a management company, particularly when the management company will be performing any type of marketing activity.[234]

State deceptive trade practices and consumer protection statutes often can be used both by the government and private citizens to challenge certain arrangements involving self-referrals and kickbacks. Like the *qui tam* provisions of the federal FCA, private litigants who prevail in cases brought under these statutes may be eligible to receive large damage awards. Similarly, some state statutes prohibit filing false claims with private insurers and may further provide insurance companies with a private right of action to recover compensatory damages or penalties.[235] In some states the waiver of copayment amounts may be

---

[231] *E.g.*, MD. CODE ANN., HEALTH OCC. §1-301(g) (2000).

[232] FLA. STAT. ANN. §456.053 (West 2000); N.Y. PUB. HEALTH LAW §238-a(1) (McKinney 2000); VA. CODE ANN. §54.1-2410 *et seq.* (Michie 2000).

[233] *E.g.*, ARIZ. REV. STAT. ANN. §32-1401(25)(ff) (West 2000); HAW. REV. STAT. ANN. §431:10C-308.7(c) (Michie 2000).

[234] *E.g.*, FLA. STAT. ANN. §458.331(l)(i), §817.505 (West 2000). *See also In re* Petition for Declaratory Statement of Magan L. Bakarania, M.D., 20 FALR 395 (Fla. Bd. of Med. 1997). *Cf. In re* Petition for Declaratory Statement of Rew, Rogers & Silver, M.D.'s, P.A., 21 FALR 4139 (Fla. Bd. of Med. 1999) (distinguishing *Bakarania*).

[235] 18 PA. CONS. STAT. ANN. §4117(g) (West 2000).

a false claim under regulations[236] or case law.[237] In some cases, the result has depended on the language of the insurance policy at issue.[238]

Because of the wide variation among state laws, it is essential to review all applicable provisions. Particularly if an arrangement involves more than one state's law, a helpful starting point may be the CMS Web site,[239] which provides a listing of many state fraud and abuse laws. Because there often is little case law or other guidance available in many jurisdictions, it may be advisable to contact the appropriate regulatory boards for further guidance. Some states also have mechanisms for obtaining formal advisory opinions on particular issues. While some states have been actively enforcing their fraud and abuse laws, there has been less evidence of enforcement in other states. However, state enforcement activities will likely increase due to increased resources, collaboration, and encouragement being provided by the federal government.

## IV. OTHER RESOURCES

There are a number of other documents published by the federal government that may be helpful to the practitioner trying to eliminate, or at least minimize, his or her client's exposure. Most of these can be accessed through the OIG's Web site.[240]

### A. Compliance Program Guidance

The OIG has published various compliance program guidance documents for hospitals,[241] clinical laboratories,[242] DME suppliers,[243] third-party medical billing companies,[244] hospices,[245] nursing facilities,[246] Medicare+Choice organizations,[247] individual and small group physician practices,[248] and home health agencies.[249]

---

[236] *See* FLA. ADMIN. CODE ANN. r. 4-153.003 (2000).

[237] Feiler v. New Jersey Dental Ass'n, 489 A.2d 1161 (N.J. Super. Ct. App. Div.), *cert. denied*, 491 A.2d 673 (1984).

[238] Kennedy v. Connecticut Gen. Life Ins. Co., 924 F.2d 698 (7th Cir. 1991).

[239] The CMS Web site relating to state law is: http://www.hcfa.gov/medicaid/fraud/mfs/default.asp.

[240] The OIG Web site is: http://oig.hhs.gov.

[241] *See* 63 Fed. Reg. 8987 (Feb. 23, 1998). For text of this guidance, see Appendix I-1.

[242] *See* 63 Fed. Reg. 163 (Aug. 24, 1998).

[243] *See* 64 Fed. Reg. 36,368 (July 6, 1999).

[244] *See* 63 Fed. Reg. 70,138 (Dec. 18, 1998).

[245] *See* 64 Fed. Reg. 54,031 (Oct. 5, 1999).

[246] *See* 65 Fed. Reg. 14,289 (Mar. 16, 2000).

[247] *See* 64 Fed. Reg. 61,893 (Nov. 15, 1999).

[248] *See* 65 Fed. Reg. 59,434 (Oct. 5, 2000). For text of this guidance, see Appendix I-2.

[249] *See* 63 Fed. Reg. 42,410 (Aug. 7, 1998). All of the OIG compliance program guidance documents are *available at* http://oig.hhs.gov/modcom/index.htm.

It is important to remember that these compliance program guidance documents are not legally binding. Rather, they have often been described as the OIG's "wish list." However, they contain descriptions of "high-risk" areas that the government is likely to scrutinize and thus should be carefully monitored by health care providers and other entities. Moreover, implementing a corporate compliance program can have various other tangible benefits for health care providers. These issues are discussed in further detail in a subsequent chapter.[250]

Various other government publications also can be helpful in identifying issues where government enforcement is particularly likely, and can provide further guidance as to how federal authorities are interpreting certain requirements. Reviewing such documents can help the attorney assist his or her client in taking a proactive stance to reduce the risk of exposure rather than simply reacting to problems after they arise. In this connection, it may be helpful to review documents such as the OIG's annual Work Plan, the Semiannual Report, and the HHS/DOJ Annual Health Care Fraud and Abuse Control Program Report. In addition, CMS's program manuals and program memoranda may contain relevant material and should be consulted.

## B. The Office of Inspector General Work Plan

The HHS OIG Work Plan,[251] summarizes the major projects the OIG intends to pursue in the coming year in each of HHS's major operating areas. The report typically lists numerous projects under such categories as hospitals, home health care, nursing home care, hospice services, physician services, DME supplies, laboratory services, ESRD, drug reimbursement, other Medicare services,[252] Medicare and Medicaid managed care, Medicaid services, Medicare contractor operations,[253] general administration, investigations, and legal counsel.[254] Within each of these areas, the OIG lists numerous issues planned for review.

For 2001, with regard to hospitals, the Work Plan FY 2001 list includes the following project areas:

- one-day stays;
- discharges and subsequent readmissions;

---

[250] See Chapter 7 (Jones *et al.*, Corporate Compliance Programs).

[251] *See, e.g.*, Office of Inspector Gen., U.S. Dep't of Health & Human Servs., Work Plan, Fiscal Year 2001, *available at* http://oig.hhs.gov/wrkpln/index.htm [hereinafter Work Plan FY 2001].

[252] This category includes topics such as Medigap insurance, outpatient diabetes self-management training services, rural health clinics, and certain community mental health centers. *See* Work Plan 2001, at 20–21.

[253] This section covers topics ranging from suspension of payments to bankrupt providers. *See* Work Plan FY 2001, at 35–40.

[254] This section includes references to many fraud and abuse topics including integrity agreements, advisory opinions, safe harbors, exclusions, and CMPs. *See* Work Plan FY 2001, at 44–46.

- PPS transfers;[255]
- related hospital and skilled nursing stays;
- uncollected copayments;
- DRG payment limits;
- outlier payments;
- 72-hour rule issues;
- outpatient PPS; and
- outpatient pharmacy and medical supplies.[256]

Home health issues include compliance programs, physician involvement in approving care, PPS system controls, and payments based on location of service.[257]

With regard to nursing homes, the OIG will be reviewing several issues including those related to

- quality assessment and assurance committees;
- the role of the medical director;
- consolidated billing requirements;
- ineligible stays in skilled nursing facilities;
- therapy services for Medicare Part B patients;
- ancillary medical supplies; and
- processes relating to survey and certification and complaints.[258]

Hospice reviews will cover plans of care, payments to nursing homes, and continuous home care.[259] Physician reviews will include physicians at teaching hospitals (the subject of the ongoing OIG national PATH enforcement initiative), reassignment, services and supplies incident to physician's services, non-physician practitioners, critical care codes, podiatry bills and services, bone density screening, and advance beneficiary notices.[260] The DME review will include payments for nebulizer drugs, and more general reviews of Medicare payments for prescription drugs.[261] With regard to ESRD, the Work Plan FY 2001 focuses on issues such as composite rate reimbursement, payment for epogen, hepatitis tests, Method II billing, and duplicate payments for nephrologist office visits.[262] Laboratory services reviews will include Clinical Laboratory Improvement Amendments of 1988 certifications, Medicare billings for cholesterol tests, and laboratory proficiency testing.[263]

---

[255] The four types of PPS transfers being reviewed include transfers between chain members and transfers during hospital mergers. *See* Work Plan FY 2001, at 2–3.

[256] *See* Work Plan FY 2001, at 1–6.

[257] *Id.* at 6–7.

[258] *Id.* at 8–11.

[259] *Id.* at 12.

[260] *Id.* at 13–15.

[261] *Id.* at 15–16.

[262] *Id.* at 17–19.

[263] *Id.* at 16–17.

Managed care issues to be examined in 2001 include the following:

- the adjusted community-rate proposal process including general and administrative costs;
- cost-based managed care plans;
- enhanced managed care payments;
- health maintenance organization (HMO) profits;
- physician incentive plans;
- additional benefits;
- prescription drug benefits;
- marketing materials;
- Medicare+Choice compliance programs;
- enrollment incentives and disincentives;
- fee-for-service costs incurred by HMO disenrollees;
- marketing and enrollment by Medicaid managed care entities; and
- emergency services for Medicaid managed care enrollees.

Medicaid services to be reviewed include payments to dually eligible beneficiaries, disproportionate share payment limits, outpatient psychiatric services, nursing facility administrative costs, community mental health services, DME reimbursement, clinical laboratory services, drug pricing and rebates, unallowable transportation costs, and payments to deceased beneficiaries.

The Work Plan FY 2001 also notes two specific investigative initiatives being conducted in cooperation with the DOJ. First, the investigation concerning hospitals that have upcoded the DRG for pneumonia claims from viral to bacterial pneumonia will continue. The OIG also will work with the DOJ to investigate PPS hospital misrepresentation of patient discharge status by which hospitals receive the full DRG reimbursement when the transferring hospital actually should be paid a lesser, per diem, amount.

In addition, the Work Plan FY 2001 indicates that the OIG expects to issue regulations implementing the CMP authorities applicable to Medicare+Choice organizations and Medicaid managed care. Also, the OIG will continue CMP enforcement activities, specifically focusing on cases involving improper conduct by managed care organizations. These are just a few of a number of recent indications that the government intends to increase its focus on managed care organizations. This topic is covered in a subsequent chapter.[264]

## C. The OIG Semiannual Report

While this document ostensibly reports on prior initiatives and enforcement actions, it also provides insight into issues likely to be of continuing concern to the OIG. For example, in the OIG Semiannual

---

[264] See Chapter 6 (Roth and Palmer, Managed Care Fraud and Abuse: Risk Areas for Government Program Participants).

Report, April 1, 2000–September 30, 2000,[265] the discussion on the 72-hour-rule national project states that $73 million has been recovered thus far from 2,799 hospitals.[266] However, the Semiannual Report goes on to indicate that 4,660 hospitals were identified as having submitted improper billings. Therefore, there are at least 2,000 additional hospitals that may be facing further enforcement action by the OIG on this issue. While some of these hospitals may have been approached already, there could well be others the OIG has yet to notify.[267] Therefore the 72-hour rule should remain on the list of any hospital's compliance priorities.

Moreover, the Semiannual Report states that "[o]ne of the most important aspects of this project is the stipulation in each settlement agreement that each hospital will assure compliance with proper billing for inpatient and outpatient services."[268] There have been several other indications that the OIG intends to devote significant resources to monitoring the performance of settlement agreements and CIAs[269] and providers should continue to monitor their current compliance.

## D. Miscellaneous

There are several other resources that can assist lawyers trying to counsel their health care clients. Notably, speeches by government officials can provide guidance as to likely agency interpretation of particular regulatory provisions or indicate changing enforcement priorities. These speeches are often given at conferences and seminars sponsored by various organizations across the country. As a practical matter, it is not feasible to attend all these meetings and there is usually no way to know in advance exactly which topics will be addressed. Fortunately, the trade press is aware of the government's propensity to use these venues and generally reports on important new developments.

The speakers often preface their remarks by noting that they are expressing their personal views and, in any event, such semiofficial pronouncements cannot make new law. Nevertheless, in light of all

---

[265] SEMIANNUAL REPORT APR.–SEPT. 2000, *supra* note 2.

[266] *Id.* at 9.

[267] Similarly, with regard to other national initiatives, the Semiannual Report indicates that the OIG is investigating the coding for pneumonia at over 100 hospitals, and only 22 hospitals have settled as of September 2000. SEMIANNUAL REPORT APR.–SEPT. 2000, *supra* note 2, at 11. With regard to the Hospital Outpatient Laboratory Project, the SEMIANNUAL REPORT APR.–SEPT. 2000 states that more hospitals also are expected to execute settlement agreements in the future. The discussion of the PPS Patient Transfer Project indicates that CMS is preparing a Program Memorandum to address these types of overpayments. Since the OIG claims to have identified $429 million in overpayments relating to this issue and has settled with only three hospitals for under $3 million, numerous other hospitals face exposure in this area.

[268] SEMIANNUAL REPORT APR.–SEPT. 2000, *supra* note 2, at 9.

[269] *See, e.g.*, Frequently Asked Questions Related to OIG Corporate Integrity Agreements, *available at* http://oig.hhs.gov/cia/ciafaq1.htm.

the complexities and ambiguities in the laws and regulations, these comments can provide helpful guidance.

## V. CONCLUSION

Simply identifying the applicable health care fraud and abuse requirements in what appears to be a typical commercial transaction can be a challenge, particularly for those who do not specialize in health care law. This book is intended both to serve as a useful starting point and to provide more advanced, practical guidance for any attorney handling arrangements that could implicate one or more of the various laws and regulations relating to health care fraud and abuse. This chapter is directed at those with less background in this area, and has endeavored to provide an overview of many of the more important subjects, references, and resources in the field. The subsequent chapters, which address a number of related subjects in considerable detail, will be particularly helpful for the experienced health care attorney as well as for those whose expertise lies in other areas.

As the statistics and other data in this chapter indicate, all those individuals and entities involved in the health care industry, as well as their attorneys, potentially face a significant degree of exposure if they fail to comply with any one of the complex laws and regulations relating to health care fraud and abuse. While many of these laws cannot be violated absent improper intent, other statutory schemes impose a form of strict liability. Various government agencies now have extensive funds and personnel available to investigate and prosecute those who fail to fully comply with these provisions, and the penalties can be enormous. However, the government is also making efforts to help the industry come into compliance through initiatives such as the issuance of advisory opinions, special fraud alerts, special advisory bulletins, and compliance program guidance documents.

Fraud and abuse enforcement actions are not likely to diminish significantly at any time in the foreseeable future. In fact, state agencies and private payers seem to be getting more actively involved in health care fraud audits, investigations, and prosecutions. Many segments of the health care industry have been subject to criticism for fraudulent or abusive practices over the past decade, including hospitals, nursing homes, hospices, and home health agencies. The government is likely to continue to scrutinize these types of providers, and there are signs that activities undertaken by certain other health care groups, such as physicians and pharmaceutical manufacturers, will face increasing review in the future. Moreover, government focus on quality-of-care cases also seems likely to increase.

The best protection for any health care entity, and for those who do business with them, is to be sure their attorney is very well informed about the current laws, regulations, and interpretations relevant to this area. This in-depth knowledge is also essential for the attorney involved in a health care transaction or case, so he or she will not face exposure.

# 2

# Federal Physician
# Self-Referral Restrictions*

*Thomas S. Crane, J.D., M.H.S.A. The author gratefully acknowledges the substantial assistance provided by his colleague, M. Daria Niewenhous, J.D.

The views expressed in this chapter are the personal views of the author and do not represent the formal position of Mintz, Levin, Cohn, Ferris, Glovsky and Popeo, P.C., any other individual attorneys at the firm, or any of its clients. The author expressly reserves the right to advocate freely other positions on behalf of clients.

# I. INTRODUCTION

For over two decades, the Social Security Act has criminalized physician self-referral through the Federal health care program anti-kickback statute.[1] Congress's original concern in enacting the anti-kickback statute was to prevent fraud and abuse that might result from a variety of business and professional arrangements involving individuals in a position to influence patient referrals. In 1989, however, Congress developed another approach to the problem by enacting a sweeping, targeted federal restriction on physician self-referrals. Specifically, the federal Medicare/Medicaid self-referral statute pro-

---

[1]Social Security Amendments of 1972, Pub. L. No. 92-603, 86 Stat. 1329 (1972) (originally codified at 42 U.S.C. §1395nn; presently codified at 42 U.S.C. §1320a-7b(b)). (See Appendix A-1 for full text of the anti-kickback statute.)

hibits a physician from referring Medicare/Medicaid patients for designated health services (DHS) to entities with which the physician (or an immediate family member) has a financial relationship unless the relationship is permitted by one of the enumerated exceptions to the statute.[2]

From inception to the present, the federal Medicare/Medicaid self-referral statute has undergone considerable change and has been subject to volumes of interpretative writings. Proponents of self-referral restrictions maintain that physicians' medical judgments as to where and when to refer patients are corrupted, however subtly, by their financial relationships with referral sources, thereby negatively affecting the quality and price of health care services and patient care. Among the many deleterious effects of self-referral, according to these proponents of restrictions, is that physicians with financial arrangements will order unnecessary services that result in increased costs to third-party payers.

Conversely, critics of restrictions on physician self-referral argue that self-referral arrangements may improve the quality of patient care because the financial arrangement fosters a stronger working relationship between the physician and the entity providing the item or service. This relationship works to assure that the entity provides superior health care services because entities with a reputation for providing substandard services are likely to lose money. In addition, critics argue that prohibiting a physician from referring patients to an entity may make physicians hesitant to invest their own time and money in certain projects. Accordingly, certain necessary medical items and services may not become available and a vital source of funding no longer will be available in the health care market.

Regardless of this ongoing debate, the federal Medicare/Medicaid self-referral statute continues to have a significant impact on the delivery and structure of health care in the United States.[3]

## II. Historical Background

### A. Self-Referral Studies

Congress recognized a need for the federal Medicare/Medicaid self-referral statute as a result of the findings of numerous studies regarding financial arrangements between physicians and health care entities.

---

[2]Ethics in Patient Referrals Act of 1989, Omnibus Budget Reconciliation Act of 1989 (OBRA 1989), Pub. L. No 101-239, §6204, 103 Stat. 2106 (1989) (codified at 42 U.S.C. §1395nn). (See Appendix B-1 for full text of the physician self-referral statute.)

[3]In addition, certain states have enacted laws that prohibit or restrict physician self-referrals. These state laws are outside the scope of this chapter. Because these laws vary considerably as to their scope and penalties, however, practitioners need to review them closely.

## 1. Medicare Catastrophic Coverage Act of 1988

In 1988, Congress enacted the Medicare Catastrophic Coverage Act of 1988.[4] Although subsequently repealed by Congress,[5] the Catastrophic Coverage Act would have expanded Medicare coverage of intravenous (IV) drug therapies while simultaneously prohibiting home IV providers from providing services to Medicare or Medicaid beneficiaries referred by physicians who had ownership interests in, or received compensation from, the home IV provider. The Catastrophic Coverage Act also required the Office of Inspector General (OIG) of the Department of Health and Human Services (HHS) to perform a study of ownership or compensation arrangements between physicians and entities providing Medicare covered services (the OIG Study). The conference report for the Catastrophic Coverage Act revealed that Congress was seeking the OIG Study to address concerns regarding physician self-referral arrangements that might have existed beyond the scope of home IV therapy benefits.[6]

## 2. The OIG Study

The OIG Study was issued on April 30, 1989, and contained findings on numerous issues, including the variety and scope of self-referral arrangements and the potential for such arrangements to lead to overutilization of health care services.[7] After providing an overview of several other studies regarding physician ownership,[8] the OIG Study focused on physician investments in independent clinical laboratories, independent physiological laboratories, and durable medical equipment (DME) suppliers. Overall, the OIG Study found that 12 percent of

---

[4] Medicare Catastrophic Coverage Act of 1988, Pub. L. No. 100-360, 102 Stat. 683 (1988).

[5] Medicare Catastrophic Coverage Repeal Act of 1989, Pub. L. No. 101-234, 103 Stat. 1979 (1989).

[6] H.R. CONF. REP. NO. 100-661 (1988), *reprinted in* 1988 U.S.C.C.A.N. 923.

[7] OFFICE OF INSPECTOR GEN., U.S. DEP'T OF HEALTH & HUMAN SERVS., REPORT TO CONGRESS, *Financial Arrangements Between Physicians and Health Care Businesses*, No. OA-12-88-01410, *reprinted in* Medicare & Medicaid Guide (CCH) ¶37,838, at 19,925–19,938 [hereinafter OIG Study].

[8] *Id.* at 19,927. The OIG Study cited to the following studies: Mich. Dep't of Social Servs., Med. Servs. Admin., *Utilization of Medicaid Laboratory Services by Physicians With / Without Ownership Interest in Clinical Laboratories: A Comparative Analysis* (June 9, 1981) (finding that Michigan Medicaid recipients referred by physician-owners had an average of 41% more tests than those referred by non-owners); Division of Health Standards & Quality, Region V, Health Care Fin. Admin., Dep't of Health & Human Servs., *Diagnostic Clinical Laboratory Services in Region V*, #2-05-2004-11 (May 1983) (finding that patients of practice related laboratories have a higher incidence of service per patient than patients of non-practice-related laboratories) Med. Affairs Div., Blue Cross & Blue Shield of Mich., *A Comparison of Laboratory Utilization and Payout to Ownership* (May 9, 1984) (finding that laboratories owned by physicians provided 20% more services than the average for all laboratories and 40% more services than non-physician-owned laboratories).

the physicians who billed the Medicare program had ownership or investment interests in entities to which they made patient referrals.[9] The OIG Study found a prevalence of physician investments in a wide range of health-related businesses other than the independent clinical and physiological laboratories and DME suppliers that were the focus of the OIG Study, including home health agencies, hospitals, nursing homes, ambulatory surgical centers, and health maintenance organizations.[10] Moreover, the OIG Study found that, nationally, at least 25 percent of independent clinical laboratories, 27 percent of independent physiological laboratories, and eight percent of DME suppliers were owned in whole or in part by referring physicians.

As it pertains to utilization, the OIG Study stated that patients of physician-owned independent clinical laboratories received 45 percent more clinical laboratory services than all Medicare patients in general.[11] The OIG estimated that this increased utilization of clinical laboratory services by patients of physician-owners cost the Medicare program $28 million in 1987. Patients of physician-owned independent physiological laboratories received 13 percent more physiological laboratory services than the national Medicare average. Patients of physicians who owned or invested in DME suppliers, however, did not use any more DME than all Medicare patients in general.

Of note is that neither the OIG Study, nor the vast majority of subsequent studies, attempted to evaluate the effects of physician ownership on the quality of care or outcomes. However, many researchers used the utilization variable as a proxy for quality. Thus, an inference exists that quality of care may be suspect where utilization disparities appear to be explained only by self-referral. Of course, such inferences may well be rebutted by other patient care measures.

In what remains the only reported study that examines self-referrals related to compensation arrangements, as opposed to ownership interests, the OIG Study also found that eight percent of Medicare physicians had compensation arrangements with entities to which they referred patients.[12] These compensation arrangements varied from space rental agreements and consulting agreements to management service contracts. The OIG did not attempt to examine the effects of such compensation arrangements on the utilization of services.

Based on the results of the OIG Study, the OIG recommended that the Health Care Financing Administration (HCFA), now the Centers for Medicare and Medicaid Services (CMS),[13] pursue necessary legisla-

---

[9] OIG Study at 19,931.

[10] *Id.* at 19,931–932.

[11] *Id.* at 19,933–934.

[12] *Id.* at 19,932.

[13] As of July 1, 2001, the former Health Care Financing Administration (HCFA) was renamed the Centers for Medicare and Medicaid Services (CMS). For the purposes of this chapter, references will be to CMS.

tive and regulatory channels to require entities billing Medicare to disclose to the program the names of physician-owners and physician-investors, and to require claims submitted by all entities providing services under Medicare Part B to contain the names and provider numbers of referring physicians.[14] To address overutilization problems by physician-owners and -investors, the OIG Study also urged legislators and administrators to pursue the following six options:

1. implement a post-payment utilization review program by carriers directed at physicians who own or invest in other health care entities;
2. require physicians to disclose financial interests to patients;
3. improve enforcement of the Federal health care programs antikickback statute;
4. institute a private right of action for anti-kickback cases;
5. prohibit self-referral arrangements involving specific types of health care entities in which physicians have a financial interest; and
6. prohibit physicians from referring to any entity in which they have a financial interest.

## 3. The Florida Study

In the same year that the OIG Study was released, the Florida legislature required the Florida Health Care Cost Containment Board (HCCB) to conduct a special study of joint venture arrangements between health care providers. The Florida legislature required the HCCB to conduct specific studies that would identify, analyze, and evaluate the impact of ownership and compensation interests on referrals by persons who provide health care. Moreover, the HCCB was required to submit recommendations that would work to strengthen enforcement of Florida anti-kickback laws and coordinate interagency regulation of joint venture relationships in the health care industry. The HCCB issued a series of three final reports detailing the results of its study (the Florida Report).[15]

In 1991, Volume I of the Florida Report stated that "[o]f the eight states covered by the [OIG] study, Florida had the highest percentage of physicians involved in joint ventures. Medicare patients of physician owners in Florida received 40 percent more lab tests, 12 percent more diagnostic imaging tests, and utilized 16 percent more durable medical equipment than the general population of Florida Medicare beneficiaries."[16] In general, the HCCB's findings revealed that physician ownership of health care businesses providing diagnostic testing or similar ancillary services was common in Florida. The HCCB reported:

---

[14] OIG Study at 19,936–937.

[15] FLA. HEALTH CARE COST CONTAINMENT BD., JOINT VENTURES AMONG HEALTH CARE PROVIDERS IN FLORIDA, Vol. I (Jan. 1991), Vol. II (Sept. 1991), Vol. III (Oct. 1991).

[16] *Id.*, Vol. I, at iv–v.

[M]ore than three-fourths of the responding ambulatory surgical facilities and about 93 percent of the diagnostic imaging centers are owned either wholly or in part by physicians. Almost 80 percent of the responding radiation therapy centers, more than 60 percent of the responding clinical laboratories and nearly 40 percent of the responding physical therapy and/or rehabilitation facilities also report physician owners. Furthermore, about 20 percent of the responding durable medical equipment businesses, as well as close to 13 percent of the home health agencies are owned by physicians.[17]

The HCCB also reported that a high percentage of patients who were referred to a physician-owned health care facility were referred to that facility by the physician-owner. As a result of its findings, the HCCB recommended that the Florida legislature consider prohibiting physician owners from referring patients to the four specific facility types that the HCCB identified as being problematic—clinical laboratories, diagnostic imaging centers, physician therapy/rehabilitation centers, and radiation therapy centers.[18]

## B. Legislative and Regulatory History

On August 10, 1988, Representative Fortney "Pete" Stark (D-Cal.) addressed the issue of physician self-referrals by introducing a bill, H.R. 5198, "to amend Title XVIII of the Social Security Act to provide civil monetary penalties and other remedies for certain improper referral arrangements for services provided under the Medicare program."[19] This bill would have barred physician referrals for all Medicare covered services; the bill ultimately formed the basis for the Ethics in Patient Referrals Act of 1988, introduced by Representative Stark, and enacted on December 19, 1989.[20] Partially as a result of the OIG Study that found elevated numbers of referrals only for clinical laboratory services, however, congressional negotiations in 1989 narrowed the scope of the legislation to apply only to referrals for clinical laboratory services.

In his remarks to the House of Representatives in 1988 introducing his original bill, Representative Stark described his frustration with the failure of the anti-kickback statute to stop physician self-referrals even though the anti-kickback statute is a "sweeping law prohibiting payment of kickbacks for patient referrals under Medicare . . . [that] is clear on its face[.]"[21] He noted that providers of medical services, in spite

---

[17] *Id.*

[18] *Id.*, Vol. III, at 23. The Florida legislature subsequently enacted the Florida Patient Self-Referral Act of 1992, which prohibits a health care provider from referring a patient for "designated health services" (clinical laboratory services, physical therapy services, comprehensive rehabilitative services, diagnostic imaging services, and radiation therapy services) to an entity in which the health care provider is an investor or has an investment interest. *See* FLA. STAT. ANN. §456.653.

[19] Ethics in Patient Referrals Act of 1988, H.R. 5198, 100th Cong. (1988).

[20] Ethics in Patient Referrals Act of 1989, Omnibus Budget Reconciliation Act of 1989 (OBRA 1989), Pub. L. No. 101-239, §6204, 103 Stat. 2106 (1989) (codified at 42 U.S.C. §1395 nn).

[21] 134 Cong. Rec. E2724-02 (daily ed. Aug. 11,1988) (statement of Rep. Stark).

of the anti-kickback statute, had continued to develop and promote "a variety of new forms of business organization specifically intended to secure patient referrals from physicians."[22] With respect to joint ventures with physicians in particular, Representative Stark complained that, "lawyers advising health care clients have recognized that joint ventures with physicians are potentially within the scope of Medicare's anti-kickback law, but have argued that such ventures are nonetheless permissible if (i) there is no explicit requirement that physician investors make referrals and (ii) dividend payments do not vary in proportion to the number of referrals made by the physician investor."[23]

Finally, in support of the bill, Representative Stark explained the two major shortcomings of the anti-kickback statute as being "the enormous difficulty involved in proving to the satisfaction of a judge in a criminal or civil enforcement action that a particular arrangement is deliberately structured to induce referrals[,]"[24] and the OIG's inability to adequately enforce the anti-kickback statute due to a severe lack of resources and shortage of investigators.

Congressman Stark's solution was the Ethics in Patient Referrals Act. On introducing the bill in 1998, he remarked that

> what is needed is what lawyers call a bright line rule to give providers and physicians unequivocal guidance as to the types of arrangements that are permissible and the types that are prohibited. If the law is clear and the penalties are severe, we can rely on self-enforcement in the great majority of the cases.
> [My bill] provides this bright-line rule.[25]

As a result of Representative Stark's dedication to the issue of physician self-referral, the federal Medicare/Medicaid self-referral statute is commonly referred to as the "Stark law," or "Stark I" to distinguish it from the 1993 amendments discussed below and known as "Stark II."[26] Stark I provided that for services furnished on or after January 1, 1992, a physician with a financial relationship with an entity that furnishes clinical laboratory services (or a physician with an immediate family member who has such a relationship) may not make a referral to that entity for clinical laboratory services that are reimbursable by Medicare unless certain exceptions are met.

HCFA, now CMS, published a proposed regulation implementing Stark I on March 11, 1992.[27] The final Stark I regulation was published on August 14, 1995, and became effective on September 13, 1995.[28]

---

[22] *Id.*

[23] *Id.*

[24] *Id.*

[25] *Id.*

[26] Stark I was amended by §4207(e) of the Omnibus Budget Reconciliation Act of 1990 (OBRA 1990) to clarify certain definitions and reporting requirements regarding physician ownership and referral, and to provide an additional exception to the prohibition. *See generally* Pub. L. No. 101-508, 104 Stat 1388 (Nov. 5, 1990).

[27] 57 Fed. Reg. 8588 (Mar. 11, 1992).

[28] 60 Fed. Reg. 41,914 (Aug. 14, 1995).

In 1993, Congress significantly amended the Stark law as part of the Omnibus Budget Reconciliation Act of 1993 (OBRA 1993).[29] Specifically, Stark II expanded the scope of Stark I to cover referrals for numerous DHS in addition to clinical laboratory services, and included referrals for services payable under the Medicaid program. In addition, Stark II significantly amended many of the statutory definitions and exceptions enacted in Stark I.

Stark II, applicable to DHS other than clinical laboratory services, generally went into effect for referrals made after December 31, 1994. The effective date for those provisions of Stark II that amended the definitions and exceptions contained in Stark I, however, was generally made retroactive to January 1, 1992.

On January 9, 1998, CMS issued a proposed rule, Medicare and Medicaid Programs: Physicians' Referrals to Health Care Entities With Which They Have Financial Relationships.[30] CMS also published a final rule to implement the Stark law advisory opinion process on January 9, 1998.[31] This rule was promulgated pursuant to the Balanced Budget Act of 1997 (BBA), which required the Secretary of HHS to issue written advisory opinions regarding whether a particular referral relating to a designated health service (other than clinical laboratory services) is prohibited by the Stark law.[32] The BBA directed the Secretary to apply to the Stark advisory opinion process, to the extent practicable, the rules governing advisory opinions interpreting the anti-kickback, civil monetary penalty, and Medicare exclusion statutes that the OIG promulgated pursuant to the Health Insurance Portability and Accountability Act of 1996[33] and published in February 1997.[34]

## III. FEDERAL RESTRICTIONS ON PHYSICIAN SELF-REFERRALS

## A. Stark II Final Rule

### 1. Introduction

On January 4, 2001, CMS released the long-awaited final regulation for Stark II.[35] The final rule, which included a 90-day comment period, represented the first of two phases of regulations to be issued by CMS. The agency extended this comment period to June 4, 2001, and on June 1, 2001, the Health Law Section of the American Bar Associa-

---

[29] Omnibus Budget Reconciliation Act of 1993, Pub. L. No. 103-66, §13562, 107 Stat. 312 (1993).

[30] 63 Fed. Reg. 1659 (Jan. 9, 1998).

[31] 63 Fed. Reg. at 1646.

[32] Pub. L. No. 105-33, §4314, 111 Stat. 251, *codified at* 42 U.S.C. §1395nn(g)(6).

[33] Pub. L. No. 104-191, 100 Stat. 1936 (1996).

[34] 63 Fed. Reg. at 1647; *see* 42 C.F.R. part 1008 (containing the OIG's procedures for advisory opinions under the anti-kickback statute).

[35] 66 Fed. Reg. 856–965 (Jan. 4, 2001) (see Appendix B-3).

tion filed detailed comments on the Phase I regulations.[36] The final rule gave as its effective date one year from publication, January 4, 2002, except for one section relating to physician referrals to home health agencies, which is effective February 5, 2001. In addition, in a subsequent notice, CMS extended the effective date, subject to an additional comment period, of the part of the final rule regulating percentage compensation arrangements.[37] While it remains to be seen if significant changes to the final rule will be made, delay in implementation of both phases of the final rule appears likely.

In drafting the final rule, HHS has clearly attempted to extensively re-examine the Stark law's statutory language and legislative history, to carefully reconsider the January 1998 proposed rule, and to closely review industry's concerns about the proposed rule and the Stark law itself. HHS stated that it wanted to avoid the "undue disruption" of common financial arrangements, yet not adversely impact the delivery of services to Medicare beneficiaries.[38] HHS also stated that it intended where possible to issue clear bright-line rules, in keeping with the goals Representative Stark specifically set in 1988, when he first introduced the bill that eventually came to be known by his name.[39] Toward these goals, HHS tried to interpret the prohibitions narrowly and the exceptions broadly, focusing on financial relationships that may result in overutilization. By interpreting the Stark law in this manner, HHS interpreted the reach of the Stark law as narrowly as possible, consistent with the statutory language and congressional intent.

Of note, although not publicly acknowledged, is the understanding that the OIG provided substantial technical assistance to CMS in drafting the final rule. This assistance is clear, as the final rule contains many indications of OIG policies and enforcement concerns. Because of the role of the OIG in working with CMS, and the official clearance of the final rule by the Secretary of HHS, reference is made to the final rule as drafted by HHS, although CMS is officially responsible for the final rule and enforcement of the Stark law.

HHS issued the final rule in two parts: Phase I implemented a majority of the provisions of the Stark law, with certain exceptions and related definitions, as applied to the Medicare program. The principal portions of the Stark law deferred to Phase II were the reporting requirements, sanctions provisions, and application to the Medicaid program. In addition, Phase II will also incorporate comments concerning Phase I. Although in the preamble to the Phase I rules, HHS states formally that it is deferring implementation of a final rule regarding the well-known Section 1877(c), (d), and (e) ownership and compensation exceptions (e.g., the employee and personal services exceptions), the

---

[36] The Health Law Section's comments are reprinted in THE HEALTH LAW. (Sept. 2001) (Special Edition).

[37] See *infra* Section III.B.2.f.i.

[38] 66 Fed. Reg. at 860.

[39] 134 Cong. Rec. E2724-02 (daily ed. Aug. 11, 1988) (statement of Rep. Stark).

rule itself appears to leave intact existing regulations applicable to Stark I and clinical laboratory services that implement these ownership and compensation provisions. Therefore, these provisions are arguably incorporated into the Stark II final rule and will become applicable for all DHS.

In the preamble to the final rule, HHS promises that Phase II will be issued "shortly." This promised timeframe must be understood in context. The Stark I law was enacted in 1989 and a final rule was not implemented until 1995. The Stark II law was enacted in 1993 with an effective date of January 1995, but the proposed rule was not issued until January 1998. This final rule was issued in January 2001 and only implements Phase I. Thus, a significant passage of time prior to the issuance of Phase II can be anticipated.

### 2. Highlights of the Final Rule

The final rule injects a substantial dose of common sense and an understanding of the realities of the effect of the Stark law on the enormously complex health care market. On balance, HHS appears to have taken commentators' concerns to heart and has introduced a variety of adjustments and amendments offering greater clarity and, in several instances, increased protections for legitimate arrangements.

HHS appears to have taken a strategic straddling position on a statute that some CMS officials had quietly hoped they would not need to implement because of its complexities and the lack of departmental resources. The issuance of the rule in two phases, coupled with the delay in the effective date of the first phase for a full year from date of publication, and even then without two key enforcement weapons—reporting obligations and sanctions—make it seem as though HHS is offering a trial balloon or "beta testing" of a liberalized set of rules that has some chance of being palatable to providers and Congress. Certainly, HHS was looking over its shoulder at the handful of attempts by House committee leaders from both parties to significantly rollback or amend major provisions of the Stark law. So while this final rule contains important provisions that will need to be understood and complied with, the outcome of self-referral enforcement is a long way from final.

#### a. Effective Date

Two competing forces raised questions concerning the actual effective date of the Stark law and final rule. In a September 29, 2000, letter to Representative Stark, the Department of Justice (DOJ) announced that it had over 50 matters under investigation involving possible violations of the Stark law that were brought by whistleblowers under the *qui tam* provisions of the False Claims Act (FCA).[40] Presum-

---

[40]The False Claims Act is discussed extensively in Chapter 3 (Salcido, The False Claims Act in Health Care Prosecutions: Application of the Substantive, *Qui Tam*, and Voluntary Disclosure Provisions). The *qui tam* provisions appear at 31 U.S.C. §3730. See Appendix C-1 for full text of the False Claims Act.

ably, such actions are premised on the theory that Stark II became effective in January 1995.

On the other hand, one of President Bush's first actions on January 20, 2001, was to issue a memorandum calling for the 60-day postponement of all published rules not yet effective.[41] Although the practical and legal effects of this order were not clear, it further clouds an already murky situation. Whatever the various forces within the administration determine to be the actual effective date, without question whistleblowers and their counsel will continue to bring FCA cases based on the statutory effective date and their view that the Stark law is clear on its face.

### b. Four Significant Interpretations / Exceptions

The final rule contains several original provisions or revised interpretations of the Stark law, including four significant interpretations and/or exceptions that taken together provide significant relief and flexibility to providers.

1. HHS has introduced a knowledge standard that limits the enforcement of the Stark law to "knowing" violations as defined in the final rule.[42] This will prevent unfair enforcement of the statute where non-compliance with an exception is de minimus or unintended. The consequence of this approach is to introduce uncertainty, because an examination of intent is now required. Ironically, HHS has determined that Representative Stark's promise of clear bright-line rules is illusory and ultimately not achievable.[43]

2. In a sweeping original interpretation, HHS has determined that a "referral" does not take place when physicians refer patients for services the physicians personally perform.[44] This elimination of "pure self-referrals" can apply to services physicians perform anywhere, e.g., in their offices or in the professional component of a hospital service.

3. HHS has introduced a fair market value exception and related definition that generally permits (under certain guidelines) payments based on a per use, per service, per-click, or per-time-period basis, but does not permit many common percentage compensation arrangements because they violate the requirement that payments be set in advance.[45] In addition, the requirements for this exception have been significantly liberalized from the proposed rule.

---

[41] 66 Fed. Reg. at 7702.

[42] 66 Fed. Reg. at 864–65, 958–59; *see, e.g.*, 42 C.F.R. §411.353(e).

[43] 66 Fed. Reg. at 864–65.

[44] 66 Fed. Reg. at 871–73; 42 C.F.R. §411.351 (see definition of "referral").

[45] 66 Fed. Reg. at 876–79; 42 C.F.R. §411.354(d).

4. HHS has also defined "indirect compensation arrangements" and created a related exception.[46] The concept of indirect compensation could apply to a large number of arrangements that must be analyzed to determine compliance with the definition and the exception. Along with the fair market value exception, this compensation exception, despite its unnecessarily complex structure, will provide significant relief, and these two exceptions will likely become the primary compensation exceptions to which providers will turn. As a result, these two exceptions will substantially diminish the effect of any Phase II rule with respect to the implementation of the remaining statutory compensation exceptions.

### c. New Regulatory Exceptions

The final rule also contains important changes to statutory definitions and exceptions, and creates regulatory exceptions in the following areas:

- designated health services,
- in-office ancillary services,
- managed care,
- academic medical centers,
- erythropoietin (EPO) or other prescription drugs furnished by end-stage renal disease (ESRD) facilities, and
- non-cash gifts or benefits of minimal value.

### d. Key Statutory Terms

The final rule also addresses key statutory terms and definitions of DHS including:

- A person or entity is generally considered to be furnishing DHS if it is the person or entity to which CMS makes payment for the DHS.[47]
- Unexercised stock options and unsecured loans are not ownership interests.[48]
- "Under arrangement" services provided by physician-owned providers need only comply with the compensation exceptions.[49]
- Under certain rules, a compensation arrangement may be conditioned on referrals.[50]
- Many of the DHS are clearly defined by Current Procedural Terminology (CPT) or HCFA Common Procedure Coding System (HCPCS) codes.[51]

---

[46] 66 Fed. Reg. at 865–70; 42 C.F.R. §411.354(c)(2).

[47] 66 Fed. Reg. at 943; 42 C.F.R. §411.351 (see definition of "entity").

[48] 66 Fed. Reg. at 870; 42 C.F.R. §411.354(b)(3).

[49] 66 Fed. Reg. at 942; 42 C.F.R. §411.354(c).

[50] 66 Fed. Reg. at 876–77; 42 C.F.R. §411.354(d)(4).

[51] 66 Fed. Reg. at 922–23, Attachment at 963–65.

- Included within radiology and other imaging services are the technical and professional components of the service, but excluded are invasive procedures.[52]
- Outpatient prescription drugs include all such drugs covered under Medicare Part B.[53]

Each of these important developments is discussed more fully below.

## B. The Prohibition on Physician Self-Referrals and Key Statutory Terms

### 1. *The Basic Prohibition*

The Stark law[54] provides that, unless certain enumerated exceptions are met:

[I]f a physician (or an immediate family member of such physician) has a financial relationship with an entity specified in paragraph (2) [of the Stark law], then—

(A) the physician may not make a referral to the entity for the furnishing of designated health services for which payment otherwise may be made under [the Medicare program], and

(B) the entity may not present or cause to be presented a claim under [the Medicare program] or bill to any individual, third-party payer, or other entity for designated health services furnished pursuant to a referral prohibited under [this provision].[55]

The Stark law further specifies that:

[A] financial relationship of a physician (or an immediate family member of such physician) with an entity specified in this paragraph [(2)] is—

(A) except as provided in [the exceptions applicable to both ownership and compensation arrangements and to only ownership or investments interests], an ownership or investment interest in the entity, or

(B) except as provided in [the exceptions applicable to compensation arrangements], a compensation arrangement . . . between the physician (or an immediate family member of such physician) and the entity.

An ownership or investment interest . . . may be through equity, debt, or other means and includes an interest in any entity that holds an ownership or investment interest in an entity providing the designated health service.[56]

---

[52] 66 Fed. Reg. at 927–28; 42 C.F.R. §411.351 (see definition of "radiology and certain other imaging services").

[53] 66 Fed. Reg. at 937; 42 C.F.R. §411.351 (see definition of "outpatient prescription drugs").

[54] Unless otherwise noted, all references will be to the Stark law as currently enacted. Practitioners must note that if they are analyzing physician relationships with clinical laboratory service providers, for which the Stark I regulation is final and binding, they may need to consult the provisions of the Stark I law. This analysis is especially important if the conduct in question occurred prior to 1995. If the conduct occurred subsequent to January 1, 1995, practitioners may want to analyze the arrangement under both the Stark I regulation and the Stark II law and regulation.

[55] 42 U.S.C. §1395nn(a)(1).

[56] 42 U.S.C. §1395nn(a)(2).

## 2. Key Statutory Terms

The Stark law contains a definitions section further clarifying many of these terms and providing special rules, including a definition of the terms "compensation arrangement," "remuneration," and "referral."[57]

The final rule expands the existing Stark I regulation applicable to clinical laboratory services, 42 C.F.R. Section 411 Subpart J, to the entire list of DHS. While the prohibitions seem relatively straightforward on paper, on closer examination of key terms, certain nuances become evident.

The final rule revises and fully develops the key statutory terms "referral," "entity," "financial relationship," "ownership or investment interest," "remuneration" and "compensation arrangement." In addition, HHS introduces a "knowledge" or scienter element. On the whole, the final rule provides significant flexibility and relief to providers.

### a. Referral

As in the proposed rule, the term "referral" is broadly defined in the final rule and can be direct or indirect, meaning that physicians would be considered to have made referrals if they caused, directed, or controlled referrals made by others.[58] A referral can be in any form, including—but not limited to—any written, oral, or electronic means of communication. A referral can also be made in a plan of care and does not require that physicians send patients to particular entities or indicate in the plan of care that DHS should be performed by particular entities.[59]

One of the most significant interpretations in the final rule is the HHS determination that the term "referral" excludes services personally performed by the referring physician.[60] (Similarly, HHS revised the definition of "entity" to clarify that the referring physician him- or herself is not an entity for purposes of the statute.)[61] Because there are so many situations where one component of a referral involves a pure self-referral for services personally performed by the referring physician, this interpretation removes a substantial amount of conduct from the ambit of the Stark law. For example, any personally performed service a physician provides in his or her office or at a hospital is not covered by the Stark law under this interpretation. Examples of personally performed services at a hospital include the professional component of cardiac catheterization and lithotripsy. For the most part, these services are physician services, although as discussed below, the professional component of a radiology service is deemed to be a DHS. Referrals still take place when physicians refer patients to other members of their

---

[57] *See generally* 42 U.S.C. §1395nn(h).

[58] 66 Fed. Reg. at 871; 42 C.F.R. §411.351.

[59] *See id.*

[60] *See id.*

[61] 66 Fed. Reg. at 943; 42 C.F.R. §411.351.

group practices or to other entities for DHS, including technical components of radiology services or hospital services themselves.

HHS raised the question regarding referrals within a group practice when an employee of the referring physician performs the service. In most cases, such referrals will be permitted under the substantially broadened in-office ancillary services exception.[62] Consequently, CMS noted that it was soliciting comments as to whether, and under what conditions, services performed by a physician's employees could be treated as the physician's personally performed services.[63]

By statute, a referral does not include certain requests, pursuant to a consultation by pathologists, radiologists, and radiation oncologists.[64] A "consultation" is separately defined to mean a request by another physician documented in the patient's medical record follow-up, by a written report to the treating physician.[65] HHS clarifies that the term "referral" is broader and separate from coverage and payment rules for a consultation.[66]

The final rule specifies that a physician's prohibited financial relationship will not generally be imputed to his or her group practice, its members, or its staff.[67] Although HHS attempted to clarify these issues here, many questions were left unanswered by virtue of what is not in the final rule.

### b. Entity

To implicate the Stark law, the referral must be to an entity furnishing DHS. The term "entity" is, again, notable for what it does not include. Most of the definition remained unchanged from the proposed rule, but the final rule made clear that an entity did not include the referring physicians themselves, but did include their medical practices.[68] A person or entity is generally considered to be furnishing DHS if it is the person or entity to which CMS makes payment for the DHS, directly, upon assignment on the patient's behalf, or upon reassignment pursuant to CMS's reassignment rules.[69] The preamble also clarifies that neither medical device manufacturers nor drug manufacturers are "entities" for purposes of the statute because they do not furnish prescription drugs.[70] However, a pharmacy that delivers outpatient prescription drugs directly to patients would be an entity for such purposes.[71] As discussed in Section VII., below, this revised definition of "entity" has important ramifications for managed care.

---

[62] 66 Fed. Reg. at 880–82; 42 C.F.R. §411.355(b).

[63] 66 Fed. Reg. at 872.

[64] 66 Fed. Reg. at 873; 42 C.F.R. §411.351.

[65] 66 Fed. Reg. at 873–74; 42 C.F.R. §411.351.

[66] 66 Fed. Reg. at 873.

[67] 66 Fed. Reg. at 903, 958; 42 C.F.R. §411.353(a).

[68] 66 Fed. Reg. at 943, 953; 42 C.F.R. §411.351.

[69] *See id.*

[70] *See id.*

[71] *See id.*

## c. Financial Relationship

A "financial relationship" can be through an ownership or investment interest or compensation arrangement.[72] Surprisingly, HHS took the position that an ownership or investment interest is a subset or type of compensation arrangement.[73] However, a financial arrangement qualifying under an ownership exception need not also qualify under a compensation exception. Both ownership interests and compensation arrangements may be either direct or indirect.[74]

## d. Ownership or Investment Interest
### i. Direct Ownership or Investment Interest

The final rule confirms that an ownership or investment interest may be through equity debt or "other means," and includes an interest in an entity that holds an ownership or investment interest in any entity that furnishes DHS.[75] However, an ownership or investment interest in a subsidiary is neither ownership nor investment in the parent corporation nor in any other subsidiary, unless the subsidiary corporation itself holds an interest in the parent or such other subsidiary. Beyond the core definition, the final rule clarifies a number of issues.

An ownership or investment interest will include stock, partnership shares, and limited liability company memberships, as well as loans, bonds, or other financial instruments that are secured by an entity's property or revenue. An unsecured or nonconvertible loan or a loan with no other indicia of ownership, however, will not be treated as an ownership interest. Note that if a physician or an entity owned by a physician in whole or in part provided any type of secured financing to another entity, the physician will have an ownership interest in the debtor, not a compensation arrangement.

The final rule clarified what is *not* an ownership or investment interest, such as: an interest in a retirement plan, stock options and convertible securities until the options are exercised or the securities converted to equity, an unsecured loan, and an "under arrangements" contract between a hospital and an entity owned by a physician or physician group.[76] In the preamble, CMS indicated that although under arrangement contracts could reasonably be construed as creating prohibited ownership interests in part of a hospital, they will be analyzed as compensation arrangements, not ownership interests.[77]

The final rule also reconfirmed that an ownership or investment interest that meets an ownership exception need not also qualify for a compensation arrangement exception with respect to profit distribu-

---

[72] 66 Fed. Reg. at 864, 958; 42 C.F.R. §411.354(a).

[73] 66 Fed. Reg. at 870.

[74] 66 Fed. Reg. at 864, 958; 42 C.F.R. §411.354(a).

[75] 66 Fed. Reg. at 958; 42 C.F.R. §411.354(b).

[76] 66 Fed. Reg. at 958; 42 C.F.R. §411.354(b)(3).

[77] 66 Fed. Reg. at 942, 958; 42 C.F.R. §411.354(b)(3) & (c).

tions, dividends, interest payments, and the like. However, the final rule indicated that an ownership or investment interest could be viewed as a type of compensation arrangement. CMS noted in the preamble that ownership interests that do not fall within an ownership exception would create compensation arrangements that are "deemed to take into account the volume or value of referrals."[78]

### ii. Indirect Ownership or Investment Interest

As noted above, in the final rule CMS substantially revised its approach to indirect financial relationships. Abandoning the very broad criteria referenced in the proposed rule, the final rule articulated tests for when an indirect relationship will trigger the Stark prohibition and established a knowledge requirement to avoid unfair application of the statute's sanctions when an entity has no reason to know that a DHS referral is tainted. The final rule provides:

(i) An indirect ownership or investment interests exist if—

(A) Between the referring physician (or immediate family member) and the entity furnishing DHS there exists an unbroken chain of any number (but no fewer than one) of persons or entities having ownership or investment interests between them; and

(B) The entity furnishing DHS has actual knowledge of, or acts in reckless disregard or deliberate ignorance of, the fact that the referring physician (or immediate family member) has some ownership or investment interest (through any number of intermediary ownership or investment interests) in the entity furnishing the DHS.

(ii) The entity furnishing DHS need not know, or act in reckless disregard or deliberate ignorance of, the precise composition of the unbroken chain or the specific terms of the ownership or investment interests that form the links in the chain.[79]

The principal substantive change to the indirect ownership test was the introduction of the knowledge element. An unsuspecting DHS entity will not be sanctioned for billing for services referred by a physician with an unknown indirect equity interest. However, the final rule made clear that the circumstances under which the DHS entity can claim ignorance are limited.

### e. Remuneration

This term is relevant to compensation arrangements. The final rule tracks language from the anti-kickback statute and broadly defined "remuneration" to mean "any payment or other benefit made directly or indirectly, overtly or covertly, in cash or in kind."[80] The Stark law, however, excepts from the definition of the term remuneration the following: forgiveness of amounts owed for inaccurate or mistakenly

---

[78] 66 Fed. Reg. at 877.

[79] 66 Fed. Reg. at 865, 958–959; 42 C.F.R. §411.353(c)(2).

[80] 42 U.S.C. §1395nn(h)(1)(B). *Compare* 42 U.S.C. §1320a-7b(b); 42 C.F.R. §411.351.

performed tests or procedures, or the correction of minor billing errors; furnishing of items, devices, or supplies used solely to collect, transport, process, or store specimens for the entity furnishing the items, or used solely to order or communicate the results of tests or procedures for the entity; and certain payments made by insurers to physicians.[81]

### f. Compensation Arrangement

A "compensation arrangement" includes any arrangement involving remuneration, direct or indirect, between a physician (or an immediate family member) and an entity. In this section, discussion will focus on direct compensation arrangements and the requirements commonly found in compensation exceptions regarding payments set in advance, not based on the volume or value of referrals, or other business generated between the parties, and compensation conditioned on referrals. In Section IV.E. below, we discuss the definition of "indirect compensation arrangement" together with the indirect compensation exception. The definition of a compensation arrangement is very broad. Virtually any exchange of remuneration between a physician and an entity could suffice.

Many of the Stark law compensation arrangement exceptions require that the compensation not take into account the "volume or value of referrals" and, in some cases, that the compensation not take into account "other business generated between the parties." CMS clarified the meaning of these often-used phrases, and also discussed its interpretation of the phrase "set in advance," in a section of the final rule entitled "Special Rules on Compensation." Each of these terms is addressed below.

### i. Set in Advance

The final rule provides that compensation will be considered "set in advance" if the aggregate compensation or a time-based or per unit of service-based (whether per use or per service) amount is set in advance in sufficient detail in the initial agreement between the parties so that the amount can be objectively verified. The payment amount must be fair market value compensation for services or items actually provided, not taking into account the volume or value of referrals or other business generated by the referring physician at the time of the initial agreement or during the term of the agreement. Percentage compensation arrangements in which compensation is based on fluctuating or indeterminate measures or in which the arrangement results in the seller receiving different payment amounts for the same services from the same purchaser do not constitute compensation set in advance, subject to additional rulemaking and a delayed effective date of January 4, 2003.[82]

The final rule clarified that the aggregate or total amount of payment need not be set in advance, and that compensation may be based

---

[81] 42 C.F.R. §411.351.

[82] 66 Fed. Reg. at 959; 42 C.F.R. §411.354(d)(1); 66 Fed. Reg. at 60,155.

on a per use or per service basis if the payment per use or per service is set in advance.[83]

The commentary to the final rule included a question concerning whether percentage compensation arrangements meet the volume or value standard. CMS responded that the following arrangements would *not* meet the set-in-advance requirement: payments based on a percentage of gross revenues, payments based on a percentage of collections, and payments based on a percentage of expenses.

### ii. Volume or Value of Referrals

The final rule provided guidance as to what types of payment methodologies do not take into account the volume or value of referrals:

> Compensation (including time based or per unit of service-based compensation) will be deemed not to take into account the "volume or value of referrals" if the compensation is fair market value for services or items actually provided and does not vary during the course of the compensation agreement in any manner that takes into account referrals of DHS.[84]

In the final rule, CMS permitted per click or unit-of-service payments, even when the physician receiving the payment is the referring physician. The final rule provided that such compensation will be deemed as not taking into account the volume or value of referrals if the compensation is fair market value and the per unit price does not vary during the course of the agreement in any manner that takes into account referrals of DHS. Thus, a physician may lease equipment to a hospital and receive "per use" rental payments, even on procedures performed on patients referred by the physician-owner, provided that the per use rental payments are fair market value, do not vary over the term of the lease, and meet the other requirements of the lease exception.

### iii. Other Business Generated Between the Parties

Some compensation arrangement exceptions require that compensation not be determined in a manner that takes into account other business generated between the parties. The final rule defined "other business generated between the parties" as follows:

> Compensation (including time-based or per unit of service-based compensation) will be deemed to not take into account "other business generated between the parties" as long as the compensation is fair market value and does not vary during the term of the agreement in any manner that takes into account referrals or other business generated by the referring physician, including private pay health care business.[85]

Thus, where an exception provides that compensation must not be determined in a manner that takes into account any other business generated by the referring physician (as in the fair market value exception), the compensation (including any per service payments) may

---

[83] *See id.*

[84] 66 Fed. Reg. at 959; 42 C.F.R. §411.354(d)(2).

[85] 66 Fed. Reg. at 959; 42 C.F.R. §411.354(d)(3).

not vary over the term of the agreement due to other private-pay business generated by the referring physician. Note that CMS stated that the other-business-generated restriction applied only to those exceptions in which it expressly appeared.

### iv. Compensation Conditioned on Referrals to a Particular Provider

In the final subsection to the special rules on compensation, CMS clarified that a physician's compensation may be conditioned on the physician's referrals of patients to particular providers. Such arrangements, however, must meet the following conditions:

1. the arrangement must be in writing;
2. the compensation must be set in advance and consistent with fair market value;
3. the arrangement must comply with an exception for ownership/investment interests or compensation arrangements; and
4. the referral requirement may not apply when the patient expresses a different choice of provider, the patient's insurance determines the provider, or the referral in the physician's judgment is not in the best medical interest of the patient.[86]

When these requirements are met, arrangements will not run afoul of the volume or value standard solely because the arrangement requires the physician to refer the patient to a particular provider as a condition of payment (e.g., where an employer or a managed care contract requires referrals to certain providers). While CMS believed that payments tied to referral requirements were potentially abusive, it concluded that precluding such referral requirements would have had far-reaching effects on managed care arrangements and group practices.[87]

### g. Knowledge Standard

HHS recognized the draconian effect of denying payments when there were unintentional or technical violations of one of its complicated rules. For example, a minor compensation arrangement with a referring physician could require a hospital to have to repay *all* Medicare revenues related to that physician's admissions or services for the period of noncompliance. Consequently, in one of the most significant provisions of the final rule, HHS added a scienter or knowledge requirement. Payment may be made for a service made pursuant to an otherwise prohibited referral if the entity did not have actual knowledge or act in reckless disregard or deliberate ignorance of the identity of the referring physician.[88] Elsewhere in the final rule, similar knowledge standards are imposed to prevent the application of the statute unless the person or entity submitting the claim knew or should have

---

[86] 66 Fed. Reg. at 959; 42 C.F.R. §411.354(d)(4).

[87] 66 Fed. Reg. at 878.

[88] 66 Fed. Reg. at 958; 42 C.F.R. §411.353(e)(1).

known of the situation.[89] This knowledge element is consistent with the term "knowing" as applied under other federal laws, such as the False Claims Act and the civil monetary penalty law.[90]

This knowledge standard does not generally impose an affirmative obligation on providers, absent some information that would alert a reasonable person to inquire or investigate whether an indirect financial relationship with a referring physician exists. Instead, providers are required to make reasonable inquiries when possessing facts that could lead a reasonable person to suspect the existence of an indirect financial relationship.[91] The reasonable steps to be taken, the preamble contends, will depend on the circumstances.[92]

Many practitioners hope that the addition of the knowledge standard will provide welcome relief by preventing the Stark law from being applied unfairly. Nonetheless, it represents the ultimate repudiation of Representative Stark's original promise of regulating physician self-referrals throughout the health care landscape with bright-line rules. However alluring such a concept is, HHS appeared to have recognized that bright-line rules could bring arbitrary enforcement with significant financial consequences to providers. In contrast, most will agree that the HHS approach preserves the underlying principles of the statute and will achieve more effective enforcement, but at the expense of bright-line rules, in that Stark law compliance analysis will involve subjective inquiry into the parties' state of mind.

## C. Legal Analysis Under the Stark Law

For purposes of a legal analysis under the Stark law, the essential questions are:

1. whether the relationship with a physician constitutes a prohibited financial relationship;
2. whether there will be any referrals of Medicare or Medicaid patients by the physician for any of the DHS; and
3. whether there are any applicable exceptions.

Of critical importance is the fact that a violation of the Stark law can occur if the financial relationship with the entity is wholly independent of the physician's referrals, whereas the anti-kickback statute requires proof of a nexus between the financial relationship and the referrals. The second issue, namely whether there are or will be any referrals of Medicare or Medicaid patients by the physician for DHS, is

---

[89]*See, e.g.,* 66 Fed. Reg. at 958–59; 42 C.F.R. §411.354(b)(5) & (c)(2).

[90]The knowledge or scienter requirement is expressed in both the civil monetary penalty law, 42 U.S.C. §1320a-7a(a), and the False Claims Act, 31 U.S.C. §§3729–3733, as "knows or should know." See Appendix D-1 for full text of the civil monetary penalty statute and Appendix C-1 for full text of the False Claims Act.

[91]66 Fed. Reg. at 865.

[92]*Id.*

a question of fact. As will be discussed below, it is not always easy to determine whether a referral has taken place. Because of the complicated prohibitions or restrictions of the Stark law exceptions, these two predicate questions must be analyzed closely to determine if the Stark law is initially applicable.

The next level of analysis is a determination as to whether the arrangement complies with one of the exceptions. Critical to this analysis is an understanding of (1) the definition of DHS published in the final rule and (2) the intent of HHS in crafting these definitions.

## D. Expansion of Designated Health Services

As noted above, Stark II expanded the physician self-referral restrictions from clinical laboratory services to all statutorily specified DHS. Specifically, DHS include:

- clinical laboratory services;
- physical therapy services;
- occupational therapy services;
- radiology, including magnetic resonance imaging, computerized axial tomography scans, and ultrasound services;[93]
- radiation therapy services and supplies;
- parenteral and enteral nutrients (PEN), equipment, and supplies;
- outpatient prescription drugs;
- DME and supplies;
- prosthetics, orthotics, and prosthetic devices and supplies;
- home health services; and
- inpatient and outpatient hospital services.[94]

### 1. *Current Procedural Terminology and HCFA Common Procedure Coding System Codes*

In an effort to reduce confusion regarding which services constitute DHS, HHS took a different approach by defining the entire scope of a number of DHS according to the CPT and HCPCS codes commonly associated with those DHS and familiar to the provider community.[95] Specifically identified by CPT and HCPCS codes in an attachment to the final rule (but not appearing in the *Code of Federal Regulations*) are clinical laboratory services, physical therapy, occupational therapy, radiology and certain other imaging services, and radiation therapy services.[96] Any future changes to this list of codes will be reflected in the

---

[93] Section 152 of the Social Security Act Amendments of 1994 (SSA 1994) amended the list of designated health services, effective January 1, 1995, to clarify that this DHS was not meant to include all diagnostic services. *See also* 42 U.S.C. §1395nn(h)(6); 42 C.F.R. §411.351.

[94] 66 Fed. Reg. at 940; 42 C.F.R. §411.351.

[95] 66 Fed. Reg. at 922–23.

[96] 66 Fed. Reg. at 963–65.

annual addendum to the final rule concerning payment policies under the physician fee schedule rule. Additionally, an updated list will be posted on HCFA's Web site: www.hcfa.gov (or CMS's Web site: www.cms.gov). According to HHS, the published list of codes will be controlling in all cases.[97]

Because these DHS are defined by specific CPT and HCPCS codes, the need for providers to properly code and document services becomes even more crucial. For this reason, parties entering into an agreement for DHS may want to list any relevant codes within the agreement. Also, because miscoding may implicate Stark, the party contracting for the DHS should strongly consider requiring the DHS provider to indemnify for expenses resulting from any claims or actions related to DHS miscoding.

CMS noted that under the final rule the definitions for the remaining DHS are clear enough not to warrant including any relevant CPT or HCPCS codes in the attached list of codes.[98] These DHS include: DME and supplies; parenteral and enteral nutrients, equipment, and supplies; prosthetics, orthotics, and prosthetic devices and supplies; home health services; outpatient prescription drugs; and inpatient and outpatient hospital services. Important features of these categories of DHS are discussed below.

## 2. Radiology and Certain Other Imaging Services

As discussed above, listed CPT and HCPCS codes define the categories of radiology and other imaging services, as well as radiation therapy services. It is important to note that HHS reiterated that both the professional component and the technical component of any diagnostic test or procedure using X-rays, ultrasound, or other imaging services, computerized axial tomography, or magnetic resonance imaging are considered part of DHS.[99] However, the final rule also defined these services as *not* constituting a referral where the referring physician is the interpreting physician.

To resolve confusion created by its use of the term "invasive radiology procedure" in the Stark II proposed rule, HHS revised its definition of "radiology and certain other imaging services" in the final rule to exclude X-ray, fluoroscopy, and ultrasound services that are themselves invasive procedures, such as cardiac catheterizations and endoscopies, requiring insertion of a needle, catheter, tube, or probe.[100] Because invasive radiologists are often referring physicians, this exclusion effectively removed this subspecialty from the ambit of the Stark law. HHS also specifically excluded from this category nuclear medicine services, certain covered preventive screening procedures (such as screening mammography) that are subject to CMS-imposed

---

[97] 66 Fed. Reg. at 955–56; 42 C.F.R. §411.351.

[98] 66 Fed. Reg. at 922.

[99] 66 Fed. Reg. at 923.

[100] 66 Fed. Reg. at 931, 955–56; 42 C.F.R. §411.351.

frequency limits that mitigate the potential for abuse, and radiology procedures that are integral to the performance of, and performed during, a nonradiology medical procedure.[101]

### 3. Clinical Laboratory, Physical Therapy, and Occupational Therapy Services

The clinical laboratory and occupational therapy services that constitute DHS are included in the list of CPT and HCPCS codes attached to the final rule.[102] CMS specified that it considered the professional components of laboratory tests to be DHS when such components are included in the attached codes.[103] CMS defined physical therapy services according to HCPCS codes; the selected codes are intended to include those services that are traditionally regarded as physical therapy.[104] Also, to clarify the meaning of speech-language pathology services, CMS set out specific codes that correspond to these services.[105] Because they overlap, codes for physical therapy, occupational therapy, and speech-language pathology services are grouped together under the attached list of codes.

### 4. Durable Medical Equipment

No significant changes were made to the definition of DME under the final rule, which generally followed the Medicare Part B coverage criteria for DME.[106] However, CMS acknowledged that there had been frequent confusion regarding the definition of this designated health service as to whether a given item was considered DME or a prosthetic, prosthetic device or orthotic. In response to this confusion, CMS recommended consulting the DME, prosthetic/orthotics, and supplies fee schedule; HCPCS codes pertaining to certain miscellaneous items; and explanations provided in the January 1998 Stark II proposed rule. In the proposed rule, CMS specifically noted that items or services that might involve equipment generally viewed as DME, but not reimbursed as DME under Medicare Part B, such as DME used in a physician's office for diagnostic or therapeutic purposes, would not be included in the Stark II DME definition.[107]

### 5. Parenteral and Enteral Nutrients, Equipment, and Supplies and Prosthetics, Orthotics, and Prosthetic Devices and Supplies

All HCPCS level 2 codes for these services are DHS.[108] CMS (formerly HCFA) explained that prosthetic device implants performed in

---

[101] 66 Fed. Reg. at 928; 42 C.F.R. §411.351.

[102] 66 Fed. Reg. at 963–65.

[103] 66 Fed. Reg. at 922.

[104] 66 Fed. Reg. at 924; 42 C.F.R. §411.351.

[105] 66 Fed. Reg. at 925.

[106] 66 Fed. Reg. at 953; 42 C.F.R. §411.351.

[107] 66 Fed. Reg. at 932.

[108] 66 Fed. Reg. at 933, 963–65.

a Medicare-certified ambulatory surgical center (ASC) by the referring physician or a member of the referring physician's group practice are permitted under a regulatory exception not found in prior rules (see Section IV.B.3., below). Likewise, eyeglasses and contact lenses are permitted under a specific regulatory exception (see Section IV.B.6., below).

### 6. Home Health Services

Effective February 5, 2001, CMS removed the five percent ownership limit and the $25,000 limit on financial or contractual relationships.[109] This change will allow home health agencies to pay physician medical directors more than $25,000 provided these arrangements meet a relevant compensation exception.

### 7. Outpatient Prescription Drugs

Under the final rule, all outpatient prescription drugs covered by Medicare Part B, including injectibles, constitute DHS.[110] HHS clarified that, unless otherwise directed, discounts related to drugs provided by a physician in the physician's office do not need to be passed along to the Medicare program.[111] Similarly, certain vaccinations, immunizations, and preventive screening tests subject to CMS-imposed frequency limits were also excepted.[112]

### 8. Inpatient and Outpatient Hospital Services

Inpatient and outpatient services provided to a hospital patient, whether provided by the hospital or provided under arrangement with another entity, are considered DHS.[113] The final rule stated that inpatient and outpatient hospital services provided under arrangement, such as lithotripsy and cardiac catheterization services are specifically included within this DHS category.[114] However, the impact of this determination was substantially diminished by the HHS determination that such under arrangement services need only meet a compensation exception;[115] and another HHS determination that professional services personally furnished by the referring physician are not part of a hospital service nor otherwise constitute a referral.[116]

---

[109] 66 Fed. Reg. at 936.
[110] 66 Fed. Reg. at 937–38; 42 C.F.R. §411.351.
[111] 66 Fed. Reg. at 938–39.
[112] 66 Fed. Reg. at 939, 961; 42 C.F.R. §411.356(h).
[113] 66 Fed. Reg. at 941–42; 42 C.F.R. §411.351.
[114] 66 Fed. Reg. at 941; 42 C.F.R. §411.351.
[115] 66 Fed. Reg. at 942; 42 C.F.R. §411.354(c).
[116] 66 Fed. Reg. at 942; 42 C.F.R. §411.351.

## IV. Stark Law Exceptions

### A. Statutory Ownership and Compensation Exceptions

There are a number of statutory exceptions to the ownership and compensation arrangement prohibitions. If the Stark law is triggered because of a financial relationship, the arrangement must qualify for a specific statutory or HHS-created exception to allow physicians to refer Medicare and Medicaid patients for DHS at entities with which they have financial relationships. The Stark law exceptions fall into three categories:

- both ownership and compensation arrangements;
- ownership arrangements only; and
- compensation arrangements only.

As a general matter, to permit patient referrals a financial relationship must necessarily satisfy the criteria of only one exception relevant to the type of financial relationship. Nonetheless, it is critical to ensure that all aspects of arrangements with referring physicians are analyzed because a single arrangement will often involve multiple financial relationships. For example, a hospital could arrange with a referring physician to use his or her space and services on a consulting basis, which would implicate the space rental and personal services exceptions, or a physician-employee could be paid a salary and stock options, which would implicate the employee compensation and ownership exceptions.

Statutorily exempt from both the ownership and compensation arrangement proscriptions are the following:

- personal physician services;
- in-office ancillary services; and
- prepaid health plans.

Each of these arrangements has specific requirements to qualify for the exceptions, which are discussed below.

### 1. Physician Services

The Stark law allowed an exception for physician services[117] provided personally by or under the personal supervision of another physician in the same group practice as the referring physician.[118] In the preamble to the final rule, HHS stated that it believed this exception to be of "limited application."[119] The exception was intended to cover

---

[117] The term "physicians' services" means professional services performed by physicians, including surgery, consultation, and home, office, and institutional calls. 42 U.S.C. §1395x(q); 42 C.F.R. §411.355(a).

[118] *See* 42 U.S.C. §1395nn(b)(1); *see also* 42 C.F.R. §411.355(a).

[119] 66 Fed. Reg. at 879.

only services provided by physicians, not services performed by non-physicians, even when furnished under physician supervision, such as ancillary or "incident to" services.[120]

The Stark law provided a detailed definition of the term "group practice," discussed in Section IV.A.2.b., below (regarding the in-office ancillary services exception).

### 2. Group Practice and In-Office Ancillary Services

The in-office ancillary services exception is one of the most difficult exceptions to understand and to apply, and yet it is one of the most important. Its importance lies in the fact that it permits arrangements that may be barred under other exceptions, most notably, the ownership exceptions.

#### a. Definition of Group Practice

The Stark law requires a group practice to meet five requirements, including a predicate, definitional requirement. The Stark law defined a group practice as "a group of 2 or more physicians legally organized as a partnership, professional corporation, foundation, not-for-profit corporation, faculty practice plan, or similar association" in which each group physician:

- provides substantially the full range of services that he or she routinely provides utilizing the resources of the group;
- provides, bills, and collects for substantially all services through the group;
- shares expenses and income from the practice, which are distributed in accordance with pre-determined methods;
- does not receive directly or indirectly compensation based on the volume or value of the physician's referrals, except through a permitted profit-sharing or productivity bonus arrangement;
- personally conducts at least 75 percent of the group's physician-patient encounters, and
- meets other regulatory standards.[121]

The definition of a group practice is relevant for compliance with the physician services and in-office ancillary services exceptions, whose requirements can be summarized in six categories, discussion of which follows immediately below.

##### i. Single Legal Entity

The final rule broadened the types of arrangements that qualify under the "single legal entity" test to include multi-entity legal structures.[122] The final rule provided that the entity may be organized by physicians, health care entities, or other persons or entities (including,

---

[120] *See* 63 Fed. Reg. at 1695; *see also* 66 Fed. Reg. at 880.

[121] 42 U.S.C. §1395nn(h)(4); 42 C.F.R. §411.352.

[122] 66 Fed. Reg. at 956; 42 C.F.R. §411.352(a).

but not limited to, physicians individually incorporated as professional corporations). The entity may not be organized or owned by another medical practice that is an operating physician practice, even if the medical practice meets the final rule's requirements for a group practice. Furthermore, a single legal entity does not include informal affiliations of physicians formed to share profits for referrals, or separate group practices under common ownership or control through another entity. The final rule also expanded the single-legal-entity test to include entities owned by a single physician, provided, however, that the group must have at least two physicians who are members, whether as employees or as direct or indirect owners.[123]

### ii. Members of the Group

A "member of the group" is defined to include any physician who owns or is employed by the group practice, but excludes independent contractors.[124] However, in an important shift from the proposed rule, the final rule provided that independent contractors may supervise the furnishing of DHS as physicians in the group practice, and under such circumstances may receive profit shares and productivity bonuses.[125]

### iii. The "Full Range of Services" Test

Group practice members must provide substantially the full range of patient care services. Patient care services include all services a physician performs that address the medical needs of specific patients or patients in general or benefit the group practice.[126]

### iv. The "Substantially All" Test

The "substantially all" test requires that at least 75 percent of patient care services of the group practice members must be furnished within the group.[127] HHS modified the requirements of this standard by permitting groups to adopt various methods for determining compliance. The final rule established criteria for measuring compliance.

HHS eliminated a requirement that group practices attest to compliance with this provision. Instead, the final rule merely requires that supporting documentation verifying compliance with this test must be made available to the Secretary on request.[128]

### v. The Unified Business Test

The final rule created a more flexible requirement that generally permits a group practice to use cost-center and location-based accounting with respect to services that are not DHS.[129] Many forms of

---

[123] 66 Fed. Reg. at 957; 42 C.F.R. §411.352(b).

[124] 66 Fed. Reg. at 954; 42 C.F.R. §411.351.

[125] 66 Fed. Reg. at 957; 42 C.F.R. §411.351 (see definition of "physicians in the group practice").

[126] 66 Fed. Reg. at 955; 42 C.F.R. §411.351.

[127] 66 Fed. Reg. at 904–905, 959; 42 C.F.R. §411.352(d).

[128] 66 Fed. Reg. at 910; 42 C.F.R. §411.352(d)(2).

[129] 66 Fed. Reg. at 957; 42 C.F.R. §411.352(f).

cost-center and location-based accounting are permitted, provided that the compensation formulas with respect to DHS revenues otherwise meet the requirements of the law.

To meet this test, a group practice must also be organized and operated on a bona fide basis as a single integrated business enterprise with legal and organizational integration. Essential elements are: centralized decision making by a body representative of the practice that maintains effective control over the group's assets and liabilities; consolidated billing, accounting, and financial reporting; and centralized utilization review.[130]

The group's overhead expenses and income must be distributed in accordance with methods "previously determined." The final rule treats the distribution method as "previously determined" (or determined in advance) if it is determined prior to receipt of payment for the services giving rise to the overhead expense or the production of income.[131] This approach permits groups to adjust their methodologies prospectively as often as they deem appropriate. A compensation method that directly relates to the volume or value of DHS referrals, or is retroactively adjusted, would violate the statute.

### vi. Compensation, Profit Shares, and Productivity Bonuses

Compensation, including time-based or per unit of service-based compensation is permissible if the compensation is fair market value and does not vary during the term of the agreement in any manner that takes into account the volume or value of referrals of DHS.[132] The final rule provides that a physician's compensation may be conditioned on the physician's referrals to a particular provider, practitioner, or supplier, as long as the arrangement is pursuant to an agreement fixing compensation to fair market value for the term of the agreement, complies with the applicable exception to the referral prohibition in the final rule, and allows for patient and third-party payer choice, and exercise of the physician's independent medical judgment.[133]

Member physicians and independent contractors who qualify as "physicians in the group" may be paid productivity bonuses based directly on their personal productivity (this includes "incident to" services).[134] Bonuses may not, however, be based directly upon referrals for DHS that are performed by someone else.[135] Nor may they be determined in any manner that is directly related to the volume or value of referrals by the physician for DHS.[136] The final rule provides examples of permissible compensation formulas.[137]

---

[130] *See id.*

[131] 66 Fed. Reg. at 957; 42 C.F.R. §411.352(e).

[132] 66 Fed. Reg. at 958; 42 C.F.R. §411.354(d).

[133] 66 Fed. Reg. at 959; 42 C.F.R. §411.354(d)(4).

[134] 66 Fed. Reg. at 957; 42 C.F.R. §411.352(i).

[135] 66 Fed. Reg. at 957; 42 C.F.R. §411.352(i).

[136] 66 Fed. Reg. at 957; 42 C.F.R. §411.352(i).

[137] 66 Fed. Reg. at 957; 42 C.F.R. §411.352(i)(3).

With regard to distributions of profit shares, the Stark law allows group practice members to receive shares of the overall profits of the group as long as those profits are unrelated to the volume or value of referrals.[138] The final rule defined "share of the overall profits" as meaning a share of the entire profits derived from DHS of the entire group or any component of the group that consists of at least five physicians.[139] The final rule specifies permissible methods for distributing overall profits.[140]

Group practices are not required to use the illustrated methods set forth for distribution of productivity and overall profit shares. Other methods are acceptable provided they are reasonable, objectively verifiable, and indirectly related to referrals. The group practice must maintain, and make available to the Secretary upon request, supporting documentation regarding the methodology used to calculate productivity bonuses and profit shares.[141]

### b. In-Office Ancillary Services Exception

#### i. Scope of Designated Health Services That Can Be In-Office Ancillary Services

Under the final rule, services are designated to be "furnished" under the exception in the location where the service is actually performed on the patient or when an item is dispensed to a patient in a manner that is sufficient to meet Medicare billing and coverage rules.[142] The DME exception now includes crutches, canes, walkers, and folding manual wheelchairs, provided they meet certain conditions.[143]

Under the final rule, the in-office ancillary services exception includes an exception allowing physicians or group practices to furnish blood glucose monitors and a starter set of strips and lancets if these practitioners furnish outpatient diabetes self-management training to patients receiving such monitors.[144] This change is in addition to allowing the furnishing of external ambulatory infusion pumps (other than pumps that are PEN equipment or supplies) as in-office ancillary services covered by the exception.[145]

#### ii. Direct Supervision

Although the deletion of the employment requirement in Stark II is clear on its face, the meaning of the term "directly supervised by" required congressional clarification in the conference report: "The conferees intend that the requirement for direct supervision by a physician would be met if the lab is in a physician's office which is personally

---

[138] 66 Fed. Reg. at 957; 42 C.F.R. §411.352(i)(2).

[139] 66 Fed. Reg. at 957; 42 C.F.R. §411.352(i)(2)(iii).

[140] 66 Fed. Reg. at 957; 42 C.F.R. §411.352(i)(2).

[141] 66 Fed. Reg. at 957–58; 42 C.F.R. §411.352(i)(4).

[142] 66 Fed. Reg. at 959–60; 42 C.F.R. §411.355(b)(5).

[143] 66 Fed. Reg. at 960; 42 C.F.R. §411.355(b)(4).

[144] 66 Fed. Reg. at 960; 42 C.F.R. §411.355(b)(4)(i).

[145] 66 Fed. Reg. at 960; 42 C.F.R. §411.355(b).

supervised by a lab director, or a physician, even if the physician is not always on site."[146] Surprisingly, the commentary in the final Stark I regulation concluded: "We believe that this explanation provides no insight into Congress's purpose in using the term 'direct supervision.'"[147] After reexamining the Stark law's legislative history, HHS recognized that Congress never intended to impose a physical presence requirement in the strictest sense. Rather, according to the preamble, Congress sought to establish a nexus between the referring physician and the individual performing the ancillary services with the intent of limiting the exception to services that are truly ancillary to the referring physician's medical practice.[148] Consequently, the direct-supervision requirement is met under the final rule merely by complying with the supervision requirements under applicable Medicare and Medicaid payment or coverage rules for the specific services at issue.[149]

The final rule recognized that the supervising physician need not be a formal member of the group, but merely a physician in the group practice.[150] Thus, owners and employees of the group practice, as well as independent contractors, qualify for this purpose.

### iii. Building Requirements

In general, an in-office ancillary service must be furnished in either the same building where the group practice provides professional services or in a centralized building where offsite DHS are furnished. HHS defined "same building" to include a structure with, or combination of structures that share, a single street address as assigned by the U.S. Postal Service.[151]

Due to the easing of the direct-supervision requirement, HHS inserted a stricter interpretation of the location standards "to ensure an adequate nexus between in-office ancillary designated health services and the physician's core medical practice."[152] The more significant revision to the location standard required the referring physician (or another physician who is a member of the same group practice) to provide in the same building substantial physician services unrelated to the provision of DHS.[153]

This same-building-location requirement has been liberalized in two ways. First, HHS has backed off significantly from its previous position, and is now permitting shared facilities under certain constraints. Secondly, the space in the building in which the DHS is provided need not be adjacent to the space in which other services are provided.[154]

---

[146] H.R. Conf. Rep. No. 103–213 (1993).

[147] 60 Fed. Reg. 41,914, 41,962 (Aug. 14, 1995).

[148] 66 Fed. Reg. at 885–87.

[149] 66 Fed. Reg. at 885, 959; 42 C.F.R. §411.355(b)(1).

[150] *Id.*

[151] 66 Fed. Reg. at 956; 42 C.F.R. §411.351.

[152] 66 Fed. Reg. at 888.

[153] 66 Fed. Reg. at 959; 42 C.F.R. §411.355(b)(2)(i).

[154] 66 Fed. Reg. 952.

With respect to the centralized building standard, the space must be used exclusively by the group.[155] In other words, the facility must be wholly owned by the group practice or leased by the group on a full-time basis (24 hours per day, 7 days per week). This requirement precludes shared facilities in these buildings.

### iv. Billing Requirements

To meet the billing standard, DHS must be billed by one of the following:

1. the physician performing or supervising the service;
2. the group practice in which such physician is a member;
3. with respect to services performed or supervised by the supervising physician, the group practice if such physician is a physician in the group practice; or
4. an entity that is wholly owned by the referring or supervising physician or the referring or supervising physician's group practice.[156]

For purposes of the billing requirement, "wholly owned" does not include joint ventures between group practices and individual group-practice physicians or joint ventures that include other providers or investors that do not qualify as wholly owned entities. The billing number used for billing must be "assigned to the group," and groups "may have, and bill under, more than one Medicare billing number, subject to any applicable Medicare program restrictions."[157] Finally, specific rules are provided for groups using third-party billing companies.

An area of concern that remains unaddressed under the Stark law is how this billing requirement works in a corporate-practice-of-medicine state where the professional corporation is owned by a physician and provides physician services, but another entity owned by a hospital provides ancillary services.[158] In some of these situations it may be possible to argue that the billing number is assigned to the group.

### 3. Prepaid Health Plans

The Stark law also provides an exception for services furnished to enrollees of certain types of prepaid health plans.[159] In its analysis of the statutory prepaid health plan ownership and compensation exception, HHS was faced with two principal problems in trying to avoid the unintended disruption of many physician arrangements with health maintenance organizations (HMOs) or managed care organizations (MCOs). First, HHS wanted to ensure that it generally permitted physician ownership of network-type HMOs or MCOs, provider-sponsored

---

[155] 66 Fed. Reg. at 952; 42 C.F.R. §411.351.

[156] 66 Fed. Reg. at 960; 42 C.F.R. §411.355(b)(3).

[157] 66 Fed. Reg. at 960; 42 C.F.R. §411.355(b)(3)(v).

[158] 66 Fed. Reg. at 894.

[159] 42 U.S.C. §1395nn(b)(3); 42 C.F.R. §411.355(c).

organizations (PSOs), and independent practice associations (IPAs).[160] Secondly, the statutory prepaid health plan exception does not protect physician arrangements involving commercial or employer-provided group plans—typically the so-called commercial product paralleling the Medicare MCO product—that include some Medicare retiree members.[161] HHS resolved the first major problem by more clearly defining the party that is furnishing DHS.[162] HHS resolved the second major problem by creating a compensation risk-sharing exception, which will be discussed in this section (see Section IV.A.3.b., below).[163]

As with other parts of the final rule, HHS is deferring its treatment of Medicaid managed care plans until Phase II.

### a. The Prepaid Plan Exception

The prepaid health plan exception protects ownership and compensation arrangements for "services furnished by an organization (or its contractors or subcontractors) to enrollees of one of the [designated] prepaid health plans (not including services provided to enrollees in any other plan or line of business offered or administered by the same organization)."[164] The Medicare+Choice regulation amended the Stark I regulation regarding specifically protected prepaid health plans to include, for example, certain Medicare+Choice plans, health care prepayment plans, demonstration project MCOs, and Public Health Service Act-qualifying HMOs.[165]

In defining the term "entity," the final rule clarifies that the entity that will be deemed to be furnishing DHS as a general matter is *not* the HMO, MCO, PSO, IPA, or similar entity under contract with other entities directly furnishing DHS. Rather, a person or entity is considered to be furnishing DHS if it is the person or entity to which Medicare payment is made for the DHS, directly or upon assignment on the patient's behalf.[166] Thus, a prepaid health plan, or an MCO, PSO, or IPA with which the health plan contracts directly or indirectly for services to plan enrollees, will only be considered to be furnishing DHS when the services are provided directly through an employee or otherwise, so that Medicare payment is made to the plan for DHS directly, upon assignment on the patient's behalf, or pursuant to a valid reassignment under Medicare reassignment rules; or when services are provided by a supplier employed by the plan or the plan operates a facility able to accept reassignment from the supplier under Medicare reassignment rules.[167] HHS believed that this change made it possible for physicians to hold ownership interests in most types of network IPAs and MCOs, as most

---

[160] 66 Fed. Reg. at 912.

[161] 66 Fed. Reg. at 913.

[162] 66 Fed. Reg. at 912–14.

[163] 66 Fed. Reg. at 913.

[164] 66 Fed. Reg. at 960; 42 C.F.R. §411.355(c).

[165] 66 Fed. Reg. at 960; 42 C.F.R. §411.355(c).

[166] 66 Fed. Reg. at 912; 42 C.F.R. §411.351.

[167] 66 Fed. Reg. at 912; 42 C.F.R. §411.351.

do not provide DHS directly, but rather contract with others for the delivery of services to enrollees. However, in limited situations in which the prepaid health plan will be deemed to be the DHS provider, CMS noted that physicians with an ownership interest in the prepaid health plan would be prohibited from referring patients to that entity for DHS absent an applicable exception.[168]

The final rule makes clear that this exception protects providers, suppliers, and other entities—the "downstream providers"—that provide, either under direct or indirect contract, DHS to enrollees of protected Medicare prepaid health plans.[169] Thus, a physician may refer a patient for DHS covered by the protected Medicare prepaid health plans to an MCO that has a Medicare managed care contract or to any entity, provider, or supplier furnishing the services under a contract or subcontract with the MCO. As noted above, this exception and the explicit language of the final rule only protect services furnished to enrollees of one of the protected prepaid health plans. It does not, however, protect "pull through" patients, i.e., other Medicare beneficiaries served by that prepaid health plan or provider pursuant to a commercial product.

### b. Risk-Sharing Compensation Exception

Because there are so many commercial or employer-provided MCO arrangements that serve Medicare beneficiaries, HHS determined that additional protection was needed for managed care incentive compensation (for example, withholds, bonuses, and risk pools not protected by either the employment or personal services exceptions).[170] Therefore, the final rule created a risk-sharing compensation exception for compensation pursuant to a risk-sharing arrangement (including, but not limited to, withholds, bonuses, and risk pools) between an MCO or an IPA and a physician (either directly or indirectly through a subcontractor) for services provided to enrollees of a health plan.[171] Specifically, the exception applies to the following four types of prepaid health plans providing services to individuals enrolled in the plan:

1. health plans that have entered into a Medicare risk-sharing contract under Section 1876 of the Social Security Act;[172]

---

[168] 66 Fed. Reg. at 913.

[169] 66 Fed. Reg. at 911.

[170] 66 Fed. Reg. at 912–13.

[171] 66 Fed. Reg. at 912–13; 42 C.F.R. §411.357(n).

[172] *See* 42 U.S.C. §1395mm. Note, however, that pursuant to §4001 of the Balanced Budget Act of 1997, health plans that have entered into a Medicare "risk sharing" contract under §1876 of the Social Security Act will automatically transition into the Part C Medicare+Choice program. "Beginning January 1, 1998, section 1876 risk-based contractors will be paid under a new Medicare+Choice payment methodology rather than the current AAPCC method in section 1876(a), and will be subject to certain other Medicare+Choice provisions. Upon publication, the Secretary will no longer accept new 1876 risk applications." *Operational Policy Letter, HCFA Center for Health Plans and Providers*, OPL No. 55 (Sept. 5, 1997). Presumably, the protection afforded §1876 plans under the Stark law will transfer over to similar Medicare+Choice plans.

2. health plans that provide medical and other health services on a prepayment basis pursuant to Section 1833(a)(1)(A) of the Social Security Act;[173]
3. health plans that receive payment from the Medicare program pursuant to enumerated types of demonstration projects; and
4. federally qualified HMOs.

While HHS defined the term "health plan" in the same manner as the federal anti-kickback statute safe harbor, the final rule text did not define the term "risk sharing," and the preamble made clear that this term was specifically intended to be broader than the same term used in the federal anti-kickback statute risk-sharing safe harbors (Section 1001.952(t) and (u)).[174] The arrangement, however, may not violate the federal anti-kickback statute or any law or regulation governing billing or the submission of claims, and, as with the prepaid health plan exception, the "pull through" of non-enrollees (i.e., traditional Medicare fee-for-service patients) is not protected.

This exception is unique among those in the Stark law, because it is limited only to referrals of certain patients—those who are enrolled in a prepaid health plan. The exception does not apply to referrals of Medicare or Medicaid fee-for-service patients for DHS.[175]

## B. New Regulatory Exceptions for Ownership and Compensation

The Stark law grants the Secretary the regulatory authority to create additional exceptions for ownership and compensation financial relationships where the Secretary determines, and specifies in regulations, that such relationships do not pose a risk of program or patient abuse. These exceptions are known as "(b)(4)" exceptions because of the statutory authority of Section 1877(b)(4) of the Social Security Act. This authority is important because it provides CMS with its only opportunity to grant relief for both ownership and compensation arrangements. Thus for example, services permitted under (b)(4) can be joint ventured with referring physicians.

Because the Stark law is intended to cover those specific services that Congress determined are or could be subject to abuse, HHS created in the final rule limited exceptions for those few services or circumstances that HHS determined, as required by law, posed a limited risk of abuse and were necessary to promote continuous patient care. These ownership and compensation exceptions are in addition to the statutory exceptions discussed above for in-office ancillary services and prepaid health plans. The exceptions set forth in the final rule include:

- certain clinical laboratory services furnished by ASCs, ESRD facilities, or hospices;

---

[173] *See also* 42 U.S.C. §1395*l*(a)(1)(A).

[174] 66 Fed. Reg. at 914.

[175] 66 Fed. Reg. at 911.

- academic medical centers;
- implants at ambulatory surgical centers;
- EPO or other dialysis-related prescription drugs furnished in or by an ESRD facility;
- preventive screening tests, vaccinations, and immunizations; and
- eyeglasses and contact lenses following cataract surgery.

## 1. *Clinical Laboratory Services Furnished by Ambulatory Surgical Centers, End-Stage Renal Disease Facilities, or Hospice Services*

The final rule excepts from the Stark law prohibition clinical laboratory services furnished in ASCs, ESRD facilities, or hospice services, provided that payments for those services are included in the applicable rate (the ASC rate, the ESRD composite rate, or as part of the per diem hospice charge, respectively).[176]

## 2. *Academic Medical Centers*

Under certain conditions, referred services provided by an academic medical center are excepted from the Stark law prohibition. HHS has created an exception for academic medical centers because of the unique symbiotic relationship among faculty, medical centers, and teaching institutions and the educational and research roles of faculty, and because the flow of funds and referrals within academic medical settings do not easily fit within other exceptions.[177]

For the academic medical center exception to apply, referring physicians must be full-time or substantial part-time employees of the academic medical center, have faculty appointments at the affiliated medical school, and provide substantial academic or clinical teaching services for which they are compensated under their employment relationships. This exception is not intended to cover physicians providing only occasional teaching services and who are more appropriately considered community physicians. As with the other exceptions, all payments to physicians must be at fair market value and not based in any way on referrals. This exception does not prevent, however, productivity bonuses based on services physicians personally perform or other business generated by the referring physician within the academic medical center.

HHS intended for this exception to apply to "genuine" academic medical settings.[178] Accordingly, the exception requires that all transfers of money between components of the academic medical center directly or indirectly support the missions of teaching, indigent care, research, or community service.[179] Furthermore, there must be a bona

---

[176] 42 C.F.R. §411.355(d).

[177] 66 Fed. Reg. at 916.

[178] 66 Fed. Reg. at 916.

[179] 66 Fed. Reg. at 916; 42 C.F.R. §411.355(e)(1)(iii)(A).

fide affiliation between the medical center components as evidenced by a written agreement.[180]

While HHS may have intended for this exception to provide some relief for academic medical center arrangements that did not quite fit within other exceptions under the Stark law, this exception is limited in its scope and does not address many legitimate arrangements. For example, it only covers employed physicians at teaching hospitals, medical schools, faculty practice plans, or departmental professional corporations, but may not fully protect affiliated group practices or physician-hospital organizations with non-employed clinical faculty— by far the more common arrangement between physicians and academic medical centers. In addition, reflecting the increased concerns over fraud and abuse in clinical and sponsored research, any monies given to a referring physician for research must be used solely to support bona fide research.[181]

### 3. Implantation of Devices at Ambulatory Surgical Centers

The final rule creates an exception to permit referring physicians or members of the referring physician's group practice to perform prosthetic device implants in Medicare-certified ASCs.[182] The exception applies to implants, including, but not limited to, cochlear implants, intraocular lenses, and other implanted prosthetics, implanted prosthetic devices, and implanted DME that meet the following conditions:

- The implant is furnished by the referring physician or a member of the referring physician's group practice in a Medicare-certified ASC with which the referring physician has a financial relationship.
- The implant is implanted in the patient during a surgical procedure performed in the same ASC where the implant is furnished.
- The arrangement for the furnishing of the implant does not violate the federal anti-kickback statute.
- Billing and claims submission for the implants complies with all federal and state laws and regulations.
- This exception does not apply to any financial relationships between the referring physician and any entity other than the ASC in which the implant is furnished to and implanted in the patient.

CMS created this exception to protect surgeons who refer patients needing implantable devices to an ASC in which the surgeon has an ownership interest. In the absence of a special rule, no other existing exception applies in this situation because many of these devices are billed outside of the bundled ASC rate. CMS believed that the exclusion

---

[180] 66 Fed. Reg. at 916–17; 42 C.F.R. §411.355(e)(1)(iii)(B).

[181] 66 Fed. Reg. at 917; 42 C.F.R. §411.355(e)(1)(iii)(C).

[182] 66 Fed. Reg. at 934; 42 C.F.R. §411.355(f).

of these implants will not increase the risk of overutilization beyond what was already presented by the surgeon's Part B physician fee. CMS also noted that, as a practical matter, the absence of an applicable exception allowing implantation of these items at ASCs would result in these procedures moving to more costly hospital settings.[183]

This exception is limited to its explicit terms; it does not protect items implanted in other settings. As to implants provided in other settings or those that otherwise do not meet the conditions of this exception, other exceptions may still apply.

### 4. EPO or Other Prescription Drugs Furnished in or by an End-Stage Renal Disease Facility

HHS created an exception for erythropoietin (EPO) and certain other drugs required for dialysis when furnished by an ESRD facility.[184] HHS created this exception in part because of its determination that, due to the strict utilization and coverage criteria for EPO furnished as part of ESRD services, the exception poses a limited risk of abuse and was necessary to avoid disruption of patient care. However, HHS noted in the preamble that it would continue to monitor such exceptions and revisit the exclusions to prevent abuse if it deems it necessary.[185] Significantly, HHS determined that Congress did not intend to prevent physician ownership of ESRD facilities. Any physician investments in a home dialysis supply company, such as a "Method II" supply company, or other entity that supplies EPO to ESRD facilities or patients pursuant to a contractual relationship with an ESRD facility do not fall under this exception. In other words, physicians may not have an ownership interest in any dialysis facility subsidiary furnishing these services unless an ownership exception is met.

### 5. Preventive Screening Tests, Immunizations, and Vaccines

The final rule included an exception for certain legislatively mandated preventive screening and immunization services that are subject to CMS-imposed frequency limits (that it believes mitigate the potential for abuse) and are paid based on a fee schedule.[186] Preventive screening tests, immunizations, and vaccines that are covered by Medicare and identified by CPT and HCPCS codes meet this exception if the following conditions are satisfied:

- The preventive screening tests, immunizations, and vaccines are subject to CMS-mandated frequency limits and are reimbursed by Medicare based on a fee schedule.
- The arrangement for the provision of the preventive screening tests, immunizations, and vaccines does not violate the federal anti-kickback statute.

---

[183] 66 Fed. Reg. at 934.
[184] 66 Fed. Reg. at 937–38; 42 C.F.R. §411.355(g).
[185] 66 Fed. Reg. at 923.
[186] 66 Fed. Reg. at 961; 42 C.F.R. §411.355(h).

- Billing and claims submission for such tests, immunizations, and vaccines complies with all federal and state laws and regulations.
- The preventive screening tests, immunizations, and vaccines must be covered by Medicare and must be listed on the HCFA (or CMS) Web site and in annual updates.

### 6. Eyeglasses and Contact Lenses Following Cataract Surgery

The final rule created an exception for eyeglasses and contact lenses that are prescribed after cataract surgery.[187] The exception applies when the following conditions are met:

- The glasses or contact lenses are provided in accordance with Medicare coverage and payment provisions set forth in 42 C.F.R. Sections 410.36(a)(2)(ii) and 414.228.
- The arrangement for the furnishing of the glasses or contact lenses does not violate the federal anti-kickback statute.
- Billing and claim submission for the eyeglasses or contact lenses complies with all federal and state laws and regulations.

CMS created this exception in response to comments urging the exclusion of eyeglasses and contact lenses from the definition of prosthetic devices. CMS noted in the commentary that Medicare coverage of eyeglasses and contact lenses is unique in that it is limited to one pair of either item after each cataract surgery and is available to any patient who has had this surgery. In addition, the Medicare-approved amount of payment does not vary based on the expense of a particular pair of glasses or contact lenses. Accordingly, CMS created this exception because it sees little opportunity or incentive for a physician either to under- or overutilize these items in the Medicare program.

## C. Statutory Ownership Exceptions

As noted above, HHS stated formally in the preamble to the final rule that it was deferring until Phase II implementation of a final rule for the statutory ownership and compensation exceptions contained in Section 1877(d) and (e) of the Stark law (for example, employee and personal services exceptions).

This discussion of these exceptions will focus on the statute and Stark II proposed rule. However, at least until Phase II is implemented, it appears that, in the interim, existing regulations applicable to Stark I that implement these exceptions remain intact, and therefore arguably are incorporated into the Stark II final rule and will become applicable to all DHS.

### 1. Publicly Traded Securities

Ownership of publicly traded securities is not a "financial relationship" for purposes of the Stark law if the requirements of the ex-

---

[187] 66 Fed. Reg. at 936; 42 C.F.R. §411.355(i).

ception are met.[188] Acceptable ownership is defined as ownership of investment securities, shares, bonds, debentures, notes, or other debt instruments that may be purchased on terms generally available to the public and that are listed on the New York Stock Exchange, the American Stock Exchange, or any regional exchange in which quotations are published on a daily basis, or foreign securities listed on a recognized foreign, national, or regional exchange in which quotations are published on a daily basis.[189] Alternatively, the securities may be traded under an automated interdealer quotation system operated by the National Association of Securities Dealers.[190]

CMS's comments in the Stark II proposed rule shed some light on the ownership or investment interest exception. The Stark II proposed rule would clarify language in the Stark I regulation regarding the exception for physician ownership of investment securities purchased on the open market, that, although ambiguous, seemed to suggest that the terms on which the physician obtained the interest must be generally available to the public, thus precluding private placement "roll ups" that eventually became publicly traded.[191] The Stark II proposed rule would make it clear that roll-ups do not qualify because this exception applies only if, "at the time the physician or family member obtained the securities, they *could* be purchased on the open market, even if the physician or family member did not actually purchase the securities on those terms."[192]

In addition, the corporation must have had, at the end of its most recent fiscal year, or on average during the previous 3 fiscal years, stockholder equity exceeding $75 million.[193] Moreover, ownership of shares in a regulated investment company as defined in Internal Revenue Code Section 851(a) is exempt from the provisions of the Stark law if such company had, at the end of its most recent fiscal year, or on average during the previous 3 fiscal years, total assets exceeding $75 million.[194]

## 2. Hospitals in Puerto Rico, Rural Providers, and Hospital Ownership

The Stark law contains a statutory exception applying to DHS provided by hospitals located in Puerto Rico.[195] In addition, the Stark law exempts DHS furnished by entities in rural areas if substantially all of those designated services furnished by such entities are provided to individuals residing in those rural areas.[196]

---

[188] *See* 42 U.S.C. §1395nn(c); *see also* 42 C.F.R. §411.356.

[189] *See* 42 U.S.C. §1395nn(c)(1); *see also* 42 C.F.R. §411.356(a).

[190] *See* 42 U.S.C. §1395nn(c)(1)(A); *see also* 42 C.F.R. §411.356(a).

[191] 63 Fed. Reg. at 1698.

[192] *Id.* (emphasis in original).

[193] 42 U.S.C. §1395nn(c)(1)(B).

[194] *See* 42 U.S.C. §1395nn(c)(2); *see also* 42 C.F.R. §411.356(b).

[195] 42 U.S.C. §1395nn(d)(1).

[196] 42 U.S.C. §1395nn(d)(2).

The exception for hospital ownership applies to DHS provided by the hospital if the following two criteria are met: the referring physician who is an investor of the hospital is authorized to perform services at the hospital; and the physician's ownership or investment interest is in the hospital itself and not merely in a subdivision of the hospital.[197]

CMS's comments in the Stark II proposed rule indicated that the hospital ownership exception would cover only DHS furnished by the hospital, and not services furnished by any other health care providers that the hospital owns, such as a hospital-owned home health agency or skilled nursing facility (SNF).[198] This interpretation appears to create the anomaly that if a physician has an ownership interest in a hospital, the physician can refer a patient to the hospital laboratory if it is a department of the hospital, but not if it is a legally separate, but wholly owned subsidiary. This approach is also inconsistent with CMS's interpretation of indirect financial relationships, i.e., relationships established through intermediate parties, no matter how many steps removed, because the physician's indirect financial relationship with a hospital subsidiary is not severed by the exception that covers the physician's direct investment interest in the hospital.

## D. Statutory Compensation Exceptions

As noted above, HHS formally stated in the preamble to the final rule that it is deferring implementation of a final rule until Phase II for the statutory compensation exceptions contained in Section 1877(e) of the Stark law. These statutory compensation exceptions include those for:

- rental of office space or equipment;
- bona fide employment arrangements;
- personal services arrangements;
- physician incentive plans;
- remuneration unrelated to the provision of designated services by a hospital;
- physician recruitment;
- isolated transactions;
- certain group practice arrangements by a hospital; and
- payments by physicians for items or services.

This discussion of these exceptions will focus on the statute and Stark II proposed rule. However, the existing regulations applicable to Stark I that implement these exceptions appear to remain intact, and therefore, arguably are incorporated into the Stark II final rule and will become applicable to all DHS.

---

[197] *See* 42 U.S.C. §1395nn(d)(3); *see also* 42 C.F.R. §411.356(c)(1).
[198] 63 Fed. Reg. at 1698.

Prior to a discussion of these statutory exceptions, two general areas of concern for practitioners should be noted. First, CMS did not address in the Stark II proposed rule the provision contained in the Stark law related to the concept of commercial reasonableness. Specifically, a few of the compensation exceptions imposed on the definition of fair market value an additional requirement that the compensation arrangement be "commercially reasonable," even if no referrals are made. If this requirement were to be interpreted literally, a provider could not lease space from a physician unless the lease would make economic sense, even if the renting physician made no referrals at all. A more reasonable interpretation that has been widely accepted would be to require that the lease meet certain business bona fides, such as being open to the public and being advertised with the expectation that the provider achieve referrals from physicians other than the renting physician.

The second analytical difficulty for practitioners relates to the flow of money in a compensation arrangement. Practitioners first should determine which is the most appropriate compensation exception to meet based on whether money or compensation is flowing from the physician to the entity, or from the entity providing the service to the physician. As discussed more fully below (see Section IV.D.8.), there is a liberal exception under the Stark law for payments by a physician. Where possible, practitioners will want to rely on this exception. The problem with this approach is that many of the Stark law compensation exceptions are written to apply to arrangements with physicians regardless of the direction of the flow of money. Consequently, it would appear reasonable for providers to be able to choose the exception under which they will seek protection. In the Stark II proposed rule, however, CMS foreclosed this approach by requiring compliance first with the other compensation exceptions before a provider can rely on the payments-by-a-physician exception.[199]

## 1. Rental of Office Space or Equipment

### a. Office Space

Office space rental arrangements are exempted from the Stark law if the lease is set out in writing and signed by the parties, is for a term of at least 1 year, and specifies the premises covered by the lease. In addition, the space rented cannot exceed that which is reasonable and necessary for the legitimate business purposes of the rental and must be used exclusively by the lessee when being used by the lessee, except that in the case of space rentals, the lessee may make payments for the use of space consisting of common areas if such payments do not exceed the lessee's pro rata share of expenses for such space. The rental charges over the term of the lease must be set in advance, be consistent with fair market value, and not be determined in a manner that

---

[199] 63 Fed. Reg. at 1703.

takes into account the volume or value of any referrals or other business generated between the parties. Moreover, the space lease must be commercially reasonable even if no referrals were made between the parties.[200]

The legislative history of Stark II contains an unequivocal statement as to congressional intent with respect to the space rental exception (as well as the equipment rental exception discussed below):

> [T]he conferees intend that charges for space and equipment leases may be based on daily, monthly, or other time-based rates, or rates based on units of service furnished, as long as the amount of the time-based or units of service rates does not fluctuate during the contract period based on the volume or value of referrals between the parties to the lease or arrangement.[201]

The Stark II proposed rule does not appear to amend in any way the rental exception to the Stark law, although CMS explained its position that capital leases under which the lessee acquires title to the property at the end of the lease term go beyond the scope of the Stark law's rental exception.[202] The Stark II proposed rule also indicated that equipment leased on a "click fee" basis (i.e., where a fee is charged each time the equipment is used) may qualify under the rental exception.[203] Yet because the compensation under this exception may not reflect the volume or value of the physician's own referrals, CMS has indicated that click fees for patients who are referred for DHS by a lessor-physician will not qualify as permissible rental fees under the Stark law because a physician's compensation cannot reflect the volume or value of referrals.[204] As discussed in Section III.B.2.f.ii., above (volume or value of referrals), CMS abandoned this analysis in the Stark II final rule.

Parenthetically, it is clear that click fees do not meet the requirements of the anti-kickback statute safe harbor for equipment leases because the aggregate compensation under such leases must be set in advance.

### b. *Equipment*

The exception for equipment rental is substantially similar to the exception for space leases. Specifically, payments made by a lessee of equipment to the lessor of the equipment for the use of the equipment are excepted from the Stark law if the equipment lease is set out in writing, signed by the parties, and specifies the equipment covered by the

---

[200] *See* 42 U.S.C. §1395nn(e)(1)(A). In addition, the space lease must meet such other requirements as the Secretary of HHS may impose by regulation as needed to protect against program or patient abuse. As of January 4, 2001, the Secretary of HHS had not imposed any additional standards.

[201] H.R. CONF. REP. OF THE COMM. ON THE BUDGET TO ACCOMPANY H.R. 2264, at 814 (Aug. 4, 1993).

[202] 63 Fed. Reg. at 1714.

[203] *Id.*

[204] *Id.*

lease. The equipment rented or leased may not exceed that which is reasonable and necessary for the legitimate business purposes of the lease or rental and must be used exclusively by the lessee when being used by the lessee. In addition, the equipment lease must provide for a term of rental or lease of at least 1 year, and the rental charges over the term of the equipment lease must be set in advance, be consistent with fair market value, and not be determined in a manner that takes into account the volume or value of any referrals or other business generated between the parties. Finally, the equipment lease must be commercially reasonable even if no referrals were made between the parties.[205]

### 2. Bona Fide Employment Arrangements

The Stark law also exempts any amount paid by an employer to a physician employee[206] (or an immediate family member of such physician employee) who has a bona fide employment relationship with the employer for the provision of services if: the employment is for identifiable services, the amount of the remuneration under the employment is consistent with the fair market value of the services, and the remuneration is not determined in a manner that takes into account (directly or indirectly) the volume or value of any referrals by the referring physician. The remuneration must be provided pursuant to an agreement that would be commercially reasonable even if no referrals were made to the employer, and the employment must meet such other requirements as the Secretary of HHS may impose by regulation as needed to protect against program or patient abuse.[207]

According to CMS's comments in the Stark II proposed rule, remuneration paid by an employer to a physician in the form of a productivity bonus based on services performed personally by the physician is not prohibited as long as the bonus is not directly related to the volume or value of a physician's own referrals.

An important distinction to bear in mind is the difference between the employee compensation exception under the Stark law and the employee compensation safe harbor under the anti-kickback statute. The employee compensation safe harbor permits payment for referrals, whereas the Stark law employment compensation exception does not.

---

[205] 42 U.S.C. §1395nn(e)(1)(B). In addition, as with space leases, the equipment lease must meet such other requirements as the Secretary of HHS may impose by regulation as needed to protect against program or patient abuse. As of January 4, 2001, the Secretary of HHS had not imposed any additional standards.

[206] As it pertains to the term "employee," the Stark law states that "[a]n individual is considered to be 'employed by' or an 'employee' of an entity if the individual would be considered to be an employee of the entity under the usual common law rules applicable in determining the employer-employee relationship (as applied for purposes of section 3121(d)(2) of [the Internal Revenue Code of 1986])." 42 U.S.C. §1395nn(h)(2).

[207] *See generally* 42 U.S.C. §1395nn(e)(2).

## 3. Personal Service Arrangements

The personal service arrangements exception under the Stark law permits a physician to receive compensation from an entity with which the physician has a financial relationship and that provides DHS to the physician's Medicare or Medicaid patients, provided that the arrangement is set out in writing, signed by the parties, specifies the services covered by the arrangement, and covers all of the services to be provided by the physician (or an immediate family member of such physician) to the entity. In addition, the aggregate services contracted for may not exceed those that are reasonable and necessary for the legitimate business purposes of the arrangement; the term of the arrangement must be for at least 1 year; and the compensation to be paid over the term of the arrangement must be set in advance, not exceed fair market value, and not be determined in a manner that takes into account the volume or value of any referrals or other business generated between the parties, except pursuant to a physician incentive plan (PIP).

Finally, the services to be performed under the arrangement may not involve the counseling or promotion of a business arrangement or other activity that violates any state or federal law and the arrangement must meet such other requirements as the Secretary of HHS may impose by regulation as needed to protect against program or patient abuse.[208] As discussed in Sections IV.D.1.a. and III.B.2.f.ii., above, in the final rule CMS has accepted "per use" or "per service" arrangements. In the Stark II proposed rule, CMS indicated that it would interpret this exception to permit a physician or family member to perform the services, or these individuals may enter into an agreement to provide the services through technicians or others whom they employ.

Although CMS would retain the requirement that personal service contracts be for a term of 1 year, it is noteworthy that under the Stark II proposed rule, CMS indicated that it would recognize and accept such contracts even if they contain certain types of termination clauses that would effectively render the contracts to be for a term of less than 1 year.

The personal service arrangements exception permits compensation to be determined in a manner that takes into account referrals if the arrangement is pursuant to a qualifying PIP. A PIP is defined as "any compensation arrangement between an entity and a physician or physician group that may directly or indirectly have the effect of reducing or limiting services provided with respect to individuals enrolled with the entity."[209] Effective September 13, 1995, the Stark I regulation incorporated this definition and the statutory requirements into the applicable sections of the *Code of Federal Regulations*.[210] The Stark II pro-

---

[208] *See generally* 42 U.S.C. §1395nn(e)(3)(A). As of January 4, 2001, the Secretary of HHS had not imposed any additional standards. *See also* 42 C.F.R. §411.357(d).

[209] *See generally* 42 U.S.C. §1395nn(e)(3)(B).

[210] *See generally id.*; 42 C.F.R. §411.351; 42 C.F.R. §411.357(d)(2).

posed rule would retain this definition, but would revise the Stark I regulation as follows:

> The August 1995 final rule incorporated section 1877(e)(3)(B)(i) into our regulations at §411.357(d)(2). Because of the establishment at §417.479 of requirements concerning incentive plans, this proposed rule would revise §411.357(d)(2). It would replace the reference to requirements established by the Secretary under section 1876(i)(8)(A)(ii) of the Act with a reference to the requirements of §417.479. We would also reverse the order of paragraphs (ii) and (iii) of §411.357(d)(2) because we believe this order reflects a more logical progression. In addition, we would delete existing §411.357(d)(3), which contains a time-sensitive provision related to personal services arrangements that, based on the statute, is now obsolete.[211]

This regulatory exception requires that no specific payment is made directly or indirectly under the plan as an inducement to reduce or limit *medically necessary services* provided with respect to a specific individual *enrolled with the entity.*[212] If the plan puts the physician or physician group at substantial financial risk, as determined by the Secretary under Section 1876(i)(8)(A)(ii) of the Social Security Act, then the plan has to meet specified regulatory requirements.[213] Finally, on request, the entity must provide CMS with access to descriptive information regarding the plan.[214]

Under the second prong of this exception, "substantial financial risk" occurs when a PIP places a physician or physician group at risk for amounts greater than 25 percent of such physician's or physician group's total potential compensation for covered services *and* if the risk is based on the use or cost of referral services.[215]

The PIP exception under the Stark law precludes the incentive plan from reducing or limiting "medically necessary services provided with respect to a specific individual."[216] Experts in the industry generally believe that an incentive plan needs strong utilization review and quality assurance components to ensure that medically necessary services are not denied.

In the Stark II proposed rule, it is clear that CMS would apply the PIP exception to the prohibition on compensation based on volume or value of referrals only when the entity making payments is an HMO or other insurer that enrolls patients.[217] Thus, this exception would appear to have limited application in light of the prepaid health plan exception.

---

[211] 63 Fed. Reg. at 1669.

[212] 42 U.S.C. §1395nn(e)(3)(B)(i)(I).

[213] 42 U.S.C. §1395nn(e)(3)(B)(i)(II).

[214] 42 U.S.C. §1395nn(e)(3)(B)(i)(III).

[215] *See generally* 42 C.F.R. §417.479(f); *see also* 42 U.S.C. §1395mm(i)(8)(A)(ii).

[216] 42 U.S.C. §1395nn(e)(3)(B); 42 C.F.R. §411.357(d)(2)(i).

[217] *See generally* 63 Fed. Reg. at 1712.

## 4. Remuneration Unrelated to the Provision of Designated Health Services by a Hospital

The Stark law also exempts remuneration that is provided by a hospital to a physician if such remuneration does not relate to the provision of DHS.[218] This exception is a good reminder that remuneration that is unrelated to the provision of DHS can run afoul of the Stark law unless a specific exception is met. This exception, as well as the ownership exception for hospitals, demonstrates the special status Congress has afforded hospital providers under the Stark law.

## 5. Physician Recruitment

The physician recruitment exception to the Stark law protects remuneration that is provided by a hospital to a physician for the purpose of inducing the physician to relocate to the geographic area served by the hospital to become a member of the medical staff of the hospital, if certain conditions are met. Specifically, the physician may not be required to refer patients to the hospital; the amount of the remuneration under the arrangement may not be determined in a manner that takes into account (directly or indirectly) the volume or value of any referrals by the referring physician; and the arrangement must meet such other requirements as the Secretary of HHS may impose by regulation as needed to protect against program or patient abuse.[219]

The Stark II proposed rule would not amend or modify the criteria for the physician recruitment exception. CMS indicated, however, that recruitment payments made by a hospital to physicians living in the hospital's geographic area—so-called "cross-town" recruiting—also may be protected under the proposed fair market value compensation exception. CMS has specifically solicited comments from the health care community regarding how to define "geographic area."

## 6. Isolated Transactions

The Stark law provides an exception for isolated financial transactions, such as a one-time sale of property or practice, if the amount of the remuneration is consistent with the fair market value of the property or practice and is not determined in a manner that takes into account (directly or indirectly) the volume or value of any referrals by the referring physician. Thus, it is this exception that must be met for purchases of physician practices. This provision also requires that the remuneration be provided pursuant to an agreement that would be commercially reasonable even if no referrals were made to the employer or buyer, and that the transaction meet such other requirements as the Secretary of HHS may impose by regulation as needed to protect against program or patient abuse.[220]

---

[218] 42 U.S.C. §1395nn(e)(4).

[219] *See generally* 42 U.S.C. §1395nn(e)(5).

[220] *See generally* 42 U.S.C. §1395nn(e)(6); *see also* 42 C.F.R. §411.357(f).

The Stark II proposed rule clarified the language in the Stark I final rule, revising the definition of "isolated transaction" to make clear that a transaction involving a single payment is required, and that long-term or installment payments will not qualify for this exception.[221] Thus, some type of third-party financing is generally required for purchases of physician practices.

### 7. Certain Group Practice Arrangements by a Hospital

This exception applies to certain arrangements between a hospital and a physician group under which DHS are provided by the group but are billed by the hospital if: (1) with respect to services provided to an inpatient of the hospital, the arrangement is pursuant to the provision of inpatient hospital services under Section 1861(b)(3) of the Social Security Act; (2) the arrangement began before December 19, 1989, and has continued in effect without interruption since such date; (3) with respect to DHS covered under the arrangement, substantially all of such services furnished to patients of the hospital are furnished by the group under the arrangement; (4) the arrangement is pursuant to an agreement that is set out in writing and that specifies the services to be provided by the parties and the compensation for services provided under the agreement; (5) the compensation paid over the term of the agreement is consistent with fair market value and the compensation per unit of services is fixed in advance and is not determined in a manner that takes into account the volume or value of any referrals or other business generated between the parties; (6) the compensation is provided pursuant to an agreement that would be commercially reasonable even if no referrals were made to the entity; and (7) the arrangement between the parties meets such other requirements as the Secretary of HHS may impose by regulation as needed to protect against program or patient abuse.[222]

### 8. Payments by Physicians for Items or Services

The Stark law protects payments made by a physician for items or services (other than clinical laboratory services) if they are furnished at a price that is consistent with fair market value.[223] Such financial arrangements can qualify under this exception even if they are not in writing, are for a period of less than 1 year or are not commercially reasonable. Given the obvious simplicity of these requirements, it is an attractive exception under which to seek protection.

In the Stark II proposed rule, CMS probably sensed the broad appeal of this exception and tried to narrow its scope by permitting its use only where a more specific exception does not apply.[224] The Stark

---

[221] 63 Fed. Reg. at 1669.

[222] *See generally* 42 U.S.C. §1395nn(e)(7).

[223] *See* 42 U.S.C. §1395nn(e)(8); *see also* 42 C.F.R. §411.357(i).

[224] 63 Fed. Reg. at 1670, 1725.

II proposed rule, however, does not provide any clear criteria to guide practitioners in this area.

## E. Indirect Compensation Arrangement Definition and Exception

One of the more significant features of the final rule is CMS's recognition that the statute either does not reach or does not adequately protect indirect compensation arrangements. As a result, CMS has both crafted a different definition of "indirect compensation arrangement" and created a broad exception for such arrangements.

### 1. Definition of Indirect Compensation Arrangement

The final rule defined indirect compensation as containing three elements:

- the unbroken chain test,
- the volume or value test, and
- the knowledge requirement.

#### a. Unbroken Chain Test

The first element requires, as between the referring physician and the entity furnishing DHS, "an unbroken chain of any number (but not fewer than one) of persons or entities that have financial relationships between them."[225] This first element is met if there is an unbroken chain of any type of financial relationship from the DHS entity to the referring physician, regardless of the form or purpose of the payments or their relationship to the DHS referrals.

It is unclear whether this unbroken chain test takes into account the structure of direct exceptions under the Stark law. If one of the financial relationships in the chain fits within a direct ownership or direct compensation arrangement exception, then according to the language of the statute, the relationship "shall not be considered" either an ownership interest or a compensation arrangement. Thus, any financial relationship that fits within a direct compensation or ownership exception breaks the chain and effectively ends the need for further analysis of the indirect relationship.

#### b. Volume or Value Test

The second element in the definition is the volume or value test, which reads:

> The referring physician . . . receives aggregate compensation from the person or entity in the chain with which the physician . . . has a direct financial relationship that varies with, or otherwise reflects, the volume or value of referrals or other business generated by the referring physician for the entity furnishing the DHS. If the financial relationship between the physician . . . and the person or entity in the chain with which

---

[225] 66 Fed. Reg. at 958–59; 42 C.F.R. §411.354(c)(2)(i).

the referring physician . . . has a direct financial relationship is an ownership or investment interest, the determination whether the aggregate compensation varies with, or otherwise reflects, the volume or value referrals or other business generated by the referring physician for the entity furnishing the DHS will be measured by the nonownership or noninvestment interest closest to the referring physician . . . (For example, if a referring physician has an ownership interest in company A, which owns company B, which has a compensation arrangement with company C, we would look to the aggregate compensation between company B and company C for purposes of this paragraph[ ]).[226]

Thus, it appears that if total payments under the arrangement rise or fall based on the volume or value of referrals, it is an indirect compensation arrangement that will trigger the referral prohibition unless it complies with an exception. In applying this test, CMS has departed from the requirement announced in the proposed rule that providers must trace payments. Instead, the focus of this second element under the final rule's test is the direct financial relationship with the referring physician, i.e., the last financial relationship in the chain. The only exception occurs when the direct financial arrangement with the referring physician is an ownership or investment interest; in that case the analysis moves up the chain until the first compensation arrangement is found. In the example of a group practice's medical director contract with a hospital, one must first look to the direct financial arrangement with the physician, in this case the physician's financial interest in the group practice. If that relationship is an ownership interest, the analysis moves upstream to the hospital's compensation arrangement with the group practice.[227]

Once the reference point of the direct financial arrangement is found, the next step in the analysis is whether that compensation arrangement involves aggregate compensation that varies with or otherwise reflects the volume or value of referrals or business otherwise generated. If it does, and the other definitional elements are met, an indirect compensation arrangement exists.

Given this test, virtually all service contracts between hospitals and physician groups will trigger the indirect compensation arrangement analysis. When physicians have an ownership interest in the group, the compensation arrangement between the hospital and the group will be the focus of the volume or value analysis. If the physicians do not own the group, the volume or value test will be applied to the physicians' compensation from the group to determine whether it varies with or otherwise reflects their referrals to the hospital.

---

[226] 66 Fed. Reg. at 959; 42 C.F.R. §411.354(c)(2)(ii).

[227] Similarly, in the case of "under arrangement" services between hospitals and physician-owned service providers, the analysis is of the compensation between the hospital and the service provider. The regulation elsewhere makes clear that physician-owned "under arrangement" providers do not have an ownership interest in the hospital, and need only comply with a compensation exception.

### c. Knowledge

The third element is a knowledge requirement similar to the one that applies to the overall regulation. For an indirect compensation relationship to exist, the entity furnishing DHS must have "knowledge" that the referring physician's compensation "varies with, or otherwise reflects, the value or volume of referrals or other business generated by the referring physician for the entity furnishing the DHS."[228] CMS's intent in this third element is to prevent the unfairness of imposing what would be draconian sanctions when the DHS provider is not aware of the nature of the indirect compensation arrangement. As noted above, the knowledge element here does not impose an affirmative duty on providers to investigate. CMS maintains, however, that the DHS entity must make a reasonable inquiry when it has reason to suspect a financial relationship exists. The nature of such an inquiry is undefined, but CMS suggests that reasonable inquiry by the DHS entity may include obtaining, in good faith, a written assurance from the referring physician or the entity from which the referring physician receives direct compensation that the physician's aggregate compensation is not based on the volume or value of referrals to the DHS entity.[229]

## 2. Exception for Indirect Compensation Arrangements

If an indirect compensation arrangement is found to exist, DHS referrals are prohibited unless the arrangement fits within a compensation exception that protects indirect relationships. The exception that will be most frequently called upon for this purpose is the indirect compensation exception. This exception has three elements that virtually parallel the fair market value exception.

1. The compensation received by the referring physician (or immediate family member) is fair market value for services and items actually provided, not taking into account the value or volume or referrals or other business generated by the referring physician for the entity furnishing DHS.
2. The compensation arrangement is set out in writing, signed by the parties, and specifies the services covered by the arrangement, except in the case of a bona fide employment relationship between an employer and an employee; in that case the arrangement need not be set out in a written contract, but must be for identifiable services and be commercially reasonable even if no referrals are made to the employer.
3. The compensation arrangement does not violate the anti-kickback statute or any laws or regulations governing billing or claims submission.[230]

---

[228] 66 Fed. Reg. at 959; 42 C.F.R. §411.354(c)(2)(iii).

[229] 66 Fed. Reg. at 866.

[230] 66 Fed. Reg. at 962; 42 C.F.R. §411.357(p).

For purposes of this exception, CMS indicated in the commentary to the final rule that in determining whether compensation takes into account the value or volume of referrals by the referring physician to the DHS entity, the "volume or value of referrals" and "other business generated" tests will be applied, permitting time-based or unit-of-service-based payments, even when the physician has generated the payment through a DHS referral. Therefore, per service or per use compensation arrangements can fit under this exception as long as the payments are fair market value for the items or services provided (i.e., do not include any additional amount that might be attributable to the volume or value of referrals), and the payments do not vary during the term of the compensation arrangement in any manner that takes into account referrals to the DHS entity.

> [W]e want to clarify that ownership or investment interests that are not protected under [the ownership exceptions] (and are therefore compensation arrangements . . .) are deemed to take into account the value or volume of referrals. We believe this view is consistent with the general prohibition on investment and ownership interests in the statute.[231]

In the final analysis, the concept of indirect compensation could apply to a large number of arrangements. Each such arrangement must be analyzed to determine whether it fits within the indirect compensation arrangement definition and/or the corresponding exception.

### 3. Joint Ownership

Another noteworthy issue is the final rule's analysis of joint ownership. CMS noted in the commentary that it abandoned the interpretation set forth in the proposed rule that joint ownership alone does not create a financial relationship between or among the joint owners. Instead, the agency indicated that the test for indirect financial relationships should be used to determine whether joint ownership arrangements pass muster.

Unfortunately, CMS gives no guidance as to how to apply the indirect ownership or the indirect compensation tests to joint ownership arrangements. Given that an ownership interest in a subsidiary does not create an ownership interest in the parent, joint ownership should not create an indirect ownership interest between the co-owners. Applying the test for indirect compensation arrangements to joint ownership, one would look "through" the physician's ownership interest in the joint venture and apply the volume or value test to the compensation arrangements, if any, between the joint venture and any DHS provider. Thus, an indirect compensation arrangement could be created in the case of a hospital-physician joint venture if the hospital had a compensation arrangement with the joint venture and the compensation the hospital paid the venture varied with or otherwise reflected the value of physician owner's referrals to the hospital.

---

[231] 66 Fed. Reg. at 877.

## F. Fair Market Value Exception

The final rule defined "fair market value" as the value in an arm's-length transaction that is consistent with the price that would result from bona fide bargaining between well-informed parties who are not otherwise in a position to generate business with each other. The definition also specifies that the fair market price will usually be the price at which other, similar bona fide sales have been consummated in the same market.[232]

The preamble made clear that the contracting parties bear the burden of establishing the fairness of any agreement.[233] That stated, CMS is willing to accept any commercially reasonable valuation method. A list of comparable transactions in the marketplace or an appraisal from a qualified independent expert should be satisfactory. CMS noted, however, that the fair market value standard indicates that compensation may not take into account the volume or value of referrals or other business between the parties. CMS asserts that this volume or value restriction may preclude the use of comparables involving entities or other physicians in a position to refer patients or generate business. As a practical matter, this restriction would almost seem to prohibit using any comparables from the health care industry. Thus, at least in the case of rural communities, CMS recognized that this restriction may require the use of alternative valuation methodologies.

Fair market value in the context of a lease of office space or equipment is defined as the value of rental property for general commercial purposes without taking into account the intended use of the property. The definition further specifies that a lease of office space may account for the lessor's cost of developing, upgrading, or maintaining the property, but may not take into account any potential additional value that may result from the proximity between the lessor and lessee and the resulting convenience of making patient referrals from the lessor to the lessee.[234]

The fair market value compensation exception created under HHS's statutory authority to create exceptions that do not pose a risk of program abuse should prove very valuable to physicians and entities seeking to set up a business relationship.[235] This exception itself is relatively straightforward, and incorporates the volume or value restrictions discussed above. The exception will protect arrangements in which, among other things, compensation paid to a physician is set in advance, is consistent with fair market value, and does not take into account the value or volume of referrals or other business generated by the referring physician. As with other Stark exceptions, the arrangement must involve a transaction that is commercially reasonable. Commercial reasonable-

---

[232] 66 Fed. Reg. at 953; 42 C.F.R. §411.351.

[233] 66 Fed. Reg. at 944–45.

[234] 66 Fed. Reg. at 953–54; 42 C.F.R. §411.351.

[235] 66 Fed. Reg. at 961–62; 42 C.F.R. §411.357(*l*).

ness is determined by viewing the transaction in the context of the particular business in which the parties are involved.

Many of the constraints parties face when drafting contracts under Stark have been loosened by the fair market value compensation exception. For example, the written contracts need not be for a year as long as the parties enter into only one arrangement for the same items or services during the course of the year. An arrangement made for less than 1 year may be renewed any number of times, although the terms and the compensation may not change. Additionally, in the final rule HHS dropped a particularly burdensome requirement in the proposed fair market value compensation exception that all other arrangements between the parties must be cross-referenced in the agreement.

The fair market value exception requires parties to be sure that the arrangement either meets a safe harbor under the federal anti-kickback statute, has been approved by the OIG under an advisory opinion, or does not violate the federal anti-kickback statute.[236] Because none of the safe harbors under the federal anti-kickback statute permit arrangements for less than 1 year or permit payments based on a per use or per service basis, the arrangement must comply with the federal anti-kickback statute for this exception to apply. The bright lines that HHS attempted to draw in the final rule have become somewhat blurred by this requirement. Most arrangements will have to be subject to a full analysis under the federal anti-kickback statute, particularly in regard to the parties' intent, to determine that the arrangement does not violate the federal anti-kickback statute.

## G. Other New Compensation Exceptions

Previous discussions have examined compensation exceptions related to risk-sharing arrangements (see Section IV.A.3.b., above), indirect compensation (see Section IV.E., above), and fair market value arrangements (see Section IV.F., above). Responding to concerns that an entity to which such physicians refer (referral recipients) providing even noncash gifts or benefits of minimal value to physicians or their families could create a compensation arrangement that would bar such referrals, the final rule establishes three new exceptions to the compensation arrangement referral ban for qualifying gifts and benefits that the rule's drafters believe will not lead to overutilization.

### 1. Non-Monetary Compensation

The first of these three exceptions applies to gifts or benefits provided by a referral recipient to a physician. To comply, the gift or benefit (1) must not be in cash or a cash equivalent; (2) must not exceed $300 in value in any year; (3) must not be determined so as to take into account the volume or value of referrals or other business generated by referring physicians; (4) must not be solicited by physicians or their

---

[236] 42 C.F.R. §411.357(*l*)(5).

practices; and (5) must not violate the federal anti-kickback statute.[237] One major implication of this exception is that professional courtesies in the form of health care items or services offered to physicians for free, or at a discount not passed on to Medicare, will restrict the ability of physicians to refer unless the value falls below the specified amounts.

### 2. Medical Staff Incidental Benefits

This second exception applies to incidental benefits other than cash or cash equivalents provided by a hospital to a member of its medical staff.[238] The types of benefits that might fall within this exception include reduced or free parking, free computer/Internet access, and meals. In general, this exception requires that the benefits must be used on the hospital's campus and offered to all medical staff members without regard to the volume or value of referrals.[239] In addition, the benefits must be offered only during the periods when staff members are making rounds or performing other hospital or patient-related duties, and must be reasonably related to the hospital's medical services.[240] The benefits must also be consistent with benefits offered to medical staff members by hospitals in the local region, and not exceed $25.00 per occurrence.[241] HHS does not believe that medical transcription services commonly provided by hospitals are of nominal value.[242] Finally, as with many other exceptions, the compensation arrangement must not violate the federal anti-kickback statute.[243]

### 3. Compliance Training

The third exception is very narrow and applies to compliance training provided by a hospital to a referring physician who practices in the community, and requires that such training must either cover the basic elements of a compliance program or the specific rules of a federal health care program.[244] Thus, a qualifying general training program can focus on training-related policies and procedures, training of staff, or internal monitoring and reporting, while a qualifying specific program should focus, for example, on such requirements as billing, coding, medical necessity, and unlawful referral arrangements.

It is surprising that such a narrow exception that appears to barely give credence to the OIG's stated encouragement for voluntary compliance would be issued. As important as hospital compliance training is, it is hard to understand why HHS would only formally recognize com-

---

[237] 66 Fed. Reg. at 961; 42 C.F.R. §411.357(k).

[238] 66 Fed. Reg. at 962; 42 C.F.R. §411.357(m).

[239] 66 Fed. Reg. at 962; 42 C.F.R. §411.357(m)(1) & (m)(3).

[240] 66 Fed. Reg. at 962; 42 C.F.R. §411.357(m)(2) & (m)(4).

[241] 66 Fed. Reg. at 962; 42 C.F.R. §411.357(m)(5) & (m)(6).

[242] 66 Fed. Reg. at 921.

[243] 66 Fed. Reg. at 921; 42 C.F.R. §411.357(m)(8).

[244] 66 Fed. Reg. at 921; 42 C.F.R. §411.357(o).

pliance programs by this part of the health care community. This rule is also unnecessarily narrow in that it only protects compliance training activities, but does not appear to protect assistance to physicians in regard to many other compliance program components about which the OIG has gone on record as being necessary for effective compliance programs, including, for example, the creation of policies and self-audits.

## V. Miscellaneous

### A. Reporting Requirements

The Stark law requires that every entity providing covered items or services for which payment may be made under Medicare or Medicaid must provide CMS with information concerning the entity's ownership, investments, and compensation arrangements. This information includes the covered items and services the entity provided, and the names and unique physician identification numbers of all physicians with an ownership or investment interest (as described in the Stark law), or with a compensation arrangement (as described in the Stark law), in the entity, or whose immediate relatives have such an ownership or investment interest or who have such a compensation relationship with the entity.[245]

Failure to comply with the reporting requirements can subject the violating entity to a civil monetary penalty of up to $10,000 for each day in which the report was to have been made.[246] The Stark law states that such information must be provided in such form, manner, and at such times as the Secretary of HHS shall specify. This part of the Stark law is being deferred to Phase II of the final rule. Thus, a review of prior regulations is needed for guidance.

The Stark I regulation provides that entities must submit the requisite information on a form prescribed by CMS within 30 days of the request, and that all changes to that information must be submitted to CMS within 60 days from the date of the change.[247] Specifically, HCFA Form 96, effective January 1, 1992, and entitled "Clinical Laboratory Financial Relationships with Physicians," is a Medicare carrier survey requiring disclosure of the financial relationships between entities furnishing clinical laboratory services and physicians. Similarly, HCFA Form 97, also effective January 1, 1992, is a Medicare fiscal-intermediary survey requiring disclosure of financial relationships between physicians and hospital and facility-based clinical laboratories. Although both forms contain a box indicating that a

---

[245]*See generally* 42 U.S.C. §1395nn(f). The Stark law reporting requirement does not apply to DHS provided outside the United States or to entities that CMS determines provide services for which payment may be made under this title very infrequently.

[246]42 U.S.C. §1395nn(g)(5).

[247]42 C.F.R. §411.361.

form is being used to update previous information, and indeed the instructions to these forms indicate that such updating is required, CMS has informally indicated that it is not requiring providers of clinical laboratory services to update these forms as financial relationships change.

While final regulations with respect to reporting requirements await Phase II of the final rule, in the Stark II proposed rule CMS acknowledged that it is still in the process of developing the statutorily prescribed reporting process and the necessary forms. Until that time, CMS has stated that physicians and entities are not required to report. CMS also proposed to amend the regulation to specify that entities need report changes to the requested information only once every year, as opposed to within 60 days of the date of the change. CMS also proposes to amend the reporting regulations to specify that all financial relationships must be reported, even if those relationships satisfy an exception to the Stark law. (The existing regulations permit an entity not to report a financial relationship if the entity determines that the financial relationship satisfies the requirements of an exception.)

In the Stark II proposed rule, CMS acknowledged that it is still in the process of developing the statutorily prescribed reporting process and the necessary forms, and that until it completes this process, physicians and entities are not required to report.[248] CMS proposed to amend the reporting regulations in three ways: by specifying that entities need only report changes to the requested information once a year, instead of within 60 days of the date of the change; by specifying that all financial relationships must be reported, even if those relationships satisfy an exception to the Stark law (the existing regulations permit an entity not to report a financial relationship if the entity determines that it satisfies the requirements of certain exceptions); and by developing a streamlined reporting system that does not require entities to retain and submit large quantities of data (this in response to public comments that the reporting requirements may be impossible for large corporations to satisfy).[249]

When CMS develops a form for reporting this information, it will publish the form as a proposed notice in the *Federal Register* and solicit comments.[250]

## B. Relationship to Medicaid

With the enactment of Stark II in 1993, Congress extended aspects of the Stark law to the Medicaid program. Rather than specifically prohibiting Medicaid referrals, however, Stark II amended the Social Security Act to deny federal financial participation (FFP) to state Medicaid programs for DHS furnished pursuant to a physician referral that would have resulted in denial of payment under Medicare.[251] Con-

---

[248] 63 Fed. Reg. at 1703.

[249] *See generally* 63 Fed. Reg. at 1703–1704.

[250] *See* 63 Fed. Reg. at 1704.

[251] 63 Fed. Reg. at 1704.

sequently, state Medicaid agencies must implement, in large measure, the Stark law as it applies to referrals for services payable under Medicaid.

Phase II will address Section 1903 of the Stark law, which extends aspects of the statute to the Medicaid program. The Stark II proposed rule would implement the Medicaid aspects of the self-referral prohibition by:

- denying FFP to a state for expenditures for DHS furnished to an individual on the basis of a physician referral that would have resulted in a denial of payment under the Medicare rules;
- interpreting "referral" in the Medicaid context to cover a physician's request for a Medicaid-covered DHS comparable to a Medicare-covered service;
- giving the definition of a DHS under a state Medicaid plan precedence when it differs from the definition of a DHS under the Stark law (except when including those services would run counter to the underlying purpose of the legislation);
- applying the Medicare definition of physician to Medicaid programs (expanding the Medicaid definition of physician to include osteopaths, podiatrists, optometrists, chiropractors, and similar practitioners);
- providing that states may obtain advisory opinions from CMS as to whether a physician's referrals are prohibited by the proposed Stark II regulations for the purpose of limiting FFP; and
- expanding the program integrity requirements under Medicaid to require that Medicaid providers submit information concerning their financial relationships with physicians, including financial relationships that the provider believes fall within a statutory or regulatory exception.[252]

## C. Sanctions

For any entity found to have violated the Stark law, CMS may deny payment for any DHS provided and require refunds of all amounts collected by such entity.[253]

This authority to deny payment makes strict compliance with the statutory exceptions mandatory. Moreover, if a long-standing relationship that violates the Stark law is uncovered, for example in due diligence, the financial exposure can be enormous because all Medicare and Medicaid revenues the provider has derived from referrals from physicians with nonconforming financial relationships are potentially subject to recoupment.

Additionally, violators also may be excluded from the Medicare program and/or state health care programs, including Medicaid. More

---

[252] 63 Fed. Reg. at 1704–1705.

[253] 42 U.S.C. §§1395nn(g)(1) & (2).

importantly, however, violators are subject to civil sanctions including civil monetary penalties of up to $15,000 for each bill or claim presented or caused to be presented for a service that a person knows or should have known payment may not be made, and up to $100,000 for each arrangement or scheme (such as a cross-referral arrangement) that the physician or entity knows, or should have known, has the principal purpose of assuring referrals by the physician to a particular entity that, if directly made, would be in violation of the Stark law.[254]

At the time the Stark law was enacted, the OIG's civil monetary penalty law (CMP) did not specifically define the term "knows or should know," but the phrase was understood to mean a negligence standard.[255] Pursuant to Section 231(d) of HIPAA,[256] however, Congress amended the CMP to define "knows or should know" as requiring proof that the person acted in "deliberate ignorance" of the truth or falsity of the claim or in "reckless disregard"—the same scienter requirement as under the False Claims Act.[257] Although Congress did not directly amend the Stark law or the numerous other provisions of the Social Security Act containing civil monetary penalty provisions, it appears reasonable to argue that Congress in fact intended to have this reckless-disregard scienter requirement apply uniformly to all CMP proceedings where the term "knows or should know" appears. HHS will address sanctions in Phase II of the final rule.

## D. Relationship to the Anti-Kickback Statute

Although the Stark law and the anti-kickback statute are intended to combat the same perceived harms, the two provisions must be analyzed separately. In enacting Stark I, congressional conferees stated that:

> [t]he conferees wish to clarify that any prohibition, exemption, or exception authorized under this provision in no way alters (or reflects on) the scope and application of the anti-kickback provisions in section 1128B of the Social Security Act. The conferees do not intend that this provision should be construed as affecting, or in any way interfering with, the efforts of the Inspector General to enforce current law, such as cases described in the recent Fraud Alert issued by the Inspector General. In particular, entities, which would be eligible for a specific exemption, would be subject to all of the provisions of current law.[258]

The following are the significant differences between the two provisions. First, a violation of the Stark law occurs without proof of ille-

---

[254]42 U.S.C. §§1395nn(g)(3), (4).

[255]See H.R. REP. No. 391, at 533–34 (1987), commenting on legislative change from "knows or has reason to know" to "knows or should know" contained in §4118(e)(1) of OBRA 1987 (Pub. L. No. 100-203).

[256]Pub. L. No. 104-191, §231(d), *codified at* 42 U.S.C. §1320a-7a(i)(7).

[257]42 U.S.C. §1320a-7a(i)(7).

[258]H.R. CONF. REP. No. 386, at 856 (1989).

gal intent, and thus it is a strict liability offense.[259] In other words, if there is a financial relationship between an entity and a physician, and the physician refers Medicare or Medicaid patients to the entity for designated services, then the arrangement *must* fall within one of the statutorily defined exceptions to avoid violating the self-referral prohibition. Thus, strict compliance with statutory exceptions is mandatory.

In contrast, the failure of an arrangement to fall within one of the safe harbors of the anti-kickback statute—the models for many of the Stark law's exceptions—does not mean necessarily that the arrangement is illegal. A separate analysis should be conducted to determine if there was prohibited intent to induce referrals through payment of remuneration. Thus, compliance with the anti-kickback statute's safe harbors is voluntary.

Other significant differences are set forth below:

- The Stark law applies only to prohibited referrals under the Medicare and Medicaid programs, whereas the anti-kickback statute applies to all federally funded health care programs.[260]
- The Stark law regulates conduct within a physician's own practice, whereas the anti-kickback statute has never been interpreted by a court to apply to a referral to oneself.
- The Stark law regulates physician compensation, whereas the anti-kickback statute generally does not, with the exception that the safe harbors specify that compensation must be at fair market value.
- The Stark law prohibits paying bona fide employees for referrals, whereas the anti-kickback statute does not.
- The Stark law applies only to relationships between physicians and entities, whereas any two parties may violate the anti-kickback statute.
- The Stark law prohibits only referrals, whereas the anti-kickback statute prohibits wider forms of misconduct, including, inter alia, arranging for and/or recommending the purchase of items or services.
- The principal remedy under the Stark law is denial of payment, whereas the anti-kickback statute is principally a criminal felony prohibition.
- The principal remedy of denial of payment under the Stark law applies only to the provider billing for the service rendered pursuant to a prohibited referral under the Stark law, whereas both parties to an illegal kickback arrangement are equally vulnerable.

---

[259]As discussed in Section V.C., above (regarding sanctions), it is arguable that civil monetary penalties may be imposed on violator(s) of the Stark law only on proof that the violator(s) knew or should have known that a claim was submitted for a service for which payment may not be made, or that the violator(s) acted in reckless disregard.

[260]42 U.S.C. §1320a-7b(b).

Clearly, in some of these cases the ambit of the Stark law is broader than that of the anti-kickback statute, and in other cases it is narrower. Because of these significant differences, it is imperative that practitioners conduct a separate analysis of the applicability of both statutes to a financial relationship.

## E. Stark Law Advisory Opinion Final Rule

In 1989, the House of Representatives voted as part of its consideration of Stark I to authorize an advisory opinion process that would permit a case-by-case review of an arrangement where providers can demonstrate that the services would otherwise be unavailable, be more convenient based on reduced travel time, and be provided at a lower unit charge and lower overall cost to the Medicare program than comparable services.[261] This approach was rejected by the conferees and lay dormant until 1996—despite commentary urging action[262]—when Congress authorized advisory opinions under the anti-kickback statute.[263] The OIG's implementing regulation in 1997 adopted just such a case-by-case approach.

The BBA extended the advisory opinion process to the Stark law in response to the health care industry's justifiable confusion concerning the parameters of the self-referral prohibition. The advisory opinion final rule[264] established a process for seeking guidance as to whether existing or proposed arrangements violate the Stark law, but it also imposed what could be very difficult criteria for the requests, certain risks, and somewhat onerous burdens on the parties seeking advisory opinions.

In general, based on the congressional directive in the BBA, CMS has patterned the advisory opinion final rule after the OIG anti-kickback advisory opinion regulations, including similar limitations, timing, and procedural rules.[265] The most significant difference between the two advisory opinion processes is that in the anti-kickback advisory opinion process, the OIG has adopted a case-specific approach whereby it is free to waive certain safe harbor standards or impose additional requirements on a particular transaction. In contrast, the advisory opinions to be issued under the Stark law will analyze merely whether a transaction falls within the statute and, if so, whether it also satisfies the criteria for one of the exceptions. Thus, the advisory opinions under the Stark law potentially could be much narrower and have less utility than those issued under the anti-kickback statute.

---

[261] H.R. CONF. REP. NO. 386, at 847–48.

[262] *See, e.g.,* T.S. Crane, *The Problem of Physician Self Referral Under the Anti-Kickback Statute: The Hanlester Network Case and the Safe Harbor Regulation,* 268 JAMA, 85, 90 (1992).

[263] Pub. L. No. 104-191, §205, *codified at* 42 U.S.C. §1320a-7d(b).

[264] *See generally* 63 Fed. Reg. 1646 (Jan. 9, 1998).

[265] *See generally id.* (For regulations on the Stark law advisory opinion process, see Appendix G-4 on disk accompanying this volume.)

Given the clear mandate of Congress to follow the OIG's process, CMS's rigid approach in the advisory opinion final rule appears to fall well short of fulfilling its statutory mandate.

A Stark law advisory opinion is available only for existing or soon-to-be consummated arrangements. A party submitting a request must certify that all of the information provided is true and correct, and that it intends in good faith to enter into the arrangement if it does not already exist.[266] CMS will not provide an opinion regarding hypothetical or generalized arrangements.[267] Once the advisory opinion is issued, it is binding upon the Secretary and the requesting party.[268] Although the Secretary retains the authority to revoke an opinion after its issuance, the requesting party does not have any recourse if it is not satisfied with the result.[269] In addition, there is a risk of sanctions following any adverse advisory opinion. CMS has indicated that it will use the information disclosed in the process against the requesting party and others in subsequent civil, criminal, or administrative actions.

Despite a lack of explicit statutory authority, the advisory opinion final rule specifies that CMS will charge a fee equal to the costs incurred in responding to the request, and CMS is not obligated to estimate these costs in advance.[270] CMS estimated that the cost will be approximately $75 per hour, and that the total cost of an opinion will depend on the complexity of the arrangement and the quality of the submission.[271] The advisory opinion final rule provides that CMS will generally issue an opinion within 90 days after the request has been formally accepted, unless the request involves complex legal issues or highly complicated fact patterns; in that case, CMS will respond to the request "within a reasonable time period."[272] By contrast, the anti-kickback advisory opinion regulations require that the OIG issue an opinion not later than 60 days after receiving a request.[273]

Once a Stark law advisory opinion has been issued, it will be made available promptly for public inspection, but will be legally binding only on the HHS and the requesting party, and only with respect to the specific conduct of the requesting party.[274] CMS will not be bound with respect to the conduct of any third party, even if the conduct of that party appears similar to the conduct that is the subject of the opinion.[275]

---

[266] 63 Fed. Reg. at 1649.

[267] *See id.*

[268] *See* 63 Fed. Reg. at 1653.

[269] *See* 63 Fed. Reg. at 1652–53.

[270] *See* 63 Fed. Reg. at 1650.

[271] *See id.*

[272] *See* 63 Fed. Reg. at 1652.

[273] 42 U.S.C. §1320a-7d(b)(5)(B).

[274] 63 Fed. Reg. at 1653.

[275] *See id.*

## VI. Conclusion

The Stark law is the natural child of the budget reconciliation process of the 1980s where Congress saw excesses in the health care business environment and an executive branch it believed needed to be micromanaged. The result was a sweeping per se prohibition of most then-existing forms of self-referral, coupled with regulation of physician compensation relationships with outside referral sources, referrals within physicians' practices, and physician compensation in virtually any setting. All of this was set in motion in Stark I and II with little discretion granted to the executive branch to modify by regulation onerous requirements or requirements rendered meaningless by the sweeping changes in the health care system since the statute's enactment. Although the final rule injects common sense into the Stark law, the outcome of self-referral enforcement is a long way from being final, and Representative Stark's promise of "clear bright-line rules" remain elusive.

# 3

# The False Claims Act in Health Care Prosecutions: Application of the Substantive, *Qui Tam,* and Voluntary Disclosure Provisions*

*Robert Salcido, Akin, Gump, Strauss, Hauer & Feld, L.L.P., Washington, D.C.

111

# I. Introduction

Over the past decade, the health care community has witnessed dramatic changes in the government's efforts to enforce its fraud and abuse laws. For example, fraud alerts regarding prohibited kickback arrangements[1] and the expansion of the Stark law[2] have demonstrated the government's commitment to policing health care transactions. The most dramatic development, however, measured by dollars recovered, has been the government's enforcement of the False Claims Act (FCA).

---

[1] *See, e.g.*, 59 Fed. Reg. 65,372 (Dec. 19, 1994); 60 Fed. Reg. 40,847 (Aug. 10, 1995); 61 Fed. Reg. 30,623 (June 17, 1996).

[2] *See* 42 U.S.C. §1395nn. For extensive discussion of the Stark law restrictions, see Chapter 2 (Crane, Federal Physician Self-Referral Restrictions); for full text of the Stark law, see Appendix B-1.

The FCA is the government's "primary litigative tool for combating fraud."[3] The FCA empowers both the Attorney General and private persons to institute civil actions to enforce the Act.[4] The FCA imposes liability on those who, inter alia, "knowingly" present, or cause to be presented, "a false or fraudulent claim for payment."[5] "Knowingly," at a minimum, is defined to mean that the provider acted in "deliberate ignorance" or in "reckless disregard" of the truth or falsity of the information.[6]

Under the *qui tam* provisions of the FCA, private persons, known as relators, may enforce the Act by filing a complaint, under seal, setting forth allegations of fraud committed against the government.[7] The government, while maintaining the complaint under seal, investigates the allegations.[8] If the government determines that the allegations have merit, the Department of Justice (DOJ) intervenes in the action, unseals the complaint, and assumes primary responsibility for prosecuting the claim.[9] If the government believes the claim lacks merit, it declines to intervene, in which case the *qui tam* plaintiff may elect, but is not obligated, to prosecute the action.[10] If the government intervenes and prevails on the merits, it is awarded treble damages plus a $5,000 to $10,000 penalty for each false claim submitted;[11] the relator receives, under most circumstances, 15 to 25 percent of the government's recovery (depending on his or her contribution to the action) plus reimbursement of reasonable legal fees and expenses.[12] If the government does not intervene in the action, the relator's statutory recovery is between 25 to 30 percent of the government's recovery plus reimbursement of reasonable legal fees and expenses.[13]

---

[3] United States *ex rel.* Kelly v. Boeing Co., 9 F.3d 743, 745 (9th Cir. 1993) (quoting Senate Judiciary Committee, False Claims Amendments Act of 1986, S. REP. NO. 345 (1986), *reprinted in* 1986 U.S.C.C.A.N. 5266) [hereinafter S. REP. NO. 99-345].

[4] 31 U.S.C. §3730. The False Claims Act is codified at 31 U.S.C. §§ 3729–3733. (See Appendix C-1 for full text of the Act.)

[5] 31 U.S.C. §3729(a)(1).

[6] 31 U.S.C. §3729(b).

[7] 31 U.S.C. §3730(b)(2). *Qui tam* "is an abbreviation for *qui tam pro domino rege quam pro seipso,* which means 'he who is as much for the king as for himself.'" United States *ex rel.* Springfield Terminal Ry. v. Quinn, 14 F.3d 645, 647 n.1 (D.C. Cir. 1994) (emphasis added) (citation omitted).

[8] 31 U.S.C. §3730(b)(3).

[9] 31 U.S.C. §3730(b)(4) and (c)(1).

[10] 31 U.S.C. §3730(b)(4)(B).

[11] For violations committed on or after Sept. 29, 1999, the defendant is liable for treble damages plus penalties ranging from $5,500 to $11,000 per claim. *See* Civil Monetary Penalties Inflation Adjustment, 64 Fed. Reg. 47,099, 47,103–47,104 (1999) (to be codified at 28 C.F.R. pt. 85). However, the statute also contains voluntary disclosure provisions under which a provider's exposure to liability is limited to double the government's damages and civil penalties.

[12] 31 U.S.C. §§3729(a) and 3730(d)(1). Under §3730(d)(1), if the relator's action is primarily based upon specified types of information, his or her recovery is capped at 10 percent.

[13] 31 U.S.C. §3730(d)(2).

Before 1986, the FCA languished in relative disuse.[14] In 1986, outraged by scandals plaguing the Department of Defense (DOD), Congress revamped the FCA by expanding the scope of its scienter standard.[15] Congress also modernized FCA penalty provisions to increase the government's recovery amounts, allowing from double to treble damages and from $2,000 per claim to $5,000 to $10,000 per claim in civil monetary penalties.[16] Congress also liberalized the FCA's *qui tam* provisions by eliminating the broad jurisdictional bar, increasing the amount of the whistleblower's bounty, and expanding the relator's right to participate in the action.[17]

As a result of Congress's expansion and liberalization of the FCA, the government's recoveries under the FCA have skyrocketed, totaling more than $4 billion over the last decade.[18] The health care indus-

---

[14] *See, e.g.,* S. REP. NO. 99-345 at 4 n.10, *reprinted in* 1986 U.S.C.C.A.N. at 5269 (pointing out that in fiscal year 1984 the DOJ received 2,850 fraud referrals, but had filed only 21 complaints based on those referrals).

[15] At the time of the 1986 amendments, the rule of the Fifth, Sixth, Ninth, and Eleventh Circuits was that to establish an FCA violation the government must prove that the defendant acted with specific intent to defraud the government. *See* United States v. Davis, 809 F.2d 1509, 1512 (11th Cir. 1987); United States v. Aerodex, Inc., 469 F.2d 1003, 1007 (5th Cir. 1972); United States v. Mead, 426 F.2d 118 (9th Cir. 1970); United States v. Ueber, 299 F.2d 310 (6th Cir. 1962). Conversely, the Seventh, Eighth, and Tenth Circuits and the Court of Claims had held that an intent to deceive was not necessarily a requisite element of proof under the pre-1986 Act. *See* United States v. Hughes, 585 F.2d 284, 287–88 (7th Cir. 1978); United States v. Cooperative Grain & Supply Co., 476 F.2d 47, 56 (8th Cir. 1973); Fleming v. United States, 336 F.2d 475, 479 (10th Cir. 1964); Miller v. United States, 550 F.2d 17, 23 (Ct. Cl. 1977). In 1986, Congress clarified that "no proof of specific intent to defraud" was required to establish a violation of the statute—and that liability extended to those whose acted with "reckless disregard" or in "deliberate ignorance" of the truth or falsity of the information. 31 U.S.C. §3729(b).

[16] *See, e.g.,* United States v. Hill, 676 F. Supp. 1158, 1165–68 (N.D. Fla. 1987) (describing Congress's 1986 amendments to the FCA).

[17] *See* United States v. Northrop Corp., 59 F.3d 953, 964–69 (9th Cir. 1995) (describing Congress's goals in amending the *qui tam* provisions of the FCA); *see generally* Evan Caminker, *The Constitutionality of* Qui Tam *Actions*, 99 YALE L.J. 341 (1989); *see* Robert Salcido, *Screening Out Unworthy Whistleblower Actions: An Historical Analysis of the Jurisdictional Bar to* Qui Tam *Actions Under The False Claims Act*, 24 PUB. CONT. L.J. 237 (1995) (setting forth the history underlying the 1986 amendments to the *qui tam* provisions of the FCA) [hereinafter cited as Salcido, *Screening Out Unworthy Whistleblower Actions*].

[18] The DOJ, in a press release issued on February 24, 2000, reported that it had received more than $3.5 billion in whistleblower litigation. *See* http://www.usdoj.gov/opa/pr/2000/february/ 079civ.htm. Since that time, the DOJ has recovered $731 million in its settlement with Columbia/ HCA. *See In re* Columbia/HCA Healthcare Corp. Qui Tam Litigation, No. 99-3288, et al., 2001 U.S. Dist. LEXIS 11482 (D.D.C. Aug. 7, 2001). Further, on November 2, 2000, DOJ announced that it had recovered $1.5 billion under the FCA during the past fiscal year (October 1, 1999, to September 30, 2000); of this amount, approximately $1.2 billion stemmed from recoveries under the *qui tam* provisions of the FCA. *See* http://www.usdoj.gov/opa/pr/2000/November/ 641civ.htm. Health care fraud cases topped the list of annual recoveries, totaling more than $840 million. *Id.*

try has been especially hard hit, with every sector—hospitals,[19] fiscal agents,[20] peer review organizations,[21] physicians,[22] researchers,[23] laboratories,[24] home health agencies,[25] long-term care facilities,[26] and

---

[19] *See, e.g.*, United States *ex rel*. Dhawan v. New York Med. College, 252 F.3d 118 (2d Cir. 2001); United States v. Texas Tech Univ., 171 F.3d 279 (5th Cir. 1999); Hindo v. University of Health Scis./The Chicago Med. Sch., 65 F.3d 608 (7th Cir. 1995); Covington v. Sisters of the Third Order of St. Dominic of Hanford, Cal., No. 93-15194, 1995 U.S. App. LEXIS 20370 (9th Cir. July 13, 1995); United States *ex rel*. Obert-Hong v. Advocate Health Care, No. 99 C 5806, 2001 U.S. Dist. LEXIS 3767 (N.D. Ill. Mar. 27, 2001); United States *ex rel*. McCarthy v. Straub Clinic & Hosp., 140 F. Supp. 2d 1062 (D. Haw. 2001); United States *ex rel*. Mathews v. HealthSouth Corp., 140 F. Supp. 2d 706 (W.D. La. 2001); United States *ex rel*. Cherry v. Rush-Presbyterian/St. Luke's Med. Ctr., No. 99 C 06313, 2001 WL 40807 (N.D. Ill. Jan. 16, 2001); United States *ex rel*. Goodstein v. McLaren, No. 97-CV-72992-DT, 2001 U.S. Dist. LEXIS 2917 (E.D. Mich. Jan. 3, 2001); United States *ex rel*. Chandler v. Hektoen Inst., 118 F. Supp. 2d 902, 903 (N.D. Ill. 2000); United States *ex rel*. Amin v. George Washington Univ., 26 F. Supp. 2d 162 (D.D.C. 1998); United States *ex rel*. Thompson v. Columbia/ HCA Healthcare, 20 F. Supp. 2d 1017 (S.D. Tex. 1998); United States *ex rel*. Cox v. Iowa Health Sys., 29 F. Supp. 2d 1022 (S.D. Iowa 1998).

[20] *See, e.g.*, United States *ex rel*. Stinson, Lyons, Gerlin & Bustamante, P.A. v. Prudential Ins., 944 F.2d 1149 (3d Cir. 1991).

[21] *See, e.g.*, United States *ex rel*. McCoy v. California Med. Review, Inc., 723 F. Supp. 1363 (N.D. Cal. 1989).

[22] *See, e.g.*, United States *ex rel*. Hochman v. Nackman, 145 F.3d 1069 (9th Cir. 1998); United States *ex rel*. Bidani v. Lewis, No. 97 C. 6502, 2001 U.S. Dist. LEXIS 260 (N.D. Ill. Jan. 11, 2001); United States v. Cabrera-Diaz, 106 F. Supp. 2d 234 (D.P.R. 2000); United States v. Krizek, 859 F. Supp. 5 (D.D.C. 1994), *aff'd in part, rev'd in part*, 111 F.3d 934 (D.C. Cir. 1997), *on remand*, 7 F. Supp. 2d 56 (D.D.C. 1998), *remanded*, 192 F.3d 1024 (D.C. Cir. 1999).

[23] *See, e.g.*, United States *ex rel*. Cantekin v. University of Pittsburgh, 192 F.3d 402 (3d Cir. 1999); United States *ex rel*. Berge v. Trustees of Univ. of Ala., 104 F.3d 1453 (4th Cir.1997); United States v. University of Tex. M.D. Anderson Cancer Ctr., 961 F.2d 46 (4th Cir. 1992).

[24] *See, e.g.*, United States *ex rel*. LaCorte v. SmithKline Beecham Clinical Labs., 149 F.3d 227 (3d Cir. 1998); United States *ex rel*. Downy v. Corning, Inc., 118 F. Supp. 2d 1160 (D.N.M. 2000); United States *ex rel*. Kneepkins v. Gambro Healthcare, Inc., 115 F. Supp. 2d 35 (D. Mass. 2000); United States *ex rel*. Ramona Wagner v. Allied Clinical Lab., 1995 Medicare & Medicaid Guide (CCH) ¶43,142 (S.D. Ohio 1995).

[25] *See, e.g.*, United States *ex rel*. Russell v. Epic Healthcare Management Group, 193 F.3d 304 (5th Cir. 1999); United States v. Estate of Rogers, No. 1:97CV461, 2001 WL 818160 (E.D. Tenn. June 28, 2001); United States *ex rel*. Waris v. Staff Builders, Inc., No. 96-1969, 1999 U.S. Dist. LEXIS 15247 (E.D. Pa. Oct. 4, 1999); United States *ex rel*. Smith v. First Am. Health Care of Georgia, No. 1:97-CV-780, 1999 U.S. Dist. LEXIS 6181 (W.D. Mich. Apr. 26, 1999); United States *ex rel*. Okeke v. Home Care Servs., Inc., No. 3:97-CV-2738-H, 1999 U.S. Dist. LEXIS 5177 (N.D. Tex. Apr. 9, 1999); United States *ex rel*. Joslin v. Community Home Health of Maryland, Inc., 984 F. Supp. 374 (D. Md. 1997); United States v. American Health Enters., Inc., No. 94-CV-450-RCF, 1996 U.S. Dist. LEXIS 7494 (N.D. Ga. Apr. 29, 1996).

[26] *See, e.g.*, United States v. NHC Healthcare Corp., 115 F. Supp. 2d 1149 (W.D. Mo. 2000); United States *ex rel*. Swan v. Covenant Care, Inc., No. C-97-3814, 1999 U.S. Dist. LEXIS 15287 (N.D. Cal. Sept. 21, 1999); United States *ex rel*. Eaton v. Kansas Healthcare Investors, 22 F. Supp. 2d 1230 (D. Kan. 1998); United States v. Chester Care Ctr., No. 98 CV-139, 1998 U.S. Dist. LEXIS 4836 (E.D. Pa. Feb. 4, 1998).

suppliers and billing services,[27] among others—having been the target of an FCA action.

Moreover, it is projected that recoveries over the next decade will increase dramatically. Specifically, one private group has estimated that the government, from 1996 to 2006 (the second decade since the amendments to the FCA), will recover more than $21 billion.[28] Certainly, the government's recent intensive efforts—such as the PATH (Physicians at Teaching Hospitals) Project (in which the government reviews billing practices at teaching hospitals to determine whether hospitals billed for services performed by teaching physicians and not by residents) and the 72-Hour Project (in which the government reviews hospitals that allegedly billed for outpatient diagnostic services immediately before a patient's admission)—demonstrate the government's resolve to enforce the FCA's provisions.

This chapter discusses three areas of FCA jurisprudence that those within the health care community are likely to confront.

- Section II examines the FCA's substantive elements. By reviewing these elements, a provider may ascertain the likelihood that its practices will be subject to FCA liability.
- Section III addresses the *qui tam* provisions of the FCA, focusing specifically on the public disclosure jurisdictional bar defense to *qui tam* actions. This jurisdictional bar has spawned a remarkable diversity of case law and presents those accused of a violation with a potential defense.
- Section IV covers the Department of Health and Human Services (HHS), Office of the Inspector General (OIG), Voluntary Disclosure Program, which offers providers that may have violated the FCA a significant opportunity to limit their exposure to liability for penalties.

## II. CONSTRUCTION OF THE "FALSE" AND "KNOWING" ELEMENTS OF THE FALSE CLAIMS ACT

There are several contexts in which a potential FCA action can arise: a provider may receive a contact or demand letter from the DOJ;[29] a provider may be the subject of a *qui tam* action; or a provider

---

[27]*See, e.g.*, United States *ex rel.* Glass v. Medtronic, Inc., 957 F.2d 605 (8th Cir. 1992); United States *ex rel.* Franklin v. Parke-Davis, 147 F. Supp. 2d 39 (D. Mass. 2001); United States v. Gericare Med. Supply, Inc., No. 99-0366-CB-L, 2000 U.S. Dist. LEXIS 19661 (S.D. Ala. Dec. 11, 2000); United States *ex rel.* Trim v. McKean, 31 F. Supp. 2d 1308 (W.D. Okla. 1998); Luckey v. Baxter Healthcare Corp., 2 F. Supp. 1034 (N.D. Ill. 1998), *aff'd*, 183 F.3d 730 (7th Cir. 1999).

[28]*See False Claims Act*, 66 FED. CONT. REP. 229 (Sept. 16, 1996).

[29]Historically, the DOJ's letters to persons reflecting its belief that a provider may have violated the law were known as "demand" letters because the DOJ often demanded payment in exchange for not filing a lawsuit. As a result of Congress's concern regarding the DOJ's abusive use of the FCA, the DOJ has promised to modify its

may identify a practice that has resulted in the erroneous submission of claims. No matter what the context, however, the provider will need to evaluate the elements underlying the FCA to determine its potential liability.

To establish a violation of the FCA, the plaintiff generally must establish a number of elements. Specifically, the plaintiff generally must prove that:

1. the "person";[30]
2. "present[ed]" or "cause[d] to be presented";[31]

---

approach and simply notify the provider regarding its possible breach of the FCA (rather than demand payment) and invite the provider to respond to the DOJ's inquiry. These letters are now known as "contact" letters. *See, e.g.*, Memorandum From Eric H. Holder, Jr., Deputy Attorney General to All United States Attorneys, All First Assistant United States Attorneys, All Civil Health Care Fraud Coordinators in the Offices of United States Attorneys and All Trial Attorneys in the Civil Division, Commercial Litigation Section (June 3, 1998). (For text of the Holder Memorandum, see Appendix C-2.)

[30] According to the Senate Judiciary Committee's report on its bill, the word "person" is to be construed broadly:

> The False Claims Act reaches all parties who may submit false claims. The term "person" is used in its broad sense to include partnerships, associations, and corporations—*United States v. Hanger One, Inc.*, 563 F.2d 1155, 1158 (5th Cir. 1977); *United States v. Nat'l Wholesalers, Inc.*, 236 F.2d 944 (9th Cir. 1956)—as well as States and political subdivisions thereof. *Cf. Ohio v. Helvering*, 292 U.S. 360, 370 (1934); *Georgia v. Evans*, 316 U.S. 153, 161 (1942); *Monell v. Dep't of Soc. Serv. of N.Y.*, 436 U.S. 658 (1978).

*See* S. REP. NO. 345 at 8, *reprinted in* 1986 U.S.C.C.A.N. 5266, 5273. Recently in Vermont Agency of Natural Res. v. United States, 529 U.S. 765 (2000), the Supreme Court ruled that in *qui tam* actions in which the United States does not intervene, states are not "persons" and therefore cannot be subject to liability. For a discussion of the case law, see Robert Salcido, FALSE CLAIMS ACT & THE HEALTHCARE INDUSTRY: COUNSELING & LITIGATION §2:01 (American Health Lawyers Ass'n 1999) [hereinafter Salcido, FALSE CLAIMS ACT COUNSELING]; *see also* Robert Salcido, FALSE CLAIMS ACT & THE HEALTHCARE INDUSTRY: COUNSELING & LITIGATION: NOV. 2000 SUPP. §2:01 (American Health Lawyers Ass'n 2000) [hereinafter Salcido, FALSE CLAIMS ACT COUNSELING: NOV. 2000 SUPP.].

[31] Generally, if an individual did not direct or authorize the submission of a claim, a court will not find the individual liable for presenting or causing the submission of a false claim under the FCA. *See, e.g.*, United States *ex rel*. Shaver v. Lucas Western Corp., 237 F.3d 932, 933 (8th Cir. 2001) (the court found that the relator, who alleged that the defendant employer had been ordered by a state worker's compensation board to pay the relator's medical bills but failed to do so which resulted in those claims being submitted to the Social Security Administration and Medicare, did not state a cause of action because the relator "did not allege that [the defendant] affirmatively instructed [the relator] to submit his medical bill claims to the government; he alleged merely that [the defendant] refused to pay the bills. Even assuming the truth of [the relator's] allegation that [the defendant] 'knew' [the relator] would submit such bills to Medicare, [the defendant] cannot be said to have 'caused' [the relator's] medical bill claims to be submitted to the government") (citations omitted); United States *ex rel*. Kinney v. Hennepin County Med. Ctr., 2001 WL 964011 at *9–*10 (D. Minn. Aug. 22, 2001) (when emergency room physicians did not instruct or control the representations that a medical center made regarding claims for ambulance transport fees, the physicians could not have "caused" the submission of false

3. "a false or fraudulent";
4. "claim," "record or statement";[32]
5. "knowingly";
6. to "the United States [g]overnment";[33] that was
7. "material"[34] to the government's determination to pay.[35]

---

claims under the FCA); United States *ex rel.* Piacentile v. Wolk, Medicare & Medicaid Guide (CCH) 1995 ¶43,028 (E.D. Pa. 1995). However, a person will "cause" another to submit a false claim if she instructs the person to do so. *See, e.g.*, United States v. Mackby, No. 99-15605, 2001 U.S. App. LEXIS 18478 at *13 (9th Cir. Aug. 18, 2001) (where defendant had instructed office manager and billing service to use an inaccurate provider identification number on claim forms "he caused the claims to be submitted with false information" and hence the "causation element was established by a preponderance of the evidence"). For a discussion of the case law, see Salcido, FALSE CLAIMS ACT COUNSELING, *supra* note 30, §2:02.

[32] The word "claim" generally is construed to be a demand for money or property of the United States that results in the United States suffering immediate financial detriment. *See, e.g.*, United States v. McNinch, 356 U.S. 595 (1958); United States *ex rel.* Windsor v. Dyncorp, Inc., 895 F. Supp. 844 (E.D. Va. 1995). For a discussion of the case law, see Salcido, FALSE CLAIMS ACT COUNSELING, *supra* note 30, §2:04.

[33] The FCA requires that the claim be submitted to "an officer or employee of the United States Government or a member of the Armed Forces of the United States." The Senate Judiciary Committee stated that the provision applies whenever payment will result in a loss to the United States government:

> A claim upon any Government agency or instrumentality, quasi-governmental corporation, or nonappropriated fund activity is a claim upon the United States under the act. In addition, a false claim is actionable although the claims or false statements were made to a party other than the Government, if the payment thereon would ultimately result in a loss to the United States. *United States v. Lagerbusch*, 361 F.2d 449 (3rd Cir. 1966); *Murray & Sorenson, Inc. v. United States*, 207 F.2d 119 (1st Cir. 1953). For example, a false claim to the recipient of a grant from the United States or to a State under a program financed in part by the United States, is a false claim to the United States. *See*, for example, *United States ex rel. Marcus v. Hess*, 317 U.S. 537 (1943); *United States ex rel. Davis v. Long's Drugs*, 411 F. Supp. 1114 (S.D. Cal. 1976).

S. REP. NO. 99-345 at 10, *reprinted in* 1986 U.S.C.C.A.N 5266, 5275.

[34] *See, e.g.*, United States *ex rel.* Harrison v. Westinghouse Savannah River Corp., 176 F.3d 776 (4th Cir. 1999). In *Harrison*, the relator alleged that the defendant had submitted claims that were not authorized under the terms of its contract with the federal government, but the defendant pointed out that the government had a copy of the contract and could best judge whether its work was unauthorized. The court agreed with the defendant and dismissed the relator's claim. Specifically, the court pointed out that the government "was aware of the terms of the contract—it could have objected to the inclusion of procedure development costs if it had believed that such work was not authorized. [The relator] does not allege that [the defendant] tried to conceal the nature of the work. Thus, [the relator's allegations] do not involve any material falsity, if any falsity at all." *See also* United States *ex rel.* Lamers v. City of Green Bay, 168 F.3d 1013, 1019 (7th Cir. 1999) (holding that even if defendant's representation "was an outright lie," the lie would be immaterial if defendant's practices had conformed (unbeknownst to defendant) with the underlying regulation); United States *ex rel.* Berge v. Trustees of Univ. of Ala., 104 F.3d 1453, 1461–62 (4th Cir.) (rejecting the relator's claim that the defendant had made false representations to the government to obtain federal grant funds by identifying the relator as a post-doctoral graduate stu-

Two elements are discussed in detail in this chapter: the "false or fraudulent" and the "knowing" elements. These two elements of the substantive provisions of the FCA have produced the most litigation. Also set forth below is a discussion of defenses to the charge that a claim is false or fraudulent and that the provider knew the claim was false.

---

dent when in fact she was a doctoral candidate because such a misrepresentation would not be material to the government's decision of whether to fund a multimillion dollar grant since the government would be interested in the internationally respected scientists working on the project and not an unknown graduate student), *cert. denied*, 522 U.S. 916 (1997); United States v. Robbins, 207 F. Supp. 799, 807 (D. Kan. 1962) (finding that the government cannot charge that it was defrauded by the false representations of another party where it has made an independent investigation prior to paying any money to defendants); United States v. Goldberg, 158 F. Supp. 544, 548 (E.D. Pa. 1958) (same); *cf.* United States v. Board of Educ. of Union City, 697 F. Supp. 167 (D.N.J. 1988). For a discussion of the case law, see Salcido, FALSE CLAIMS ACT COUNSELING, *supra* note 30, §2:07; *see also* Salcido, FALSE CLAIMS ACT COUNSELING: NOV. 2000 SUPP., *supra* note 30, §2:07.

[35] Specifically, courts have found subsection (a)(1), the prohibition on false claims, to have the following elements: that a claim for payment or approval was presented or caused to be presented to the government; that the claim was false or fraudulent; and that the defendant knew that the claim was false or fraudulent. *See* United States v. Mackby, No. 99-15605, 2001 U.S. App. LEXIS 18478 at *7–*8 (9th Cir. Aug. 18, 2001); United States *ex rel.* Rosales v. San Francisco Hous. Auth., No. C-95-4509, 2001 WL 370176 at *2 (N.D. Cal. Mar. 26, 2001); Luckey v. Baxter Healthcare Corp., 2 F. Supp. 2d 1034, 1044 (N.D. Ill. 1998), *aff'd*, 183 F.3d 730 (7th Cir. 1999); *but see* Hutchins v. Wilentz, Goldman & Spitzer, No. 98-6248, 2001 U.S. App. LEXIS 12833 at *10 (3d Cir. June 13, 2001) (adding additional element that the "United States suffered damages as a result of the false or fraudulent claim") (citations omitted); United States v. United Techs. Corp., 51 F. Supp. 2d 167, 195 (D. Conn. 1999) (same); United States *ex rel.* Mikes v. Straus, 84 F. Supp. 2d 427, 432 (S.D.N.Y. 1999) (same). To establish a violation of subsection (a)(2), the prohibition on false statements, the government or whistleblower must prove that the defendant presented or caused a third party to present a claim for payment or approval, that the claim was false or fraudulent, that the defendant presented or caused the claim to be presented knowing it was false or fraudulent, and that the defendant made or used a false statement that the defendant knew to be false and that was causally connected to the false claim. *See* United States *ex rel.* Aakhus v. Dyncorp, Inc., 136 F.3d 676, 682 (10th Cir. 1998); *but see* United Techs. Corp., 51 F. Supp. 2d at 195–96 (adding additional element that "the United States suffered damages as a result"); *Straus*, 84 F. Supp. 2d at 432 (same). To prove a violation of subsection (a)(3), the plaintiff must prove that the defendant conspired with one or more persons to get a false or fraudulent claim allowed or paid by the United States, that one or more conspirators performed any act to effect the object of the conspiracy, and that the government suffered losses as a result of the claim. United States *ex rel.* Durcholz v. FKW Inc., 997 F. Supp. 1159, 1173 (S.D. Ind. 1998), *aff'd*, 189 F.3d 542 (7th Cir. 1999); United States v. Hill, 676 F. Supp. 1158, 1173 (N.D. Fla. 1987); *see also* Blusal Meats, Inc. v. United States, 638 F. Supp. 824, 828 (S.D.N.Y. 1986), *aff'd other grounds*, 817 F.2d 1007 (2d Cir. 1987); *Straus*, 84 F. Supp. 2d at 432; *but see* United States *ex rel.* Wilkins v. North Am. Constr. Corp., 101 F. Supp. 2d 500, 525–26 n.14 (S.D. Tex. 2000) (refusing to find that the elements to a conspiracy violation under the FCA requires proof of damages, noting that it was "clear" that "the damages element of the *Blusal Meats* test is erroneous" and that the "better rule has two elements . . . the plaintiff must show: (1) the defendant conspired with one or more persons to get a false or fraudulent claim allowed or

## A. Defining "Falsity" Under the FCA

To establish liability under the FCA, the government or whistle-blower must establish that the claim was false or fraudulent. Although the FCA does not define what constitutes a false claim, general case law provides some parameters. Discussed below are cases in which courts found that a defendant did submit a false claim and cases in which courts found that there was no falsity. These cases offer some guidance to providers in determining whether their practices may fairly be characterized as false or fraudulent.

### 1. Cases Establishing Falsity

There are two general types of health care claims that the government considers false. One type includes claims in which the provider furnishes inaccurate or misleading information to the government to obtain payment or approval of a claim. These claims include upcoding, claiming payment for services not rendered, or explicitly certifying compliance with specific rules with which the provider did not in fact comply. The second type concerns instances in which a provider omits information from a claim or "implicitly" certifies compliance with rules, but does not actually adhere to those rules. Both types of cases are addressed below.

#### a. Literal Falsity

*United States v. Lorenzo*[36] and *United States ex rel. Thompson v. Columbia/HCA Healthcare*[37] present situations in which courts found health care claims or statements to be literally false.

In *Lorenzo*, a dentist performed a cancer examination of the oral cavity of the head and neck as part of a general examination. The dentist billed the service to Medicare as a "limited consultation" although the Medicare statute and regulations preclude providers from billing for routine examinations and from billing for dental services that are limited to the treatment of the teeth. The court held that the dentist's claims were false because they "were prepared in such a way as to dis-

---

paid by the United States; and (2) one or more conspirators performed any act to effect the object of the conspiracy") (citation omitted); United States *ex rel.* Atkinson v. Pennsylvania Shipbuilding Co., No. 94-7316, 2000 U.S. Dist. LEXIS 12081 at *27 (E.D. Pa. Aug. 24, 2000) (same). Finally, to establish a violation of subsection (a)(7), the plaintiff must prove that there is a record or statement, that is false, that is "known" to be false, and is used to "conceal, avoid, or decrease" an "obligation to pay or transmit money or property." *See, e.g., Dyncorp, Inc.*, 136 F.3d at 681–82; United States *ex rel.* Lamers v. City of Green Bay, 998 F. Supp. 971, 996–97 (E.D. Wis. 1998), *aff'd on other grounds*, 168 F.3d 1013 (7th Cir. 1999); *cf.* United States v. Raymond & Whitcomb, 53 F. Supp. 2d 436, 444–45 (S.D.N.Y. 1999) (adding additional element that the government suffer damage). *See generally* Salcido, FALSE CLAIMS ACT COUNSELING: NOV. 2000 SUPP., *supra* note 30, §§2:04, 2:08, 2:09.

[36] 768 F. Supp. 1127 (E.D. Pa. 1991).

[37] 20 F. Supp. 2d 1017, 1046–47 (S.D. Tex. 1998).

guise a routine dental checkup as a limited consultation consisting of 'a cancer examination of the oral cavity [of the] head and neck.' "[38]

In *Columbia / HCA Healthcare*, a hospital explicitly certified that the services in its cost report complied with Medicare laws, regulations, and program provisions, including the provisions outlawing kickbacks. The relator alleged that the hospital violated the anti-kickback statute. The court held that the hospital's certification was false if the hospital in fact breached the anti-kickback law.[39]

---

[38] 768 F. Supp. at 1131. *See also* United States v. Mackby, No. 99-15605, 2001 U.S. App. LEXIS 18478 at *8–*12 (9th Cir. Aug. 18, 2001). There the Ninth Circuit ruled that the defendant clinic had submitted a false claim when, in providing physical therapy, it inserted the provider identification number (PIN) of a physician who did not perform or supervise the service rather than the physical therapist in independent practice who did perform the service. Specifically, the court reasoned: "While the purpose of box 24k [on the HCFA-1500 claim form] is not specified on the form itself, Medicare bulletins sent to the . . . Clinic state that the box is to be used for the PIN of the performing physician or supplier. Placing [the doctor's] PIN in box 24k indicated that [the doctor] was the performing physician or supplier and therefore constituted a false statement. Box 33 is clearly labeled as requiring the PIN or group number of the physician or supplier providing the treatment, and [the doctor] was neither of these. Therefore, placing his PIN number in this box was a false statement as well." *Id.* at *9–*10. Moreover, the court rejected the defendant's contention that the claims were not false because the underlying services were actually rendered because "a claim may be false even if the services billed were actually provided, if the purported provider did not actually render or supervise the service." *Id.* at *8 (citation omitted).

[39] *Columbia/HCA Healthcare*, 20 F. Supp. 2d at 1046–47. *See also* United States *ex rel.* Kneepkins v. Gambro Healthcare, Inc., 115 F. Supp. 2d 35, 43 (D. Mass. 2000) (accepting theory of FCA liability based on violation of the anti-kickback statute); *but see* United States *ex rel.* Franklin v. Parke-Davis, 147 F. Supp. 2d 39, 55 (D. Mass. 2001) (rejecting the relator's claim that the defendant violated the FCA because it violated the anti-kickback statute, because the "Relator has failed to allege that physicians either expressly certified or, through their participation in a federally funded program, impliedly certified their compliance with the federal anti-kickback statute as a prerequisite to participating in the federal program. This Count fails for a different reason as well. [The defendant] argues that no False Claims Act anti-kickback case has ever extended the 'false certification' or the 'false implied certification' theory to cover claims filed, not by the Defendant, but by third parties. While Defendant's payment of kickbacks may well be illegal, a claim under the FCA will fail unless Relator alleges that [the defendant] caused or induced a doctor and/or pharmacist to file a false or fraudulent certification regarding compliance with the anti-kickback statute"). Courts have ruled that violations of the Stark law could trigger a violation of the False Claims Act. *See, e.g.*, United States *ex rel.* Goodstein v. McLaren, No. 97-CV-72992-DT, 2001 U.S. Dist. LEXIS 2917 at *14–*15 (E.D. Mich. Jan. 3, 2001) ("Under Stark, if a physician has a specified financial relationship with an entity, the physician may not make referrals to the entity for the furnishing of designated health services[.] 42 U.S.C. § 1395nn(a)(1). The Government's complaint alleges that defendants [which included a professional limited liability company that employed nine physicians who provide orthopedic services and a realty company that the physicians controlled that leased space to a defendant McLaren Regional Medical Center and made referrals to the Medical Center] have a financial relationship with McLaren in violation of Stark, and that defendants referred patients to McLaren for physical therapy and occupational therapy in violation of Stark. As it is conceivable that a set of facts could be proven in support of the Government's allegations, dismissal under

When a provider submits expressly false information to the government, the provider clearly may be subjected to FCA liability. Literal falsity cases, like those discussed above, are relatively straightforward. To state a cause of action, the government or whistleblower must demonstrate that some information is false. In determining whether the information is in fact false, there must be a comparison made to some benchmark. For example, the services of the dentist in *Lorenzo* were found to be false when compared to the rules and regulations governing the Medicare program because the services were not consultations, but were instead general examinations. Similarly, in *Columbia / HCA*, the representation that the hospital complied with the rules and regulations governing the program was false when the facts, if proven, demonstrated the opposite.[40] Inevitably, the government or whistle-

---

12(b)(6) is not warranted"); Gublo v. Novacare, Inc., 62 F. Supp. 2d 347, 355 (D. Mass. 1999) ("A number of courts . . . have recognized that the submission of a false certification of compliance with the Stark Law in order to qualify for Medicare reimbursement can constitute a false claim under the FCA") (citations omitted); United States *ex rel*. Pogue v. American Healthcorp., Inc., 914 F. Supp. 1507 (M.D. Tenn. 1996). Similarly one court recently found that providers' false certification on their cost report that they were unrelated to the management company in compliance with HCFA (CMS) regulations could constitute a false claim and support a cause of action under the FCA. *See* United States v. Estate of Rogers, No. 1:97CV461, 2001 WL 818160 at *6 (E.D. Tenn. June 28, 2001) (ruling that "FCA liability may not be based merely on noncompliance with statutes and regulations. FCA liability for a false certification will lie only if compliance with a statute or regulation was a prerequisite to gaining a benefit, and the defendant affirmatively certifies such compliance. Where the government has conditioned payment of a claim upon a claimant's certification of compliance with a statute or regulation, a claimant submits a false or fraudulent claim within the purview of the FCA when the claimant falsely certifies compliance with that statute or regulation").

[40]*But see* United States *ex rel*. Scott v. Dr. Eugene, No. 99-117 DOC (Eex) (C.D. Cal. Dec. 19, 2000). In *Scott*, the relator alleged that a defendant hospital had submitted false cost report certifications because, contrary to its representation that it had adhered to all program rules and regulations, it had in fact breached the anti-kickback law. The court rejected the relator's contention and questioned whether, because of its breadth, a cost report certification could serve as a predicate to an FCA action. Specifically, the court reasoned: "[I]t is not clear that the cost reports are relied on by the government to the extent required for a FCA allegation. The compliance certification is quite broad, requiring the signer to state that the report is in compliance with all the many and complex laws and regulations governing Medicare. This compliance certification may be so broad that it cannot stand as a basis for a false claim act allegation. Without reliance, the Cost-Report cannot serve as a basis for an FCA claim, even if false." *Id*. at 9. *Cf*. United States *ex rel*. Sharp v. Consolidated Medical Transport, Inc., No. 96 C 6502, 2001 U.S. Dist. LEXIS 13923 (N.D. Ill. Sept. 4, 2001). In *Consolidated Medical Transport*, the district court ruled that the relators could predicate an FCA claim based upon a violation of the anti-kickback act only if they could adequately plead that the United States would have refused to tender payment had it known of the violation. *See id*. at *29–*30 ("plaintiffs must plead (and ultimately prove) that had the government known about the kickback scheme, it would have refused payment of the claims and, further, that the defendants were aware that this was the case when they engaged in their fraudulent conduct. It does not make sense to the court to hold, as relators suggest, that defendants which certify compli-

blower proves falsity by showing an objective gap between the representation that was submitted and what the representation would have been if it were truthful. Thus, for example, if the government contends that a Current Procedural Terminology (CPT) code a physician claims is false, the government must identify what code the physician should have used to properly represent the services furnished to the patient. Similarly, if a provider certifies compliance with a rule or regulation, the government must show that the provider did not in fact comply with the pertinent rule or regulation. As is noted in detail below, when the plaintiff cannot prove the existence of such a gap—because, for example, the defendant complied with all regulatory guidance or contractual provisions in submitting the claim, or the regulatory guidance is so amorphous that no gap between what was claimed and what should have been claimed can be demonstrated—the plaintiff's claim must necessarily fail because it cannot demonstrate falsity.

### b. Falsity by Omission or Implicit Certification

The following health care cases illustrate where the line should be drawn when determining whether FCA claims can be false by omission or can be "implicitly" false because of the violation of a rule or regulation that is not specifically referenced in the claim itself.

A hospital in *Covington v. Sisters of the Third Order of St. Dominic of Hanford, California,*[41] received inflated payments from its intermediary because the intermediary designated the hospital as an urban rather than rural hospital. The hospital believed that it had received an inflated payment and corresponded with the intermediary regarding the error. In reviewing the issue of falsity in this situation, the court noted, in dicta, that the receipt and deposit of government funds the hospital knew to have been mistakenly paid could constitute a false claim.

The relator in *United States ex rel. Pogue v. American Healthcorp, Inc.,*[42] alleged that physicians referred their Medicare and Medicaid patients to a medical center in violation of the federal anti-kickback and self-referral statutes. Although the claims themselves were not false in that the services were actually rendered and medically necessary, the relator contended that the submission of the claims was

---

ance with the Medicare laws while secretly maintaining a kickback arrangement, automatically violate the FCA. If the certification in question has no bearing on the government's decision to pay the claims, there is no reason why it should trigger liability under the FCA. However, if the relators can show that the alleged scheme is in fact an illegal kickback scheme, and that the government would have barred claims had it known of the existence of the underlying scheme, a violation of the FCA would be proven. Under these circumstances, the alleged facts would constitute a fraudulent scheme materially bearing on the government's decision to pay the claims submitted to it").

[41]No. 93-15194, 1995 U.S. App. LEXIS 20370 (9th Cir. July 13, 1995).

[42]914 F. Supp. 1507 (M.D. Tenn. 1996).

fraudulent because the defendants "implicitly" stated that they had complied with all statutes, rules, and regulations governing Medicare when they submitted the claims. The court held that the FCA "was intended to cover not only those situations in which the claims themselves are false but also those situations in which a claimant engages in fraudulent conduct with the purpose of inducing payment of the government." Thus, the relator "may bring his claim under the [FCA] . . . if he can show that Defendants engaged in the fraudulent conduct with the purpose of inducing payment from the government. If Defendants' fraudulent conduct was not committed with the purpose of inducing payment from the government, that conduct does not operate to taint their Medicare claims and render the claims false or fraudulent under the [FCA]."[43]

In *United States v. NHC Healthcare Corp.*,[44] the government alleged that two residents at the defendant nursing home did not receive care that satisfied Medicare and Medicaid program standards. Specifically the government contended that "these residents developed pressure sores, incurred unusual weight loss, were in unnecessary pain . . . and ultimately died because of this care." The defendant contended that the claims it submitted to the government were not false or fraudulent and that it could not have known that the claims were false and that such contentions could not generate liability under the FCA. The court rejected the defendant's contentions, ruling that as a condition of receiving a per diem payment "the care facility agrees in principle to 'care for its residents in such a manner and in such an environment as will promote maintenance or enhancement of the quality of life.' 42 U.S.C. §1396r(b) (quotation from Nursing Home Reform Act which all Medicare and Medicaid recipients are required to adhere to). Therefore, the Court holds that in order for the Plaintiff to prove that it was fraudulently billed for the care given to the two residents at issue in this lawsuit it must demonstrate that the patients were not provided the quality of care which promotes the maintenance and the enhancement of the quality of life."[45]

---

[43] *Id.* at 1513.

[44] 115 F. Supp. 2d 1149 (W.D. Mo. 2000).

[45] The district court conceded that the standard it established was "amorphous" and "in need of further clarification." *Id.* at 1153. However it noted that "at this stage of the litigation the plaintiff need . . . only plead a sufficient cause of action" and that the court "cannot say as a matter of law that no set of facts which could be reasonably demonstrated by the Government could not result in FCA liability." *Id.* at 1153–54. The court concluded that it "may indeed be a very difficult burden of proof for the Government to show that the Defendant did not provide the minimum level of care necessary under its obligation to the United States, but difficulty in proving a cause of action should not bar the cause from even being litigated." *Id.* at 1154. Finally, significantly, the district court distinguished its ruling from the district court's ruling in United States *ex rel.* Mikes v. Straus (discussed *infra* note 48). The court reasoned that in *Straus* the district court ruled that the "dispute as to the proper standard of care for [the] billed procedures did not rise to the level of a fraudulent claim under the

In *United States v. Regents of University of California*,[46] a university and researchers submitted applications for federally funded grants to conduct an original project and for continuing research. After the relator, a scientist, questioned some of the results of the experiments, a retraction was published regarding some of the experiments. The relator alleged that the defendants submitted false claims by not disclosing the retraction in their subsequent application for federal grants. The court held that the defendants did not submit false claims to the government because the FCA "does not impose liability for omissions unless the defendant has an obligation to disclose the omitted information." Because there was no statutory or regulatory duty to inform the government of the retraction, the omission could not form the basis of FCA liability.[47]

In *United States ex rel. Mikes v. Straus*,[48] the relator alleged that the defendants violated the FCA because the services they furnished were not "of a quality which meets professionally recognized standards of health care," citing 42 U.S.C. Section 1320c-5(a). The relator alleged that the defendants, when providing patients with spirometry tests to measure the speed and volume of exhalation, did not use a three-liter syringe to calibrate the equipment or check calibration on a daily basis and after the equipment was moved, contrary to the recommended standards of the American Thoracic Society (ATS). The court held that there was no basis to the relator's theory that the

---

FCA" while in the *NHC Healthcare Corp.* case the government "argues that it paid the Defendant for complete care of these elderly patients (the standard of care) and the Defendant failed to meet this standard by knowingly failing to perform all necessary acts." *Id.* at 1155. Hence the billing dispute in *NHC Healthcare Corp.* was "not **how** the Defendant turned, bathed, administered drugs to, and fed the two residents in question, but **whether** the Defendant did these things at all." *Id.* (emphasis in original). The court pointed out that it "would not find a cognizable claim under the FCA if the United States simply disagreed with a reasonable medical or care treatment administered by the Defendant. In that case, the Defendant would obviously be innocent of fraud in its billing practices, but rather it would simply be at odds with the entity that pays the treatment it provided." *Id.* at 1153.

[46]912 F. Supp. 868, 883–85 (D. Md. 1995); *see also* United States *ex rel.* Berge v. Trustees of Univ. of Ala., 104 F.3d 1453, 1461 (4th Cir. 1997) (the "omission of [the researcher's] name from an abstract submitted as part of the progress report cannot possibly be material. In the first place, NIH [the National Institute of Health] did not even require the inclusion of her name, or anyone's name. There can only be liability under the [FCA] where the defendant has an obligation to disclose omitted information.") (citation omitted), *cert. denied*, 522 U.S. 916 (1997).

[47]*Regents of Univ. of Cal.*, 912 F. Supp. at 883–85.

[48]84 F. Supp. 2d 427 (S.D.N.Y. 1999); *see also* United States *ex rel.* Mikes v. Straus, 78 F. Supp. 2d 223 (S.D.N.Y. 1999) (in supplemental opinion, the court pointed out, in light of objections raised by the government in an amicus brief, that the basis for its decision was that the defendants did not execute any certification that "explicitly or implicitly[ ] suggest[s] that the spirometry machines used to measure patients' lung function had been calibrated in accordance with standards that the Government has neither promulgated nor adopted in any statute, regulations or manual governing Medicare").

defendants had implicitly certified compliance with all rules governing the Medicare program. That theory should only apply, according to the court, when the alleged breach "lies at the core of its agreement with the Government, or, in more practical terms, where the Government would have refused to pay had it been aware of the claimant's non-compliance."[49] The court concluded that the relator did not demonstrate that the defendants' compliance with the ATS standard was at the core of their agreement with the United States because she did not set forth any evidence that the government conditioned payment on such compliance, and the HCFA-1500 form, on which the defendants requested payment, did not expressly mandate compliance.[50]

Finally in *United States ex rel. Swafford v. Borgess Medical Center*,[51] the relator alleged that the defendants had billed for interpreting venous ultrasound studies although they only reworded the vascular technician's worksheet summary reporting results as either negative or negative with abnormality and did not review the technician's hard data (video tape results). The relator contended that this practice breached the FCA because it constituted substandard care. The court ruled that there was no basis to the relator's theory because the defendants' compliance with the statutory or regulatory authority was not so essential for reimbursement that if the government had been aware of the defendants' noncompliance it would have refused payment.

When a provider submits expressly false information to the government, it clearly may be subject to FCA liability. A more difficult issue is determining when a provider may be liable for submitting

---

[49] 84 F. Supp. 2d at 435.

[50] *See also* Lum v. Vision Serv. Plan, 104 F. Supp. 2d 1237 (D. Haw. 2000). In *Lum* the relator alleged that a company that contracted to provide vision care services through a managed care delivery system that provided services to Medicaid beneficiaries had breached the FCA because contrary to its contract with the health plan stating that it would comply with all applicable federal and state laws, rules, and regulations, it breached the law because it charged adult patients a $7.00 co-payment. *Id.* at 1238–39. The defendant contended that it did not submit any "false" statement or claim because the bill it submitted to the managed care plan contained billing data and calculations only and contained no express statement of compliance with any law or contract. The court concurred with the defendant. Specifically, it held:

> There was nothing false about the bills. The bills did not impose the $7 co-payment. Nor did the bills promise compliance with any law. The bills merely contained billing information. The False Claims Act attaches liability to false and fraudulent claims for payment, not to underlying activity that is allegedly fraudulent. . . . Accordingly, violations of laws, rules, or regulations alone do not create False Claims Act liability.

*Id.* at 1241 (citations omitted). The court's decision in *Lum* could be important to other health care companies in providing a potential defense when they subcontract with managed care organizations and are accused of breaching the FCA although they submitted bills that are accurate on their face.

[51] 98 F. Supp. 2d 822 (W.D. Mich. 2000).

false information by omission. On one hand, a plaintiff may contend, as in *Pogue* or *NHC Healthcare Corp.*, that whenever a provider that seeks Medicare or Medicaid reimbursement violates one of the program's myriad rules and regulations, and fails to inform the government of the breach, the provider submitted false claims by omission because if the provider had disclosed the breach, the government would not have paid the claim. On the other hand, a defendant may contend, as in *University of California, Mikes*, and *Swafford*, that there is no falsity unless the falsity is intrinsic to the allegedly false document and the provider has an affirmative legal (as opposed to moral or social) duty to disclose the information. As set forth below, the latter view best conforms to the statutory language, the case law, and the FCA's purpose.

The FCA's language demonstrates that Congress intended that the alleged falsity exists in the document itself and that the FCA not be applied as a "superlaw" to enforce all rules and regulations in existence at the time the claim or statement was submitted. Subsections 3729(a)(1) and (a)(3) of the FCA apply to false claims; subsection (a)(2) applies to false statements that are used "to get" a false claim paid or approved; and subsection (a)(7) applies to false statements or records that are used to decrease an obligation to pay or transmit money. Congress's focus thus was directed toward specific types of statements and claims. It did not simply mandate that any false or fraudulent conduct or act be subject to liability under the statute.[52] Hence, an assessment of whether liability attaches must be limited to an examination of the statement or claim itself and a determination of whether any overt representation is false, and not a broad-based inquiry into whether the defendant committed some unrelated improper act or breached some undefined standard.

The majority of cases have rejected the theory that claims can be tainted or implicitly false, requiring instead that the falsity appear on the face of the claim or statement. For example, courts have historically refused to apply the FCA when the defendants may have engaged in fraudulent conduct but that conduct was not embodied in any discrete claim.[53] More recently, the Ninth Circuit embraced this

---

[52] *See, e.g.*, United States v. Rivera, 55 F.3d 703, 709 (1st Cir. 1995) (the FCA "attaches liability, not to the underlying fraudulent activity or to the government's wrongful payment, but to the 'claim for payment'. . . . This focus on the claim for payment appears to reflect a congressional judgment that fraud by government contractors is best prevented by attacking the activity that presents the risk of wrongful payment. . .").

[53] *See, e.g.*, United States *ex rel.* Weinberger v. Equifax, 557 F.2d 456, 461 (5th Cir. 1977) (the defendant did not engage in fraudulent conduct when it was unclear whether its conduct violated a statute and the defendant was not required to certify that its conduct conformed with the questioned statute); United States v. Bausch & Lomb Optical Co., 131 F.2d 545 (2d Cir. 1942) (because the defendant had never certified to the government that its bid was competitive, it did not submit

view in *United States ex rel. Hopper v. Anton*.[54] In that case, the relator alleged that the defendant had violated the regulations governing
the Individuals With Disabilities Education Act (IDEA), and thus its
claims for IDEA funds were actionable under the FCA. The Ninth Circuit rejected this contention, ruling that the regulatory violation did
not result in FCA liability because "[v]iolations of law, rules or regulations alone do not create a cause of action under the FCA" and in this
action the defendant did not certify that it had complied with all IDEA
regulations in order to receive payment.[55] Furthermore, additional case
law has limited the broad-based falsity-by-omission theory by ruling
that a provider's adherence to other laws or regulations is only pertinent
when the provider expressly certifies compliance with those laws[56] or

---

false claims to the government even if it had "been guilty of unlawful conduct in
eliminating competitors"), *aff'd*, 320 U.S. 711 (1943); United States v. Shaw, 725 F.
Supp. 896 (S.D. Miss. 1989) (court ruled that although a bribe paid to influence loan
approval may have "tainted" the underlying application for the loan, the "bare fact
that bribes were involved . . . does not necessarily lead to the further conclusion that
false or fraudulent claims were made in connection with each of the loan applications or preapplications"); United States *ex rel*. Hughes v. Cook, 498 F. Supp. 784,
787–88 (S.D. Miss. 1980) (although physicians may not have complied with the
technical requirements of Mississippi medical licensure law—specifically, that they
file their license with the office of the Clerk of the Circuit Court within their local-
ity within 60 days of issuance—the relator could not bring an FCA action because
the physicians committed no fraud and did "nothing but submit perfectly appropriate Medicaid claims after performing valuable and necessary medical services");
United States v. Farina, 153 F. Supp. 819, 822 (D.N.J. 1957) (even if manufacturer
had conspired with government representative to ensure that manufacturer submitted a lower bid than competitor, there was no violation of the FCA if the representation was not incorporated into any claim).

[54]91 F.3d 1261, 1266 (9th Cir. 1996), *cert. denied*, 519 U.S. 1261 (1997).

[55]*Id*. at 1266. *See also* United States *ex rel*. Siewick v. Jamieson Science & Eng'g,
214 F.3d 1372, 1376 (D.C. Cir. 2000) (rejecting the relator's assertion that the defendant's claims were implicitly false because the defendant had hired a former government employee who assisted the company in obtaining additional government
contracts in violation of 18 U.S.C. §207 (a criminal statute aimed at "revolving door"
abuses by former government employees) because the relator "points to nothing suggesting that [the defendant company] was required to certify compliance with § 207
as a condition of its contract. Thus his claim of implied certification fails"). As the
Ninth Circuit pointed out, however, a provider's violation of another regulation may
result in FCA liability when a provider specifically certifies that it has adhered to that
regulation. *Id*. at 1267; *see also* United States *ex rel*. Fallon v. Accudyne Corp., 880 F.
Supp. 636, 638 (W.D. Wis. 1995) (a company's false certification that it has complied
with environmental laws results in FCA liability). Under these circumstances, there
is no implicit falsity. Instead, the falsity is explicit on the face of the claim form, and
the violator thereby has been expressly notified of its duties and the probable penalties stemming from the transgression.

[56]*See, e.g*., Luckey v. Baxter Healthcare Corp., 2 F. Supp. 2d 1034, 1045 (N.D. Ill.
1998) ("[a] finding of a false implied certification under the FCA for every request for
payment accompanied by a failure to comply with all applicable regulations, without more, improperly broadens the intended reach of the FCA"), *aff'd*, 183 F.3d 730
(7th Cir. 1999); United States *ex rel*. Durcholz v. FKW Inc., 997 F. Supp. 1143, 1156
(S.D. Ind. 1998) ("a failure to adhere to agency policy, without more, does not necessarily violate the FCA") (citation omitted).

when the provider has an express duty to disclose information to the government as part of the submission of the claim.[57]

Cases holding that claims or statements can be implicitly false because of the violation of some unrelated statute or regulation relied upon a mistaken reading of FCA precedent and a misunderstanding of the FCA legislative history. The district court in *Pogue*[58] offered the most comprehensive account of the basis for imposing FCA liability for a violation of another statute or regulation. However, the *Pogue* court's reasoning was flawed. The court cited to *Ab-Tech Construction, Inc. v. United States*[59] and *United States v. Incorporated Village of Island Park*[60] to provide support for the theory, yet the defendants in both cases also had submitted false statements to the government on which the government relied.[61] Moreover, the legislative history the court cited is similarly inapposite.[62] Although the Senate Judiciary Committee Report stated that the FCA reached "each and every claim submitted under a contract, loan guarantee, or other agreement which was originally obtained by means of false statements or other corrupt or fraudulent conduct, or in violation of any statute or applicable regulation," this reference merely encompasses situations in which a

---

[57] United States *ex rel.* Berge v. Trustees of Univ. of Ala., 104 F.3d 1453, 1461 (4th Cir.), *cert. denied*, 522 U.S. 916 (1997); United States *ex rel.* Milam v. Regents of the Univ. of Cal., 912 F. Supp. 868 (D. Md. 1995).

[58] 914 F. Supp. 1507 (M.D. Tenn. 1996). One misapplication of this broad theory in the health care context occurs when the government alleges that each claim that a provider submitted is false because the provider knew that it had violated some unrelated regulation. For example, in United *States ex rel. Aranda v. Community Psychiatric Ctrs.,* 945 F. Supp. 1485 (W.D. Okla. 1996), a district court ruled that the government stated a cause of action by alleging that the provider "implicitly certif[ied] that it was abiding by applicable statutes, rules and regulations" that required that patients be provided "appropriate quality of care and a safe and secure environment" although the provider knew that in fact it was not providing an appropriate quality of care and a safe and secure environment. Similarly, in *United States ex rel. Sanders v. East Ala. Health Care Auth.,* 953 F. Supp. 1404 (M.D. Ala. 1996), a district court ruled that the relator stated a cause of action by alleging that the provider's claims were false because they were based on an improperly obtained certificate of need that allowed the provider to operate and receive reimbursement for additional beds.

[59] 31 Fed. Cl. 429 (1994), *aff'd*, 57 F.3d 1084 (Fed. Cir. 1995).

[60] 888 F. Supp. 419 (E.D.N.Y. 1995).

[61] In *Ab-Tech*, the company had falsely stated that it understood Small Business Administration (SBA) program requirements and that it would comply with those requirements as a basis for continuing eligibility. Notwithstanding these representations, the defendant failed to adhere to SBA rules by not disclosing the company's association with another company. 31 Fed. Cl. at 432. In *Island Park*, to obtain HUD funds, the defendants had falsely stated that persons would not be excluded from the subsidized housing program on the basis of race. 888 F. Supp. at 439–40. Thus, these were not cases in which an entity was held liable under the FCA for violating a separate regulation, but because, at least in part, the entity had submitted false statements to the government.

[62] 914 F.2d at 1511.

provider made a false statement to obtain subsequent payment on a claim (e.g., a provider represents a false net worth on a loan application) or when adherence to other regulations or statutes is built into the specific certification signed by the defendant (e.g., a provider certifies on a claim that it has adhered to a particular government rule or regulation). Both of those examples include situations in which the FCA is properly invoked. There is no support, however, for the broader proposition that violation of a rule or regulation, when a provider does not certify compliance with the rule or regulation in the first instance, may result in the submission of implicitly false claims under the FCA.[63]

---

[63]*But see* Shaw v. AAA Eng'g & Drafting Inc., 213 F.3d 519 (10th Cir. 2000). There the Tenth Circuit expressly found that the language and structure of the FCA supported the theory of "implicitly" false claims. Specifically the court wrote:

> Additionally, the language and structure of the FCA itself supports the conclusion that, under 31 U.S.C. §3729(a)(1), a false implied certification may constitute a "false or fraudulent claim." This interpretive conclusion flows from a distinction between the language of §3729(a)(1) and that of §3729(a)(2). Under §3729(a)(2), liability is premised on the presentation of a "false record or statement to get a false or fraudulent claim paid or approved." Section 3729(a)(1), however, requires only the presentation of a "false or fraudulent claim for payment or approval" without the additional element of a "false record or statement." *See United States ex rel. Fallon v. Accudyne*, 921 F. Supp. 611, 627 (W.D. Wis. 1995) (Fallon II) (noting this distinction between §3729(a)(1) and §3279(a)(2); cf. *United States ex rel. Aakhus v. Dyncorp, Inc.*, 136 F.3d 676, 682–83 (10th Cir. 1998) (concluding that there needs to be a specific statement by the contractor to support a cause of action under §3729(a)(2)). Thus, FCA liability under §3729(a)(1) may arise even absent an affirmative or express false statement by the government contractor.

*Id.* at 531–32; *see also* United States *ex rel.* Wright v. Cleo Wallace Ctrs., 132 F. Supp. 2d 913, 926 (D. Colo. 2000) ("After fully reviewing the Tenth Circuit's opinion in *Shaw*, I conclude that if a person who knowingly submits claims to the government for the purpose of acquiring federal Medicaid funds while not in compliance with all relevant laws, rules and regulations may constitute a false claim under the FCA, even without an affirmative or express false statement of such compliance") (citation omitted). The distinction between false statements or reports and false claims has existed since the FCA was initially passed in 1863. *See, e.g.,* Act of March 2, 1863, ch. 67, 12 Stat. 696 (proscribing the submission of "false, fictitious, or fraudulent" claim, on the one hand, and "any false bill, receipt, voucher, entry, roll, account, claim, statement, certificate, affidavit, or deposition" to obtain approval or payment on such claim, on the other hand). It is hard to imagine that Congress in 1863, when it drew this distinction between various types of false statements and claims, had as its purpose that the false claims prong of the provision was intended to reach "implicitly false claims," that is claims that had no falsity on their face, while the false statement prong of the provision would reach claims that contained some false statement on their face. The more likely basis for the distinction, instead, is that the term "claim" is a term of art that captures only submissions to the United States that is a demand for money or property and causes the United States immediate financial detriment and that not all false statements or reports satisfy that criteria and thus Congress created a second prong to proscribe the submission of such false statements when they are used to get a false claim paid. *See* McNinch v. United States, 356 U.S. 595 (1958) (interpreting the word "claim" in this fashion); *see also* Salcido, Fᴀʟsᴇ Cʟᴀɪᴍs Aᴄᴛ Cᴏᴜɴsᴇʟɪɴɢ, *supra* note 30, §2:04

Limiting when one can be liable for falsity by omission to include only those instances in which a provider certified compliance with specific rules or regulations or when the provider had a specific legal duty to disclose is sensible. To extend the FCA beyond situations in which a provider expressly lies to obtain governmental benefits undermines not only the statutory language, but also the purpose of the FCA. The FCA was intended to operate as a remedial, not penal, statute.[64] However, to apply the FCA, with its treble damages and civil monetary penalty provisions, when the provider does not have clear notice that the conduct breaches some objective standard is to apply the FCA in a highly punitive, and perhaps unconstitutional, fashion.

### 2. Cases in Which Courts Refused to Find That Defendant Submitted False or Fraudulent Claims or Statements

There are several discrete categories of cases in which courts generally will find that the defendant's claims are not false. For example, if the provider's practices conform with the regulations or cannot be shown to be objectively false, the FCA plaintiff cannot prove falsity as a matter of law and its claim must be dismissed.

#### a. Literal Compliance

In *United States ex rel. Cox v. Iowa Health Systems*,[65] the relator, an air ambulance pilot, alleged that by converting nautical miles to statute miles various health care entities falsified the number of miles flown to yield a higher number and hence higher reimbursement. The defendants contended that no rule or regulation required medical care providers to measure air ambulance mileage in nautical miles rather than statute miles. The court held that the relator could not state a cause of action because the relator failed to "identify any law, regulation, or other source suggesting federal medical programs expected air ambulance mileage claims to be in nautical miles rather than statute miles."[66]

---

(describing the historical development of the word "claim"). Indeed, the Tenth Circuit's reasoning in *Shaw* based upon "the language and structure of the FCA" is a good example of how construing statutory language without the benefit of reviewing the long and detailed history underlying the provision can yield a potentially erroneous conclusion.

[64]*See, e.g.*, S. REP. NO. 99-345 at 6–7, *reprinted in* 1986 U.S.C.C.A.N. at 5271–72; *see also* 132 CONG. REC. 22,336 (Sept. 9, 1986) (In the course of explaining the amendments, Rep. Fish, who was an original sponsor of the legislation, pointed out: "It should be stressed, Mr. Speaker, that we are dealing with a civil—not criminal—statute. The False Claims Act is remedial in nature. The reason for my emphasis on this point is that considerable confusion has been prompted by judicial decisions that have treated the False Claims Act as if it were a criminal statute. . . . These cases, in part, are the reason why I introduced the administration's package.").

[65]29 F. Supp. 2d 1022 (S.D. Iowa 1998).

[66]*Id.* at 1026.

Of course, whenever a defendant's practices conform to the rules and regulations of a government program, the defendant's submission of claims and statements cannot be false or fraudulent as a matter of law.[67] In this sense, providers that institute comprehensive compli-

---

[67] United States *ex rel*. Hochman v. Nackman, 145 F.3d 1069, 1073–74 (9th Cir. 1998) (no falsity when defendants' acts conformed with VA payment guidelines); United States *ex rel*. Lindenthal v. General Dynamics Corp., 61 F.3d 1402, 1412 (9th Cir. 1995) (whistleblower's FCA claims for payment based on work that satisfied contractual obligations "could not have been 'false or fraudulent' within the meaning of the [False Claims Act]"); United States *ex rel*. Glass v. Medtronic, Inc., 957 F.2d 605, 608 (8th Cir. 1992) (a statement cannot be false or fraudulent under the FCA when the statement is consistent with regulations governing program); United States *ex rel*. Bidani v. Lewis, No. 97 C 6502, 2001 U.S. Dist. LEXIS 9204 at *14–*16 (N.D. Ill. June 29, 2001) (rejecting relator's claim that defendants breached the FCA because they breached the assignment rules by receiving payment rather than the patient because the relator "points to no regulation requiring that the patient also sign a separate assignment form nor any evidence that defendants were aware that they were violating any regulation. Since relator has not provided evidence (or a sufficient argument) in support of his assignment claim, he will not be permitted to file an amended complaint raising that claim"); United States *ex rel*. Mathews v. HealthSouth Corp., 140 F. Supp. 2d 706, 710–11 (W.D. La. 2001) (rejecting the relator's claim that the defendant rehabilitation hospital's cost report certification was false because it failed to comply with "[m]edicare regulations and criteria [that] require" rehabilitation hospitals "to provide to all patients intensive rehabilitation service, which is defined as a minimum of three hours of therapy a day, five days a week," when the relator could not point to any such mandate in a statute or regulation and hence had "failed to allege a fraudulent course of conduct or falsity in connection with [defendant's] certification of compliance in its . . . annual cost reports"); United States *ex rel*. Ben-Shlush v. St. Luke's-Roosevelt Hosp., 97 Civ. 3664 (LAP), 2000 U.S. Dist. LEXIS 3039 (S.D.N.Y. Mar. 10, 2000) (the court rejected the relator's contention that the defendant had falsely certified to the government that it had an adequate written plan of discharge for plaintiff because "a review of the regulations cited by plaintiff does not support his position" in that plaintiff did not cite "any regulations mandating certification to HHS regarding discharge planning" or "specify any information to be included in such a plan" and thus "plaintiff's allegations do not support a False Claims Act claim"); United States *ex rel*. Swafford v. Borgess Med. Ctr., 98 F. Supp. 2d 822, 827 (W.D. Mich. 2000) (the court rejected the relator's allegation that defendant physicians breached their certification that the services they provided were "personally furnished" by them or by an "employee under [their] personal direction" when they billed for interpreting venous ultrasound studies by merely rewording the vascular technologist's worksheet summary when the technologist reported the results as either negative or negative with abnormality (and did not review the technologist's hard copy data [video tape results]) because no regulations mandated that the physicians must review the hard copy data to bill for the interpretations); United States *ex rel*. Gathings v. Bruno's Inc., 54 F. Supp. 2d 1252 (M.D. Ala. 1999) (the court rejected the relator's allegation that the defendants, which were pharmacies, defrauded the government by charging lower dispensing fees for Blue Cross-Blue Shield patients than they did for Medicaid patients contrary to a contractual provision mandating that the Medicaid program be charged the same amount as the general public because the defendants' practice did not breach any Medicaid standard regarding the amount of the dispensing fees); United States *ex rel*. LaCorte v. SmithKline Beecham Clinical Labs., No. 96-1380 *et al.*, 1999 U.S. Dist. LEXIS 13036 (E.D. La. Aug. 20, 1999) (the court dismissed relator's allegation that defendant submitted false claims when it billed the government for a price higher than it billed its best customers because the

ance programs should achieve substantial cost savings because implementing measures to ensure that their practices conform to the law should dramatically minimize the risk that they will become the subject of a successful FCA lawsuit.

### b. Non-Objective False Claims

A company in *Luckey v. Baxter Healthcare Corp.*[68] certified that it would utilize test methods that provide accurate and reliable results. The relator contended that the company's testing procedures were scientifically unsound and should be improved. The court ruled that the relator could not demonstrate that the company's certification was false because the relator could not point to any contract or regulation that required a specific type of testing and because "[c]ourts have consistently declined to find that a contractor's exercise of scientific or professional judgment as to an applicable standard of care falls within the scope of the FCA."[69]

In *United States v. Estate of Rogers,*[70] the government contended that the defendants had submitted false cost reports and claims seeking reimbursement for management fees that were not properly reimbursable costs because the defendant home health agencies were related to the defendant management company within the meaning of Medicare's rules and regulations. The defendants claimed that the government could not predicate an FCA action on Medicare's related-party rules because they had acted within a reasonable interpretation of those rules. Specifically, the defendants claimed that the Medicare "related party" rules and regulations are complex, subjective, and difficult to understand and apply and that the FCA was not enacted to punish persons for merely disagreeing with the federal government over the meaning of administrative regulations. The court rejected the defendants' contention. The court ruled that with "regard to the specific element of falsity under the FCA, it is immaterial whether the defendants did or did not make reasonable interpretations of the applicable HCFA rules and regulations governing the related-party issues. . . . [T]he defendants' contention that they made a reasonable interpretation of HCFA's related-party rules and regulations only goes to the scienter element and whether the defendants acted 'knowingly' as defined

---

relator could not point to any "statute or regulation imposing the obligation it asserts defendant has breached" and the "statute does not state that providers must charge Medicare the lowest rate billed to anyone"); United States *ex rel.* Joslin v. Community Home Health, 984 F. Supp. 374, 379 (D. Md. 1997) (where defendants' practices conformed with the law "any representation to the Federal Government . . . is correct . . . and did not violate the FCA"); United States *ex rel.* Milam v. Regents of the Univ. of Cal., 912 F. Supp. 868, 883 (D. Md. 1995) ("as a matter of law . . . False Claims Act liability cannot be imposed on the basis of a literally true statement.").

[68] 2 F. Supp. 2d 1034 (N.D. Ill. 1998), *aff'd*, 183 F.3d 730 (7th Cir. 1999).

[69] *Id.* at 1047–48.

[70] No. 1:97CV461, 2001 WL 818160 (E.D. Tenn. June 28, 2001).

in 31 U.S.C. § 3729(b). The factual issue of scienter is a matter for the jury to determine at trial."[71]

As noted earlier, to establish falsity under the FCA, it is not sufficient to demonstrate that the provider's practices could have or should have been better. Instead, the plaintiff must demonstrate that an objective gap exists between what the defendant represented and what the defendant would have stated had the defendant told the truth. At times, it is difficult to establish that such a gap exists because the government certification, contract, or guidelines call for the provider to exercise discretion. For example, in *Luckey v. Baxter Healthcare Corp.*, the government rule to which the company certified compliance mandated the use of testing methods that provide accurate and reliable results. There is a wide spectrum involving subjective judgment between adopting perfect test procedures and minimally compliant procedures. As long as the defendant's practices were anywhere along that spectrum, it could not be deemed to have submitted false certification because its certification would satisfy its legal duty. Accordingly, under such circumstances, courts will rule that the defendant's claim or statement is not false or fraudulent.[72] However, as the *Rogers* case illustrates, where the rule or the regulation does not call for an exercise of discretion and can be determined with judicial precision, then the court in the first instance will determine whether the claim is

---

[71] In *Estate of Rogers*, the district court adopted the reasoning the Ninth Circuit had applied in *United States ex rel. Oliver v. Parsons Corp.,* 195 F.3d 457 (9th Cir. 1999), *cert. denied*, 530 U.S. 1228 (2000). There the Ninth Circuit held that the falsity element could not be bypassed by merely demonstrating that the underlying contractual provision is ambiguous or that defendant acted in accordance with a reasonable interpretation of the regulation. *See* 195 F.3d at 463 n.3 (noting that the "amicus brief submitted by the Government correctly points out the potential problem created by embracing a 'reasonable interpretation' exception to the 'falsity' of a claim. A defendant could submit a claim, knowing it is false or at least with reckless disregard as to falsity, thus meeting the intent element, but nevertheless avoid liability by successfully arguing that its claim reflected a 'reasonable interpretation' of the requirements").

[72] *See, e.g.,* Hagood v. Sonoma County Water Agency, 81 F.3d 1465, 1477 (9th Cir. 1996) ("How precise and how current the cost allocation needed to be in light of the [Water Supply Act's] imprecise and discretionary language was a disputed question within the [government]. Even viewing [the relator's] evidence in the most favorable light, that evidence shows only a disputed legal issue; that is not enough to support a reasonable inference that the allocation was *false* within the meaning of the False Claims Act") (emphasis added); United States *ex rel.* Anderson v. Northern Telecom, Inc., 52 F.3d 810, 815–16 (9th Cir. 1995); Wang v. FMC Corp., 975 F.2d 1412, 1421 (9th Cir. 1992) ("Proof of one's mistakes or inabilities is not evidence that one is a cheat. . . . Without more, the common failings of engineers and other scientists are not culpable under the Act. . . . The Act is concerned with ferreting out 'wrongdoing,' not scientific errors.") (citation omitted); United States *ex rel.* Milam v. Regents of the Univ. of Cal., 912 F. Supp. 868 (D. Md. 1995); United States *ex rel.* Boisjoly v. Morton Thiokol, Inc., 706 F. Supp. 795, 810 (N.D. Utah 1988) ("[The certification] reflects an engineering judgment. . . . It is clearly not a statement of fact that can be said to be either true or false, and thus cannot form the basis of a FCA claim.").

false as a matter of law and, if the defendant's acts are inconsistent with the legal requirements underlying the government's program, a jury will determine whether the defendant acted with the requisite intent to submit the false claim or statement.

## B. The FCA "Knowing" Standard

Falsity alone is insufficient to impose FCA liability; the provider must have "knowingly" submitted the false claim. The FCA defines "knowing" and "knowingly" to mean that a person: "(1) has actual knowledge of the information; (2) acts in deliberate ignorance of the truth or falsity of the information; or (3) acts in reckless disregard of the truth or falsity of the information."[73] The FCA further provides that "no proof of specific intent to defraud is required."[74]

Consistent with the terms "reckless disregard" and "deliberate ignorance," the legislative history indicates that Congress was generally concerned about two types of conduct that some courts had concluded were not actionable under the pre-1986 FCA. The first type involved instances in which a provider submitted claims in a sloppy, unsupervised fashion without due care regarding the accuracy of the claim (i.e., reckless disregard).[75] The second type concerned instances in which a provider deliberately refused to learn additional facts that, if learned, would disclose that the claim was inaccurate (i.e., deliberate ignorance).[76]

---

[73] 31 U.S.C. §3729(b).

[74] *Id.*

[75] *See, e.g.*, 132 CONG. REC. 20,535–36 (Aug. 11, 1986). Specifically, Sen. Grassley pointed out:

> While the committee expressed in its report accompanying S. 1562 that mistake, inadvertence or mere negligence in the submission of a false claim would not be actionable under the bill, concerns stemming mainly from the Government contracting community, were raised that such examples of mere negligence might be construed as grossly negligent acts.
>
> To address those concerns, I, along with the other sponsors of this bill, have agreed to return to a "reckless disregard" standard, but only with the express qualification that "no proof of specific intent is required." Our intent in returning to the reckless disregard standard is only to assure that mere negligence, mistake, and inadvertence are not actionable under the False Claims Act. In doing so, we reconfirm our belief that reckless disregard and gross negligence define essentially the same conduct and that under this act, reckless disregard does not require any proof of an intentional, deliberate, or willful act.

[76] *See, e.g.*, S. REP. NO. 99-345 at 6–7, *reprinted in* 1986 U.S.C.C.A.N. 5271–72 ("the Government is unable to hold responsible those corporate officers who insulate themselves from knowledge of false claims submitted by lower-level subordinates. The 'ostrich-like' conduct which can occur in large corporations poses insurmountable difficulties for civil false claims recoveries. . . . [T]he Committee does believe the civil False Claims Act should recognize that those doing business with the Government have an obligation to make a limited inquiry to ensure the claims they submit are accurate.").

Below are descriptions of cases in which courts have applied the deliberate ignorance and reckless disregard elements of the FCA. Also addressed are cases in which courts have concluded that the provider did not act knowingly because, for example, the conduct was merely negligent and did not rise to the level of knowledge required by the FCA, the relevant regulatory guidance was ambiguous, the government knew and approved of the potential overpayment, or the defendant relied upon a sound legal theory in submitting the claim. These cases also help health care providers confronting a possible billing discrepancy assess whether to disclose the wrongdoing to the OIG pursuant to its Voluntary Disclosure Program or whether they are simply liable for an overpayment and need only reimburse the government's fiscal agent. Furthermore, a review of the FCA intent standard gives health care providers guidance as to what specific steps they may take to minimize the risk that a government enforcement action or a viable *qui tam* action will be filed.

### 1. Reckless Disregard

In *United States v. Krizek,*[77] a psychiatrist with a small practice delegated the task of billing services to his wife and a billing clerk. The wife and clerk assumed the doctor furnished a 50-minute psychotherapy session unless they were told otherwise. The wife believed that "it was fair and appropriate to use the [50-minute] code as a rough approximation of the time spent, because on some days, an examination would last up to two hours and [she] would still bill [the 50-minute code]." The court noted that the "net result of this system, or more accurately 'nonsystem,' of billing was that on a number of occasions, [staff] submitted bills for . . . psychotherapy sessions"[78] but the psychiatrist "could not have spent the requisite time providing services." The court held that the submitted claims exceeding a set hourly threshold per day were false and had been submitted in reckless disregard of their truth or falsity.[79]

---

[77] 859 F. Supp. 5 (D.D.C. 1994), *aff'd in part, rev'd in part,* 111 F.3d 934 (D.C. Cir. 1997).

[78] *Id.* at 11.

[79] Although the defendant psychiatrist claimed that he was at worst merely "negligent" and emphasized the "ma and pa" nature of his small practice, the court nonetheless imposed liability, ruling that the psychiatrist

> failed utterly in supervising [his] agents in their submissions of claims on his behalf. As a result of his failure to supervise, [the physician] received reimbursement for services which he did not provide. These were not "mistakes" nor merely negligent conduct. Under the statutory definition of "knowing" conduct, the Court is compelled to conclude that the defendants acted with reckless disregard as to the truth or falsity of the submissions. As such, they will be deemed to have violated the False Claims Act.

In affirming the district court's ruling, the D.C. Circuit stated that "the best reading of the Act defines reckless disregard as an extension of gross negligence." The court ruled that the defendants' conduct had reached that standard:

In *United States ex rel. Trim v. McKean*,[80] a national billing company submitted claims on behalf of emergency department physicians. The company required its coders to code 40 charts per hour and instructed them to bill based upon the services provided rather than the documentation provided in the charts. The company's billing manual stated that lower-level acuity codes rarely were appropriate because the services involved the emergency department. Comparison with national statistics revealed that the company billed at levels consistently higher than the average. The company instructed coders not to use certain International Classification of Diseases (9th Revision) (ICD-9) codes that would result in lower reimbursements and to use a CPT 52-modifier to notify its physician-clients that documentation was insufficient to support the level of service the coder actually assigned, which resulted in a higher charge being passed on to the government. As in *Krizek*, the court found that the company had submitted claims with knowledge of their falsity or in reckless disregard of their falsity.

In *United States v. Mackby*,[81] defendant, a nonphysician owner of a physical therapy clinic, used the provider identification number of his father, a physician who did not perform services at the clinic, when presenting health care claims to the government. The defendant claimed that he did not knowingly submit false claims to the government because he had asked his office manager to contact Medicare to find out about the appropriate payment rules and had also, on two occasions, requested that the clinic's billing number be changed to a physical therapist who worked at the clinic but that the request was denied. The court ruled that the defendant submitted claims in reckless disregard or in deliberate ignorance of the law. Specifically, the court reasoned: defendant "was the managing director of the clinic. He was responsible for day-to-day operations, long-term planning, lease

---

We are also unpersuaded by the Krizeks' argument that their conduct did not rise to the level of reckless disregard. The District Court cited a number of factors supporting its conclusion: Mrs. Krizek completed the submissions with little or no factual basis; she made no effort to establish how much time Dr. Krizek spent with any particular patient; and Dr. Krizek "failed utterly" to review bills submitted on his behalf. *Krizek*, 859 F. Supp. at 13. Most tellingly, there were a number of days within the seven-patient sample when even the shoddiest recordkeeping would have revealed that false submissions were being made—those days on which the Krizeks' billing approached twenty-four hours in a single day. On August 31, 1985, for instance, the Krizeks requested reimbursement for patient treatment using the 90844 code thirty times and the 90843 code once, indicating patient treatment of over 22 hours. *Id.* at 12. Outside the seven-patient sample the Krizeks billed for *more* than twenty-four hours in a single day on three separate occasions. *Krizek*, 909 F. Supp. at 34. These factors amply support the District Court's determination that the Krizeks acted with reckless disregard.

111 F.3d at 942.

[80] 31 F. Supp. 2d 1308 (W.D. Okla. 1998).

[81] No. 99-15605, 2001 U.S. App. LEXIS 18478 (9th Cir. Aug. 18, 2001).

and build-out negotiations, personnel, and legal and accounting oversight. It was his obligation to be familiar with the legal requirements for obtaining reimbursement from Medicare for physical therapy services, and to ensure that the clinic was run in accordance with all laws. His claim that he did not know of the Medicare requirements does not shield him from liability. By failing to inform himself of those requirements, particularly when twenty percent of [the] Clinic's patients were Medicare beneficiaries, he acted in reckless disregard or in deliberate ignorance of those requirements, either of which was sufficient to charge him with knowledge of the falsity of the claims in question."[82]

A significant development in the 1986 FCA amendments was Congress's clarification that specific intent to defraud the government is not an essential element for liability under the FCA. Prior to the 1986 amendments, a defendant could escape liability by demonstrating that although the claims were erroneous (i.e., false), there was no liability because the provider did not consciously intend to cheat the government.[83] As *Krizek*, *Trim*, and *Mackby* illustrate, the government or relator can now prevail in a claim by pointing to the defendant's practices that perhaps were not tailored toward the submission of truthful claims even if the defect resulted from a lack of supervision or due care rather than an express desire to cheat the government. Therefore, given these judicial decisions, those who delegate responsibility for billing and claims processing without providing any controls aimed toward ascertaining the truthfulness of the claims being submitted may be at risk under the reckless-disregard portion of the FCA's standard for acting knowingly.[84]

---

[82] *Id.* at *14–*16 (citation omitted).

[83] *See, e.g.,* United States v. Davis, 809 F.2d 1509 (11th Cir. 1987); United States v. Mead, 426 F.2d 118 (9th Cir. 1970).

[84] *See also* United States v. Cabrera-Diaz, 106 F. Supp. 2d 234 (D.P.R. 2000). In *Cabrera-Diaz*, the United States filed a motion for a judgment of default. The district court concluded that the defendants were liable under the FCA because an audit conducted by the fiscal agent demonstrated that 455 of the 461 sampled claims "had been overstated, falsely reported, unsupported or undocumented." *Id.* at 238. As a result of this error rate, the district court concluded that the defendants either had actual knowledge or acted in reckless disregard or deliberate ignorance of the truth or falsity of the information in submitting claims to the United States:

> Th[e audit] demonstrates that Dr. Cabrera, the anesthesiologist that billed Medicare for this [sic] services, and Arbona, his billing secretary, had either actual knowledge or constructive knowledge of the falsity, in that they acted in reckless disregard of the truth, or certified information (anesthesia time) in support of the claims with neither personal knowledge of its accuracy nor reasonable investigative efforts. It appears that either they acted with actual knowledge that the information was false, or hided [sic] behind a shield of self-imposed ignorance. Dr. Cabrera cannot escape liability on the basis of lack of knowledge of the fraud when he has purposefully turn the blind eye of [sic] the conduct of Arbona, his subordinate.

## 2. Deliberate Ignorance

A dissenting opinion in *Covington v. Sisters of the Third Order of St. Dominic of Hanford, California*[85] describes the FCA's deliberate ignorance standard. There, a hospital learned in 1984 that it was receiving overpayments because its intermediary mistakenly applied an incorrect geographical factor to compute the hospital's Medicare reimbursement. Although hospital officials knew of the overpayments and the likely source of the problem between 1984 and 1987, they merely asked the intermediary for the basis for its calculation rate and did not notify the intermediary until October 1987 that they had in fact been receiving inflated reimbursements. Contrary to the view of the majority of the panel, which affirmed the district court's refusal to grant summary judgment to the relator on the grounds that a better factual record needed to be developed, the dissent noted that the "behavior clearly satisfies the gross negligence standard of deliberate indifference to the truth" because all parties were sure that the source of the overpayments was an urban coding error and hospital officials refrained from informing the intermediary "and continued to benefit from the windfall funding that accrued due to the error."[86]

Congress inserted a deliberate ignorance standard into the FCA in 1986 when it amended the statute's intent standard. Congress's apparent goal was to capture within the scope of the statute those instances in which providers, when confronted with potential "red flags," avoided obtaining additional information that would reveal whether the claim was in fact truthful.[87] Unlike the recklessly disregardful conduct standard, which does not require willful conduct, the

---

*Id. Cf.* United States *ex rel.* Norbeck v. Basin Elec. Power Coop., 2001 WL 432211 at *7 (8th Cir. Apr. 30, 2001). In *Norbeck* the court refused to aggregate various overcharges into an FCA violation. Specifically, the court noted that "the district court's reliance on the 'small edges' taken by [the defendant] in the various areas of cost computation cannot support its decision. The district court found that all of [the defendant's] other overcharges were just 'simple contract breaches'. . . . But . . . the mere misinterpretation of a contract cannot be the basis of a False Claims Act violation. All of these other 'simple contract breaches', therefore, cannot provide evidence of a knowing violation of the Act") (citation omitted).

[85] No. 93-15194, 1995 U.S. App. LEXIS 20370 (9th Cir. July 13, 1995).

[86] *Id.* at *25. As to other facts that could have been developed, the majority of the panel noted: "We do not know how extensive the overpayments were compared to the hospital's total budget. If the overpayments were substantial, [the hospital] personnel should perhaps have taken dramatic action quickly. If the overpayments were relatively steady but small, the actions of [the hospital officials] might well have been all that one would expect. Because the record is silent, we cannot conclude as a matter of law that [the hospital] personnel acted knowingly, recklessly or with deliberate ignorance in accepting the overpayments." *Id.* at *13–*14.

[87] *See generally* H.R. REP. NO. 99-660, at 2, 20–21 (1986) [hereinafter H.R. REP. 99-660]; 132 CONG. REC. 22,339 (Sept. 9, 1986) (providers are liable when they ignore "red flags" and "play 'ostrich'" by burying "their heads in the sand to insulate themselves from the knowledge a prudent person should have before submitting a claim to the Government") (statement of Rep. Berman).

deliberate ignorance standard, by its plain meaning, requires at a minimum that the person intentionally—"deliberate[ly]"—refrain from obtaining additional information. As *Covington* illustrates, on becoming cognizant of a potential billing problem involving a significant amount of money, it is important for the provider to try to determine the precise basis of the overpayment, because failing to do so may increase the chances of being accused of deliberately ignoring those circumstances. In the current fraud enforcement environment, ignorance is no longer bliss.

### 3. Defenses Demonstrating Lack of Knowledge

The government has a heavy burden in demonstrating that claims are false or fraudulent and that a provider knowingly submitted such claims. As the U.S. Supreme Court has cautioned, the FCA is "not designed to reach every kind of fraud practiced on the Government."[88] This is because the statute, which the Senate Judiciary Committee characterized at the time of the 1986 legislative amendments as being remedial in nature, could conceivably be applied in a penal fashion.[89] Thus, some courts have strictly construed the statute's false or fraudulent and knowing elements.[90]

---

[88] United States v. McNinch, 356 U.S. 595, 599 (1958).

[89] In amending the Act's knowledge standard, the Senate Judiciary Committee pointed out the following:

> As a civil remedy designed to make the Government whole for fraud *losses*, the civil False Claims Act currently provides that the Government need only prove that the defendant knowingly submitted a false claim. However, this standard has been construed by some courts to require that the Government prove the defendant had actual knowledge of fraud, and even to establish that the defendant had specific intent to submit a false claim. . . .The Committee believes this standard is inappropriate in a civil remedy. . .
> The Committee's interest is not only to adopt a more uniform standard, but a more appropriate standard for *remedial* actions.

S. Rep. No. 345 at 6–7, *reprinted in* 1986 U.S.C.C.A.N. at 5271–72 (emphasis added). *But see* United States v. Halper, 490 U.S. 435, 449 (1989). In that case, the defendant defrauded the government of $585 but was subjected to statutory civil penalties of $130,000. The Supreme Court found that the double jeopardy clause could be implicated in the "case such as the one before us, where a fixed-penalty provision subjects a prolific but small-gauge offender to a sanction overwhelmingly disproportionate to the damages he has caused." *Cf.* Hudson v. United States, 522 U.S. 93 (1997).

[90] *See* United States *ex rel.* Weinberger v. Equifax, 557 F.2d at 460 (5th Cir. 1977) ("The penal nature of the statute requires careful scrutiny to see if the alleged misconduct violates the statute"); United States v. Bottini, 19 F. Supp. 2d 632, 640 (W.D. La. 1997) ("The statute is penal in nature and must be strictly construed"), *aff'd without op.*, 159 F.3d 1357 (5th Cir. 1998); United States *ex. rel.* Pogue v. American Healthcorp, Inc., 914 F. Supp. at 1511 (M.D. Tenn. 1996) (Because of possible penal application of statute, "a number of courts have denied application of the False Claims Act in particular situations, although a claimant has engaged in fraudulent conduct.") Further, the Supreme Court recently emphasized that merely an application of the treble damage and civil penalty provision of the FCA could result in a penal application of the statute. *See* Vermont Agency of Natural Res. v. United States, 529 U.S. 765, 120 S. Ct. 1858, 1869–70 (2000) ("[T]he current version of the FCA imposes dam-

Following are a number of defenses that parties have used to disprove a FCA plaintiff's theory that a provider knowingly submitted a

---

ages that are essentially punitive in nature. . . . Although this Court suggested that damages under an earlier version of the FCA were remedial rather than punitive . . . that version of the statute imposed only double damages and a civil penalty of $2,000 per claim . . . the current version, by contrast, generally imposes treble damages and a civil penalty of up to $10,000 per claim. . . . The very idea of treble damages reveals an intent to punish past, and to deter future, unlawful conduct, not to ameliorate the liability of wrongdoers") (citations, footnotes, and internal quotation omitted). Besides the effect on the construction of the FCA's knowledge standard, the characterization of the FCA as a penal statute will have a number of other effects in interpreting the provisions of the FCA. For example, courts will apply Rule 9(b) more literally and strictly in FCA jurisprudence, see generally United States v. Cheng, 184 F.R.D. 399, 401 (D.N.M. 1998) (pointing out that courts "must be particularly attentive to the heightened pleading requirement in a case brought under the False Claims Act since the Act carries heavy penal consequences"); *see also* Salcido, FALSE CLAIMS ACT COUN-SELING: NOV. 2000 SUPP., *supra* note 30, §3:09 (discussing application of Rule 9(b) to the FCA); courts will be less inclined to apply vicarious liability, see United States v. Southern Md. Home Health Servs., 95 F. Supp. 2d 465, 468–69 (D. Md. 2000) (when the recovery sought by the Government is substantially higher than its actual losses, an employer is not vicariously liable under the FCA for wrongful acts undertaken by a non-*managerial* employee unless the employer had knowledge of her acts, ratified them, or was reckless in its hiring or supervision of the employee); courts will be less inclined to apply the FCA against local governmental entities, see United States *ex rel.* Garibaldi v. Orleans Parish Sch. Bd., 244 F.3d 486, 491, 493 (5th Cir. 2001) ("[O]ne potion of the Supreme Court's opinion in *Stevens* does provide us with some guidance. The False Claims Act imposes punitive damages on those who violate it. This is contrary to the well-settled presumption that governments, including local governments, are not subject to punitive damages. . . . We are convinced that the punitive damages regime of the False Claims Act discussed above reflects a congressional intent that the term 'person' in the liability provisions of the False Claims Act not include local governments") (citations and footnotes omitted); United States *ex rel.* Honeywell v. San Francisco Hous. Auth., No. C 99-1936, 2001 U.S. Dist. LEXIS 9743 at *5 (N.D. Cal. July 12, 2001) (applying presumption against imposition of punitive damages on governmental entities and noting that in "*Stevens*, the Supreme Court held that FCA claims can not be brought against states or state agencies. In so doing, it explicitly resolved the dispute over whether the current version of the FCA—which mandates treble damages—is compensatory or punitive, finding it to be the latter"); United States *ex rel.* Dunleavy v. County of Delaware, No. 94-7000, 2000 U.S. Dist. LEXIS 14980 at *16 (E.D. Pa. Oct. 12, 2000) ("Justice Scalia's explicit reference to the damage provision of the FCA as 'essentially punitive in nature', rendering it inappropriate 'in light of the presumption against the imposition of punitive damages on governmental entities', has a significant impact on the present matter. . . . Under the *Stevens* rationale, the FCA imposes mandatory damages that are punitive in nature that may not be brought by a *qui tam* relator against a county") (citation omitted); United States *ex rel.* Chandler v. Hektoen Inst. for Med. Research, 118 F. Supp. 2d 902, 903 (N.D. Ill. 2000) (holding that "the County is immune from prosecution under the FCA because it is immune from any award or claim for punitive damages"); *but see* United States *ex rel.* Rosales v. San Francisco Hous. Auth., No. C-95-4509, 2001 WL 370176 at *15–*35 (N.D. Cal. Mar. 26, 2001) (ruling that FCA applied against a municipal corporation because congressional intent was that such corporations would be subject to liability under the FCA); *cf.* United States *ex rel.* K&R Ltd. Partnership v. Massachusetts Hous. Fin. Agency, No. 99-1343, 2001 U.S. Dist. LEXIS 11367 at *5–*12 (D.D.C. July 30, 2001) (applying Eleventh Amendment analysis to false claim.[91] Specifically, defendants may demonstrate that they were no more than negligent in confirming entitlement to government funds; that the government knew and approved of the questioned transactions; that the regulatory guidance underlying payment was ambiguous; or that the defendants reasonably relied upon legal opinions in claiming reimbursements.

### a. Merely Negligent Conduct Does Not Result in Liability Under the FCA

In *Hindo v. University of Health Sciences / The Chicago Medical School*,[92] a medical school was informed by the Department of Veterans Affairs (VA) that although there were no guarantees, funding for radiology residents would likely be approved. On the basis of this representation, the medical school included two radiology residencies in its submissions to the national resident matching program. During the academic year, the radiology residents worked at a VA-funded hospital that did not protest their presence. The medical school requested funding for the residents and received payment from the VA-funded hospital. Subsequently, when the VA-funded hospital learned that it had mistakenly made payment for the radiology residents because it had not received authorization from the VA, it demanded—and received—reimbursement from the medical school for the overpayment. The court held that although the medical school may have been negligent in not ascertaining whether funding had been approved before it invoiced the VA-funded hospital, the medical school did not commit fraud against the government because it believed, based on the VA's prior assurances and the fact that the residents were permitted to work full time during the academic year, that funding had in fact been authorized.

---

determine whether public agency was an arm of the state and concluding that because agency was not an arm of the state it was a "person" for purposes of the FCA); finally, courts will be less inclined to apply the FCA's treble damages and civil penalty provisions because the penal application of these provisions could run afoul of the Excessive Fines Clause, see United States v. Mackby, No. 99-15605, 2001 U.S. App. LEXIS 18478 at *21–*24 (9th Cir. Aug. 18, 2001) ("We conclude the civil sanctions provided by the False Claims Act are subject to analysis under the Excessive Fines Clause because sanctions represent a payment to the government, at least in part, as punishment. Inquiry must be made, therefore, to determine whether the payment required by the district court is so grossly disproportionate to the gravity of [the defendant's] violation as to violate the Eighth Amendment. . . . [And] [w]e conclude that the FCA's treble damages provision is, like the statutory penalty provision, not solely remedial and therefore subject to an Excessive Fines Clause analysis under the Eighth Amendment. Accordingly, we remand to the district court for its consideration of the question whether a treble damage award in this case would be unconstitutionally excessive") (citation omitted); *see also* Salcido, FALSE CLAIMS ACT COUNSELING, *supra* note 30, §3:05; *see also* Salcido, FALSE CLAIMS ACT COUNSELING: NOV. 2000 SUPP., *supra* note 30, §3:05.

[91] Of course, some of these defenses may also be used to disprove the falsity element of the FCA.

[92] 65 F.3d 608 (7th Cir. 1995).

There are occasions on which a provider may mistakenly fail to confirm entitlement to federal funds. However, Congress expressly provided that mere negligence is not actionable under the FCA.[93] Thus, in instances in which the plaintiff's contention is simply that the defendant's business practices could or should have been more efficient or effective, the plaintiff cannot state a cause of action under the FCA.[94]

---

[93] 132 CONG. REC. 20,536 (Aug. 11, 1986) (Congress settled upon the "reckless disregard" standard "to assure that mere negligence, mistake, and inadvertence are not actionable under the False Claims Act") (statement of Sen. Grassley).

[94] *See, e.g.,* United States *ex rel.* Hochman v. Nackman, 145 F.3d 1069, 1074 (9th Cir. 1998); Luckey v. Baxter Healthcare Corp., 2 F. Supp. 2d 1034, 1049 (N.D. Ill. 1998) (even if defendant's certifications were false because its testing procedures did not ensure pure plasma, its certifications did not result in FCA liability because they were the product of "defendant's good faith professional opinion or judgment" and the FCA "prevents [the] Court from converting what at best can be called [defendant's] negligence into a lie"), *aff'd,* 183 F.3d 730 (7th Cir. 1999). Other, non–health-care cases similarly demonstrate that the government may not predicate FCA liability on the submission of mistaken claims. *See, e.g.,* United States *ex rel.* Norbeck v. Basin Elec. Power Coop., 2001 WL 432211 at *7 (8th Cir. Apr. 30, 2001) (even if an accounting error were committed, that does not necessarily result in FCA liability because even "if the district court was correct that the $99.5 million should have somehow been applied directly to debt charged to [the governmental entity], it provides no evidence that the audit team knew or acted in reckless disregard of the possibility that its assumption was incorrect. The audit team's deliberate choice of this assumption cannot be fraud if they honestly believed it was a correct assumption, and the district court does not point to any evidence suggesting that was the case"); *see also* United States *ex rel.* Rueter v. Sparks, 939 F. Supp. 636 (C.D. Ill. 1996), *aff'd mem.,* 111 F.3d 133 (7th Cir. 1997). In *Rueter,* the relator alleged that the defendants had misreported his time and wages on certified payroll records because the defendants reported that he received $18 per hour to perform his work operating heavy equipment when, for approximately one half hour per day, he received a rate of only $8 per hour because for that half hour he performed maintenance work on that equipment. The district court concluded that, at most, the defendants were merely negligent in reporting the time and wages as required by the Davis-Bacon Act and related statutes. The court noted that the government, during previous audits, had never informed the defendants that their method of reporting time and wages was erroneous and that the company did not receive guidance from the government on the proper method of reporting maintenance hours until several years after it had performed work on the government contract that was the subject of the lawsuit. *See generally* Haynes v. United States Through Food & Nutrition Serv., 956 F. Supp. 1487 (E.D. Ark. 1995), *aff'd,* 106 F.3d 405 (8th Cir. 1997). In *Haynes,* the district court ruled that the owner of a general store could not be held responsible for the acts of managers of the store, the owner's mother and aunt, who improperly purchased food stamps because he had no knowledge that they had illegally acquired, possessed, or redeemed food stamps. The court rejected the government's contention that the owner had "turned his back" to avoid learning of the misdeeds, ruling that at most the owner "could be said to have been negligent in failing to more closely monitor the store's compliance with the Food Stamp Act since his name remained on the license despite his lack of further involvement in running the store. Nonetheless, any negligence on his part would not rise to the level of 'reckless disregard.' Given that the store is run by his mother and aunt, it is conceivable that [he] would not have felt the need to monitor the business as closely as he might otherwise have done."

## b. The Government Cannot Predicate an FCA Action on Ambiguous Regulatory Guidance

*United States v. Krizek* [95] provides an example of when regulatory ambiguity eliminates FCA exposure. There the government contended that CPT code 90844 required 45 to 50 minutes of face-to-face patient contact. A psychiatrist, who admitted that he did not code according to the amount of face-to-face time he spent with patients, contended that the code only required that he work on cases for that period of time and could include time spent reviewing charts, speaking with relatives, and similar activities without direct patient contact. The court held that because the CPT itself, during the relevant time frame, did not use the term "face to face," and the CPT itself was "ambiguous," the government could not state a FCA cause of action. [96]

The myriad, cumbersome rules governing state and federal health care programs are not a model of clarity. At times prudent health care providers will attempt in good faith to comply fully with the rules, but because of the inherent ambiguity in the rules, will act in accordance with an incorrect interpretation of the law. Under these circumstances, as *Krizek* illustrates, the provider will have a viable defense under the FCA if, notwithstanding the ambiguity of the rules, the actions in question are consistent with a plausible interpretation of the law. [97]

---

[95] 859 F. Supp. 5, 9–10 (D.D.C. 1994), *aff'd in part, rev'd in part*, 111 F.3d 934 (D.C. Cir. 1997).

[96] The court further pointed out:

> The Court will not impose False Claims Act liability based on such a strained interpretation of the CPT codes. The government's theory of liability is plainly unfair and unjustified. Medical doctors should be appropriately reimbursed for services legitimately provided. They should be given clear guidance as to what services are reimbursable. The system should be fair. The system cannot be so arbitrary, so perverse, as to subject a doctor whose annual income during the relevant period averaged between $100,000 and $120,000 dollars, to potential liability in excess of 80 million dollars.

*Id.* at 9–10. However, although the court did not find the defendants guilty on this claim, the court did nonetheless find that the defendants had violated the FCA as a result of submitting an excessive—erroneous—number of claims to the government (i.e., because of inadequate office procedures the defendant psychiatrist had billed, on occasion, for more than 20 hours of services within a 24-hour period). *Id.* at 12.

[97] *Id.* at 10–11 (footnote omitted). *See also* Hagood v. Sonoma County Water Agency, 81 F.3d 1465, 1477 (9th Cir. 1996) (when statute grants government discretion to allocate costs, contractor's reliance on the government's exercise of discretion in allocating costs does not render claim false because all that existed was proof of "a disputed legal issue," which is not enough "to support a reasonable inference" that the claim "was *false* within the meaning of the False Claims Act") (emphasis added); United States v. Data Translation, Inc., 984 F.2d 1256 (1st Cir. 1992) (when supplier's actions conformed with industry practice and were otherwise reasonable, the government could not state a cause of action under the FCA); United States *ex rel.* Swafford v. Borgess Med. Ctr., 98 F. Supp. 2d 822, 831–32 (W.D. Mich. 2000) (where the relator had contended that to bill for an "interpretation or reading" of the "results of the test" of ultrasound studies, the defendant physicians must

### c. *Government Knowledge May Provide a Defense*

In *United States ex rel. Bennett v. Genetics & IVF Institute*,[98] the defendant's contract with the state mandated that the defendant conduct two tests in providing paternity testing. However, the defendant only conducted one test because the DNA test it utilized, unlike the type of test originally contemplated, did not scientifically require a second test to ensure accuracy. Because the defendant had openly disclosed to the government what its practice would be (i.e., that it would only conduct one test), the court ruled that the government's knowledge undermined the relator's claim that the defendant acted with the requisite intent to violate the FCA.

At times a provider's conduct may not be entirely consistent with the government's rules and regulations. If the provider discloses the discrepancy to the government and attempts to resolve the issue, it is less likely that the provider will be accused of attempting to deceive the government because those who actually attempt to defraud or deceive the government typically do not inform the government in advance of their actions. For example, it is difficult to contend that a provider acted recklessly or in deliberate ignorance when it informed the government of its actions and attempted to create a dialogue regarding the matter. Thus, although the government-knowledge defense is not a dispositive defense to FCA liability because it is the provider's knowledge—and not necessarily the government's—that matters, proof of government knowledge tends to demonstrate that the provider did not act with the requisite intent to violate the FCA.[99]

---

do more than merely rely upon the findings of the technician and independently review the supporting data from which the technician arrived at her conclusions, the court rejected the relator's claim because it found that those terms were undefined and ambiguous and that the relator's position "devolves to a dispute over the meaning of the terms governing the delivery of the professional component of physicians services" and that such a "legal dispute is . . . insufficient" to establish FCA liability); United States v. Napco Int'l, Inc., 835 F. Supp. 493, 498 (D. Minn. 1993) (because underlying regulation was ambiguous, the court would not permit the government to apply "an interpretative afterthought by the agency" against the contractor in a FCA action).

[98] No. 98-2119, 1999 U.S. App. LEXIS 27911 (4th Cir. Oct. 28, 1999).

[99] *See also* United States *ex rel.* Durcholz v. FKW, Inc., 189 F.3d 542, 545 (7th Cir. 1999) ("If the government knows and approves of the particulars of a claim for payment before that claim is presented, the presenter cannot be said to have knowingly presented a fraudulent or false claim. In such a case, the government's knowledge effectively negates the fraud or falsity required by the FCA."); United States *ex rel.* Butler v. Hughes Helicopters, Inc., 71 F.3d 321 (9th Cir. 1995) (where the contractor disclosed to the Army various nonconforming tests and the Army officials on site had approved of the tests, the government's knowledge defeated any inference that the defendant "knowingly" presented false claims to the government); Wang *ex rel.* United States v. FMC Corp., 975 F.2d 1412, 1421 (9th Cir. 1992) (that the government knew of the defendant's "mistakes and limitations, and that [defendant] was open with the Government about them, suggests that while [defendant] might have been groping for solutions, it was not cheating the Government in its effort.").

### d. The Defendants' Reliance on Sound Legal Theory Negates Inference of Fraud

*United States ex rel. Hochman v. Nackman*[100] provides an example of this defense. There the VA had permitted scarce-specialty pay for physicians who practice in high-demand fields. According to the applicable VA guidelines, the physician must work in the specialty area to obtain such pay. However, according to the applicable VA policy handbook, the physician must use the specialty in direct patient care to obtain the pay. The defendants argued that the physician earned the pay because he worked the requisite time within his specialty area by creating preoperative and postoperative procedures and supervising other physicians, although he did not work in direct patient care. The court held that the relators did not state a cause of action under the FCA. "Absent evidence that the defendants knew that the [guidelines] on which they relied did not apply, or that the defendants were deliberately indifferent to or recklessly disregardful of the alleged inapplicability of those provisions, no False Claims Act liability can be found" because to "take advantage of a disputed legal question, as may have happened here, is to be neither deliberately ignorant nor recklessly disregardful."[101]

In *United States ex rel. Bidani v. Lewis*,[102] the defendant doctor owned a dialysis facility that provided outpatient home dialysis ser-

---

[100] 145 F.3d 1069 (9th Cir. 1998).

[101] *Id.* at 1073–74 (internal quotation and citation omitted). *See* United States *ex rel.* Siewick v. Jamieson Science & Eng'g, 214 F.3d 1372 (D.C. Cir. 2000). In *Siewick*, the relator asserted that the defendants' claims were implicitly false, because the defendant company had hired a former government employee who assisted the company to obtain government contracts in violation of 18 U.S.C. §207, a criminal statute aimed at "revolving door" abuses by former government employees. *Id.* at 1374–75. The court ruled that even if the relator's contention that a violation of §207 nullified the parties' contract, rendering each claim submitted under the contract to be false, the relator could not prove that the defendant "knowingly" breached the FCA because the legal effect of a breach of §207 to the parties' contract was one of "only legal argumentation and possibility" and "opinion" and hence could not result in a violation of the FCA. *Id.* at 1378. *See also* United States *ex rel.* Hagood v. Sonoma County Water Agency, 929 F.2d 1416, 1421 (9th Cir. 1991). In that case, the court pointed out that although the defendant may have relied on a legal theory that a statute did not govern its contract with the government (and thus, contrary to the relator's claim, it had properly allocated costs on its contract with the government), the Ninth Circuit found that the defendant's defense, if proven, would be dispositive:

> What is crucial—and what must be proven at trial—is that the [defendant] knew that the information was false. . . . Innocent mistake is a defense to the criminal charge or civil complaint. So is mere negligence. The statutory definition of "knowingly" requires at least "deliberate ignorance" or "reckless disregard." To take advantage of a disputed legal question, as may have happened here, is to be neither deliberately ignorant nor recklessly disregardful.

*Cf.* Harrison v. Westinghouse Savannah River Co., 176 F.3d 776, 792 (4th Cir. 1999).

[102] No. 97 C 6502, 2001 U.S. Dist. LEXIS 260 (N.D. Ill. Jan. 11, 2001), *reh'g granted in part, denied in part,* 2001 U.S. Dist. LEXIS 9204 (N.D. Ill. June 29, 2001).

vices commonly known as "Method I" and a dialysis supply company that would contract with dialysis patients to provide necessary dialysis equipment and related supplies for self-administered home dialysis under a program commonly known as "Method II." The defendant doctor and his dialysis facility would refer patients to his dialysis supply company for participation in the Method II program. The defendant doctor and his companies had fully apprised their lawyers of the structure of the arrangement and had never been informed that the arrangement was unlawful until the Stark law became operational, at which time the arrangement ceased. The relator contended that the defendant doctor and his companies breached the FCA because the referrals breached the anti-kickback statute and that they breached the FCA because the dialysis supply company did not qualify as a proper supplier because of the doctor's common ownership of both companies. The court ruled that the relator could not prove that the defendants acted with the requisite intent to violate the FCA because, based on advice of counsel, they had a good faith belief that the arrangement complied with the applicable laws and regulations.[103]

At times, the law underlying a claim for reimbursement will be subject to dispute. As *Hochman* illustrates, when a provider acts in accordance with one interpretation of the law, even if the government

---

[103] Specifically, in granting summary judgment to the defendants, the court reasoned that because of the level of communications flowing from the defendants to their attorneys regarding Medicare rules and regulations, the relator could not prove that the defendants "knowingly presented or knowingly caused to be presented any false Medicare claims":

> The undisputed evidence establishes that [the defendant doctor] sought the advice of attorneys in purchasing [the hospital's] dialysis facility, incorporating [the dialysis supply company] and [the facility company], and regarding the operations of [the supply company] as a dialysis supplier. The attorneys, who also did the incorporation work for [the supply company and the facility], were fully aware of the ownership relationship between the two entities and that one functioned as a Method I dialysis facility and one as a Method II dialysis supplier. There is no indication that [the defendant doctor] hid from the attorneys any pertinent facts regarding the ownership relationship. [The defendant doctor] was continually advised that his operations were lawful and, when advised of changes in applicable statutes and regulations, [he] accordingly revised his conduct. When finally advised that the ownership relationship would be unlawful under a new statute [i.e., the Stark law], [the supply company] ceased operations before the new statute went into effect. The only reasonable inference that can be drawn from the undisputed evidence is that [the defendant doctor] (and the entities he controlled) had no actual knowledge during the pertinent time period that the common ownership either prohibited [the defendant doctor] from referring patients to [the supply company] or that [the supply company] failed to qualify as a dialysis supplier because of the common ownership. Neither can it be inferred that [the defendant doctor] deliberately ignored or acted in reckless disregard of the truth. Therefore, it cannot be found that [the defendant doctor] knowingly presented or knowingly caused to be presented any false Medicare claims and defendants are entitled to summary judgment on the remaining FCA claims.

2001 U.S. Dist. LEXIS 260 at *35–*36.

or whistleblower may tenably point to some other equally applicable provision of law, the FCA plaintiff is unlikely to succeed. Similarly, as *Bidani* illustrates, if a provider's actions are based on a legal opinion, it is unlikely that the provider's conduct could be actionable under the FCA. A similar application of these principles was applied in *Tyger Construction Co. v. United States*.[104] There the court rejected the government's contention that the FCA reached "false" legal opinions. In that case, the plaintiff had submitted a number of claims to the government, some of which were based on legal theories, specifically that its construction work complied with the contract specifications and that the project was substantially complete.[105] The government filed a counterclaim alleging violations of the FCA. The court struck those paragraphs of the government's counterclaim that did not allege misrepresentations of fact but misrepresentations of law:

> The principle is fundamental that fraud cannot be predicated upon the mere expression of an opinion. . . . Attaching FCA liability to expressions of legal opinion would have an impermissibly stifling effect on the legitimate presentation of claims. Indication is absent that Congress intended to penalize disputes over contract liability.[106]

Accordingly, as these cases demonstrate, in formulating a defense to an FCA action, the defendant should focus on the precise basis of

---

[104] 28 Fed. Cl. 35 (1993).

[105] *Id.* at 56.

[106] *Id.* at 56 (internal quotation, footnote, and citation omitted). The court, however, did note that the legal opinion must be grounded in fact. For example, one could not assert based on a legal theory that the project was substantially completed when ground had not been broken. *Id.* at 56 n.29. *Cf.* United States v. Medco Physicians Unlimited, No. 98 C 1622, 2001 WL 293110 (N.D. Ill. Mar. 26, 2001). There the person signing the cost report had affixed an addendum to the cost report stating that the disputed meal and transportation costs had been included in the cost report because he believed that such inclusion was consistent "with regulations issued in February, 1994." *Id.* at *3. The court found that the person's statement was knowingly false because, when challenged, he could not "cite to any regulations in 1994" that supported his contention. *See also* United States v. Estate of Rogers, No. 1:97CV461, 2001 WL 818160 at *5 (E.D. Tenn. June 28, 2001) (rejecting defendants' contention that the government's complaint should be dismissed because when they certified that the home health agencies were not related to the management company they relied upon their legal opinion based upon their reasonable interpretation of Medicare regulations "because a statement or certification to HCFA [(CMS)] and the [(fiscal intermediary)] that the [home health agencies] and [the management company] were not related is a statement of fact and not purely the expression of legal opinions. . . . When the [home health agencies] stated they were unrelated to [the management company] for purposes of applying HCFA's [(CMS's)] regulations, they in effect said that the [home health agencies] were not to a significant extent associated or affiliated with [the management company], and that [the management company] did not control the [home health agencies]. These are essentially statements of fact. In determining whether the [home health agencies] and [the management company] were related under 42 C.F.R. § 413.17, factual issues concerning associations, affiliations, common ownership and control must be resolved").

the government's claim to determine whether the government can discharge its burden of proving a knowing violation of the FCA. In the health care context, if the relator or the government is contending that the defendant knowingly submitted a false claim because another code better fits the service, as occurred in *Krizek*,[107] the defendant should probe into the underlying regulatory basis supporting use of the code. If it can show that its use of the code was reasonable, or at least subject to good-faith disagreement, then the defendant likely will prevail. Moreover, even if the government can show that the claim is in fact false, the defendant may prevail if it can demonstrate that it did not knowingly submit a false claim by retracing each of its steps and proving that it had a reasonable—albeit mistaken—basis to believe that it was entitled to payment.[108]

## III. Defending Against *Qui Tam* Actions

### A. The Public Disclosure Jurisdictional Bar to *Qui Tam* Actions

When the DOJ prosecutes an FCA action on its own, a provider generally receives notice that an FCA action may be looming. For example, before instituting an action against a provider, the DOJ usually will inform the provider that the government believes that the provider may have violated the FCA and invites the provider to respond. *Qui tam* actions are different in that a defendant may be brought into court without advance notice and may be subjected to legal action by a private individual rather than the federal government.

As noted earlier, after the informer files a *qui tam* action, the DOJ investigates to determine whether to intervene. In such actions, much turns on whether the government chooses to intervene. When the government declines to intervene, which occurs in the vast majority of *qui tam* cases, the FCA action generally does not result in any governmental recovery. Historically, as of November 1999, the DOJ intervened in approximately 21 percent of all cases.[109] Yet in those 21 percent of cases in which the government had intervened, the government recovered

---

[107]*See, e.g.*, United States v. Krizek, 859 F. Supp. 5 (D.D.C. 1994), *aff'd in part, rev'd in part*, 111 F.3d 934 (D.C. Cir. 1997), *on remand*, 7 F. Supp. 2d 56 (D.D.C. 1998), *remanded*, 192 F.3d 1024 (D.C. Cir. 1999) (see discussion *supra* note 95); *see also* United States *ex rel.* Glass v. Medtronic, Inc., 957 F.2d 605, 608 (8th Cir. 1992) (a statement cannot be false or fraudulent under FCA when the statement is consistent with Medicare rules).

[108]*See, e.g.*, Hindo v. University of Health Scis./The Chicago Med. Sch., 65 F.3d 608 (7th Cir. 1995), *and* United States *ex rel.* Hagood v. Sonoma County Water Agency, 929 F.2d 1416 (9th Cir. 1991); *see generally* Salcido, False Claims Act Counseling: Nov. 2000 Supp., *supra* note 30, §§2:03, 2:05.

[109]According to statistics issued in November 1999, the DOJ had investigated in or otherwise pursued 462 cases and declined in 1,673. (The remainder were under investigation.) *See Qui Tam* Statistics (*available at* http://www.taf.org).

$2.9 billion, whereas in the 79 percent of cases in which the government had declined to intervene,[110] recovery amounted to only $410 million. Thus, the 79 percent of cases in which the government did not intervene contributed only about 13 percent to the government's total recoveries.

The strategies used to handle *qui tam* actions will vary substantially depending on whether the government has intervened. If the government intervenes after conducting an extended investigation, it has done so because it believes that it has uncovered evidence that establishes a violation of the FCA. These actions typically result in a settlement, and, as is reflected in the statistics discussed above, all very large settlements have occurred only in those actions in which the government has intervened. When the government declines to intervene, the parties usually engage in protracted discovery before the action is tried, settled, or dismissed. As noted, relators' recoveries in cases in which the government did not intervene have been relatively small.

Whether the government intervenes, litigation under the FCA generally proceeds as in any other civil case. However, one defense merits discussion because it has resulted in the dismissal of a substantial number of actions. This defense is based on the FCA's public disclosure jurisdictional bar, which proscribes lawsuits "based upon" public information unless the relator is the "original source" of that information.[111] This defense is a procedural one directed solely at the relator. Thus, it is especially useful in those actions in which the government does not intervene because by eliminating the relator, the defendant eliminates the lawsuit.[112]

---

[110] *Id.*

[111] 31 U.S.C. §3730(e)(4). There are three other lesser-known jurisdictional bars in §3730(e). Subsection (e)(1), in pertinent part, bars suits "brought by a former or present member of the armed forces . . . arising out of such person's service in the armed forces." Subsection (e)(2) bars actions "against a Member of Congress, a member of the judiciary, or a senior executive branch official if the action is based on evidence or information known to the government when the action was brought." Subsection (e)(3), in pertinent part, bars all persons from bringing an action if the government had already brought a civil suit or administrative action involving monetary penalties. Another jurisdictional bar, in §3730(b)(5), prohibits relators from intervening in or bringing a related action that is based on the facts underlying a pending action.

[112] However, where this defense is available, it should be asserted even in those actions in which the government intervenes. Under the statute, if the government obtains a recovery, the relator is entitled to reasonable attorneys' fees and costs. 31 U.S.C. §3730(d)(1). In some actions, relators have incurred more than $1 million dollars in attorneys' fees. *See, e.g., United States ex rel.* Taxpayers Against Fraud v. General Electric Co., 41 F.3d 1032 (6th Cir. 1994) (the district court awarded the relator more than $2.3 million in attorneys' fees; the Sixth Circuit remanded the action so the district court could find additional facts to determine whether the award was reasonable). Thus, although in those cases in which the government is a party the successful assertion of the public disclosure jurisdictional bar defense will result merely in the relator's dismissal, and not the government's, the relator's dismissal, nonetheless, will save the defendant the substantial expense of compensating the relator's counsel.

The public disclosure jurisdictional bar is examined in detail below. A study of the case law informs a relator's counsel of when an action should not be undertaken because it would be barred and instructs defense counsel on the circumstances under which the relator may successfully be ousted from the action.

## B. History of the *Qui Tam* Public Disclosure Jurisdictional Bar

Understanding the proper application of the public disclosure jurisdictional bar requires a detailed study of its history. Initially, when Congress enacted the FCA in 1863, the statute contained no jurisdictional bar.[113] In 1943, after a series of abuses in which private persons filed *qui tam* actions based expressly on public information, Congress revamped the statute to preclude such lawsuits.[114] Specifically, Congress provided that no action could be filed based on information in the government's possession.[115] This jurisdictional bar applied even if the relator was the original source of the information in the government's "possession."[116]

When the Senate and House Judiciary Committees initially considered amending the jurisdictional bar in 1986, both proposed language that would have expressly permitted persons to bring lawsuits based on public information.[117] As initially proposed, the jurisdictional bar would have permitted actions based on public information if the federal government failed to act on that information within six months of its disclosure.[118] The committees believed that such modification was necessary because DOJ files were stuffed with referrals it had received from other governmental agencies, but had failed to process.[119]

---

[113] Act of March 2, 1863, ch. 67, §4, 12 Stat. 698 (1863). *See also* Salcido, FALSE CLAIMS ACT COUNSELING, *supra* note 30, §1:01.

[114] Act of December 23, 1943, 57 Stat. 608, *recodified in* 31 U.S.C. §3730; Salcido, FALSE CLAIMS ACT COUNSELING, *supra* note 30, §1:02.

[115] *Id.* (no *qui tam* action can be brought "based upon evidence or information in the possession of the United States . . . at the time such suit was brought").

[116] *See, e.g.*, United States *ex rel.* State of Wisconsin v. Dean, 729 F.2d 1100, 1103 (7th Cir. 1984); Pettis *ex rel.* United States v. Morrison-Knudsen Co., 577 F.2d 668, 669 (9th Cir. 1978) ("[W]e conclude that jurisdiction is lacking even when an informer prior to bringing suit supplies the government with the information which under [the *qui tam* provisions] invokes the bar"); Safir v. Blackwell, 579 F.2d 742 (2d Cir. 1978); United States v. Aster, 176 F. Supp. 208 (E.D. Pa. 1959), *aff'd*, 275 F.2d 281 (3d Cir. 1960).

[117] *See* S. REP. NO. 99-345, at 43 (proposed §3730(e)(4)); H.R. REP. 99-660, at 2–3 (1986) (proposed §3730(b)(5)).

[118] *Id.*

[119] S. REP. NO. 99-345, at 4, 8, *reprinted in* 1986 U.S.C.C.A.N. 5269, 5273 (the Senate report noted that "available Department of Justice records show most fraud referrals remain unprosecuted and lost public funds, therefore remain uncollected" and that a "resource mismatch" exists between the federal government and large contractors who may marshal the efforts of large legal teams).

This provision, however, was not enacted. Instead, rather than permitting persons to file actions based on public information, Congress opted to prohibit such actions unless the whistleblower was the original source of the publicly disclosed information.[120] If the information is not in the public domain, there is no assurance that the government is aware of the information and is acting as needed to further the public interest. Hence, *qui tam* actions are permitted. But, if the information is in the public domain, *qui tam* actions are barred unless the relator was the government's source of the information. The basis for using a public disclosure as a trigger in activating the bar is that when the allegations or transactions of fraud have been publicly disclosed, the whistleblower's action does not advance the public interest, but hinders it, because the government is compelled to share a portion of its recovery with a whistleblower who merely republishes public allegations.[121] Once allegations are public, citizens rely on the government to proceed with the action, and if the government does not do so, they have the power to hold the government accountable through the political process. By drawing the line here, Congress ensured that *qui tam* actions would augment the government's recoveries in FCA actions and, at the same time, eliminate *qui tam* actions when such actions were not needed to protect the federal fisc.[122]

---

[120] 31 U.S.C. §3730(e)(4).

[121] *See, e.g.*, Findley v. FPC-Boron Employees' Club, 105 F.3d 675, 685 (D.C. Cir.) ("Once the information is in the public domain, there is less need for a financial incentive to spur individuals into exposing frauds. Allowing *qui tam* suits after that point may either pressure the government to prosecute cases when it has good reasons not to or reduce the government's ultimate recovery"), *cert. denied*, 522 U.S. 865 (1997); United States *ex rel.* Dhawan v. New York City Health & Hosp. Corp., No. 95 Civ. 7649 (LMM), 2000 U.S. Dist. LEXIS 15677 at *11 (S.D.N.Y. Oct. 24, 2000) ("In cases where the information that forms an FCA action is public, the opportunity for abuse of process is maximized. Section 3730(e)(4) is intended to bar parasitic lawsuits based upon publicly disclosed information in which would be relators seek remuneration although they contributed nothing to the exposure of the fraud") (citation and internal quotation omitted), *aff'd*, 252 F.3d 118 (2d Cir. 2001); United States v. CAC Ramsay, 744 F. Supp. 1158, 1159 (S.D. Fla. 1990) ("Congress intended to bar parasitic *qui tam* suits, that is, lawsuits based on public information" because "it will usually serve no purpose to reward a relator for bringing a *qui tam* action if the incident of fraud is already a matter of public knowledge by virtue of 'public disclosure'"), *aff'd mem.*, 963 F.2d 384 (11th Cir. 1992); *see also* Seal 1 v. Seal A, No. 98-56447, 2001 U.S. App. LEXIS 15044 at *7 (9th Cir. July 5, 2001) ("The compensation available to relators . . . encourages parasitic lawsuits in which those with no independent knowledge of fraud use information already available to the government to reap rewards for themselves without exposing any previously unknown fraud"); United States *ex rel.* Phipps v. Comprehensive Community Dev. Corp., No. 99 Civ. 5172, 2001 U.S. Dist. LEXIS 9949 at *16 (S.D.N.Y. July 18, 2001) (the public disclosure bar "is intended to bar 'parasitic lawsuits' based upon publicly disclosed information in which would-be relators seek remuneration although they contributed nothing to the exposure of the fraud") (citations and internal quotation omitted).

[122] *See, e.g.*, *Findley*, 105 F.3d at 680–81 ("After ricocheting between the extreme permissiveness that preceded the 1943 amendments and the extreme restrictiveness

A comparison of three of the FCA's jurisdictional bars—subsections 3730(b)(5), (e)(3), and (e)(4)—further illuminates Congress's purpose in creating the public disclosure jurisdictional bar. Under subsection 3730(e)(4), Congress forces would-be whistleblowers to report fraud before it is publicized. If a relator fails to report the information before publication, the suit would be barred unless the relator was the government's informant; that is, the original source of the information. Under subsection 3730(e)(3), Congress, in addition to other procedures, forces relators to race the government to the courthouse by prohibiting any *qui tam* action after the government files a civil lawsuit or administrative civil money penalty proceeding based on the allegations or transactions underlying the government's action. If the government files first, the relator is barred even if the underlying facts were not publicly disclosed and even if the relator was an original source. Under subsection 3730(b)(5), Congress pits relators against each other in a race to the courthouse by prohibiting all actions based on facts underlying a pending action. As in subsection 3730(e)(3), subsection 3730(b)(5) applies even if the pending action is not public (e.g., the action is under court seal) and even if the relator in the subsequent action would otherwise qualify as an original source. The reason that subsections 3730(b)(5) and 3730(e)(3) are broader than subsection 3730(e)(4)—that is, applying even if the underlying allegations or transactions are not public and even if the relator was the original source of the information—is that once a *qui tam* lawsuit has been filed (subsection 3730(b)(5)) or once the government is a party to a proceeding (subsection 3730(e)(3)), no *qui tam* action is necessary for the government to enforce its rights effectively.

The primary purpose underlying the creation of each of these various "races" in the FCA is to compel whistleblowers to disclose perceived wrongdoing to the government at the earliest possible moment.[123]

---

that followed, Congress again sought to achieve the golden mean between adequate incentives for whistleblowing insiders with genuinely valuable information and discouragement of opportunistic plaintiffs who have no significant information to contribute on their own.") (internal quotations and citations omitted).

[123] *See, e.g.*, H.R. REP. NO. 660, at 23 ("[t]he purpose of the *qui tam* provisions of the False Claims Act is to encourage private individuals who are aware of fraud being perpetrated against the Government to bring such information forward"); S. REP. No. 345, at 14, *reprinted in* 1986 U.S.C.C.A.N. at 5279 (amendments intended to reward those who "bring . . . wrongdoing to light"); *see also* United States *ex rel.* Jones v. Horizon Healthcare Corp., 160 F.3d 326, 335 (6th Cir. 1998) ("the *qui tam* provisions were intended not only to block freeloading relators, but also to inspire whistleblowers to come forward as soon as possible") (citation omitted); *Findley*, 105 F.3d at 685 ("the *qui tam* provisions of the FCA were designed to inspire whistle-blowers to come forward promptly with information concerning fraud so that the government can stop it and recover ill-gotten gains"); United States *ex rel.* Devlin v. California, 84 F.3d 358, 362 (9th Cir. 1996) ("the purpose of the FCA . . . aims at ferreting out fraud by encouraging persons with first-hand knowledge of alleged wrongdoing to come forward"); United States *ex rel.* Barth v. Ridgedale Elec. & Eng'g, 44 F.3d 699, 704 (8th Cir. 1995) ("the clear intent of the Act . . . is to encourage private individuals who are aware of

Accordingly, in construing the scope of subsection (e)(4), courts should be mindful that *qui tam* actions are designed only to provide a mechanism by which the government may obtain useful information so that it may protect its interests; they should not be viewed as a means to enrich private individuals and their counsel.[124] Thus, whenever the information underlying the complaint is publicly available and the relator did not furnish the information to the government before that disclosure, the relator should be barred from proceeding. Although, as noted in detail below, some courts have reached this conclusion,[125] other courts have taken an unduly expansive view of the statute, such that if whistleblowers merely demonstrate that they were unaware of the public information, they may proceed with the action.[126] This interpretation serves to enrich relators (and their counsel) but does not appropriately enrich the government whose recovery is reduced by the relator's share.

## C. Case Law Construing the Public Disclosure Jurisdictional Bar

As enacted, the public disclosure jurisdictional bar provides in part:

> (4)(A) No court shall have jurisdiction over an action under this section based upon the public disclosure of allegations or transactions in a criminal, civil, or administrative hearing, in a congressional, administrative, or Government Accounting Office [sic] report, hearing, audit, or investigation, or from the news media, unless the action is brought by the Attorney General or the person bringing the action is an original source of the information.[127]

---

fraud against the government to bring such information forward at the earliest possible time and to discourage persons with relevant information from remaining silent") (citations omitted); United States *ex rel.* Wang v. FMC Corp., 975 F.2d 1412, 1419–20 (9th Cir. 1992); United States *ex rel.* Dick v. Long Island Lighting Co., 912 F.2d 13, 18 (2d Cir. 1990); *cf.* United States *ex rel.* LaCorte v. SmithKline Beecham Clinical Labs., 149 F.3d 227, 234 (3d Cir. 1998) ("[I]nterpreting section 3730(b)(5) as imposing a broader bar furthers the Act's purpose by encouraging *qui tam* plaintiffs to report fraud promptly. . . . In addition, . . . duplicative claims do not help reduce fraud or return funds to the federal fisc, since once the government knows the essential facts of the fraudulent scheme, it has enough information to discover related frauds.") (citation omitted).

[124] *See, e.g.*, United States v. Health Possibilities, P.S.C., 207 F.3d 335, 340 (6th Cir. 2000) ("The FCA is not designed to serve the parochial interests of relators, but to vindicate civic interests in avoiding fraud against public monies") (citations omitted); United States v. Northrop Corp., 59 F.3d 953, 968 (9th Cir. 1995) ("The private right of recovery created by the provisions of the FCA exists not to compensate the *qui tam* relator, but the United States. The relator's right to recovery exists solely as a mechanism for deterring fraud and returning funds to the federal treasury").

[125] *See, e.g.*, *Findley*, 105 F.3d at 685.

[126] *See, e.g.*, United States *ex rel.* Siller v. Becton Dickinson & Co., 21 F.3d 1339 (4th Cir. 1994).

[127] 31 U.S.C. §3730(e)(4)(A).

Almost all circuit courts have now construed the bar's various provisions. As the Ninth Circuit explained in *United States ex rel. Lindenthal v. General Dynamics Corp.*, to invoke the public disclosure jurisdictional bar successfully, the defendant must establish four elements:

1. that there has been a "public disclosure"
2. of "allegations or transactions"
3. in a "criminal, civil, or administrative hearing, in a congressional, administrative, or Government [General] Accounting Office report, hearing, audit, or investigation, or from the news media," and
4. that the relator's action is "based upon" that public disclosure.[128]

If these four elements are satisfied, then relators may proceed only if they are an original source. To be an original source, relators must have direct and independent knowledge of the allegations and must have voluntarily provided to the government before publication the information underlying the action. Counsel defending *qui tam* actions should become fully familiar with the body of case law summarized below to determine whether the public disclosure defense is applicable and, if so, which facts should be probed during discovery to maximize the likelihood of a successful defense.

### 1. Meaning of "Public Disclosure"

Courts have disagreed in their construction of the term "public disclosure." The Third and Second Circuits have formulated the broadest interpretation of the word "public," finding that information is public when it is communicated to a stranger to the fraud. The Ninth Circuit has restricted that interpretation, finding that information is not public, even if revealed to a stranger to the fraud, if that stranger has no incentive to disseminate the information to others. The Seventh Circuit has ruled that disclosures to the federal government, if made to appropriate individuals, can be considered public disclosures.

#### a. The Majority Rule: Information Is Public If It Is Disclosed to a Stranger to the Fraud

Two cases illustrate the majority rule. In *United States ex rel. Stinson, Lyons, Gerlin & Bustamante, P.A. v. Prudential Ins. Co.*,[129] a person learned by reviewing a document during discovery in an unrelated state court litigation that a provider allegedly had defrauded the federal government. Although the document was not filed with the state court, the court found the document to have been publicly dis-

---

[128] 61 F.3d 1402, 1409 (9th Cir. 1995).
[129] 944 F.2d 1149, 1155 (3d Cir. 1991).

closed. Similarly, in *United States ex rel. Fine v. Advanced Sciences, Inc.*,[130] a person became aware of a federal government audit, which had not been publicly disclosed, indicating that a company had defrauded the government. That person informed another person of that information and thus the court ruled that the information had been publicly disclosed.

Congress did not define the term "public." Instead, it chose to effectuate the term by reference to specific types of information revealed during hearings, contained in government reports, audits, or investigations, or disseminated through the news media. If the allegations or transactions are divulged through any of these means, the information is public. Congress did not place any restriction on the term and did not, for example, mandate that the information must reach a mass audience or be read by specific individuals. Instead, Congress adopted a general rule that any allegation or transaction revealed through any of the statutorily approved mechanisms is sufficient to put the government on notice of the fraud and hold it accountable should it fail to act.

Consistent with this purpose, the majority of courts have broadly defined the word "public" to encompass any information that is disclosed to a person who is a "stranger to the fraud."[131] Thus, the Third Circuit in *Stinson* held that a "public disclosure" in a "hearing" had occurred when the relevant information was disclosed to one person, the relator, who had received the information pursuant to his discovery request in a state court proceeding.[132] Similarly, the Second Circuit, in *United States ex rel. John Doe v. John Doe Corp.*,[133] held that a "public disclosure" of a government "investigation" had occurred when government investigators had merely interviewed "innocent" employees of the target company regarding allegations of fraud.

After *John Doe*, the Second Circuit took this rule a step further in *United States ex rel. Kreindler v. United Technologies*[134] by holding

---

[130] 99 F.3d 1000 (10th Cir. 1996).

[131] *See, e.g.*, United States *ex rel.* John Doe v. John Doe Corp., 960 F.2d 318 (2d Cir. 1992); United States *ex rel.* Stinson, Lyons, Gerlin & Bustamante, P.A. v. Prudential Ins. Co., 944 F.2d 1149, 1155 (3d Cir. 1991); *cf.* United States *ex rel.* Springfield Terminal Ry. v. Quinn, 14 F.3d 645, 652–53 (D.C. Cir. 1994) (no public disclosure results from "the discovery process conducted between two private litigants" when that information is not filed with the court) (dictum) (citations omitted); United States *ex rel.* Hagood v. Sonoma County Water Agency, 929 F.2d 1416, 1419 (9th Cir. 1991) (no public disclosure occurs merely as a result of internal government debate regarding defendant's acts); United States *ex rel.* Williams v. NEC Corp., 931 F.2d 1493 (11th Cir. 1991) (same).

[132] 944 F.2d at 1155.

[133] 960 F.2d at 323. The basis for the court's ruling was that once innocent employees have learned of the allegations, the government could not defer taking action on the claim by throwing a "cloak of secrecy" over the fraud and thus no whistleblower action was needed. *Id.*

[134] 985 F.2d 1148, 1159 (2d Cir. 1993).

that not only is information public if it reaches a single individual (i.e., a stranger to the fraud), but that it is also public if it is simply accessible to the public.[135] Accordingly, in that case, the court found that although the relator was prohibited under a confidentiality agreement from disclosing information it had obtained in discovery, the information nonetheless was public because it was on file with the court and thus "it was available to anyone who wished to consult the court file."[136]

Under this expansive reading of the word, "public" means not just information released to the public, but also information merely available to the public. The implication is that the public disclosure jurisdictional bar possibly reaches all documents or information in any repository from which it may be obtained by the general public.[137]

### b. Ninth and Tenth Circuits' Limitations on the Stranger-to-the-Fraud Rule: Requiring an Incentive to Reveal the Information or an Affirmative Disclosure

In *United States ex rel. Schumer v. Hughes Aircraft*,[138] the government issued an audit report critical of the defendant's accounting practices and released the report to the defendant's and the prime contractor's employees. The defendant contended that the disclosure of the audit report to innocent employees and other strangers to the fraud constituted a public disclosure and that the audit report was a "public" document because it could be obtained under the Freedom of Information Act. The U.S. Court of Appeals for the Ninth Circuit held that the disclosure was not a public disclosure. Rather, any disclosures to the company and its prime contractor were merely disclosures within a "private sphere" because those companies had no economic incentive to further publicize the results of the audit report.

---

[135] *See also* United States *ex rel*. Branhan v. Mercy Health Sys. of Southwest Ohio, No. 98-3127, 1999 U.S. App. LEXIS 18509 at *5 (6th Cir. Aug. 5, 1999) (HCFA (CMS) report was publicly disclosed because it would be "available to anyone who requested it") (citations omitted); United States *ex rel*. Phipps v. Comprehensive Community Dev. Corp., No. 99 Civ. 5172, 2001 U.S. Dist. LEXIS 9949 at *17 (S.D.N.Y. July 18, 2001) ("If information is equally available to the relator as it is to strangers to the fraud transaction had they chosen to look for it, then there is public disclosure") (citations omitted).

[136] *Id.*

[137] For example, under this broad reading of the public disclosure jurisdictional bar, all repositories of public information that may contain information relating to fraud against the government, such as cost reports submitted to fiscal intermediaries to verify hospital Medicare costs or documents on file with contracting officers regarding government construction or manufacturing projects, could be deemed to be public disclosures. As noted below, however, although this type of information may qualify as public, it may not contain information specific enough to qualify as allegations or transactions under the Court of Appeals for the District of Columbia's test in United *States ex rel. Springfield Terminal Ry. v. Quinn*, 14 F.3d 645 (D.C. Cir. 1994). In that instance, the public disclosure jurisdictional bar would not apply.

[138] 63 F.3d 1512 (9th Cir. 1995), *rev'd on other grounds*, 520 U.S. 939 (1997).

The Ninth Circuit specifically rejected the Second and Third Circuits' broad interpretation of the word "public," holding that even if a stranger to the fraud receives the information, there are pockets of "private spheres" within the public domain in which individuals have no incentive to disseminate the information further and hence the information is not public. This interpretation of "public" is not supported by the plain meaning of the word and would result in a tedious, cumbersome process in every case because courts would have to inquire into how a particular recipient of information would handle that information on its receipt. Limiting the inquiry to whether a stranger to the fraud has received the information will more likely result in uniform results and will furnish courts with an objective test for determining whether they have jurisdiction over the action. Thus, the Third Circuit's formulation in *Stinson* and the Second Circuit's holding in *John Doe* offer better interpretations of the term "public" than *Schumer*.[139]

Additionally, in *Schumer*, the Ninth Circuit, criticizing the Third Circuit's holding in *Stinson*, reasoned that the public disclosure juris-

---

[139] *Id.* at 1518. The court believed that its ruling was consistent with the statutory purpose because Congress specifically intended that the relators be able to bring lawsuits when the government possessed identical information. *Id.* at 1519. The court relied, in part, on statements in the Senate Judiciary Committee's report. *Id.* However, the court's reliance on the Senate report undermines the reliability of its holding because the draft jurisdictional bar the Senate Judiciary Committee referenced in its report was substantially narrower than the one that Congress ultimately passed. *Compare* S. REP. NO. 99–345, at 43 (setting forth draft §3730(e)(4)), *with* 31 U.S.C. §3730(e)(4) (the provision as passed); *see generally* Salcido, *Screening out Unworthy Whistleblower Actions, supra* note 17, at 250–60. As the Third Circuit pointed out in another context, extreme care must be exercised when relying on the FCA's legislative history because "[t]he bill that eventuated in the 1986 amendments underwent substantial revisions during its legislative path. This provides ample opportunity to search the legislative history and find some support somewhere for almost any construction of the many ambiguous terms in the final version." United States *ex. rel.* Stinson v. Prudential Ins. Co., 944 F.2d at 1154. Indeed, to the extent that the audit report was released to the prime contractor (a stranger to the fraud), under the plain language of the statute, which requires only that the information be public, the Ninth Circuit should have found that there had been a public disclosure of the audit report. The statute, unlike the court's ruling, contains no exception for public disclosures within private spheres. Indeed, recently the Ninth Circuit limited its application of *Schumer* in Seal 1 v. Seal A, No. 98-56447, 2001 U.S. App. LEXIS 15044 (9th Cir. July 5, 2001), where the court ruled that U.S. Attorneys' Office disclosure of information to a single person (the relator) qualified as a "public" disclosure of a governmental investigation. The court reasoned: "Disclosure of information to one member of the public, when that person seeks to take advantage of that information by filing an FCA action, is public disclosure. It may not be public disclosure as to some other member of the public who independently comes upon information already possessed by the government and disclosed to a single person . . . and who then files an FCA action based on the information independently obtained. But it is public, as to [the relator], in the sense necessary to the sensible operation of § 3730(e)(4)(A). Because it was disclosed to an outsider to the investigation who now seeks to profit from it as an FCA relator, it was publicly disclosed to that person." *Id.* at *18.

dictional bar applied only to actual disclosures, not theoretical disclosures, and thus the fact that the audit report theoretically was obtainable under the Freedom of Information Act was inconsequential under the FCA.[140] The Tenth Circuit, in *United States ex rel. Ramseyer v. Century Healthcare Corp.*,[141] later similarly interpreted the term "public disclosure" narrowly to require an "affirmative" act of disclosure to a third party.

The relator in *Ramseyer*[142] alleged that she became aware of the defendants' submission of false claims for Medicaid reimbursement while she was employed at the defendants' mental health facility. The state, independent of the relator's efforts, had conducted an inspection and audit of the defendants' facilities and, in a subsequent report, detailed the same Medicaid compliance problems that the relator had discovered in the scope of her employment.[143] Three copies of the audit report were made; two remained within the agency's files, and the third was sent to the defendants. The defendants contended that because the relator's lawsuit was similar to the information contained in the state's audit, which had not been publicly disseminated to anyone but the defendants, the action was based on an audit and therefore barred under the statute.[144]

The Tenth Circuit rejected this contention, ruling that the agency's knowledge of the fraud and the internal circulation of the report did not constitute public disclosures because "mere possession" of information by an individual or an entity without additional "affirmative" disclosure "does not amount to 'public disclosure.' "[145] Furthermore, the court concluded that although the information was potentially available to the public on request, the public disclosure requirement "signifies more than the mere theoretical or potential availability of information."[146] Instead, to be publicly disclosed, "the allegations or transactions on which a *qui tam* suit is based must have been made known to the public through some affirmative act of disclosure."[147]

The Tenth Circuit thus concurred with the Ninth Circuit, and disagreed with the Second and Third Circuits, holding that the mere availability of the information to the public is not sufficient to trigger application of the public disclosure jurisdictional bar, but that the information must have actually been obtained by an innocent member

---

[140] 63 F.3d at 1520.

[141] 90 F.3d 1514, 1516–17 (10th Cir. 1996).

[142] *Id.* at 1519.

[143] *Id.*

[144] *Id.*

[145] *Id.* at 1521.

[146] *Id.* at 1519 (citation omitted).

[147] *Id.*

of the public.[148] However, these cases can be reconciled by reference to the specific mechanism of disclosure. In both *Stinson* and *Kriendler*, the public disclosure occurred in connection with court proceedings, whereas the material in *Schumer* and *Ramseyer* concerned government reports. By their very nature, court proceedings (unless restricted) are public, and anyone may freely witness proceedings or copy court records. Government reports, however, unless specifically requested by the general public, are merely maintained in files and cannot be easily accessed by the public or the news media unless they have some prior knowledge of the information.[149]

### c. Disclosures to Federal Government Are Public

In *United States v. Bank of Farmington*,[150] a government official received a subpoena related to state court litigation. He then called one party, a bank, to inquire into the basis for the subpoena and the bank informed the official that it failed to disclose a guarantee on a federal guaranteed loan. The Seventh Circuit held that the bank's disclosure to the government official of its failure to disclose the guarantee on the loan constituted a public disclosure of that information.

The *Bank of Farmington* case involves a slight variation on the public disclosure test in that it involved a disclosure to the government. In construing the public disclosure jurisdictional bar, the court

---

[148]*Id.* at 1519. Although the Tenth Circuit has required that an affirmative act of disclosure to the public occur, it has also ruled that disclosure to a single individual is sufficient to trigger the bar. *See* United States *ex rel.* Fine v. MK-Ferguson Co., 99 F.3d 1538, 1545 (10th Cir. 1996) (court dismissed action by former OIG auditor because government's audit report had been sent to the state of Oregon); United States *ex rel.* Fine v. Advanced Scis., Inc., 99 F.3d 1000, 1005 (10th Cir. 1996) (court dismissed action by former OIG auditor because the auditor had discussed the underlying allegations with another person (i.e., a stranger to the fraud) before filing his action); *cf.* United States *ex rel.* Fallon v. Accudyne Corp., 921 F. Supp. 611, 624–25 (W.D. Wis. 1995) (court rejected the defendants' contention that notices of deficiency transmitted by state agency to one defendant constituted a public disclosure because there was "no evidence that the non-compliance notices sent as a result of routine inspections were received, viewed or disclosed by or to anyone other than [defendant]" and the "mere creation of such a document by a state agency does not constitute [a] public disclosure within the intended meaning of § 3730(e)(4)(A)").

[149]*See, e.g.,* United States *ex rel.* Dunleavy v. County of Delaware, 123 F.3d 734 (3d Cir. 1997). In *Dunleavy,* the court had to consider whether a report a county submitted to the federal government had been publicly disclosed because citizens could possibly obtain the report. The court pointed out that it had held previously in United States *ex rel.* Stinson, Lyons, Gerlin & Bustamante, P.A. v. Prudential Ins., 944 F.2d 1149 (3d Cir. 1991), that a document's potential availability was sufficient to trigger the bar and that in the instant action, the state administrative report was potentially available to others under the Freedom of Information Act. However, the court distinguished the two cases by pointing out that *Stinson* "dealt with information produced on the public record in connection with litigation while here we are concerned with reports that may be filed away without the receiving agency being put on notice that there is any reason to give them close attention." *Id.* at 746 (footnote omitted).

[150]166 F.3d 853 (7th Cir. 1999).

ruled that the bank's disclosure to the government employee qualified as a public disclosure because the information was "disclosed . . . to a competent public official."[151] The court found that the disclosure of information to a competent public official about an alleged false claim submitted to the government qualifies as a public disclosure "when the disclosure is made to one who has managerial responsibility for the very claims being made."[152] The court pointed out that this construction accords "with a standard meaning of 'public,' which can also be defined as 'authorized by, acting for, or representing the community.' 12 OED, at 779. Disclosure to an official authorized to act for or represent the community on behalf of government can be understood as public disclosure."[153]

The court pointed out that this interpretation also effectuated the purpose of the provision:

> The point of public disclosure of a false claim against the government is to bring it to the attention of the authorities, not merely to educate and enlighten the public at large about the dangers of misappropriation of their tax money. Disclosure to the public at large is a step in lowering the jurisdictional bar precisely because it is likely to alert the authorities about the alleged fraud. After investigation, they can take the proper steps to deal with it—prosecution, settlements involving repayment of funds, or whatever may be called for in the particular case. Since a public official in his official capacity is authorized to act for and to represent the community, and since disclosure to the public official responsible for the claim effectuates the purpose of disclosure to the public at large, disclosure to a public official with direct responsibility for the claim in question of allegations or transactions upon which a *qui tam* claim is based constitutes public disclosure within the meaning of §3730(e)(4).[154]

---

[151] *Id*. at 861.

[152] *Id*.

[153] *Id*.

[154] *Id*. In essence, the court established a sliding scale regarding the type of disclosures that would be deemed "public." For example, the court noted that disclosures "to officials with less direct responsibility might still be public disclosure if the disclosure is public in the commonsense meaning of the term as 'open' or 'manifest' to all." *Id*. (citation omitted). Further, the "more open a disclosure is, the less any public official need be specifically informed. If it is sufficiently open, no official need to specifically informed. The more likely the competent official is to be apprised of the relevant facts by a disclosure, the less 'public,' in the sense of open or manifest to all, it need be. If the disclosure is made, as here, to precisely the public official responsible for the claim, it need not be disclosed to anyone else to be public disclosure within the meaning of the Act." *Id*. (footnote omitted). *Accord* United States *ex rel*. Cherry v. Rush-Presbyterian/ St. Luke's Med. Ctr., No. 99 C 06313, 2001 WL 40807 at *3 (N.D. Ill. Jan. 16, 2001) (hospital's voluntary disclosure of inappropriate billing practices to the U.S. Attorney's Office, the FBI, and HCFA (now CMS) "constitutes 'public disclosure' for FCA purposes"); *see also* United States *ex rel*. O'Keeffe v. Sverdup Corp., 131 F. Supp. 2d 87, 92 (D. Mass. 2001) (because the Environmental Impact Statements/Reports "was co-authored by the United States Department of Transportation, any transactions or allegations contained therein would also implicate the jurisdictional bar of

On the one hand, the test in *Bank of Farmington* appears to be too broad in that one could contend that one purpose of the 1986 amendments was to eliminate the 1943 government knowledge bar and that the *Farmington* decision resuscitated that bar.[155] Such a contention, however, is faulty on two grounds. First, the primary purpose of the amendments, as noted above, was not merely to repeal the government knowledge bar but to create a means by which the federal government would receive pertinent information at the earliest possible time and reward the informant. The government's receipt of the information puts it on the trail of fraud, and under those circumstances it should not have to share its recovery with a so-called whistleblower who merely repeats to the government what it already knows.[156] Second, a major reform of the 1986 amendments in correcting and amending the 1943 government knowledge jurisdictional bar was to permit actions by relators who were an original source to go forward. Relators who are original sources—those, for example, who would have disclosed their information to the government before the bank in *Bank of Farmington*—could still bring an action even if the government subsequently learned of the information from another source. Thus, *Bank of Farmington* strikes a balance between eliminating those actions that do not advance the government's interest because the information repeats what it has already learned, while not precluding those actions in which persons divulge new, significant information to the government and thus further the government's interest.

## 2. *"Allegations" or "Transactions" of Fraud*

Courts have ruled that not only must the information underlying the complaint be in the public domain but also that the information must be of a specific type: it must set forth either the "transactions" or the "allegations" underlying the complaint. Courts have attempted to simplify the analysis into a basic formula, known as the "X + Y = Z" test. This section first discusses the case that formulated the $X + Y = Z$ test, *United States ex rel. Springfield Terminal Railway v. Quinn*,[157] and then considers the application of the test in cases in which the

---

§ 3730(e)(4)(A)") (citation omitted); United States *ex rel.* Coleman v. Indiana, No. 96-714-C-T/G, 2000 U.S. Dist. LEXIS 13666 at *30–33 (S.D. Ind. Sept. 19, 2000) (Indiana's submission of state plans qualified as public disclosures to the federal government and the government's "letters approving the State Plans constitute administrative reports").

[155] *See, e.g.,* United States *ex rel.* Dunleavy v. County of Delaware, 123 F.3d 734, 745–46 (3d Cir. 1997).

[156] Some district courts had similarly ruled that information transmitted from state agencies or private persons to the federal government constitute public disclosures because the information is sufficient to put the government on the trail of alleged wrongdoing. *See, e.g.,* United States *ex rel.* Long v. SCS Bus. & Tech. Inst., 999 F. Supp. 78, 87–88 (D.D.C. 1998), *rev'd on other grounds*, 173 F.3d 870 (D.C. Cir. 1999); United States *ex rel.* Alexander v. Dyncorp, Inc., 924 F. Supp. 292, 299 (D.D.C. 1996).

[157] 14 F.3d 645 (D.C. Cir. 1994).

information in the public domain does not specifically identify any individual defendant.

### a. Overview of the X + Y = Z Test

The relator in *Springfield Terminal Railway* alleged that an arbitrator appointed by the National Mediation Board had billed the government for services not actually rendered. The relator first learned of the underlying evidence during discovery in a previous lawsuit. Because of its own involvement in the arbitration, the relator recognized that the arbitrator had no arbitral function to perform on several of the days for which he sought payment. The relator later confirmed its suspicions by conducting its own investigation (e.g., calling numbers listed on the arbitrator's telephone records, which it had obtained during discovery in the previous litigation). On these facts, the appellate court for the District of Columbia held that the information disclosed did not constitute " 'allegations or transactions' within the meaning of the FCA jurisdictional bar." In "order to disclose the fraudulent *transaction* publicly, the combination of $X$ and $Y$ must be revealed, from which readers or listeners may infer $Z$, i.e., the conclusion that fraud has been committed."[158] The information in the public domain did not concern allegations or transactions because all that was in the public domain was the untrue set of facts (i.e., the alleged misrepresentations submitted by the arbitrator), whereas the relator supplied the missing pieces (i.e., the true set of facts). Thus, because both $X$ and $Y$ were not in the public domain, there were not sufficient allegations or transactions in the public arena to bar the *qui tam* action.

Other courts have followed this $X + Y = Z$ formulation.[159] The $X + Y = Z$ test has set the standard for determining whether a lawsuit is based on allegations or transactions in a hearing, report, audit, investigation, or the news media. The *Springfield* court believed that this reading was consistent with the FCA's purpose because otherwise "[m]any potentially valuable *qui tam* suits would be aborted prematurely by a reading of the jurisdictional provision that barred suits when the only publicly disclosed information was itself innocuous."[160]

---

[158] *Id.* (emphasis added).

[159] *See, e.g.,* United States *ex rel.* Foundation Aiding the Elderly v. Horizon West Inc., No. 99-17539, 2001 U.S. App. LEXIS 20365 at *7–*8 (9th Cir. Sept. 13, 2001); United States *ex rel.* Jones v. Horizon Healthcare Corp., 160 F.3d 326, 331 (6th Cir. 1998); United States *ex rel.* Dunleavy v. County of Delaware, 123 F.3d 734, 741 (3d Cir. 1997); United States *ex rel.* Findley v. FPC-Boron Employees' Club, 105 F.3d 675, 687 (D.C. Cir.), *cert. denied*, 522 U.S. 865 (1997); United States *ex rel.* Rabushka v. Crane Co., 40 F.3d 1509, 1512 (8th Cir. 1994); United States *ex rel.* O'Keeffe v. Sverdup Corp., 131 F. Supp. 2d 87, 94 (D. Mass. 2001); United States *ex rel.* Downy v. Corning, Inc., 118 F. Supp. 2d 1160 (D.N.M. 2000); United States *ex rel.* Pogue v. American Healthcorp., Inc., 977 F. Supp. 1329, 1337–38 (M.D. Tenn. 1997).

[160] *Id.* at 654. The court concluded that one may determine whether the information is specific enough to trigger the bar by whether the material was sufficient to

*b. Application of the* X + Y = Z *Test When Information in the Public Domain Does Not Identify the Defendant*

In *United States ex rel. Cooper v. Blue Cross & Blue Shield of Florida, Inc.*,[161] the relator was a Medicare beneficiary who noticed that Medicare paid a claim for which his employer's health plan was responsible. Believing this practice was improper, the relator informed the government of the practice, including the identity of the party, Blue Cross Blue Shield of Florida (BCBSF), that allegedly engaged in the fraudulent conduct. Subsequently, the General Accounting Office (GAO) issued a report stating that Medicare intermediaries failed to monitor payments to hospitals under Medicare secondary payment (MSP) laws. Further, the report stated that insurers serving as Medicare intermediaries had a conflict of interest when they also served as primary insurers because their financial interest would dictate that the Medicare program pay claims that they could pay as primary insurers. The pertinent GAO report did not identify BCBSF and did not trigger the public disclosure jurisdictional bar, the court held, because "the report [did] not allege that BCBSF in its capacity as a primary insurer actually engaged in wrongdoing." Accordingly, the "report does not constitute a 'public disclosure of allegations or transactions' that BCBSF knowingly violated MSP laws."[162]

In *United States ex rel. Findley v. FPC-Boron Employees' Club*,[163] the relators attempted to obtain a contract to service certain vending machines at a Bureau of Prisons facility. By attending a preproposal conference, the relators learned that an employees' club operated some machines at the facility. The relators questioned the legality of this practice and filed a lawsuit against all employees' clubs of the Bureau of Prisons and DOJ. However, a 1952 Comptroller General opinion, a 1974 Senate report, and a 1986 Federal Circuit opinion had all questioned the legality of retention of such funds by employees'

---

enable the DOJ "to investigate the case and to make a decision whether to prosecute"; that is, "whether the information conveyed [to the government] could have formed the basis for a government decision on prosecution, or could at least have alerted law-enforcement authorities to the likelihood of wrongdoing. . . ." *Id.* (quoting United States *ex rel.* Joseph v. Cannon, 642 F.2d 1373 (D.C. Cir. 1981)). For a general description of the application of the X + Y = Z test, see Salcido, FALSE CLAIMS ACT COUNSELING, *supra* note 30, §3:05.

[161] 19 F.3d 562 (11th Cir. 1994) (per curiam).

[162] *Cooper*, 19 F.3d at 567; *see also Downy*, 118 F. Supp. 2d at 1166 ("It is apparent that in the Tenth Circuit cases, a particular alleged wrongdoer had been identified in the public disclosures or would be readily identifiable given the information in those disclosures, and a specific explanation of the alleged wrongdoing had been provided."); United States *ex rel.* Butler v. Magellan Health Servs., 74 F. Supp. 2d 1201, 1210–11 (M.D. Fla. 1999) (refusing to apply the public disclosure jurisdictional bar to defendants that were not named in the publicly disclosed state court action but who were named in the *qui tam* action); United States *ex rel.* Stinson, Lyon, Gerlin & Bustamante, P.A. v. Provident Life, 721 F. Supp. 1247 (S.D. Fla. 1989).

[163] 105 F.3d 675 (D.C. Cir. 1997), *cert. denied*, 522 U.S. 865 (1997).

clubs. Therefore, it was held that the allegations underlying the lawsuit had been publicly disclosed although the publicly disclosed material did not identify the specific defendants. The court pointed out that given the information in the public domain, one would only need to identify employees' clubs that provide vending services on federal property to question the appropriateness of the arrangement. The court ruled that the relators' complaint was barred because all it added was "the identity of particular employees' clubs engaged in the questionable and previously documented generic practice" and that their "conclusory allegations offer at best collateral information; they do not introduce elements of new wrongful transactions or material elements to the publicly disclosed transaction."[164]

The $X + Y = Z$ formulation does not yield mathematical certainty. As the above examples illustrate, one difficult issue is defining the specific degree of match that must exist between the allegations or transactions in the public domain and those in the complaint—or, at an even more basic level, determining whether the information in the public domain must identify the particular defendant. On the one hand, if generic allegations in the public domain suffice to trigger the public disclosure jurisdictional bar, then given the multitude of government investigatory reports and hearings, a number of *qui tam* suits would be barred even under circumstances in which the government could not be expected to have at least constructive notice of the particular practices of a specific party. On the other hand, if generic allegations do not trigger the bar, nothing prevents opportunistic

---

[164]*See also* United States v. Alcan Elec. & Eng'g, Inc., 197 F.3d 1014, 1019 (9th Cir. 1999) (where publicly disclosed document alleged that union had conspired "with local contractors" by deducting set amount from workers' paychecks and remitting that amount back to the union in violation of federal law, the relator's subsequent *qui tam* action was based on the public document although the defendants were not expressly mentioned in the public document because the public document "alleged a narrow class of suspected wrongdoers—local electrical contractors who worked on federally funded projects over a four-year period," who were required "by statute to file certified payrolls with the government on a weekly basis," and hence "the government, as regulator and owner, presumably would have ready access to documents identifying those contractors" and "makes it highly likely that the government could easily identify the contractors at issue") (footnote omitted); United States *ex rel.* Fine v. Sandia Corp., 70 F.3d 568, 572 (10th Cir. 1995). In *Sandia*, a GAO report and a congressional hearing reported that at least two of the nine national laboratories had used funds that were allocated for research involving the storage and disposal of radioactive waste for discretionary research. In his *qui tam* complaint, the relator alleged that one, Sandia National Laboratory, had specifically engaged in this practice. *Id.* at 571. The court ruled that the relator's action was barred by virtue of the information in the public domain. The court distinguished *Sandia* from *Cooper* by pointing out the ease with which the government and the public could identify the responsible individuals: "When attempting to identify individual actors, little similarity exists between combing through the private insurance industry in search of fraud and examining the operating procedures of nine, easily identifiable, DOE-controlled, and government-owned laboratories. *Cooper* is inapplicable to this case." *Id.* at 572.

whistleblowers from usurping public information for private gain (and thereby depriving the government of its rightful recovery) by naming a specific party not mentioned in the public information. For example, if the government issues a report that points out that several providers within an industry breached a regulatory provision and the report did not name the specific parties because they were still under investigation, it would not take much for an enterprising relator (or even a purported "insider") to file a lawsuit claiming that a particular provider committed that specific regulatory breach. If the court were to find that the relator's allegations differed from those in the public domain simply because the relator named the defendant while the public information did not, then the relator would never have to prove that he or she was the original source because the information was not publicly disclosed. Such a result would subvert the purposes underlying the public disclosure jurisdictional bar by substantially minimizing the government's recovery while adding nothing to the government's knowledge regarding the conduct.

In close cases, the proper response to this issue inevitably turns on whether the public information is sufficient to permit the government to identify the "individual actors engaged in the fraudulent activity."[165] A close analysis of both *Cooper* and *Findley* is useful because these courts, although they arrived at opposite conclusions, both were correct given the factual situation each confronted.

In *Cooper*, as is noted above, the court ruled that because the publicly disclosed material did not identify the specific defendant, the publicly disclosed information did not trigger the public disclosure jurisdictional bar.[166] There, the relator identified specific information that he believed demonstrated that a particular defendant violated the FCA and named the precise intermediary that he thought was responsible for the misconduct. Accordingly, the court ruled that the information in the public domain, which did not identify the specific defendant, did not bar the relator's action, which named the specific defendant and tied the defendant to the allegedly fraudulent conduct and was reported to the government before any disclosure of the information. In short, the relator's action was based on particular facts, not a legal theory, and the relator contributed specific facts that were not fairly ascertainable from the public material.

Conversely, in *Findley*, the D.C. Circuit ruled that although the information in the public domain did not identify the specific defendant, the relators' action was barred because the information in the public domain was specific enough that the government could have easily identified the individual actors engaging in the alleged misconduct. In *Findley*, the relators relied on a theory regarding the appropriateness of employees' clubs sharing in the profits from vending

---

[165] *See, e.g., Sandia*, 70 F.3d at 572; *Cooper*, 19 F.3d at 566.
[166] 19 F.3d at 566.

machines on government premises. From this public material, the court concluded, the government and the public could identify all entities engaged in misconduct by simply inquiring into whether an employees' club operated vending machines and retained the profits. Thus, in *Findley*, unlike *Cooper*, the suit was based on the theory, not the particular defendant-specific facts, and given that the theory was already in the public domain, the relators' action was properly barred since the relators were not the original source of that information.

Finally, in applying the statutory language regarding allegations or transactions of fraud, care must be taken to effectuate the statutory intent of eliminating opportunistic lawsuits. As the Tenth Circuit pointed out in *United States ex rel. Precision Co. v. Koch Industries*,[167] a relator's action is barred even if the relator identified additional facts after the essential allegations or transactions were disclosed. Otherwise, relators (and their counsel) could "with a little artful pleading" circumvent the public disclosure jurisdictional bar by adding one or more new facts that are different from the material in the public domain and assert that their action is therefore somehow different from the information in the public domain. Once the essential allegations or transactions are in the public domain, the government could easily undertake the same type of factual investigation.[168] Therefore, the relator's action does not add information of value. Unless the relator is an original source of the information, the action should be dismissed.

### 3. Hearing, Audit, Report, or Investigation

It is not enough that information be publicly disclosed. Rather, the defendant must also show that the disclosure arose from "a criminal, civil, or administrative hearing, in a congressional, administrative, or Government [General] Accounting Office report, hearing, audit or investigation, or from the news media."[169] As the Ninth Circuit pointed out, under this provision, "public disclosure can occur in one of three categories of fora: (1) in a 'criminal, civil, or administrative hearing,' (2) in a 'congressional, administrative, or Government Accounting Office report, hearing, audit, or investigation,' or (3) in the 'news media.' "[170]

The vast majority of courts have ruled that Congress did not intend the words "hearing," "audit," "report," "investigation," or "news

---

[167] 971 F.2d 548, 552 (10th Cir. 1992).

[168] *Cf.* United States *ex rel.* Devlin v. California, 84 F.3d 358 (9th Cir. 1996) (relators' efforts to confirm the allegations did not provide relators with direct knowledge of the allegations and hence permit relators to qualify as original sources because any federal investigator could have performed the same work based upon the information in the public domain).

[169] 31 U.S.C. §3730(e)(4).

[170] A-1 Ambulance Serv. v. California, 202 F.3d 1238, 1243 (9th Cir. 2000) (citation omitted).

media" to be mere examples but intended that these terms comprise the exclusive means through which the underlying information may be publicized. If the publicly disclosed material did not arise from a hearing, audit, investigation, or report or from the news media, the court is unlikely to invoke the public disclosure jurisdictional bar.[171]

However, courts have defined what constitutes a hearing, audit, report, or investigation in different ways. The courts have split on two significant issues. The first is whether the audit, report, or investigation must be federal or whether such publicized state material qualifies. The second is whether the pertinent audit, report, or investigation must be completed and issued to trigger the jurisdictional bar.

### a. State Reports, Audits, or Investigations

In *United States ex rel. Dunleavy v. County of Delaware*,[172] the defendant county was responsible for disclosing a report—a grantee

---

[171] *See, e.g.*, United States ex rel. Dunleavy v. County of Delaware, 123 F.3d 734, 744 (3d Cir. 1997) ("The prevailing view is that this list constitutes an exhaustive rendition of the possible sources. We agree. . . ."); United States ex rel. John Doe v. John Doe Corp., 960 F.2d 318, 323 (2d Cir. 1992) ("Section 3730(e)(4)(A) furnishes an exclusive list of the ways in which a public disclosure must occur for the jurisdictional bar to apply") (citation omitted); United States ex rel. Williams v. NEC Corp., 931 F.2d 1493, 1499–500 (11th Cir. 1991) ("The list of methods of 'public disclosure' is specific and is not qualified by words that would indicate that they are only examples of the types of 'public disclosure' to which the jurisdictional bar would apply. Congress could easily have used 'such as' or 'for example' to indicate that its list was not exhaustive. Because it did not, however, we will not give the statute a broader effect than that which appears in its plain language"); United States ex rel. LeBlanc v. Raytheon Co., 913 F.2d 17, 20 (1st Cir. 1990) (the public disclosure bar "does not deny jurisdiction over actions based on disclosures other than those specified, contrary to what the district court seemed to maintain"); United States ex rel. Stinson, Lyons, Gerlin & Bustamante, P.A. v. Blue Cross, 755 F. Supp. 1040, 1050 (S.D. Ga. 1990) ("The plain meaning of the statute compels the conclusion that the language following the term 'public disclosure' *does* limit that phrase") (emphasis added) (citation omitted); *but see* United States ex rel. Stinson, Lyons, Gerlin & Bustamante, P.A. v. Prudential Ins., 736 F. Supp. 614, 621 (D.N.J. 1990) ("After careful consideration of the above precepts, the Court finds it reasonable to read 'public disclosure' as a general phrase not specifically limited by the enumerated examples in the remainder of the statute, and thus, it easily encompasses allegations such as those in issue in this case, public disclosures during civil discovery"), *aff'd on other grounds*, 944 F.2d 1149 (3d Cir. 1991). However, as the Tenth Circuit recently ruled, although the statute establishes an exclusive list of the sources for the disclosure (i.e., hearings, report, investigation, audit, or news media), these sources are not the only means by which a public disclosure can occur. *See* United States ex rel. Fine v. Advanced Scis., Inc., 99 F.3d 1000 (10th Cir. 1996). Thus, where a person repeats to a stranger to the fraud information contained in a nonpublicly disseminated audit report, a public disclosure of the report has occurred. *Id.* at 1004 (the statute "defines the sources of allegations and transactions which trigger the bar but it does not define the only means by which [a] public disclosure can occur"); *cf.* Seal 1 v. Seal A, No. 98-56447, 2001 U.S. App. LEXIS 15044 at *11–*12 (9th Cir. July 5, 2001) (noting the Tenth Circuit's ruling in *Advanced Sciences* and declining to decide whether the list of types of disclosures set forth in §3730(e)(4)(A) "is exhaustive").

[172] 123 F.3d 734 (3d Cir. 1997).

performance report—to the federal government. The court noted that this report was the only document in the public domain that disclosed the transactions underlying the complaint. The report revealed that the defendant county had breached its duty to report the sale of property and to remit funds to the Department of Housing and Urban Development. The court held that a document cannot qualify as an administrative report unless it was prepared or issued by the federal government. The court reasoned that the words "report, hearing, audit, or investigation" were modified by the words "congressional, administrative, or Government [General] Accounting Office." Because the term "administrative" otherwise would be susceptible to many meanings, the court concluded that it would apply the doctrine of noscitur a sociis (i.e., a word gathers its meaning from the words around it). Applying this doctrine, the court reasoned that an "administrative report" includes only federal administrative reports, not state administrative reports, because the surrounding words "Congress" and "Government [General] Accounting Office" are "entities of our federal government."[173]

The Third Circuit ruled in *Dunleavy* that a state report does not constitute an administrative report under the public disclosure jurisdictional bar. In addition to its argument based on the statutory language, the court believed that this interpretation was supported by policies underlying the statute. First, the court noted that those who prepare reports typically control the underlying information. Accordingly, when a state or local government prepares a report, there is no assurance that the federal government has access to the information needed to detect the fraud in question.[174] Second, the court pointed out that a substantial purpose of the 1986 legislative amendments to the FCA was to eliminate the existing jurisdictional bar (i.e., the government-knowledge bar, which prohibited *qui tam* actions based on information in the government's possession).[175] If the bar applied to information state or local governments supplied to the federal government without any additional disclosure, the government-knowledge

---

[173] *See also* United States *ex rel.* Hansen v. Cargill, Inc., 107 F. Supp. 2d 1172, 1180 (N.D. Cal. 2000) ("the Court concludes that the phrase 'administrative . . . report, hearing, audit or investigation' in the second category of FCA fora does not include non-federal agency actions. To hold otherwise would lead to the anomalous result that disclosure of a state administrative report implicates the FCA jurisdictional bar while disclosure of a state legislative report—a report which is neither congressional, administrative or from the General Accounting Office—does not raise the jurisdictional bar. The Court declines to read the statute to compel such a nonsensical result"); United States *ex rel.* Garibaldi v. Orleans Parish Sch. Bd., 21 F. Supp. 2d 607, 614–15 (E.D. La. 1998), *vacated on other grounds,* 244 F.3d 486 (5th Cir. 2001); *cf.* United States *ex rel.* Devlin v. County of Merced, No. 95-15285, 1996 U.S. App. LEXIS 17681, at *7 (9th Cir. July 11, 1996) (court applied public disclosure jurisdictional bar to state audit report that had been disseminated "to individuals, community and advocacy groups, and to various other interested parties throughout California").

[174] 123 F.3d at 745–46.

[175] *Id.*

bar would, contrary to congressional design, be revived because an action would be barred merely because information was in the federal government's possession.[176]

This ruling, however, if applied in a general fashion, could easily undermine the purposes of the public disclosure jurisdictional bar. If the case is read broadly as holding that all state administrative reports (and presumably, under the court's logic, audits or investigations) are not subject to the bar because they are not federal reports, a primary purpose of the FCA would be undermined because relators would be empowered to parrot the results of widely disseminated state reports or investigations regarding fraud (e.g., Medicaid fraud) and nonetheless be permitted to proceed with their parasitic *qui tam* actions merely because the federal government had not issued the pertinent material and the information was not reported in the news media.[177]

*b. Final Issuance or Completion of Report, Audit, or Investigation*

The relator in *United States ex rel. Williams v. NEC Corp.* was a government attorney who prepared a report analyzing bidding on telecommunications contracts, that he then submitted to his supervising officer, the Office of the Staff Judge Advocate, and the Office of General Counsel. The court commented that the report was not an administrative report under the FCA because the relator's "report on bidding practices was *not issued* by Congress, an administrative agency, or out of the Government [General] Accounting Office," and hence "is not a 'public disclosure' within the meaning of section 3730(e)(4)(A)."[178]

In *United States ex rel. Foust v. Group Hospitalization & Medical Services,* the Office of Personnel Management (OPM) was investigating whether participating plans (including nondefendants) were properly crediting discounts they received from providers when reporting costs incurred in covering persons under the Federal Employees Health Benefits Program. In conjunction with this review, the government issued an audit inquiry—a formal notice sent pursuant to an existing audit regarding the defendants' handling of provider dis-

---

[176]*Id.*

[177]As the Ninth Circuit noted in *A-1 Ambulance Servs. v. California,* 202 F.3d 1238 (9th Cir. 2000), as to the three forums, the term "hearing" is both in the first—"criminal, civil, or administrative *hearing*"—and in the second—"congressional, administrative, or Government Accounting Office *report, hearing,* audit, or investigation" while the term "*report*" is only in the second of the forums. 202 F.3d at 1243 (emphasis added). The court reasoned that this is one explanation for the court's ruling in *United States ex rel. Dunleavy v. County of Delaware,* 123 F.3d 734 (3d Cir. 1997), that "report" only applies to federal reports because while the first of the forums covered public disclosures by federal or state courts or agencies, the second of the forums covered only public disclosures by federal government agencies. *Id.* at 1244–45.

[178]931 F.2d 1493 (11th Cir. 1991) (emphasis added).

counts. The relators contended that there was no audit because there was no final or draft audit report. The court held that because an "audit is a 'formal or official examination and verification of books of account'[] Webster's Third New International Dictionary 143 (1993)," and it "is clear from the government's declarations and exhibits that OPM was in fact undertaking *an audit* of certain . . . activities by . . . the participating plans. . . , the procedure undertaken by OPM to look into the defendants' handling of provider discounts constituted an administrative audit."[179]

The question posed above is whether there is a tacit requirement that the audit, report, or investigation be completed and/or formally issued by an administrative agency to trigger the public disclosure jurisdictional bar. The clear response must be that no such finality is required. A relator can usurp a draft report or audit as easily as a completed report or audit. Moreover, the fact that the government is preparing such material is proof that the government is aware of the fraud and no *qui tam* action is needed. Rather, a *qui tam* action at that point would likely only reduce the government's potential recovery as it would have to share a substantial percentage of the recovery with the relator. Therefore, any draft or otherwise incomplete but public report, audit, or investigation that reveals allegations or transactions of misconduct should be sufficient to trigger the public disclosure jurisdictional bar.

### 4. "Based Upon" a Public Disclosure

In *United States ex rel. Jones v. Horizon Healthcare Corp.*,[180] the relator learned of possibly fraudulent conduct of her employer during the course of her employment. After she was terminated, she filed an action under the state whistleblower protection law (which publicly disclosed the underlying allegations) before filing her *qui tam* suit. The Sixth Circuit held that the relator's lawsuit was based upon the earlier state court action, although the basis for her *qui tam* lawsuit was her personal knowledge, because all that is required to trigger the bar is that the allegations or transactions in a complaint mirror the information in the public domain and not that relators actually derive their information from the public information.

In *United States ex rel. Siller v. Becton Dickinson & Co.*,[181] the relator, who was employed by Scientific Supply Inc. (SSI), a distributor of the defendant's supplies, filed a *qui tam* action after SSI brought a lawsuit alleging that the defendant had wrongfully terminated its distributorship agreement because SSI was prepared to disclose to the government that the defendant was overcharging the government. The relator contended that the allegations underlying his *qui tam*

---

[179] 26 F. Supp. 2d 60, 70 (D.D.C. 1998) (emphasis added).

[180] 160 F.3d 326, 335 (6th Cir. 1998).

[181] 21 F.3d 1339 (4th Cir. 1994).

complaint were based upon personal experience and independent investigation, and that he had not read SSI's complaint until the defendant brought the action to his attention in its motion to dismiss the complaint. The defendant contended that the relator's action was based upon SSI's complaint, and that the relator was not an original source. The Fourth Circuit held that the relator's action would not be based upon allegations of fraud in the public domain if the relator could prove that he learned of the allegations independent of the public disclosure.[182]

As illustrated by the contrast between *Jones* and *Siller*, there is a split in the circuits regarding the meaning of the term "based upon" in the public disclosure jurisdictional bar. The issue arises when there has been a public disclosure of allegations or transactions of fraud contained in or resulting from a hearing, audit, report, investigation, or news media account, but the relator claims ignorance of the public information or claims that the information was obtained from another source. Under these circumstances, the issue is whether the relator's action can be "based upon" the public information if the relator in fact did not know of that information.

Initially, it appeared that this issue would be significant in FCA jurisprudence, requiring resolution by the Supreme Court. However, since *Siller* was decided, all other circuits have disagreed with its reasoning.[183] These subsequent decisions better accord with the FCA's structure, history, and policy.

First, a narrow construction of "based upon"—requiring that a relator actually derive his or her information from public information—

---

[182] Specifically, the court concluded:

> Section 3730(e)(4)(A)'s use of the phrase "based upon" is, we believe, susceptible of a straight forward textual exegesis. To "base upon" means to "use as a basis for." *Webster's Third New International Dictionary* 180 (1986) (definition No. 2 of verb "base"). Rather plainly, therefore, a relator's action is "based upon" a public disclosure of allegations only where the relator has actually derived from that disclosure the allegations upon which his *qui tam* action is based. Such an understanding of the term "based upon," apart from giving effect to the language chosen by Congress, is fully consistent with section 3730(e)(4)'s undisputed objective of preventing "parasitic" actions, *see, e.g., Stinson, supra,* at 1154, for it is self-evident that a suit that includes allegations that happen to be similar (even identical) to those already publicly disclosed, but were not actually derived from those public disclosures, simply is not, in any sense, parasitic.

*Id.* at 1348.

[183] *See, e.g.,* United States *ex rel.* Mistick PBT v. Housing Auth., 186 F.3d 376, 385–88 (3d Cir. 1999), *cert. denied,* 529 U.S. 1018 (2000); United States *ex rel.* Biddle v. Board of Trustees of Stanford Univ., 161 F.3d 533 (9th Cir. 1998), *cert. denied,* 526 U.S. 1066 (1999); United States *ex rel.* McKenzie v. BellSouth Telecomms., Inc., 123 F.3d 935, 940 (6th Cir. 1997), *cert. denied,* 522 U.S. 1077 (1998); United States *ex rel.* Findley v. FPC-Boron Employees' Club, 105 F.3d 675 (D.C. Cir.), *cert. denied,* 522 U.S. 865 (1997); *cf.* United States v. Bank of Farmington, 166 F.3d 853, 863 (7th Cir. 1999) (noting in dicta that the "Fourth Circuit's interpretation of 'based upon' is the better on the grounds of plain meaning and public policy").

would eliminate the original source exception.[184] The FCA's original source exception permits relators to bring actions based upon public information if they have direct and independent knowledge of the alleged fraud. If "based upon" were construed to mean "derived from" as *Siller* contends, then the relator could still pass the public disclosure jurisdictional bar by obtaining direct and independent knowledge of the allegations after having already learned of the information from a public source.[185] Courts have noted that Congress's imposition of such a requirement would make little sense because once information is in the public domain, anyone, including the government, could conduct the same investigation.[186] As the circuit court pointed out in *Findley*, a better reading of "based upon" is that the term is used as a "proxy for whether the relator's complaint merely parrots what is already in the public domain" which, if it does, would "lead[] logically to a subsidiary inquiry into whether the relator had obtained the information in his complaint independently *prior to* the disclosure."[187] Relators who learn of information before public disclosure and deliver that information to the government constitute the class of whistleblowers that Congress intended to benefit from the FCA.

Second, the courts have pointed out that "based upon" had an established meaning under the FCA that was not repealed *sub silincio* when Congress amended the statute in 1986. Specifically, courts have noted that the jurisdictional bar prior to 1986 had prohibited actions "*based upon* evidence or information in the possession of the United States" and that in applying this test, courts had implicitly rejected any interpretation of the phrase "based upon" that required relators to have obtained their information from governmental files, but instead construed the provision more broadly to apply whenever information from relators mirrored the information in the possession of the government.[188] As the D.C. Circuit pointed out in *Findley*, no evidence existed in either the language of the FCA or the legislative history of the 1986 amendments that in amending the jurisdictional bar Congress intended to change the established meaning of "based upon."[189]

Third, as mentioned previously, the purpose of the public disclosure jurisdictional bar is not merely to ferret out truly parasitic lawsuits. Rather, Congress intended to create incentives to encourage individuals to come forward at the earliest opportunity with informa-

---

[184]*See Stanford Univ.*, 161 F.3d at 538 (citing Salcido, *Screening out Unworthy Whistleblower Actions*, 24 Pub. Cont. L.J., *supra* note 17, at 272–73); *Findley*, 105 F.3d at 683 (citing Salcido, *Screening Out Unworthy Whistleblower Actions*, 24 Pub. Cont. L.J., *supra* note 17, at 272–73).

[185]*Findley*, 105 F.3d at 683.

[186]*See, e.g., id.*

[187]105 F.3d at 683 (emphasis added).

[188]*See, e.g., id.* at 684 (emphasis added).

[189]*Id.* at 684–85.

tion regarding possible fraud.[190] "Once the information is in the public domain, there is less need for a financial incentive to spur individuals into exposing fraud."[191] Furthermore, rewarding relators for merely republishing public information only serves to reduce the government's ultimate recovery because relators are entitled to a portion of any recovery.

In *Siller*, the Fourth Circuit based its reading on a dictionary definition of the term.[192] However, such a definition does not account for the historical meaning attributed to the term as used in the jurisdictional bar and, more significantly, the Fourth Circuit did not explain how its interpretation makes sense in light of the structure of the statute. Furthermore, the Fourth Circuit unduly confined the purpose of the statute to preventing parasitic lawsuits. An interpretation requiring only that the complaint mirror the allegations or transactions in the public domain to potentially trigger the bar best effectuates Congress's purpose and maximizes the government's recovery while minimizing the social costs occasioned by the filing of unnecessary *qui tam* actions.[193]

## 5. *The Original Source Provisions*

If each of the four elements of the public disclosure jurisdictional bar is satisfied, then relators must prove that they are an original source or the action will be barred. In defining "original source," the statute provides as follows:

---

[190] See *supra* note 123.

[191] *Id.* at 685.

[192] 21 F.3d at 1349.

[193] Finally, no matter which "based upon" test a court ultimately adopts, it is important to note that *each* separate cause of action in the complaint must be evaluated under that test. Thus, for example, if one separate cause of action is not based in any part upon publicly disclosed material, then that cause of action is not subject to dismissal—even if other causes of action are dismissed under the public disclosure jurisdictional bar. *See, e.g.*, United States *ex rel.* Merena v. SmithKline Beecham Corp., 205 F.3d 97, 102 (3d Cir. 2000) ("What happens under these provisions if a relator files a multi-claim suit and some, but not all, of the claims fall into one of [the jurisdictional bars]? The plaintiff's decision to join all of his or her claims in a single lawsuit should not rescue claims that would have been doomed by section (e)(4) if they had been asserted in a separate action. And likewise, this joinder should not result in the dismissal of claims that would have otherwise survived. Thus, in applying section (e)(4), it seems clear that each claim in a multi-claim complaint must be treated as if it stood alone"); United States *ex rel.* Settlemire v. District of Columbia, 198 F.3d 913 (D.C. Cir. 1999) (The relator "correctly points out that each count of fraud alleged in a *qui tam* action is considered separately under the jurisdictional bar provision") (citation omitted); United States *ex rel.* Koch v. Koch Indus., No. 91-CV-763-K(J), 1999 U.S. Dist. LEXIS 16637 (N.D. Okla. Sept. 27, 1999) ("Nothing in . . . § 3730(e)(4) suggests that a relator must qualify as an original source with regard to an allegation in a *qui tam* complaint that is not based upon a publicly disclosed allegation"); United States *ex rel.* Aflatooni v. Kitsap Physicians Servs., 163 F.3d 516 (9th Cir. 1999); Wang v. FMC Corp., 975 F.2d 1412 (9th Cir. 1992).

(4)(A) No court shall have jurisdiction . . . based upon the public disclosure of *allegations or transactions* . . . unless the action is brought by the Attorney General *or the person bringing the action is an original source of the information.*
(B) For purposes of this paragraph, "original source" means an individual who has direct and independent knowledge of *the information* on which the allegations are based and has *voluntarily* provided *the information* to the Government before filing an action under this section which is based *on the information.*[194]

Thus, to qualify as an original source, relators must satisfy three conditions: they must possess direct knowledge of the information on which the allegations are based; possess independent knowledge of the information on which the allegations are based; and provide the information voluntarily to the government before the information has been publicly disclosed.

Courts have offered various interpretations of these provisions. However, largely as a result of Judge Wald's analysis in *United States ex rel. Findley v. FPC-Boron Employees' Club,*[195] there is a possibility that future court interpretations will be more uniform, making it less likely that relators will be able to forum shop by filing in circuits that broadly construe the original source provision.[196] Specifically, *Findley* defined, for the first time, when precisely the informer must obtain direct and independent knowledge and provide the information to the government. On the basis of the statutory language, the court concluded that a relator must obtain his or her knowledge and provide the information to the government before its public disclosure.

### a. Timing of the Relator's Knowledge and Disclosure of Information

Courts have split regarding whether the relator must voluntarily disclose the information underlying the action before that information is publicly disclosed to qualify as an original source.

---

[194]The statutory references to "information" are italicized here because, as noted below, the word plays an important role in some courts' construction of the original source provision.

[195]105 F.3d 675 (D.C. Cir.), *cert. denied,* 522 U.S. 865 (1997).

[196]The statute provides that the plaintiff may file the action "in any judicial district in which the defendant or, in the case of multiple defendants, any one defendant can be found, resides, transacts business, or in which any act proscribed by section 3729 occurred." 31 U.S.C. §3732(a). Thus, a relator has great discretion as to where to file. He or she can file in any district in which a defendant can be found, resides, or transacts business or where the alleged proscribed act occurred (which could be interpreted to mean where the claim was made or where the claim was processed and paid by the United States). Furthermore, when there are multiple defendants, this discretion is substantially magnified because a number of unrelated defendants could be brought into one judicial district in which one person happens to transact business. *Cf.* United States *ex rel.* Merena v. SmithKline Beecham Corp., 114 F. Supp. 2d 352, 372 (E.D. Pa. 2000) (noting that "because of inter-circuit conflicts as to [the] interpretation" of the original source provision, "litigants and litigants' attorneys [are forced], wherever possible, to attempt to choose the most favorable jurisdiction; i.e., 'forum shop'. This should not have to occur when actions are filed under a federal statute that should be applied and interpreted uniformly throughout the land.")

The relators in *Findley*[197] alleged that government employees' clubs that earn revenue from vending services on federal property violated the FCA by retaining monies owed to the government. The relators claimed that they first learned of the allegedly unlawful practice when they attended a preproposal conference to discuss a Bureau of Prisons request for proposals to service certain vending machines at a federal prison camp. The court found that a 1952 Comptroller General opinion, a 1974 Senate report, and a 1986 Federal Circuit decision had questioned the legality of the practice and that the practice had been publicly disclosed. The court held that the relators could not qualify as an original source because they did not have direct and independent knowledge of the information in the public domain and did not voluntarily provide that information to the government before the information was publicly disclosed.

The relator in *United States ex rel. Bidani v. Lewis*[198] alleged, in part, that one defendant had violated the FCA because he violated the Medicare anti-kickback law by referring patients to a corporation that he owned. The defendants contended that the relator could not qualify as an original source because the pertinent defendant's ownership interest was publicly disclosed in state court litigation before the relator provided the information to the federal government. The court held that the original source provision "only requires that information be provided [to the government] prior to filing an FCA action" and not that "the information be provided [to the government] prior to any public disclosure of the information."[199] Therefore, the relator qualified as an original source of the allegation although he did not furnish the information to the government before its publication in the state court proceeding.[200]

---

[197] 105 F.3d 675 (D.C. Cir.), *cert. denied*, 522 U.S. 865 (1997).

[198] No. 97-C6502, 1998 U.S. Dist. LEXIS 20647 (N.D. Ill. Jan. 3, 1999).

[199] *Id.* at *17.

[200] *See also* United States *ex rel.* Coleman v. Indiana, No. 96-714-C-T/G, 2000 U.S. Dist. LEXIS 13666 at *45 (Sept. 19, 2000); *SmithKline Beecham Corp.*, 114 F. Supp. 2d at 358 ("The statute merely requires that a relator, in order to qualify as an 'original source', have direct and independent knowledge of the information on which the allegations are based and have 'voluntarily provided the information to the Government before filing an action under this section.' 31 U.S.C. §3730(e)(4)(B). The statute by its express wording, at least, makes no other temporal requirement as to when the information must be provided to the government. Had the statute intended an additional requirement that the voluntary disclosure occur before there is any public disclosure, the statute could easily have so stated quite plainly and simply.") (footnote omitted); United States *ex rel.* Butler v. Magellan Health Servs., 74 F. Supp. 2d 1201, 1211–12 (M.D. Fla. 1999); United States *ex rel.* Johnson v. Shell Oil Co., 33 F. Supp. 2d 528, 542 (E.D. Tex. 1999) (refusing to rule that the relators must disclose their information to the government before the time in which the information is publicly disclosed because "adding a temporal requirement . . . could discourage citizen involvement, even when the citizen has direct and independent knowledge of fraud").

The D.C. Circuit's decision in *Findley* comes closest to making sense of the statutory language, implementing the legislative history, and effectuating the statutory purpose. As to the statutory language, initially, any fair characterization of who is an original source must include the notion that the person was the first to report the information. As the Ninth Circuit pointed out in *Wang v. FMC Corp.*,[201] the informer is the person who breaks the conspiracy of silence, not the one that mimics public information:

> The paradigm *qui tam* plaintiff is the "whistleblowing" insider. . . . *Qui tam* suits are meant to encourage insiders privy to a fraud on the government to blow the whistle on the crime. In such a scheme, there is little point in rewarding a second toot. . . .
>
> If, however, someone *republishes* an allegation that already has been publicly disclosed, he cannot bring a *qui tam* suit, even if he had "direct and independent knowledge" of the fraud. He is no "whistleblower." A "whistleblower" sounds the alarm; he does not echo it. The Act rewards those brave enough to speak in the face of a "conspiracy of silence," and not their mimics. . . . Because he had no hand in the original public disclosure of the [defendant's] troubles, [the relator's] claim regarding the [defendant] is blocked by the jurisdictional bar of section 3730(e)(4)(A).[202]

Furthermore, a reading of the statutory language that requires the informer to have direct and independent knowledge of the publicly disclosed information and provide it to the government is the only reading, as the D.C. Circuit pointed out in *Findley*, that harmonizes subparagraphs (A) and (B).[203] Subparagraph (A) mandates that the relator be "an *original source* of the information." The phrase "of the information" must have meaning; otherwise Congress could easily

---

[201] 975 F.2d 1412 (9th Cir. 1992).

[202] *Id.* at 1419–20 (emphasis added). The Sixth Circuit, in *United States ex rel. McKenzie v. BellSouth Telecomms.*, 123 F.3d 935 (6th Cir. 1997), concurred with the D.C. Circuit's ruling. In *BellSouth*, the Sixth Circuit noted:

> We find it difficult to understand how one can be a "true whistleblower" unless she is responsible for alerting the government to the alleged fraud before such information is in the public domain. Therefore, we adopt the approach of the District of Columbia Circuit and conclude that, to be an original source, a relator must inform the government of the alleged fraud before the information has been publicly disclosed.

The court further reasoned that its ruling was based on the policy of the statute because it rewarded persons who broke the conspiracy of silence and penalized those who merely repeated public information:

> Anyone who alerts the government and is a "true whistleblower" deserves any reward that may be obtained by pursuing a *qui tam* action under the FCA. However, the individual who sits on the sidelines while others disclose the allegations that form the basis of her complaint should not be able to participate in any award. This would be contrary to the purpose of the statute.

*Id.* at 942–43.

[203] 105 F.3d at 690.

have omitted the language without changing the meaning of the jurisdictional bar. The question is—what information? The only information referenced in the subparagraph is the allegations or transactions
that are publicly disclosed. Thus, a plain reading of subparagraph (A)
is that the person must be "an original source of the [allegations or
transactions]" that were publicly disclosed.

Moreover, an analysis of subparagraph (B) confirms this interpretation. Each use of the word "information" in subparagraph (B)
refers back to the allegations or transactions that were publicly disclosed. Therefore, that provision, when read in light of subparagraph
(A), would read as follows: For purposes of this paragraph, "original
source" means an individual who has direct and independent knowledge of the information (separate discrete transactions or allegations,
i.e., the $X + Y$ or the $Z$) on which the publicly disclosed allegations are
based and has voluntarily provided the information (again, the separate discrete transactions or allegations, i.e., the $X + Y$ or the $Z$) to the
government before filing an action under this section which is based
on the information (the separate discrete transactions or allegations,
i.e., the $X + Y$ or the $Z$).

This is the only reading of the provision that harmonizes subparagraphs (A) and (B) and makes use of each word of the public disclosure
jurisdictional bar. Further, to read the last clause of subparagraph (B)
as the district court did in *Bidani* would render it meaningless. That
provision requires that the original source voluntarily provide the information to the government before filing an action based on that information. When relators file actions, they are required to file statements
of material evidence with the government.[204] Because relators must
submit the materials to the government at the time of filing, it would
make no sense to require that they also submit the same information to
the government before filing the action (e.g., 5 minutes prior to filing).[205]
It does make sense, however, to require that relators provide the infor-

---

[204] 31 U.S.C. §3730(b)(2).

[205] *See, e.g, Findley*, 105 F.3d at 690–91. As the court pointed out:

> We previously noted that the government notice part of the "original source"
> exception may appear extraneous in light of the statute's filing provisions,
> which require cases to be filed under seal for a period of at least sixty days and
> served only on the government. The "original source" government notification
> provision is not superfluous, however, for it serves an entirely different pur-
> pose from the statute's filing and government notice provisions. By protecting
> a party who initially exposes fraud to the government, Congress "corrected"
> the holding of *United States ex rel. Wisconsin v. Dean*. Once the information
> has been publicly disclosed, however, there is little need for the incentive pro-
> vided by a *qui tam* action. Thus, the only reading of the statute that accounts
> for the requirement that an "original source" voluntarily provided informa-
> tion to the government before filing suit, and Congress' decision to use the
> term "original source" rather than simply incorporating subparagraph (B)'s
> description into subparagraph (A), is one that requires an original source to
> provide the information to the government prior to any public disclosure.

mation to the government before publication. The government then can use the information to investigate before defendants are prematurely tipped off by the public disclosure and can promptly undertake any remedial actions needed to minimize their losses.

The legislative history also supports this reading. In discussing the original source provision, both the primary Senate sponsor and the primary House sponsor stated that to qualify as an original source the person must be the source of the subsequent disclosure of the information. Senator Grassley stated that "a *qui tam* action based solely on public disclosures cannot be brought by an individual . . . who had not been an *original source to the entity that disclosed the allegations.*"[206] Representative Berman stated that "[o]nce the public disclosure of the information occurs through one of the methods referred to above, then

---

*See also* United States *ex rel.* Ackley v. International Business Machines, 76 F. Supp. 2d 654, 667 (D. Md. 1999) (holding that the relator's assertion that he could satisfy the original source provision by disclosing his information to the government seconds before filing "leads to an obviously absurd result since, at the time of the filing of the complaint, a formal written disclosure statement must also be filed. It makes no sense at all to require what might be a disclosure, oral or written, to be made a few seconds before a written one is required to be filed"). Other courts have required that the relator prove that she provided her information to the United States prior to filing the action. *See* United States *ex rel.* Cherry v. Rush-Presbyterian/St. Luke's Med. Ctr., No. 99 C 06313, 2001 WL 40807 at *5 (N.D. Ill. Jan. 16, 2001) (ruling that the relator could not satisfy the voluntary requirement when she did not establish that she provided the information to the government prior to filing the action); United States *ex rel.* Coleman v. Indiana, No. 96-714-C-T/G, 2000 U.S. Dist. LEXIS 13666 at *46–*47 (S.D. Ind. Sept. 19, 2000) (ruling that the relator's action should be dismissed because the relator did not prove that he disclosed his information to the government prior to the time he filed his action) (citations omitted). Further, the Tenth Circuit ruled that even if an attorney makes a pre-suit disclosure to the United States, the disclosure will be deemed inadequate to satisfy the original source mandate that information be provided to the government prior to suit if the relator's attorney withheld the identity of the relator and the purported defendants. *See* United States *ex rel.* King v. Hillcrest Health Ctr., No. 00-6158, 2001 U.S. App. LEXIS 19820 at *21–*23 (10th Cir. Sept. 7, 2001) ("The narrow question raised on appeal is whether a relator qualifies as a 'source' if in making his pre-filing disclosure he withholds his identity and the identities of the potential defendants. The identities of the accuser and the accused are information, *i.e.* essential elements of the fraud transaction, on which the *qui tam* allegations are based. As for the information about the fraudulent schemes that was disclosed, there is little question that the government's ability to analyze and assess it was hampered, if not blocked, by this omission of identities. To withhold the identities of the relator and perpetrator deprives the government of key facts necessary in its efforts to confirm, substantiate or evaluate the fraud allegations. Without the identities, the information behind the allegations essentially remains in the relator's possession and undisclosed to the government, and what has been disclosed could be said to be little more than a hypothetical account given by an attorney").

[206] 132 CONG. REC. 20,536 (1986) (emphasis added). Presumably, the reason Sen. Grassley used the word "entity" rather than "government" is that at the time he made these statements a person could qualify as an original source if the person had "voluntarily informed the Government or the news media prior to an action filed by the Government." *Id.* at 20,531. The words "news media" subsequently were struck, and relators instead were required to supply their information solely to the government.

only a person who qualifies as an 'original source' may bring the action. A person is an original source if he had some of the information related to the claim *which he made available to the government or the news media in advance of the false claims being publicly disclosed.*"[207] The legislative history thus is consistent with the statutory language mandating that the original source be the person that supplies the pertinent information to the government before its public disclosure.

Finally, the district court's ruling in *Bidani* ignores the primary purpose of the provision. Both the legislative history and several cases make clear that the purpose of the *qui tam* provisions is to ensure that the federal government learns of misconduct at the earliest possible time.[208] Once the government learns of this information, it may take remedial action and minimize its potential losses. Contrary to this purpose, the district court's ruling in *Bidani* will encourage possible whistleblowers to wait in the hope that damages will mount and their bounty will increase.

In *Bidani*, the court apparently arrived at the erroneous conclusion because of the language in subparagraph (B), which provides that the relator must "voluntarily provide[] the information to the Government before filing an action under this section which is based on the information." If this clause were read without reference to the section as a whole, one might conclude that the relator must merely provide the information prior to the lawsuit, *not* prior to the public disclosure. The focus of the clause, however, is not on when the relator must furnish the information to the government; that issue is dealt with in subparagraph (A), which provides that the relator must be "an original source of the [publicly disclosed] information." The focus instead is on when the relator must voluntarily provide the information to the government. Obviously, any relator who desires success will voluntarily provide the government with information after filing an action. The purpose of the clause is only to clarify that the relator also must voluntarily provide information supporting the allegations to the government before filing the action. Because the district court's ruling in *Bidani* is so contrary to the FCA's language and purpose, it is unlikely to be followed by other courts.[209]

---

[207] 132 CONG. REC. 29,322 (1986) (emphasis supplied).

[208] See *supra* note 123 (citing cases).

[209] The majority of courts have expressly followed *Findley* and ruled that a relator must disclose his or her information to the government before the allegations or transactions are publicly disclosed. *See* United States *ex rel.* Jones v. Horizon Healthcare Corp., 160 F.3d 326, 335 (6th Cir. 1998); United States *ex rel.* McKenzie v. BellSouth Telecomms., 123 F.3d 935, 942 (6th Cir. 1997); *see also* United States *ex rel.* Eaton v. Kansas Healthcare Investors, 22 F. Supp. 2d 1230, 1236 (D. Kan. 1998) ("two circuit courts have interpreted [the provision] to mean that an original source must provide the government with the information prior to any public disclosure. . . . The court believes that the Tenth Circuit would likely adopt this requirement.") (citations omitted); United States *ex rel.* Hafter v. Spectrum Emergency Care, 9 F. Supp. 2d 1273,

### b. The Nature of the Relator's Knowledge: The "Direct" and "Independent" Requirements

Below is the definition of "direct" that courts have used and an analysis of court decisions requiring relators to possess a certain threshold of direct knowledge before filing actions. This is followed by a discussion of the second qualification on the nature of information a relator must possess to be an original source—the "independent" requirement.

#### i. When Knowledge Is "Direct"

In *United States ex rel. Stinson, Lyons, Gerlin & Bustamante, P.A. v. Prudential Insurance Co.,*[210] the relator, a law firm, obtained in a prior state court lawsuit two documents that the relator believed demonstrated that the defendant had violated federal law. The court held that the relator did not have direct knowledge, pointing out that a dictionary defined "direct" as "marked by absence of an intervening agency, instrumentality, or influence; immediate." The court ruled that the relator's knowledge was not direct because it was dependent on two intermediaries—the employee who drafted the questioned documents and the discovery procedure by which the documents were produced.

Following the Third Circuit's decision in *Stinson*, courts have almost universally ruled that a relator must have firsthand information to satisfy the direct knowledge requirement. Indeed, one essentially must be the employee on the shop floor.[211] The Third Circuit

---

1280–81 (D. Kan. 1998), *aff'd other grounds*, 190 F.3d 1156 (10th Cir. 1999). Furthermore, two circuits, in cases decided before *Findley*, similarly ruled that the information must be disclosed before the public disclosure, but they reached this result on different grounds. *See* United States *ex rel.* Wang v. FMC Corp., 975 F.2d 1412, 1419–20 (9th Cir. 1992); United States *ex rel.* Dick v. Long Island Lighting Co., 912 F.2d 13, 18 (2d Cir. 1990). In *Long Island Lighting*, the Second Circuit based its ruling on subparagraph (A)'s language that the relator must be the original source of the information, meaning that the relator be the source to the entity that made the disclosure. As the D.C. Circuit pointed out in *Findley*, this formulation is slightly wrong in that it would permit the relator to qualify if the relator merely disclosed the information to the news media when the statute requires that the relator disclose the information to the government. In *Wang*, the Ninth Circuit agreed with the Second Circuit—the relator must be the source to the entity that made the disclosure—based upon the inherent meaning of "original source." The Fourth Circuit in United States *ex rel.* Siller v. Becton Dickinson & Co., 21 F.3d 1339 (4th Cir.), and the Eleventh Circuit in Cooper v. Blue Cross & Blue Shield of Fla., 19 F.3d 562, 568 n.13 (11th Cir. 1994), rejected the Second and Ninth Circuits' rulings regarding the "source" requirement; the Fourth and Eleventh Circuits ruled, however, prior to the D.C. Circuit's decision in *Findley*, and thus it is unclear whether those circuits would want to revisit their rulings in light of *Findley*. In any event, notwithstanding the slight differences in their formulations of the rule, four circuits have clearly required that a relator must disclose his or her allegations or transactions before this information is publicly disclosed.

[210] 944 F.2d 1149 (3d Cir. 1991).

[211] *Id.* at 1160; *see also* Grayson v. Advanced Management Tech., 221 F.3d 580, 583 (4th Cir. 2000) (relators, who were lawyers who had represented their client in an administrative proceeding when they learned of the alleged misconduct by read-

supported its construction of "direct" by noting that the legislative history indicated that the only persons qualified to be original sources are those "individuals who are close observers or otherwise involved in the fraudulent activity."[212]

### ii. The Level of Direct Knowledge Relators Must Possess

The relators in *United States ex rel. Springfield Terminal Railway v. Quinn*[213] through an unrelated civil lawsuit obtained payment vouchers and telephone records a federal arbitrator had submitted to the government to obtain reimbursement. The relators, who were participants in the arbitration proceeding, investigated by calling the numbers on telephone records and learned that the arbitrator had billed the government for activities unrelated to the arbitration pro-

---

ing a complaint filed by another party, did not have direct knowledge because they "at best verified" the other party's information and such "conduct is insufficient to render [them] original sources" nor did they "become 'original sources' due to their 'specialized' experience as government contract lawyers"); United States *ex rel.* Fine v. MK-Ferguson Co., 99 F.3d 1538, 1548 (10th Cir. 1996) (relator's allegations are not based on direct knowledge when they "are derivative of the facts uncovered" by others); United States *ex rel.* Fine v. Advanced Scis., Inc., 99 F.3d 1000, 1007 (10th Cir. 1996) (same); United States *ex rel.* Devlin v. State of Cal., 84 F.3d 358 (9th Cir. 1996) (the relators did not have direct knowledge because they had received information underlying action from an insider although they had conducted some independent investigation after learning of the allegations from the insider); United States *ex rel.* Barth v. Ridgedale Elec. & Eng'g, Inc., 44 F.3d 699, 703 (8th Cir. 1995) ("a person who obtains secondhand information from an individual who has direct knowledge of the alleged fraud does not himself possess direct knowledge and therefore is not an original source under the Act") (citation omitted); United States *ex rel.* Kreindler & Kreindler v. United Techs. Corp., 985 F.2d 1148, 1159 (2d Cir. 1993) (the relator did not have direct knowledge because he received the core facts from the defendant); United States *ex rel.* Dhawan v. New York City Health & Hosp. Corp., No. 95 Civ. 7649 (LMM), 2000 U.S. Dist. LEXIS 15677 at *13–17 (S.D.N.Y. Oct. 24, 2000) (the relators, who were hospital officials who alleged that their hospital had paid inflated rates to other hospitals for staffing services and that their concerns resulted in an internal audit being conducted that confirmed their suspicions, lacked direct and independent knowledge because the "original source" to the fraud would be "the auditor that investigated, reported and uncovered the alleged fraudulent claims submitted for reimbursement" and not the relators who did not discover any information upon which the fraud allegations are based or make any first-hand observations of such fraud during the course of their employment), *aff'd*, 252 F.3d 118 (2d Cir. 2001); United States *ex rel.* Hansen v. Cargill, Inc., 107 F. Supp. 2d 1172, 1182–85 (N.D. Cal. 2000); *cf.* United States *ex rel.* Cooper v. Blue Cross & Blue Shield of Fla., 19 F.3d 562, 568 (11th Cir. 1994) (per curiam) (the relator possessed direct knowledge when his investigation triggered the government's investigation); United States *ex rel.* Springfield Terminal Ry. v. Quinn, 14 F.3d 645, 656–57 (D.C. Cir. 1994) (the relator possessed direct knowledge when it made the public disclosure itself after conducting its own investigation); Wang v. FMC Corp., 975 F.2d 1412, 1417 (9th Cir. 1992) (the relator had direct knowledge because he saw the transactions with "his own eyes" and his knowledge was "unmediated by anything but [his] own labor"). For a detailed analysis of the cases, see Salcido, FALSE CLAIMS ACT COUNSELING, *supra* note 30, §3:05; *see also* Salcido, FALSE CLAIMS ACT COUNSELING: NOV. 2000 SUPP., *supra* note 30, §3:05.

[212] 944 F.2d at 1154, 1160.

[213] 14 F.3d 645 (D.C. Cir. 1994).

ceedings. The relators then publicly disclosed this allegation by adding a claim to the lawsuit that the arbitrator had inaccurately billed the government and later filed a *qui tam* action based upon the same allegation. The court held that the relators had direct knowledge of the allegation of fraud because they learned of the fraud through their "own efforts and experience, which in this case included personal knowledge of the arbitration proceedings and interviews with individuals and businesses identified in the telephone records."[214]

In *United States ex rel. Hafter v. Spectrum Emergency Care, Inc.*,[215] a lawyer handling a medical malpractice action contacted a physician regarding the practices of the defendants, companies that managed emergency departments. The physician was the medical director of a company that contracted with a hospital for the provision of emergency department services. The physician stated that the companies providing the management services directed physicians in their practice of medicine and engaged in improper billing practices. His latter contention was based on information he had heard from another physician. On the basis of this information, the lawyer amended the malpractice claim to assert that the defendants also had violated the Texas Medical Practices Act. The physician then filed a *qui tam* action. The defendants asserted that the physician's action was barred under the public disclosure jurisdictional bar and the court agreed, ruling that it was based on the allegations in the malpractice action (a public disclosure). Further, the physician-relator did not qualify as an original source because his knowledge was indirect in that he had no firsthand knowledge of how the management company prepared its claims.

The relator in *United States v. Daniel F. Young, Inc.*[216] was an owner of a company who learned through an investigation that a former customer and another individual had defrauded the government. The government criminally prosecuted those contractors. Through that investigation, the relator suspected that another company and two of its employees had similarly defrauded the government. The relator then filed a *qui tam* action in which he named as John Doe defendants the additional contractors he suspected of misconduct. A grand jury then returned an indictment against some of these John Doe defendants. The relator amended his *qui tam* complaint to name these persons directly as defendants. The court found that the relator did not have sufficient direct knowledge regarding the allegations because, in part, his initial allegations regarding that scheme could not survive a challenge under Rules 9(b) and 11 of the Federal Rules of Civil Procedure.

The more difficult issue regarding the direct element is how much direct knowledge relators must have, or, stated another way, what is

---

[214]*Id.* at 658.

[215]9 F. Supp. 2d 1273 (D. Kan. 1998), *aff'd*, 190 F.3d 1156 (10th Cir. 1999).

[216]909 F. Supp. 1010 (E.D. Va. 1995).

the minimum threshold of direct knowledge relators must possess? For example, if some information is traceable to public information, but the relator also witnessed directly other facts that are material to the claim, does he or she have sufficient direct knowledge to proceed with the action?

The most liberal construction of this requirement is set forth by the D.C. Circuit in *Springfield*. There, the court ruled that the original source provision did not require that the relator have direct knowledge of all the vital ingredients of the fraudulent transaction. Instead, the relator could proceed if she had direct knowledge of one element of the transaction. Applying the same $X + Y = Z$ test it used in determining whether the allegations or transactions were in the public domain (i.e., $X$ is the misrepresented facts, $Y$ is the true state of facts, and $Z$ is the allegation of fraud), the court concluded that the relator needed to have direct knowledge of only one element of the transaction, either the $X$ or the $Y$, to have direct knowledge under the original source provision. Thus, in that case, where the relator lacked direct knowledge of the $X$ element (the untrue state of facts—the payment vouchers and telephone logs produced in discovery) but had direct knowledge of the $Y$ element (the true state of facts—that, based on the relator's interviews and personal knowledge, the arbitrator did not perform the functions for which he billed), the court ruled that the relator qualified as an original source.[217] The court concluded that the relator's knowledge was direct because it would be "[r]are" for the relator to have direct knowledge of the $X$ element because that "would almost always have been disclosed to the government independently by the alleged defrauder."[218] Thus, "in light of the aims of the statute, . . . 'direct and independent knowledge of information on which the allegations are based' refers to direct and independent knowledge of *any* essential element of the underlying fraud transaction (e.g., $Y$)."[219]

Two district courts, however, have developed more restrictive tests. *Hafter* requires that relators have direct knowledge of both the $X$ and the $Y$ transactions of fraud, and *Young* mandates that based on their personal knowledge, relators have enough direct knowledge to satisfy Rules 9(b) and 11 of the Federal Rules of Civil Procedure. The *Hafter* ruling makes the best use of the statutory language and, together with *Young*, best effectuates the statutory purpose of the public disclosure jurisdictional bar by limiting *qui tam* actions to those instances when there has been a public disclosure in which the relator brings significant, useful information to the government's attention.

Specifically, in *Hafter*, the district court pointed out that the D.C. Circuit in *Springfield* simply ignored the statutory language. In *Hafter*,

---

[217] 14 F.3d at 656–57.

[218] *Id.* at 657.

[219] *Id.* (emphasis added).

the relator, like the relator in *Springfield*, knew the Y element—the true state of affairs (i.e., that billing problems existed)—but did not know the X element—the misrepresented state of affairs (i.e., the actual claims the defendants submitted to the government). Applying the plain language, the court ruled that the relator "must demonstrate that he had some direct and independent knowledge as to all the essential elements of the claim."[220] The court pointed out that the statute "does not provide that all that is necessary is that the relator have 'direct and independent knowledge of *some of* the information on which the allegations are based'. . . . [T]here is no indication in the language of the statute that the supporting information need only provide a fraction of the necessary elements of the allegations."[221]

Furthermore, the district court in *Young* required that the relator not only have firsthand (i.e., "direct") knowledge, but also that "the nature and quantum of knowledge" be sufficient to withstand a challenge under Rules 9(b) and 11 of the Federal Rules of Civil Procedure. If the relator's action is based on a public disclosure and his or her knowledge of the underlying information is not specific enough to withstand such a challenge, but is based upon additional investigation the government conducted (even if the relator initially tipped off the government regarding the wrongdoing), the relator's action will be dismissed.[222] The district court pointed out that to permit the relator to proceed absent sufficient knowledge

> would be tantamount to encouraging citizens to initiate parasitic lawsuits feeding entirely off government information, or to run to the government with only a suspicion of fraud in the hope that they might later be able to win the relator status by riding piggyback on information subsequently developed by a government investigation. Although the *qui tam* provisions of § 3730 are designed to encourage citizens with actual knowledge of fraud to come forward, they are plainly not designed to result in government agencies pursuing fishing expeditions at the behest of suspicious citizens. Moreover, the FCA is not designed to have the government function as a sort of free private investigator to help persons achieve *qui tam* relator status and the resulting opportunity of financial gain.[223]

---

[220] 9 F. Supp. 2d at 1278.

[221] *Id.* at 1277 (citation omitted).

[222] 909 F. Supp. at 1022–23. The relator did not proceed against the defendants named initially because the government had waived civil prosecution against some of the defendants who were criminally prosecuted and another defendant did not participate in any federally funded contracts. *Id.* at 1015.

[223] *Id.* at 1022 (emphasis added). The United States similarly takes this position in litigation, asserting that if the relator's initial complaint and statement of material evidence, unaided by any information in the public domain, cannot satisfy Rule 9(b) or 11, then the relator is not entitled to any statutory recovery. *See, e.g.*, Brief of the United States in Response to Motion of Relators for Determination of Relators' Share and Motion to Dismiss Relators as to "Automated Chemistry" Allegations (filed Dec. 22, 1997), *in* United States *ex rel.* Merena v. SmithKline Beecham Corp., No. 93-5974

### c. When Knowledge is "Independent"

The Department of Energy OIG in *United States ex rel. Fine v. MK-Ferguson Co.*[224] conducted an audit of a contractor's charges for a construction project. The relator did not work directly on the audit, but he did help draft the final report. The audit was circulated to the state of Oregon, which had a cooperative agreement with the Department of Energy regarding the project. Hence, the government report was publicly disclosed. The relator contended, however, that he was an original source, but the court disagreed, ruling that the relator did not have direct and independent knowledge. Independent knowledge is knowledge that is not secondhand. Because the relator's knowledge regarding the underlying conduct was derivative of the facts uncovered by others, the relator's knowledge was not independent and he did not qualify as an original source.

Numerous courts have ruled that the independent knowledge requirement is separate from the direct knowledge requirement.[225] If direct knowledge means knowledge gained by the relator's own efforts and not acquired from the labors of others,[226] then what could "independent" mean? Initially, courts ruled that "independent" meant that the relator must have knowledge independent of the public information.[227] Although that certainly is true, that definition is inconsistent

---

(E.D. Pa. July 21, 1997); *see generally* Robert Salcido, *The Government Declares War on* Qui Tam *Plaintiffs Who Lack Inside Information: The Government's New Policy To Dismiss These Parties In False Claims Act Litigation*, 13 HEALTH LAW. 1 (A.B.A., Oct. 2000) (describing the government's position that non-insider relators should be dismissed when the statement of material evidence they supply to the government could not satisfy FED. R. CIV. P. 9(b)). The Ninth Circuit, however, in United States v. Northrop Corp., 5 F.3d 407 (9th Cir. 1993), ruled that the relator need not possess direct and independent knowledge of all of the allegations to satisfy the original source requirements. In *Northrop Corp.*, the government, on investigating the relator's complaint, uncovered totally unrelated allegations of fraud, which it publicized in an indictment. The relator then amended his complaint to include these unrelated allegations of fraud. *Id.* at 408–09. The court ruled that the relator could base his action on those allegations about which the relator had no direct or independent knowledge if his initial tip triggered the government's subsequent discovery of the additional fraud. *Id.* at 411. The district court in United States v. Daniel F. Young, Inc, 909 F. Supp. 1010 (E.D. Va. 1995), criticized *Northrop Corp.* as perhaps "open[ing] the *qui tam* door too wide" in that a "complainant might well win [] relator status merely by communicating to the government, 'I think something fishy is going on in connection with Government Contract A and Contractor B,' and then relying on the evidence of fraud, if any, disclosed by a subsequent government investigation." 909 F. Supp. at 1021–22.

[224] 99 F.3d 1538 (10th Cir. 1996).

[225] *See* United States *ex rel.* Springfield Terminal Ry. v. Quinn, 14 F.3d 645, 656 (D.C. Cir. 1994) (citing cases).

[226] *See, e.g.*, United States *ex rel.* Fine v. Advanced Scis., Inc., 99 F.3d 1000, 1006–07 (10th Cir. 1996); United States *ex rel.* Hafter v. Spectrum Emergency Care, Inc., 9 F. Supp. 2d at 1276.

[227] *See, e.g.*, *Springfield Terminal Ry.*, 14 F.3d at 656 ("'Independent knowledge' is knowledge that is not itself dependent on public disclosure") (citation omitted).

with the structure of the statute. If a relator is required to have direct knowledge of the information before its public disclosure—as the better reading of the statute requires—the relator's knowledge will always be independent of the public disclosure.

The best interpretation of the term—and the one that fits most neatly within the structure of the statute—requires that the relator's information not be independent of the publicly disclosed information but that the relator's knowledge be independent of any other person or source. For example, there may be instances in which a person has direct knowledge (e.g., he or she witnessed the misconduct on the shop floor), but he or she may not appreciate the extent of the misconduct or may not understand that the conduct resulted in the submission of false or fraudulent claims, but is given the remaining pieces of the puzzle by another person. Under those circumstances, the person's knowledge would be direct, but not independent, because it is dependent on another source. Thus, the formulation of the rule the Tenth Circuit applied in *MK-Ferguson* is correct.[228] Furthermore, this reading effectuates the statutory purpose of limiting *qui tam* actions after informa-

---

[228] *See also Advanced Scis.*, 99 F.3d at 1007 ("to be independent, the relator's knowledge must not be derivative of the information of others, even if those others may qualify as original sources") (citation omitted); *Hafter*, 9 F. Supp. 2d at 1276–77 (same); *cf.* United States *ex rel.* Mistick PBT v. Housing Auth., 186 F.3d 376, 388–89 (3d Cir. 1999) (relator's knowledge could not qualify as "direct and independent" knowledge when it could not identify the defendant's alleged misrepresentation without obtaining information under FOIA); United States v. Bank of Farmington, 166 F.3d 853, 864–65 (7th Cir. 1999) (relator's knowledge could not qualify as "direct and independent" when it was dependent upon a disclosure the defendant had made to a government employee); *but see* United States v. Lamers, 168 F.3d 1013, 1018 (7th Cir. 1999) (the relator's knowledge qualified as independent although it had learned of defendant's alleged misrepresentations by virtue of a FOIA request because the relator's investigation of the defendant assisted the government). Other courts have dismissed relators' claims when they have obtained essential information regarding the alleged misconduct from public sources after the lawsuit is filed. *See, e.g.*, United States *ex rel.* Waris v. Staff Builders, Inc., No. 96-1969, 1999 U.S. Dist. LEXIS 15247 (E.D. Pa. Oct. 4, 1999). In *Waris*, the relator's initial complaint was dismissed under Fed. R. Civ. P. 9(b) for failure to plead fraud with particularity. *Id.* at *5. The relator then used public information (such as information he obtained under FOIA) to amend his complaint. *Id.* at *10–11. The court ruled that when the relator's initial complaint was deficient and the relator could only correct the deficiency by reference to public information, the relator could not qualify as an original source. *Id.* at *21–22; *see also* United States *ex rel.* Branhan v. Mercy Health Sys., No. 98-3127, 1999 U.S. App. LEXIS 18509, at *4–7 (6th Cir. Aug. 5, 1999) (same). When determining whether the relator did in fact possess the requisite information, the court will look at the relator's initial complaint. *See* United States *ex rel.* Ackley v. International Business Machines Corp., 76 F. Supp. 2d 654, 660 (D. Md. 1999) (in evaluating whether the relator's action is based upon publicly disclosed allegations or transactions, the court will limit its review primarily to the relator's initial complaint and his or her initial disclosure statement because this is the information that was "framed before any possible distortions associated with discovery" and hence is the "most reliable evidence" of whether the relator's action is based upon public information and "what, if any, did he have direct and independent knowledge of before filing suit?").

tion is publicly disclosed to true informers (i.e., those who witnessed or participated in the conduct and understand its significance). Limiting actions to this narrow category of true whistleblowers is appropriate because, as numerous courts have found, once information is in the public domain "no incentive for a private *qui tam* suit is needed."[229]

### d. The "Voluntary" Requirement

One relator in *United States ex rel. Barth v. Ridgedale Electric & Engineering*[230] was an electrician who claimed that his employer had failed to pay the prevailing wages required under the Davis Bacon Act. The relator did not report the fraud himself; instead, a business representative of the union reported the allegations to a government investigator. The investigator then interviewed the relator, who subsequently filed a *qui tam* action. The news media had reported the allegations before the relators filed their *qui tam* action. The relator contended that he voluntarily provided information to the government because he cooperated with the government once he was contacted, but the court disagreed, finding that the relator did not voluntarily provide the information to the government because the government, not the relator, initiated the contact. The court ruled that to permit such an action would undermine "the clear intent of the Act which is to encourage private individuals who are aware of fraud against the government to bring such information forward at the earliest possible time and to discourage persons with relevant information from remaining silent."[231]

The relator in *United States ex rel. Fine v. Chevron, U.S.A.*,[232] was a Department of Energy OIG auditor who claimed that he had uncovered evidence of contractor fraud in the course of his duties as an OIG agent. The court ruled that the information underlying the action had been publicly disclosed and that the relator did not qualify as an original source where he did not voluntarily provide the information to the government because he had a legal duty as an OIG agent to disclose the information to the government.[233]

---

[229] *MK-Ferguson Co.*, 99 F.3d at 1546 (citation omitted).

[230] 44 F.3d 699 (8th Cir. 1995).

[231] *Barth*, 44 F.3d at 704; *cf.* United States *ex rel.* Stone v. AmWest Sav. Ass'n, 999 F. Supp. 852, 857 (N.D. Tex. 1997) (relator who received immunity from prosecution and brought information during the government's criminal fraud investigation, did not "voluntarily" provide the information to the government because the term is interpreted to mean "uncompensated" or "unsolicited," not "uncompelled") (citations omitted).

[232] 72 F.3d 740 (9th Cir. 1995) (en banc).

[233] *See also* United States v. Board of Trustees of Stanford Univ., 161 F.3d 533 (9th Cir. 1998) (same); United States *ex rel.* Schwedt v. Planning Research Corp., 39 F. Supp. 2d 28, 36 (D.D.C. 1999) (relator "performed a management role that obligated him to alert superiors to any suspicions of contractor wrongdoing that threatened to impede development of the [product]"); *cf.* United States v. A.D. Roe Co., Inc., 186 F.3d 717 (6th Cir. 1999), *vacating* United States *ex rel.* Burns v. Roe Co., 919 F. Supp. 255 (W.D. Ky. 1996).

Only a few courts have construed the "voluntary" provision of the statute. These courts have interpreted the word broadly and found that when the government initiated contact with the relator or the relator had a legal obligation to disclose the information, the information was not voluntarily furnished to the government. These rulings effectuate the statutory purpose of the FCA. If the government compels a person to speak or even initiates contact with a person (with the option that if the person does not cooperate it can compel that person's testimony), no incentive is needed to lure the person to provide information. The person has come to the government's attention. Any bounty would only nullify the taxpayer's right to obtain a full recovery. The only person who should obtain the bounty is the whistleblower who goes to the government.

## D. Developing Evidence That Supports Application of the Public Disclosure Jurisdictional Bar

The public disclosure jurisdictional bar is not, of course, the only nonsubstantive defense that defendants have raised to dismiss *qui tam* actions—but it has been the most successful.[234] As outlined in the

---

[234] Among other procedural defenses that have been tried with mainly negative results are the following:

- *Dismissal based on relator's failure to file the action under seal or breach of the seal. Compare* United States *ex rel.* Lujan v. Hughes Aircraft Co., 67 F.3d 242 (9th Cir. 1995) (failure to abide by statute's mandatory seal provision does not per se require dismissal of action), *with* United States *ex rel.* Pilon v. Marietta Corp., 60 F.3d 995, 1000 (2d Cir. 1995) (dismissing action because relator did not file complaint under seal); Erickson *ex rel.* United States v. American Inst. of Bio. Scis., 716 F. Supp. 908 (E.D. Va. 1989) (same).
- *Dismissal because action is brought by government employee.* There is no automatic bar to a government employee filing a *qui tam* action. However, courts, at times, have read the public disclosure jurisdictional bar broadly to eliminate such actions. *See* United States *ex rel.* Fine v. MK-Ferguson Co., 99 F.3d 1538 (10th Cir. 1996); United States *ex rel.* Fine v. Advanced Scis., Inc., 99 F.3d 1000 (10th Cir. 1996); United States *ex rel.* Fine v. Chevron, U.S.A., 72 F.3d 740 (9th Cir. 1995) (dismissing former government employee under original source provision) (en banc); United States *ex rel.* LeBlanc v. Raytheon Co., 913 F.2d 17, 20 (1st Cir. 1990); United States *ex rel.* Holmes v. Consumer Ins. Group, No. 99-D-665, 2000 WL 33115680 (D. Colo. Dec. 20, 2000); *cf.* United States v. A.D. Roe Co., Inc., 186 F.3d 717 (6th Cir. 1999), *vacating* United States *ex rel.* Burns v. Roe Co., 919 F. Supp. 255 (W.D. Ky. 1996); United States *ex rel.* Tipton v. Niles Chem. Paint, No. C98-5177RJB, 1999 U.S. Dist. LEXIS 21604 (W.D. Wash. May 6, 1999); *but see* United States *ex rel.* Williams v. NEC Corp., 931 F.2d 1493 (11th Cir. 1991) (no jurisdictional bar on government employees filing a *qui tam* action based on facts obtained through their government employment).
- *Dismissal because relator signed a broad release prior to filing the action.* United States v. Northrop Corp., 59 F.3d 953 (9th Cir. 1995) (prefiling release of *qui tam* claim could not be enforced to bar subsequent *qui tam* action); United States *ex rel.* DeCarlo v. Kiewit, 937 F. Supp. 1039 (S.D.N.Y. 1996) (same); United States v. American Healthcorp, Inc., 1995 Medicare & Medicaid Guide (CCH) ¶43,681 (M.D. Tenn. Sept. 14, 1995) (same), *reh'g granted and*

discussion above, the relator contemplating filing an action and the attorney defending one should quickly ascertain what information underlying the action is in the public domain. As the case law instructs, this can be accomplished by:

- reviewing all news media reports involving the affected company or industry that may have raised similar allegations;
- examining all government reports, such as OIG or GAO reports, that have been issued and may have covered the same transactions raised in the complaint;
- determining whether the government has previously investigated allegations similar to those identified in the complaint and whether the government has publicly disclosed its findings; and
- inquiring of the relator whether he, she, or any person he or she knows has been involved in other litigation that covered the same subject matter.

Of course, by unearthing publicly disclosed allegations and transactions of fraud, the defendant has no guarantee of success. For example, counsel must still grapple with whether the action in question is "based upon" those disclosures and whether the relator is an "original source" of the information. However, such information may provide the defendant with a viable, proven defense.

## IV. PREEMPTING FCA ACTIONS: THE OFFICE OF INSPECTOR GENERAL'S VOLUNTARY DISCLOSURE PROGRAM

If providers become aware of conduct that they believe may subject them to liability under the FCA, and they are interested in possibly preempting any *qui tam* action that may be filed, the OIG's voluntary disclosure program may be the most attractive option.

---

*order vacated on other grounds*, 914 F. Supp. 1507 (M.D. Tenn. 1996). *But see* United States *ex rel.* Hall v. Teledyne Wah Chang Albany, 104 F.3d 230 (9th Cir. 1997) (release enforced when government had full knowledge of relator's charges and had investigated them before relator and defendant had executed their release).

- *Dismissal because* qui tam *statute is unconstitutional.* The Supreme Court ruled that relators have constitutional standing to file *qui tam* actions. *See* Vermont Agency of Natural Res. v. United States, 529 U.S. 765 (2000). Moreover, several circuits have ruled that the relator's ability to institute litigation on behalf of the United States does not unconstitutionally infringe upon the Executive Branch's duties under Article II's Take Care Clause, which commands that the Executive "take Care that the Laws be faithfully executed." *See* United States *ex rel.* Riley v. St. Luke's Episcopal Hosp., 252 F.3d 749 (5th Cir. 2001); United States *ex rel.* Kelly v. Boeing Co., 9 F.3d 743, 747–59 (9th Cir. 1993); United States *ex rel.* Kreindler & Kreindler v. United Techs. Corp., 985 F.2d 1148, 1153–55 (2d Cir. 1993); United States *ex rel.* Taxpayers Against Fraud v. General Electric Co., 41 F.3d 1032 (6th Cir. 1994).

## A. The Voluntary Disclosure Process

The preliminary issue for a provider in determining whether to submit a voluntary disclosure is to first determine whether there is a potential violation of the FCA. If, as described earlier in this chapter,[235] a strong defense exists, such as that the provider acted within a good-faith interpretation of ambiguous regulatory guidance or at most was merely mistaken, then, as the OIG pointed out in its recent Voluntary Disclosure Protocol, the provider need not submit a voluntary disclosure.[236] However, if reasonable, responsible government officials could deem the conduct to be unlawful, then the conservative approach would be to report the conduct. Indeed, if such conduct did occur, the OIG believes that the provider has an affirmative duty to disclose the misconduct. Specifically, the OIG has stated:

> [A]s participants in the Federal health care programs, health care providers have an ethical and legal duty to ensure the integrity of their dealings with these programs. This duty includes an obligation to take measures, such as instituting a compliance program, to detect and prevent fraudulent, abusive and wasteful activities. It also encompasses the need to implement specific procedures and mechanisms to examine and resolve instances of non-compliance with program requirements. Whether as a result of voluntary self-assessment or in response to external forces, health care providers must be prepared to investigate such instances, assess the potential losses suffered by the Federal health care programs, and make full disclosure to the appropriate authorities.[237]

---

[235] See text at notes 92–108.

[236] Specifically, the OIG pointed out that its program "is intended to facilitate the resolution of only matters that, in the provider's reasonable assessment, are potentially violative of Federal criminal, civil or administrative laws." 63 Fed. Reg. 58,399–58,400 (Oct. 30, 1998). The OIG further provided:

> Matters exclusively involving overpayment or errors that do not suggest that violations of law have occurred should be brought directly to the attention of the entity (e.g., a contractor such as a carrier or an intermediary) that processes claims and issues payment on behalf of the Government agency responsible for the particular Federal health care program (e.g., HCFA [(CMS)] for matters involving Medicare). The program contractors are responsible for processing the refund and will review the circumstances surrounding the initial overpayment. If the contractor concludes that the overpayment raises concerns about the integrity of the provider, the matter may be referred to the OIG. Accordingly, the provider's initial decision of where to refer a matter involving non-compliance with program requirements should be made carefully.

*Id.* at 58,400–401.

[237] 63 Fed. Reg. at 58,400. *See also* the OIG's Compliance Program Guidance for Hospitals, 63 Fed. Reg. 8987, 8998 (Feb. 23, 1998) (pointing out that if the hospital learns of "misconduct [that] may violate criminal, civil or administrative law, then the hospital promptly should report the existence of misconduct to the appropriate governmental authority") (footnote omitted).

If, after discovering the misconduct, providers determine that they must submit a voluntary disclosure, they will first make initial disclosures to the OIG's Assistant Inspector General for Investigative Operations. Under the OIG guidelines, providers must, in addition to other procedures, identify who is making the disclosure, describe the matter being disclosed, explain why they believe that their conduct may have violated the law, describe whether there are any pending governmental inquiries pending against the company, and certify that their submissions contain truthful information.[238]

After submitting the initial disclosure, it is anticipated that the provider will conduct an internal review regarding the matter and submit the results of the investigation to the OIG. The OIG generally will agree, "for a reasonable period of time, to forego an investigation of the matter if the provider agrees that it will conduct the review in accordance with the Internal Investigation Guidelines and the Self-Assessment Guidelines. . . ."[239] On completing an internal review, the provider submits a final report. The report should additionally contain a written narrative that identifies the questioned conduct in detail; describe how the practice was identified; describe remedial efforts the provider undertook to stop the inappropriate conduct and to prevent its recurrence, including any disciplinary action taken against corporate officials and employees; estimate the monetary impact of the incident or practice upon federal health care programs; and certify that the report is truthful.[240]

After the provider submits its report, the government performs a verification investigation of the disclosed matter. "The extent of the OIG's verification effort will depend, in large part, upon the quality and thoroughness of the internal investigative and self-assessment reports."[241] The OIG noted that it "will use the validated provider self-assessment report in preparing a recommendation to DOJ for resolution of the provider's False Claims Act or other liability."[242]

---

[238] *Id.* at 58,401. Failure to disclose this precise information is not fatal to the submission of a voluntary disclosure but will likely delay resolution of the matter. *Id.* at 58,400 ("Failure to conform to each element of the Protocol is not necessarily fatal to the provider's disclosure, but will likely delay the resolution of the matter").

[239] *Id.* at 58,401. The OIG also noted, however, that a provider should not conduct its internal review when it learns of an "ongoing fraud scheme within its organization." *Id.* at 58,400 ("[A] provider that uncovers an ongoing fraud scheme within its organization immediately should contact the OIG, but should not follow the Protocol's suggested steps to investigate or quantify the scope of the problem. If the provider follows the Protocol in this type of situation without prior consultation with the OIG, there is a substantial risk that the Government's subsequent investigation will be compromised."). Presumably, when whether the matter in fact concerns "an ongoing fraud scheme within the organization," is not clear, the OIG will give the provider guidance on the issue after the provider submits an initial disclosure and at that time advise the provider whether to refrain from conducting an internal review.

[240] *Id.* at 58,401–403.

[241] *Id.* at 58,403.

[242] *Id.* at 58,402.

## B. Benefits and Risks of Submitting a Voluntary Disclosure

Any provider that submits a voluntary disclosure ventures into uncharted terrain. Indeed, the OIG expressly refuses to give any advance assurance regarding how the provider will be treated once it submits the disclosure.[243] Because of this uncertainty, providers have been reluctant to submit voluntary disclosures.[244] Set forth below are some of the specific risks a provider incurs when submitting a disclosure and some of the incentives the government furnishes those that submit disclosures.

---

[243] *See, e.g.,* 63 Fed. Reg. 58,399–58,400 (Oct. 30, 1998). Specifically, the OIG noted:

> Because a provider's disclosure can involve anything from a simple error to outright fraud, the OIG cannot reasonably make firm commitments as to how a particular disclosure will be resolved or the specific benefit that will enure to the disclosing entity. In our experience, however, opening lines of communication with, and making full disclosure to, the investigative agency at an early stage generally benefits the individual or company. In short, the Protocol can help a health care provider initiate with the OIG a dialogue directed at resolving its potential liabilities.

[244] For example, according to a recent press release from the OIG, from May 1995 to October 1998, "[f]ew providers took advantage" of the OIG's pilot Voluntary Disclosure Program—which applied to health care providers in the home health and nursing home industries, and medical suppliers to these providers, in the five states with the highest Medicare expenditures (California, Florida, New York, Texas, and Illinois)—with 20 providers making self-disclosures and 4 being accepted. *See* http://www.hhs.gov/oig/modcomp/disclosenews.htm. Since the OIG has issued its "new, more flexible self-disclosure protocol" that is open to all health care providers that obtain federal funds, "55 providers have self-disclosed with 50 being accepted into the program." *Id.* Furthermore, to make the existing program more attractive, HHS's Inspector General, in an open letter to the health care community, offered additional reforms such as reversing its previous policy that all self-disclosing entities must agree to enter into a Corporate Integrity Agreement (CIA) and agree to exclusion if they breach the terms of the CIA. *See* http://www.hhs.gov/oig/modcomp/openletter.htm. Specifically, the Inspector General stated that "[i]f the self-disclosing provider has demonstrated that its compliance program is effective and agrees to maintain its compliance program as part of the False Claims Act settlement, we may not even require a CIA." *Id.* Factors the Inspector General will use in determining whether to impose a CIA include: "the scope and seriousness of the misconduct, the risk of recurrence, whether the disclosed matter was identified and reported as a result of the provider's compliance measures and the degree of the provider's cooperation during the disclosure verification process." *Id.* Moreover, the Inspector General stated that even in those cases where a CIA must be imposed, the OIG may determine that "the provider may need to make only limited changes to its existing policies and procedures to meet most of the requirements of the CIA." Finally, the OIG stated that "a provider that has made an appropriate self-disclosure and has demonstrated sufficient trustworthiness may lead [the OIG] to conclude that [it] can sufficiently safeguard the programs through a CIA without the exclusion remedy for a material breach. Therefore, [the OIG] will forego the exclusion remedy in appropriate self-disclosure cases." Moreover, the OIG has issued additional guidance setting forth specific examples of when an entity has made a voluntary disclosure and, as a result of the disclosure, the OIG has declined to impose any CIA on the provider. *See* Self-Disclosure of Provider Misconduct: Assessment of CIA Modifications, *available at* http://www.hhs.gov/oig/cia/assessment.htm.

## 1. Risks of Disclosure

The submission of a voluntary disclosure is not without risk. Of greatest concern is that the government itself, a friendly adversary at the start of a voluntary disclosure proceeding, may turn hostile and threaten to file an action based on the conduct underlying the disclosure and/or accuse the provider of submitting a false disclosure statement because the provider did not fully disclose the entire scope of the misconduct.[245] A provider can reduce the likelihood of government prosecution by ensuring that its disclosure report does in fact disclose, not conceal, the misconduct in question. The disclosure should include all material facts underlying the provider's internal investigation. If witnesses or documents reveal that the provider withheld material facts, the government will accuse the provider of submitting a false report and, at a minimum, become more aggressive in its negotiations.

A secondary concern is that an employee will file a *qui tam* action based on the provider's internal review or, if an employee is disciplined as a result of misconduct that contributed to the need to submit a voluntary disclosure, the disciplined or discharged employee may challenge the employer's actions.[246] Because of recent developments in the interpretation of the public disclosure jurisdictional bar, it is less likely that an employee can appropriate the results of an internal investigation to file a *qui tam* action.[247] However, a provider should use only highly trusted employees to assist in an internal investigation and should ensure that the voice of each, to the extent possible, is incorporated into the final product.[248]

---

[245] In this regard, the OIG in its guidelines points out that "the intentional submission of false or otherwise untruthful information, as well as the intentional omission of relevant information, will be referred to DOJ or other Federal agencies and could, in itself, result in criminal and/or civil sanctions, as well as exclusion from participation in the Federal health care programs." 63 Fed. Reg. at 58,403.

[246] Once a provider discovers that its employees have engaged in wrongdoing, it often will initiate specific disciplinary measures against those who participated in the misconduct. Indeed, as part of its report to the government, the provider must "[d]escribe any disciplinary action taken against corporate officials, employees and agents as a result of the disclosed matter." *See* 63 Fed. Reg. at 58,402.

[247] *See* Salcido, *The Use of Voluntary Disclosures to Pre-Empt* Qui Tam *Actions Under the False Claims Act: An Analysis of the* Bank of Farmington *Case and the OIG's Voluntary Disclosure Program*, 27 HEALTH L. DIG. 3 (American Health Lawyers Ass'n Apr. 1999). Indeed, in one case, a district court dismissed the relator's allegations in a *qui tam* action that stemmed from a hospital's voluntary disclosure to the government pursuant to the FCA's public disclosure bar. *See* United States *ex rel.* Cherry v. Rush-Presbyterian/St. Luke's Med. Ctr., No. 99 C 06313, 2001 WL 40807 (N.D. Ill. Jan. 16, 2001).

[248] Because of the persistent threat that other related or unrelated litigation may develop in which the facts found during the course of the internal investigation may be relevant, providers should ensure that all privileges, to the extent possible, are preserved. Regarding confidentiality, the OIG provides the following in its guidelines:

> In the normal course of verification, the OIG will not request production of written communications subject to the attorney-client privilege. There may

## 2. *Incentives for Disclosure*

Although the risks mentioned above are tangible and must be seriously evaluated any time a provider submits a voluntary disclosure, the government's enforcement history of the FCA's voluntary disclosure provision demonstrates that the disclosing provider substantially minimizes its criminal, civil, and administrative liability. By submitting a disclosure, a provider may effectively eliminate any risk of being criminally prosecuted as a result of the misconduct that forms the basis of the voluntary disclosure. The government has not had a practice of instituting criminal proceedings against providers as a result of voluntary disclosures.[249]

Furthermore, a provider substantially minimizes potential civil exposure if the government accepts a voluntary disclosure. As noted previously, the FCA empowers the court to reduce a party's liability to double, rather than treble, damages when the party submits a valid disclosure and to limit civil penalties to $5,000 per claim rather than

---

be documents or other materials, however, that may be covered by the work product doctrine, but which the OIG believes are critical to resolving the disclosure. The OIG is prepared to discuss with provider's counsel ways to gain access to the underlying information without the need to waive the protections provided by an appropriately asserted claim of privilege.

63 Fed. Reg. at 58,403. However, even if the government concurs that the material is privileged, courts are likely to rule that the company waived any privilege by disclosing the information to the government. *See, e.g., In re* Columbia/HCA Healthcare Corp. Billing Practices Litig., 192 F.R.D. 575, 579 (M.D. Tenn. 2000) ("Clients who wish to selectively disclose privileged documents and the entity to whom they wish to disclose the documents cannot negate a waiver simply by agreeing to do so. . . . Accordingly, the Court holds that even in the context of a government investigation, voluntary disclosure of privileged materials to the government constitutes a waiver of the attorney-client privilege to all other adversaries."). Some of the work-product material the OIG requests access to are summaries of interviews that are conducted pursuant to the internal investigation. Specifically, it requests the following:

A list of all individuals interviewed, including each individual's business address and telephone number, and their positions and titles in the relevant entities during both the relevant period and at the time the disclosure is being made. For all individuals interviewed, provide the dates of those interviews and the subject matter of each interview, as well as summaries of the interview. The health care provider will be responsible for advising the individual to be interviewed that the information the individual provides may, in turn, be provided to the OIG. Additionally, include a list of those individuals who refused to be interviewed and provide the reasons cited.

63 Fed. Reg. at 58,403.

[249] For example, under the DOD Voluntary Disclosure Program, as of Feb. 18, 1992, of the 249 contractors who had made Voluntary Disclosures, the DOJ had criminally prosecuted only 4, and in each of those cases the government claimed that it was investigating the company before the disclosure. *See* William F. Pendergast & Marc S. Gold, *Surviving Self-Governance: Common Interests Approach to Protecting Privileges under the DOD Voluntary Disclosure Program*, 22 PUB. CONT. L.J. 1 95, 201–03 (1993) [hereinafter Pendergast & Gold, *Surviving Self-Governance*].

the statutory maximum of $10,000 per claim.[250] Additionally, the DOJ in many cases has exercised its discretion to refrain from recovering any civil penalties under the statute (i.e., it has unilaterally capped its recovery at double damages and has not applied the civil penalty provision of $5,000 to $10,000 per claim) against providers to encourage the submission of additional disclosures. If this practice is continued under the OIG's voluntary disclosure program, providers will have considerable incentive to submit disclosures because it is the civil monetary penalty provision of the statute that often imposes the larger element of liability.

Finally, a provider substantially reduces the likelihood that the OIG will institute any exclusion action against it as a result of the misconduct that formed the basis of the voluntary disclosure.[251] However, even in the unlikely event that the government undertakes an administrative action against the provider, submission of the disclosure will likely result in the government's limiting the duration of the exclusion because of the provider's demonstrated willingness to institute corrective action and exercise self-governance.

## V. Conclusion

The 1986 amendments to the FCA transformed the rules for all health care providers. By deputizing all employees as bounty hunters and offering them huge financial incentives to disclose misconduct, the statute almost ensures that any large-scale questionable or fraudulent practice will be reported to the government.

However, health care providers can easily modify their practices as needed to meet this challenge. They can—and should—develop internal compliance programs that will assist them in identifying fraud before they become embroiled in costly litigation. Providers should familiarize themselves with court interpretations of the FCA to ensure that their practices conform to its standards. They should also develop procedures to disclose questionable practices to the government to preempt the government or private persons from instituting actions against them. By taking these steps, a health care provider can substantially reduce the likelihood that it will confront allegations that it has defrauded the government under the FCA.

---

[250]*See* 31 U.S.C. §3729(a). *See also* 132 Cong. Rec. 28,581 (1986) (The False Claims Act provides a procedure "for corporations to come forward when they discover fraud within their midst. When corporations follow these procedures in cooperating with the Government, the court may impose not only the lesser level of damages, but also a lesser level of penalty.") (statement of Sen. Grassley).

[251]*See* Pendergast & Gold, *Surviving Self-Governance* at 201–03. In nonbinding guidelines regarding the circumstances under which the OIG will exercise its discretion to impose a permissive exclusion on a provider, one factor the OIG considers is whether the provider brought "the activity in question to the attention of the appropriate Government officials prior to any Government action, e.g., was there any Voluntary Disclosure regarding the alleged wrongful conduct?" 62 Fed. Reg. 67,392–67,393 (Dec. 24, 1997).

# 4

# Practical Considerations for Defending Health Care Fraud and Abuse Cases*

*Patric Hooper, Hooper, Lundy & Bookman, Inc., Los Angeles, California.

# I. THE EVOLVING NATURE OF HEALTH CARE FRAUD AND ABUSE ENFORCEMENT

To understand the current realities of defending parties accused of health care fraud or abuse, it is important to be aware of how enforcement activities have evolved. That evolution provides a critical context for understanding current enforcement practices.

## A. The Early Days

Fraudulent and abusive practices in health care are as old as the practice of health care itself. Historic purveyors of snake-oil remedies were not tolerated in the towns of the Old West any more than fraudulent and abusive practitioners are tolerated throughout the country today. The sheriffs and marshals of the Old West were in many ways as vigilant as government enforcement agencies are now in regulating health care. However, rather than exercising government health care program exclusionary authority, the town marshal simply ran the snake-oil salesman out of town with a stern warning never to return. Today, such action would be construed as a permanent exclusion implemented by an executive agency officer without due process—a scenario many perceive as not dissimilar to some current enforcement initiatives.

More recently, however, as the practice of health care became more regulated, state licensing authorities assumed the bulk of the responsibility for protecting consumers from questionable health care practitioners. Through such licensing authority, states were able to safeguard the public against fraudulent, abusive, and unprofessional conduct by licensees, including physicians, hospitals, and other health care providers.

In addition to state licensing regulation, health care professional and trade organizations established codes of conduct and ethics to govern their members. Private accreditation agencies also policed the health care industry. Government agencies often incorporated the credentialing processes of the private associations and accreditation agencies to help regulate the health care industry. Of course, general criminal and civil law sanctions against fraudulent and abusive business and professional practices, such as criminal actions for theft, have been available to federal and state prosecutors for years.[1] Until relatively recently, however, those sanctions typically were reserved for the most egregious cases of fraud and abuse.

## B. Medicare and Medicaid

Health care fraud and abuse did not receive national attention until the establishment of the Medicare and Medicaid programs in 1965.[2] Because the creation of these programs caused the federal and state governments to become major purchasers of health care services, and because of ever-increasing federal and state expenditures for Medicare and Medicaid services, it is not surprising that Congress established specific Medicare and Medicaid fraud and abuse laws in

---

[1] *See, e.g.*, CAL. PENAL CODE §487. *See* People v. Brown, 61 Cal. App. 3d 476, 478 (1976) (physician prosecuted for grand theft for filing false claims with Medi-Cal).

[2] Title XVIII and Title XIX of Social Security Act, as added July 30, 1965, Pub. L. No. 89-97, §102(a), *codified at* 42 U.S.C. §§1395 *et seq.*, 1396 *et seq.*

1972.[3] The 1972 laws were aimed at preventing unlawful kickbacks, bribes, and rebates as well as other types of fraudulent and abusive practices affecting the federal Medicare and Medicaid programs.

To appreciate Congress's original intent, the 1972 laws must be considered in the context in which they were enacted. Although the Medicare and Medicaid programs were then, as now, substantial in their scope, Congress mandated that the programs not interfere with the practice of medicine.[4] Additionally, the Secretary of the Department of Health and Human Services (HHS), then the Secretary of Health, Education, and Welfare, was instructed to consider existing third-party payer principles and practices in determining Medicare and Medicaid payment principles and practices.[5] However, unlike other third-party payers that often paid providers based on the providers' customary charges, Congress intended to impose limits on the amounts Medicare and Medicaid would pay providers.[6] For example, Congress established across-the-board limits on Medicare and Medicaid reimbursement for inpatient hospital services.[7]

In 1972, Congress also had an early opportunity to review the breadth and complexity of the Medicare and Medicaid payment rules. After reviewing them, Congress realized that there were likely to be payment disputes regarding the interpretation of the Medicare statutes and regulations. Therefore, it created a specialized administrative agency tribunal, the Provider Reimbursement Review Board (PRRB), as the first step in adjudicating such disputes.[8] State Medicaid agencies also developed specialized administrative appeal processes for state Medicaid programs.[9]

The contemporaneous enactment of the law establishing the PRRB and the Medicare and Medicaid fraud and abuse statutes is a significant historical development that should not be overlooked. As emphasized later, complex Medicare and Medicaid payment disputes, although originally intended to be resolved through administrative agency adjudicatory processes because of the intricacy and enormous volume of the governing rules, have now become the regular source of health care fraud and abuse enforcement actions.[10]

---

[3] Social Security Act Amendments of 1972, Pub. L. No. 92-603, §§242(b)–(c), 278(b)(9), 86 Stat. 1419 (codified as amended at 42 U.S.C. §§1395nn(b), 1396(h)).

[4] 42 U.S.C. §1395.

[5] 42 U.S.C. §1395x(v)(1)(A).

[6] *See, e.g.,* SENATE FIN. COMM., S. REP. NO. 92-1230 (1972).

[7] *See, e.g.,* 42 U.S.C. §1396b(i)(3) (imposing limit based on provider's customary charges).

[8] 42 U.S.C. §1395oo (Pub. L. No. 103-66, §13503(c)(2) (1993)).

[9] *See, e.g.,* CAL. WELF. & INST. CODE §14171.

[10] The courts have described the Medicare and Medicaid payment process and rules as "among the most completely impenetrable texts within human experience" and as "baffling." *See* Rehabilitation Ass'n of Va. v. Kozlowski, 42 F.3d 1444, 1450 (4th Cir. 1994); Beverly Community Hosp. Ass'n v. Belshe, 132 F.3d 1259, 1266 (9th Cir. 1977).

## C. The Late 1970s and 1980s

Because of a perceived need for stronger antifraud weapons, Congress enacted substantial amendments to the Medicare and Medicaid fraud and abuse statutes in 1977.[11] The 1977 amendments were intended not only to strengthen the government's enforcement abilities but also to alleviate concerns about the vagueness of the 1972 laws. Violations of the Medicare and Medicaid fraud and abuse statutes also were upgraded from misdemeanors to felonies, demonstrating congressional seriousness regarding the issue.[12]

Although early enforcement actions under the Medicare and Medicaid fraud and abuse statutes were prosecuted by U.S. Department of Justice (DOJ) criminal attorneys—thus helping to ensure that prosecutions were limited to circumstances involving genuine fraud and abuse—it quickly became obvious that the concept of fraud and abuse in health care could be subject to considerable definitional debate. It is important to note that in response to this possibility of overly broad definitions of health care fraud, the courts emphasized in early cases that they were not interested in "refereeing" ethical conflicts within the health care industry. Instead, they would decide only whether specific conduct violated specific criminal laws. Thus, for example, the U.S. Court of Appeals for the Fifth Circuit articulated in *United States v. Porter*[13] a clear distinction between issues of ethics and issues of fraud and abuse in health care and confirmed that the court's function was not to evaluate medical ethics but to decide legal issues.

Shortly after *Porter* was decided by the Fifth Circuit, Congress again amended the Medicare and Medicaid fraud and abuse laws to incorporate an express scienter (i.e., state of mind) requirement to ensure that criminal penalties were not imposed for acts undertaken without criminal intent.[14] The scienter or intent requirement was, and continues to be, critical in the defense of health care fraud and abuse cases, whether criminal, civil, or administrative agency actions. Simply put, under most laws a provider cannot be guilty of fraud or abuse in any forum without some proof of wrongful intent.

## D. Deregulation

In the late 1970s and early 1980s, primary responsibility for federal agency enforcement of Medicare and Medicaid fraud and abuse laws rested with the U.S. Health Care Financing Administration (HCFA)[15]— now the Centers for Medicare and Medicaid Services (CMS)—the

---

[11] Medicare-Medicaid Anti-Fraud and Abuse Amendments, Pub. L. No. 95-142, 91 Stat. 1175, 1182 (1977).

[12] 42 U.S.C. §1320a-7b.

[13] 591 F.2d 1048, 1058 (5th Cir. 1979).

[14] Omnibus Budget Reconciliation Act of 1980, Pub. L. No. 96-499, 94 Stat. 2599.

[15] As of July 1, 2001, the former Health Care Financing Administration (HCFA) was renamed the Centers for Medicare and Medicaid Services (CMS). For the purposes of this discussion, references typically will be to CMS.

agency within HHS responsible for the day-to-day operation of the Medicare and Medicaid programs. CMS attorneys drafted several important opinion letters in the late 1970s and early 1980s interpreting some of the more vague concepts of the Medicare and Medicaid fraud and abuse laws (e.g., the Medicare/Medicaid anti-kickback provisions).[16] These opinion letters, which were circulated widely within the health care industry, constituted realistic, practical analyses that coincided with the government's movement toward deregulating the health care industry. For example, CMS opined that health care joint ventures in which physicians had ownership in ancillary service providers such as clinical laboratories did not violate the Medicare/Medicaid anti-kickback statute per se, even though physician owners could benefit financially by referring business to such providers.[17]

In the early 1980s, as a means of curbing costs, the Reagan administration insisted that the health care industry operate more like a business than it had. For example, certificate of need laws, which were thought by some to be anticompetitive, were abolished in various states, allowing the forces of free enterprise to determine the best and the most efficient use of health care resources. In 1983, Congress established the Medicare Prospective Payment System (PPS) to encourage hospitals to control their own expenditures, which no longer would be generally subsidized by the Medicare program.[18]

In the laissez faire atmosphere of the 1980s, most health care providers furnished services on a fee-for-service basis, under which their revenues depended primarily on the volume of services provided. In the health care industry, unlike manufacturing industries, financial efficiency and productivity are measured in terms of "patient days" and "patient visits" rather than number of products manufactured. Medicare and Medicaid cost accounting uses patient days and charges as the means for identifying Medicare and Medicaid activity in hospitals and other patient-care settings. Therefore, providers' internal and external financial analyses projected health care revenues in terms of patient days, patient visits, or patient charges. Health care businesses relied on such projections to perform feasibility studies and other financial analyses. In future years, however, these data would come to be viewed suspiciously by enforcement agencies. The agencies often consider these data to be evidence of wrongful intent to encourage the referral of health care business.

Competition was not welcomed by all members of the health care industry. Many health care providers had been successful, in large part, because of the absence of traditional competitive forces. The continued

---

[16]42 U.S.C. §1320a-7b(b). For text of the anti-kickback statute, see Appendix A-1.

[17]*See* B. Tully, *Federal Anti-Kickback Law* §1500:0607 (BNA's Health L. & Bus. Series 2001). Although a large number of informal interpretive opinions were written, no official or unofficial compendium of these letters exists.

[18]42 U.S.C. §1395ww(d) (Pub. L. No. 98-21, §601(e), 97 Stat. 65, 152–62 (1983)).

viability of some providers was threatened by increased competition. In instances in which a new, competing provider would affect the patient days, patient visits, or patient charges of another provider, the affected provider had every reason to view such competition negatively. This was especially true of business practices designed to encourage changes in patient referral patterns.

## E. Office of Inspector General

In the mid-1980s, CMS (then HCFA) stopped issuing interpretations of health care fraud and abuse laws, including the Medicare/Medicaid anti-kickback statute. Primary responsibility for enforcement of the Medicare and Medicaid fraud and abuse laws shifted to the HHS Office of Inspector General (OIG).[19] In 1987, the OIG's authority was boosted significantly by Congress, which gave the OIG the authority to enforce health care fraud and abuse laws (including the anti-kickback statute) by excluding guilty providers from the Medicare and Medicaid programs through an administrative agency process.[20] Until that time, the remedy for violations of the anti-kickback statute was exclusively judicial, and it was enforced at the discretion of the DOJ. After enactment of the 1987 legislation, however, the OIG no longer had to convince a busy prosecutor from the U.S. Attorney's Office to prosecute a case of suspected wrongdoing. Instead, the OIG could unilaterally seek to impose substantial penalties through the HHS administrative process.

Congress also recognized in the 1987 amendments that the breadth of the statutory language in the Medicare and Medicaid fraud and abuse laws had created uncertainty among health care providers as to which commercial arrangements were legitimate and which were not. Thus, Congress authorized the Secretary of HHS to develop "safe harbor" regulations specifying those practices that, regardless of underlying intent, would not be prosecuted.[21] The Secretary, in turn, delegated the development of these safe harbors to the OIG.[22]

Significantly, neither Congress nor the Secretary of HHS expressly delegated any authority to the OIG to establish regulations or other policy-defining acts prohibited by the Medicare and Medicaid fraud and abuse statutes. Although the OIG was thus empowered by the safe harbor legislation to identify practices that would *not* be prosecuted under the anti-kickback statute, regardless of their legality or

---

[19] 42 U.S.C. §§3521 *et seq. See also* Office of Inspector Gen., U.S. Dep't of Health & Human Servs., Statement of Organizations, Functions and Delegations of Authority, 50 Fed. Reg. 45, 48 (Oct. 31, 1985).

[20] Pub. L. No. 100-93, §2, 101 Stat. 680–86 (1987) (codified at 42 U.S.C. §1320a-7(b)(7)).

[21] Medicare and Medicaid Protection Act of 1987, Pub. L. No. 100-93, §14, 101 Stat. 680 (codified at 42 U.S.C. §1320a-7b(b)(3)).

[22] 59 Fed. Reg. 37,202 (July 21, 1994).

illegality, the OIG was not authorized to make laws announcing or defining what it perceived to be illegal practices under the Medicare and Medicaid fraud and abuse statutes.

The OIG has, nevertheless, undertaken continuing responsibility for determining what is illegal and what is not illegal under the Medicare and Medicaid fraud and abuse laws. To do so, it has issued "fraud alerts," "management advisories," and other general pronouncements that purport to interpret and construe the fraud and abuse laws.[23] Because the OIG is an enforcement agency, it is not surprising that its pronouncements often are skewed toward an expansive interpretation of prohibited acts.

Understanding the role of the OIG's pronouncements is important in defending health care fraud and abuse cases. Since the late 1980s, the OIG has occupied an extremely important position in the hierarchy of both federal and state enforcement agencies. Additionally, the OIG has led a number of investigatory initiatives focusing on health care practices that previously have been considered benign by many members of the health care industry. Moreover, the OIG is maintaining a constant vigil to ensure that CMS and other administrative agencies are not allowing any unnecessary health care dollars to be left available for providers. For example, the OIG routinely suggests ways that CMS could reduce payments to providers.[24]

## F. The *Hanlester* Case

The *Hanlester* case, which culminated in a 1995 decision by the U.S. Court of Appeals for the Ninth Circuit in *Hanlester Network v. Shalala*,[25] illustrates how the rules of acceptable conduct in health care are changing dramatically as a result of enforcement activities.

Because of the *Hanlester* case's notoriety and the fact that the OIG considered it to be an important test case for its enforcement of the Medicare and Medicaid fraud and abuse laws, specifically the anti-kickback statute, the facts and circumstances of the *Hanlester* case are used for illustration throughout this chapter. Additionally, the case's history parallels the increase in enforcement activities in health care.

The Hanlester Network, a partnership, was established in the mid-1980s to create freestanding independent clinical laboratories to compete for clinical laboratory testing business referred from physicians' offices and clinics. The Hanlester Network principals hoped to ensure the laboratories' success by offering laboratory ownership to physicians

---

[23] *See, e.g.*, Special Fraud Alert: Joint Venture Arrangements (Aug. 1989), 59 Fed. Reg. 65,372 (Dec. 19, 1994); Financial Arrangements Between Hospitals and Hospital-Based Physicians, OIG Mgmt. Advisory Rep. No. OEI-09-89-00330 (Oct. 1991). For text of these documents, see Appendix F on disk accompanying this volume.

[24] See, for example, Memorandum From Office of Inspector Gen. to Health Care Financing Admin. (Nov. 16, 1998), recommending "corrective audits" regarding testing by hospital outpatient department laboratories.

[25] 51 F.3d 1390 (9th Cir. 1995).

who were in a position to refer specimens to the Hanlester Network laboratories.

Although this type of joint venture arrangement had been generally determined to be lawful in the past, as evidenced by earlier CMS opinion letters, the OIG believed that many joint ventures possessed "suspect" criteria that caused them to violate the anti-kickback statute. The OIG also believed that the proliferation of health care joint ventures was bad public policy. Thus, in 1989, in addition to issuing a special health care fraud alert announcing the criteria of suspect joint ventures, the OIG issued a barrage of investigative subpoenas to obtain information about other potentially suspect joint ventures and continued addressing Congress and others about the evils of physician self-referral, as epitomized by joint ventures such as the Hanlester Network.[26]

## II. SOURCES OF HEALTH CARE FRAUD AND ABUSE INVESTIGATIONS

By the late 1980s, fear had beset the health care industry, particularly those providers that had heeded the government's earlier messages about the need for competition in the industry and had set out to compete using common business practices. This fear was fueled by three federal appellate court cases, *United States v. Greber, United States v. Kats,* and *United States v. Bay State Ambulance & Hospital Rental Service,* that were interpreted by the OIG and many health care attorneys as stating that if any purpose of a health care transaction was to encourage patient referrals, the transaction was unlawful if it was motivated by any form of remuneration.[27] This overly expansive interpretation of the holdings in *Greber, Kats,* and *Bay State Ambulance* ignored the well-established distinction in criminal law between a defendant's motive for doing an act and the defendant's intent in doing the act. In short, motive is not controlling if the defendant lacked the requisite wrongful intent. Thus, for example, when *Hanlester* reached the Ninth Circuit, the court concluded that the *Hanlester* defendants lacked wrongful intent even though they structured their business transactions so that physician owners were actively encouraged to refer Medicare and Medicaid patient specimens to Hanlester Network laboratories.

By the late 1980s, the subject of health care fraud and abuse had become central to the health care industry. Although the topic previously was only a minor part of health care law seminars, by the late 1980s it was dominant. The health care media also gave priority to the

---

[26]59 Fed. Reg. at 65,372.

[27]United States v. Greber, 760 F.2d 68 (3d Cir.), *cert. denied,* 474 U.S. 988 (1985); United States v. Kats, 871 F.2d 105 (9th Cir. 1989); United States v. Bay State Ambulance & Hosp. Rental Serv., 874 F.2d 20 (1st Cir. 1989).

issue, which made the problem well known throughout the health care industry. Indeed, almost anyone in the industry knew of either someone being investigated or someone about to be investigated. This created an environment fertile for producing many new fraud and abuse investigations in the years to come.

## A. Internal Sources

Although there are no precise statistics on the subject, many experienced health care fraud practitioners believe that a substantial percentage of health care fraud and abuse investigations start with disgruntled current or former employees. Almost every confrontation between a health care employer and employee has the potential to develop into an allegation of fraud or abuse. Employer–employee issues, which used to be the exclusive province of human resources officers and labor lawyers, now require the involvement of a health care lawyer. Wrongful discharge complaints in health care commonly involve contentions of fraud and abuse. Employees and others are encouraged to become whistleblowers by the prospect of substantial bounties offered under federal and state false claim laws and the special protections afforded to employee whistleblowers.[28]

The OIG and other enforcement agencies are well aware of the value of disgruntled current and former employees as sources of information regarding health care fraud and abuse allegations. Investigative agencies seek the identities of former employees early in health care investigations, hoping to find cooperative witnesses.

In addition to disgruntled employees, internal sources of fraud allegations include medical staff physicians and other professionals affiliated with providers. Disputes over treatment practices and policies may easily expand into charges of fraud and abuse. Medical staff members also are becoming false claims *qui tam* relators more now than they have been in the past. Allegations of wrongdoing often develop out of business disputes between professionals.

Other sources of fraud and abuse reporting, which may not be wholly internal, are friends, lovers, and relatives. Not only may an office romance turned sour become the subject of a charge of sexual harassment, it also may give rise to a health care fraud and abuse investigation. One important early health care fraud and abuse case arose between two physician brothers associated with a prestigious medical clinic. Whether that action was motivated by longstanding sibling rivalry, actual good-faith concern about the clinic's billing practices, or some combination of the two is not known. However, the consequence of the resulting investigation was significant to the clinic involved.

More recently, a potentially important federal health care fraud and abuse investigation relied heavily on the testimony of the father in

---

[28]*See* Federal Civil False Claims Act, 31 U.S.C. §§3729 *et seq.*; CAL. GOV'T CODE §12652.

a longstanding and very personal father-son dispute. The government relied heavily on the father's testimony during the trial of the case.[29] This example also illustrates the tactics used by some health care fraud and abuse investigators who, according to the father, requested that he not contact his son to discuss the charges being investigated.

## B. External Sources

The *Hanlester* case began when a marketing representative mistook a competing laboratory owner for a prospective physician investor. The competing laboratory owner deceived the Hanlester marketing representative by telling her he was a physician interested in investing in the Hanlester laboratories rather than disclosing the truth (i.e., that he was the owner of a competing laboratory with no interest in investing). The competing laboratory owner provided a congressional staff member with a copy of his surreptitiously tape-recorded conversation with the Hanlester Network employee, which eventually made its way to the OIG. The OIG considered the tape-recorded conversation to be critical evidence of wrongdoing in the Hanlester Network investigation.

Medicare fiscal intermediaries and carriers are also important external sources of information in health care fraud and abuse investigations. These organizations employ fraud and abuse specialists who scrutinize transactions to identify fraud and abuse. Carrier and intermediary auditors also may serve that purpose. Because CMS has defined abusive practices as including inappropriate billings caused by a provider's misunderstanding of Medicare policy,[30] it can be expected that Medicare fiscal intermediaries and carriers will be even more active in searching out fraud and abuse than they have been.

More recently, federal and state health care facility surveyors have been "deputized" to report fraud and abuse to government enforcement agencies. Although the regulatory surveyors traditionally have limited their role to monitoring a provider's compliance with licensing and certification (i.e., health and safety) requirements, survey teams, such as the multidisciplinary teams involved in the so-called "wedge audits" of Operation Restore Trust, will be increasing their focus on fraud and abuse.[31]

Additionally, patients themselves may complain of perceived fraud and abuse. The government has undertaken substantial efforts to educate Medicare beneficiaries about fraud and abuse. The government's hope is that patients will become knowledgeable about and comfortable with reporting incidents of alleged fraud and abuse.

Finally, under the Health Insurance Portability and Accountability Act of 1996 (HIPAA), HHS is required to implement the Medicare

---

[29]United States v. Mackby, 261 F.3d 821 (9th Cir. 2001).

[30]*See, e.g.*, 42 C.F.R. §455.2.

[31]*See* Press Release, U.S. Dep't of Health & Human Servs., Secretary Shalala Launches New "Operation Restore Trust" (May 20, 1997).

Integrity Program,[32] which expands HHS's authority to contract with private parties to perform so-called "integrity activities." These private contractors perform medical fraud and utilization review, cost report audits, and other investigatory activities to fight fraud and abuse.

## C. Importance of Determining the Source of Disclosed Information

Obviously, those who report health care fraud and abuse perform a very important role in the investigation and prosecution of health care fraud and abuse cases. Such persons are entitled to protection so that they and others are not deterred from reporting instances of fraud and abuse. However, because of the possibility of hidden agendas, it is important for a party under investigation to identify the source of the government's information as early as possible.

Competitors may be motivated to exaggerate anecdotal information. Patients may not be reliable because they may lack the competence necessary to evaluate instances of fraud or abuse. On more than one occasion, patients have complained to government authorities about a lack of medical testing when the testing in question actually had been performed on them. Patients simply did not realize that the test or tests had been performed.

The government often will not know a critical fact about the trustworthiness or motives of a person providing information. Such a fact could affect the reporting person's credibility and the accuracy of that person's information. For example, in the Spectra Laboratories investigation (involving a San Francisco-area clinical laboratory), the person who reported the alleged fraud and abuse was a "professional" whistleblower who regularly pursued actions against his employers shortly after being employed. Information about the frequent "problems" with each of his many employers discovered by this whistleblower was relevant not only to the reliability of the information being supplied by him to the government, but also to the issue of whether he simply was repeating something already known to the government.

The identity of the reporting person might eventually be disclosed or become obvious. For example, if a reporting party has filed a false claims action, his or her identity will be revealed when the *qui tam* complaint is unsealed. The *qui tam* plaintiff is then subject to the same discovery obligations of any other plaintiff. However, where the reporting party does not become a plaintiff, his or her identity may remain unknown.

## III. ENFORCEMENT AND INVESTIGATIVE AGENCIES

Now that health care fraud and abuse has become a priority for federal and state law enforcement agencies, myriad public and private en-

---

[32]Pub. L. No. 104-191, §202, 110 Stat. 1936 (1996), *codified at* 42 U.S.C. §1395ddd.

forcers are getting involved. Advocating the prevention and prosecution of fraud and abuse in health care is a particularly popular political cause. Cracking down on health care fraud and abuse is not only popular, but the subject gives federal and state policy makers a way to divert attention from other, more difficult problems facing the health care system, such as health care rationing. In fact, major cost savings are routinely projected in both federal and state health care budgets as a result of anticipated recoveries from fraud and abuse investigations.[33]

Because so many different government agencies are involved in health care fraud and abuse investigations, identifying precisely which agency is conducting an investigation is important but often difficult. Identifying the agency is important for a number of reasons, including, for example, determining the fundamental question of whether the investigating agency actually has the authority to regulate the conduct under review. A simple illustration is a case in which a local enforcement agency of limited jurisdiction (e.g., a county attorney) attempts to enforce a state law against a party located outside of the enforcement agency's geographic jurisdiction. It should not be assumed that anyone with a badge has the authority to investigate allegations of health care fraud and abuse. To the contrary, there may be substantial limitations on the authority of a particular investigating agency.

## A. Federal Enforcement Agencies

As noted above, since the establishment of the Medicare and Medicaid programs, the federal government has been increasingly active in health care fraud and abuse investigation and law enforcement. One of the most important federal enforcement and investigation agencies is the HHS OIG. The OIG has assumed primary responsibility for enforcing Medicare and Medicaid fraud and abuse laws throughout the United States. Although the OIG may act as an investigatory agency for another federal agency (e.g., the DOJ) in a particular matter, the OIG has its own authority to enforce the Medicare and Medicaid fraud and abuse laws through various administrative agency proceedings, including exclusion proceedings and civil monetary penalty proceedings.

Other federal agencies, such as the U.S. Department of Defense (DOD), also have enforcement and investigatory units. The DOD's Criminal Investigative Services is an important investigatory agency in the health care industry because of Tricare, formerly the Civilian Health and Military Program of the Uniformed Services (CHAMPUS). Tricare uses civilian health care providers to furnish services to the dependents of active and retired military personnel. The Tricare program is an especially important payer of mental health services, which have been a frequent target of health care fraud and abuse enforcement activities.

---

[33]*See* U.S. Gen. Accounting Office, Medicare: Health Care Fraud and Abuse Control Program Financial Report for Fiscal Year 1997, at 5 (1998) (tracing contributions made to Medicare trust fund for fiscal year 1997).

The Federal Employees Health Benefits Program, which insures approximately 9 million federal employees, also has become active in health care fraud and abuse investigations. The Office of Program Management, the agency responsible for administering the program, has independent authority to debar fraudulent and abusive providers without waiting for Medicare or some other government payer to do so. The Railroad Retirement Board exercises similar authority on behalf of the beneficiaries of the Railroad Retirement Insurance Program.

The Federal Bureau of Investigation (FBI) is also extremely active in health care fraud and abuse investigations now that health care fraud and abuse has become a high priority to the federal government. FBI agents have been newly hired or reassigned throughout the country to investigate health care fraud and abuse allegations. Significantly, the FBI may be involved in both criminal and civil investigations and also may be used to investigate health care fraud in programs other than government health care programs.[34] For example, if it is suspected that health care fraud or abuse may have been accomplished by the use of the U.S. Postal Service (USPS), the FBI is authorized to investigate for mail fraud, even if only private health care payers are allegedly damaged.

Similarly, when mail fraud is suspected, USPS inspectors have been assigned to investigate health care fraud and abuse. Although USPS inspectors typically do not take lead roles in such investigations, they provide additional resources to the federal government.

The DOJ maintains criminal and civil health care fraud and abuse units. The Washington, D.C., office often coordinates with local offices in investigating (and often ultimately prosecuting) health care fraud and abuse. And, now that the government suspects the presence of organized crime, the Organized Crime Sections of the DOJ are also investigating health care fraud and abuse.

Additionally, health care fraud and abuse also has become of great interest to the Internal Revenue Service, with respect to nonprofit providers of health care services, and to the Federal Trade Commission, with respect to the enforcement of federal antitrust laws.

## B. State Enforcement and Investigative Agencies

Whereas Medicare, Tricare, and other public programs are wholly federal programs, Medicaid is a combined federal/state program that is administered at the state level by a single state Medicaid agency in each state. In most states, the single state agency is the state's health or social services department, which is required to be the exclusive authority under federal law to administer the state Medicaid program in that state.[35]

---

[34] For discussion of the increasing role of the FBI in health care fraud enforcement, see Chapter 1, at Section I.C. (Baumann, An Introduction to Health Care Fraud and Abuse).

[35] 42 C.F.R. §431.10.

In addition to the single state Medicaid agency, Medicaid-participating states typically have Medicaid Fraud Control Units. Such units often are located in the state prosecuting attorney's office, which in many states is the state attorney general. Although most Medicaid Fraud Control Units are authorized to prosecute criminal health care fraud and abuse cases, they also have the right to pursue civil actions against providers suspected of fraud and abuse. Medicaid Fraud Control Units employ their own investigators, who may work jointly with other state or federal investigators.

Because of the widespread interest in the enforcement of health care fraud and abuse laws, other state agencies are also becoming involved in investigation and enforcement activities. Thus, a state controller or a state insurance commissioner might initiate his or her own independent health care fraud and abuse investigations. Similarly, state professional licensing agencies, such as state medical boards, also are investigating and enforcing laws against health care fraud and abuse. For example, such licensing agencies are construing acts of alleged excessive billing to constitute unprofessional conduct, which could give rise to disciplinary action against the licensee.[36]

At the local level, district attorneys and other local government prosecutors, such as city attorneys, are enforcing state health care fraud and abuse laws. Special health care fraud sections have been and are continuing to be established for the local investigation and enforcement of health care fraud and abuse.

## C. Private Enforcers

Private insurance companies are no longer content to let government enforcement agencies investigate and enforce allegations of health care fraud and abuse. Instead, they now are aggressively conducting their own independent investigations. Of course, private investigators do not have the authority or the breadth of enforcement weapons available to them that the public agencies have. However, it can be expected that such private enforcers will be even less mindful of due process and fairness than their public agency counterparts.

Another private force that may be significant is the shareholders of health care companies. They may initiate shareholder derivative actions when stock values fall as a result of government investigations, arguing that the company failed to deal with incidents of fraud and abuse appropriately, thus damaging the value of the company's stock and causing them considerable financial harm.[37]

---

[36] For example, California licensing authorities have relied on §§2227 and 2261 of the California Business and Professional Code to argue that improper billing practices constitute "unprofessional conduct."

[37] For further discussion of such shareholder derivative lawsuits, see Chapter 8, at Sections II.B. and III. (Baumann & McDavid, Potential Liabilities for Directors and Officers of Health Care Organizations).

Also, as mentioned earlier, the Medicare Integrity Program permits HHS to contract with private parties to perform investigatory activities.[38] This may present problems of fairness and due process similar to those encountered with private insurance investigations.

Regarding private enforcers, it must be emphasized that *qui tam* relators are acting on behalf of the government, not as private citizens, when they file false claims actions. At least one court[39] initially concluded that Congress lacked the constitutional authority to provide such private relators with the requisite standing to enforce the False Claims Act[40] and has thus declared the *qui tam* relator provisions of the federal False Claims Act to be unconstitutional. However, that decision was reversed on rehearing.

## IV. Enforcement Weapons

As identified above, there are various federal, state, local, and private enforcement agencies affecting the health care industry. The identity of the enforcement agency may have a significant effect on the agency's jurisdiction and ability to search for and obtain evidence. Equally important as identifying the agency conducting an investigation is identifying the particular laws and regulations that the agency may enforce against the target of an investigation.

### A. Federal Criminal Laws

#### 1. General Criminal Laws

Federal criminal law prohibits a variety of acts that are not unique to the health care industry. Such general criminal laws as mail fraud and money laundering may be applied to participants in health care fraud schemes just as they may be applied in other industries. For example, a false entry in a Medicare patient's chart can violate the criminal prohibition against making false statements to the federal government.[41]

#### 2. Health Care–Specific Criminal Statutes

However, there also are specific federal criminal statutes uniquely governing health care activities. The Medicare/Medicaid anti-kickback statute is a special health care criminal statute that has been used in a variety of federal criminal actions to prevent offering, paying, soliciting, or receiving kickbacks for the referral of health care business.

---

[38] *See supra* text accompanying note 32.

[39] See the district court's decision in United States *ex rel.* Riley v. St. Luke's Episcopal Hosp., 196 F.3d 514 (5th Cir.), *reh'g en banc granted,* 196 F.3d 561 (5th Cir. 1999), *rev'd,* 252 F.3d 749 (5th Cir. 2001). *Qui tam* relators may not maintain false claims actions against public entities. *See* United States *ex rel.* Garibaldi v. Orleans Parish Bd., 244 F.3d 486 (5th Cir. 2001).

[40] 31 U.S.C. §§3729 *et seq.*

[41] 18 U.S.C. §1001.

### 3. Health Insurance Portability and Accountability Act of 1996 (HIPAA)

HIPAA implemented the most sweeping amendments to the federal health care fraud laws to date. The Act created five new federal health care fraud crimes. First, HIPAA prohibits executing or attempting to execute a scheme or artifice to defraud or to fraudulently obtain money or property of any health care benefit program.[42] Second, HIPAA prohibits embezzling, stealing, misapplying, or converting money, property, premiums, or other assets of a health care benefit program.[43] Third, HIPAA prohibits making false statements or concealing material facts in connection with the delivery of or payment for health care benefits, items, or services.[44] Fourth, HIPAA prohibits willfully obstructing, preventing, misleading, or delaying, or attempting to do so, the communication of information or records relating to a federal health care fraud offense to a criminal investigator.[45] Finally, HIPAA also prohibits disposing of assets to enable a person to become eligible for Medicaid.[46]

In addition to adding the new health care fraud crimes listed, HIPAA expanded existing money laundering, asset forfeiture, and fraud injunction statutes to cover federal health care offenses. The 1996 act also expanded the scope of the "specified unlawful activity," which forms the predicate for a money-laundering violation under 18 U.S.C. §1956, to include any act or activity constituting an offense involving the federal health care laws.[47] In addition, the 1996 amendments expanded the anti-kickback statute to other federal health care programs such as Tricare.[48]

Most important, however, is that four of the five new criminal statutes created by the 1996 Act apply to any health care benefit program, including any private health care plan or contract that affects commerce, thus bringing private insurance plans and contracts within the provisions of the new health care criminal statutes.[49]

## B. State Criminal Laws

As with the federal laws, general state criminal laws may be used to prosecute health care fraud and abuse. For example, in California, the state Medicaid Fraud Control Unit routinely charges the owners of independent clinical laboratories with grand theft in connection with alleged overbilling of the Medi-Cal program.

---

[42] 18 U.S.C. §1347 (Pub. L. No. 104-191, §242, 110 Stat. 1936 (1996)). For text of §1347, see Appendix E-2.

[43] 18 U.S.C. §669 (Pub. L. No. 104-191, §243).

[44] 18 U.S.C. §1035 (Pub. L. No. 104-191, §244). For text of §1035, see Appendix E-1.

[45] 18 U.S.C. §1518 (Pub. L. No. 104-191, §245).

[46] 42 U.S.C. §1320a-7b(a)(6) (Pub. L. No. 104-191, §217).

[47] Pub. L. No. 104-191, §§246, 247, 249.

[48] *Id.* §204, *codified at* 42 U.S.C. §1320a-7b.

[49] *Id.* §241(a) (amending the definition of "health care benefit program").

Additionally, there are specific state health care criminal laws. Various states have enacted their own versions of the Medicare/Medicaid anti-kickback laws, which may be applicable to certain specific payers, such as state Medicaid payers or workers' compensation programs, or to all payers in general.[50]

Many of the state health care criminal laws are modeled after specific federal health care criminal laws. However, it should not be assumed that a state law is consistent with the related federal law. For example, Section 14107.2 of the California Welfare and Institutions Code, which purports to be modeled after the federal Medicare/Medicaid anti-kickback statute, does not contain the specific scienter requirements or the "inducement" factor required by the federal law. These omissions could arguably raise constitutional issues. However, one court has rejected this argument.[51]

Similarly, although states have expressly adopted the Medicare/Medicaid anti-kickback statute as a model, many have not expressly incorporated the federal regulatory safe harbors,[52] which are intended to alleviate the uncertainty and overbreadth of the federal law. It has yet to be determined whether the federal safe harbors would protect a defendant in a state court prosecution under a state anti-kickback law that does not expressly incorporate the federal safe harbors.

## C. Federal Civil Laws

Once again, although there are various generic statutes that may be applied in a federal civil health care fraud and abuse case, the most important and widely used civil statute is the federal False Claims Act.[53] Indeed, most major civil enforcement actions and health care settlements have been brought under that act.

Although the elements of a civil False Claims Act action are dealt with extensively elsewhere in this volume,[54] two aspects of such actions are mentioned briefly here because of their practical implications. The first is the attempt by the federal government and private *qui tam* relators to expand the breadth of the False Claims Act by trying to redefine "false claims" to include any violation of any law or regulation governing a health care provider. A common example is the allegation that a purported violation of the Medicare/Medicaid anti-kickback statute necessarily gives rise to false claims with respect to all services provided by the payer of the kickback. The courts generally have not

---

[50] *See, e.g.,* CAL. BUS. & PROF. CODE §650; CAL. WELF. & INST. CODE §14107.2.

[51] California v. Duz-Mor Diagnostic Lab., 68 Cal. App. 4th 654 (1998).

[52] CAL. WELF. & INST. CODE §14107.2.

[53] 31 U.S.C. §§3729 *et seq.*

[54] For in-depth discussion of the False Claims Act, see Chapter 3 (Salcido, The False Claims Act in Health Care Fraud Prosecutions: Application of the Substantive, *Qui Tam*, and Voluntary Disclosure Provisions). For text of the Act, see Appendix C-1.

supported this position. Instead, they have held that more must be proven than simply a violation of the anti-kickback law.[55]

The second practical element pertains exclusively to false claims actions initiated by private *qui tam* relators. The government is well aware of various generic allegations of health care fraud and abuse in the health care industry, as various agencies have published fraud alerts and other documents describing fraudulent activities. Indeed, at most health care seminars, speakers routinely identify areas of suspected fraud and abuse. It is unlikely that Congress intended such publicly disclosed and generally known allegations to constitute the type of whistleblowing that is to be encouraged and rewarded by the provisions of the False Claims Act.

When a *qui tam* relator's false claims action appears to repeat common fraud and abuse themes, defense counsel will want to consider pursuing the issue of public disclosure because the relator's suit will have to be dismissed if the allegations are shown to be so generally well known that the relator must be doing nothing more than repeating previous allegations.[56]

In addition to seeking relief under the federal False Claims Act, federal enforcement agencies typically add causes of action for common law fraud and unjust enrichment to supplement false claims allegations. However, false claims allegations generally remain the primary focus of federal civil actions.[57]

## D. State Civil Remedies

Many states have their own false claims acts. For example, the California False Claims Act[58] is modeled after the federal False Claims Act. Note again, however, that when a state statute is modeled after a federal statute, it is arguable whether interpretations of the federal statute, such as federal court cases and agency interpretations, should be persuasive in interpreting the state law.

In addition to using false claims statutes, state health care enforcement agencies also are actively using state unfair competition laws to remedy and enjoin health care fraud and abuse.[59] Because unfair competition statutes are broadly written and traditionally interpreted expansively by the courts, such statutes provide state and local enforcement agencies with potentially wide authority. However, as a practical matter, if the enforcement agency is not able to prove the

---

[55] *See, e.g.,* United States *ex rel.* Thompson v. Columbia/HCA Healthcare Corp., 125 F.3d 899 (5th Cir. 1997).

[56] *See* United States *ex rel.* Findley v. FPC-Boron Employees' Club, 105 F.3d 675 (D.C. Cir. 1997).

[57] For discussion of the civil Stark law restrictions, see Chapter 2 (Crane, Federal Physician Self-Referral Restrictions). For text of the Stark law, see Appendix B-1.

[58] CAL. GOV'T CODE §12651.

[59] CAL. BUS. & PROF. CODE §§17200 *et seq.*

wrongfulness of the underlying conduct, it is unlikely that a court or jury will be persuaded to characterize the conduct as constituting unfair competition.

Additionally, it is questionable whether a court or jury would find a party liable for unfair competition if the party is able to establish that the practice engaged in was common for the industry. Although the plea of "everybody's doing it" generally is not an effective defense, the fact that a major segment of the industry engages in the practice could have a major effect on the determination of whether the competition is unfair.

The state courts also have been the forum of choice when private health care parties become enmeshed in disputes over the legality of their financial arrangements. For example, a hospital that owns a medical office building may refuse to continue to honor its lease obligations to its physician tenants because it fears that the favorable rental terms may be construed as disguised kickbacks. Such action has given rise to civil lawsuits over the issue of whether the contract is unenforceable because it is illegal. Indeed, substantial case law is being developed from such controversies.[60]

## E. Federal Administrative Agency Remedies

As discussed in Section I.E., above, one of the most significant aspects of the 1987 amendments to the Medicare and Medicaid Act was the provision authorizing the HHS OIG to bring administrative actions against health care providers as a remedy to curb health care fraud and abuse. Thus, in *Hanlester*, the OIG did not have to convince the U.S. Attorney's Office to bring criminal proceedings against the Hanlester Network principals. Rather, after the local U.S. Attorney declined to prosecute, the OIG was able to initiate its own proceedings in the form of an administrative exclusion proceeding.

The administrative remedy of exclusion is extremely significant because most health care providers rely heavily on Medicare, Medicaid, and other government payers for their revenues. Without such revenues, most providers would not be able to continue to provide services. In addition to the far-reaching impact of such exclusion actions, the OIG is able to maintain an action in HHS's own quasi-adjudicative forum, which places respondents at substantial risk of an adverse result.

The OIG also has the authority to assess and impose civil monetary penalties against a health care provider in an administrative proceeding to enforce the fraud and abuse laws. Although the civil monetary penalty provisions are very similar to those of the federal False Claims Act, the fact that they can be implemented through an administrative proceeding, which ultimately is subject only to somewhat limited judicial review, is very important.[61]

---

[60]*See, e.g.,* Vana v. Vista Hosp. Sys., No. 233623 (Riverside County, Cal. Super. Ct., Oct. 25, 1993).

[61]*See* 42 C.F.R. §§1003.100–.128.

## 1. Limited Judicial Review

Indeed, the OIG has assumed that because Congress authorized it to enforce the health care fraud and abuse laws through exclusion and civil monetary penalties, it may determine the rules governing the administrative proceedings.[62] For example, the OIG takes the position in such cases that its initial determinations are presumed to be valid and are subject to somewhat limited review by the administrative law judges and the appellate board charged with presiding over exclusion and civil monetary penalty proceedings. The OIG's attempt to limit the authority of the HHS administrative law judges is especially troublesome because the HHS administrative law judges typically are the only adjudicators who actually view the witnesses and evidence and function as de novo decision makers.

Another extremely important practical consequence of the OIG's authority to remedy fraud and abuse through administrative proceedings is that the final agency decision is subject to a limited standard of judicial review.[63] Adverse factual findings must be upheld by a reviewing court if they are supported by any competent evidence in the record. Although the courts are the final arbiters of the correct interpretation of the law, the OIG typically will argue that a reviewing court must give substantial deference to the agency's interpretation of the governing statutory and regulatory provisions.

Because of the limited nature of judicial review, it is very important that a defendant prevail at the administrative hearing level regarding civil exclusion and monetary penalty remedies. However, as was the case in *Hanlester*, it is possible to prevail on judicial review under the appropriate circumstances when the terms of a statute are at issue and factual findings are not being challenged.

In addition to the exclusion and civil monetary penalty provisions of the federal law, the Secretary of HHS and the heads of other government programs (e.g., the director of the Tricare program) may impose other administrative remedies. For example, a provider's Medicare or Tricare certification may be removed through an administrative proceeding.[64]

## 2. Suspension of Payments

Often, a more troubling result is the temporary suspension of payment by government payers in cases of suspected fraud or abuse. The federal government, through the Medicare fiscal intermediary or carrier, has the authority to suspend payments to a provider temporarily.[65] The temporary suspension of payments can, and often does, have devastating cash flow consequences to a provider. And, as a practical

---

[62] *See* 42 C.F.R. §1005.21(h).

[63] *See, e.g.,* 42 U.S.C. §1320a-7(f).

[64] *See, e.g.,* 42 C.F.R. §489.53.

[65] 42 C.F.R. §405.371.

matter, it is difficult to challenge a temporary suspension of payments because of the temporary nature of the action and the lack of a formal administrative review process or the availability of judicial review of the suspension action.

Similarly, a Medicare fiscal intermediary or carrier may subject a provider's claims to "special review" for issues such as medical necessity. Although payment technically is not suspended under these prepayment reviews, the reviews can cause payments to be slowed to a point at which a provider eventually may be unable to operate because of cash flow problems. Once again, such prepayment review is considered a temporary remedy, and thus it is difficult to prevent such action through administrative or legal proceedings. Rather, informal methods of resolution may be the most efficient way to stop or lessen the duration of such action. The key is to satisfy the Medicare fiscal intermediary or carrier that no recoupment of an overpayment is necessary because of corrective actions taken by the provider.

## F. State Administrative Agency Remedies

Once again, it is important to note that state Medicaid agencies and other state agencies possess their own authority, similar to that of federal administrative agencies, to impose civil monetary penalties and suspend a provider from the state's Medicaid program. As with federal administrative agency actions, such state action generally is subject to full administrative review and limited judicial review.

Similarly, state agencies have the authority to suspend payments, such as Medicaid payments, temporarily.[66] However, it is important to emphasize that because the Medicaid program is a federal/state program, any action undertaken by any state agency ultimately is subject to compliance with federal Medicaid laws and regulations. Thus, for example, if, as in the case of *Doctor's Medical Laboratory, Inc. v. Connell*,[67] a state controller, who is not part of the single state Medicaid agency, decides to suspend Medicaid payments to a provider, the action arguably must comply with the provisions of the governing federal Medicaid law as well as any independent state law.

Although state licensing boards, such as state medical boards, traditionally have restricted their activities to monitoring the quality of services furnished by professionals and other licensees, there is a growing trend to broaden the authority of these professional licensing boards to include taking action against professionals and others involved in excessive billing or other abusive financial practices. For example, the California Medical Board considers such practices to be "unprofessional conduct," which purportedly authorizes it to take disciplinary action against a licensee.[68]

---

[66] 42 C.F.R. §455.23.

[67] 69 Cal. App. 4th 891 (1999).

[68] CAL. BUS. & PROF. CODE §§2227, 2261.

Such action by licensing boards provides private payers with a dangerous weapon for alleged payment errors by physicians and other health care professionals with respect to private-pay patients. For example, private insurers may report examples of suspected fraud and abuse to state licensing agencies, which are not limited to policing the provision of services to public sector patients.

## G. Identifying the Remedy Threatened by the Enforcement Agency

Federal and state enforcement agencies, as well as private parties, have a variety of remedies available to them to prevent and punish health care fraud and abuse. Unfortunately, especially at the early stages of an investigation, it is not always easy to determine the particular remedy being threatened. In fact, many times parallel proceedings are being considered. For example, the government may be reviewing the facts for both False Claims Act purposes and a potential exclusion proceeding. Therefore, it is not unusual for the Civil and Criminal Divisions of the DOJ to be investigating the very same conduct and threatening both a civil False Claims Act action and a criminal indictment.

The subject of defending potentially parallel proceedings is complicated and beyond the scope of this chapter. Perhaps it is sufficient to say, however, that a potential defendant may have different rights with respect to the investigation or prosecution of different agencies and remedies. Obviously, for example, the target of a criminal prosecution has constitutional rights that might be unavailable to a defendant in an administrative proceeding involving the termination of the defendant's provider agreement.

Moreover, as a practical matter, the government usually is not especially helpful in identifying the types of remedies threatened. To the contrary, as a matter of strategy, the government often prefers to be vague about the breadth and nature of an investigation and the remedies that ultimately might be sought. Although there obviously is good reason for such vagueness at the onset of an investigation, there is little justification for the government's continued lack of clarity about its purposes as the investigation progresses.

## V. HEALTH CARE PRINCIPLES BEING ENFORCED

## A. Hierarchy

At the risk of being elementary, it is worth emphasizing that not every written statement of health care payment or coverage is binding on the public, nor does every rule or guideline cited by a government investigator as a basis for taking action constitute a proper interpretation of the law. Health care lawyers must be vigilant to ensure that they are advising their clients correctly. In a field in which the statutes are amended annually, and the governing regulations are changed even more often, every analysis of every health care dispute should begin with a review of the statutes and regulations. In fact, even a periodic review of the U.S. Constitution is helpful to remind lawyers that the OIG is *not* a constitutional office.

As is the case with many complex regulatory areas, Congress established the general statutory principles governing the Medicare and Medicaid programs and left most of the responsibility for the details to the Secretary of HHS. This is true of the Tricare program as well. However, surprisingly, in some areas of Medicare and Medicaid law, Congress has spoken very specifically and has delegated no discretion to the Secretary of HHS or to any other administrative agency to establish alternative interpretations of the governing statutes.

Government health care investigators seldom are aware of the actual provisions of the governing statutes. They, like the industry, tend to focus on the "rules" that provide the day-to-day interpretations of the "law." Those rules typically are found in the many CMS manuals, Medicare fiscal intermediary and carrier bulletins, and other informal guidelines, such as the American Medical Association's (AMA's) *Current Procedural Terminology* (CPT) *Code Manual*. These informal guidelines often are vague and inconsistent.

As a result, for example, although an enforcement agency may be convinced that an independent clinical laboratory billing Medicare for a laboratory test ordered by an end-stage renal disease (ESRD) dialysis unit constitutes unlawful billing (because the laboratory test presumably is subject to the confusing and esoteric Medicare "50–50" rule), it is questionable whether the governing Medicare statute allows HHS to establish such a rule in the first place because the statute compels an independent clinical laboratory to bill for all laboratory testing it performs, subject to certain exceptions that do not include ESRD laboratory testing.

## B. Importance of Reviewing All the Rules

It simply is not possible to discuss or even list in this chapter all of the rules that might be applicable to a health care dispute involving, for example, the Medicare program. However, unless substantial effort is made to identify and reconcile all of the potentially applicable rules to a given set of facts, it is not possible to be certain that all the rules are being considered.

Fortunately, Congress publishes its policies through statutes. However, when a statute is vague, or even when it appears to be clear, considerable assistance in interpreting Congress's intent may be gathered from the statute's legislative history. Although the Secretary of HHS publishes formal regulations in the *Code of Federal Regulations*, their sheer volume can be overwhelming. Yet, this volume must be mastered because of the surprisingly specific details set forth within the regulations.

Once one extends his or her research and information gathering beyond the statutes and regulations, the task becomes more complex.

Researching Medicare, Medicaid, and Tricare policies is a triple-tiered process. The statutes form the first layer, the regulations form the second, and the other guidelines and rules the third.

## 1. Informal Guidelines

CMS publishes many manuals containing thousands of very important rules interpreting the hundreds of Medicare statutes and regulations. These include, for example, the *Medicare Coverage Issues Manual* (HCFA Publication 6); *State Operations Manual* (HCFA Publication 7); *Hospital Manual* (HCFA Publication 10); *Home Health Agency Manual* (HCFA Publication 11); *Skilled Nursing Facility Manual* (HCFA Publication 12); *Medicare Intermediary Manual* (HCFA Publication 13); *HCFA Carriers Manual* (HCFA Publication 14); *Provider Reimbursement Manual* (HCFA Publication 15); *Medicare Peer Review Organization Manual* (HCFA Publication 19); *Hospice Manual* (HCFA Publication 21); the *Regional Office Manual* (HCFA Publication 23); and *Renal Dialysis Facility Manual* (HCFA Publication 29). CMS also issues Medicare intermediary letters and other program memoranda. Medicare intermediaries and carriers, in turn, issue bulletins and local medical review policies.

These informal interpretations and guidelines are not promulgated according to applicable federal rule-making requirements. Thus, they may be established on an ad hoc basis without consideration of public input. Yet, such guidelines are commonly relied on by government enforcement agents as the basis for health care false claims and other allegations.

That these principles have not been promulgated as formal regulations raises the important question of whether they even can be relied on by government enforcement agents.[69] However, regardless of the outcome of that issue, such guidelines also may be of questionable substantive validity because they often contain requirements not set forth in the statutes and regulations they purport to interpret.

In addition to relying heavily on interpretations developed by the government, enforcement agencies also rely on so-called rules established by private organizations, such as the AMA's CPT codes, noted above, which are incorporated as rules for billing Medicare.[70] In fact, noncompliance with the CPT codes often is alleged as the basis for False Claims Act actions.

## 2. Agency Adjudicative Decisions

Although enforcement agencies rely heavily on informal rules and guidelines to judge the conduct of health care providers for purposes of

---

[69] In Cedars-Sinai Med. Ctr. v. Shalala, 125 F.3d 765, 766 (9th Cir. 1997), the court suggested that violation of such a rule could give rise to a false claim. However, in United States *ex rel.* Swafford v. Borgess Med. Ctr., 98 F. Supp. 2d 822, 828 (W.D. Mich. 2000), the court refused to base liability on a provision of the *Medicare Carriers' Manual.*

[70] See discussion at 65 Fed. Reg. 13,082, 13,087 (Mar. 10, 2000).

determining whether fraud or abuse has occurred, they may be unaware of the interpretations given these provisions by agency adjudicators such as the Medicare PRRB and HHS's administrative law judges. For example, enforcement agencies recently have been aggressively challenging items claimed by providers on Medicare cost reports, such as advertising and marketing costs. Enforcement agencies often consider claiming such costs to be abusive or even fraudulent. However, there is a well-established history of debate over the allowability of these advertising-type costs. Significantly, the federal courts, reviewing PRRB and CMS decisions several years ago, allowed such costs, using the reasoning that the costs were incurred for the purpose of alerting patients who suffer from alcoholism to the need and availability of treatment, an activity related to patient care.[71]

Similarly, for many years, a provision of the Medicare *Provider Reimbursement Manual* was interpreted by Medicare fiscal intermediaries as prohibiting psychiatric hospitals from claiming the direct and indirect costs of providing education services to children and adolescent patients as allowable Medicare costs.[72] CMS and its fiscal intermediaries considered these costs to be particularly nonallowable given that there are few, if any, child and adolescent Medicare patients in psychiatric hospitals.

There is little doubt that if issues such as these, which have been the subject of disputes before the PRRB since its inception, were viewed by enforcement agencies today, the agencies would be inclined to characterize the claiming of such costs as fraudulent or abusive.

However, notwithstanding CMS and its fiscal intermediaries' positions and their reliance on a provision of the Medicare *Provider Reimbursement Manual*, the PRRB and reviewing federal courts, applying the governing Medicare statutory and regulatory provisions, concluded that Medicare was, in fact, required to share in such costs notwithstanding the fact that education services were seldom, if ever, furnished to Medicare patients.[73]

The point to be emphasized is that the government's reliance on informal rules must be scrutinized very closely for both consistency with the actual law (the Medicare statutes and regulations) and internal consistency. Moreover, health care lawyers cannot ignore the considerable body of quasi-judicial determinations that have dealt with many of the rules relied on by government enforcement agencies.

### 3. Other Pronouncements

In addition to official government guidelines and quasi-judicial decisions, additional government pronouncements are being relied on by government and private parties in connection with health care fraud

---

[71]*See* Advanced Health Sys. v. Schweiker, 510 F. Supp. 965 (D. Colo. 1981).
[72]*See* PRM-I §2104.5.
[73]Vista Hill Found. v. Heckler, 767 F.2d 556 (9th Cir. 1985).

and abuse enforcement and compliance issues. For example, fraud alerts issued by the OIG are considered by many to be the equivalent of binding regulations. However, these fraud alerts are nothing more than the viewpoints of government enforcement agencies, specifically the OIG, as to how they would like to see the fraud and abuse laws interpreted. As such, they are no different from the opinions of a police officer or investigator on how the law should be interpreted.

Similarly, model compliance programs issued by the OIG are not binding laws or regulations.[74] Indeed, they have no legal effect. However, government and even some industry spokespersons are seemingly affording the terms of such documents the dignity of formal regulations. Such a reaction, especially among lawyers, is especially confounding, because they are trained during the early days of law school to give little effect to nonbinding pronouncements. It is indeed strange that health care lawyers give more weight to the musings of OIG officials than to dicta in a Supreme Court decision.

## C. Impact of the Rules

The importance to be attached to fraud alerts, model compliance plans, and even the terms of out-of-court settlement agreements depends on the role of the health care lawyer in a particular situation. If the lawyer is advising a client about structuring a particular transaction or engaging in other future activities, the lawyer naturally will give substantial deference to these informal government pronouncements because they are helpful to the client that wishes to structure its activities as much as possible in accordance with the pronouncements even though they may not be legally binding. A client can hardly be accused of possessing wrongful intent if it has attempted to adhere not only to formal, legally binding government policies, such as formal regulations, but also to nonbinding pronouncements and interpretations. However, for the lawyer defending a client in a fraud and abuse investigation or action, the informal pronouncements should be challenged to the extent the enforcement agency is relying on an informal pronouncement in its investigation and potential prosecution.

A final comment on informal pronouncements and interpretations: arguably, although informal pronouncements and interpretations are not binding on the public, including members of the health care industry, such interpretations and pronouncements should be binding on a government agency. Thus, for example, when an enforcement agency is pursuing a False Claims Act investigation against a provider because a physician has used the Medicare billing number of another affiliated physician to bill for services, the issue may involve nothing more than

---

[74]*See, e.g.,* OIG Compliance Program Guidance for Hospitals, 63 Fed. Reg. 8987 (Feb. 23, 1998); OIG Compliance Program Guidance for Clinical Laboratories, 62 Fed. Reg. 9435 (Mar. 3, 1997), *as revised in* 63 Fed. Reg. 45,076 (Aug. 24, 1998); OIG Compliance Program Guidance for Home Health Agencies, 63 Fed. Reg. 42,410 (Aug. 7, 1998).

a technical violation of the Medicare provisions prohibiting reassignment of Medicare claims. Under a provision of a CMS manual, the violation of the reassignment rules in such a situation may not even give
rise to an overpayment. Thus, such an act can hardly be said to constitute a false claim.

## D. Private Party Interpretations, Practices, and Codes of Conduct

As enforcement agencies have become more aggressive and have
publicized their successful investigations and prosecutions, health care
lawyers and consultants have grown increasingly more conservative in
interpreting the governing law. For example, a scenario that is somewhat common in health care shows how health care policy making is
evolving. A government lawyer from the OIG responds to a question
from the audience at a seminar by relying on a recently issued OIG
fraud alert to opine that a particular practice could constitute fraudulent or abusive activity. Health care lawyers and media representatives attending this seminar publish the OIG lawyer's opinion in
subsequent newsletters and articles. When repeated often enough, the
OIG lawyer's opinion becomes virtually a new standard of conduct.

This characterization of health care fraud and abuse policy making is not merely anecdotal. Indeed, during the *Hanlester* administrative hearings, to try to support its position, the OIG relied on articles
written by private health care lawyers who quoted informal pronouncements and statements made by the OIG. Fortunately for the *Hanlester*
defendants, the HHS administrative law judge who heard the case was
aware of the authorities of law he was obligated to follow, which did not
include the OIG's "wish list" of prohibited activities.

Advice and opinions by private lawyers obviously are not the law.
However, as with reliance on informal government pronouncements
and interpretations, a client's reliance on a private lawyer's advice and
opinion regarding a particular activity may be very important in determining the intent element of an allegedly wrongful act.

The related issue of the relevance of widespread industry practice
is questionable. It is likely that every health care lawyer has heard that
a client undertook a particular action because everyone in the industry,
or perhaps more important, all of the client's competitors, are engaging
in the same practice. Although industry practices may be some evidence
of a standard of care, if the industry practice is illegal, the practice is still
illegal. However, as with reliance on informal government pronouncements and interpretations and reliance on the advice and opinions of
private counsel, reliance on industry practice may be relevant to the intent issue for a party involved in a health care fraud and abuse investigation or proceeding. This is particularly true when the defendant can
demonstrate that he or she relied not only on the industry practice itself but also on the government's knowledge of and acquiescence to the
practice. For example, when a laboratory is able to show that its billing

practices were known to and approved by the government's fiscal intermediary, the practices can hardly be characterized as false.[75]

Formalized industry standards, including ethical and other standards established by professional organizations and trade associations, also may be evidence of a standard of conduct. Most certainly, if a particular practice is considered to be ethical or consistent with the standards established by a professional organization or a trade association, such evidence is, at the very least, relevant to the intent element of a defense in a fraud and abuse case.

The *Hanlester* proceedings provide an example of the relevance of such standards.[76] The *Hanlester* defendants were able to establish that, during the period involved in that case, the AMA did not consider physician ownership in clinical laboratories to be unethical. They also pointed out that the legislative history supporting the Medicare/ Medicaid anti-kickback statute indicated that the statute was intended to prohibit wrongful acts of the type considered to be unethical by professional organizations. Thus, although the determination of whether a particular act is fraudulent or abusive should not depend on questions of ethics, the fact that the act being scrutinized is consistent with the ethical standards of the profession may be important.

## VI. Government Investigatory Strategies

### A. Overview

Health care fraud and abuse enforcement agencies typically conduct investigations using a variety of tools to obtain information. Although some tactics are common, other tools available vary according to the severity of the suspected fraud and abuse. For example, if criminal conduct is suspected, the government may seek a search warrant to inspect and seize records and other documents (or even an arrest warrant).

To obtain a search warrant, the enforcement agency seeking the warrant must involve either a court or grand jury. However, under Section 248 of HIPAA, DOJ attorneys may now issue investigative demands, in the form of subpoenas duces tecum, to obtain information without convening a grand jury or requesting permission from a judge.[77] Although this process does not have the force and effect of a search warrant, federal attorneys are now using it to conduct preliminary investigations in cases in which there is no need for a search warrant.

In addition to the criminal processes described above, government enforcement agencies have available a variety of other mechanisms to obtain information for an investigation. For example, the HHS OIG often issues subpoenas for information. In False Claims Act investiga-

---

[75] *See* California v. Duz-Mor Diagnostic Lab., 68 Cal. App. 4th 654, 672–73 (1998).

[76] Hanlester Network v. Shalala, 51 F.3d 1390 (9th Cir. 1995).

[77] Pub. L. No. 104-191, §248, *codified* at 18 U.S.C. §3486.

tions, in addition to having subpoena authority, U.S. attorneys have the ability to issue civil investigatory demands, which enable them to depose potential witnesses in an investigation in which a *qui tam* complaint has not yet been unsealed.[78]

Moreover, because health care is a regulated business, government regulators generally are permitted to inspect health care facilities and the offices of health care practitioners during reasonable business hours without obtaining any special permission or using any special investigatory instrument. Generally, Medicare, Medicaid, and other government and private third-party payers require providers to agree to make records and other information available as a condition of program participation.[79] Government payers, including Medicare, may impose substantial penalties on a provider that refuses to cooperate with a request for an inspection or review of records.

## B. Enforcement Agency Interviews

Generally, most government interviews in health care fraud and abuse investigations are conducted informally. Although the government has procedures available to compel the testimony of a particular person under particular circumstances, the government seldom is required to resort to those procedures. Thus, persons generally are free to choose not to be interviewed by enforcement agents. However, in the health care field, persons are reluctant to refuse to be interviewed by government officials and, thus, often willingly agree to talk with investigating agents. Health care personnel are accustomed to assisting government regulators and might not wish to appear defensive. Of course, potential targets of possible criminal investigations cannot be compelled to testify because of the privilege against self-incrimination under the Fifth Amendment.

The informal interview process can be filled with risk and potential negative consequences. Just as compliance programs have become standard in the health care industry, regularly advising employees of the possibility of government investigations should also be a standard business practice. Employees should be advised that they might be contacted during nonworking hours by government enforcement agents and investigators who will ask them questions about their jobs and their employer's business practices. Employees should be informed that they may request identification from the investigator and that although they have the right to speak to an investigator, they also have the right not to speak or to speak with the investigator at a different time. Moreover, they have the right to have counsel or other persons present during the interview.

Experience shows that the presence of counsel at interviews helps to ensure the accuracy of the subsequently developed investigative re-

---

[78] 31 U.S.C. §3733.
[79] 42 C.F.R. §489.53.

port. Thus, to the extent possible, defense counsel should attempt to be present at all interviews conducted during an investigation. Additionally, it is good practice to conduct such interviews at a neutral location. Interviews at a person's place of employment can be disruptive and embarrassing, whereas interviews at government agents' offices can be intimidating.

Interviews generally are not tape recorded by investigators, although interviews may be recorded with the permission of the agent. Instead, the investigator takes notes of the interview and ultimately prepares investigatory reports including information from the interview. The investigatory reports contain the impressions of the investigator rather than a verbatim record of the discussion that actually occurred. Because interview reports typically are not shown to interviewees immediately after their interviews, they may not be a reliable means of refreshing the memories of those persons interviewed. However, these reports often are used for that purpose by the government. Thus, it is important that the interviewee and other persons present during an interview take notes of the discussion or be debriefed regarding the details of the interview if no one other than the interviewee and the investigator were present at the interview.

Without such record, contemporaneous notes, or a debriefing, an interviewee who becomes a witness may rely inappropriately on the possibly unfounded impressions of the investigator. As a result, an interviewee's subsequent testimony based on the investigator's written interview report may be very different from the actual discussion that occurred during the original interview itself.

Enforcement agencies conduct extensive interviews with disgruntled employees and competitors and other persons who may have reason to be hostile toward a provider under investigation. Under those circumstances, it is unusual for defense counsel to be present during such interviews. As a result, a party under investigation may not know the substance of such interviews until actual proceedings begin.

In addition to being excluded from interviews of disgruntled employees and competitors, a party under investigation also will probably not be present during government interviews of patients and their families, who enforcement agencies are now actively interviewing in connection with investigations. This absence from interviews of patients, especially very elderly, confused, or incompetent patients, may be extremely prejudicial to a provider. Counsel must explore the circumstances surrounding such interviews if an enforcement agency intends to rely heavily on them in making investigatory findings. For example, it is not unusual for a patient to believe that a particular procedure, such as one of several laboratory tests, was not performed when, in fact, the procedure actually was performed.

Unfortunately, government investigators are not always fair or truthful. Indeed, when examined about investigatory techniques during the *Hanlester* proceedings, the OIG investigator who had conducted various interviews in that case admitted during the administrative hearing that she had made statements during interviews that were not completely accurate. She indicated that she was trained to use misstatements as an investigatory technique "to obtain the truth." For example, the OIG investigator began some interviews by asking the interviewee whether he or she would be "surprised" if the investigator had a tape recording of the interviewee's previous unspecified conversations. The investigator admitted that she asked this question even though she did not have such tape recordings because she had been taught that this technique helps to ensure the truthfulness of the content of the interview.

Investigators might also respond to a proposed interviewee's inquiry about the need for an attorney to be present during an interview by indicating that an attorney is only necessary if the interviewee has something "to worry about." Investigators might also inform interviewees that they are not the focus of the government's investigation when, in fact, an interviewee later becomes the target of an enforcement action.

It appears that aggressive investigators will use virtually any tactic short of physical intimidation to further their investigation. And, when they have a preconceived notion of the results of the investigation, those methods can border on coercion. For example, in the false claims action of *United States v. Mackby*,[80] the target of a fraud and abuse investigation reported that his own father was told not to talk to him about the father's interview with the investigator.

In some cases, interviews also may be used as the bases for seeking search warrants. When an investigator's impressions of an interview are biased or clearly inconsistent with the truth of the interview, improper consequences may follow. For example, in a state Medicaid fraud investigation, a state police officer relied almost exclusively on a misstatement of a state surveyor to obtain a search warrant to conduct an unjustified search of a laboratory owner's home.

These types of abuses will continue so long as health care enforcement agencies reward overzealous investigators and take no adverse actions against investigators who act inappropriately or dishonestly. The safeguards embodied in the system, such as the requirement that a magistrate issue a search warrant only if there is probable cause to believe a crime has occurred, are effective only if government enforcement agents act in good faith.

## C. Document Production

Most health care fraud and abuse investigations depend heavily on documentary evidence. As discussed in Section VI.A., above, enforcement agencies have a variety of procedures available to compel the production of documents, including computerized information and data. Given the broad enforcement authority delegated to agencies such as

---

[80] 261 F.3d 821 (9th Cir. 2001).

the OIG, challenging such authority may not be the best use of legal resources. With rare exceptions, courts will confirm the authority of enforcement agencies to compel the production of documents.

However, because the government has such general authority does not mean that there can be no limits on document requests. For example, if documents are seized pursuant to a valid search warrant, the warrant must define with some precision the scope of the documents that may be seized. Additionally, statutory and common law protections, such as attorney–client privilege, protect many documents from being produced. Yet, it is not uncommon for privileged documents to be seized during a search. Therefore, as a standard business practice, privileged documents should be maintained separately from nonprivileged documents if possible.

A practical comment regarding the seizure of documents, including computer information: The seizure of such documents can devastate a health care provider's continuing operations. Thus, a provider is not being overly cautious if it retains duplicates of important documents at an off-site location. Although enforcement agencies typically allow a party eventual access to documents seized pursuant to a search warrant, it is often extremely inconvenient to obtain copies of such documents in a timely and convenient manner.

When search warrants are not used to obtain documents, there typically is more flexibility. For example, absent unusual circumstances (such as when the government suspects potential altering of documents), copies of documents ordinarily are acceptable to an investigating agency. The attorneys for most government enforcement agencies also are willing to discuss reasonable requests to narrow the scope of documents requested. Furthermore, although subpoenas typically provide for a relatively short return period, extensions are routine. Staggered production of documents often is permitted.

Defense counsel should exercise the same degree of care regarding document production that would be used in responding to any investigation by a government enforcement agency. For example, because the information requested and produced may contain trade secrets, it is appropriate to identify and label such documents as "trade secrets" so the documents are not inadvertently released inappropriately.

## VII. RESPONDING TO AN INVESTIGATION

### A. Understanding the Government's Interests

Government agencies at all levels are convinced that fraud and abuse are widespread in the health care industry.[81] Presently, little can

---

[81] According to government statistics, 10% of every health care dollar spent is wasted on fraud and abuse. *See* Pamela H. Bucy, *Health Care Reform and Fraud by Health Care Providers*, 38 VILL. L. REV. 1003 (1993) (citing PROSPECTIVE PAYMENT ASSESSMENT COMM'N, REPORT AND RECOMMENDATION TO THE CONGRESS 15 (1993)).

be done to convince them otherwise. However, counsel's knowing and responding to the goals and interests of the various enforcement agencies may assist clients.

Government investigations are undertaken with cost–benefit goals in mind. For example, HHS has indicated that the Operation Restore Trust antifraud program collected $23 for every $1 spent.[82] Not surprisingly, the government wants to get the most for its money. Thus, the more expensive an investigation, the greater the return the government expects. Therefore, if after assessing the facts and the law applicable to a particular situation, defense counsel believes that liability exists, it may be unwise to require the government to incur substantial additional costs that may be avoided through cooperative fact-finding.

Other factors motivating government enforcement agencies are more political. For example, the OIG may have an interest in demonstrating that CMS or the Medicare fiscal intermediaries or carriers are not adequately enforcing the governing payment principles in a particular area. The OIG has issued numerous reports critical of CMS's administration of the Medicare and Medicaid programs.[83] This criticism has not been overlooked by CMS. The resulting interagency tension may provide positive opportunities to defense counsel under appropriate circumstances. For example, because many fraud and abuse investigations are based on complicated Medicare and Medicaid rules that are being interpreted for the first time by the government enforcement agencies, knowledgeable CMS employees may be an important source of unbiased, independent information that may be important to present to the lawyer for the enforcement agency.

The political issue is also important in state and local matters. For example, a state attorney general or state insurance commissioner may have political reasons to discredit other state officials charged with the administration of Medicaid or another health care program. Thus, if an enforcement agency headed by a political foe of the head of the agency charged with administering the state health care program becomes overly aggressive, the latter agency may have a motive for agreeing with the position being advocated by defense counsel to deter the overly aggressive enforcement agency.[84]

## B. Communicating With Enforcement Agents and Their Attorneys

As with many areas of the law, one of the most important assets of an effective health care defense attorney is his or her credibility with

---

[82] *See* Office of Inspector Gen., U.S. Dep't of Health & Human Servs., SEMIANNUAL REPORT, OCT. 1, 1994–MAR. 21, 1995, at 23 (1995).

[83] *See, e.g.*, Office of Inspector Gen., U.S. Dep't of Health & Human Servs., Audit of HCFA's FY 1997 Financial Statements (1998).

[84] The controller of the state of California, a Democrat, repeatedly criticized the enforcement practices of the former state attorney general, a Republican, in the 1990s.

the opposing party. This is particularly true of the health care industry, in which government regulators must continue to interact with clients even after an investigation is over. If the regulators or their attorneys decide that defense counsel's representations cannot be relied on, the negotiation process (and even the litigation process) can be damaged, to the detriment of the client.

Civility is almost as important as credibility. Although a client may obtain temporary satisfaction from an attorney's outburst at the government's lawyer, little is achieved in the long run. Notwithstanding the anxiety and hostility engendered by an investigation, defense counsel does little to advance the client's cause by insulting or attempting to intimidate enforcement agency employees and their attorneys. Indeed, rather than helping the client, inappropriate tactics can injure the client in the long run.

However, lack of courtesy, consideration, or manners should not be confused with the aggressive representation of a client's case. A favorable settlement or litigation outcome cannot be expected unless the enforcement agency knows the defendant's counsel will use all ethical tactics available to protect his or her client.

## C. Explaining the Client's Position

An unfortunate consequence of the ongoing crackdown on health care fraud and abuse is that persons unfamiliar with health care laws, regulations, practices, and procedures sometimes are given substantial authority to make critical decisions. Not surprisingly, these persons are not always equipped to make those determinations. For example, many government lawyers, without any health care experience, must rely on investigators who also may have very little, if any, health care experience to assess allegedly suspicious circumstances.

The health care industry is not analogous to the defense industry or the savings and loan industry. Many issues in health care do not lend themselves to clear-cut answers. For example, issues of medical necessity involve subjective judgments for which there might be no "true" answer. However, government enforcement agency lawyers and investigators commonly view the health care industry as being the same as other industries and are predisposed to be skeptical of pleas of good-faith confusion or misunderstanding as possible defenses to alleged acts of fraud or abuse.

Health care lawyers can play an important role in educating government attorneys and investigators about the rules and practicalities governing health care. For example, they can place perceived problems in their proper context for government enforcement agency lawyers and investigators to avoid automatic adverse reactions. Means for doing so include submitting position papers and using outside consultants and even persons within CMS or other health care regulators to help educate the government representatives.

## D. Position Papers

Preparing position papers during the investigatory stages of a fraud and abuse case serves not only to communicate the client's position to the government but also to prepare the lawyer for further proceedings. Such documents set forth the facts, policies, and laws that might be favorable to the client. Of course, the preparation process works both ways: Not only does it prepare the client's attorneys, it also alerts the government's attorneys and investigators to the strategies that ultimately may be used if the investigation is not settled short of formal proceedings. Nevertheless, on balance, the advantages of submitting position papers generally outweigh the disadvantages. Almost without exception, government attorneys are very receptive to position papers.

As with other communications, credibility is critical in the preparation of position papers. Overstating or misrepresenting the facts or the law may be overlooked temporarily, but ultimately the true facts will surface, and damaged credibility is difficult to repair.

## E. The Context Concept

Using position papers and other communications to place suspect practices in the appropriate context and perspective is imperative. For example, enforcement agencies recently have been characterizing some quality-of-care issues as areas of potential fraud and abuse. For example, at seminars, enforcement officials graphically portray, through slide presentations, evidence of nursing home care that appears so poor that billing for the services could arguably constitute a false claim.

Most individuals who have represented providers of skilled nursing facility services have encountered instances in which the delivery of care at a facility is below minimum standards. Existing enforcement mechanisms are in place to remedy these serious problems. However, it is also a very sad fact that elderly patients admitted to nursing facilities often spend the remainder of their lives at those facilities. Sometimes, during the end stage of a disease, symptoms are present that would be distasteful to anyone when viewed outside of the context of the nursing facility. As systems begin to fail before a person's death, the body begins to deteriorate rapidly, and, even with the best of care, the last days of a patient's life may be unpleasant.

In a Los Angeles County coroner's inquest of several years ago, the coroner examined a 102-year-old nursing facility patient who had developed decubitus (bedsores) that rapidly deteriorated in degree, requiring debridement. When a Stage III or Stage IV decubitus is debrided, the resulting open sore is painfully ugly. For a patient with debrided decubitus who is 102 years old and whose life systems are failing, the result can be deadly, as was the case with this patient. Yet, the fact that the patient died with Stage IV decubitus did not automatically reflect poor care. To the contrary, the evidence at the coroner's inquest showed that the care furnished to the patient before death was more than adequate. Thus, the death was deemed to be accidental rather than death at the hands of another. However, if this episode had been taken out of context and if photographs of the patient had been circulated, there is little doubt that one could conclude that subquality care was given.

Another relatively common example of allegedly deficient care at a nursing facility occurs when medications are given to patients without physician orders. When considered in the abstract, this allegation appears to be extremely serious. Indeed, it can evoke visions of ill-intentioned nurses drugging recalcitrant patients to control them. However, when placed in context, this allegation may mean no more than that after a patient's longstanding renewed orders for a certain medication had expired without the facility obtaining a signed order renewing the prescription on a particular date, the medicine was nevertheless given to the patient by the attending nurse. This can happen in the best of facilities, and it may occur because the patient's physician has either failed to visit the patient on a timely basis or simply overlooked signing a telephone order for the medication. Surveyors might cite the facility for "medications being given without orders," which, although literally true, may not accurately describe the situation. When placed in its proper context, the decision to provide the medication without a signed order was probably neither wrongful nor harmful. Although the "letter of the law" might have required the facility to cease giving the medication until a signed order was obtained, the absence of a signed order should not result in the facility being denied payment for the services provided. In fact, *not* administering a medication might have resulted in harm to the patient.

Financial issues also must be placed in their appropriate context. Giving enforcement lawyers and investigators an overview of the background and circumstances surrounding a perceived problem can be very beneficial for a client. For example, as indicated earlier, marketing and advertising costs are now being scrutinized closely by enforcement agencies, which often come to the unfounded conclusion that such costs should not be reimbursed by the government under a cost-based reimbursement system. However, there is a substantial history of such costs being considered necessary indirect costs of patient care.

Another example of an issue pursued by enforcement agencies out of its proper context is a hospital or other health care provider's claims for losses on the sale of depreciable assets under the reasonable-cost reimbursement system. In 1997, government enforcement agencies indicated their skepticism about the validity of Medicare reimbursement for substantial losses that were occurring on the sale of facilities. This investigatory concern clearly was spurred by an increase in Medicare reimbursement for losses claimed by providers following the disposal of health care assets.[85]

---

[85] *See OIG Report: Medicare Losses on Hospital Sales*, MEDICARE & MEDICAID GUIDE (CCH) ¶45,444 [1997-2].

Although such sales and the corresponding losses may have increased Medicare expenditures, the Medicare rules allowing losses on the bona fide disposal of hospitals and their assets have existed since the beginning of the Medicare program.[86] Indeed, when it was more typical of assets to be sold for a profit, as was the situation in the majority of cases until relatively recently, the government applied those rules to recapture excessive depreciation paid for past years based on the gain on sale. The very same regulations that allowed the government to recapture depreciation for a gain on sale required the government to share in the additional reimbursement owed a provider when assets were sold at a loss. If such losses are perceived by policy makers to be a problem, the remedy is legislation, not prosecution. Indeed, in 1997 Congress legislated away gains and losses on sales of depreciable health care assets.[87]

Another example of the need to place suspicious facts in the appropriate context so as to enable the government to respond appropriately is the pervasive misconception that independent clinical laboratories essentially dictate the laboratory tests ordered by physicians for Medicare, Medicaid, and other government patients. According to national investigations, such as the National Health Laboratories investigation, the government believes that laboratory marketing employees, at the direction of the laboratory owners, arbitrarily add unnecessary tests to the menu of laboratory tests on requisition sheets supplied to physicians to "trick" them into ordering excessive laboratory testing for their patients.[88] For example, the government accused National Health Laboratories of surreptitiously adding ferritin testing to the laboratory requisition sheets of their client physicians without informing the physicians that when a laboratory profile containing ferritin was ordered the laboratory would perform the ferritin test and bill separately for it.

Regardless of the merits of the government's position and suspicions in general, it does not necessarily follow that the routine ordering of ferritin testing is always an unlawful ploy by laboratories to increase Medicare and other payer revenues through the delivery of medically unnecessary laboratory testing. For example, patients suffering from ESRD have chronic health care problems that often include anemia. Thus, ferritin testing for these patients on a regular basis is medically necessary under virtually any definition of the term. Therefore, for ESRD patients, the routine ordering of ferritin testing may be very appropriate.

---

[86] See 42 C.F.R. §413.134 and its predecessor, 42 C.F.R. §405.415 (1970).

[87] *See* Balanced Budget Act of 1997, Pub. L. No. 105-33, §4404(a), 111 Stat. 251, *codified at* 42 U.S.C. §1395x(v)(1)(O).

[88] Press Release, Dep't of Justice, NHL Will Pay $100 Million to Settle Longest Fraud Case Ever (Dec. 18, 1992).

## F. Explaining Industry Terms and Practices

In addition to placing events and actions in context, it also may prove helpful to interpret and explain common terms or jargon used by health care providers that may cause unnecessary suspicion. As in other industries, members of the health care industry often use terms or phrases that, when taken out of context, may sound suspicious.

An example that became known in one FBI investigation was the use of the term "back office." Physicians often refer to the "front office" and the "back office" of their premises to distinguish office administrative activities occurring in or near the waiting room area from bookkeeping and other activities that are performed elsewhere in the facility. However, when an investigating agent obtains an internal memo that refers to adjustments to the physician's financial records to be made in the "back office," suspicion can arise.

Mistaken interpretations of dialects and foreign languages can be made by investigating agents. Wiretapped telephone conversations have been translated incorrectly, causing substantial unjustified harm to persons being investigated. Defendants who are members of ethnic minorities are especially vulnerable to such mistakes in interpretation or translation.

Additionally, just as members of the health care industry are not experts in law enforcement, law enforcement employees are not experts in health care. Enforcement agencies thus may be unnecessarily troubled by the application of common business practices to the delivery of health care, even though the industry has been encouraged by the government to be more businesslike to try to lower costs and increase competition. This fact became obvious in the *Hanlester* proceedings.

Although the Hanlester Network Laboratories were established when the Reagan administration was encouraging competition in the health care industry, the enforcement agency in that case, the HHS OIG, characterized many of the business practices used by the Hanlester Network as improper. An important example was the government's criticism of the Hanlester Network's practice of monitoring the referral patterns of physicians who used the Hanlester Network Laboratories. When laboratory usage decreased for a particular physician, the Hanlester Network's medical director was instructed to contact the physician to discuss why usage had decreased. The OIG concluded that such contacts, in and of themselves, were unlawful attempts to interfere with the referring physicians' medical judgment by forcing them to order more tests than they believed to be medically necessary.

However, at the administrative hearing, it became obvious that there were legitimate reasons why the laboratory medical director contacted physicians when their laboratory usage decreased. For example, if usage had decreased because a physician became dissatisfied with the service he or she was receiving from the laboratory, the contact by the medical director was believed to be a good method for trying to resolve the problem. Ironically, the OIG's model compliance guidelines for independent clinical laboratories now require independent clinical laboratories to monitor the ordering of laboratory services by physicians.[89] Yet, in *Hanlester*, this practice was considered to be suspect, and evidence of illegal kickback activity.

Enforcement agency lawyers and investigators must be made aware that the health care industry is competitive and there is nothing unlawful or immoral about using common business practices to compete effectively. Although there is little case law in the area, one aspect of the decision of the U.S. Court of Appeals for the Ninth Circuit in *Hanlester* that often is overlooked is the court's conclusion that Hanlester Network's practice of encouraging physicians, including physician owners, to use Hanlester Network Laboratories was *not* unlawful.[90]

## VIII. Impact of Investigations

### A. Timing

Members of the health care industry are extremely troubled by the disruption caused by the length and breadth of health care fraud and abuse investigations. Because of the nature of its role in serving the public, the health care industry is particularly sensitive to adverse publicity, and an investigation alone may be enough to destroy a health care provider. For example, in the *Hanlester* case, shortly after the government had begun its investigation of the three Hanlester Network laboratories, there was so much fear and apprehension on the part of referring physicians that the laboratories essentially went out of business.

Fairness requires that internal guidelines or legislation be developed to establish deadlines for the completion of health care fraud and abuse investigations. The statute of limitation periods that exist (e.g., 6 years to initiate a false claims action, which may be extended up to 10 years under certain circumstances) simply do not provide a sufficient safeguard.

### B. Publicity

Health care lawyers disagree regarding the amount of information that should be shared with employees of a health care provider under investigation for fraud and abuse. Some believe that the dissemination of information should be carefully controlled among a very small group of persons within the organization. Others believe that virtually all employees should be made aware of an ongoing investigation so they will not be surprised if they are asked to be interviewed by a government investigator one evening when they return home from work.

---

[89] OIG Compliance Program Guidance for Clinical Laboratories, 62 Fed. Reg. 9435 (Mar. 3, 1997), *as revised in* 63 Fed. Reg. 45,076 (Aug. 24, 1998).

[90] Hanlester Network v. Shalala, 51 F.3d 1390, 1398 (9th Cir. 1995).

The fact is, once a full-fledged investigation is under way, there is very little that can be gained from attempting to limit all information about the investigation to select employees. The rumors and innuendos that will circulate as part of normal office gossip may be much worse than the reality. Thus, the better practice is to inform employees of the existence of the investigation without speculating about the details or disclosing privileged information. Owners and shareholders also must be informed. And, of course, public company disclosure requirements also must be adhered to carefully.

Controlling publicity outside of the organization is difficult. Although the official policy of enforcement agencies generally prohibits comments on an ongoing investigation, word of such investigations often becomes public. The health care media may become aware of an investigation even before the general media.

There is not a great deal that can be done to respond to the publicity generated by a health care fraud and abuse investigation. Typically, statements such as "The company intends to cooperate fully in the investigation" are issued. Some parties prefer to take a more active role with the media. Although such an approach may be therapeutic, it is important to remember that media outlets are in business to sell their products or generate advertising dollars, not necessarily to tell the truth or even to present a balanced story.

One tool that has been used successfully in some cases is the press release. Press releases typically are not edited as much as interviews. However, if a health care provider wishes to avoid the possible negative consequences of editing, the provider should consider purchasing advertising space, as advertisements generally are not subject to editorial changes or comments.

## C. Effect on Business

The publicity from an investigation not only has an effect on the public and the employees of a health care provider but, more important, it also has an effect on the provider's customers. If the provider is an independent clinical laboratory, for example, its primary customers are referring physicians. Obviously, referring physicians may be reluctant to use a laboratory that is under suspicion of fraudulent or abusive practices. Similarly, patients naturally become wary when their local hospital or physician is under investigation. Potential merger partners and investors are affected as well.

Competitors who learn of an investigation may use that information to attempt to gain a competitive advantage. For example, in the highly competitive laboratory industry, marketers commonly mention the existence of investigations to physicians they are pursuing as customers. If a provider believes that negative statements are being circulated by competitors, efforts should be made to inform customers of the truth and, if necessary, to discourage competitors from making untrue statements. In extreme situations, lawsuits for trade libel, for example, may be an effective remedy.

In short, investigations present a substantial public relations challenge. Inevitably, an investigation will injure a provider. However, an investigation need not destroy a provider's business. Indeed, some companies, such as Tenet Healthcare (formerly known as National Medical Enterprises), have used the investigation process as a tool to create a state-of-the-art compliance program.

## D. Cash Flow Consequences

In addition to the consequences of investigations discussed above, the government has authority to affect payments (e.g., temporary suspension of payments or exclusion) made to a provider being investigated for fraud or abuse. When the government has reliable evidence that fraud or abuse has occurred, Medicare and Medicaid payments may be temporarily withheld pending the outcome of the investigation. This authority is not without limits, however. The government is not allowed to withhold as much money as it likes for as long as it likes. Rather, there are certain minimal procedural requirements that are afforded a provider under investigation.[91] Nevertheless, any withholding can cause significant disruption to the operations of a provider that is substantially dependent on Medicare and Medicaid revenues.

If the government threatens such withholding, the lawyer for the provider should make certain that the procedural requirements of the regulations are strictly followed. Additionally, there may be ways the provider can satisfy the government's questions and concerns about the potential for recovering any overpayments. Such tactics may affect the government's decision regarding withholding of payments. For example, offering to provide the government with a letter of credit could satisfy the government's concerns in some situations.

## IX. Settlement Considerations

Many more health care fraud and abuse investigations are settled than litigated. While published statistics do not appear to exist, trials are relatively rare. The substantial array of remedies available to the government if it is successful in litigation creates a powerful incentive for a provider to settle a dispute short of litigation. Obviously, the decision to settle depends on the unique facts of each case. Moreover, the terms of a settlement vary with the circumstances of the specific case. However, there are some common considerations, which are discussed in more detail below.

## A. Collateral Consequences

The collateral consequences of settling a health care fraud and abuse case can be significant. For example, if a party settles a state health care fraud and abuse investigation by pleading "no contest" to a

---

[91]*See, e.g.*, 42 C.F.R. §§455.23, 405.371.

misdemeanor count of paying a kickback to obtain health care services, the provider may receive a fairly light criminal sentence, such as a minimal fine and a minimal period of probation. However, the consequences of the no contest plea are nevertheless substantial and far-reaching.

First, the no contest plea to a one-count misdemeanor involving health care fraud and abuse will automatically cause the provider to be excluded from the Medicare, Medicaid, and other state and federal health care programs for a minimum of 5 years.[92] Such program exclusion prevents the provider or any future employer of the provider from billing such government programs for any services delivered by the excluded provider. Because most health care providers are extremely dependent on revenues from government payers, this automatic exclusion is thus a very significant collateral consequence of a plea agreement.

In addition, the provider's professional license likely will be subject to discipline under most state laws.[93] As with Medicare and Medicaid program exclusion, a no contest plea is treated the same as a guilty plea and conviction under most state professional licensing statutes. The relevant licensing authorities can be expected to take action against the provider's professional license some time after the court disposes of the criminal settlement.

There are a variety of other practical consequences that may result from a no contest plea. For example, if the provider is a physician, he or she may be subject to disclosure requirements that could affect his or her medical staff privileges, private third-party payer contracts, independent practice association arrangements, and even his or her malpractice insurance coverage.

## B. Binding the Government

When settlement is contemplated, the attorney for the defendant must try to bind as many government agencies as possible through the terms of the settlement agreement. For example, if the U.S. Attorney's Office is contemplating a federal False Claims Act action based on the facts of an investigation, the attorney for the provider being investigated should attempt to reach agreement with the civil and criminal sections of the U.S. Attorney's Office or DOJ and with the Medicaid Fraud Control Unit of any state in which the provider performs services. The OIG and other federal payers, such as the Tricare program, also should be bound by the terms of the settlement agreement. Unless bound, the OIG could initiate exclusion proceedings or seek civil monetary penalties through the administrative process based on the same facts that gave rise to the settlement with the U.S. Attorney's Office.

It is virtually impossible, as a practical matter, to bind all potential enforcement agencies and regulators when settling a dispute over a particular set of facts. However, the inability to bind every possible

---

[92] 42 U.S.C. §1320a-7(a)(3).

[93] CAL. BUS. & PROF. CODE §2236.

future prosecutor or regulator should not stop a party from settling if the major enforcement agencies have agreed to be parties to the settlement. Indeed, the argument can be made that a state attorney general signing a settlement agreement on behalf of the state Medicaid Fraud Control Unit binds a local district attorney in the same state.

In addition to binding as many parties to a settlement as possible, there are other techniques to minimize the collateral consequences of settlements. For example, in the hypothetical situation above, if the corporate entity, rather than the individual owner of the corporate entity pleaded no contest to a misdemeanor, only the corporate entity would automatically be excluded from the Medicare and Medicaid programs. Although the owner arguably may be subject to a permissive exclusion proceeding, the likelihood of that occurring can be reduced by having the appropriate government agencies provide in the settlement agreement that no permissive exclusion will be pursued.

## C. Settlement Goals

The exact terms of a settlement will vary depending on the bargaining positions of the government and the provider under investigation. Early on in the settlement negotiations, the government should be able to disclose whether one of its goals is to force the provider out of business. If the government does not have as its goal the termination of the business or practice of the provider under investigation, the terms of the settlement can help to ensure the provider's continued viability.

Although most government demand letters threaten staggering financial remedies and penalties, the enforcement agencies are practical enough to know that a provider's ability to pay is a significant factor in determining the ultimate financial terms of a settlement agreement. Thus, not only should the lawyer for the provider focus on rationalizing the client's behavior, but he or she also should address the client's ability to satisfy the government's financial demands. In short, even if the enforcement agency could clearly prove allegations that would give rise to a judgment involving tens of millions of dollars, it would be foolish for the government to reject a settlement proposal that included an admission of wrongdoing simply because the settling party was unable to pay the requested tens of millions of dollars.

In this regard, there are various ways to structure a settlement so that payment of the settlement amount does not force the provider into bankruptcy, such as providing for installment payments over time. However, the government will want to be secure about its ability to collect settlement payments from the settling party if terms other than immediate payment are agreed to. For example, the government may insist on settlement terms that protect it in the event of a provider's subsequent bankruptcy.

The government's primary goal in a particular case may be deterrence. It may want to send a message to the industry. Recognizing this goal, a settling party may be able to minimize other consequences of a settlement by agreeing to stop practices that are the government's targets at the time.

Just as the investigation process is lengthy (e.g., investigations can drag on for years), so too is the settlement process. Settling a health care fraud and abuse case may result in a party's actually incurring more time and higher expenses than litigating. However, considerations such as adverse publicity may dictate against litigation.

## D. Life After a Settlement

One of the most important matters that often is not fully appreciated by a party to a settlement agreement is that the party must be able to live with the terms of the settlement agreement long after the anxiety created by the investigation has passed. Thus, although a party to a settlement agreement may be willing to stop engaging in various activities and practices to reach settlement, ceasing such practices and activities may ultimately incapacitate the health care provider. Moreover, typically, the terms of a settlement agreement are required to be binding on the successors and assigns of the party. A settlement agreement with onerous terms may make it extremely difficult to sell a company.

As part of most settlement agreements, the private party is required to implement a corporate integrity agreement containing specific requirements that otherwise might not be binding on the provider. For example, third-party consultants may have to be hired to review billing practices. The terms and conditions of an integrity agreement will typically require substantial expenditures for ongoing monitoring activities and staffing (e.g., a compliance officer must be hired, and compliance policies and procedures established).[94]

On the other hand, the terms of the settlement agreement and any accompanying integrity program may be used to the settling party's advantage by specifically defining those practices that the enforcement agency considers to be appropriate. Therefore, from a public relations standpoint, customers of the settling provider can be assured that the practices engaged in by the settling party are appropriate, because they have been "blessed" by the government. This could give the customers of the settling party comfort that they otherwise might not have when doing business with a competitor.

## X. Litigation Defense Strategies

### A. Importance of the Fundamentals

As discussed previously, health care fraud and abuse enforcement agencies have a range of remedies that can apply in a variety of settings

---

[94]*See* Barbara Frederickson, *Corporate Integrity Agreements Impose Additional Obligations on Providers*, 1 J. Health Care Compliance 26–27 (1999). For a detailed discussion of corporate integrity agreements, see Chapter 7, at Section III.C. (Jones *et al.*, Corporate Compliance Programs).

against a provider accused of fraud and abuse. For example, numerous criminal acts (e.g., making false statements) can be prosecuted in federal and state courts. Civil actions, such as civil false claims proceedings, also may be pursued in both federal and state courts. Additionally, administrative remedies, such as exclusion proceedings and the imposition of civil monetary penalties, may be sought through administrative proceedings.

Although different substantive and procedural rules are applicable to the various remedies in different settings, health care fraud and abuse cases generally require the government to prove that a wrongful act has been committed by someone with a wrongful intent. Surprisingly, these two fundamental elements are overlooked in many cases.

### 1. Necessity of Prohibited Act or Omission

Significantly, the law governing the health care industry, like the law governing other industries or areas, is contained in federal and state statutes and duly enacted agency regulations. The law is not made by administrative agencies through the issuance of informal guidelines or by enforcement agencies through the issuance of model compliance programs or fraud alerts. Nor is the law established through the terms and provisions of settlement agreements between health care organizations and the government. And, most definitely, the law is not created by statements made by government enforcement officers at seminars and by health care lawyers repeating those statements. Notwithstanding these facts, it is common for government enforcement agencies to base investigations and potential prosecutions on alleged violations of Medicare intermediary letters, bulletins, and other informal guidelines.

The starting point for any defense strategy must be an analysis of the statutes and regulations governing the activity and practices under investigation. If it is determined that the government is relying on a guideline published in a Medicare manual or bulletin, an initial analysis of the statutory and regulatory authority for the guideline is mandatory. It is possible that the guideline that the government contends has been violated lacks statutory or regulatory support. In such a situation, it is questionable whether the conduct that violates the guideline can be considered to be prohibited by the law.[95]

Of course, not only must a guideline be authorized by an agency's enabling statute and regulations, but it also must be written clearly enough to give adequate notice to members of the health care industry. Ambiguous guidelines, like ambiguous regulations and statutes, cannot be used as the basis for a successful health care fraud or abuse prosecution. Thus, a Medicaid "Bulletin" that is vague about the grouping of laboratory tests for billing purposes may not support a false claims action.[96]

---

[95] It is fundamental that an administrative agency guideline must be consistent with the agency's enabling statutes and formal regulations. *See, e.g.,* National Med. Enters. v. Bowen, 851 F.2d 291 (9th Cir. 1988).

[96] *See* California v. Duz-More Diagnostic Lab., 68 Cal. App. 4th 654 (1998).

## 2. Necessity of Wrongful Intent

Almost without exception, some form of scienter or wrongful intent must be established before any adverse action can be taken against a defendant. For example, although there is ongoing debate over the nature of the intent required to violate the federal anti-kickback statute, it generally is agreed that some wrongful intent is required. The intent requirement serves the very important purpose of protecting persons from being punished or sanctioned for innocent acts and omissions. Although much emphasis is placed by enforcement agencies on prohibited acts or omissions, little attention is paid to the mental state necessary to constitute a violation of the law for purposes of imposing some form of remedy or penalty.

When an act or omission is not inherently nefarious, which may often be the case in a health care fraud and abuse situation, common law and statutory law ordinarily require the government to prove some type of wrongful intent before any substantial penalty or sanction may be imposed. For example, in *Hanlester*, where there was nothing inherently nefarious about the clinical laboratory making profit distributions to the laboratory owners on the basis of their ownership percentages, the government was required to prove wrongful intent before the profit distributions could be said to constitute prohibited kickbacks under the federal Medicare/Medicaid anti-kickback statute. Under the Ninth Circuit's decision in *Hanlester*, the wrongful intent required to be proven was that the defendants knew what they were doing and that what they did violated the anti-kickback statute. Although other cases have not insisted on such a strict definition of scienter, they continue to require that defendants know their acts are unjustifiable or wrongful before the defendants can be deemed to possess the requisite wrongful intent necessary to violate the federal anti-kickback statute and other health care criminal laws.[97]

Similarly, a scienter requirement is necessary under the federal False Claims Act. To constitute an actionable false claim, a party must knowingly present a false or fraudulent claim to the federal government. Although reckless disregard of the truth also satisfies the intent requirement of the False Claims Act, innocent mistakes, good-faith disagreements over the interpretation of the law, and even negligence do not give rise to False Claims Act liability.[98]

Because health care regulatory requirements, especially Medicare regulatory requirements such as coding instructions for payment, often are complex and frequently vague, payment disputes will arise. However, not all alleged overpayments constitute false claims. In fact, not all alleged overpayments constitute genuine overpayments. Where reason-

---

[97] *See, e.g.*, United States v. Neufeld, 908 F. Supp. 491 (S.D. Ohio 1995) (rejecting the *Hanlester* analysis); United States v. Jain, 93 F.3d 436 (8th Cir. 1996) (requiring no "heightened mens rea").

[98] *See* United States *ex rel.* Hagood v. Sonoma County Water Agency, 929 F.2d 1416, 1421 (9th Cir. 1991).

able minds differ regarding the interpretation of a particular requirement and where the party has submitted a bill in good-faith reliance on
a reasonable interpretation of the rule, it is questionable whether there
would be any False Claims Act liability if it turns out that the interpretation relied on is ultimately deemed to be erroneous.[99]

There are also a variety of examples in health care in which a particular business practice not only is widespread in the industry but also
is a practice that the government historically has permitted through acquiescence. For example, the industry-wide practice of clinical laboratories giving discounts to physician customers when performing testing
for private-pay patients has been known to the federal and state governments for years. The government also knows that this practice continues because the laboratories seek to encourage physicians to use the
laboratories for all of their testing needs, including for Medicare and
Medicaid patients. Although there has been considerable debate over
the propriety of the practice, the government has not taken the position
that the practice is illegal per se. Thus, a clinical laboratory charged by
a state attorney general with violating a state Medicaid anti-kickback
statute (modeled after the federal anti-kickback statute) for giving discounts to physicians was able to defend itself successfully in a state
court unfair competition action on the grounds that the laboratory objectively and subjectively believed that the physician discounting practice was lawful.[100]

The intent issue is very fact specific. The same type of act may or
may not give rise to some type of liability depending on the unique circumstances of a case and the defendant's thought processes. Although
the intent requirement will not, and should not, protect someone who
intends to defraud or abuse health insurance programs, it is an important safeguard against overzealous or mistaken enforcement in situations in which someone acting in good faith misinterprets a complex or
confusing regulation.

### 3. Necessity of Agency Authority to Act

In addition to the two fundamental concepts discussed above, a
defense lawyer should be certain that the enforcement agency that is
threatening to act against his or her client does, in fact, possess the
legal authority required to take the action threatened. An agency may
not always have the right to initiate a particular action it threatens.

First, local prosecutors, such as district attorneys, county prosecutors, and city prosecutors, have a legitimate interest in ensuring that
health care fraud and abuse do not occur within their jurisdictions. However, most state laws do not allow a district attorney from one county to
prosecute allegedly wrongful acts committed in another county by a res-

---

[99] *See* United States *ex rel.* Hochman v. Nackman, 145 F.3d 1069, 1073 (9th Cir.
1998) ("superficially plausible" interpretation may negate wrongful intent).

[100] California v. Duz-Mor Diagnostic Lab., 68 Cal. App. 4th 654 (1998).

ident of the other county. This limit applies whether the local prosecutor is attempting to apply a state law or a local ordinance.

Second, some agencies that are accustomed to exercising considerable state statutory and constitutional authority in other areas may lack authority over health care programs. For example, under the federal Medicaid law, only the state agency designated as the single state Medicaid agency is authorized to administer the Medicaid program within that state.[101] Administration of the program includes the promulgation of policies and procedures governing such matters as auditing and determining overpayments made to providers. Although a state controller ultimately may have state statutory and even state constitutional authority to audit and determine the correctness of state payments, that authority may be restricted or inapplicable with respect to auditing and determining the correctness of Medicaid payments.

It must be assumed that the limits imposed on the federal and state enforcement agencies and regulators are intended for valid reasons. Thus, when an enforcement agency threatens to exceed those limits, defense counsel is justified in insisting on strict adherence to the limits.

## B. Other Practical Defense Concepts

### 1. Stressing the Facts

The most important defenses to fraud and abuse allegations are generally found within the facts of the case. If there are compelling facts to explain or justify a client's actions, a court will be more likely to interpret the governing law in favor of the client. There is no substitute for good facts.

In health care fraud and abuse prosecutions, special facts may strengthen a client's defense. For example, although it is no defense to argue that other providers are performing the same act, if the reality is that the practice for which a party is being prosecuted is widespread in the industry, that fact is bound to have some practical effect on a judge or jury so long as the act is not inherently nefarious.

In the *Hanlester* proceedings, the fact that physicians throughout the country possessed ownership interests in laboratories and other health care providers to which they referred their patients was not lost on the administrative law judge or the Ninth Circuit. It is hard for a decision maker to ignore such a fact, especially if it means that tens of thousands of physicians must be considered felons if they have violated the federal anti-kickback law as result of such self-referral arrangements.

Similarly, the fact that an activity that is being prosecuted was reviewed and "approved" by the defendant's attorney may be beneficial. Most government enforcement agencies will consider this "advice of

---

[101] 42 C.F.R. §431.10.

counsel" evidence to be very problematical to the successful prosecution of the case. Whether considered to be relevant to the intent element or some other element necessary to prove liability, the advice of defense counsel can be very useful.

As discussed earlier in the chapter, because of the sheer volume of regulations, guidelines, and other informal interpretations applicable to health care activities, inconsistent agency interpretations regarding a particular practice are not unusual. Although the interpretations may not have the legal authority to bind the federal or state governments under a theory of equitable estoppel, the existence of contrary interpretations tends to negate any wrongful intent if a party has relied on those interpretations. Contrary agency interpretations also tend to show the arbitrariness of a particular interpretation even if a party has not relied on the interpretation.

Finally, unlike some administrative agency matters in which the complexity of an issue favors the government, complexity favors the defendant in enforcement actions. In short, the more confusing the requirements alleged to have been violated, the more likely the court or jury will sympathize with the defendant.

## 2. Burden of Proof Requirements

Appreciating and applying the appropriate burden of proof and determining the correct quantum of evidence necessary to satisfy the burden of proof are as important in defending health care fraud and abuse cases as they are in any other type of litigation. Although these issues must be resolved differently in different actions depending on the forum, it is accurate to state in general that the enforcement agency typically has the initial burden of producing evidence to establish a prima facie case in most actions. Of course, in a criminal action, the government has not only the burden of going forward with the evidence but also the burden of proving beyond a reasonable doubt each element of a crime.

The importance of requiring the government to satisfy its burden of proof cannot be overemphasized. Enforcement agencies are not used to having to do so in most health care fraud enforcement investigations because of the willingness of health care providers to settle and resolve potential disputes short of litigation. Although no defense attorney can expect to present the defendant's entire case through the prosecution witnesses, it is possible in health care fraud and abuse cases to cast substantial doubt on the viability of the government's case before the defendant's side of the case is even presented. In other words, defense counsel should attempt to use the government's presentation as an opportunity to question the government's case. Issues such as the inconsistency of agency interpretations are particularly effective when presented during the cross-examination of government witnesses.

## 3. Credibility of Defendant

Notwithstanding the above, the most critical evidence in a health care fraud and abuse case can be the testimony of the defendant.

Whereas typical criminal defense strategies may caution against calling a defendant to testify at his or her own trial, in health care fraud and abuse cases, the judge and jury will likely expect to hear from the defendant. Therefore, if defense counsel doubts the credibility of the defendant or has other reasons for being concerned about the impact of the defendant testifying at trial, this factor alone may encourage settling the case short of trial or of attempting to prevail through summary judgment motions.

As with any case, the defendant's credibility is critical. If the defendant is believable and can sincerely persuade the trier of fact that he or she was acting in good faith and without any wrongful intent in performing the allegedly wrongful acts, the government will have a difficult time prevailing in most fraud and abuse cases. On the other hand, if the trier of fact believes the defendant is not trustworthy and not credible about any aspect of his or her testimony, regardless of how relevant or immaterial, the government's case will be strengthened significantly.

### 4. Limited Judicial Review

Unlike most criminal and civil litigation, the defense of health care fraud and abuse cases often originates with administrative hearings within federal or state agencies. In other words, as in *Hanlester*, the only "trial" at which witnesses actually testified and were observed by the trier of fact occurred before the assigned HHS administrative law judge. As a consequence of the case being tried administratively, the extent of judicial review was limited.

Under well-established principles of administrative law, judicial review of federal and state agency adjudication typically is restricted to a review of the legal determinations made by the agency. Among the legal issues to be resolved is whether the findings made by the agency decision maker are supported by substantial evidence. This is a very deferential level of review, similar to the review an appellate court performs of the factual findings of a trial court.

At the judicial review level of an agency decision, evidence in addition to that presented during the administrative hearing typically is not permitted. The reviewing court ordinarily must limit the scope of its review to the evidence presented during the administrative hearing, which is presented to the court in the form of an administrative record.

In situations in which judicial review of a final agency decision following a hearing must be sought initially from the lower level of the court system, such as the federal district court in OIG exclusion cases, appellate review of the district court's decision is not limited. Because the federal district court is limited to reviewing the administrative record of the agency proceedings and determining questions of law, the appellate court standard and scope of review are the same as the lower court's. For example, no special deference is owed to the lower court's determinations of law. The practical result is that if the final agency decision is adverse to the provider, and if the district court upholds that adverse decision, as was the situation in *Hanlester*, there is still a chance of prevailing before the appellate court if there are compelling legal arguments that can be presented.

Of course, in cases in which an enforcement action is initiated in a federal or state court rather than in an administrative hearing, the trial judge and jury have the same responsibilities they do in any case. Appellate review of a trial court or jury's verdict is also the same as in other cases.

## XI. CURRENT ENFORCEMENT PRIORITIES

To deter health care fraud and abuse, the government enforcement agencies periodically publish their enforcement priorities. The annual work plans issued by the OIG, for example, outline that office's priorities, which often dictate federal enforcement priorities in general.

Additionally, the government regularly advises the health care industry of areas of concern in its model compliance programs. The following risk areas are identified in the OIG's model compliance program for hospitals:

- billing for items or services not actually rendered;
- providing medically unnecessary services;
- upcoding (using a billing code that provides for higher payment than that for the services actually performed);
- diagnosis-related group (DRG) creep (using a DRG code that provides for higher payment than the accurate patient DRG code);
- outpatient services rendered in connection with inpatient stays;
- teaching physician and resident requirements for teaching hospitals;
- duplicate billing;
- false cost reports;
- unbundling;
- billing for discharge in lieu of transfer;
- patients' freedom of choice;
- failure to refund credit balances;
- hospital incentives that violate the anti-kickback statute or other similar federal or state statutes or regulations;
- joint ventures;
- financial arrangements between hospitals and hospital-based physicians;
- Stark physician self-referral laws;
- knowing failure to provide covered services or necessary care to members of a health maintenance organization; and
- patient dumping.[102]

---

[102] 63 Fed. Reg. 8987 (Feb. 23, 1998).

Because many of these risk areas apply not only to hospitals but also to other types of providers, the OIG's descriptions and definitions contained in the hospital model compliance plan are instructive. For example, billing for services not actually rendered is defined as submitting a claim that represents that the provider performed a service, all or part of which was not performed. According to the OIG, this form of billing fraud occurs in many health care entities, including hospitals and nursing homes, and represents a significant part of the OIG's investigative caseload.

According to the OIG, a claim requesting payment for medically unnecessary services "intentionally" seeks reimbursement for a service that is not warranted by the patient's current and documented medical condition. The OIG points out that a physician must certify on every CMS claim form that the services provided were medically necessary for the health of the beneficiary.[103]

The practice of upcoding is defined by the OIG as the use of a billing code that provides a higher payment rate than the billing code that actually reflects the services furnished to the patient. The OIG also points out that upcoding has been a major focus of its enforcement efforts.[104] The OIG includes the concept of DRG creep as a type of upcoding. DRG creep is the practice of billing using a DRG code that provides a higher payment rate than the DRG code that accurately reflects the service furnished to the patient.[105]

Hospitals that submit claims for nonphysician outpatient services that were already included in the hospital's inpatient payment under the Medicare Prospective Payment System are considered by the OIG to be submitting duplicate claims. Duplicate billing is also considered to occur when a hospital submits more than one claim for the same service or the bill is submitted to more than one primary payer at the same time. Although the OIG recognizes that such duplicate billing can occur as a result of simple error, it indicates that systematic or repeated double billing may be viewed as a false claim, particularly if any overpayment is not promptly refunded.[106]

The submission of false cost reports usually is limited to certain Medicare Part A providers such as hospitals, skilled nursing facilities, and home health agencies. The OIG refers to one of its audit reports concerning the purported mischaracterization by providers of fringe benefits and general and administrative costs as allowable costs. The OIG also indicates an awareness of practices in which hospitals and other providers inappropriately shift certain costs to cost centers that are below their Medicare reimbursement cap and shift costs not related to Medicare to Medicare-allowable cost centers.[107]

---

[103] *Id.* at 8990 n.14.

[104] *Id.* at n.15.

[105] *Id.* at n.16.

[106] *Id.* at nn. 17, 18.

[107] *Id.* at n.19.

The practice of submitting bills piecemeal or in fragmented fashion to maximize the reimbursement for various tests or procedures that must be billed together is the "unbundling" referred to by the OIG as a risk area for hospitals and other providers. The unbundling issue is most commonly found in billing for laboratory services, but it also may occur in other areas such as fragmenting global billings.[108]

Examples of arrangements that may run afoul of the anti-kickback statute given by the OIG include excessive payment for medical directorships, free or below-market rents or fees for administrative services, interest-free loans, and excessive payment for intangible assets in physician practice acquisitions.[109] Other equally troubling areas to the OIG with respect to the anti-kickback statute include the proliferation of business arrangements that may violate the anti-kickback statute, such as those that generally are established between persons in a position to refer business and those providing items or services for which a federal health care program pays.[110] These are the same joint ventures that the OIG warned about in its 1989 fraud alert, which became the subject of the *Hanlester* proceedings.[111]

The OIG also continues to warn hospitals and other providers about financial arrangements with hospital-based physicians that compensate physicians for less than the fair market value of services they provide to the hospital or require physicians to pay more than fair market value for services provided by the hospital. The OIG issued a management advisory report regarding this topic in October 1991.[112]

In addition to the risk areas described in the model compliance plan for hospitals, other areas of health care have been targeted for special scrutiny. According to recent OIG work plans, these include the home health care industry in general, ambulance services, partial hospital services, physician evaluation and management coding, and prescription drug services.

With the increase in managed care programs, the government is shifting considerable resources to investigating managed care companies and arrangements.[113] Managed care companies that structure capitation payments in a way that encourages physicians to withhold treatment or offer incentives to limit services could be subject to investigation.

---

[108] *Id.* at n.20.

[109] *Id.* at n.23.

[110] *Id.* at n. 24.

[111] Special Fraud Alert: Joint Venture Arrangements (Aug. 1989), 59 Fed. Reg. 65,372 (Dec. 19, 1994). For text of this document, see Appendix F-11 on disk accompanying this volume.

[112] Financial Arrangements Between Hospitals and Hospital-Based Physicians, OIG Mgmt. Advisory Rep. No. OEI-09-89-00330 (Oct. 1991). For text of this document, see Appendix F-17 on disk accompanying this volume.

[113] *See* Office of Inspector Gen., U.S. Dep't of Health & Human Servs., Compliance Program Guidance for Medicare+Choice Programs, *published in* 64 Fed. Reg. 61,893 (Nov. 15, 1999).

Managed care plans may be victimized by providers with whom they contract. Providers may submit false financial status reports or falsify quality reports and make misrepresentations about secondary payers. Evidence of providers falsifying patient encounter data to bolster increases in capitation payments and even to disguise underutilization of services also has been discovered.

As with fee-for-service arrangements, substantial fraud and abuse risk arises from the marketing practices of managed care plans. Payments to marketing agents to enroll new members are often commission driven, which may create an incentive for marketers to misrepresent plan services.[114]

By monitoring government enforcement initiatives, providers and other members of the health care industry may keep informed of areas of priority for enforcement agencies. However, it is not enough simply to know about such enforcement priorities. Steps must be taken to avoid future problems and correct past problems in these areas. This is precisely why health care compliance programs are needed.[115]

## XII. CONCLUSION

Although the government enforcement agencies perceive that health care fraud and abuse have increased significantly in terms of the dollars paid out because of fraud and abuse, there is at least anecdotal evidence that fraudulent and abusive practices have not actually increased, but rather, the ever-changing definition of fraud and abuse is creating the perception of increasing fraudulent and abusive practices.[116] Payment practices that previously would have generated an overpayment assessment at most are now being subjected to investigation by enforcement agencies for fraud and abuse.

Concern on the part of some members of the health care industry about continued changes in the definition of fraud and abuse is not unwarranted. Indeed, in a December 1997 Clarification issued by CMS to Section 7500 of the *Medicare Carriers Manual*, Medicare carriers are instructed that their medical review programs must ensure that all payments made by the Medicare program are appropriate, accurate, and consistent with Medicare policy. Obviously, this is a perfectly appropriate goal of any medical review program. However, the 1977 amendment also states as follows:

---

[114] For comprehensive coverage of fraud and abuse risks in the managed care context, see Chapter 6 (Roth & Palmer, Managed Care Fraud and Abuse: Risk Areas for Government Program Participants).

[115] For discussion of effective corporate compliance programs, see Chapter 7 (Jones *et al.*, Corporate Compliance Programs).

[116] In fact, the OIG has conceded that its estimate of approximately $20.3 billion in overpayments during fiscal year 1997 could be the result of problems ranging from inadvertent mistakes to outright fraud and abuse. *See* Office of Inspector Gen., U.S. Dep't of Health & Human Servs., Audit of HCFA's 1997 FY Financial Statements, n.12 (1998).

Problem areas identified will represent a continuum of intent for those providers involved. For example, some inappropriate billing will be the result of provider misunderstandings or failure to pay adequate attention to Medicare policy. Other incidents of inappropriate billing will represent calculated plans to knowingly acquire unwarranted payment. *Either case* results in abusive billing practices.

Before the December 1997 amendment, inappropriate billings that were the result of a provider misunderstanding or a failure to pay adequate attention to Medicare policy were not considered to be examples of abuse. Indeed, under the governing Medicare statutes, regulations, and manual provisions, in situations in which there is a provider misunderstanding of a billing requirement, the liability for overpayments resulting from the misunderstanding could be waived under appropriate circumstances.[117] The December 1997 verification not only makes such waiver unlikely, it also suggests that a misunderstanding may be construed as billing abuse by enforcement agencies.

In the resulting enforcement environment in which virtually any mistake can be construed by an enforcement agency as fraudulent or abusive conduct, it is absolutely critical that lawyers defending health care clients accused of fraud and abuse be mindful of the importance of fundamental principles of law, such as the supremacy of statutes and regulations over guidelines, and be certain that they are able to apply the appropriate historical and factual context to allegations of possible fraud and abuse.

---

[117] 42 U.S.C. §§1395gg, 1395pp.

# 5

# Legal Issues Surrounding Hospital and Physician Relationships*

---

*Dennis M. Barry, Vinson & Elkins L.L.P., Washington, D.C.

## I. Background on the Nature of Relationships Between Hospitals and Physicians and the Factors Affecting Those Relationships

As we begin the next century, relationships between hospitals and physicians are often complex, but are founded in mutual dependence. In the first half of the twentieth century, many hospitals were established, owned, and operated by physicians. These facilities often operated as an extension of physician practices. If any such hospitals continue to exist now, they are rare. Hospitals require too much capital and too much management time for an individual physician to want to undertake the responsibilities of operating a hospital facility. Just as hospital ownership is no longer commonly held by physicians (other than small interests as limited partners), hospital management is generally entrusted to professionals whose training concentrates on facility and personnel management rather than the clinical management of patients.

Hospitals need physicians. Under state law, only a physician can order hospital services; literally no services can be furnished by a hospital without the order of a physician (or in limited instances, the order of certain other "mid level" health professionals).[1] Physicians are not ignorant of their importance to a hospital's financial viability. Commonly, physicians will remind hospital administrators that millions of dollars in hospital charges arise from patients the physicians have admitted. But hospital dependence on physicians is not limited to reliance on referrals and orders made by physicians. The accreditation standards of the Joint Commission on Accreditation of Healthcare Organizations (JCAHO), as well as the Medicare conditions of participation, require hospitals to have physicians on their governing boards, a medical director who is a physician, an organized medical staff, and physician control of many medical functions.[2]

Hospital dependence on physicians is not one-sided; many physicians cannot function without hospitals. Notwithstanding occasional unflattering portraits of physicians as being interested solely in their wealth or their egos, what motivates most physicians more than anything else is seeing that their patients are treated as effectively as possible. In this era, that level of care requires a hospital. A hospital is necessary not just for the availability of 24-hour nursing service but also because only a large institution can afford the immense capital expenditures for services that are accepted as necessary. For example, magnetic resonance imaging (MRI) is now routinely ordered but the machines and their sites require capital expenditures well in excess of $1 million. While the price tag for an MRI is a dramatic illustration of the cost of capital equipment, it is not unique. Mid-size community hospitals routinely spend $10 million or more a year on new capital equipment.

A physician's dependence on a hospital varies greatly, depending on the physician's specialty. Indeed, there is an increasing trend for some family practice physicians to avoid treating their patients in hospitals. When their patients require admission, family practitioners may refer patients to a "hospitalist." Other physician specialties rely heavily on the availability of hospital services. For example, surgeons conduct most surgeries in hospitals, particularly the more complicated or dangerous procedures that cannot be done on an outpatient basis. A

---

[1] The categories of various "physician extenders" such as nurse practitioners and physician assistants who have been afforded increased stature and power in recent years, including the power to order certain services, do not, at least yet, have any material effect on the virtually exclusive control physicians have in determining what health care services shall be furnished.

[2] JOINT COMMISSION ON ACCREDITATION OF HEALTHCARE ORGANIZATIONS, HOSPITAL ACCREDITATION STANDARDS GO.2.2, MS.3.1 (2000); 42 C.F.R. §§482.12, 482.22.

cardiac surgeon relies on the skills of the operating room team, including specialty nurses, perfusionists, and anesthesiologists (including certified registered nurse anesthetists supervised by anesthesiologists) to furnish a very high level of service expertly. Thus, surgeons and other physicians will lobby hospitals to purchase certain types of equipment and hire qualified personnel so that the physician can furnish services using that equipment and personnel—services they otherwise would be unable to perform. Some physician specialties, such as pathologists, anesthesiologists, and radiologists, work almost exclusively in hospitals. Unlike their counterparts in private practice, hospital-based physician specialists are dependent on hospitals to practice their specialties.

The growth of managed care has also affected relationships between hospitals and physicians. Managed care payers often seek to contract with an existing network for the obvious reason that it is much easier to have a single contract than to try to assemble a network of multiple individual contracts with separate physician practices. Thus, it is advantageous for physicians to join a larger group, and one way to do so is to become affiliated with a network. Sometimes a hospital controls the network. One reason that physicians may affiliate with a network, which has hospital involvement, is the need for capital. Managed care payers often try to shift risk to contracting physicians and providers. Bearing that risk requires access to capital, and even physicians with handsome incomes often have very little capital, or at least insufficient capital compared to the amount needed to bear risk in the world of managed care. Managed care also reduces a physician's discretion in ordering services in terms of both the volume and nature of services ordered, as well as the choice of service providers. Thus, in some markets, it is more important for a hospital to have contracts with managed care payers than good relationships with referring physicians, because the payer controls where the services will be furnished.

Relationships between hospitals and physicians are obviously affected by the relative balance of power between the parties. This relationship is subject to the rules of supply and demand, with physicians in overbedded urban areas with multiple hospitals having much more power than physicians practicing in areas with a single hospital. Moreover, there simply are cultural differences among various parts of the country, so that physicians are treated with more deference in some areas than in others.

Physician and hospital relationships can run the gamut from the physician having no direct economic connection to the hospital to the hospital being the sole source of the physician's income. For example, there often is no direct economic or contractual relationship between hospitals and physicians. Physicians, as members of the hospital's "voluntary" medical staff, admit patients and order services in their sole discretion, and may serve on more than one voluntary medical staff at a time. As voluntary medical staff members, physicians may also serve on various hospital medical staff committees and on hospital boards of directors.[3] It is also common for hospitals to have limited contractual relationships with physicians. For example, a hospital may lease to a physician space in an adjacent medical office building. Hospitals also commonly pay physicians to assume medical director responsibilities in various departments, but these physicians continue to spend the bulk of their time and derive the bulk of their income from their private practices. Finally, there are situations in which physicians are employed by, or contract with, a hospital on a full-time basis, and are solely dependent on the hospital for their incomes.

## II. LEGAL ISSUES

A host of legal issues can come into play in the relationships between physicians and hospitals including:

- medical staff bylaw rights and responsibilities;
- contractual duties, obligations, and remedies;
- malpractice liability and vicarious liability;
- EMTALA[4] compliance;
- antitrust laws as they affect exclusive contracts;
- state laws on the corporate practice of medicine and fee splitting;
- federal and state laws barring illegal remuneration or kickbacks;[5]
- limitations applicable to federally tax-exempt organizations, including the bars on inurement and private benefit;[6]
- federal Stark law and state laws barring certain financial relationships between physicians and entities from which they order services;[7] and
- Medicare reimbursement requirements.

The purpose of this chapter is not to explore these areas in depth, but rather to illustrate the practical impact these laws have on relationships between hospitals and physicians, so that lawyers can try at the outset to structure relationships to comply with the law and, in the event of an unfortunate occurrence, minimize the resulting costs and disruptions.

---

[3] In nonprofit corporations, the board of directors may often be called the board of trustees. Regardless of name, it is the governing board of the hospital.

[4] Emergency Medical Treatment and Active Labor Act, 42 U.S.C. §1395dd; implementing regulations at 42 C.F.R. §489.24.

[5] 42 U.S.C. §1320a-7b(b); *and, e.g.*, ALA. CODE §22-1-11(b) & (c); N.J. STAT. ANN. §30:4D-17(c); VA. CODE §32.1-315(A) & (B). (See Appendix A-1 for full text of the anti-kickback statute.)

[6] 26 U.S.C. §501(c)(3).

[7] 42 U.S.C. §1395nn; *e.g.*, FLA. STAT. ANN. §483.245(1).

## III. RELATIONSHIPS WITH PHYSICIANS WHO ARE VOLUNTARY MEMBERS OF THE MEDICAL STAFF

### A. Medical Staff Membership

#### 1. Open Staff

Medical staff bylaws are created by the medical staff, but must be approved by the hospital board of directors.[8] Statutory, regulatory, and accreditation standards govern how the medical staff is organized and the way its bylaws and related documents are drafted.[9] Although the medical staff may resist admitting particular individuals or classes of individuals to the medical staff, the hospital bears the responsibility and liability for any illegal or wrongful conduct.

A threshold issue in regard to medical staff bylaws is who is entitled to admission to the medical staff. In some states, provisions of the medical staff bylaws are deemed to be contractual, and provisions concerning who may join the staff are viewed as open offers.[10] Thus, physicians or other practitioners who meet the requirements set forth in the medical staff bylaws must be admitted to membership. Medicare conditions of participation also require hospitals to open their medical staffs to qualified physicians,[11] although many teaching hospitals condition membership on a willingness to assume teaching responsibilities, and hospitals may enter "exclusive" contractual arrangements that limit other physicians' opportunities for admission to the medical staff.

#### 2. Open Staff and Exclusive Contracts

Sometimes one or more physicians already on the medical staff may oppose the admission of a new member to the medical staff who may interfere with their "exclusive" contract to furnish services at the hospital in a particular specialty. On occasion, there is no exclusive con-

---

[8] JOINT COMMISSION ON ACCREDITATION OF HEALTHCARE ORGANIZATIONS, HOSPITAL ACCREDITATION STANDARDS, MS.2.1 (2000).

[9] *See* Health Care Quality Improvement Act of 1986, 42 U.S.C. §§11101 *et seq.*; Americans With Disabilities Act of 1990, 42 U.S.C. §§12101 *et seq.*; Hospital Survey and Construction Act of 1946 (Hill-Burton Act), 42 U.S.C. §§291 *et seq.*; Fair Credit Reporting Act, 42 U.S.C. §§1681 *et seq.*; 42 C.F.R. §§482.12, 482.22; JOINT COMMISSION ON ACCREDITATION OF HEALTHCARE ORGANIZATIONS, HOSPITAL ACCREDITATION STANDARDS (2000).

[10] *See, e.g.*, Strauss v. Peninsula Reg'l Med. Ctr., 916 F. Supp. 528, 536 (D. Md. 1996) (stating that Maryland law is well settled that hospital bylaws are enforceable contracts); Islami v. Covenant Med. Ctr., 822 F. Supp. 1361, 1370–71 (N.D. Iowa 1992) (recognizing a split of authority in the states on this issue, the court found that the majority view that a hospital's medical staff bylaws constitute a contract between the hospital and the medical staff is in accord with Iowa law); Gonzalez v. San Jacinto Methodist Hosp., 880 S.W.2d 436 (Tex. App.-Texarkana 1994, writ denied); *contra* Zipper v. Health Midwest, 978 S.W.2d 398, 416 (Mo. Ct. App. 1998) (holding that hospital bylaws are not contracts under Missouri law due to lack of consideration); Robles v. Humana Hosp. Cartersville, 785 F. Supp. 989 (N.D. Ga. 1992).

[11] 42 C.F.R. §482.22.

tract, but physicians already on staff want to protect themselves from competition. In either case, the physician seeking medical staff membership may complain that denial of such membership violates antitrust laws. Exclusive contracts are, by definition, a restraint of trade, but in virtually all cases, they have been upheld by the courts.[12] The courts have found that legitimate needs for 24-hour coverage and quality assurance, as well as other hospital and patient concerns, override the limited restraint on trade caused by the exclusivity provisions.[13]

If a hospital has exclusive arrangements, it is preferable for those arrangements to be reflected in contracts, even if no monetary consideration flows from the hospital to the physicians. Exclusive contracts, with appropriate recitations of the legitimate need for exclusivity, facilitate exclusion of practitioners who seek to join the staff. In addition, medical staff bylaw provisions allowing for an open staff should be qualified to avoid the appearance of a conflict between the bylaws and the terms of an exclusive contract. Similarly, exclusive contracts should be drafted so that termination or non-renewal of the contract terminates medical staff appointments and clinical privileges and cannot be contested by physicians or physician groups through the medical staff appeal procedures. Exclusive contracts should also make clear that when contracts and medical staff bylaws conflict, contracts prevail. All of these provisions should also be a part of the medical staff bylaws.

### 3. Osteopaths and Podiatrists

In some parts of the country, the medical community itself holds strong prejudices against certain types of practitioners. For example, allopathic trained physicians (M.D.s) may hold great disdain for osteopathic trained physicians (D.O.s). Similarly, some physicians hold podiatrists in low regard. Some states, however, have laws requiring hospitals to accept osteopathic physicians or podiatrists on their medical staffs.[14]

## B. Credential Review and Corrective Action

### 1. Verification of Credentials and Checking Available Databases

Hospitals absolutely must verify that any physician seeking medical staff membership has the required credentials for membership,

---

[12] *See, e.g.*, Beard v. Parkview Hosp., 912 F.2d 138 (6th Cir. 1990) (holding that exclusive contract for provision of radiological services did not violate antitrust law); Dos Santos v. Columbus-Cuneo-Cabrini Med. Ctr., 684 F.2d 1346, 1352 (7th Cir. 1982) (finding that a plaintiff can only prevail on an exclusive dealing arrangement "by showing that the agreement in question results in a substantial foreclosure of competition in an area of effective competition, that is, in a relevant market"); Nilavar v. Mercy Health Sys. W. Ohio, 142 F. Supp. 2d 859 (S.D. Ohio 2000) (dismissing plaintiff's tying claims based on an exclusive contract); *Gonzalez*, 880 S.W.2d 436 (holding hospital is entitled to enter into an exclusive services contract).

[13] Jefferson Parish Hosp. Dist. No. 2 v. Hyde, 466 U.S. 2, 104 S. Ct. 1551 (1984).

[14] *See, e.g.*, 225 ILL. COMP. STAT. 62/5 (osteopaths); *e.g.*, CAL. HEALTH & SAFETY CODE §1316 (1998) (podiatrists).

including a degree from an accredited medical school, satisfactory completion of a residency program, and a currently valid license to practice in the state in which the hospital is located (and in the state(s) where the physician has an office). In addition, hospitals must check the National Practitioner Data Bank (NPDB)[15] to determine if there have been adverse actions with respect to the physician. The hospital should also verify that the physician has not been excluded from any government health care program.

### 2. Physician Malpractice Insurance

Many hospitals require physicians to carry adequate malpractice insurance as a condition of medical staff membership, which offers some limited assurance of quality as a demonstration of a physician's insurability. Physician malpractice insurance also offers protection for the hospital. If a physician is uninsured, it is much more likely that an injured patient will sue the hospital as a "deep pocket," and assert that the hospital had been negligent in permitting the physician to practice at the facility.

### 3. Hospital Duty to Deal With Problem Practitioners

A hospital's obligations do not lapse upon credentialing a new member of the medical staff. Should a hospital become aware of incidents or conduct that reflect on a physician's ability to treat patients with an acceptable level of skill and in accordance with community and hospital standards of care, the hospital must take corrective action. If a hospital negligently admits a physician to its medical staff or fails to take appropriate corrective action with respect to a physician who the hospital knew or should have known was not practicing appropriately, the hospital can be held liable for the damage caused by the physician's negligence.[16]

On the flip side, physicians who are denied privileges or have their privileges revoked often initiate antitrust litigation against the hospital. Although some circuit courts have ruled that a hospital cannot conspire (as prohibited under the Sherman Act §1[17]) with its medical

---

[15] 42 U.S.C. §11135. The information in this data bank is considered confidential and is not available to the public. The information from the NPDB is available only to state licensing boards, hospitals and other health care entities, professional societies, certain federal agencies, and others as specified by law. *See* Health Resources and Servs. Admin., U.S. Dep't of Health & Human Servs., National Practitioner Data Bank/Healthcare Integrity and Protection Data Bank, *available at* http://www.npdb.com.

[16] Darling v. Charleston Cmty. Mem'l Hosp., 33 Ill.2d 326, 211 N.E.2d 253 (Ill. 1965), *cert. denied*, 86 S. Ct. 1204 (1966); *see also* Johnson v. Misericordia Cmty. Hosp., 301 N.W.2d 156 (Wis. 1981) (holding hospital liable for failing to establish procedures to determine a physician's competence when granting privileges, in particular, for failing to check the National Practitioner Data Bank).

[17] 15 U.S.C. §1.

staff,[18] other circuit courts have held otherwise.[19] For this reason, it is important that medical staff bylaws, as well as bylaws of the health care entity, clearly state that the medical staff is a constituent part of the hospital and not a separate entity. This tension between a hospital's duty to deal with problem practitioners and the threat of antitrust litigation was one of the reasons the Health Care Quality Improvement Act was enacted. This law provides antitrust immunity for peer review activities that meet specific standards.[20]

## C. Corrective Action Under the Medical Staff Bylaws

At such time as a hospital learns that a physician may not be practicing in a manner consistent with hospital[21] or community standards, the hospital must take corrective action to protect itself pursuant to its medical staff bylaws. The corrective action need not necessarily be termination of medical staff privileges. In many instances, medical staff bylaws permit a lesser sanction, such as additional training, monitoring on a case-by-case basis by a respected member of the medical staff, or some other appropriate measure tailored to meet the observed problem.

If there is a dispute with the physician whose conduct is in question, JCAHO requires the hospital to have an appeal mechanism in the medical staff bylaws affording the physician an opportunity to present his or her side of a case.[22]

Government health care programs such as Medicare and Medicaid can exclude practitioners.[23] As a general rule, if practitioners are excluded from one governmental health care program, they will be excluded from all of them.[24] If practitioners are excluded, no services ordered by those practitioners are covered.[25] Hence, if a physician who is

---

[18] *See* Balaklaw v. Lovell, 14 F.3d 793 (2d Cir. 1994); Oksanen v. Page Mem'l Hosp., 945 F.2d 696 (4th Cir. 1991), *cert. denied*, 11 S. Ct. 973 (1992).

[19] *See* Bolt v. Halifax Hosp. Med. Ctr., 851 F.2d 1273 (11th Cir. 1988), *aff'd*, 980 F.2d 1381 (11th Cir. 1993); Oltz v. St. Peter's Cmty. Hosp., 861 F.2d 1440 (9th Cir. 1988), *rev'd on other grounds*, 19 F.3d 1312 (1994).

[20] 42 U.S.C. §11111(a).

[21] If it is not careful in its advertising or other public statements, a hospital can be held to a standard of care above that of the community standard of care. For example, if a hospital holds itself out as furnishing only "the highest quality of patient care," a plaintiff's attorney may try to rely on that puffery as creating a warranty or otherwise setting a standard above the community standard of care. Denton Reg'l Med. Ctr. v. LaCroix, 947 S.W.2d 941, 946 (Tex. App.-Ft. Worth 1997, rev. denied) (alleging that hospital was negligent for "representing to the public that it provided the highest quality anesthesia care when, in fact, it only provided unsupervised CRNAs").

[22] JOINT COMMISSION ON ACCREDITATION OF HEALTHCARE ORGANIZATIONS, HOSPITAL ACCREDITATION STANDARDS, MS.5.2 (2000).

[23] 42 U.S.C. §1320a-7.

[24] 42 C.F.R. §1001.601.

[25] 42 C.F.R. §1001.1901; *see also* Office of Inspector Gen., U.S. Dep't of Health & Human Servs., Special Advisory Bulletin, The Effect of Exclusion From Participation in Federal Health Care Programs (Sept. 1999), *available at* http://www.os.dhhs.gov/progorg/oig/frdalrt/effected.htm, and as Appendix F-14 on disk accompanying this volume.

a member of a hospital's voluntary medical staff is excluded from Medicare, but retains medical staff membership and privileges, the physician may order services for which the hospital will not be paid. This is an unacceptable position for a hospital for two reasons.

First, whatever conduct the physician engaged in to merit exclusion may very well be conduct that is relevant to the physician's fitness to remain on the medical staff. Second, regardless of the merits of the physician's exclusion from government health care programs, a hospital should not place itself in the position of being barred from billing for services ordered by that practitioner. Therefore, it is preferable for a hospital to have a procedure in its medical staff bylaws permitting summary suspension of privileges when a practitioner is excluded or suspended from one or more governmental health care programs.

If adverse action is taken against a physician by a hospital, or if the physician resigns from the medical staff under threat of such action, the hospital is legally obligated to report the matter to the NPDB.[26] Failure to report can result in sanctions against the hospital.[27]

## D. Physician Attestation of Accuracy of Medicare Diagnoses

Under the Medicare prospective payment system for hospital inpatient services, the level of payment is determined by the diagnosis-related group (DRG) to which the patient's case is assigned. The DRG assignment is determined by the patient's principal and secondary diagnoses, as well as procedures performed. Medicare payment regulations previously required physicians to acknowledge in writing that diagnosis information had been entered correctly for each Medicare discharge. That requirement was eliminated in 1995 and replaced by the requirement that every physician, on entering into medical staff membership or before admitting patients, must sign a single acknowledgment that the hospital keeps on file for as long as the physician is on the medical staff. By signing the acknowledgment, a physician attests to the diagnoses and procedures in the medical record and recognizes that he or she is liable for the misrepresentation or falsification of that information.[28]

## E. Physician Coverage of the Emergency Room

Historically, many hospitals arranged for emergency room coverage by rotating the obligation through members of the medical staff. Now such an arrangement for basic coverage of the emergency room is the exception. In most cases, hospitals employ or contract with specialists experienced in emergency medicine to staff emergency rooms. However, hospitals still often rely on members of the voluntary medical staff

---

[26] 45 C.F.R. §60.9.

[27] 42 C.F.R. §1003.102(b)(5).

[28] 42 C.F.R. §412.46.

for specialist services required by emergency room patients. For example, a hospital that holds itself out as handling major trauma will need to have available the services of a neurologist, orthopedist, and similar specialists. Under the obligations created by EMTALA, a hospital must accept certain referrals of emergency patients from other hospitals and failure to accept such patients can subject the refusing hospital to termination of its participation in Medicare and fines up to $50,000.[29] One problem that arises is that a hospital may violate its EMTALA obligations because a member of its voluntary medical staff refuses to honor his or her agreement to be on-call.[30] A hospital needs a mechanism, through its medical staff bylaws, or otherwise, to deal with this potential problem.

## F. Perquisites for Members of the Medical Staff

At most hospitals, physicians enjoy modest perquisites by reason of their medical staff membership. For example, hospitals have routinely offered professional courtesy to physicians on the medical staff and members of their immediate families. Hospitals have also routinely furnished to physicians on the medical staff free parking in a lot convenient to the hospital entrance, cafeteria discounts, coffee and donuts in the physician lounge, and occasional entertainment. Even items that seem innocuous raise potential problems under various fraud and abuse laws including the Stark law.[31] Under the Stark law, a hospital may not bill Medicare or Medicaid for services ordered by a physician with a financial relationship with the hospital. Unwitting violations subject a hospital to nonpayment for the services; violations when the hospital knew or should have known of the prohibited financial relationship can also result in a civil monetary penalty (CMP) of up to $15,000 per occurrence.[32] "Financial relationship" is defined with sufficient breadth as to encompass any remuneration given by a hospital to a physician.[33] Thus, it is necessary to fit within an exception to the law to avoid the risk of draconian penalties.

---

[29] 42 U.S.C. §1395dd(d)(1)(A); 42 C.F.R. §1003.102(c); *see also* Office of Inspector Gen., U.S. Dep't of Health & Human Servs., Special Advisory Bulletin on the Patient Anti-Dumping Statute, 64 Fed. Reg. 6135 (Nov. 10, 1999) (see Appendix F-13 on disk accompanying this volume).

[30] *See* St. Anthony Hosp. v. Office of Inspector Gen., Doc. No. A-2000-12, Dec. No. 1728 (HHS Departmental Appeals Bd., Appellate Div.), MEDICARE & MEDICAID GUIDE (CCH) ¶120,147 (Jun. 5, 2000), *aff'g* Office of Inspector Gen. v. St. Anthony Hosp., Doc. No. C-98-460, CR 620 (HHS Departmental Appeals Bd., Civil Remedies Div.), MEDICARE & MEDICAID GUIDE (CCH) ¶120,101 (Oct. 5, 1999) (holding hospital violated EMTALA when its on-call surgeon told a community hospital emergency room physician seeking to transfer a critical patient that he was "not interested" in taking the case).

[31] 42 U.S.C. §1395nn. See generally Chapter 2 (Crane, Federal Physician Self-Referral Restrictions), and Appendix B-1 for full text of the Stark law.

[32] 42 U.S.C. §1395nn(g)(3).

[33] 42 U.S.C. §1395nn(a)(2), (h)(1).

Phase I of the Stark II final rules issued by the Health Care Financing Administration (HCFA), now the Centers for Medicare and Medicaid Services (CMS),[34] on January 4, 2001, created two new exceptions for perquisites to physicians. The first is a non-monetary compensation exception that exempts from the Stark II ban non-cash or cash equivalent items or services up to an aggregate yearly amount of $300.[35] This compensation cannot take into consideration the volume or value of referrals or other business generated by the referring physician, cannot be solicited by the physician, and cannot violate the anti-kickback statute. Unlike the proposed Stark II rule for de minimis compensation, there is no per gift limit or requirement that such compensation be made available to all similarly situated individuals.[36] The second is a new exception for medical staff incidental benefits. This provision exempts non-cash or cash equivalent items or services given to a member of the medical staff when used on the hospital campus if they are:

- offered to all members of the medical staff and do not consider the volume or value of referrals or other business generated between the parties;
- offered only when staff are making rounds or performing other duties for the hospital;
- reasonably related to or facilitate the provision of medical services at the hospital;
- consistent with what other hospitals offer;
- less than $25 value for each occurrence (e.g., each meal); and
- not in violation of the anti-kickback statute.[37]

## 1. Professional Courtesy

Many hospitals commonly engage in "insurance only" billing for members of the medical staff and their immediate families. CMS recognizes in the Phase I final rule that some of these arrangements would qualify for the non-monetary compensation exception, but others would not.[38] CMS says it is considering an exception for these arrangements and will address professional courtesy discounts in Phase II of this rulemaking.[39]

---

[34] As of July 1, 2001, the former Health Care Financing Administration (HCFA) was renamed the Centers for Medicare and Medicaid Services (CMS). For the purposes of this discussion, however, references typically will be to CMS.

[35] 66 Fed. Reg. 856, 961 (Jan. 4, 2001) (codified at 42 C.F.R. §411.357(k)). CMS has decided that the aggregate amount of $300 will not be adjusted for inflation. 66 Fed. Reg. at 921.

[36] 62 Fed. Reg. 1646, 1725 (Jan. 9, 1998).

[37] 66 Fed. Reg. at 962 (codified at 42 C.F.R. §411.357(m)) (for text of regulations under Stark I and II, see generally Appendix B). The anti-kickback statute is codified at 42 U.S.C. §1320a-7b(b) (for text of the anti-kickback statute, see Appendix A-1).

[38] 66 Fed. Reg. at 922.

[39] *Id.*

## 2. *Entertainment*

It is also common for hospital management to entertain members of the medical staff at lunches, dinners, or golf outings. If total charges for meals, green fees, tips, and similar fees for physicians (and their spouses, if present) exceed $300 per year, the Stark exception for non-monetary compensation would not apply.

## 3. *Parking*

The proposed Stark regulation distinguished between furnishing parking to physicians while they are seeing patients at the hospital and furnishing spaces to physicians regardless of whether they are seeing patients in the hospital at the time:

> It is our [CMS] view that, while a physician is making rounds, the parking benefits both the hospital and its patients, rather than providing the physician with any personal benefit. Thus, we do not intend to regard parking for this purpose as remuneration furnished by the hospital to the physician, but instead as part of the physician's privileges. However, if a hospital provides parking to a physician for periods of time that do not coincide with his or her rounds, that parking could constitute remuneration.[40]

This distinction was formally recognized in the elements to the new exception created for medical staff incidental benefits in the Phase I final rule. Parking provided to all members of the medical staff for times they are making rounds or performing other duties at the hospital would fall under this new exception.[41]

## 4. *Compliance Training*

Another new exception in the Phase I final rule was created for compliance training. CMS believes that these programs are beneficial and pose little risk of fraud or abuse.[42] These programs will be exempt as long as they are provided to physicians who practice in the local community and are conducted in the local community.[43]

## G. Physician Hospital Organizations

Physician hospital organizations (PHOs) are joint ventures between hospitals and members of their medical staffs.[44] The principal purpose is to have a ready-made network to contract with managed care payers. Often, physicians in a PHO with a hospital have no other financial relationship with the hospital. In ideal circumstances, PHOs

---

[40] 63 Fed. Reg. at 1714.

[41] 66 Fed. Reg. at 921.

[42] *Id.*

[43] *Id.* at 962 (codified at 42 C.F.R. §411.357(o)).

[44] *See generally*, NATIONAL HEALTH LAWYERS ASS'N, 3 HEALTH LAW PRACTICE GUIDE §34:2, at 34-3 (West 1998).

offer hospitals and members of their medical staffs the opportunity to work together to support each other and provide their communities with cost-effective medical services. On behalf of all of its members, the PHO contracts with managed care payers, handles utilization review, and may bear some risk under capitation arrangements. Unfortunately, these goals are often difficult to achieve because of legal or practical limitations. Several fundamental legal problems arise with PHOs under (1) tax law limitations on tax-exempt organizations; (2) antitrust laws barring monopolies; (3) antitrust laws barring price setting and agreements to act in concert; and (4) state laws defining the business of insurance.

### 1. *Capital Requirements and the Need to Avoid Hospital Subsidization of Physician Members*

PHOs do not require immense amounts of capital because they own no medical equipment, can rent the premises they need, do not need to employ medical personnel, and do not furnish services directly. What they do is negotiate and contract with third-party payers, engage in utilization review including case management, and may bear some risk under capitation arrangements. In addition, PHOs are not established with the expectation of making a profit, but instead the intent is to provide members greater revenues through greater volume and cost savings or to preserve existing market shares. For a start-up period of 3 years or more, PHOs often lose money. Thus, although capital needs are not great, there is a need for a capital contribution of several hundred thousand dollars at the outset and during the start-up period.

In the ideal model, physicians in the aggregate hold equal ownership, make equal capital contributions, and have a vote equal to the hospital. In the real world, however, physicians are often reluctant to invest sufficient capital to fund half of the capital needs of the PHO. Serious inurement and private benefit issues arise if a tax-exempt hospital subsidizes physician capital contributions by making larger investments for equal ownership and power.[45] Sometimes, this problem can be solved by having the hospital hold more than half ownership, with minority physician shareholder protections such as super majority requirements when certain actions are taken.

As the PHO matures, particularly if it has been successful, the issue of its capital needs may continue to arise. For example, some joint ventures between hospitals and physicians have gone beyond contracting with managed care payers, and have obtained licenses as HMOs or insurance companies. To ensure sufficient reserves to satisfy state insurance commissioners requires immense amounts of capital. In such instances, success in enrolling patients is a mixed blessing because it will raise the reserve requirements. In several such ventures, the hospital has bought out all or a portion of physician interests. Of course,

---

[45] There also are Stark law and anti-kickback issues.

such buyouts have to be at fair market value and satisfy an appropriate Stark exception, such as the exception for isolated transactions.[46]

## 2. Antitrust Issues

In a large, highly competitive market, there is not much concern that a relatively small percentage of physicians joining together in a network is monopolization. But in smaller markets with only one or two hospitals, there is a risk of being accused of monopolization if too many physicians become involved in a PHO and will only contract with managed care payers through a PHO. This issue needs to be considered not only in regard to all physicians generally, but also on a specialty-by-specialty basis. Some PHOs provide that physician members are free to contract with a managed care payer separately from the PHO, but only after presenting the opportunity to the PHO. The extent to which this ameliorates potential monopolization issues depends on the facts and circumstances of each PHO and the market.

An antitrust issue inherent in virtually all PHOs is the extent to which they may negotiate on behalf of otherwise independent members. If members have bound themselves not to deal with payers other than through the PHO, there is a risk that the arrangement will be treated as an impermissible boycott. Moreover, virtually any delegation to the PHO by independent physician members to negotiate prices on their behalf can raise risks of illegal price fixing. The safest structure is one in which the PHO acts solely as a messenger between the managed care payer and independent physicians.[47]

## 3. Business of Insurance

To engage in the business of insurance, an entity must be licensed as an insurance company under state law. Hospitals and PHOs do not normally pursue this avenue because as many as several million dollars must be set aside in reserves. Thus, engaging in the business of insurance is not a practical option for most PHOs. The business of insurance generally assumes the entity is accepting risk. In many states, insurance commissioners find the types of risks that PHOs think they want to accept fit within the definition of the "business of insurance."

---

[46] 42 C.F.R. §411.357(f). This exception will be addressed in Phase II rulemaking. The buyout would also have to be structured so as not to violate the anti-kickback statute.

[47] *See generally*, U.S. DEP'T OF JUSTICE & FEDERAL TRADE COMM'N, STATEMENTS OF ANTITRUST ENFORCEMENT POLICY IN HEALTH CARE (Aug. 28, 1996), *reprinted in* 4 TRADE REG. REP. (CCH) ¶ 13,153, *available at* http://www.ftc.gov/reports/hlth3s.htm; James H. Sneed & David Marx, Jr., Antitrust: Challenge of the Health Care Field 75-92 (National Health Lawyers Ass'n, 1990). *See* Memorandum From Kenney Shipley, Chair, Health Plan Accountability Working Group, National Ass'n of Insurance Commissioners, to All Commissioners, Directors, and Superintendents (Aug. 10, 1995).

## H. Including Physicians Who Are Voluntary Members of the Medical Staff in a Wide-Area Computer Network Tied to the Hospital

A number of hospitals now give physicians on the voluntary medical staff access to their wide-area computer network. By connecting physician offices to the hospital's network, the physician will be able to schedule patients for procedures more easily, approve orders sooner and more efficiently, communicate with the hospital and other physicians by e-mail, gain access to clinical databases to assist in determining the best treatment of a patient, obtain demographic information for his or her own billing, and otherwise interface more efficiently and effectively with the hospital. To provide these benefits, a hospital may find it easier to furnish the physician with a computer, modem, and other hardware and software. The obvious issue is whether doing so constitutes remuneration to the physician and presents a problem under the triple threat of the Stark law, the anti-kickback statute, and the limitations applicable to tax-exempt organizations.

The answer to these questions requires an analysis of precisely what hardware, software, or other items or services the hospital furnishes to physicians. In virtually all instances, the benefits to the hospital itself, or to hospital care for its patients, are apparent. For example, if a physician reviews test results by computer, enabling the patient to be discharged sooner, the hospital avoids increased costs from a longer stay, and the patient can return home or proceed sooner to the next level of care. But there are ancillary benefits of such arrangements as well. To the extent that the physician can use the equipment for purposes unrelated to the hospital or hospital patients, there is not much question that the physician has received a benefit. In some instances, that benefit may be incidental and immaterial; but in other instances, it could be substantial. To avoid legal problems, the hospital may either install in physician offices dummy terminals that are only capable of interfacing with the hospital mainframe or charge the physician fair market value for the non-hospital-related use of the equipment. The charge need relate only to the value to the physician apart from the benefit to the hospital or the hospital's patients. This risk area has been discussed in the preambles to both the anti-kickback safe harbors and the Stark regulations,[48] and more generally in other guidance materials, including a Special Fraud Alert.[49]

CMS recognized in the Phase I final Stark rules that free computer/Internet access for physicians benefits hospitals and patients because it facilitates accurate recordkeeping and provides physicians with ac-

---

[48] 56 Fed. Reg. 35,952, 35,978 (1991) (distinguishing between a computer that only prints out laboratory test results and a regular personal computer that can be used for other purposes); 62 Fed. Reg. 1646, 1693–94 (Jan. 9, 1998).

[49] 59 Fed. Reg. 65,372, 65,377 (Dec. 19, 1994).

cess to cutting-edge medical information.[50] It was this type of benefit that CMS intended to protect when it promulgated an exception for medical staff incidental benefits. It seems today that the risk of prosecution of a hospital for installing a terminal in a physician's office that can access the hospital mainframe and the Internet would be low. However, it is important to note that in the two advisory opinions issued by the OIG regarding the provision of telemedicine equipment to physicians, the OIG found that the arrangements implicated the antikickback statute but would not be prosecuted for several reasons, including the reason that the lease agreements satisfied the equipment rental safe harbor.[51]

## I. Medicare Prohibition on Unbundling

When Congress enacted the prospective payment system for hospitals, one of its concerns was that while full DRG payment could be made to hospitals, entities other than hospitals could submit additional charges for the hospitalized patient. Hence, Congress amended the law to bar anyone, except hospitals and physicians (and now certain other allied health professionals such as certified nurse anesthetists), from billing for services furnished to Medicare hospital patients. The exception for professional billing is solely for services personally furnished by physicians or mid-level professionals.[52] This is called the "prohibition against unbundling." Some physicians use their own equipment or personnel in treating hospital patients. Nothing in the law prohibits this practice. However, physicians may not charge Medicare for their equipment or personnel services. For example, a physician directing a staff nurse to take equipment to a hospital and administer a diagnostic test to a patient may not bill for any service other than interpretation of that test. If Medicare is billed for services other than test interpretation, in this case, the physician and the hospital are subject to CMPs, and the hospital is also at risk of termination of its provider agreement.

Accordingly, hospitals must ensure that neither physicians nor anyone else bill Medicare for services furnished to hospital patients, other than services personally performed by a physician or other mid-level professional falling within an exception to the prohibition against unbundling. If outside suppliers furnish other than separately billable professional services to hospital patients, the hospital may pay for such services and bill Medicare.[53]

---

[50] 66 Fed. Reg. 921, 856 (Jan 4, 2001).

[51] U.S. Dep't of Health & Human Servs., OIG Advisory Op. No. 98-18 (Nov. 25, 1998), *available at* http://www.hhs.gov/oig/advopn/1998/ao98_18.htm; OIG Advisory Op. No. 99-14 (Dec. 28, 1999), *available at* http://www.hhs.gov/oig/advopn/1999/ao99_14.htm.

[52] 42 U.S.C. §1395cc(a)(1)(H); 42 C.F.R. §489.20(d); *see also* 53 Fed. Reg. 29,486 (Aug. 5, 1988) (Hospital PPS Proposed Rule); 63 Fed. Reg. 47,552, 47,555–559 (Sept. 8, 1998) (Hospital PPS Final Rule).

[53] Although the service will be included on the hospital's bill to Medicare, under the DRG system, there will not be any additional payment to the hospital unless the patient is a cost outlier.

Because Stark II treats all inpatient and outpatient hospital services for Medicare and Medicaid patients as designated health services subject to Stark II referral and billing prohibitions, when a physician orders these services it will be necessary for the financial arrangements between the physician and the hospital to qualify for an exception under Stark II. It is possible to structure a permissible compensation arrangement under Stark II whereby the hospital pays the physician on a per service or per unit of time basis for performing these services, provided that the per service or per unit of time payment is agreed to in advance and constitutes the fair market value of the services actually provided by the physician, not taking into account the volume or value of any of the physician's referrals to the hospital or other business generated by the physician for the hospital.[54]

## J. Physician Use of Hospital Clinic Space

Some hospitals operate their own clinics. Those clinics may qualify as hospital outpatient departments or may simply operate as physician offices. Medicare payment differs depending on whether the site is a hospital-based outpatient department. Many other payers do not make that distinction and will pay for the services as if they were furnished in a physician office. When a hospital operates a clinic, the hospital must ordinarily collect payments to cover its costs from either third-party payers or from the physicians practicing at that site. The failure to do so raises issues under the Stark law, the limitations applicable to tax-exempt hospitals, and the anti-kickback statute.

When a hospital-operated clinic operates as a hospital outpatient department,[55] there are two charges, one for physician services and another for hospital technical component services. The hospital's charge is recorded regardless of whether the patient received any ancillary tests; this technical component charge covers all costs except services personally furnished by the physician or other mid-level professional who may bill independently. Medicare honors the hospital's bill, but because it is paying the hospital for overhead costs ordinarily deemed to be included in the physician's fee, Medicare will reduce the physician payment for services furnished in a hospital outpatient department.[56] This reduction is referred to as the "site of service" differential and its application is triggered when the physician indicates on the face of the bill that the site of service was a hospital outpatient setting.

Medicare is almost unique among third-party payers in honoring a hospital facility charge for clinic services. Most other payers will not pay the hospital bill, but will pay the physician bill without any reduction for a site of service differential. In such instances, the hospital must obtain payment from the physician for the use of its facilities for

---

[54] 42 C.F.R. §411.354(d).

[55] 42 C.F.R. §413.65, *published in* 65 Fed. Reg. 18,434, 18,538 (Apr. 7, 2000).

[56] 42 C.F.R. §414.22(b)(5)(A).

which payment is included as an undifferentiated part of the payment to the physician from non-Medicare payers. If the hospital fails to do so, it is furnishing value in-kind to the physician, which constitutes a "financial relationship" within the meaning of the Stark law, and the transaction will not ordinarily fit within an exception. For the same reason, the transaction poses risks under tax laws applicable to tax-exempt hospitals. Finally, the transaction could be viewed as a kick-back to the extent that there is evidence of intent to induce or reward the physician for referring patients to the hospital.

When a hospital-operated clinic is not treated for Medicare purposes as a hospital outpatient department, the same issue exists, except it pertains to all payers, not just Medicare. For the reasons discussed above, it is critical for a hospital to obtain fair market value payment from physicians for the space, personnel, and other items or services furnished to them. Such payments should be able to fit within the Stark exception for payment of fair market value compensation by physicians for items or services.[57]

There may be one circumstance in which a hospital could furnish clinic space to physicians at no charge. In some remote parts of the country or in inner city areas, it is difficult to persuade physicians to maintain offices or even visit. If there is demonstrated difficulty in obtaining physician services, a hospital may furnish clinic space at no charge to a physician as fair compensation for physician availability and travel time in coming to the site. Assuming that the facts are consistent with the claim of physician shortage and there is no evidence of any improper intent to motivate referrals, both anti-kickback and tax-exempt organization problems should be eliminated. However, it remains unclear as to whether there might still be Stark law problems in such a case.

## IV. CONTRACTUAL RELATIONSHIPS WITH PHYSICIANS

### A. Generally Applicable Limitations Arising From Tax-Exempt Status Can Be the Basis for Intermediate Sanctions Under the Internal Revenue Code

The Internal Revenue Service (IRS) perceives that hospitals are prone to furnish benefits to physicians for admitting patients who bring in revenues beyond payment of fair market value for necessary services. However, the only weapon that the IRS had historically to deal with violations of the limitations on tax-exempt hospitals was revocation of the hospital's tax-exempt status. The severity of the penalty meant that it was rarely used. To make the threat of enforcement of the prohibitions on tax-exempt organizations engaging in transactions resulting in inurement or private benefit more credible, Congress amended the law to

---

[57] 42 U.S.C. §1395nn(e)(8); 42 C.F.R. §411.357(i).

permit the imposition of intermediate sanctions for violations of these prohibitions.[58]

The intermediate sanctions provisions impose an excise tax whenever a Section 501(c)(3) public charity or a Section 501(c)(4) organization provides an excess benefit (e.g., unreasonable compensation, a bargain sale or lease, or other non–fair market value transaction) to or for the benefit of a "disqualified person." The amount of the tax is initially 25 percent of the excess benefit provided to the disqualified person, but if the transaction is not timely corrected, a second-tier tax of 200 percent of the excess benefit is imposed.[59] In addition, a 10 percent excise tax (up to a per-transaction maximum of $10,000) is imposed on any individual organization manager for the tax-exempt organization who approves or participates in the transaction knowing it to be an excess benefit transaction.[60] In each case, the excise tax is imposed on the individuals involved and not on the organization itself. The IRS published temporary regulations in January 2001 to address an array of interpretational issues related to the intermediate sanctions statute, some of which are summarized below.[61]

### 1. Definition of "Disqualified Persons"

One of the major uncertainties regarding intermediate sanctions has been precisely who would be a "disqualified person" subject to the rules. The statute provides simply that a disqualified person is a person who is in a position to exercise substantial influence over the affairs of the applicable tax-exempt organization at any time during a 5-year look-back period, as well as family members of a disqualified person and certain 35 percent controlled entities.[62] The temporary regulations add considerable meat to these statutory bones. In this regard, the temporary regulations specifically identify certain persons who hold the following powers, responsibilities, or interests as having substantial influence over the affairs of a tax-exempt organization. These include:

- any individual who serves as a voting member on the governing body of the organization;
- any individual or individuals who have the power or responsibilities of the president, chief executive officer, chief operating officer, treasurer or chief financial officer of an organization, regardless of title; and

---

[58]Taxpayers Bill of Rights 2, Pub. L. No. 104-168, §1311, 110 Stat. 1452 (1996) (codified at 26 U.S.C. §4958).

[59] 26 U.S.C. §§4958(a)(1), (b).

[60] 26 U.S.C. §§4958(a)(2), (d)(2).

[61] 66 Fed. Reg. 2144 (Jan. 10, 2001) (considered temporary because they only have a 3-year duration—from Jan. 10, 2001, to Jan. 9, 2004—and the IRS will continue to refine these regulations).

[62] 26 U.S.C. §4958(f)(1).

- any person who has material financial interest in certain provider-sponsored organizations in which a tax-exempt hospital participates.[63]

The temporary regulations also identify categories of persons deemed not to have substantial influence over the affairs of a tax-exempt organization. These categories include any employee who receives economic benefits from the organization that are less than what a highly compensated employee earns,[64] who is not otherwise defined in the proposed regulations as a disqualified person or identified as having substantial influence, and who is not a substantial contributor to the organization.[65]

Apart from these more specific rules, the temporary regulations provide that the determination of whether a person has substantial influence over the affairs of an organization is based on all relevant facts and circumstances.[66] Under the temporary regulations, some of the facts and circumstances tending to show that a person has substantial influence over the affairs of an organization are that:

- the person is the founder of the organization;
- the person is a substantial contributor to the organization;
- the person's compensation is based on revenues derived from activities of the organization that the person controls;
- the person has authority to control or determine a significant portion of the organization's capital expenditures, operating budget, or compensation for employees;
- the person has managerial authority;
- the person owns a controlling interest in a corporation, partnership, or trust that is defined as a disqualified person; or
- the person is in legal terms a non-stock entity controlled by a disqualified person.

There are also several factors that tend to show no substantial influence over the organization:

- the person has taken a vow of poverty;
- the person is an independent contractor who merely provides professional advice and does not have decision-making authority;
- the direct supervisor of the person is not a disqualified person;
- the person participates in no management decisions affecting the whole or discrete parts of the organization; or
- any preferential treatment offered to a person based on a contribution is offered to all other donors making a similar donation.

---

[63] 66 Fed. Reg. at 2160 (codified at 26 C.F.R. §53.4958-3T).

[64] As defined under 26 U.S.C. §414(g).

[65] 66 Fed. Reg. at 2160–61.

[66] *Id.* at 2161.

Any physician on a hospital's board of directors, or who has been on the board in the last 5 years, is a disqualified person. Other physicians may also be disqualified persons, as illustrated by the following IRS examples:

- A cardiologist employed by a tax-exempt hospital is a disqualified person when the cardiologist is managerial head of the department and has authority to allocate the budget for that department, including authority to determine employee compensation.
- A radiologist employed by a tax-exempt hospital in a non-managerial capacity is *not* a disqualified person when the radiologist does not receive revenue-based compensation from activities he controlled and has no authority to control or determine any significant portion of the hospital's capital expenditures, operating budget, or employee compensation.
- A management company of a whole hospital joint venture with a tax-exempt hospital participant is a disqualified person when the management company is given broad discretion to manage the joint venture's day-to-day operations.[67]

## 2. Definition of Reasonable Compensation

Under the temporary regulations, compensation for the performance of services is reasonable, and thus does not confer an excess benefit, only if it is an "amount that would ordinarily be paid for like services by like enterprises under like circumstances."[68] Generally, the circumstances to be considered are those existing on the date the contract for services was made, with special rules taking into account any material modification and certain termination rights with respect to the contract. However, when reasonableness of compensation cannot be determined based on circumstances existing on the date the contract for services was made, then the determination of whether the compensation is reasonable is made based on all facts and circumstances, up to and including circumstances as of the date of payment. Compensation under the proposed regulations includes all items provided by a tax-exempt organization in exchange for the performance of services by a disqualified person, regardless of whether cash or non-cash compensation and (subject to some exceptions) whether taxable or nontaxable compensation.

## 3. Rebuttable Presumption That a Transaction Is Not an Excess Benefit

The temporary regulations state that a compensation arrangement between a tax-exempt organization and a disqualified person is presumed to be reasonable—and a transfer of property, a right to use property, or any other transaction with a disqualified person is presumed

---

[67] *Id.* at 2162.

[68] *Id.* at 2166 (codified at 26 C.F.R §53.4958-4T(b)).

to be at fair market value—if three conditions are satisfied: (1) the compensation arrangement or terms of transfer are approved by the organization's governing body or a committee of the governing body composed entirely of individuals who do not have a conflict of interest with respect to the arrangement or transaction; (2) the governing body, or committee thereof, obtained and relied on appropriate comparability data prior to making its determination; and (3) the governing body or committee adequately documented the basis for its determination concurrently with making that determination.[69] The IRS may rebut this presumption "only if it develops sufficient contrary evidence to rebut the probative value of the comparability data relied upon by the authorized body."[70] It is highly advisable for hospitals to take the steps to fit within this safe harbor whenever entering into transactions with physicians who may be disqualified persons.

### 4. Rules for Revenue-Sharing Transactions

Under the intermediate sanctions statute, the IRS has authority to promulgate regulations that address whether certain revenue-sharing transactions with disqualified persons (e.g., compensation based in whole or in part on the revenues of one or more activities of the tax-exempt organization) result in inurement, and therefore constitute an excess benefit transaction.[71] The IRS proposed rules in 1998 to govern these transactions, but due to the overwhelming number of conflicting comments on this issue, did not publish rules governing these transactions in the temporary regulations. The IRS indicated that it may issue proposed rules on this topic in the future, but in the meantime, revenue-sharing transactions will be evaluated under the general rules for excess benefit transactions.[72]

## B. Hospitals Often Lease Space to Physicians

Physicians often prefer office space in or near a hospital for the convenience of seeing and treating hospitalized patients. Hospitals also benefit from this close proximity because physicians who are nearby are readily available to patients if needed. In addition, a hospital may believe that a physician is more likely to admit patients to it instead of a competitor if it is more convenient for the physician to do so. For all of these reasons, most hospitals have at least one, if not more, professional office buildings on or near campuses owned by the hospital or a hospital affiliate.

Again, the trinity of legal issues—limitations on tax-exempt organizations, the Stark law, and the anti-kickback statute—is of concern. For all of these issues, there is a simple solution: The hospital must lease space at fair market value.

---

[69]*Id.* at 2167–68 (codified at 26 C.F.R. §53.4958-6T).

[70]*Id.* at 2168.

[71]26 U.S.C. §4958(c)(2).

[72]66 Fed. Reg. at 2153.

The Office of Inspector General of the U.S. Department of Health and Human Services (OIG) created a safe harbor under the anti-kickback statute for leases of space. The requirements of the safe harbor are:

1. The lease agreement must be set out in writing and signed by the parties.
2. The lease must specify the premises it covers.
3. If the lease is intended to provide the lessee with access to the premises for periodic intervals of time, rather than on a full-time basis, it must specify exactly the schedule of such intervals, their precise length, and the exact rent for such intervals.
4. The term of the lease must be for not less than 1 year.
5. The aggregate rental charge must be set in advance, be consistent with fair market value in arm's length transactions and not be determined in a manner that takes into account the volume or value of any referrals or business otherwise generated between the parties for which payment may be made in whole or in part under Medicare or a state health care program.
6. The amount of space rented must not exceed that reasonably necessary to accomplish a commercially reasonable business purpose.[73]

A transaction that does not fit within a safe harbor does not necessarily violate the anti-kickback statute; failure to fit within a safe harbor simply means that the parties do not have absolute assurance that the transaction will not be challenged. Depending on the nature of the transaction, the parties often can have a very high level of comfort without precisely fitting within a safe harbor. However, the safe harbor for leases of space is so easily met, there is usually no reason not to do so.

Because a lease is a financial relationship under the Stark law, physician leases of hospital-owned space must necessarily meet an exception to Stark. Unlike the safe harbor for leases under the anti-kickback statute, the need to meet a Stark exception when there is a financial relationship between a hospital and a referring physician is not optional. The requirements for the Stark exception for leases of space are:

1. The agreement must be set out in writing, signed by the parties, and specify the premises covered by the lease.
2. The term of the agreement must be for at least 1 year.
3. The space rented or leased must not exceed that which is reasonable and necessary for the legitimate business purposes of the lease or rental and must be used exclusively by the lessee, except that the lessee may pay for the use of space consisting of common areas if those payments do not exceed the lessee's

---

[73] 42 C.F.R. §1001.952(b). (For text of the safe harbor, see Appendix A-2.)

pro rata share of expenses based on the ratio of the space used exclusively by the lessee to the total amount of space (other than common areas) occupied by all persons using the common areas.

4. The rental charges over the term of the lease must be determined in advance and be consistent with fair market value.

5. The charges must not be determined in a manner that takes into account the volume or value of any referrals or other business generated between the parties.

6. The agreement must be commercially reasonable even if no referrals were made between the lessee and the lessor.[74]

There is no specific IRS regulation for leases between tax-exempt hospitals and physicians, but the general principles of the prohibition against inurement and private benefit require that the lease be at fair market value. The IRS does consider the leasing of office space to a physician as a related activity and a tax-exempt hospital is not subject to the tax on unrelated business taxable income (UBTI) for lease payments.[75]

Thus, the key determinants of compliance under the three statutes of greatest concern are the determination and collection of rent at fair market value. In the abstract, fair market value (or fair rental value) is the amount negotiated between a willing landlord and a willing tenant when neither is coping with exigent circumstances.[76] In almost all instances, fair market value can be expressed in a range, not a single amount. A hospital is well advised to obtain contemporaneous documentation for its files showing that the amounts at which it is leasing to physicians are within the range of fair market value. Usually, a real estate broker in the community with access to market information can explain in writing the basis for arriving at an estimate of fair market value. Fair market value is not necessarily related to cost. It is quite possible that cost may be greater than fair market value. Thus, the recovery of cost is not necessarily the measure of fair market value.

In some instances when hospitals examine their compliance with Stark and other applicable laws, they discover that leases entered into years ago or by prior management do not satisfy requirements of the law because the rent is too low. If a significant portion of time remains in the lease term, this presents a problem to the hospital. Physicians have often been more sympathetic than one might expect to renegotiating an increased rent in the middle of a lease term. In other instances, however, physicians refuse to renegotiate the rent and rely on what

---

[74] 42 U.S.C. §1395nn(e)(1).

[75] *See* Rev. Rul. 69-463, 1969-2 C.B. 131; Rev. Rul. 69-464, 1969-2 C.B. 132; Priv. Ltr. Rul. 84-52-099.

[76] 63 Fed. Reg. 1659, 1686, 1721 (Jan. 9, 1998); 56 Fed. Reg. 35,952, 35,972 (July 29, 1991). But see the Stark Phase I regulations for a somewhat different definition. 42 C.F.R. §411.351. (For text of the Stark Phase I regulations, see Appendix B-3.)

they believe to be a binding obligation under state law. In such a case, the hospital could seek a declaratory judgment that the lease is not enforceable because it violates the anti-kickback statute, in that the low rent had been offered to the physician in exchange for referrals.[77] This is a risky strategy because voiding the contract involves admitting a violation of a federal criminal statute.

If rent is too low, but the intent was not to reward or induce the physician to refer patients to the hospital, there is no violation of the anti-kickback statute. However, there remains a problem under the Stark law. The only cure, apart from renegotiating fair market rental, is for the physician not to refer or admit Medicare or Medicaid patients to the hospital.

For Medicare cost-reporting purposes, costs associated with hospital space leased to physicians are not allowable.[78] This is of virtually no significance for most acute care hospitals because such cost reimbursement accounts for a small percentage of total payments to hospitals. However, this remains a relevant consideration for some hospitals.[79]

## C. Leases of Equipment

On occasion, a hospital leases equipment from a physician. It is not uncommon for physicians to lobby hospitals to purchase certain pieces of equipment. If hospitals fail to do so, physicians may make the purchase themselves and be able to perform procedures that they otherwise would have to refer to other physicians at other facilities. However, physicians may not recover equipment costs from Medicare or most other payers. As explained in Section III.I., above, under the Medicare prohibition against unbundling, physicians may charge Medicare only for services furnished personally to hospitalized patients. Thus, physicians may not charge Medicare for use of equipment when patients are hospitalized.

While most other payers do not have a similar rule, the cost of equipment used by physicians in hospitals is not usually reflected in "usual and customary" fee schedules or in other fee schedules negotiated by payers. Thus, for physicians to recover the cost of equipment purchased and used for hospital patients, physicians must look to hospitals for payment. One avenue for equipment cost recovery is through lease transactions in which hospitals pay physicians on a per procedure basis for the use of the equipment.

---

[77]*See* Polk County v. Peters, 800 F. Supp. 1451 (E.D. Tex. 1992) (physician defended against hospital claim by asserting illegality of contract under anti-kickback statute).

[78]PROVIDER REIMBURSEMENT MANUAL, Pt. I §2108.5.

[79]*E.g.*, critical access hospitals in rural areas, psychiatric hospitals, and rehabilitation hospitals which continue to be cost-reimbursed. In addition, there are a few Blue Cross plans that continue to pay cost reimbursement using the Medicare principles of reimbursement.

Because an owner/lessor physician is also the physician most often using the equipment covered by the lease, the amount of rent paid is closely tied to the volume of the physician's referrals. CMS has clarified in its preamble comments to the Stark II regulations that hospitals are permitted to pay per service or per unit of time rental fees to physicians leasing equipment, notwithstanding the fact that physician lessors make referrals to use the equipment at hospitals, provided that rental payments are agreed to in advance, constitute fair market value rent for the equipment, and do not vary over the lease term.[80] It is important to note, however, that in determining whether the rental amount meets the fair market value standard, the parties must look to comparable equipment leasing arrangements that do not involve lessors who are referring physicians.[81] According to CMS, if such information is not available, the parties must set the rental amount based on other relevant factors (for example, the cost of the equipment) that do not take into account that the physician lessor is a source of referrals.[82]

However, such a lease will not meet the equipment rental safe harbor to the anti-kickback statute because the aggregate contract price cannot be set in advance for per procedure leases.[83] This problem was raised by commentators and addressed in the final safe harbor rules. Although the OIG recognized that this requirement would be a problem for as-needed arrangements, it found the requirement necessary to prevent abusive arrangements and reminded commentators "that safe harbors do not define the scope of legal activities under the anti-kickback statute."[84] These arrangements can still be lawful as long as payments are not made to induce referrals.

## D. Medical Director Agreements

Hospitals commonly compensate medical directors, not just for services to the hospital as a whole, but also for individual departments. Indeed, Medicare requires a hospital to have medical directors for psychiatric units and rehabilitation units.[85] Thus, there is nothing wrong with compensating physicians for services as medical directors. Yet in some situations, compensation to medical directors has been characterized as payment for referrals, not for medical director duties. Thus, there necessarily must be a demonstrable need for the physician's medical director services and compensation paid for those services must be at fair market value.

---

[80] 66 Fed. Reg. 856, 876 (Jan. 4, 2001); 42 C.F.R. §411.354(d)(1).

[81] *Id.*

[82] 66 Fed. Reg. at 876–77.

[83] 42 C.F.R. §1001.952(e).

[84] 64 Fed. Reg. 63,518, 63,526 (Nov. 19, 1999). The anti-kickback statute is codified at 42 U.S.C. §1320a-7b(b) (see Appendix A-1 for full text of the anti-kickback statute).

[85] 42 C.F.R. §§412.27(d)(2), 412.29(f).

Two Stark exceptions cover medical directors. First, a hospital can employ a medical director, full-time or part-time, as long as the amount paid is fair market value, does not relate to the volume or value of referrals made by that physician, and is paid pursuant to a commercially reasonable agreement that specifically identifies the services rendered.[86]

As a practical matter, however, most medical directors serve as independent contractors and not as employees. The Stark exception for personal services agreements also can come into play; the exception requires:

1. The arrangement must be set out in writing, signed by the parties, and specify the services covered by the arrangement.
2. The arrangement must cover all of services to be furnished by the physician (or an immediate family member of the physician) to the entity.
3. The aggregate services contracted for must not exceed those that are reasonable and necessary for the legitimate business purposes of the arrangement.
4. The term of the arrangement must be for at least 1 year.
5. The compensation to be paid over the term of the arrangement must be set in advance, must not exceed fair market value, and, except in the case of a physician incentive plan, must not be determined in a manner that takes into account the volume or value of any referrals or other business generated between the parties.
6. The services to be furnished under the arrangement must not involve counseling or promotion of a business arrangement or other activity that violates any state or federal law.[87]

A similar safe harbor exists under the anti-kickback statute.[88] One difference between the safe harbor exception and the Stark exception is that the anti-kickback safe harbor requires that the specific times for part-time service be stated. That constraint is impractical for medical director arrangements. Although there is no legal guarantee that an arrangement meeting the Stark exception would not be viewed as violating the anti-kickback statute, in most situations compliance with the Stark exception should give the parties a high level of comfort that there is not a material anti-kickback risk.

Three elements must be satisfied to demonstrate that a medical director's compensation is set at fair market value: the amount per hour (or however the unit of service is defined) must be reasonable, the amount of time used must be necessary, and that the time paid is the amount of time actually spent must be documented. Fortunately, a reasonable amount of data is available on physician compensation. At the

---

[86] 42 U.S.C. §1395nn(e)(2).
[87] 42 U.S.C. §1395nn(e)(3).
[88] 42 C.F.R. §1001.952(d).

low end of the scale are the Medicare reasonable compensation equivalents (RCEs). The RCEs are used to evaluate the allowability of physician compensation. The original RCEs were set at the median, and have been updated only to 1997, and even then use a methodology yielding a low percentage increase.[89] Compensation above the RCEs is common and RCEs do not define fair market value.

Justifying the need for the medical director services goes hand-in-hand with showing that the services are actually furnished. Any situation with more than one medical director for a single department is likely to be viewed with suspicion. If such arrangements exist, hospitals should be especially thorough in demonstrating the necessity for the arrangements.

Documentation of medical director services is also important. For Medicare cost reporting purposes, a provider may not claim costs for physician compensation unless the provider has time records or other verifiable documentation showing that the physician actually worked the time for which compensation has been claimed.[90] With the declining importance of cost reimbursement, many hospitals do not insist that compensated physicians maintain the time records required to claim reimbursement. However, those records could be very useful if the government ever challenged, for purposes of the Stark exception or otherwise, whether the amount paid to a physician was fair market value.

## E. Employing and Contracting With Physicians for the Provision of Patient Care Services

Many hospitals seek to employ or contract with physicians to furnish not just medical director services, but to provide direct patient care. Hospitals do this for a number of reasons. One is to provide physician services in an underserved geographic area. For a charitable hospital to meet its mission to furnish health care services to the community it serves, it sometimes must retain physicians directly. Hospitals may also place physicians in outlying communities to expand the hospital's service area. Some hospitals seek control over physicians to facilitate the negotiation of managed care contracts. Directly controlling a network of physicians is much easier to manage, both legally and practically, than dealing through a PHO for managed care contracts.

### 1. Federal Compliance Issues

From a federal compliance perspective, employing physicians is the simplest way to avoid risk. The anti-kickback statute has an express exception for employees.[91] Similarly, the Stark exception for employees is very simple and requires only that the employment be bona fide and

---

[89] 62 Fed. Reg. 24,483 (May 5, 1997).

[90] 42 C.F.R. §415.60(g)(1).

[91] 42 U.S.C. §1320a-7b(b)(3)(B); *see also* 42 C.F.R. §1001.952(i).

compensation be at fair market value and not tied to the volume or value of referrals (but it can be tied to personal productivity).[92] The Stark exception for personal services contracts is also fairly easy to comply with although it is more formal, as discussed in Section IV.D., above. The personal services exception is sometimes limiting in that it requires that the term of the agreement be a minimum of 1 year. But even that is not a problem if the arrangement can fit within the general fair-market-value exception appearing in the Stark II, Phase I final rule allowing arrangements for less than 1 year if they are renewed with the same terms.[93]

The difficulty with most situations in which hospitals employ or contract with physicians for the provision of medical services in hospital-operated clinics is that the vast majority of such clinics lose money. Losing money can raise the inference that physicians are being paid too much, i.e., that they are making more money than they would make in their own private practices. If physicians are paid more than they would make in private practice, there is a serious problem under the Stark law, a problem of inurement or private benefit under the applicable IRS law for tax-exempt hospitals, and a potential risk of being accused of violating the anti-kickback statute. Accordingly, it is necessary to determine why the practice is losing money and whether the physician is being paid too much in comparison with market data or if other factors are causing the loss.

Hospital-owned clinics have higher costs than physician offices for several reasons. First, many hospitals have greater expectations for what the space should look like, where it should be located, and how it should be furnished. While physicians often tolerate a cramped, poorly decorated space, most hospitals avoid that type of cost savings for image reasons. Second, clinic personnel are often paid at a level comparable to hospital scales for comparably qualified personnel. Those compensation levels usually are substantially in excess of what physician offices normally pay. Similarly, the Employee Retirement Income Security Act (ERISA) usually requires that hospitals offer the same benefit packages to clinic and hospital employees, and those benefits are almost always more generous than those typically offered by physicians. Thus, the costs of hospital operation of physician practices are greater than costs that physicians typically incur on their own.

In addition, revenue may suffer in hospital-operated practices. Hospital clinics are more likely to accept indigent and Medicaid patients. Usually, fewer ancillary services will be furnished in practices operated by hospitals because of the greater efficiency of sending patients to the hospital rather than duplicating those services in clinics. Thus, revenue for such ancillary services that is often captured in physician practices, and that under Stark may properly be distributed to

---

[92] 42 U.S.C. §1395nn(e)(2); 42 C.F.R. §411.357(c).

[93] 66 Fed. Reg. 856, 917–19, 961–62 (Jan. 4, 2001) (codified at 42 C.F.R. §411.357(*l*)).

physicians as long as the basis for distribution is not the volume or value of referrals from any individual physician, is not captured in hospital-operated clinics. Prevailing compensation levels for physicians reflect profits on ancillary services. Although hospitals may not pay physicians for referrals for ancillary services, there is no requirement to pay less than fair market value compensation for physician services furnished in a hospital-owned practice.

An issue related to hospital operation of physician practices is hospital acquisition of physician practices. In the 1990s, hospitals commonly acquired physician practices and the amounts paid often included payments for goodwill and other intangible assets. "Goodwill" is the value of a business based on future profitability. The problem that some hospitals encountered in acquiring physician practices was that they paid considerable amounts for the goodwill of practices that did not produce any net income. This left open the question of whether the amount paid was in excess of fair market value, which posed problems under the Stark law, the tax-exempt hospital restrictions, and the anti-kickback statute.

Physician practice acquisitions by hospitals can fit within the isolated transaction exception to the Stark law provided that the amount paid is fair market value, it does not directly or indirectly take into account the volume or value of referrals, the agreement would be commercially reasonable, and "there are no additional transactions between the parties for 6 months after the [sale of the practice]."[94] Goodwill is not the only intangible asset acquired in most transactions; hospitals also acquire the value of an ongoing business that includes an assembled workforce, telephone listing, arrangements for space and with vendors, and similar business assets. Hospitals establishing practices on their own would have to duplicate all of these items, and therefore, reasonable value should be attributed to these items. In addition, hospitals should be certain to obtain written valuations of acquired practices prepared by experts familiar with physician practice value. The nature of the appraisal is discussed below in connection with IRS treatment of physician practice acquisitions.

The OIG has created a safe harbor for physician acquisition of other physician practices, but specifically refrained from extending that safe harbor to hospital acquisition of physician practices in most cases.[95]

The IRS has also been concerned that hospitals may pay too much to acquire physician practices, but does not otherwise object to such transactions. In determining the appropriate valuation for physician practice acquisitions, the IRS wants to see appraisals based on the future expected income stream from the practice after physician com-

---

[94] 42 C.F.R. §411.357(f).

[95] 42 C.F.R. §1001.952(e), 56 Fed. Reg. 35,952, 35,975 (July 29, 1991). In 1999, the safe harbor was extended to cover hospital acquisition of physician practices located in a health professional shortage area (HPSA) under certain circumstances.

pensation has been paid.[96] This discounted cash flow methodology, of course, presumes that there will be profit from acquired practices. There are at least two crucial elements in the valuation process, the first of which concerns assumptions used to estimate expected future income such as payer rates, patient volume, the impact of managed care, and physician compensation and other costs. The second element is the imputed interest rate applied to discount future expected income, which will be driven by prevailing interest rates and the risk associated with physician practices.

### 2. State Corporate Practice of Medicine Prohibitions

The greater problem for either employment or independent contractor arrangements arises under state statutes barring the corporate practice of medicine.[97] The underlying purpose of these statutes is to bar nonlicensed laypersons from interfering in the medical judgment of licensed physicians. In the era when managed care personnel freely make clinical judgments (but "only" on what is covered and not what should be done clinically), this doctrine may seem quaint, but it is a very serious legal issue in some states. In so-called "corporate practice states," physicians may be barred in any way from sharing income from professional services with any non-physician. Thus, even an arrangement in which the hospital contractually states that it will not interfere with a physician's medical judgment may be illegal in some states if the physician's revenue is assigned or shared with the hospital or any other non-physician.

There are several ways to deal with the corporate practice issue. Some hospitals and physicians choose to ignore the problem. In some states, the employment of physicians is a common practice that has continued for many years without challenge. In these instances, the principal risk of ignoring the doctrine may be that the contract between the hospital and physician is found to be void as a matter of public policy. This occurred initially in *Holden v. Rockford Memorial Hospital*,[98] where a court barred enforcement of the noncompetition clause in a physician's contract with the hospital by invoking the corporate practice doctrine to void the contract. Although that particular case was reversed on

---

[96] Internal Revenue Serv., U.S. Dep't of Treasury, *Exempt Organizations Continuing Professional Education Technical Instruction Program Textbook 2001.*

[97] *See, e.g.,* TEX. REV. CIV. STAT. ANN. art. 4495b, §3.08(12), (15). A summary of corporate practice limitations, by state, can be obtained from both Catherine I. Hanson, Vice President, General Counsel, California Medical Association ("Summary of State Positions on the Corporate Practice of Medicine Bar") and Cameron Dobbins of Dobbins, Fraker, Tennant Joy & Perlstein ("Survey of State Laws Relating to the Corporate Practice of Medicine").

[98] 678 N.E.2d 342 (Ill. App. Ct. 1997), *vacated by* 688 N.E.2d 309 (Ill. 1997), *on remand to* 692 N.E.2d 374 (Ill. App. Ct. 1998). *See also* Berlin v. Sarah Bush Lincoln Health Ctr., 688 N.E.2d 106 (Ill. 1997) (initially finding entire agreement unenforceable under corporate practice of medicine doctrine, but ultimately the court found a licensed hospital, whether for-profit or nonprofit, is exempt from prohibition of corporate practice of medicine).

appeal, the nonenforceability of an agreement with a physician is a potential risk in a number of states.

Ignoring the corporate practice doctrine in some states would be foolhardy. In Texas, for instance, violation of the bar on the corporate practice of medicine is a criminal offense and physicians can also lose their licenses. Even if the only sanction is the physician's loss of license, one can imagine that the physician might seek damages from both the hospital and the hospital's lawyer who drafted the agreement.

Some states have created exceptions to the corporate practice doctrine for separate entities controlled by nonprofit hospitals. For example, in Texas, so-called "5.01(a) corporations" may employ physicians provided that the organization is a nonprofit corporation, organized for a specific medical purpose, and organized and incorporated by persons licensed by the Texas State Board of Medical Examiners.[99]

Another tool to deal with the corporate practice problem is a management agreement with an independent physician practice, through which the hospital manager controls the space and other aspects of the practice to achieve management goals without employing physicians or contracting for physician services. But even these arrangements could possibly be viewed as violating the corporate practice prohibition if the management fee is closely tied to physician revenue.

### 3. Medicare and Medicaid Prohibitions on the Reassignment of Revenue

Both Medicare and Medicaid statutes bar the reassignment of revenue by a physician, supplier, or provider unless an exception to that prohibition is satisfied.[100] (The first assignment of revenue is deemed to be from the patient to the provider, physician, or supplier although that assignment may be required by law.) Thus, absent an exception, physicians may not arrange for reimbursements for treating Medicare patients to be paid to any other entity.

The first question in analyzing a potential reassignment issue is whether there actually is a "reassignment" of revenue as defined by Medicare and Medicaid. The definition of "reassignment" is not a limited legal definition but covers powers of attorney, and any situation in which someone other than the physician has control over payment.[101] Reassignment occurs in any instance in which a hospital directly receives and controls Medicare and Medicaid payments.

When reassignments occur, the next question is whether they fit within an exception[102] to the general prohibition. Hospitals may qual-

---

[99] Tex. Rev. Civ. Stat. Ann. art. 4495b, §5.01(a).

[100] 42 U.S.C. §§1395g(c), 1396a(a)(32).

[101] Medicare Carriers Manual, Pt. III, §§3060A, C. The definition of "reassignment" does not include those situations in which someone other than the physician is authorized to simply endorse a government check "for deposit only" and deposit it in an account controlled solely by the physician.

[102] The exceptions are set forth at Medicare Carriers Manual, Pt. III, §3060B.

ify for several exceptions. One broadly applicable exception exists when physicians are in an employment relationship with the entity receiving the reassignment; physicians may always reassign their payments to employers. A second exception applies when physicians reassign payments to hospitals for services furnished at the hospital. By its terms, however, that exception is limited to services furnished on certified hospital premises. Usually, a physician will have an office outside the hospital and will see patients there as well. Services in off-premises offices can also fit within the exception for services furnished in clinics. Again, however, the exception is limited to services furnished on-site. If physicians provide services to patients elsewhere, such as in nursing facilities, and are not employed by hospitals, payments for those services provided in neither hospital-owned clinics nor on hospital premises do not technically fit within an existing exception to the prohibition against reassignment.

An issue that emerged in the late 1990s involved hospital contracts with commercial companies to furnish emergency room physician coverage to the hospital. Typically, those commercial companies required their contractor physicians to assign revenue to them. These arrangements did not fit within any existing exception.

Although the prohibition against reassignment has existed for many years, it has not been enforced vigorously. Indeed, the Medicare Carriers Manual suggests that the proper enforcement is to inform the physician that the assignment is not proper and if the arrangement is not changed within a reasonable period of time, to withhold payments.[103] Nothing in the Manual suggests that a violation of the prohibition against reassignment is a false claim or otherwise sanctionable with any of the multiple CMPs in the law. However, the OIG has alleged that violations of the prohibition against reassignment are actionable as false claims.[104]

## F. Hospital-Based Physicians

Hospitals routinely employ or contract with physicians for pathology and radiology services, as well as anesthesiology and the reading of

---

[103] MEDICARE CARRIERS MANUAL, Pt. III, §§3060.13A, B.

[104] United States *ex rel.* Schwartz v. Coastal Healthcare Group, No. 99-3105, 2000 WL 1595976, 232 F.3d 902 (Oct. 26, 2000) (unpublished table decision) (affirming dismissal of a physician's *qui tam* suit alleging Coastal violated the anti-assignment provisions of 42 U.S.C. §1395u(b)(6), which constitutes the making of false or fraudulent claims); Office of Inspector Gen., U.S. Dep't of Health & Human Servs., *Health Care Fraud Report Fiscal Year 1997*, *available at* http://www.usdoj.gov/01whatsnew/hcf-fraud2.htm (addressing false claims submitted through billing firms generally, and Coastal Healthcare Group specifically); Office of Inspector Gen., U.S. Dep't of Health & Human Servs., Statement of Lewis Morris, Assistant Inspector Gen. for Legal Affairs, Medicare: Third-Party Billing Companies, Testimony Before the House Committee on Commerce, Subcommittee on Oversight and Investigations (Apr. 6, 2000), *available at* http://oig.hhs.gov/testimony/00406fin.htm.

electrocardiograms (EKGs). Contractual arrangements may extend to other departments, such as nuclear medicine and various subsets of radiology, such as radiation therapy if separate from the radiology department. The terms of such contracts typically ensure the hospital of coverage at all times when coverage is needed (e.g., during normal business hours with on-call availability for emergencies); define what the hospital will make available to physicians, such as office space and certain equipment; define physician services for patients (e.g., interpretation of all diagnostic images within certain performance parameters); define physician duties within the hospital, such as the development of departmental policies, training of hospital personnel, and performance of quality assurance functions within the department; address who is entitled to revenue from the physicians' services for patients; provide for exclusivity with the physician group; and set forth monetary compensation, if any, that one party will pay to the other.

## 1. *Exclusivity*

As noted in Section III.A.2., above, exclusivity provisions of many hospital-based physician contracts may be challenged by physicians outside the group trying to obtain work. The overwhelming weight of authority has upheld exclusivity provisions in hospital contracts,[105] although it is still wise to recite in the contract the reasons exclusivity is appropriate, such as to ensure 24-hour coverage and consistent quality. Because both radiology and pathology are viewed as hospital functions, albeit with a physician element, the hospital needs accountability in those departments more than elsewhere, and accountability is more easily obtained when a single person or entity is responsible.

Challenges to exclusivity arise not just from outsiders trying to get in, but also from a physician or physician group who had an exclusive contract that has been terminated. Notwithstanding that they benefited from exclusivity for many years, some groups view the benefits of such arrangements quite differently when they are on the outside looking in. Physicians in such instances may attempt to challenge termination of their exclusive contract as tantamount to termination of medical staff privileges and appeal through the medical staff bylaw appeal process. It is unseemly that physicians should be able to enjoy the benefits of an exclusive contract and then subsequently challenge a hospital's determination to award an exclusive arrangement for the same department to another group. To prevent this scenario, many hospitals use what is referred to as a "go quietly" clause in their contracts with hospital-based physicians. As the name implies, these provisions bind contracting physicians not to use the medical staff bylaw appeal process to contest the termination of the contract.

---

[105] *See, e.g.,* Jefferson Parish Hosp. Dist. No. 2 v. Hyde, 466 U.S. 2 (1984); Korshin v. Benedictine Hosp., 34 F. Supp. 2d 133 (N.D.N.Y. 1999); Ezekwo v. American Bd. of Internal Med., 18 F. Supp. 2d. 271, 278 (S.D.N.Y. 1998); Finkelstein v. Aetna Health Plans of N.Y., 1997 WL 419211, at *4–5 (S.D.N.Y. July 25, 1997), *aff'd,* 152 F.3d 917 (2d Cir. 1998).

Interestingly, Joint Commission Hospital Accreditation Standard MS.5.14.3 provides that "[w]hen physicians or other individuals eligible for delineated clinical privileges are engaged by the hospital to provide patient care services pursuant to a contract, their clinical privileges to admit or treat patients are defined through medical staff mechanisms."[106] The intent of the standard is that a specified medical staff mechanism defines the clinical privileges of individuals with whom the hospital contracts to admit or treat patients.[107]

## 2. Kickbacks

An exclusive contract for a hospital department can be a valuable franchise. Virtually every hospital patient undergoes diagnostic imaging, and most surgical patients require anatomic pathology services. Physician fees for interpreting the diagnostic images or reading slides of tissue removed surgically can be lucrative. Some hospitals have sought to extract value for the franchise for physician services in these departments. Some rumored schemes have not been subtle at all and include required "donations" from the physician group to the hospital, or a rebate of a stated percentage of the physician's collected revenue. Other schemes are a bit more refined and may include a requirement that physicians use the hospital billing service at a fee that is well above prevailing market rates for similar services. The OIG views such arrangements as illegal kickbacks from physicians to hospitals in exchange for all of the hospital radiology or pathology physician work.[108]

The OIG has also criticized arrangements in which hospital-based physicians are not required to give anything to the hospital but are required to furnish certain services without compensation. For example, pathologists are expected to train clinical laboratory personnel, calibrate equipment, and engage in other quality assurance activities in the laboratory. To the extent that such services have value and the hospital provides no consideration for these services, the anti-kickback statute may be implicated. However, hospitals often furnish physicians a place to work, equipment, demographic information for their billing, and other support services. Thus, the absence of cash compensation is not necessarily evidence that the hospital is obtaining kickbacks through free services in exchange for exclusive contracts.

## G. Discounts on Reference Laboratory Services

Standard hospital charges for laboratory tests usually exceed the customary charges of competing reference laboratories to physicians

---

[106] JOINT COMMISSION ON ACCREDITATION OF HEALTHCARE ORGANIZATIONS, HOSPITAL ACCREDITATION STANDARDS, MS.5.14.3 (2000).

[107] *Id.*, Intent of MS.5.14.3.

[108] Office of Inspector Gen., U.S. Dep't of Health & Human Servs., *Financial Arrangements Between Hospitals and Hospital-Based Physicians*, OEI-09-89-00330 (Oct. 1991), *available at* http://oig.hhs.gov/oei/summaries/b327.pdf. This report predated the general applicability of the Stark law to hospital services, and does not discuss Stark issues.

who refer tests for nongovernmental patients. Thus, to compete successfully in the reference testing market, hospitals must discount their laboratory charges significantly.

Some Medicare reimbursement specialists have concluded that a hospital may not discount its charges under Medicare's cost reimbursement principles. This is a myth. In fact, CMS has stated expressly that "the Medicare program cannot dictate to a provider what its charges or charge structure may be."[109]

At one time, CMS had suggested that laboratory discounts to physicians would violate the Stark law. However, Congress amended the law to create an exception for physician payments to laboratories (including hospitals acting as a reference laboratories) "in exchange for the provision of clinical laboratory services."[110]

Deep discounts to physicians in certain circumstances can still present problems. The law requires laboratories to bill Medicare and Medicaid directly for all laboratory tests, but physicians often purchase laboratory services for nongovernmental patients. Physicians presumably mark-up the charges for those tests when they bill the patient or the third-party payer. If laboratories discount physician-purchased tests with the intent of inducing physicians to refer tests for governmental patients, a concern is created under the anti-kickback statute. Thus, the issue becomes at what point are discounts to physician so deep as to be "remuneration" and not the offering of services at fair market value. Naturally, this question must be answered on the basis of the facts of each situation. Unless the market is acting irrationally (or everyone is violating the anti-kickback statute), meeting prevailing market prices for laboratory services should not ordinarily expose hospital laboratories to charges relating to the anti-kickback statute.

Discounts below the Medicare allowable fee schedule for laboratory tests can also raise the possibility that the hospital will be accused of charging Medicare an amount "substantially in excess of [its] usual charges."[111] This is a complex area, but as a general rule, most hospital reference laboratory pricing should not raise a serious risk of being viewed as violating this law.[112]

---

[109] Provider Reimbursement Manual, Pt. I, §2203.

[110] 42 U.S.C. §1395nn(e)(8).

[111] 42 U.S.C. §1320a-7(b)(6); 42 C.F.R. §1001.701(a)(1).

[112] At one time, the OIG proposed to interpret this law as requiring providers to offer "most favored nation" status to Medicare, however, in the final rule, OIG did not take that position. 62 Fed. Reg. 47,182, 47,186, 47,192 (Sept. 8, 1997), 63 Fed. Reg. 46,676, 46,681 (Sept. 2, 1998). In a letter from Kevin McAnaney, Chief, Industry Guidance Branch, Office of Inspector Gen. (Apr. 26, 2000), *available at* http://oig.hhs.gov/ak/lab.htm, the OIG interpreted "usual" charges to mean median charges. "Substantially in excess" has not been defined in statute or regulation. *See* U.S. Dep't of Health & Human Servs., OIG Advisory Op. 99-2 (Mar. 4, 1999), *available at* http://www.hhs.gov/oig/advopn/1999/ao99_2.htm; OIG Advisory Op. 98-8 (July 6, 1998), *available at* http://www.hhs. gov/oig/advopn/1998/ao98_8.pdf.

## H. Practice Management Services Furnished by Hospitals to Physicians

Some hospitals have entered into physician practice management businesses to make money and to try to make themselves indispensable to physicians. As long as hospitals charge fair market value for their services, these arrangements should not create legal problems. The Stark statute creates a broad exception for physician payments to hospitals or other entities for "items or services . . . at a price consistent with fair market value."[113] Similarly, for purposes of the anti-kickback statute and the limitations applicable to a tax-exempt organization, the permissibility of furnishing services to a physician turns on whether fair value is received in return.

## I. Academic Medical Centers

Generally, teaching hospitals as a group generate positive operating margins. In contrast, faculty practice plans often experience difficulty paying competitive compensation and operating in the black. Thus, at many sites, there is a perceived need to supplement the income of faculty practice plans and affiliated teaching hospitals are the logical source of these funds.

Donative or equity transfers from tax-exempt teaching hospitals to faculty practice plans will be barred unless the faculty practice plans are also tax exempt. If faculty practice plans in these cases are tax exempt, such transfers without consideration from hospitals are not likely to be challenged by the IRS if the plans are designed to include performance targets related to the hospital's charitable mission, i.e., the promotion of health, indigent care, medical education, and research.

The Stark II, Phase I final rule creates a new compensation exception for payments made to faculty of academic medical centers (AMCs).[114] This exception is in addition to other exceptions that may apply, such as the personal service arrangements or employment exceptions. An arrangement only needs to meet the requirements of one of these exceptions to comply with the law.

An academic medical center, for purposes of the Stark exception, consists of at least an accredited medical school, an affiliated, nonprofit, tax-exempt faculty practice plan, and an affiliated hospital where the medical staff is made up primarily of faculty members and a majority of hospital admissions are made by such physicians.[115] The requirements of the exception include:

- The referring physician must:
  - —be a bona fide, full- or substantial part-time employee of a component of the AMC;

---

[113] 42 U.S.C. §1395nn(e)(8).

[114] 66 Fed. Reg. 856, 915–17, 960–61 (Jan. 4, 2001); 42 C.F.R. §411.355(c).

[115] *Id.* at 916.

—be state-licensed; and

—provide and be compensated for substantial academic or clinical teaching services.

- The total compensation paid by all components of the AMC must:

  —be set in advance;

  —not exceed fair market value; and

  —not be determined in a way that accounts for the value or volume of referrals or other business generated.

- The AMC must:

  —only transfer money among its components that directly or indirectly supports its missions of teaching, indigent care, research, or community service, which includes patient care;

  —set out the relationship of the components in an agreement adopted by the governing bodies of each component; and

  —assure research money paid to a referring physician solely supports bona fide research.

- The arrangement cannot violate the anti-kickback statute.

One practical problem common at many AMCs is the sheer number of arrangements among the hospital, the medical school, and the faculty practice plan. These arrangements are so numerous that there is no single source of information or recordkeeping. Another problem arises when arrangements are not in writing; these impromptu arrangements must be formalized, the parties must identify financial relationships, and then each arrangement must be analyzed.

While relationships in the aggregate may be set at fair market value, individual arrangements standing by themselves may not be as easily defended. To the extent that the parties desire to move funds from the hospital to the faculty practice plan or the medical school, the easiest way to do so is to pay full fair market value for the services furnished by the physicians to the hospital. For example, at the same time that some teaching hospitals are agonizing about how they may legally transfer funds to a medical school, they are paying far less than fair market value for teaching services furnished by physicians employed by the medical school.

## J. Gainsharing

Some hospitals have expressed interest in gainsharing, which is generally understood to refer to incentive plans for physicians to reduce hospital costs and enhance productivity. Gainsharing raises significant legal issues under the Medicare program, with implications under the civil monetary penalty statute,[116] physician incentive plan

---

[116] A general provision barring incentive payments to physicians relating to reducing care to individual patients. 42 U.S.C. §1320a-7a.

regulations,[117] the Stark law,[118] the anti-kickback statute,[119] and tax-exemption issues. The tax issues, however, appear to be more manageable since a favorable ruling has been issued on gainsharing.[120]

### 1. Civil Monetary Penalties for Improper Incentive Plans

The Social Security Act prohibits hospitals from knowingly making "a payment, directly or indirectly, to a physician as an inducement to reduce or limit services provided *with respect* to individuals" entitled to Medicare and Medicaid.[121] The sanction for hospitals that pay or physicians who receive such a prohibited payment is a CMP in the amount of not more than $2,000 for each individual for whom such a payment is made. In addition, violators will be subject to a $50,000 penalty for each act and "not more than 3 times the total amount of remuneration offered, paid, solicited, or received."[122] Congress enacted this provision in response to Medicare's conversion from cost-based reimbursement to the prospective payment system (PPS). In other words, because the PPS allows a single payment for an inpatient stay, Congress and CMS worried that hospitals would attempt to discharge patients prematurely or not furnish appropriate services. Therefore, the law was amended to prohibit the inappropriate limitation or reduction of services for Medicare and Medicaid beneficiaries.[123]

The literal wording of the prohibition suggests that it refers to reduction or limitation of services to individual patients and not, specifically, to a group or class of individuals. A payment by a hospital to a physician for each Medicare patient discharged a day under the expected length of stay for the patient's DRG clearly would be improper under this law. However, it is not nearly so clear that payments to a group of physicians for the reduction in the length of stay for a large group of Medicare patients over a period of time (e.g., all discharges for the year) would violate the law. The latter example arguably does not reward the reduction of services to "individuals." The wording of the amount of the penalty supports the conclusion that the statute is directed only toward payments with respect to individual patients because the sanction is "not more than $2,000 for each such individual with respect to whom the payment is made." If incentives were paid in

---

[117] 59 Fed. Reg. 61,571 (Dec. 1, 1994); see *infra* text accompanying note 121.

[118] 42 U.S.C. §1395nn. See generally Chapter 2 (Crane, Federal Physician Self-Referral Restrictions), and Appendix B-1 for full text of the Stark law.

[119] 42 U.S.C. §1320a-7b(b). See Appendix A-1 for full text of the anti-kickback statute.

[120] *IRS Approves Gainsharing Programs in Unreleased Private Letter Rulings*, 33 DAILY TAX REP. (BNA) G-1 (1999).

[121] 42 U.S.C. §1320a-7a(b)(1) (emphasis added). See Appendix D-1 for full text of the CMP statute.

[122] 42 U.S.C. §§1320a-7a(a)(7) *et seq.*

[123] Omnibus Budget Reconciliation Act of 1986, Pub. L. No. 99-509, §9313(c), 100 Stat. 1874, 2003–04 (1986) [hereinafter OBRA 1986].

the aggregate, the penalty provision would be much more difficult to apply because the incentives do not relate directly to individuals.

Similarly, the General Accounting Office's (GAO) report of July 1986 on physician incentive plans[124] provides some insight into the government's concern about gainsharing programs. Although this report preceded the enactment of the CMP provision, it was issued after the inception of the PPS and reflects continuing concerns regarding decreased services to Medicare and Medicaid beneficiaries. The GAO provides in this report specific recommendations to reduce the risk of abuse under physician incentive plans:

- Plan payments should be based on the cost performance of a group of physicians rather than individual physicians.
- Payments should be based on physician performance over a long period of time (at least 1 year).
- Incentive payments should not be based on hospital profits resulting from the treatment of any individual patient.
- Incentive plans should include strong utilization review and quality assurance programs.

Again, although this GAO report is not a rule or regulation promulgated by CMS or OIG, it may be instructive in determining how to implement a physician incentive or gainsharing plan.

In a December 1994 proposed rule,[125] the OIG referred to the GAO report, acknowledging the existence of physician incentive plans. However, the proposed rule is virtually useless in offering guidance on which incentive plans are allowable. The proposed rule states that "it is impossible and impractical for the OIG to specifically indicate in regulations what specific criteria may make up an acceptable hospital physician incentive plan."[126] The latter statement clearly implies an acceptable incentive plan is possible. The proposed rule further indicates that each incentive plan will be evaluated on a case-by-case basis. So, although these rules have never been finalized, the OIG has stated in the preamble to the proposed rule and in the context of other laws that these arrangements may be acceptable with certain safeguards. This idea was later dispelled by the OIG, as discussed further below.

On July 8, 1999 the OIG issued a special advisory bulletin that addressed gainsharing arrangements between hospitals and physi-

---

[124] *See* U.S. GEN. ACCOUNTING OFFICE, PHYSICIAN INCENTIVE PAYMENTS BY PREPAID HEALTH PLANS COULD LOWER QUALITY OF CARE, HRO-89-29, at 26 (Dec. 12, 1988); U.S. GEN. ACCOUNTING OFFICE, REPORT TO THE CHAIRMAN, SUBCOMMITTEE ON HEALTH, COMMITTEE ON WAYS AND MEANS, HOUSE OF REPRESENTATIVES, H.R. DOC. NO. 86-103, 99TH CONG. 2D SESS. 3, MEDICARE-PHYSICIAN INCENTIVE PAYMENTS BY HOSPITALS COULD LEAD TO ABUSE (July 1986).

[125] 59 Fed. Reg. 61,571 (Dec. 1, 1994).

[126] *Id.* at 61,573 (generally approving incentive plans that do not impact direct patient care such as rewards for "timely review and completion of medical records").

cians.[127] While recognizing that gainsharing arrangements offered significant benefits, the OIG concluded that the CMP provision clearly prohibited them and called for the expeditious termination of such arrangements. Although the OIG agrees that reducing health care costs without adversely affecting patient care would be in the nation's best interest, it nonetheless believes that the plain language of the law prohibits tying reductions in items or services to payments made to physicians.

The OIG based its conclusions on the fact that when Congress wanted CMS to regulate managed care physician incentive plans it did so explicitly, but in the case of hospital-physician incentive plans a lack of statutory authorization meant Congress considered such plans to be flatly prohibited. The bulletin went on to say that the law did not require that "the prohibited payment be tied to a specific patient or to a reduction in medically necessary care."[128] Although the preamble to the 1994 proposed rules indicated CMS would engage in a case-by-case analysis of these plans, the bulletin concluded that a case-by-case analysis would be inadequate and inequitable. A little over a month after the bulletin was published, the Assistant Inspector General for Legal Affairs, Lewis Morris, published a letter affirming that hospital-physician incentive plans in managed care plans, including Medicare+Choice, were not subject to the CMP prohibition.[129] This letter was later followed by a response from the OIG to commentary in the trade press that the Department felt distorted the gainsharing bulletin.[130]

The OIG restated its position that the law prohibits "any physician incentive plan that conditions hospital payments to physicians or physician groups on savings attributable to reductions in hospital costs for treatment of fee-for-service Medicare or Medicaid patients under the physicians' clinical care."[131] It also maintained that case-by-case determinations that were mentioned in the 1994 proposed rules were only for physician incentive plans that did not involve direct patient care and that were irrelevant to the arrangements discussed in the bulletin. A warning was issued to hospitals and physicians to heed the bulletin and unwind any existing gainsharing arrangements as expeditiously as possible.

---

[127] U.S. DEP'T OF HEALTH & HUMAN SERVS., OFFICE OF THE INSPECTOR GEN., GAINSHARING ARRANGEMENTS AND CMPS FOR HOSPITAL PAYMENTS TO PHYSICIANS TO REDUCE OR LIMIT SERVICES TO BENEFICIARIES, 64 Fed. Reg. 37,985 (July 14, 1999), *available at* http://oig.hhs.gov/frdalrt/gainsh.htm.

[128] *Id.*

[129] Lewis Morris, Office of Inspector Gen., U.S. Dep't of Health & Human Servs., Letter Regarding Social Security Act §1128A(b)(1) and (2) and Hospital-Physician Incentive Plans for Medicare or Medicaid Beneficiaries Enrolled in Managed Care Plans (Aug. 19, 1999), *available at* http://oig.hhs.gov/frdalrt/gsletter.htm.

[130] D. McCarty Thornton & Kevin G. McAnaney, Office of Inspector Gen., U.S. Dep't of Health & Human Servs., *Recent Commentary Distorts HHS IG's Gainsharing Bulletin*, *available at* http://oig.hhs.gov/frdalrt/bnagain.htm.

[131] *Id.*

In a surprise turn of events, the OIG issued an advisory opinion on January 18, 2001 declining to impose sanctions on a gainsharing arrangement although it implicated both the CMP and anti-kickback statutes.[132] The proposed arrangement was for a hospital to pay a group of cardiac surgeons a percentage of hospital savings directly attributable to cost reduction measures implemented by the surgeons. The arrangement contained several safeguards to protect beneficiaries:

- the transparency of identifying the specific cost-saving actions and resulting savings will allow for public scrutiny;
- credible medical support that the cost reduction measures will not adversely affect patient care was provided;
- payments will be based on surgeries performed on all patients regardless of insurance;
- objective historical and clinical measures were used to establish a baseline threshold below which no savings would accrue to the physicians;
- written disclosures will be provided to patients;
- financial incentives will be limited in duration and amount; and
- profits will be distributed to physicians on a per capita basis mitigating any incentive for one physician to generate disproportionate cost savings.[133]

The advisory opinion also listed several features of a gainsharing plan that would heighten the risk of payments for improper reductions or limitations on services:

- lack of a direct connection between physician actions and hospital cost-savings;
- failure to identify individual cost-saving actions with specificity;
- insufficient safeguards against other actions actually accounting for any "savings";
- quality-of-care indicators of questionable validity and statistical significance; and
- no independent review of cost savings, quality of care, or other aspects of the arrangement.[134]

It now seems that the OIG is ready to recognize the validity of some hospital-physician gainsharing arrangements under very limited circumstances.

## 2. Physician Incentive Plan Regulations

When the CMP statute was originally enacted, Congress prohibited physician incentive plans by both hospitals and Medicare managed care

---

[132] U.S. Dep't of Health & Human Servs., OIG Advisory Op. No. 01-1 (Jan. 11, 2001), *available at* http://www.hhs.gov/oig/advopn/2001/ao1_01.pdf.

[133] *Id.*

[134] *Id.*

plans that encouraged physicians to reduce or limit services.[135] In 1990, Congress deleted the reference to Medicare managed care plans and created a new section of the law that allowed these plans to implement incentive plans that did not induce reduction of medically necessary care to individual patients and did not place the physician at substantial risk for the costs of services not provided by that physician.[136] CMS issued a final rule implementing these amendments on December 31, 1996.[137] In addition to prohibiting reduction of medically necessary services and placing physicians at substantial financial risk, the rules also require managed care plans to file a disclosure of all incentive plans to CMS annually.[138]

### 3. Stark Limitations on Gainsharing

In the typical hospital-physician gainsharing arrangement the hospital and participating physicians have a financial arrangement under Stark II because the hospital shares with physicians a portion of the hospital's cost savings attributable to various cost saving measures implemented by the physicians. Because the participating physicians make referrals to the hospital for inpatient and outpatient hospital services (both of which are "designated health services" covered by Stark II), the typical gainsharing arrangement will violate the Stark II referral and billing prohibitions unless a Stark II exception applies.[139]

The Stark II exceptions that potentially could apply to a typical gainsharing arrangement include exceptions for academic medical centers, personal services arrangements, fair market value arrangements, and indirect compensation arrangements.[140] If the gainsharing arrangement were between a hospital and its physician employees, the Stark II exception for employment arrangements might also be applicable.[141]

---

[135] OBRA 1986, *supra* note 123, §9313(c) (codified at 42 U.S.C. §1320a-7a).

[136] Omnibus Budget Reconciliation Act of 1990, Pub. L. No. 101-508, §§4204(a), 4731, 104 Stat. 1388, 1388-108-09, 1388-195 (1990) (codified at 42 U.S.C. §1876(i)(8)).

[137] 61 Fed. Reg. 69,034 (Dec. 31, 1996) (following the publication of a final rule with comment period on Mar. 27, 1996, and a final rule correction on Sept. 3, 1996) (codified at 42 C.F.R. §417.479).

[138] 42 C.F.R. §417.479(h).

[139] It may be possible to establish a gainsharing arrangement, which does not involve a financial arrangement between the hospital and the participating physicians. For example, if an academic medical center enters into a gainsharing arrangement whereby a portion of the academic medical center's cost savings is used to fund research activities, it is possible that the gainsharing arrangement itself would not create any financial arrangement involving the participating physicians. If no financial arrangement exists, the Stark II prohibitions do not apply. However, given the broad definition of "indirect compensation arrangements" in the Stark II regulations, 66 Fed. Reg. 856, 958–59 (Jan. 4, 2001); 42 C.F.R. §§411.354(b)(5), (c)(2), it is likely that most gainsharing arrangements will be deemed to establish a financial arrangement within the meaning of Stark II.

[140] 42 C.F.R. §§411.355(e), 411.357(d), (*l*), (p).

[141] 42 C.F.R. §411.357(c).

All of these potentially applicable Stark II exceptions provide that the compensation involved in the arrangement cannot vary with the volume or value of referrals by the physician to the entity providing designated health services (i.e., the hospital in the case of a gainsharing arrangement), and the compensation cannot take into account any other business generated by the physician for the entity providing designated health services. Unfortunately, in the typical gainsharing arrangement the hospital cost savings that produce the funds for distribution to the participating physicians does vary with the volume or value of referrals by the participating physicians. As a result, none of the potentially applicable Stark II exceptions would cover a typical gainsharing arrangement.[142]

### 4. Anti-Kickback Limitations on Gainsharing Arrangements

The anti-kickback statute prohibits offers, payments, solicitations, or receipt of any remuneration to induce referrals of items or services paid by the federal government.[143] A gainsharing arrangement could disguise remuneration from the hospital to physicians for making referrals to the hospital. The more procedures a physician refers to a hospital with a gainsharing arrangement, the more that physician stands to gain from the hospital.

The OIG has promulgated safe harbor regulations to define practices that pose little risk of fraud or abuse. For complete assurance that a gainsharing arrangement will not invoke prosecution or sanction, it must meet the personal services and management contracts safe harbor.[144] The arrangement must meet all of the following conditions to qualify:

- a term of 1 year;
- compensation must be determined in advance and paid over the term of the arrangement;
- compensation must be consistent with fair market value; and
- compensation cannot take into account the volume or value of referrals.

Any incentive plan paid on a percentage basis would not meet the requirements for this safe harbor because the amount of compensation would not be set in advance. In the absence of safe harbor protection, hospitals and physicians must rely on case-by-case evaluations.

---

[142]Although the "physician incentive plan" provisions of the Stark II personal services exception do permit payments to a physician to reduce or limit services subject to certain limitations, those provisions would not cover the typical gainsharing arrangement because the physician incentive plan provisions only apply to payments by an HMO or similar managed care entity with respect to reductions or limitations of services for the entity's enrollees. 42 U.S.C. §1395nn(e)(3)(B); 42 C.F.R. §411.357(d)(2).

[143]42 U.S.C. §1320a-7b(b). (For text of the anti-kickback statute, see Appendix A-1.)

[144]42 C.F.R. §1001.952(d).

The OIG stated in its January 2001 advisory opinion that the proposed agreement could violate the anti-kickback statute, but the OIG would not impose sanctions for several reasons.[145] First, the arrangement is limited to surgeons who are already on the medical staff, the contract term is limited to 1 year, the potential savings are capped based on the prior year's admissions, and changes in admissions based on severity, age, or payer will be monitored. Second, any incentive for an individual surgeon to generate a disproportionate cost saving is minimized because profits are distributed on a per capita basis. Finally, the particular actions that will generate cost savings are set out with specificity; payments will be limited in amount, duration, and scope; and the payments themselves seem reasonable.

### 5. Tax-Exemption Issues for Gainsharing Arrangements

In February 1999, the IRS in an unreleased private letter ruling approved a gainsharing program.[146] Specifically, the proposed program was for a limited 12-month period; the physicians would have to meet a threshold of quality care and patient satisfaction before being eligible for an award; awards would be reasonable and fair market value for the physician's efforts; reasonableness of the awards would be reviewed by an independent appraiser at the end of each year; and the hospital would continually monitor the physician's adherence to program integrity requirements.

Using existing factors for analyzing compensation plans and benefits provided to medical staff physicians, the IRS indicated that these programs must abide by the following principles:

- There can be no private inurement. Payments must be consistent with tax-exempt status and serve a real business purpose; parties must be engaged in arm's length bargaining; and payments must result in reasonable compensation.
- Payments must further a charitable purpose. Payments must bear a reasonable relationship to the charitable purpose; there must be no inurement; payments may not cause the hospital to operate for the benefit of a private interest; and payment transactions may not constitute a substantial unlawful activity.

Despite this favorable ruling from the IRS, after the release of the OIG advisory bulletin, the IRS said it would issue no further rulings without talking to HHS first to see if they had a problem with the

---

[145] U.S. Dep't of Health & Human Servs., OIG Advisory Op. No. 01-1 (Jan. 11, 2001).

[146] *IRS Approves Gainsharing Programs in Unreleased Private Letter Rulings*, 33 DAILY TAX REP. (BNA) G-1 (1999); *see also* Internal Revenue Serv., *Full Text Letter Rulings: IRS OKs Gainsharing Arrangement in Unreleased Letter Ruling*, 25 EXEMPT ORG. TAX REV. 252 (1999) (containing the full text of the unreleased letter).

arrangement.[147] Presumably, even with the favorable OIG advisory opinion, it is likely the IRS will continue to work closely with HHS to make these determinations.

## K. Physician Recruitment

### 1. Tax-Exemption Issues

Hospitals have historically offered a wide range of incentives to attract and retain physicians, such as signing bonuses and guaranteed minimum collections. In recent years, there have been two major developments affecting the physician recruitment activities of tax-exempt hospitals. The first development was the release of physician recruitment guidelines on October 17, 1994, which were attached to a closing agreement for Hermann Hospital.[148] Unlike conventional IRS guidance, these guidelines were released as an attachment to a closing agreement entered into between the IRS and a tax-exempt hospital. As one of the conditions of the closing agreement, the hospital agreed to abide by the guidelines attached to the agreement and publish them in certain tax publications. Although the guidelines have no precedential value, given their narrowness, it is relatively safe to say that a hospital recruitment program that complies with their terms is not likely to be challenged by the IRS.

On April 21, 1997, the IRS released Revenue Ruling 97-21,[149] which was the culmination of its long-awaited physician recruitment guidance project. This document varied significantly from the guidelines and threw additional light on the IRS position on physician recruitment by tax-exempt hospitals. The primary significance of the revenue ruling is that it establishes for the first time direct legal precedent that physician recruitment by tax-exempt hospitals is a perfectly appropriate charitable activity. Thus, unlike the IRS's prior informal pronouncements, including the guidelines, Revenue Ruling 97-21 can be cited by tax-exempt hospitals as authority in support of properly structured recruitment transactions.

Highlights of this important revenue ruling include the following:

- The ruling focuses on nonemployee physicians.
- The ruling maintains three longstanding IRS physician recruitment requirements: (1) there must be a demonstrable community need for a physician; (2) all incentives must be "reasonable"; and (3) the recruitment agreement must be in writing.

---

[147] Barbara Yuill, *Government Officials Discuss Gainsharing; IRS "Reluctant" to Issue Favorable Rulings,* 149 DAILY TAX REP. (BNA) G-3 (1999); *see also* 66 Fed. Reg. 2144, 2155–56 (Jan. 10, 2001) (stating in rules published 1 day before the release of the OIG Advisory Opinion on gainsharing that the IRS would not issue private letter rulings on these arrangements).

[148] *See Closing Agreement Demonstrates How IRS Will Apply Physician Recruitment Rulings,* DAILY TAX REP. (BNA) No. 200, at d8 (Oct. 19, 1994).

[149] 1997-1 C.B. 121 (Apr. 21, 1997).

- The ruling makes it clear that the IRS places substantial emphasis on a tax-exempt hospital's board of directors becoming involved in and assuming responsibility for the hospital's physician recruitment activities, and requires that each physician recruitment arrangement be approved either (1) by the hospital's full board of directors, or (2) by a designated committee or officer in accordance with recruitment guidelines established, monitored, and reviewed by the board of directors.

Revenue Ruling 97-21 does not list permissible and impermissible physician recruitment incentives, but describes five factually detailed recruitment situations and determines that four of them would not jeopardize tax exemption and one would. These examples throw light on the IRS's thought process concerning differing recruitment situations.

In the first situation described, the IRS is obviously sympathetic to the plight of rural hospitals and communities and gives them considerable latitude in physician recruitment. According to Revenue Ruling 97-21, the hospital can offer a wide range of recruitment incentives such as a signing bonus, malpractice insurance for a limited period, office space for a limited number of years at below market rent, a mortgage guarantee on the physician's home, and financial practice start-up assistance. Although signing bonuses, malpractice insurance payments, and below market rent were three recruitment incentives called into question by the IRS in the guidelines, they are permitted for a rural hospital in a health professional shortage area (HPSA). HPSAs are designed to designate geographic regions within which an inadequate number of practitioners in certain specialties practice.[150] However, that a rural hospital is not in an HPSA does not preclude it from offering a wide range of recruitment incentives, as long as it can demonstrate community need for a physician in other ways.

In the second situation, the IRS determined that given an arm's length written agreement approved by the hospital's board, a hospital in an economically depressed inner-city area with a demonstrated need for a pediatrician could offer reimbursement of moving expenses, malpractice coverage, and a private practice income guarantee for a limited number of years. However, income guarantees must be reasonable based on "national surveys regarding income earned by physicians in the same specialty."[151] Once again, the IRS makes clear that those areas with a demonstrable need for a physician will be able to offer a liberal range of physician recruitment incentives.

The third and fourth situations demonstrate that the IRS will allow incentives to physicians already in a hospital's community or on its staff (sometimes referred to as "cross-town recruiting"). In the third

---

[150] The database to determine if a particular geographic area is a designated HPSA for each specialty is *available at* http://www.bphc.hrsa.gov/dsd.

[151] Rev. Rul. 97-21, 1997-1 C.B. 121 (Apr. 21, 1997).

situation, a hospital can reimburse the physician for the cost of 1 year's malpractice insurance in return for an agreement by the physician to treat a "reasonable number of Medicaid and charity care patients for that year."[152] The IRS expressly approves of the hospital carrying out its mission to treat Medicaid and charity patients by ensuring that a physician already in the area will commit to serve these patients. In the fourth situation, the IRS approves of recruiting a diagnostic radiologist who already practices in the community and is on the staff of another hospital to replace diagnostic radiologists who are relocating to another community. If there is an arm's length agreement, approved by the board and an income amount that is reasonable, the hospital can offer a net income guarantee for the first few years that the physician works in the hospital's radiology department.

In the fifth and final situation, the IRS determined that a hospital that has knowingly and willfully paid physicians for referrals through the provision of physician recruitment incentives, in violation of the fraud and abuse statute, will lose its tax-exempt status. It is significant to note that under this scenario the hospital losing its tax-exempt status had engaged in "substantial" illegal physician recruitment activities. This suggests that the IRS is principally interested in punishing knowing, substantial violators of the law, not those who have made a good faith effort to comply with regulations.

Although it would be preferable for the IRS to provide additional recruitment scenarios, the message from the five situations discussed is quite clear. Tax-exempt hospitals will not have to fear the loss of their tax-exempt status as long as there is a demonstrable community need for recruiting a physician, the incentives offered are reasonable, the recruitment agreement is negotiated at arm's length and is in writing, and their boards and legal counsel are involved in the process.

## 2. Anti-Kickback Issues

The OIG first communicated its views concerning the anti-kickback implications of recruitment activities in a special fraud alert published in 1994 that addressed incentives offered to physicians by hospitals and listed the following examples of practices that the OIG considered suspect under the anti-kickback statute:

- payment of any sort of incentive by the hospital each time a physician refers a patient to the hospital;
- use of free or significantly discounted office space or equipment in facilities usually located close to the hospital;
- provision of free or significantly discounted billing, nursing, or other staff services;
- free training for a physician's office staff in such areas as management techniques, CPT coding, and laboratory techniques;

---

[152]*Id.*

- guarantees which provide that, if the physician's income fails to reach a predetermined level, the hospital will supplement the remainder up to a certain amount;
- low-interest or interest-free loans, or loans that may be forgiven if a physician refers patients (or some number of patients) to the hospital;
- payment of the cost of a physician's travel and expenses for conferences;
- payment for a physician's continuing education courses;
- coverage on hospital's group health insurance plans at an inappropriately low cost to the physician; and
- payment for services (that may include consultations at the hospital) that require few, if any, substantive duties by the physician, or payment for services in excess of the fair market value of services rendered.[153]

It was brought to the attention of the OIG,[154] however, that some hospitals in rural and urban underserved areas were having great difficulty attracting physicians to their communities. The OIG was concerned that beneficiaries were being denied access to quality health care in these areas. A final rule for a practitioner recruitment safe harbor was published in the *Federal Register* on November 19, 1999.[155] The intent of the safe harbor was to protect certain entities that offer inducements to entice a physician to practice in their communities from running afoul of the anti-kickback statute.[156] It was not meant to protect all physician recruitment arrangements, but only those in rural and urban underserved areas where it is difficult to recruit practitioners.

Protection under this safe harbor is limited to arrangements with new (within 1 year of completing a residency) or relocating practitioners practicing in an HPSA. HPSAs currently recognize only three types of specialties (primary care, which includes general and family practice, general internal medicine, pediatrics, and obstetrics and gynecology; dentistry; and mental health); thus, the practitioner recruitment safe harbor appears to be limited to practitioners in those specialties.

Physician recruitment agreements will be afforded safe harbor protection as long as the following nine standards are met:

1. The arrangement is set forth in a written document signed by the parties that specifies the benefits provided by the entity, the terms under which the benefits are to be provided, and the obligations of each party.

---

[153] Office of Inspector Gen., U.S. Dep't of Health & Human Servs., Special Fraud Alert (Dec. 19, 1994), *available at* http://oig.hhs.gov/frdalrt/121994.html.

[154] 64 Fed. Reg. 63,518, 63,541 (Nov. 19, 1999).

[155] 64 Fed. Reg. at 63,554; 42 C.F.R. §1001.952(n).

[156] 64 Fed. Reg. at 63,541.

2. If a practitioner is leaving an established practice, at least 75 percent of the revenues of the new practice must be generated from new patients.
3. Benefits are paid for no more than 3 years, and the terms of the agreement are not renegotiated during this 3-year period in any substantial way; however, if the HPSA ceases to be an HPSA during the term of the agreement, payments made under the agreement will continue to satisfy this paragraph as long as that agreement is in effect.
4. There is no requirement that the practitioner refer to or generate business for the entity as a condition for receiving the benefits; although the entity may require that the practitioner maintain staff privileges at the entity.
5. The practitioner is not restricted from establishing staff privileges at, referring any service to, or otherwise generating any business for any other entity of his or her choosing.
6. The amount or value of the benefits provided by the entity do not vary based on the volume or value of referrals or other business generated for the entity.
7. The practitioner agrees to treat patients receiving medical benefits or assistance under the Medicare and Medicaid programs.
8. At least 75 percent of the revenues of the new practice are generated from patients residing in an HPSA or a medically underserved area (MUA) or who are part of a medically underserved population (MUP).
9. The payment may not directly or indirectly benefit any person (other than the practitioner being recruited) or entity in a position to make or influence referrals.[157]

Thus, in the limited situations described in the safe harbor, physician recruitment arrangements would be exempt from liability under the anti-kickback statute. Some commentators to the proposed rule were concerned about how to retain practitioners after the 3-year period allowed for incentive arrangements. OIG stated in the preamble to the final rule that "[a] physician retention safe harbor may be the subject of future rulemaking."[158]

One item is worth noting. In the preamble to the final regulations, the OIG noted that the safe harbor does not protect payments to a group or solo practitioner to assist in recruiting a new physician.[159] While the OIG conceded that these types of joint recruitment arrangements could be efficient and cost-effective, there remains a concern that the recruitment benefits could be used to disguise payments for referrals. It may

---

[157] 42 C.F.R. §1001.952(n).
[158] 64 Fed. Reg. at 63,543.
[159] *Id.* at 63,544.

be possible to remain within the protection provided by the practitioner recruitment safe harbor if a hospital makes certain recruitment payments directly to the recruited physician who then may assign such payments to a group that employs the physician.

One of the primary factors in considering the risks associated with a potential physician recruitment arrangement is the status of the physician with respect to the community. Although the new practitioner recruitment safe harbor is only available for arrangements involving practice in an HPSA, the failure to qualify for safe harbor protection does not necessarily render an arrangement illegal. Compliance with the safe harbor standards above should reduce the risks associated with a physician recruitment arrangement, even if safe harbor protection would not be available because the physician would not be recruited to practice in an HPSA. It is also a good idea to include a provision in the agreement that specifically disclaims an intent to require referrals, and the hospital should not engage in any activities that could be construed as indicia of an intent to induce the physician to refer patients to the hospital.

### 3. Stark Issues[160]

A physician recruitment agreement establishes a financial relationship between the hospital and the recruited physician that implicates the Stark law. However, the statute contains an exception for remuneration provided by a hospital to recruit a physician to relocate to the geographic area and become a member of the hospital's medical staff as long as:

- the arrangement and its terms are in writing and signed by both parties;
- the physician is not required to refer patients to the hospital;
- the amount of the remuneration under the arrangement is not based on the volume or value of any referrals; and
- the physician can have staff privileges at another hospital or refer business to another entity.[161]

Physician recruitment arrangements complying with the anti-kickback safe harbor discussed above should also qualify for the Stark law exception. It should be noted, however, that the Stark law exception for physician recruitment arrangements is technically limited to physicians who are relocating to a hospital's geographic area and does not extend to physicians currently living in the hospital's area, including physicians completing residency programs at the hospital. Although in the past CMS has indicated a willingness to consider rulemaking to extend the exception to physicians completing residency programs,

---

[160]The Stark law is discussed at length in Chapter 2 (Crane, *Federal Physician Self-Referral Restrictions*).

[161]42 U.S.C. §1395nn(e)(5); 42 C.F.R. §411.357(e).

the proposed Stark II regulations specifically limit the exception to relocating physicians. However, CMS stated that payments by a hospital to retain a resident in the hospital's geographic area might be permissible under the new fair market value exception.[162] Therefore, recruitment arrangements with new physicians graduating from a graduate medical education program in the hospital's geographic area should be carefully examined to determine whether they meet the proposed fair market value exception. This issue will not be addressed again by CMS until Phase II of Stark II rulemaking.

Another interesting twist on the proposed rule for physician recruitment is that recruitment benefits must be paid to an individual physician. Thus, if a hospital wishes to pay recruitment benefits to a group that will employ the recruited physician, the physician recruitment exception may not be directly applicable. To use the physician recruitment exception, the hospital must pay the benefits to the recruited individual physician, and the physician may then assign the benefits to the employer. Where the benefits are to be paid directly to the group, the hospital must ensure that the benefits meet the fair market value exception.

---

[162]The new fair market value exception would permit compensation relationships between an entity and a physician if the arrangement: (1) is in writing, signed by the parties, and specifies all services or items to be provided; (2) specifies the timeframe for the arrangement (which may be less than 1 year); (3) specifies the compensation or the method to determine compensation under the arrangement which must be set in advance, must be consistent with fair market value, and must not be determined in a manner that considers the volume or value of any referrals (including payment for non-Medicare or Medicaid referrals) or any other business between the parties; (4) involves a transaction that is commercially reasonable and furthers the legitimate business purposes of the parties; (5) meets a safe harbor under, or is otherwise compliant with, the federal anti-kickback statute; and (6) services to be performed do not involve the counseling or promotion of a business arrangement or other activity that violates state or federal law. 66 Fed. Reg. at 962 (codified at 42 C.F.R. §411.357(*l*)).

# 6

# Managed Care Fraud and Abuse: Risk Areas for Government Program Participants*

---

*Robert L. Roth and Alicia Palmer, Crowell & Moring, LLP, Washington, D.C. The authors gratefully acknowledge the assistance of Barbara H. Ryland, Crowell & Moring, LLP, with this chapter.

# I. Introduction

## A. Managed Care Fraud and Abuse Enforcement as Outgrowth of Fee-for-Service Model

Governmental anti-fraud efforts historically have focused primarily on the fee-for-service (FFS) delivery model. Under the FFS model, the more services a provider bills, the more payment it receives. However, as more people have become enrolled in managed care organizations (MCOs), both voluntarily (e.g., Medicare) and involuntarily (e.g., Medicaid), the government has increased its scrutiny of managed care activities at both the state and federal levels. In doing so, the government has had to appreciate that managed care differs dramatically from FFS, both operationally and economically. Most fundamentally, whereas FFS payment policies can provide an incentive for providers to overtreat patients, capitated payment for a bundle of services under managed care can create an incentive for undertreatment.

Despite its appreciation of the differences in the FFS and managed care payment systems, the government has had difficulty translating its managed care concerns into a coherent enforcement policy. In fact, many initiatives of the U.S. Department of Justice (DOJ), the Office of Inspector General (OIG) of the U.S. Department of Health and Human Services (HHS), and HHS's Health Care Financing Administration (HCFA), now the Centers for Medicare and Medicaid Services (CMS),[1] have proven to be simply attempts to apply the FFS "per claim" enforcement approach to managed care. For example, one of the most active areas of government enforcement involves payments to Medicare+Choice MCOs that were allegedly improperly increased because the MCO "claimed" too many enrollees were institutionalized in a nursing facility. This is similar to an FFS per claim issue because each enrollee claimed as institutionalized will cause an increase in the MCO's payments and shows how the government has been applying the FFS per claim mindset to managed care. However, other enforcement areas are more tailored to managed care.

## B. Compliance Programs in Managed Care Organizations

In an effort to reduce both the likelihood of adverse actions and the severity of any action taken, many MCOs have adopted compliance programs voluntarily.[2] Compliance programs are designed to ensure that an MCO is meeting all legal requirements. In addition to such voluntary actions, CMS now requires that an MCO have a compliance program as a condition of participation in the Medicare+Choice program.[3] This requirement represents a turning point in the history of compliance. Previously, merely having a compliance program was seen as indicating organizational sensitivity to legal obligations. Now, the absence of an effective compliance program is, by itself, grounds for suspicion and, at the very least, a technical violation of regulations that can lead to termination of the MCO's Medicare+Choice agreement.[4] Now, the *absence* of an effective compliance program is, by itself, grounds for suspicion and, at the very least, a technical violation of regulations that can lead to termination of the provider's Medicare+Choice agreement. Although CMS has yet to provide guidance to assist Medicare+Choice MCOs in meeting the compliance program requirement, the OIG released its model compliance program guidance for Medicare+Choice

---

[1] Effective July 1, 2001, the Health Care Financing Administration (HCFA) was renamed the Centers for Medicare and Medicaid Services (CMS). For purposes of this chapter, references will be to CMS.

[2] See Chapter 7 (Jones *et al.*, Corporate Compliance Programs).

[3] 42 C.F.R. §422.501(b)(3)(vi).

[4] A sample Medicare+Choice managed care agreement is included as Appendix J-1 to this volume.

MCOs offering coordinated care programs on its Web site on November 4, 1999.[5]

This chapter reviews many of the more significant substantive issues concerning managed care fraud and abuse, primarily focusing on Medicare, but also addressing other government programs, including the Federal Employees Health Benefits Program (FEHBP). Specifically, this chapter considers the following issues that are being scrutinized by federal and state agencies:

- mandatory compliance program and disclosure requirements that apply to organizations that participate in the Medicare+ Choice program;
- the OIG's model compliance program guidance for Medicare+ Choice plans;
- applicability of the federal False Claims Act (FCA) and other federal enforcement provisions to Medicare+Choice MCOs;
- adverse actions in which denial of care has been alleged and "prompt payment" statutes allegedly have been violated; and
- marketing of Medicare and Medicaid MCOs.

## II. MANAGED CARE FRAUD AND ABUSE ENFORCEMENT EFFORTS

### A. Health Care Financing Administration/Centers for Medicare and Medicaid Services

#### 1. Comprehensive Plan for Program Integrity

On February 11, 1999, HCFA (now CMS) issued its *Comprehensive Plan for Program Integrity* (CPPI),[6] which includes a section focusing on MCOs entitled "Addressing Service Specific Vulnerabilities: Managed Care."[7] The CPPI reported that almost 7 million Medicare beneficiaries were enrolled in 450 Medicare managed care plans for which Medicare paid more than $35 billion in fiscal year (FY) 1998.[8] In the following observation in the CPPI, CMS acknowledged how incentives in managed care differ from those in FFS medicine:

> Managed care brings a shift of fraud and abuse incentives from those found with a traditional fee-for-service health care delivery program. While concerns under fee-for-service focus on over-utilization of services, under managed care, incentives are in the provision of inadequate amounts of services.[9]

---

[5]This model program was published in the *Federal Register* on November 15, 1999. *See* 64 Fed. Reg. 61,893 (Nov. 15, 1999).

[6]HEALTH CARE FIN. ADMIN., U.S. DEP'T OF HEALTH & HUMAN SERVS., COMPREHENSIVE PLAN FOR PROGRAM INTEGRITY (1999), *available at* http://www.hcfa.gov/medicare/fraud/cmpl0299.htm [hereinafter CPPI].

[7]*Id.* at 33–35.

[8]CMS (formerly HCFA) estimates that the number of Medicare managed care enrollees in 2002 will be just over 5 million. *Id.*

[9]*Id.*

The CPPI also stated that CMS's program integrity focus is on "financial as well as beneficiary-related abuses"[10] and identified four basic areas of scrutiny:

1. *Ensuring that beneficiary payment status categories are correct.* This is important because improper classification of beneficiary members "can result in substantial overpayments and increased government administrative costs associated with recoupment activities for these incorrect payments."[11] In addition, CMS recognizes that manipulation of encounter data could lead to improper risk-adjusted Medicare capitation payments.

2. *Increasing review and validation of medical charges associated with "cost" contractors.* As in FFS, so-called "cost" contractors receive more payment if they provide more services.

3. *Ensuring that beneficiaries are receiving all appropriate services, including specialty services for which a referral is required.* This is to be achieved through review of beneficiary appeals data.

4. *Ensuring that marketing efforts meet CMS requirements, including possibly more use of standardized marketing materials and CMS review of plans' sales meeting activities.*

According to the CPPI, CMS has adopted a three-part strategy to address these issues. First, CMS plans to use its authority under the Health Insurance Portability and Accountability Act of 1996 (HIPAA)[12] to contract with managed care program safeguard contractors (PSCs). CMS has stated that "managed care PSCs will allow HCFA [now CMS] to further define, prevent, and detect managed care fraud, waste and abuse ... and allow [CMS] to develop new ways to address the fraud and abuse vulnerabilities created by managed care."[13] Second, CMS has noted with pride that it has "developed a new contract for managed care plans under Medicare+Choice [that] provides a clear basis for [CMS] monitoring activities."[14] CMS also has claimed that it "will be vigilant about referring [evidence of potential fraud and abuse] to ... internal corrective or sanctioning systems and referring all potential fraud and abuse cases to the Office of the Inspector General."[15]

Third, CMS has stated that it will continue to work with states to identify and address Medicaid managed care integrity issues and has noted that "the National Medicaid Fraud and Abuse Initiative's work to develop guidelines, procedures, new approaches, and data systems to help states control Medicaid managed care fraud will continue."[16] CMS also has indicated that it will aggressively review managed care

---

[10] *Id.*

[11] *Id.*

[12] Pub. L. No. 104-191, 110 Stat. 1936.

[13] CPPI, *supra* note 6.

[14] *Id.*

[15] *Id.*

[16] *Id.*

contracts in connection with issues highlighted by reports issued by the General Accounting Office (GAO) and other government entities:

- plans' distribution of inaccurate information regarding benefits and costs in marketing materials;
- inconsistencies in plan documentation; and
- plans' failure to inform beneficiaries of their right to appeal decisions of denial of care or payment for services.

*2. Enforcement Actions Against Managed Care Organizations*

CMS has taken enforcement actions against several MCOs in recent years. For example, in August 1999, WellCare of New York suspended marketing of and enrollment in its Medicare+Choice plan after receiving notice that the plan did not meet CMS requirements regarding prompt payment of claims and effective and efficient administration of its CMS contract.[17] Similarly, in May 1999, Blue Cross and Blue Shield of Kansas City temporarily suspended marketing and enrollment for its Blue Advantage 65 and Total Health Care 65 plans, reportedly after CMS cited concerns relating to (1) deficiencies in calculating and paying interest on Medicare claims of more than 30 days from out-of-network or nonaffiliated providers, (2) deficiencies in internal processes for denying duplicate claims from providers, and (3) certain employee activities.[18]

Earlier, in April 1997, Blue Cross of Northeastern Pennsylvania's marketing and enrollment activities for its Medicare HMO were suspended after CMS determined that the HMO did not offer enhanced drug, dental, and vision benefits during the first 4 months of 1997 after promising to do so.[19] CMS also referred the matter to the OIG under the civil monetary penalties (CMPs) statute.[20] The OIG subsequently imposed CMPs of $250,000 on the HMO. In addition, in June 1998, Oxford Health Plans voluntarily suspended marketing of its Medicare HMO in four states in response to alleged deficiencies relating to (1) claims payment times, (2) interest payments on delayed claims, and (3) enrollment and disenrollment procedures.[21] The suspension was lifted to permit the plan to participate in the Medicaid program in 1999.

## B. The Office of Inspector General

The OIG has gone even further than CMS in selecting specific areas of managed care fraud and abuse on which to focus. For example,

---

[17] *News at Deadline,* MOD. HEALTHCARE, Aug. 16, 1999.

[18] *HCFA's Medicare HMO Compliance M.O.: All Bark and No Bite?,* 4 MANAGED MEDICARE & MEDICAID, No. 14 (Apr. 20, 1998). This same plan has since paid $1.9 million to the government and agreed to withdraw from the Medicare+Choice program. See *infra* Section II.B.3.

[19] *Id.*

[20] 42. U.S.C. §1320a-7a. For text of the CMP statute, see Appendix D-1.

[21] *HCFA Findings Force Oxford to Stop New Medicare HMO Enrollments,* 4 MANAGED MEDICARE & MEDICAID, No. 21 (June 15, 1998).

the OIG's FY 2001 Work Plan[22] identified numerous areas of scrutiny, many of which are discussed in the sections that follow. Many of these issues also have been the subject of audit or investigation reports issued by the OIG and are likely to be addressed in the OIG's FY 2002 Work Plan as well.[23]

## 1. General and Administrative Costs

The OIG's audit of general and administrative costs is intended to determine whether the administrative cost component of the adjusted community rate proposals (ACRPs) that are required by the Balanced Budget Act of 1997 (BBA)[24] are appropriate compared with the Medicare program's general reasonable cost principles. In its FY 1999 Work Plan,[25] the OIG expressed concern that these costs were not being allocated to Medicare beneficiaries properly, stating that "[i]nflated general and administrative costs could increase plan profits, in which case the plans would be required to return the excess to HCFA [(now CMS)], lower Medicare enrollees' premiums, offer extra benefits to enrollees, or take a reduction in Medicare payments."[26] The OIG expressed interest in seeking a cap on these costs. However, it conceded in its FY 1999 Work Plan that this would require legislative action.

## 2. Enhanced Payments

The review of enhanced payments is intended to determine whether CMS has made proper capitation payments to risk-based Medicare MCOs for beneficiaries classified as in end-stage renal disease (ESRD) status, institutionalized, or dually eligible for Medicare and Medicaid. The OIG's focus is on the accuracy of both CMS and MCO controls regarding the special-status categories warranting these enhanced payments. As discussed in more detail below, the OIG entered into corporate integrity agreements (CIAs) with two Medicare+Choice MCOs in cases in which the underlying alleged misconduct involved enhanced Medicare payments to institutionalized and dually eligible beneficiaries.

### a. Beneficiaries With End-Stage Renal Disease

The OIG has been reviewing enhanced payments to Medicare MCOs for beneficiaries with ESRD since at least 1994. Plans audited as part of this initiative include Humana, PacifiCare of Texas, and

---

[22] OFFICE OF INSPECTOR GEN., U.S. DEP'T OF HEALTH & HUMAN SERVS., WORK PLAN, FISCAL YEAR 2001 (2000), *available at* http://www.oig.hhs.gov/wrkpln/index.htm [hereinafter OIG WORK PLAN FY 2001].

[23] *See e.g.*, OIG Audit Reports A-03-98-0046 (Jan. 18, 2000); A-04-98-01188 (Aug. 16, 1999); A-07-99-01275 (June 22, 1999).

[24] Pub. L. No. 105-33, 4001, 111 Stat. 251, 308 (codified at 42 U.S.C. §1395w-24).

[25] OFFICE OF INSPECTOR GEN., U.S. DEP'T OF HEALTH & HUMAN SERVS., WORK PLAN, FISCAL YEAR 1999 (1998), *available at* http://www.oig.hhs.gov/wrkpln/index.htm [hereinafter OIG WORK PLAN FY 1999].

[26] *Id.* at 22.

Group Health Cooperative of Puget Sound. The overpayments attributable to erroneous ESRD designation, at least until August 1996, were largely due to an error in CMS's (then HCFA's) computer system, which failed to recognize ESRD termination dates. Thus, once a beneficiary was designated as an ESRD beneficiary, he or she remained in that status, regardless of whether he or she no longer met the statutory definition of an ESRD beneficiary as a result of a successful kidney transplant or the cessation of dialysis. CMS had advised MCOs in February 1995 that it was improving its ESRD payment process and would begin enforcing ESRD rules effective March 1995. CMS subsequently began recovering overpayments from MCOs by withholding funds from the plans' monthly capitation payments as follows:

- For beneficiaries who were categorized as ESRD beneficiaries after plan enrollment but no longer qualified, recoveries were made retroactively to March 1995.
- For beneficiaries who once were ESRD beneficiaries but who were not at the time of plan enrollment or for beneficiaries who never had ESRD, recoveries were made retroactively for up to 3 years.

CMS maintained that the decision to limit recoveries for the former category of beneficiaries to March 1995 was based on its determination that the payments were largely attributable to the inability of its computer system to calculate end dates for ESRD. CMS maintained that the decision to limit recoveries for the latter category to 3 years was made to reduce CMS's liability to pay disputed claims from MCOs that may have dated back several years. The OIG determined that CMS's position caused the agency to forgo collection of approximately $20.5 million in overpayments made to 71 MCOs, and the OIG strongly criticized CMS for not making recoveries at least back to 1992.

The OIG took the same position regarding the audit of Group Health Cooperative of Puget Sound, from which the OIG sought repayment of approximately $2.8 million in overpayments made between March 1992 and April 1996. Group Health challenged the OIG's starting date, maintaining that, based on CMS's (then HCFA's) instructions, a September 1993 starting date was appropriate. The OIG rejected Group Health's position, stating that the earlier date was appropriate in light of the circumstances surrounding the overpayments and "related policy decisions that are applied to fee-for-service Medicare providers."[27]

### b. Institutionalized Beneficiaries

In a 1999 report, the OIG estimated that over a 2-year period, from October 1, 1994, through September 30, 1996, risk-based MCOs

---

[27]Memorandum From June Gibbs Brown, Inspector General, U.S. Dep't of Health & Human Servs., to Bruce C. Vladek, Administrator, Health Care Financing Admin. (Apr. 16, 1997), *available at* http://oig.hhs.gov/oas/reports/hcfa/b9600001.pdf.

received more than $22 million in overpayments attributable to the erroneous classification of beneficiaries as institutionalized.[28] Thus far, at least nine MCOs have been audited as part of this initiative, including Kaiser Foundation Health Plan (Portland, Oregon); Humana Health Plan (Chicago); Medica (Minneapolis); Providence Good Health Plan (Portland, Oregon); Group Health Plan (Minneapolis); PacifiCare of California (audited twice); Group Health Cooperative of Puget Sound (Seattle); HealthCarePlan (Buffalo); and Penn State Geisinger Health Plan (Danville, Pennsylvania). Most of the overpayments resulted from inadequate internal controls at the MCOs, with the largest overpayments being attributable to computer system errors. The OIG generally has sought to recoup the overpayments identified in these audits, although it has forgone repayment in instances in which the error rate was 7 percent or less, leaving it up to the plans to report overpayments to CMS.[29]

In addition, in November 2000, United Healthcare of Illinois (UHCI) entered into an agreement to settle an action brought under the FCA and other statutes by the U.S. Attorney for the Northern District of Illinois alleging that UHCI submitted erroneous reports on the institutionalized status of some of its beneficiaries. In addition to paying $2.9 million, UHCI agreed to enter into a CIA with the OIG. Although the institutionalized status was the only special-status category for which UHCI allegedly was overpaid, the CIA requires independent review of all special-status categories.

In August 2001, Blue Cross and Blue Shield of Kansas City entered into an agreement to settle a dispute arising out of the plan's reporting of institutionalized beneficiaries. Under the agreement, the plan agreed to pay the government $1.9 million and to terminate its participation in the Medicare+Choice program effective December 31, 2001. If the plan reenters the Medicare+Choice program within 5 years after termination, it will first have to enter into a CIA with the OIG.[30]

### c. Dually Eligible Beneficiaries

The OIG has been reviewing enhanced payments to Medicare MCOs for beneficiaries who have been eligible for Medicaid for more than 5 years. In 1995, CMS (then HCFA) issued a memorandum indicating that because of reporting errors discovered at PacifiCare of Texas

---

[28] Review of Medicare Managed Care Payments for Beneficiaries With Institutional Status, OIG Report A-05-98-00046 (Apr. 19, 1999).

[29] *See* OIG Audit Reports A-03-00-00010 (Jan. 16, 2001); A-09-00-00104 (Mar. 1, 2001); A-05-97-00014 (June 22, 1998); A-05-97-00025 (June 1998); A-05-97-00013 (Apr. 1998); A-05-97-00023 (Apr. 27, 1998); A-05-97-00024 (Mar. 2, 1998); A-05-97-00009 (Jan. 20, 1998); A-10-97-00002 (Nov. 26, 1997); and A-05-94-00053 (May 30, 1995).

[30] Julius A. Karash, *Blue Cross Fined for Claims; Insurer to Exit Medicare HMO Business as Part of Settlement Agreement With Government,* KAN. CITY STAR, Aug. 10, 2001.

and Humana of Florida it was initiating nationwide reviews of enhanced payments for beneficiaries classified as dually eligible. A report accompanying that memorandum indicated that overpayment to PacifiCare, estimated to be $455,000, was addressed through the withholding of CMS's April 1995 payment to the plan.[31] The memorandum did not identify how the overpayment to Humana was addressed. However, Humana stated in its May 1999 report of first quarter 1999 results that it had reached an agreement in principle with the DOJ and HHS to settle for $15 million for claims arising from the plan's erroneous designation of beneficiaries as dually eligible in 1991 and 1992.[32]

In June 2000, Humana entered into an agreement to settle an action brought under the FCA and other statutes by the DOJ alleging that Humana erroneously identified certain Medicare beneficiaries as dually eligible (i.e., also eligible for Medicaid) during the period October 30, 1990–April 30, 1999. In addition to paying $14.5 million, Humana agreed to enter into a CIA with the OIG. It is noteworthy that although "dually eligible" was the only special-status category for which Humana allegedly was overpaid, the CIA requires independent review of all special-status categories.

### 3. Physician Incentive Plans in Managed Care Contracts

The OIG's review of physician incentive plans (PIPs) related to the March 1996 publication by CMS of its final rule requiring that managed care plans disclose any arrangements that financially reward or penalize physicians based on utilization levels.[33] The OIG's goal was to determine whether proper disclosures have been made and also to look at other clauses in these contracts that may affect quality of care.[34]

### 4. Additional Benefits

The OIG will analyze the cost of additional benefits offered by Medicare MCOs and determine the extent to which beneficiaries actually receive these benefits.

---

[31]*See* OFFICE OF INSPECTOR GEN., U.S. DEP'T OF HEALTH & HUMAN SERVS., REP. NO. A-06-94-00028, REVIEW OF MEDICARE PAYMENTS MADE TO PACIFICARE OF TEXAS, INC. (PACIFICARE), A HEALTH MAINTENANCE ORGANIZATION IN SAN ANTONIO, TEXAS (June 1995).

[32]*See* Press Release, Humana, Inc., Humana Announces First Quarter Results (May 5, 1999), *available at* www.humana.com/corporatecomm/newsroom/archive99/may5.html.

[33]61 Fed. Reg. 69,034 (Dec. 31, 1996).

[34]Regarding quality of care, the OIG's 2000 Work Plan called for assessing how HCFA (now CMS) uses and ensures the quality of Health Plan Employers Data and Information Set (HEDIS) data submitted by Medicare MCOs and how CMS uses HEDIS data to assess the performance of MCOs and how plans are held accountable for poor-quality performance. OFFICE OF INSPECTOR GEN., U.S. DEP'T OF HEALTH & HUMAN SERVS., WORK PLAN, FISCAL YEAR 2000 (1999), *available at* http://www.oig.hhs.gov/wrkplan/index.htm [hereinafter OIG WORK PLAN FY 2000].

## 5. *New Adjusted Community Rate Proposal (ACRP) Process*

The OIG will audit ACRPs at CMS's request, and at least one audit of this type has been published.[35] The BBA ACRP process was developed as a means for Medicare+Choice MCOs to present to CMS their estimates of funds needed to provide the Medicare package of covered services to enrolled Medicare beneficiaries. It was implemented by CMS in January 2000.[36] The OIG's audits focus on the propriety and accuracy of the ACRPs submitted.

In computing an ACRP to be submitted to CMS for approval, a Medicare+Choice plan must calculate an initial rate that represents the commercial premium the plan would charge its general enrollment population for the benefit package to be offered. This rate is then adjusted to account for the excess cost of covering Medicare beneficiaries. ACRPs are designed to give CMS an estimate of the cost of providing a plan's proposed benefit package. In addition, ACRPs form the basis for the monthly capitation rate paid to plans.

This new process requires that far more detailed information be submitted in support of an ACRP than was required under the Medicare risk program, and it is anticipated that it will increase plans' exposure to potential sanctions for inaccurate submissions. In addition, the Medicare+Choice regulations require that a Medicare+Choice MCO certify "as a condition for retaining (and not providing additional benefits with) payment amounts below the amount of its ACRP, that the information in its ACRP submission is accurate and fully contains the requirements in [42 C.F.R. §422.502(m)]." This certification may increase plans' exposure under applicable civil and criminal authorities for false statements to federal agencies. The OIG has been reviewing the propriety and accuracy of proposals submitted under the Medicare risk program and has sought CMPs against plans found to have submitted inaccurate proposals.

The OIG also has been reviewing the propriety of administrative costs allocated for beneficiaries enrolled in Medicare risk-based HMOs, and has made public eight reports of audits of individual MCOs by September 2001.[37] These reports identified millions of dollars in administrative costs included in ACRPs that would not be allowed under guidelines applied to Medicare cost-based MCOs and Medicare FFS carriers, intermediaries, and providers. Examples of such costs include (1) broker commissions, (2) travel and entertainment costs, (3) meals and alcoholic beverages, (4) bad debt expense, (5) charitable donations,

---

[35] *See* OIG Audit Report A-06-00-00052 (Jan. 24, 2001).

[36] OIG WORK PLAN FY 2000, *supra* note 34, at 21.

[37] OIG reports have continued to focus on financial issues regarding payments to MCOs (e.g., the failure of MCOs to factor investment income into the development of the ACRP, the alleged failure of MCOs to adequately allocate administrative services to non-Medicare cost centers). *See* OFFICE OF INSPECTOR GEN., U.S. DEP'T OF HEALTH & HUMAN SERVS., REP. No. A-14-00-00212, ADEQUACY OF MEDICARE'S MANAGED CARE PAYMENTS AFTER BALANCED BUDGET ACT OF 1997 (Sept. 18, 2000).

(6) lobbying expenses, (7) political contributions, and (8) promotional giveaways. Because there are currently no statutory or regulatory authorities governing the allowability of such costs in the ACRP process, these audits have been used by the OIG to make recommendations to CMS rather than to seek recoupment of funds from or to make recommendations to the audited plans. The OIG has, however, encouraged CMS to seek appropriate legislative changes to disallow such costs.[38]

### 6. Cost-Based Managed Care Organizations

The OIG will, at CMS's request, evaluate the integrity of the cost-reporting processes used by cost-based MCOs. CMS currently contracts with more than 30 of such MCOs, which provide services to more than 300,000 members. These MCOs file cost reports with CMS. These reports are audited to ensure that costs are properly allocated to Medicare. However, according to the OIG, they do not undergo medical reviews to ensure that only Medicare-covered service costs are included.

### 7. Managed Care Organization Profits

A review of an MCO's profitability compares the profitability of the MCO's Medicare line of business with its other lines of business. Under the terms of a Medicare risk-based contract, a Medicare+Choice MCO is required to absorb any losses incurred—and is permitted to retain any savings earned—on its Medicare line of business. The OIG will use this information to determine whether CMS needs to establish criteria regarding the profitability of Medicare risk-based MCOs.

### 8. Final Verification of Marketing Materials

The OIG will evaluate CMS's final reviews of Medicare MCO marketing materials. The OIG noted in a report issued in 2000 that one of its previous studies detailed that few 1998 marketing materials met CMS's marketing guidelines and that a GAO report found that CMS reviewers did not ensure that final marketing materials incorporated required corrections.[39] CMS responded by instituting a new policy requiring regional offices to conduct "final verifications" of beneficiary notification materials before final CMS approval.[40]

### 9. Usefulness of Medicare+Choice Performance Measures

The OIG will examine the usefulness of Medicare+Choice performance measures from the perspective of Medicare beneficiaries. Under the Medicare+Choice program, Medicare beneficiaries have a broad

---

[38] The reports did not identify the HMOs by name, but they indicated that they are located in Florida, Missouri, New York, Northwest Ohio, Pennsylvania, and the Southwest.

[39] OIG, Medicare Managed Care, 1998 Marketing Materials Report, OEI 03-98-00271 (Feb. 2000).

[40] *See* Health Care Fin. Admin. Operational Policy Ltr. No. 60 (Nov. 14, 1997).

array of options to receive services. One of the measures used for comparison is a Medicare version of the Health Plan Employers Data and Information Set submitted by Medicare MCOs. Measuring quality is difficult, according to the OIG, because consumers, purchasers, and policy makers have different interests and priorities. Accordingly, the OIG will examine how beneficiaries interpret and use the various performance measures and determine the adequacy of these measures for beneficiary decision making.

### 10. *Educating Beneficiaries About Medicare+Choice*

The OIG will evaluate the adequacy of CMS's efforts to educate Medicare beneficiaries about their options under Medicare+Choice. The BBA expanded health plan options with the creation of the Medicare+ Choice program, and these new options provide beneficiaries with greater flexibility in their health care decisions.[41] The OIG has stated that this necessitates an extensive education campaign to ensure informed choices.[42] As part of this evaluation, the OIG will assess how well beneficiaries understand the program, the variety of choices available, the implications associated with the various choices, and where to get information about the program.[43]

### 11. *Enrollment Incentives and Disincentives*

The purpose of this review is to assess the extent to which Medicare MCOs encourage the enrollment of healthy beneficiaries and discourage the enrollment of sick beneficiaries. MCOs are paid a set amount to provide all Medicare-covered services to beneficiaries enrolled in their programs. The OIG believes that under the current payment method MCOs have a financial incentive to enroll healthier beneficiaries. Although Medicare+Choice MCOs are required to enroll all eligible Medicare beneficiaries regardless of age, health status, or cost of health services needed, there is some evidence that this does not always occur. The OIG previously found that 18 percent of Medicare beneficiaries indicated that they were asked about health problems at the time of their application.[44]

### 12. *Prescription Drug Benefit*

This review is designed to provide information on the coverage of and payment for prescription drugs in Medicare MCOs. FFS Medicare generally does not pay for outpatient prescription drugs, although some drugs, such as injectables for chemotherapy and medications used with durable medical equipment, are covered. The OIG has stated that

---

[41] OIG WORK PLAN FY 2000, *supra* note 34, at 24.

[42] *Id.*

[43] *Id.*

[44] *Id.* at 25.

Medicare MCOs may place an annual cap on prescription drug benefits. The OIG will examine how this limit is calculated for each beneficiary, which drugs are included, and how drug costs are determined.[45]

### 13. Managed Care Organization Closings

This review will determine the impact on beneficiaries of closings of Medicare+Choice MCOs. In the fall of 1998, about 100 risk-based plans announced that they did not intend to renew their Medicare contracts for 1999 or that they would be reducing their service areas, and another 100 made similar announcements in 1999 for contract year 2000. The OIG will look at the impact of such withdrawals and reductions on beneficiaries' ability to access care and to obtain Medigap policies and their willingness to join or remain in Medicare+Choice MCOs.

### 14. Role of State Health Counselors

The OIG will examine the role of state Health Insurance Counseling and Assistance Program counselors in informing Medicare beneficiaries about their insurance options. These volunteer counselors receive training under programs developed though state grants authorized by the Omnibus Budget Reconciliation Act of 1990.[46] The OIG will look at how these counselors are trained and whether they provide accurate information.

### 15. Monitoring Medicare Managed Care Organizations

The OIG plans to assess the extent to which CMS has updated its process and staffing for monitoring Medicare MCO performance in light of the changes made to the risk program as a result of the advent of the Medicare+Choice program.

### 16. Beneficiary Understanding of Medicare+Choice Benefits

The OIG will assess how well Medicare beneficiaries in Medicare+Choice MCOs understand their extra benefits and financial responsibilities. The OIG has noted that in addition to the Medicare+Choice MCOs that have withdrawn from the program, many have reduced their extra benefits or increased beneficiary copayments or premiums. The purpose of this study is to examine how well beneficiaries understood these changes and determine the impact of the changes.

### 17. Medicare+Choice Compliance Programs

The OIG will examine which elements of the OIG's model compliance program guidance have been implemented by Medicare+Choice MCOs and identify the benefits and difficulties associated with their implementation.

---

[45] OIG WORK PLAN FY 2001, *supra* note 22, at 23 (available at http://www.oig.hhs.gov/wrkplan/index.htm).

[46] Pub. L. No. 101-508, §4360, 104 Stat. 1388 (1990).

## 18. Fee-for-Service Costs Incurred by Managed Care Organization Disenrollees

The OIG plans to assess the extent of and reasons for high FFS costs incurred by recent Medicare+Choice MCO disenrollees. This will update a May 1999 OIG study that found that from 1991 to 1996 disenrollees from six Medicare MCOs received inpatient services worth $224 million within 3 months of disenrollment whereas Medicare would have paid only $20 million in capitation to the MCOs had the beneficiaries not disenrolled.[47]

## 19. Disenrollee Feedback

The OIG will continue to monitor disenrollee feedback on Medicare+ Choice MCOs because prior OIG work showed that the structured survey of disenrollees from MCOs could yield insightful information regarding service access and quality, plan performance, and reasons for disenrollment and examine the extent to which CMS uses disenrollment information.

## 20. Enrollee Access to Emergency Services

Although not in the 2001 Work Plan, the 2000 Work Plan[48] indicated that the OIG would determine whether existing federal protections for access to emergency treatment are adequate as the health care delivery system increasingly relies on managed care and gatekeeping mechanisms. The anti-dumping statute,[49] which applies to all Medicare-reimbursed hospitals, restricts the way in which a hospital may transfer or deny treatment to a person who comes to the emergency room. Transfers or denials of treatment that violate the anti-dumping statute may result in sanctions, including penalties and program exclusion. The OIG will examine whether federal enforcement authorities adequately protect patients who need and seek emergency care but are prevented from receiving such care by MCO rules or hospital policies.

On November 10, 1999, the OIG published a Special Advisory Bulletin addressing the specific obligations of hospitals to render such care to managed care enrollees. Issues of concern related to managed care enrollees and discussed in the bulletin are delays in providing treatment to managed care enrollees as a result of dual staffing (i.e., the MCO places its own physician in a hospital emergency room to evaluate MCO members) and prior authorization requirements.[50]

---

[47] OFFICE OF INSPECTOR GEN., U.S. DEP'T OF HEALTH & HUMAN SERVS., REP. NO. A-07-98-01256, REVIEW OF Inpatient SERVICES PERFORMED ON BENEFICIARIES AFTER DISENROLLING FROM MEDICARE MANAGED CARE (May 14, 1999).

[48] OIG WORK PLAN FY 2000, *supra* note 34 (*available at* http://www.oig.hhs.gov/wrkpln/index.htm).

[49] For discussion of the anti-dumping statute, see *infra* Section IV.

[50] *See* Office of Inspector Gen., Health Care Financing Admin., U.S. Dep't of Health & Human Servs., Special Advisory Bulletin on the Patient Anti-Dumping Statute, 64 Fed. Reg. 61,353, 61,354 (Nov. 10, 1999). For text of the advisory bulletin, see Appendix F-13 on the disk accompanying this volume.

*21. Medicaid Managed Care*

The OIG plans to assess the following regarding Medicaid managed care:

- how well states ensure that MCOs use appropriate marketing and enrollment practices for Medicaid recipients;
- how well states use the Quality Improvement System for Managed Care standards to measure performance of Medicaid MCOs;[51]
- how successful states have been at avoiding making FFS payments for Medicaid recipients who were enrolled in a Medicaid MCO; and
- whether Medicaid MCOs are properly implementing the BBA requirement[52] that gives Medicaid MCO enrollees the right to obtain emergency care and services immediately without regard to prior authorization or the provider's contractual relationship with the MCO by properly applying the "prudent layperson" coverage standard.

## C. Corporate Integrity Agreements

On December 8, 1999, the OIG entered into its first CIA with a Medicare+Choice MCO.[53] This CIA requires Anthem Health Plans to engage an independent review organization (IRO) to review and report on all facets of Anthem's Medicare+Choice operations. The CIA includes several pages addressing Anthem's compliance activity requirements, which is somewhat surprising in light of the mandatory compliance activities required of Medicare+Choice MCOs.[54]

As discussed above, the OIG entered into two additional CIAs in 2000: one with UHCI and one with Humana. These CIAs recognize that these entities had a compliance program in place at the time they entered into the CIA. These CIAs are particularly broad in scope (embracing oversight engagements by an IRO in six different areas).

## D. U.S. Department of Justice

In addition to the managed care anti-fraud initiatives identified by CMS and the OIG, the DOJ's Special Counsel for Health Care Fraud has urged managed care industry officials to share their "perspective and expertise" as the DOJ develops its guidelines on "what does—and does not—constitute fraud in managed care."[55] Specifically,

---

[51] OFFICE OF INSPECTOR GEN., U.S. DEP'T OF HEALTH & HUMAN SERVS., THE QUALITY IMPROVEMENT SYSTEM FOR MANAGED CARE (2000).

[52] Balanced Budged Budget Act of 1997, Pub. L. No. 105-33, §4704(a), 111 Stat. 251.

[53] *See* CIA Between the Office of Inspector General, Health Care Financing Administration and Anthem Health Plans, Inc., d/b/a Anthem Blue Cross & Blue Shield of Connecticut (Dec. 8, 1999).

[54] Discussed *infra* Sections III and IV.

[55] *See* 3 Health Care Fraud Rep. (BNA) 900 (Oct. 20, 1999).

the special counsel said, "I would encourage the managed care industry . . . to provide us with your views on where to draw the line between legitimate business practices and illegal conduct." The special counsel also stated that "[l]ogic would suggest—and our recent experience confirms—that while managed care eliminates many of the incentives and opportunities to commit fraud that existed in the fee-for-service system, it also creates new incentives and opportunities for fraudulent and abusive conduct."[56]

The DOJ's Managed Care Working Group has been working with CMS, the OIG, and the Federal Bureau of Investigation "to develop a comprehensive, long-term managed care enforcement strategy, including developing clear guidance on what does and does not constitute fraud in managed care."[57] The special counsel noted that the following alleged scams currently were under investigation by the DOJ:

- "fraudulent inflation of rates charged for certain services compared to what others in the community are charged for identical services";
- "bribes paid by a subcontractor to win a government-funded managed care contract"; and
- "the intentional failure to pay providers, signing up beneficiaries after surreptitiously disenrolling them from other plans, and giving kickbacks to a parent company."[58]

The special counsel also noted that it was "interesting" that "the majority of allegations now under investigation at the DOJ do not involve underutilization, usually cited as a top risk in the managed care arena."[59]

In addition, regarding underutilization, the Office of the U.S. Attorney for the Eastern District of Pennsylvania released a statement that it was focusing attention on "improper relationships between health plans and physicians—relationships that are alleged to be driven by cost-containment at the expense of patient care. . . . These situations may lead to refusals to refer patients, requirements on doctors to discharge patients, and a failure to pay valid claims."[60] Also, according to a March 13, 2000, report in the *Philadelphia Business Journal,* this U.S. Attorney's Office indicated that it was in the process of determining whether Medicare+Choice MCOs were deliberately slowly paying or underpaying providers and whether this constitutes fraud.[61] In previous years, this U.S. Attorney's Office had

---

[56]*Id.*

[57]*Id.*

[58]*Id.*

[59]*Id.*

[60]*Id.* at 901.

[61]*See Probe on for Possible Insurer Fraud,* PHILADELPHIA BUS. J., Mar. 13, 2000, at 1.

stated that it would focus on prescription drug formularies used by MCOs to ensure that kickbacks had not been received in exchange for inclusion, or exclusion, of a particular drug from an MCO's formulary.

The U.S. Attorney's Office for the Eastern District of Pennsylvania also is looking into situations in which MCOs have improperly denied care. In 1999, it sent a questionnaire to patients' advocates and physicians' groups soliciting information about medical claims that had been denied. The Office indicated that one purpose of the questionnaire was to help identify MCOs that deny claims more frequently than others and that it will scrutinize instances in which MCO staff members deny services referred by physicians and other medical personnel for evidence of improper intent.

The DOJ has taken several enforcement actions against MCOs. For example, as stated above, Humana of Florida indicated that it had reached an agreement in principle with the DOJ and HHS to settle for $15 million claims arising out of the plan's erroneous designation of beneficiaries as dually eligible in 1991 and 1992.[62] In addition to Medicare, the DOJ has been working with the Inspector General of the Office of Personnel Management (IG-OPM) concerning managed care fraud and abuse in the FEHBP.

## E. Federal Employees Health Benefits Program

### 1. Defective Pricing Certifications in the Federal Employees Health Benefits Program

The IG-OPM has aggressively pursued the recoupment from health plans participating in the FEHBP of payments made on the basis of defective pricing certifications. The following matters have been included in these efforts:

- *Similarly sized subscriber group (SSSG) designation.* An FEHBP community-rated MCO must offer the government the same rating that it offers to SSSGs. The IG-OPM's audits often include a review of the MCO's SSSG designations, and the IG-OPM has aggressively pursued repayment of funds paid on the basis of incorrect designations.
- *Discounted market rates.* Because the OPM is entitled to the same pricing as the two SSSGs closest to a federal account, FEHBP MCOs must offer the government any discount offered to these SSSGs. Consequently, IG-OPM audits often include a review of discounts offered to SSSGs, and the IG-OPM has aggressively pursued repayment of funds paid because such discounts were not extended to OPM.
- *Rating factors.* The IG-OPM also routinely reviews the rating factors used by FEHBP MCOs to calculate rates charged to OPM

---

[62] Press Release, Humana, Inc., Humana Announces First Quarter Results (May 5, 1999), *available at* www.humana.com/corporatecomm/newsroom/archive99/html.

to ensure that such rates are consistent with those charged to the applicable SSSGs and that the OPM's rates are properly credited or discounted for benefit variances.

## 2. *Enforcement Actions Against Managed Care Organizations in the Federal Employees Health Benefits Program*

Government entities have taken several enforcement actions against MCOs that participate in the FEHBP. For example, in its *Semiannual Report to Congress, October 1, 1997–March 31, 1998,* the IG-OPM alleged that TakeCare Health Plan of Ohio owed $8.2 million to the federal government as a result of incorrect SSSG designation.[63] Similarly, in its *Semiannual Report to Congress, October 1, 1998–March 31, 1999,* the IG-OPM alleged that MD IPA and FHP-New Mexico did not give FEHBP the highest discount offered to an SSSG.[64] In addition, the IG-OPM alleged that FHP-New Mexico included in its FEHBP pricing age and sex factors not included in SSSG pricing and did not properly credit FEHBP for benefit variances and premium taxes.[65]

In May 1999, the U.S. Attorney's Office for the District of Columbia announced that PacifiCare of Oklahoma had agreed to pay $9 million to settle allegations that the plan had overcharged the FEHBP between 1990 and 1995. According to the government's press release, PacifiCare knowingly violated its certificates of community rating and market pricing in each of those years through conduct such as including in its rates amounts for state taxes on insurance premiums despite a statutory prohibition on including such taxes and giving a discount to an SSSG plan that was not extended to the FEHBP.[66]

## F. Increased State Regulatory Enforcement Efforts

In addition to these federal actions, states have been increasing their focus on the delivery of managed care services, operational issues (including "prompt payments" statutes[67]), and fraud and abuse issues. For example, in 1998, the California Department of Insurance entered into a settlement with Kaiser Foundation of California concerning coverage and payment for Viagra. This action arose under a California law that requires that an MCO cover any drug a physician deems medically necessary.[68] States also have brought actions to com-

---

[63] OFFICE OF INSPECTOR GEN., U.S. OFFICE OF PERSONNEL MGMT., SEMIANNUAL REPORT TO CONGRESS, OCTOBER 1, 1997–MARCH 31, 1998 (Apr. 1998), at 4–6.

[64] *See* OFFICE OF INSPECTOR GEN., U.S. OFFICE OF PERSONNEL MGMT., SEMIANNUAL REPORT TO CONGRESS, OCTOBER 1, 1998–MARCH 31, 1999 (Apr. 1999), at 4–6.

[65] *See id.* at 6–7.

[66] Office of the U.S. Attorney, District of Columbia, $9 Million Civil Settlement Announced in HMO Health Care Fraud Case (May 26, 1999); *PacifiCare of Oklahoma Pays $9 Million To Settle FEHBP Overcharge Allegations,* 3 Health Care Fraud Rep. (BNA) 465 (June 22, 1999).

[67] See *infra* Section VII.

[68] CAL. HEALTH & SAFETY CODE, §1367.24.

bat perceived marketing abuses. For example, after a Tennessee state audit revealed possible improper marketing practices by OmniCare Health Plan, including enrolling fictitious or ineligible individuals, the state entered into a settlement in 1995 under which OmniCare repaid the state $13.8 million.[69] Similarly, the Maryland Department of Health and Mental Hygiene imposed a fine of $55,000 on Optimum Choice, the HMO subsidiary of Mid Atlantic Medical Services, for alleged misrepresentations in its marketing when enrolling a Medicaid recipient and her five children.[70]

Most states have taken steps to require insurers to implement anti-fraud measures, such as reporting suspicious claims to state officials and developing training, detection, and procedures manuals.[71] For example, a 1994 California law requires insurers doing business in the state to establish and maintain a "special investigative unit (SIU)" to investigate possible claims of fraud and abuse. SIUs must refer fraud and abuse allegations to the state insurance department. Maxicare Life and Health Insurance Co. agreed to pay $40,000 to settle allegations that it failed to comply with this requirement. In addition, the Los Angeles-based insurance company will undergo an audit by the California Department of Insurance "to ensure current and ongoing compliance."[72] Similarly, on December 23, 1997, the New York State Insurance Department fined Oxford Health Plans $3 million for, among other violations, its alleged failure to have sufficient systems in place to prevent and uncover fraud.[73]

## III. MANDATORY COMPLIANCE PROGRAMS UNDER THE MEDICARE+CHOICE PROGRAM

In addition to general contract requirements, Medicare+Choice contractors must institute a regulatory compliance program that includes the following:

- written policies, procedures, and standards of conduct that articulate the organization's commitment to comply with all applicable federal and state standards;[74] and
- a process to ensure prompt response to detected offenses and development of corrective action initiatives.[75]

---

[69]*See Omnicare Repays Tenn. $13.8 Million in Unspent Patient Health Care Funds,* MEMPHIS COMMERCIAL APP., Nov. 8, 1995, at 1A.

[70]*See HMO Is Fined $55,000 for Tricking Poor; Medicaid Patients Enrolled Improperly in 3 Cases, State Says; Optimum Choice Appealing; One Woman Enrolled After Session Including Sex With Marketer,* BALT. SUN, Mar. 25, 1996, at 1B.

[71]*See Kirk J. Nahra, Anti-Fraud Obligations, Opportunities for Managed Care Organizations,* 3 Health Care Fraud Rep. (BNA) 641 (July 14, 1999).

[72]*See* 3 Health Care Fraud Rep. (BNA) 6 (Jan. 13, 1999).

[73]*Oxford Health Receives Fine of $3 Million,* N.Y. TIMES, Dec. 24, 1997, at D1.

[74]42 C.F.R. §422(b)(3)(vi)(A).

[75]*Id.* §422(b)(3)(vi)(G).

However, the statutory authority for the compliance program requirement is suspect because such a requirement did not exist under the Medicare risk-based HMO program. When enacting the statutes creating the Medicare+Choice program, Congress required that Medicare+Choice contract standards be based on standards established under the Medicare risk program.

It is important to keep in mind that the OIG has taken the position that 42 U.S.C. §1320a-7b(a)(3) requires disclosure in that it exposes to criminal penalty a person who has knowledge "of the occurrence of any event affecting [a person's] initial or continued right to any [government] benefit or payment . . . [and] conceals or *fails to* disclose such event with an intent fraudulently to secure such benefit or payment either in a greater amount or quantity than is due or when no such benefit or payment is authorized."[76] In the final regulation, CMS encouraged Medicare+Choice MCOs to voluntarily report misconduct identified through their compliance programs.[77]

## IV. The Office of Inspector General's Program Guidance for Medicare+Choice Managed Care Organizations Offering Coordinated Care Plans

### A. Nature of the Guidance

The OIG issued its Compliance Program Guidance for Medicare+Choice MCOs on November 4, 1999.[78] Although the Compliance Program Guidance purports to set forth numerous guidelines for Medicare+Choice MCO compliance programs, the guidelines actually are characterized as "voluntary" and simply "intended to provide assistance for [Medicare+Choice MCOs] looking for additional direction in the development and implementation of a compliance program."[79] The OIG further stated that CMS would "release an operational policy letter" (OPL) addressing compliance requirements.[80] Therefore, the OIG de-

---

[76](Emphasis added.) *See also* 18 U.S.C. §§669, 1035.

[77] 65 Fed. Reg. 40,170, 40,265 (June 29, 2000). This is a departure from the interim final Medicare+Choice rule, which had required Medicare+Choice contractors to include in their compliance programs a process for reporting credible information of violations of law by the MCO, the Medicare+Choice plan, subcontractors, or enrollees. *See* 63 Fed. Reg. 34,968, 35,014 (June 26, 1998). This requirement was not included in the final rule.

See generally Chapter 7 (Jones et al., Corporate Compliance Programs).

[78] 64 Fed. Reg. 61,893 (Nov. 15, 1999). This is the fifth in a series of documents developed by the OIG to establish compliance program guidelines for Medicare contractors and providers. The MCO Compliance Program Guidance is available on the OIG's Web site at www.hhs.gov/progorg/oig. For additional coverage of the MCO Compliance Program Guidance for Medicare+Choice Organizations, see Chapter 7, at Section III.B.7. (Jones *et al.*, Corporate Compliance Programs).

[79] 64 Fed. Reg. at 61,894.

[80] *Id.* at 61,894 n.5. This OPL has yet to be issued as of Sept. 1, 2001.

scribed the Compliance Program Guidance as only "a set of guidelines for consideration by a Medicare+Choice organization."[81]

Nevertheless, CMS and the OIG, more than likely, will use the Compliance Program Guidance as the standard against which they will evaluate Medicare+Choice MCO compliance programs. The OIG also stated that the guidelines in the Compliance Program Guidance are intended for all Medicare+Choice MCOs, regardless of size. However, throughout the Guidance, the OIG acknowledged that the level of resources and effort may vary depending on the size and nature of the Medicare+Choice MCO.

## B. Implementation of the OIG's Compliance Program Guidance

As in other compliance program guidance documents issued by the OIG, a recurrent theme throughout the Medicare+Choice MCO Compliance Program Guidance is the need for commitment to the compliance program from the organization's senior management and governing body, through both financial resources and actions. The formal commitment of the MCO's governing body must include the following elements:

1. written standards of conduct, policies, and procedures that promote and support the Medicare+Choice MCO's commitment to compliance and address specific areas of potential fraud and abuse (e.g., marketing, quality of care, data collection, illegal inducements, and patient dumping);
2. a chief compliance officer and corporate compliance committee responsible for operating and monitoring the compliance program;
3. an education and training program for all employees involved in the Medicare+Choice MCO's operations;
4. communication tools by which employees can communicate compliance issues to the compliance officer, including providing for confidentiality and anonymity;
5. audits and other compliance program evaluation and monitoring techniques;
6. consistently used and applied employee disciplinary action to enforce compliance standards; and
7. policies by which the compliance officer and/or compliance committee responds to any violation of the compliance program and initiates corrective action to prevent similar offenses.

Each of the numbered items above is discussed in detail in the compliance program and summarized below.

---

[81]*Id.* at 61,895.

## 1. Standards, Policies, and Procedures

The OIG has stressed the need for Medicare+Choice MCOs to address in their policies, standards, and practices specific areas that are vulnerable to abuse, including issues of particular concern within the HMO industry (e.g., marketing, quality of care, and illegal enrollment inducements) and any areas with which the Medicare+Choice MCO has had a history of compliance problems. Before developing written policies, each Medicare+Choice MCO should identify the minimum standards of conduct it expects from its employees. These standards of conduct establish the Medicare+Choice MCO's principal values and framework and its commitment to prevent fraud and abuse and comply with all federal and state standards. The standards of conduct are the equivalent of the Medicare+Choice MCO's fundamental values and goals.

Written policies are the mechanism by which a Medicare+Choice MCO implements its standards of conduct and creates procedures and processes to provide day-to-day guidance to its employees. The Compliance Program Guidance states that a Medicare+Choice MCO "should establish a comprehensive set of written policies addressing all applicable statutes, rules and program instructions that apply to each function or department of [the] Medicare+Choice organization"[82] and through a comprehensive risk analysis (either self-administered or performed by an independent contractor) identify and rank the various compliance and business risks the Medicare+Choice MCO may experience in its daily operations. This risk analysis and subsequent identification and ranking of risk areas should be based on applicable state and federal health care program requirements (i.e., statutes, regulations, OPLs, and other agency guidance documents) and should include a review of the Medicare+Choice MCO's history of noncompliance, if any.

Although it refers Medicare+Choice MCOs to CMS's regulations and OPLs for a comprehensive discussion of all areas that a Medicare+Choice MCO must consider and include when designing its compliance program, the Compliance Program Guidance identifies seven areas of particular concern to the OIG: (a) marketing materials and personnel; (b) selective marketing and enrollment; (c) disenrollment; (d) underutilization and quality of care; (e) data collection and submission processes; (f) anti-kickback statute and other inducements; and (g) emergency services.

### a. Marketing Materials and Personnel

In addition to meeting CMS's marketing requirements, the OIG wants Medicare+Choice MCOs to have policies regarding the completeness and accuracy of their marketing materials and marketing personnel. A Medicare+Choice MCO *should not* rely on CMS approval as the basis for claiming that its marketing materials are complete and

---

[82]*Id.* at 61,896.

accurate. Instead, it should conduct its own thorough review of its marketing materials. In addition to meeting CMS requirements, a Medicare+Choice MCO's marketing materials should contain an adequate description of its rules, procedures, and basic benefits and services and an explanation of the grievance and appeals process. These materials should also especially address the concept and role of a primary care physician and how managed care limits health care provider choices.

Because a Medicare+Choice MCO must have control over its marketing personnel to ensure that they are presenting clear, complete, and accurate information to potential enrollees and the OIG believes that control is much more likely when marketing personnel are employees of the Medicare+Choice MCO, the OIG has strongly recommended that Medicare+Choice MCOs employ their own marketing personnel rather than contract for those services. However, in the most recent iteration of the *Marketing Guide,* CMS rescinded its policy of discouraging the use of independent agents and brokers for marketing purposes.[83] The Compliance Program Guidance reiterates the OIG's and CMS's longstanding position of discouraging Medicare+Choice MCOs from using physicians as marketing agents, but if a Medicare+Choice MCO uses providers for marketing, it should develop procedures to ensure that provider promotional activities are in accordance with CMS guidelines.

### b. *Selective Marketing and Enrollment*

The Compliance Program Guidance states that each Medicare+Choice MCO should implement policies to prevent selective enrollment practices known as "cherry picking," such as asking potential enrollees medical questions before enrollment, targeting marketing plans to areas in which healthy enrollees would be more likely to be present than unhealthy enrollees (e.g., health and exercise clubs) or are difficult for disabled people to access (e.g., upper floors of buildings that do not have elevators), or providing enrollment inducements that are more attractive to healthier beneficiaries (e.g., free gym memberships or sporting lessons).[84] Other practices that should be discouraged include giving enrollment priority to newly eligible Medicare beneficiaries, tracking costs incurred by enrollees who were enrolled in different settings for use in targeting healthier enrollees in the future, reenrollment campaigns that target past plan enrollees who had low medical

---

[83] HEALTH CARE FINANCING ADMIN., U.S. DEP'T OF HEALTH & HUMAN SERVS., MANAGED CARE NATIONAL MARKETING GUIDE 49 (June 8, 2000), *available at* http://www.hcfa. gov/pubforms/86_mmc/mc86c03.htm [hereinafter MARKETING GUIDE]; HEALTH CARE FINANCING ADMIN., U.S. DEP'T OF HEALTH & HUMAN SERVS., MEDICARE MANAGED CARE MANUAL, ch. 3 §50.2 (2001) [hereinafter MMCM]

[84] 64 Fed. Reg. at 61,898. Note that CMS's marketing guidelines permit offering discounts on gym memberships as a value-added service. MARKETING GUIDE, at 46, and MMCM, at ch. 3 §50.4.

costs, and any policies that attempt to eliminate high-risk areas from the Medicare+Choice MCO's service area (i.e., gerrymandering).[85]

### c. Disenrollment

Because of disenrollment and FFS Medicare health care expenditures after Medicare+Choice disenrollment, the OIG fears that MCOs are encouraging members to disenroll to obtain more costly services under FFS Medicare. Consequently, the Compliance Program Guidance recommends that Medicare+Choice MCOs implement policies to ensure against inappropriate disenrollment and that disenrollment policies identify those rare circumstances in which medical personnel may initiate a discussion of disenrollment (e.g., when the Medicare+Choice MCO cannot provide the covered medical items or services needed by the patient).

### d. Underutilization and Quality of Care

Although not reflective of all of the types of policies that a Medicare+Choice MCO should implement to ensure quality care, the OIG has highlighted three types of policies that Medicare+Choice MCOs should develop to help address underutilization and quality of care:[86]

1. policies against physician "gag" rules;
2. policies to ensure that if a Medicare+Choice MCO uses a PIP, the PIP provides no payments to physicians to reduce or limit medically necessary services (if a PIP puts a physician or physician group at "substantial financial risk" for referral services, the Medicare+Choice MCO must (1) survey current and previously enrolled members to assess access to and satisfaction with the quality of services, (2) ensure that there is adequate and appropriate stop-loss protection, and (3) disclose to CMS certain information regarding its PIPs);[87] and
3. policies and procedures for selection of providers, including credentialing criteria such as valid license, clinical privileges in good standing, and appropriate educational requirements.

### e. Data Collection and Submission Processes

There are numerous reporting and submission requirements under the Medicare+Choice program. Therefore, Medicare+Choice MCOs should have policies that all required submissions to CMS be accurate, timely, and complete and that all appropriate reporting requirements be met. However, the Compliance Program Guidance particularly emphasizes the need for Medicare+Choice MCOs to submit accurate information when the data determine the amount of payment the Medicare+Choice MCO receives from CMS.[88] Consistent with the OIG

---

[85] 64 Fed. Reg. at 61,899.

[86] *Id.* at 61,889.

[87] See *infra* Section V.

[88] 64 Fed. Reg. at 61,900.

audit reports[89] and the OIG's FY 1998 and FY 1999 Work Plans,[90] the OIG has recommended that Medicare+Choice MCOs have two types of policies and procedures in place:

- policies and procedures to ensure that the administrative component of the adjusted community rate (ACR) is calculated accurately; and
- adequate internal controls to ensure that the status of beneficiaries is reported accurately.

The policies and procedures to ensure that the administrative component of the ACR is calculated accurately should have clearly defined criteria for claiming reimbursement for administrative costs, including that the costs do not contain any costs that are directly associated with furnishing patient care or value-added services and that they are allocated to the applicable operating component.

### f. Anti-Kickback Statute and Other Inducements

The basis of the contractual relationship between an MCO and a provider is the understanding that the MCO will funnel a stream of patients to the provider in exchange for the provider accepting the MCO's payment terms. This can implicate the federal anti-kickback statute[91] because the primary purpose of that statute is to curtail improper payment for referrals to government-funded programs. In this regard, the Compliance Program Guidance refers to the 1999 interim final rule on the risk-sharing safe harbor[92] of the anti-kickback statute, which provides protections for certain financial arrangements between MCOs (including Medicare+Choice MCOs) and entities with which they contract for health care services under which a federal health care program pays the MCO a capitated amount. However, as indicated in the rule, there are three significant limitations.

First, there is no protection from the anti-kickback statute if the payments made under the managed care agreement are part of a broader agreement to steer federal FFS business to the entity giving the discount. Second, there is no safe harbor protection for remuneration for items and services not reasonably related to the provision of health care (e.g., marketing services or services provided before a beneficiary's enrollment in a federal health plan). Third, the safe harbor applies only to MCOs that do not claim any payment from the federal government other than the capitated payment.

---

[89] The OIG audit reports are identified *infra* Section II.B.

[90] OFFICE OF INSPECTOR GEN., U.S. DEP'T OF HEALTH & HUMAN SERVS., WORK PLAN, FISCAL YEAR 1998 (1997); WORK PLAN, FISCAL YEAR 1999 (1998) [hereinafter OIG WORK PLAN FY 1999]. (The OIG Work Plans for 1998–2001 are *available at* http://www.oig.hhs.gov/wrkpln/index.htm.)

[91] 42 U.S.C. §1320a-7b(b). For text of the federal anti-kickback statute, see Appendix A-1.

[92] 64 Fed. Reg. 63,504 (Nov. 19, 1999) (codified at 42 C.F.R. §1001.952).

In addition to the safe harbor limitations described above, the OIG has recommended that Medicare+Choice MCOs have policies in place to ensure that any incentives offered to beneficiaries and potential beneficiaries do not violate the anti-kickback statute or the CMP law prohibiting beneficiary inducements, which was added by HIPAA and codified at 42 U.S.C. §1320a-7a(a)(5). Contrary to the position taken by the OIG in the proposed CMP implementing regulations issued in March 1998,[93] the OIG stated in the compliance guidance that, pending publication of the final rule implementing the new CMP, it is the OIG's belief that it is not a violation for Medicare+Choice MCOs to offer limited incentives[94] to federal health care program beneficiaries to enroll in a plan. However, the OIG believes it would be a violation of the new CMP law if the Medicare+Choice MCO or any other entity were to offer a beneficiary remuneration to use a particular provider, practitioner, or supplier once he or she were enrolled in the plan.

The OIG has since published the final CMP rule and indicated in its response to comments the same position it set forth in the Compliance Program Guidance.[95]

### g. Emergency Services

All Medicare+Choice MCOs should have policies in place to ensure that beneficiaries have appropriate access to emergency services and hospitals within the MCO's network and that the contracts with such hospitals ensure that the hospitals provide the services required under the federal anti-dumping statute[96] without regard to the patient's insurance status or any prior authorization of such insurance. These policies are even more important if a Medicare+Choice MCO, through an agreement with the hospital, places its own physician in the hospital's emergency room for the purpose of screening and treating the Medicare+Choice MCO's managed care enrollees.[97]

## 2. Record Retention

A Medicare+Choice MCO should have a record retention system that includes policies and procedures regarding the creation, distribution, retention, storage, retrieval, and destruction of documents. In addition, there are three types of documents a Medicare+Choice MCO should ensure that it creates as a part of its compliance program:

---

[93] 63 Fed. Reg. 14,393, 14,395 (Mar. 25, 1998).

[94] The anti-kickback statute prohibits the provision of cash or other monetary rebates as an inducement for enrollment in a plan. However, CMS allows Medicare+ Choice MCOs to give Medicare beneficiaries gifts valued at less than $10 that cannot be readily converted to cash. *See* 64 Fed. Reg. 61,893, 61,898 n.42 (Nov. 15, 1999).

[95] 65 Fed. Reg. 24,400, 24,407 (Apr. 26, 2000).

[96] Emergency Medical Treatment and Labor Act (EMTALA), *codified at* 42 U.S.C. §1395dd.

[97] *See* Office of Inspector Gen., U.S. Dep't of Health & Human Servs., Special Advisory Bulletin on the Patient Anti-Dumping Statute, 64 Fed. Reg. 61,353 (Nov. 10, 1999).

1. all records and documentation required by federal or state law and federal or state health care programs;
2. records listing the persons responsible for implementing each part of the compliance program; and
3. all records necessary to protect the integrity of the Medicare+ Choice MCO's compliance process and confirm the effectiveness of the program.

The third category listed above includes items such as evidence of adequate employee training, reports from the Medicare+Choice MCO's fraud and abuse hotline, results of any investigation conducted as a consequence of a hotline call, modifications to the MCO's compliance program, all written notifications to providers regarding compliance activities, and results of the Medicare+Choice MCO's auditing and monitoring efforts. Record retention policies and procedures also should specifically address electronic data and regular backup requirements.

### 3. Compliance as Part of Employee Evaluation

The Compliance Program Guidance also provides that a relevant employee's promotion of and adherence to applicable elements of the organization's compliance program be a factor in evaluating his or her performance. Furthermore, employees should be trained periodically in new compliance policies and procedures, and managers should be required to educate employees regarding applicable policies and legal requirements and the disciplinary actions that may be taken if an employee does not adhere to the compliance program.

### 4. Subcontractor Compliance

The OIG strongly has recommended that Medicare+Choice MCOs coordinate with both first-tier and downstream providers[98] to establish compliance responsibilities in addition to the contractual responsibilities required by CMS.[99] Although the draft Compliance Program Guidance recommended that, at a minimum, Medicare+Choice MCOs send a copy of their compliance program manual to all of their health care providers, the final version provides more flexibility and instead suggests that a Medicare+Choice MCO should, on request, provide its contractors with a summary of its standards of conduct and the hotline number for reporting compliance concerns.[100]

### 5. Compliance Officer

According to the OIG, each Medicare+Choice MCO should appoint a compliance officer responsible for the following functions:

---

[98] "First tier" providers are those with which the MCO contracts directly. "Downstream" providers are those with which the first-tier providers contract, but with which the MCO does not have a direct contractual relationship.

[99] *See* Health Care Fin. Admin. Operational Policy Ltr. No. 77 (Dec. 8, 1998).

[100] 64 Fed. Reg. 61,893, 61,896 (Nov. 15, 1999).

- overseeing and monitoring the implementation of the MCO's compliance program;
- reporting on a regular basis to the MCO's chief executive officer (CEO), compliance committee, and on the progress of program implementation and also providing input on ways to improve the organization's efficiency and quality of services and reduce its vulnerability to fraud, abuse, and waste;
- revising the compliance program as necessary to meet the MCO's needs and comply with any changes in applicable laws, regulations, or government policies;
- reviewing employee certifications that state that an employee has received, read, and understood the MCO's standards of conduct;
- developing, coordinating, and participating in compliance program training and education;
- ensuring through coordination with the MCO's human resources department that the MCO does not employ or contract with excluded persons or entities;
- assisting with internal compliance review and monitoring activities;[101]
- investigating and acting on compliance matters;
- developing policies and programs that encourage employees to report suspected fraud and abuse; and
- ensuring that the compliance program remains effective after its implementation.

The compliance officer should have direct access to the CEO and members of senior management and the governing body of the MCO, but the OIG does not advise having the compliance officer report to the general counsel or any type of financial officer. In addition, the compliance officer should have appropriate authority to perform all of the functions of his or her job. In addition, a compliance committee managed by the compliance officer should be established.

### 6. The Compliance Committee

The compliance committee should include individuals with a variety of skills and significant professional experience in working with quality assurance, enrollment, marketing, clinical records and auditing. The committee's responsibilities should include such tasks as assessing existing policies and procedures to ensure that they fit with the organization's regulatory environment, working with the MCO's departments as well as affiliated providers to develop standards of

---

[101] However, see Office of Inspector Gen., U.S. Dep't of Health & Human Servs., Advisory Op. No. 01-16 (Oct. 5, 2001) (permitting Medicare+Choice organization to hire excluded provider for employee development purposes).

conduct and policies and procedures to further the organization's compliance program, recommending improvements or additions to internal systems to further the organization's compliance goals, and developing and evaluating a system or systems to detect and respond to potential violations.

### 7. Compliance Training

The Compliance Program Guidance recommends both formal and informal training regarding the MCO's compliance program. Formal training should include both general sessions (i.e., designed for all employees) and specialized sessions (i.e., designed for individuals involved in the risk area addressed in a particular policy). Employee attendance at the formal training sessions should be mandatory, and employees should be required to sign a certification stating that they have read the compliance program policies and standards, understand them, and will adhere to and support the program.

Informal training and education methods suggested by the OIG include a monthly compliance newsletter and maintaining a Web site devoted to compliance issues.[102] The OIG also has encouraged Medicare+ Choice MCOs to permit contractors to participate in the organization's compliance training and to encourage contractors to develop compliance programs that complement the MCO's program.

### 8. Effective Lines of Communication

The OIG has stressed that a good compliance program must have an effective system through which employees, enrollees, or other parties can report potential violations without fear of retaliation. This can be accomplished through (1) a hotline or some other mechanism that encourages persons to report suspected fraud or abuse and (2) developing confidentiality and nonretaliation policies. In addition, the compliance officer or an authorized designee should maintain a log of reports of compliance program violations and any resulting investigation and conclusions. The compliance officer also should be available to respond to any questions regarding the application or interpretation of the compliance program and its policies and procedures.

### 9. Auditing and Monitoring

A primary function of the compliance officer and compliance committee is to monitor the effectiveness of the Medicare+Choice MCO's compliance program. One of the most effective ways to monitor compliance is through audits by internal or external auditors who have expertise in federal and state health care statutes and regulations and federal health care program requirements. Audits should focus on

---

[102] 64 Fed. Reg. at 61,905.

identified risk areas. Other monitoring techniques include sampling protocols that permit the compliance officer to identify and review variations from an established baseline, on-site visits, questionnaires (e.g., for providers, enrollees, and employees), and trend analyses. Monitoring should not only review compliance with all applicable federal and state laws, regulations, and policies, but it also should ensure the effectiveness of the compliance program itself. Reports created as a result of auditing and monitoring activities should be maintained by the compliance officer and reviewed with members of the compliance committee and senior management.[103]

## 10. Discipline

The OIG has recommended that a Medicare+Choice MCO's compliance program include policies that (1) provide for appropriate disciplinary policies that are applied consistently when an employee violates the compliance program, and (2) ensure that a Medicare+Choice MCO does not employ or contract with excluded persons or entities or with persons or entities convicted of a criminal offense related to health care.

## 11. Corrective Action

The OIG recommends that an effective compliance program should include steps to correct any identified violation of the compliance program. Such steps may include an immediate referral to criminal and/or civil law enforcement authorities, a corrective action plan, a report to the government, and/or notification to the provider of any discrepancies or overpayments, if applicable. A Medicare+Choice MCO should document clearly all of its attempts to comply with all federal and state requirements. Policies that address responses to compliance program violations should include (1) an internal investigation, (2) identification of the proper persons or entities to whom or which the violation should be reported, (3) the procedure for reporting violations, and (4) corrective actions to be taken to ensure compliance. At a minimum, the internal investigation should include interviews with appropriate personnel and a review of relevant documents. The Medicare+Choice MCO should consider hiring outside counsel, auditors, or health care experts to assist in the investigation. The investigation as well as any subsequent reports and corrective actions should be well documented.

---

[103] In performing such audits, Medicare+Choice MCOs should refer to the *Medicare+ Choice Monitoring Guide,* which was reissued by CMS in May 2001 (previously issued in 1995, 1997, and 1999). The *Guide* combines the requirements of the Part C regulations from June 1998, February 1999, and June 2000, as well as the Quality Improvement System for Managed Care (QISMC). The *Guide* "represents a comprehensive statement of [CMS]'s expectations for Medicare+Choice Organization compliance with the coordinated care plan program requirements." Memorandum From Gary Bailey, Director, Health Plan Purchasing Administration Group to Medicare+Choice Organizations (Dec. 1, 1999). CMS "strongly recommends" that Medicare+Choice organizations use the *Guide* "to identify risk areas and conduct self-audits." *Id.*

## V. Potential False Claims Act and False Statement Liability Under Medicare+Choice Contracts

The civil False Claims Act (FCA)[104] presents the most severe threat of liability for MCOs. Increased government resources and consumer awareness have led to escalated federal enforcement activities and significant monetary recoveries for fraudulent activity, some of which have been shared with private citizens. Since the mid-1980s, the federal government has recovered more than $4 billion under the FCA—more than half was collected in the last few years alone, with more than $500 million going to private citizens. Although the government has applied the FCA to managed care, for example, in the action against UHCI concerning payment for institutionalized beneficiaries,[105] the nature of managed care presents unique FCA issues, as discussed below.

### A. Culpable Parties

The FCA imposes civil liability on persons or entities who (1) knowingly present or cause to be presented to the federal government a false or fraudulent claim for payment or approval,[106] (2) knowingly use a false record or statement to get a false or fraudulent claim paid or approved[107] or to avoid or decrease an obligation to the government,[108] or (3) conspire to defraud the government by getting a false or fraudulent claim allowed or paid.[109]

In May 2000, the U.S. Supreme Court resolved conflicting circuit court holdings in deciding that states are not "persons" under the FCA.[110] The Court expressed no view on the question of whether the Eleventh Amendment to the U.S. Constitution barred FCA suits by private citizens against state entities, a moot issue given the holding, but it stated its "serious doubt" regarding that question.[111]

### B. Levels of Knowledge

The FCA definition of "knowing" does not require the government to prove that the defendant had specific intent to defraud. Rather, the government must show that the defendant (1) had actual knowledge of the falsity of the information supporting the claim or claims, (2) acted

---

[104]31 U.S.C. §3729 et seq. The FCA is discussed at length in Chapter 3 (Salcido, The False Claims Act in Health Care Prosecutions: Application of the Substantive, *Qui Tam*, and Voluntary Disclosure Provisions).

[105]*Supra* Section II.B.2.6

[106]31 U.S.C. §3729(a)(1).

[107]31 U.S.C. §3729(a)(2).

[108]31 U.S.C. §3729(a)(7).

[109]31 U.S.C. §3729(a)(3).

[110]Vermont Agency of Natural Res. v. United States *ex rel.* Stevens, 529 U.S. 765, 120 S. Ct. 1858 (2000). This case is addressed in more detail *infra* Section V.D.

[111]120 S. Ct. at 1870.

in deliberate ignorance of the truth and falsity of the information, and (3) acted in reckless disregard of the truth or falsity of the information.[112] Under this standard, communication difficulties that often occur within large MCOs in which massive exchanges of data occur daily are potential liability risks. For example, a "disconnect" that leads to an inaccurate government payment may be characterized as "reckless" even if the "disconnect" resulted from "one hand" not knowing what the "other hand" was doing.

## C. Definition of "Claim"

Under the FCA, a "claim" is any request or demand for money or property if the U.S. government provides any portion of that money or property, including reimbursement. The concept of a "claim" is fairly straightforward in the FFS system where a provider furnishes a service or supply and submits a claim for payment. However under managed care, payment is not based on submission of a claim. Rather, the government and MCO engage in massive data exchanges and the amount paid to the MCO will depend on information generated by both the MCO and the government. In an effort to "claim-ify" this process, the Medicare+Choice MCO regulations require an MCO's CEO or chief financial officer (CFO) to "request payment under the contract based on a document that certifies the accuracy, completeness, and truthfulness of relevant data that HCFA [CMS] requests."[113]

In addition, unlike the FFS system where the "per claim" penalty gives the government tremendous leverage over providers that submit high volume–low dollar value claims, even if one were to accept that the payment to an MCO is based on a "claim," these "claims" are paid only once per month. Given the relatively large dollar value of the monthly managed care claim payments, the FCA "per claim" penalty probably does not offer the government the same leverage it enjoys over high volume–low dollar value claims. This might increase the potential that an MCO could try to litigate an FCA action.

## D. Damages

Liability for violating the FCA includes penalties of between $5,500 and $11,000 for each violation, plus treble damages.[114] In addition, a violation may result in exclusion from federal health care programs.[115]

The U.S. government or a private person (referred to as a *qui tam* relator), or both, may sue under the FCA.[116] A relator who chooses to invoke the statute files an action on the government's behalf[117] and

---

[112] 31 U.S.C. §3729(b).

[113] 42 C.F.R. §422.502(*l*)(3).

[114] 31 U.S.C. §3729(a). See 18 C.F.R. §85.3 for inflation adjustment to CMPs.

[115] 42 U.S.C. §1320a-7(a) & (b).

[116] 31 U.S.C. §3730(b) & (c). For text of the FCA, see Appendix C-1.

[117] 31 U.S.C. §3730(b)(1).

can receive from 15 percent to 30 percent of the proceeds of the action or settlement of the claim.[118] In *Vermont Agency of Natural Resources v. United States ex rel. Stevens,*[119] the U.S. Supreme Court rejected a constitutional challenge of the ability of *qui tam* relators to bring suits on behalf of the government. The petitioner had alleged that *qui tam* relators do not satisfy the judicially created "injury in fact" prong of Article III's "case or controversy" requirement for federal court jurisdiction. Although the Court refused to grant relators standing either as agents[120] or on "representational" grounds,[121] it found nevertheless that relators have standing as partial assignees of the government's claim by statutory designation under the FCA.[122]

An MCO that furnishes to CMS or a state agency an attestation or other information that it knows is false also faces substantial risk of liability under federal false statement and false claim statutes, including the "health care benefits" false statement provision adopted as Section 244 of HIPAA. Section 244 makes it a felony, punishable by fines or imprisonment, to knowingly or willfully falsify or conceal a material fact; to knowingly or willfully make a materially false, fictitious, or fraudulent statement or representation; or to make or use any materially false writing or document knowing that it contains a materially false, fictitious, or fraudulent statement or entry in connection with the delivery of or payment for health care benefits, items, or services.[123]

In addition, the Secretary of HHS is authorized to (1) impose CMPs of $15,000 to $100,000 (plus, in some circumstances, double damages) and (2) suspend enrollment or payment for specified conduct, including

1. failing to substantially provide medically necessary items and services;
2. imposing premiums in excess of those permitted;
3. expelling or refusing to enroll a person in violation of the provisions of 42 U.S.C. §1395mm;
4. engaging in any practice that reasonably would be expected to have the effect of denying or discouraging enrollment (except as permitted under 42 U.S.C. §1395mm) on the basis of a person's health condition or history;
5. misrepresenting or falsifying information provided to a person, CMS, or any other entity under 42 U.S.C. §1395mm;
6. failing to comply with the prompt payment or PIP provisions of 42 U.S.C. §1395mm; or

---

[118] 31 U.S.C. §3730(d).

[119] 529 U.S. 765, 120 S. Ct. 1858 (2000).

[120] 120 S. Ct. at 1862–63.

[121] *Id.*

[122] 120 S. Ct. at 1863.

[123] *See* 18 U.S.C. §1035. This provision is notable because it applies to statements submitted to private payers as well as to federal health care programs. For text of §1035, see Appendix E-1.

7. a risk-based contractor's employment or contracting with any person or entity excluded from participation in federal health care programs for the provision of health care, utilization review, medical social work, or administrative services or the employment of or contracting with any person or entity for the direct or indirect provision of such services by or through an excluded person or entity.[124]

The Secretary also is authorized to impose CMPs of $10,000 to $50,000 per violation for a number of specified acts, including the following:

1. improperly filing claims (e.g., for services not provided, for false or fraudulent claims, or for services rendered by unqualified or excluded providers);
2. paying inducements to reduce or limit services;
3. offering inducements to Medicare or Medicaid beneficiaries if the offeror knows or should know that the inducements are likely to influence the recipient to select a particular provider of items or services;
4. contracting with an excluded person or entity; and
5. violating the anti-kickback provisions of the Social Security Act.[125]

Another provision of the Social Security Act[126] requires the exclusion from participation in federal health care programs of persons or entities convicted of specified criminal offenses related to the delivery of an item or service under the Medicare or Medicaid programs, including those who have pled guilty or entered a "no contest" plea to such charges. It also authorizes exclusion, inter alia, of persons or entities convicted of federal program fraud and abuse or other specified violations, determined to have engaged in certain prohibited activities, or of entities controlled by sanctioned individuals.

## E. Other Statutes

Other statutes potentially applicable to fraud and abuse by MCOs with criminal penalties, include, but are not limited to the following:

- the federal Health Care Program Anti-Kickback Act;[127]
- the Health Care Fraud Act;[128]
- the Obstruction of Health Care Investigations statute;[129]

---

[124] 42 U.S.C. §1395mm(i)(6)(A)(v) (competitive medical plans and risk-based and cost HMOs); 42 U.S.C. §1395w-27(g) (Medicare+Choice plans).

[125] 42 U.S.C. §§1320a-7a, 1320a-7b(b).

[126] 42 U.S.C. §1320a-7(a)–(b).

[127] 42 U.S.C. §1320a-7b(b). For text of the statute, see Appendix A-1.

[128] 18 U.S.C. §1347. For text of §1347, see Appendix E-2.

[129] 18 U.S.C. §1518

- the Theft or Embezzlement in Relation to a Health Care Benefit Program statute;[130] and
- the Racketeer Influenced and Corrupt Organizations Act (RICO).[131]

## F. Liability for Submission of Certified Rate, Enrollment, and Encounter Data

Participation in the Medicare+Choice program increases an organization's potential for FCA liability. One area of particular vulnerability for MCO false claims liability is the submission of certified rate, enrollment, and encounter data to the government. These data affect the level of reimbursement paid. The OIG currently is conducting an audit of data submissions from many plans nationwide. Although it has relied primarily on administrative processes to effectuate the repayment of funds improperly obtained through inaccurate submissions, the OIG has referred cases of potential fraud and abuse for prosecution under the FCA. Without controls to confirm that a plan lacked knowledge of errors and did not act with deliberate ignorance or reckless disregard of the possibility of errors, such referrals could greatly increase an MCO's exposure to liability. Errors relating to ACR, enrollment and encounter data, all of which must be submitted to CMS and certified by an MCO, could lead to significant false claims exposure.

### 1. Adjusted Community Rate

Before the passage of the BBA, Medicare risk-based contractors were paid on a monthly per capita basis for each enrollee. These monthly payments were known as the average payment rate, which was 95 percent of the adjusted average per capita cost (AAPCC) for each class of enrollees that CMS recognized.[132] A new payment methodology was established under Medicare+Choice that changed the definition and method of calculating the ACR.[133] A Medicare+Choice contractor's ACR represents the premium it would charge its non-Medicare enrollees for Medicare-covered services, adjusted for the greater use of services by Medicare enrollees.

#### a. Submission and Certification

Medicare+Choice plans are required to submit (1) ACRPs for both basic and supplemental benefits, (2) a description of cost sharing, (3) the actuarial value of cost-sharing or basic and supplemental benefits, and (4) a description of any additional benefits and their value. The plan's CEO must certify that the information included in its ACRP submission

---

[130] 18 U.S.C. §669.

[131] 18 U.S.C. §1961.

[132] 42 C.F.R. §471.594.

[133] 42 U.S.C. §1395w-24(f)(3).

is accurate and completely satisfies the applicable regulations.[134] Faulty certification could lead to FCA or false statement liability.

### b. Administrative Costs

The area of "administrative costs" now requires additional information, and Medicare+Choice plans must divide their administrative components into two parts: (1) an administrative-cost component and (2) one that reflects "additional revenues" (i.e., revenues collected in excess of costs incurred).[135] A Medicare+Choice organization is required to disclose projected amounts of additional revenues to CMS for each population group (i.e., commercial and Medicare) and to justify any greater additional revenue projected for its Medicare population compared with its commercial populations.

## 2. Enrollment Data

As a condition of receiving monthly Medicare+Choice payments, plans must request payment by submitting to CMS monthly reports containing required information, including new enrollments, disenrollments, and changes in institutional status of beneficiaries. The CEO or CFO also must certify the accuracy, completeness, and truthfulness of relevant data.[136] As with any certification, concern has been expressed that such certification requirements will make MCOs and their officers vulnerable to liability whenever a mistake occurs.[137]

## 3. Encounter Data

The BBA required that CMS implement a risk-adjustment methodology for payment periods beginning after January 1, 2000. Under this methodology, capitated payments are adjusted for age, gender, institutional status, and other factors, including health status.[138] To adjust for health status, CMS applies a risk factor based on encounter data captured from plans.[139] Consequently, Medicare+ Choice plans must submit and certify the accuracy and completeness of data sufficient to characterize the content and aim of encounters between Medicare enrollees and providers or suppliers.[140] In addition, the accuracy, completeness, and truthfulness of encounter data generated by a related entity, contractor, or subcontractor of the Medicare+

---

[134] 42 C.F.R. §422.502(m).

[135] 42 C.F.R. §422.310(c)(2).

[136] The Medicare, Medicaid, and SCHIP [State Children's Health Insurance Plan] Budget Refinement Act of 1999, Pub. L. No. 106-113, as amended by the Benefit Improvement and Protection Act of 2000, Pub. L. No. 106-554, requires that the risk-adjustment methodology be phased in gradually.

[137] 42 C.F.R §422.256(d).

[138] 42 C.F.R. §422.502(*l*).

[139] *Id.*

[140] 3 Health Care Fraud Rep. (BNA) 149 (Feb. 24, 1999). Director and officer liability is discussed at length in Chapter 8 (Baumann & McDavid, Potential Liabilities for Directors and Officers of Health Care Organizations).

Choice plan must be certified by that related entity or party.[141] The complexity of the data that must be submitted and the number of parties involved in compiling it increase the likelihood that inaccurate submissions and subsequent liability could result. Note, as of September 1, 2001, Medicare+Choice MCOs are only required to gather and submit hospital inpatient encounter data. Secretary Thompson has postponed the submission of outpatient encounter data until July 2, 2002.[142]

## G. Compliance Exposure Relating to Physician Risk and Incentive Plan Issues: The Federal Physician Incentive Plan Rule

On December 31, 1996, HCFA (now CMS) and the OIG issued a final rule setting forth the requirements for contracting with the Medicare and Medicaid programs that must be satisfied by prepaid health care organizations that have PIPs.[143] The PIP rule implements the Omnibus Budget Reconciliation Act of 1990 provisions enacted to limit the circumstances under which physicians would be subject to inappropriate or extreme financial incentives to deny necessary services to Medicare and Medicaid managed care patients and was made applicable to Medicare+Choice plans by the BBA.[144] Pursuant to its 1999 Work Plan, the OIG reviewed PIPs included in contracts between physicians and MCOs, as well as other related contract provisions with the potential to affect quality of care.[145]

### 1. Scope and Applicability of the Physician Incentive Plan Rule

The PIP rule applies to MCOs that contract with CMS or a state agency to arrange for or provide Medicare or Medicaid services and governs any PIP that bases incentive payments (in whole or in part) on services provided to Medicare or Medicaid beneficiaries. It encompasses physician compensation arrangements that (1) are entered into by direct contract between the physician and the MCO and (2) the MCO may enter into only indirectly through a contract with an intermediary organization. Intermediary organizations include independent practice associations, physician hospital organizations, and similar organizations, which usually are provider sponsored and provider owned. CMS may impose sanctions under the Medicare+Choice program for failure to comply with the PIP requirements[146] and has finalized but not yet implemented sanctions for failure to comply

---

[141] 42 C.F.R. §422.502(*l*).

[142] *See* Memorandum From Gary A. Bailey, Acting Director, Medicare Managed Care Group, to Medicare+Choice Organizations (May 31, 2001).

[143] 61 Fed. Reg. 69,034 (Dec. 31, 1996).

[144] *See* 42 U.S.C. §1395mm(i) (HMOs and competitive medical plans); 42 U.S.C. §1395w-22(j)(4) (Medicare+Choice plans).

[145] OIG WORK PLAN FY 1999, *supra* note 90, at 23 (available at http://www.oig. hhs.gov/wrkpln/index.htm).

[146] 42 C.F.R. §422.752(b).

with PIP retirements under the Medicaid managed care program.[147] Note that the new proposed rule contains the same requirements as 42 C.F.R. §438.700.[148]

The rule prohibits a PIP from furnishing specific payments or any other form of remuneration directly or indirectly to a physician or physician group as an inducement to limit or reduce medically necessary services provided to an individual enrollee. In addition, it limits the amount of risk that individual physicians and physician groups can assume under a PIP for the cost of services provided to Medicare or Medicaid enrollees in an MCO. It is HHS's position that an MCO is responsible for ensuring that any physician participating in its network is compensated in a manner that does not violate the rule, regardless of whether the MCO's contractual relationship with the physician is direct or indirect. PIPs include "any compensation arrangement"[149] with a physician or physician group participating in the MCO that may have the effect of reducing or limiting services provided to Medicare or Medicaid beneficiaries enrolled in the MCO.

### 2. *"Substantial Financial Risk" Triggers Additional Requirements*

"Substantial financial risk"[150] is present if risk is based (in whole or in part) on levels or costs of referral services (i.e., services ordered by a physician or by other physicians in a risk pool with that physician but furnished by other providers who are not part of a clinically integrated physician group) if the incentive arrangement has the potential to hold the physician or physician group liable for more than 25 percent of potential payments under the arrangement with the MCO or with respect to the plan's enrollees. MCOs that contract directly or indirectly with physicians who are placed at substantial financial risk are subject to stringent requirements to ensure that enrollees are not adversely affected by any PIP. The MCO must (1) ensure that there is appropriate stop-loss insurance for excess risk assumed by the physician, (2) conduct periodic surveys of current and former enrollees, and (3) inform beneficiaries of stop-loss arrangements and the results of any required enrollee satisfaction surveys.[151]

### 3. *Required Disclosures*

A Medicare+Choice MCO must furnish to CMS information about a PIP in sufficient detail to allow CMS to determine whether the plan complies with 42 C.F.R. §422.208 and whether services not furnished by the physician or physician group are covered by the PIP. If only those services provided by the physician or physician group are covered by the

---

[147] 42 C.F.R. §438.700 (implementation delayed until Aug. 16, 2002, under 66 Fed. Reg. 43,090 (Aug. 17, 2001)).

[148] *See* 66 Fed. Reg. 43,614, 43,675 (Aug. 20, 2001).

[149] 42 C.F.R. §422.208(a).

[150] *Id.*

[151] *Id.*

PIP, then disclosure of other aspects of the plan need not be made.[152] Specific disclosures to Medicaid beneficiaries also are required.

- *Disclosures to CMS.* Required disclosures to CMS include (i) the type of incentive arrangement (e.g., withholds, bonus, capitation), (ii) the percentage of the withhold or bonus, (iii) the amount and type of stop-loss protection, (iv) the panel size and whether patients are pooled, and (v) a summary of enrollee survey results for those plans required to conduct them.[153] The new Medicare+Choice regulations no longer require plans to disclose capitated data.[154]
- *Disclosures to Medicare beneficiaries.* Required disclosures to requesting beneficiaries include (i) whether the plan uses a PIP that affects the use of referral services, (ii) the type of incentive arrangement, (iii) whether stop-loss protection is provided, and (iv) a summary of enrollee survey results for those plans required to conduct them.[155]

### 4. Certified Worksheet Issues

An MCO that furnishes to CMS or a state agency physician incentive information that it knows is false faces substantial risk of liability under federal false statement and false claim statutes, including the "health care benefits" false statement provision adopted as Section 244 of HIPAA.[156] Civil false claims exposure also could exist if the MCO furnishes information in "reckless disregard" of its accuracy.[157] Thus, the MCO must be vigilant in accepting and relying on physician incentive information provided by physicians or intermediaries that it uses to demonstrate its compliance with the rule to CMS. For example, the government may challenge as unreasonable or reckless an MCO's reliance on information provided to it by a provider if the MCO has sufficient knowledge that competitor contracting practices make it unlikely that incentive plan arrangements are "comparable" enough to permit pooling.

To avoid the PIP rule's stop-loss coverage requirements, physicians and physician groups that provide information to MCOs also must understand how the rule operates, including how the rule defines financial risk and when pooling is—and is not—permitted. If false information is knowingly provided to an MCO, the physician or physician group could potentially be subject to federal false statement or false claims liability, depending on the facts and circumstances. Civil false claims liability could attach if information is given with reckless

---

[152] 42 C.F.R. §422.210.

[153] *Id.*

[154] *See* 63 Fed. Reg. 34,968, 35,002 (June 26, 1998).

[155] 42 C.F.R. §422.210(b).

[156] 18 U.S.C. §1035.

[157] *See* 31 U.S.C. §3729.

disregard to its accuracy. Likewise, information that becomes out of date as a result of material developments (e.g., loss of a contract) could pose liability if the physician or physician group continues to receive payments under the contract but knows, or should know, that the requirements of the rule are not being met because the physician or physician group has failed to provide the MCO with information that is material to compliance with the rule.

### 5. Underutilization

The PIP rule imposes an affirmative duty on an MCO to reduce the risk of underutilization of medically necessary services for enrollees. Therefore, failure to comply with the rule could give rise to the risk of civil or criminal false claims or civil program liability (e.g., program exclusion or suspension). An MCO may have difficulty defending itself against charges that it shares responsibility for the underutilization if it fails to comply with the rule. An MCO may face enhanced risk under 42 U.S.C. §§1395mm(i)(6)(A) and 1395w-27(g), which authorize the Secretary of HHS to impose CMPs on an MCO for, among other things, "failing substantially to provide medically necessary items and services that are required (under law or contract) to be provided to a Medicare enrollee, if such failure has adversely affected (or has substantial likelihood of adversely affecting) the enrollee." A pattern of noncompliance that is knowing or reckless also could give rise to false claims liability if an MCO receives a premium payment for enrollees who are not being provided with adequate care. For example, civil false claim allegations were brought against a nursing home that failed to provide necessary services to a person yet submitted claims to the government under the Medicare program for services provided.[158]

### 6. Anti-Kickback Concerns

Under the fraud and abuse provisions enacted by HIPAA, a risk-sharing arrangement that places a provider "at substantial financial risk for the cost or utilization of the items or services which the individual or entity is obligated to provide" is essentially exempt from the Medicare and Medicaid anti-kickback statute.[159] This provision will be of particular interest to "intermediary organizations" that are not "eligible organizations" under 42 U.S.C. §1395mm[160] because these or-

---

[158] *See* United States v. Tucker House Nursing Home, C.A. No. 96-1271 (E.D. Pa. 1996) (settlement resulted in the nursing home agreeing to fines and a consent order); *see also* Northern Health Facilities v. United States, 39 F. Supp. 2d 563 (D. Md. 1998).

[159] *See* HIPAA §216 (codified at 42 U.S.C. §1320a-7b(b)(3)(F)).

[160] Under HIPAA §216 (codified at 42 U.S.C. §1320a-7b(b)(3)(F)), "any remuneration between an organization and an individual or entity providing items or services, or a combination thereof, pursuant to a written agreement between the organization and the individual or entity if the organization is an eligible organization" under 42 U.S.C. §1395mm is also exempt from the anti-kickback statute. MCOs usually are eligible organizations and thus do not have to place their providers "at substantial financial risk" to come within this exemption.

ganizations often establish referral relationships between member providers that, under certain circumstances, might be viewed as suspect fee-for-referral arrangements.[161]

### 7. *Stark Self-Referral Prohibitions*

Prior to the final Stark II regulations published in January 2001,[162] the PIP rule had implications under the Stark physician self-referral prohibitions.[163] Before the final Stark II regulations added a new exception for "risk sharing" arrangements to the general self-referral prohibition, an MCO's PIP could have potentially violated the Stark law with respect to patients who had traditional fee-for-service Medicare and Medicaid coverage and were also enrolled in the MCO's commercial plans (i.e., the members were not enrolled in the MCO's Medicare+Choice or Managed Medicaid coverage). However, the final Stark II regulations recognized this unintended risk with respect to MCOs' general PIP plans and added a new risk-sharing exception to the Stark prohibitions.[164]

Under the risk-sharing exception, "compensation pursuant to a risk-sharing arrangement (including . . . withholds, bonuses, and risk pools) between a managed care organization . . . and a physician (either directly or indirectly through a subcontractor) for services provided to *enrollees* of a health plan . . ." is exempt from the Stark Law prohibition on physician compensation arrangements.[165] Thus, the risk-sharing exception exempts compensation arrangements with respect to all of an MCO's enrollees, not just Medicare+Choice or Managed Medicaid enrollees. To qualify for the Stark II risk-sharing exception, however, the risk-sharing arrangement also must not violate the Anti-Kickback Act.[166]

### 8. *Potential Benefits of Meeting the Physician Incentive Plan Requirements*

Although the PIP rule imposes potentially burdensome requirements on MCOs, the PIP rule also provides an opportunity for plans (1) to deflect criticism that managed care financial arrangements may encourage physicians to withhold necessary care and (2) to counter momentum at the state level to enact legislation limiting the use of risk-sharing or other incentive compensation arrangements. Legislation has been enacted in Maryland, for example, to limit the use of "withholds" that ultimately would reduce a physician's agreed-on compensation.[167] Referenda that would have strictly limited a man-

---

[161] See *infra* Section VI.

[162] 66 Fed. Reg. 856 (Jan. 4, 2001).

[163] 42 U.S.C. §1395nn. For detailed discussion of the Stark law, see Chapter 2 (Crane, Federal Physician Self-Referral Restrictions). For text of the statute, see Appendix B-1.

[164] 42 U.S.C. §411.357(n). See also discussion in preamble at 66 Fed Reg. at 911.

[165] 42 U.S.C. §411.357(n) (emphasis added).

[166] *Id.*

[167] MD. CODE ANN., INS. §15-113 (1999).

aged care plan's ability to use capitation methods of payment were defeated by voters in California and Oregon in 1996,[168] but these issues are likely to be reintroduced in other forms and in other states.

### 9. Gainsharing

On July 8, 1999, the OIG issued a Special Advisory Bulletin entitled "Gainsharing Arrangements and CMPs [Competitive Medical Plans] for Hospital Payments to Physicians to Reduce or Limit Services to Beneficiaries."[169] According to this Special Advisory Bulletin, "gainsharing" is a term that "typically refers to an arrangement in which a hospital gives physicians a percentage share of any reduction in the hospital's costs for patient care attributable in part to the physicians' efforts." The OIG then found that these gainsharing arrangements "provide financial incentives to reduce or limit items or services to patients" and, therefore, are subject to CMPs for violating 42 U.S.C. §1320a-7a(b)(1) and (2), which prohibits payments to induce physicians to reduce clinical services to Medicare or Medicaid patients. However, in a letter released August 23, 1999, the OIG conceded that "hospital-physician plans limited to Medicare or Medicaid beneficiaries enrolled in risk-based managed care programs subject to regulation" under the Social Security Act are not subject to CMPs.[170] Also of interest, in an opinion in early 2001, the OIG approved a physician-hospital gainsharing program.[171]

### 10. Compliance

To decrease its risk of liability, an MCO should, at the very least, be able to demonstrate that it has made efforts to ensure compliance with the PIP rule by employees as well as by physicians, physician groups, and intermediaries with which it contracts. Adherence to the PIP rule should be a part of the MCO's overall compliance program to identify program obligations and educate responsible employees, providers, and subcontractors regarding such obligations and sanctions for noncompliance. Moreover, because facts that are material to compliance with the rule may change, it is imperative that the MCO implement systems to ensure ongoing compliance with program obligations, including designating an employee or employees with responsibility for overseeing compliance in specific areas and monitoring compliance through audits and other follow-up activities.

---

[168] Cal. Prop. Nos. 214, 216 (1996); Or. Measure No. 35 (1996).

[169] Office of Inspector Gen., U.S. Dep't of Health & Human Servs., Special Advisory Bulletin on Gainsharing Arrangements and CMPs [Competitive Medical Plans] for Hospital Payments to Physicians to Reduce or Limit Services to Beneficiaries (July 8, 1999), 64 Fed. Reg. 37,985 (July 14, 1999). For text of the advisory bulletin, see Appendix F-15 on the disk accompanying this volume.

[170] Letter From Office of Inspector Gen., U.S. Dep't of Health & Human Servs. (Aug. 19, 1999), *reported in* 3 Health Care Fraud Rep. (BNA) 776–77 (Sept. 8, 1999).

[171] *See* Office of Inspector Gen., U.S. Dep't of Health & Human Servs., Advisory Op. No. 01-1 (Jan. 11, 2001).

Finally, although compliance with the PIP rule is imperative, an MCO cannot view such compliance as providing a safe harbor against potential program liability regarding underutilization or as a substitute for an overall compliance program. The PIP rule also may have a ripple effect for intermediary organizations, physician groups, and individual physicians. These entities and physicians need to understand and consider the PIP rule in their dealings with MCOs and in managing their exposure to risk under the Stark law's self-referral prohibitions and the anti-kickback law.

### 11. Enforcement Litigation

In 1999, Harris Methodist Health Plans agreed to pay $4.6 million to settle two enrollee class action lawsuits concerning the MCO's physician incentive payments. One of the suits was filed under the Employee Retirement Income Security Act of 1974 (ERISA) and alleged that Harris Methodist had breached its fiduciary duty, and the other was filed under state tort law.[172] The plaintiffs alleged that Harris Methodist failed to disclose financial incentive arrangements with physicians that could result in the limitation of medically necessary care. Under the settlement, individual plan members were eligible for payment not exceeding $50, whereas class representatives were eligible for enhanced payments.[173] These same compensation arrangements were the subject of a state court action brought by primary care physicians that resulted in Harris Methodist agreeing to pay $3.4 million in penalties and lost bonuses in an agreement with the Texas Department of Insurance.[174]

### 12. Private Class Action Litigation

Beginning October 4, 1999, a series of nationwide class action lawsuits were filed by members. Although based on various legal theories, these cases essentially alleged, in part, that the MCOs involved engaged in a "nationwide fraudulent scheme" by illegally concealing information about the restrictions on the exercise of independent medical judgment by physicians.[175] These lawsuits were brought under

---

[172]*See, e.g.,* Ingram v. Harris Methodist Health Plan, No. 98-CV-179 (E.D. Tex., *settlement filed* Oct. 12, 1999).

[173]3 Health Care Fraud Rep. (BNA) 917 (Oct. 20, 1999).

[174]2 Health Care Fraud Rep. (BNA) 662 (Sept. 9, 1998).

[175]*See* Connecticut v. Anthem Blue Cross & Blue Shield of Conn., 3:00 CV01716 (D. Conn. *filed* Sept. 7, 2000) (alleging ERISA violations for alleged failures to disclose information related to guidelines used to deny coverage and the steps necessary to submit claims and appeal denials of coverage); Price v. Humana Inc., No. 99-8763 (S.D. Fla. *filed* Oct. 4, 1999); *In re* Managed Care Litig., Case No. 1334 (S.D. Fla. *filed* Oct. 5, 1999) (consolidated class action) (alleging that Humana improperly concealed from class members that it used for claims review financial incentives that encouraged denial of claims); Romero v. Prudential Ins. Co., Case No. CV2592 (E.D. Pa. *filed* May 22, 2000) (alleging ERISA violations for failure to disclose policy that out-of-network care would not be covered if it did not meet utilization management criteria); McRaney v. United Healthcare, Case No. 200-CV-33PG (S.D. Miss. *filed* Feb. 8, 2000) (alleging misrepresentations and omissions in advertising and marketing materials).

both RICO and ERISA, as well as under various other theories and have been consolidated in the Southern District of Florida, along with other cases.[176]

The plaintiffs' allegations in these class actions generally focus on nondisclosures or misrepresentations related to coverage and treatment decisions. In addition to this multidistrict litigation, several other lawsuits have alleged that MCOs concealed from enrollees physician financial incentives to limit medically necessary care. For example, in *Ehlmann v. Kaiser Foundation Health Plan,*[177] the plaintiffs alleged that five health plans breached their fiduciary duty under ERISA by failing to disclose physician incentive arrangements. The Fifth Circuit affirmed the district court's dismissal of the breach of fiduciary claim, ruling that Congress and not the courts should impose any such duty under ERISA and that no general duty to disclose could be implied from the general fiduciary duty under ERISA. Other courts have reached different results regarding this issue.[178]

A similar case was dismissed for lack of standing and the dismissal was affirmed on appeal. In *Maio v. Aetna, Inc.,*[179] the plaintiffs had filed a civil RICO action alleging that Aetna had engaged in a fraudulent scheme to enroll members in its health plans by representing that its primary goal in providing care was to better its members' health, whereas its actual goal was financial gain. The plaintiffs alleged that their plans were worth less than what Aetna represented; in response, Aetna filed a motion to dismiss, arguing that the plaintiffs lacked standing to sue because they had sustained no actual injury as a result of Aetna's actions. Applying the test outlined by the U.S. Supreme Court in *Lujan v. Defenders of Wildlife,*[180] the district court found that there had been no actual decrease in value of the plaintiffs' health plans. According to the court, there also had been no injury related to "denial of benefits, reduction of benefits, inferior care, malpractice, negligence and breach of contract."[181] The court, in dicta, also found that "as a matter of law, it is highly doubtful that advertising one's commitment to 'quality of care' can serve as the predicate for a fraud claim."[182] The court also was not convinced that the plaintiffs had sufficiently pled the existence of a RICO enterprise. In affirming the district court, the Third Circuit found that absent "assertions of diminished benefits or care . . . [plaintiffs] cannot establish as a factual matter

---

[176]*See Aetna, Humana Class Actions Attack Common Managed Care Practices,* 3 Health Care Fraud Rep. (BNA) 928 (Oct. 20, 1999).

[177]198 F.3d 552 (5th Cir.), *cert. dismissed,* 530 U.S. 1291 (2000).

[178]*See, e.g.,* Shea v. Esensten, 107 F.3d 625 (8th Cir.) (holding that a plan administrator has a fiduciary duty to disclose all material facts affecting a plan participant's health care interest, including financial incentives), *cert. denied,* 522 U.S. 914 (1997).

[179]No. 99-1969, 1999 U.S. Dist. LEXIS 15056, 23 EB Cases 1974 (E.D. Pa. Sept. 29, 1999).

[180]504 U.S. 555 (1992).

[181]*Aetna,* 199 U.S. Dist. Lexis 15056, at *7.

[182]*Id.* at *8.

that they received anything less than what they bargained for . . . i.e., a quality health care product."[183]

As illustrated by the *Ehlmann* case discussed above, several of these class action lawsuits allege that MCOs improperly concealed from enrollees physician financial incentives allegedly used to limit the provision of medically necessary care. Courts have reached different conclusions as to whether, under ERISA's general fiduciary duty, plans have a general duty to disclose physician incentive plans.[184]

The Supreme Court has yet to rule on this issue. However, Justice Souter wrote in a footnote in *Pegram v. Herdrich*[185] that although the question was not before the Court, it could be argued that the HMO in *Pegram* was "obligated to disclose characteristics of the plan and of those who provide services to the plan, if that information affects beneficiaries' material interests."[186]

## VI. MANAGED CARE EXCEPTIONS TO THE ANTI-KICKBACK STATUTE

Section 216 of HIPAA created a new managed care exception to the Medicare and Medicaid anti-kickback provisions.[187] This exception allows (1) remuneration between a Medicare+Choice MCO and an individual or entity providing items or services pursuant to a written agreement between the parties, and (2) remuneration between an organization and an individual provider or a provider entity if the provider is at "substantial financial risk"[188] for the cost of utilization of items or services that the provider is obligated to provide, whether through a withhold, capitation, incentive pool, or per-diem payment, or any other similar risk arrangement.

### A. Negotiated Rule Making

Section 216(b) of HIPAA provided that the Secretary of HHS, through an expedited negotiated rule-making process, set standards for the new managed care exception to the Medicare and Medicaid anti-kickback provisions. Consequently, the OIG engaged in a negotiated rule-making process to develop a safe harbor regulation, and that process was completed in January 1998. The negotiation process was

---

[183] Maio v. Aetna, Inc., 221 F.3d 472, 494 (3d Cir. 2000).

[184] *See, e.g.,* Ehlmann v. Kaiser Found. Health Plan, 198 F.3d 552 (5th Cir.), *cert. dismissed,* 530 U.S. 1291 (2000); Shea v. Esensten, 107 F.3d 625 (8th Cir. 1997) (holding that a plan administrator has a fiduciary duty to disclose all material facts affecting a plan participant's health care interests, including financial incentives), *cert. denied,* 522 U.S. 914 (1997).

[185] 530 U.S. 211, 228 n.8 (2000).

[186] *Id.* at 228 n.8

[187] 42 U.S.C. §1320a-7b(b)(3)(F).

[188] *Id.*

conducted by the OIG over a 6-month period, with approximately 20 participants from the private sector (e.g., managed care and health care provider trade associations), as well as government agencies such as the DOJ. The OIG promulgated an interim final rule on November 19, 1999, that established two new safe harbors to satisfy the exception set forth in 42 U.S.C. §1320a-7b(b)(3)(F). The resulting safe harbors are relatively narrow and clearly reflect areas of concern to the OIG and other anti-fraud enforcement authorities. Despite the regulation's limited scope, the preamble includes a statement that arrangements falling outside of the safe harbors are not presumed to be illegal, but must be judged on a case-by-case basis.[189] This language clearly is aimed at the anxieties expressed by private participants to the rule making regarding the potential stigma for any arrangement that does not fall within the safe harbors. It should be noted that prior to the issuance of these new safe harbors, the OIG, in an advisory opinion, approved an arrangement whereby an independent physician association acquired an equity interest of less than 15 percent in an MCO.[190]

As noted above, the rule established two separate safe harbors, and each of these safe harbors is further broken down into two components: the first component covers arrangements directly between the managed care entity and a contractor; the second component addresses arrangements between a managed care contractor and its subcontractors.

## B. Capitated Managed Care Entity Safe Harbor

The safe harbor set forth in 42 C.F.R. §1001.952(t) extends protection from the anti-kickback statute to most managed health care program arrangements in which the federal health care programs pay on a capitated or fixed aggregate basis (e.g., certain Medicare Part C plans). Furthermore, it extends safe harbor protection to cover subcontracts with other providers and entities to provide items and services in accordance with a protected managed care arrangement. So long as the federal heath care programs' aggregate financial exposure is fixed in accordance with its contract with the MCO, such subcontracting arrangements are protected regardless of the payment methodology, subject to the following requirements: the agreement (1) is set out in writing and signed by both parties; (2) specifies the items and services covered under the agreement; (3) is for a period of at least 1 year; and (4) with the exception of certain types of MCOs and first-tier contractors, provides that the contractors and subcontractors cannot make a claim to the federal government for services covered under the agreement.

---

[189]Statutory Exception to the Anti-Kickback Statute for Shared Risk Arrangements, 64 Fed. Reg. 63,504 (Nov. 19, 1999) (interim final rule codified at 42 C.F.R. pt. 1001).

[190]*See* Office of Inspector Gen., U.S. Dep't of Health & Human Servs., Advisory Op. No. 98-19 (Dec. 14, 1998).

## C. Risk-Sharing Safe Harbor

The safe harbor set forth in 42 C.F.R. §1001.952(u) extends protection from the anti-kickback statute to those managed care arrangements that encompass substantial risk-sharing between the qualified managed care plan and its first-tier or downstream contractors. There are several requirements that have to be met for an MCO and a provider to avail themselves of this safe harbor. However, there are two major limitations. First, to qualify for this safe harbor, a provider must be at substantial financial risk for items or services provided to *federal health care program beneficiaries*. However, as the preamble candidly notes, risk-sharing arrangements that cover federal health care program beneficiaries may be covered under the other new managed care safe harbor, 42 C.F.R §1001.952(t), as discussed above. Second, providers must be at risk for the cost or utilization of items or services that they are personally "obligated to provide," which may have the effect of excluding arrangements under which a physician's compensation may be at risk for services provided by other providers. For example, risk-sharing arrangements with primary care physicians (PCPs) often base the PCP's bonus, in part, on the volume or value of referral services, such as diagnostic and lab tests ordered by the PCP, or hospital admissions authorized by the PCP. Those types of risk-sharing arrangements are not protected under this new safe harbor.

In addition to the above listed restrictions, the arrangement between the MCO and the first-tier contractor must:

1. be in writing and signed by the parties;
2. specify the items and services covered by the arrangement;
3. be for a period of at least 1 year;
4. require that the contractor participate in the MCO's quality assurance program;
5. set a payment formula that results in periodic payments that are commercially reasonable and consistent with fair market value;
6. utilize one of the following payment methodologies:
   - a periodic fixed payment per patient that does not take into account the dates services are provided, the frequency of services, or the extent or kind of services provided;
   - percentage of premium;
   - inpatient federal health care program diagnosis related groups (other than those for psychiatric services); and
   - bonus and withhold arrangements, provided that certain specified percentage thresholds and risk proportions are met and payments are reasonable given the MCO's population and utilization;
7. if there are services or items not covered under the capitated payment made by the government to the MCO, the MCO (not the contractor or provider) must submit the claims to the federal

government for reimbursement, pursuant to a valid reassignment agreement;

8. payments to contractors (first-tier and downstream) for providing or arranging for items and services for federal health plan enrollees must be identical (allowing adjustments related to utilization patterns or costs of providing services to the relevant population) for payments to contractors for providing or arranging for items and services for commercial enrollees with similar health status; and

9. if a first-tier contractor has an investment interest in the MCO, the investment interest must meet the requirements set forth in 42 C.F.R §1001.952(a)(1). The preamble notes that this requirement is intended to eliminate any concern that the contractor's substantial financial risk may be offset by returns on its ownership interest in the organization and therefore undermine protections against overutilization.

Many of the above requirements also apply to contracts between the first-tier contractor and the downstream entity (i.e., provider).

## D. Some Common Elements of Both Safe Harbors

In addition to the requirements particular to each safe harbor set forth above, the safe harbors share several common definitions and requirements:

### 1. Health Care Items and Services

The safe harbors apply only to remuneration for health care items or services (as do the previously promulgated managed care safe harbors), but for these two new safe harbors, HHS has added a definition of "items and services" that appears to broaden the term in comparison to how it is used in the rest of the regulation. "Items and services" is defined to include "items, . . . or services reasonably related to the provision of health care items, devices, supplies, or services," such as "non-emergency transportation, patient education, attendant services, social services (e.g., case management), utilization review and quality assurance."[191] Marketing and other preenrollment activities are not considered to be "items or services" that fall within this definition.[192]

### 2. No Swapping or Shifting of Financial Burden

In addition to the requirements listed above for the new safe harbors, arrangements under either 42 C.F.R §1001.952(t) or (u) (both between MCOs and first-tier contractors and first-tier contractors and downstream entities) cannot provide for "swapping" or allow a shift-

---

[191] 64 Fed. Reg. 63,504, 63,513–514 (Nov. 19, 1999) (codified at 42 C.F.R. §1001.952(t)(2)(iv) and (u)(2)(iv)).

[192] *Id.*

ing of the financial burden of the arrangement to a federal health care program.

Arrangements are excluded from the protection of both new safe harbors if the contracting parties give or receive remuneration in return "for or to induce the provision or acceptance of business (other than business covered by the arrangement) for which payment may be made in whole or in part by a federal health care program on a fee-for-service or cost basis."[193] This exclusion reflects the OIG's concern about swapping arrangements. Swapping occurs when the risk arrangement is agreed to in exchange for the right to participate in a program that provides greater compensation to the provider (e.g., a commercial preferred provider organization) but that could result in greater utilization in the FFS Medicare program.[194]

Furthermore, the parties also cannot shift the financial burden of such arrangement to the extent that increased payments are claimed from a federal health care program to cover the cost of this arrangement. As in previous regulatory issuances in which this or similar language has been used,[195] it is unclear exactly what this standard entails. At a minimum, an entity may not seek additional compensation from a federal health care program for services that were provided under the arrangement. For example, in the case of permitted Medicare co-payment waivers by hospitals (in the older safe harbor regulations), the hospital would not be able to include the waived copayment as a bad debt and thus seek additional financial benefits from the Medicare program.

## VII. PROMPT PAYMENT AND DENIAL OF CARE COMPLIANCE ISSUES

### A. Prompt Payment

There are several instances in which MCOs resemble indemnity insurers in that they simply pay claims for services provided by others. When doing so, Medicare requires its MCO contractors to pay 95 percent of "clean" claims submitted by noncontract providers within 30 days after receipt.[196] "Clean claims" are claims that (1) are not defective or lacking necessary substantiating documentation, and (2) conform to the Medicare fee-for-service definition of clean claim.[197] Failure to comply with the prompt payment requirement can result in adverse action, in-

---

[193] 64 Fed. Reg. 63,504, 63,513–514 (Nov. 19, 1999) (codified at 42 C.F.R. §1001.952(t)(1)(i)(B) and (u)(1)(i)(E)(1)).

[194] *See* Office of Inspector Gen., U.S. Dep't of Health & Human Servs., Advisory Op. No. 99-2 (Feb. 26, 1999).

[195] *See* 57 Fed. Reg. 43,906 (Sept. 23, 1992); 54 Reg. 3448 (Jan. 24, 1989); and 52 Fed Reg. 35,044 (Sept. 16, 1987).

[196] *See* 42 U.S.C. §§1395mm(f)(6)(A), 1395w-27(f).

[197] 42 C.F.R. §422.500.

cluding the imposition of intermediate sanctions or CMPs.[198] In addition, under 42 U.S.C. §1395w-27(f)(2), if prompt payment is not made by a Medicare+Choice plan, the Secretary can choose to pay these claims directly and reduce the amounts paid from the amounts due to the Medicare+Choice contractor.[199]

The issue of prompt payment also can arise under state law, and many states have enacted prompt payment statutes. For example, New York State engaged in a highly visible confrontation under the state's consumer protection laws with an MCO concerning a claims backlog that exceeded $230 million. This backlog, which included claims to contracted providers, was resolved by an agreement with the New York State Attorney General to make the payments with interest within a specific time frame.[200] Soon after this settlement, the New York legislature enacted a statute requiring insurers and MCOs to make payment within 45 days of receipt of a claim and imposing a substantial interest penalty for late payments.[201] It imposes a $100 fine on companies that have generated multiple complaints.[202] In January 1999, the New York State Insurance Department fined 12 insurers and MCOs a total of $72,200 for violating the state's prompt payment law. The largest fine of $40,900 was levied against Oxford Health Plans; smaller fines ranged from $1,000 to $2,900.[203] Actions of this sort have become common throughout the United States.[204]

Some states have recognized that a prompt payment statute that is applied to all MCOs can run afoul of ERISA. In response, Maryland's prompt payment statute, for example, states that it "applies to an insurer or nonprofit health service plan that acts as a third-party administrator" only "[t]o the extent consistent with [ERISA]."[205]

## B. Denial of Care

As discussed above, the managed care system brings to the health care industry a reversal of FFS incentives. Under FFS, providers receive financial incentives to deliver more care (e.g., extra office visits, tests, and procedures). Hence, there is concern about overutilization. In contrast, underutilization is the source of many disputes in the managed care industry. Although negotiated capitated rates may create incentives for MCOs to deny services, the managed care system is

---

[198] *See* 42 C.F.R. §§417.50, 422.752(b).

[199] *See also* 42 C.F.R. §522.520(c).

[200] *See* 6 Health Law Rep. (BNA) 32 (Aug. 7, 1997).

[201] *See* 6 Health Law Rep. (BNA) 39 (Oct. 2, 1997).

[202] *See* 3 Health Care Fraud Rep. (BNA) 77–78 (Jan. 27, 1999).

[203] *See id.*

[204] For more information on this subject, see Robert L. Roth & Margit H. Nahra, *Knowledge Is Payment: Understanding State Prompt-Payment Laws,* 55 HEALTHCARE FIN. MGMT. 37 (May 2001).

[205] *See* MD. CODE ANN., INS. §15-1005.

based on the understanding that payments are received by MCOs for enrollees to whom no services were provided during the applicable payment period.

The DOJ has stated that it will consider several factors in determining whether the denial or unavailability of services by an MCO could constitute fraud and abuse. These factors include the following:

- representations made to beneficiaries by the plan, physicians, sales representatives, customer service employees, contractors, and plan documents;
- internal records maintained by an MCO, specifically its system of tracking utilization by practice, demographics, subscriber, and outcome;
- accounting and actuarial records systems that reveal where the MCO makes its profits;
- incentives and bonuses;
- quality measurement;
- complaints made by subscribers, providers, regulators, accreditation agencies, and competitors;
- failure to follow state, federal, or professional or trade association guidelines;
- use of a system that discourages access to reviewers, such as complex voice mail systems, broken fax machines, or long delays in returning telephone calls;
- measurement systems for provider referrals that penalize those who appeal, reward those below the median in utilization, or reward a group for reduced utilization;
- testimony by trained professional reviewers or case managers about training instructions or tapes of conversations indicating that the review process is designed to deny needed care;
- lack of articulated standards;
- decisions to allow coverage regardless of the criteria when the patient has a powerful patron;
- personal benefit to individual reviewers (e.g., bonuses and promotions);
- evidence that patients did not receive promised benefits; and
- institution and practice comparative records showing that statistically similar patients are treated differently by the physician, hospital, or clinic.[206]

In May 1998, First Priority Health, a subsidiary of Blue Cross of Northeastern Pennsylvania, paid $250,000 to settle allegations that its Medicare HMO failed to add CMS-mandated (then HCFA-mandated)

---

[206]*See* 3 Health Care Fraud Rep. (BNA) 561 (June 30, 1999); 2 Health Care Fraud Rep. (BNA) 319 (May 6, 1998).

benefits to its package of services in a timely fashion.[207] The U.S. Attorney's Office for the District of Maryland filed an FCA action against, and reached a settlement with, a nursing home on charges of substandard care, marking the first time that the FCA was used in this way.[208]

Policyholders have challenged the denial of medically necessary care under state deceptive business practices laws. For example, policyholders of the Prudential Insurance Company of America filed a class action lawsuit claiming that Prudential's alleged denials of medically necessary care violated New York business laws relating to deceptive acts and practices. A New York state court upheld a trial court's decision to permit the class action to proceed.[209]

## VIII. PROHIBITED MARKETING PRACTICES UNDER MEDICARE

CMS is responsible for ensuring that Medicare beneficiaries have the proper information to make informed decisions about whether to enroll in a Medicare MCO.[210] It accomplishes this task by regulating the marketing practices of Medicare MCOs. Marketing practices have two dimensions: (1) preparation of marketing materials for mass distribution and (2) outreach activities to individual beneficiaries. CMS regulations regarding these practices are contained in the Medicare+ Choice regulations[211] and the *Medicare Managed Care National Marketing Guide*.[212] According to CMS, the purposes of the *Marketing Guide* are to:

- expedite the review process for marketing materials;
- save resources by avoiding multiple submissions of materials for preapproval;
- ensure uniform review for plans that prepare materials for use in more than one region; and
- help Medicare+Choice MCOs develop materials that will provide beneficiaries with accurate, consumer-friendly marketing information that will help them make informed choices.[213]

Medicare MCOs may not use marketing materials that have not been submitted to CMS for approval or of which CMS has disapproved,

---

[207] Kristen Hallam & Chris Rauber, *Looking for Trouble: State, Federal Investigators Seek Tips on Problem HMOs*, MOD. HEALTHCARE, Aug. 10, 1998, at 14.

[208] *See* Northern Health Facilities Inc. v. United States, 39 F. Supp. 2d 563 (D. Md. 1998); United States v. Northern Health Facilities, 25 F. Supp. 2d 690 (D. Md. 1998).

[209] Batas v. Prudential Ins. Co. of Am., 724 N.Y.S. 2d 3 (N.Y. App. Div. 2001).

[210] The OIG also addressed marketing in its draft program. 64 Fed. Reg. 61,893 (Nov. 15, 1999).

[211] 42 C.F.R. §422.80, as revised by final regulations issued June 29, 2000 (65 Fed. Reg. 40,170).

[212] MARKETING GUIDE, *supra* note 83 (available at http://www.hcfa.gov/pubforms/ 86_mmc/mc86c03.htm), as revised by the MMCM (referred to *supra* note 83).

[213] *See* MARKETING GUIDE, at Introduction.

in writing, within 45 days after their submission to CMS. The *Marketing Guide* is intended to facilitate preapproval of marketing materials and includes models for promotional materials, enrollment and disenrollment forms, notification letters, and a sample Evidence of Coverage form. Use of the "model" beneficiary notice materials is voluntary, and model beneficiary notification materials for routine beneficiary communications may be used without CMS's prior approval. However, use of "standardized" beneficiary notification materials is mandatory.[214] As with model beneficiary materials, standardized beneficiary materials for routine communications do not require CMS's prior approval.[215]

Examples of prohibited marketing practices include (1) discouraging participation on the basis of actual or perceived health status and (2) attempting to enroll beneficiaries from a high-income area without making a comparable effort to enroll beneficiaries from lower-income areas. The Medicare+Choice rules also expanded the definition of "service area," and one consideration for CMS's approval of an MCO's service area is whether the boundaries are discriminatory in effect.[216]

Generally, gifts or payments may not be made to induce healthier prospective enrollees to join a Medicare MCO.[217] However, an MCO may offer gifts provided they (1) are offered regardless of whether the potential beneficiary chooses to enroll in the plan (e.g., a gift offered to all attendees at a marketing presentation), (2) have little or no resale value, (3) are not readily converted to cash, and (4) are worth less than $15 (e.g., keychains bearing the plan's logo).[218]

MCOs may not offer rebates, dividends, or other compensation for decreased utilization of services by beneficiaries (e.g., tying reductions in premium costs to decreases in utilization of services). Nor may MCOs use monetary inducements to discourage participation on the basis of actual or perceived health status.[219] CMS does not allow door-to-door solicitation of beneficiaries when they have not contacted the MCO or invited a representative to their residence.[220] Similarly, door-to-door marketing of Medicaid HMOs and marketing at state or county offices also have been banned in all states. An MCO also may not claim recommendation or endorsement by CMS, nor may it use terms such

---

[214] MARKETING GUIDE, at 28.

[215] *Id.*

[216] 42 C.F.R. §422.2.

[217] 42 C.F.R. §417.428(b)(3).

[218] *See* MARKETING GUIDE, *supra* note 83, at 10; 42 C.F.R. §422.80; *see also* Health Care Financing Admin. Operational Policy Ltr. No. 60 (Nov. 14, 1999).

[219] 42 U.S.C. §1395w-21(h)(4)(A).

[220] *See* HEALTH CARE FIN. ADMIN., U.S. DEP'T OF HEALTH & HUMAN SERVS., MEDICARE HMO/CMP [COMPREHENSIVE MEDICAL PLANS] MANUAL, §2211(D); 63 Fed. Reg. at 35,076 (codified at 42 C.F.R. §422.80(e)(1)(iii)).

as "official U.S. government" or "Medicare" on envelopes or in other marketing or advertising materials in ways likely to result in beneficiary confusion.[221]

CMS believes that some MCOs have filled out election forms fraudulently on behalf of beneficiaries or have convinced enrollees to sign forms without explaining the form's effect.[222] Although recognizing that individuals with disabilities and those who would be physically burdened in the absence of assistance require accommodations, CMS has indicated that it prefers that the eligible individual actually fill out and sign the form.[223] CMS has refrained from totally prohibiting a Medicare+Choice MCO or an agent thereof from assisting beneficiaries in completing election forms, but the Medicare+Choice rule provides that "[p]ersons who assist beneficiaries in completing forms must sign the form and indicate their relationship to the beneficiary."[224] CMS further encourages Medicare+Choice MCOs to use neutral parties to assist in the completion of election forms.[225]

Use of providers in marketing activities raises concerns because of (1) their potential knowledge of a beneficiary's health status; (2) their general lack of familiarity with the details of the MCO's benefits; and (3) the position of patient trust that can be exploited if providers engage in marketing activities. Provider marketing also can raise concerns under the anti-kickback prohibitions.

Improper marketing practices can violate various laws. For example, CMPs may be imposed on a person or entity that offers or transfers remuneration to an individual eligible for Medicare or Medicaid that the person or entity knows or should know will likely influence the person to seek services from a particular provider or plan that are payable under Medicare or Medicaid.[226] In addition, criminal penalties can be imposed on anyone who solicits or receives remuneration to induce the referral of a Medicare or Medicaid beneficiary or to induce a person to buy, lease, order, arrange for, or recommend the purchase, lease, or ordering of an item or service paid in whole or part by Medicare or Medicaid.[227]

CMS discourages the use of providers as marketing agents by MCOs for the following reasons:

- Providers tend not to be fully aware of membership benefits and costs.

---

[221]*See* Health Care Fin. Admin. Operational Policy Ltr. No. 51 (Mar. 19, 1997); MARKETING GUIDE, *supra* note 83, at 22.

[222]63 Fed. Reg. 34,968, 34,985 (June 26, 1998).

[223]63 Fed. Reg. at 34,984.

[224]42 C.F.R. §422.60(c)(1).

[225]63 Fed. Reg. at 34,985.

[226]42 U.S.C. §1320a-7a(a)(5).

[227]42 U.S.C. §1320a-7b(b).

- Providers acting outside the role of rendering medical services might confuse the beneficiary as to when they are functioning as agents of the plan.[228]

Under the *Marketing Guide,* acceptable provider promotional activities are limited to certain circumscribed distribution, cosponsoring, and informational activities.[229] For example, a provider may (1) distribute plan brochures, but may not compare benefits among plans or take applications; (2) cosponsor an event with an MCO and/or cooperatively market an MCO, but all materials must be preapproved by CMS; (3) announce a new affiliation with an MCO to patients, but additional marketing contacts must include information on all the Medicare MCOs with which the provider contracts; and (4) furnish a complete list of Medicare-eligible patients to an MCO, but not disclose coverage, age, or health status. A provider *may not* (1) furnish other MCO membership lists or (2) send out information to patients listing the MCOs with which the provider contracts and/or comparing the benefits of different MCOs with which they contract using materials preapproved by CMS. A provider must also consider legal issues associated with capitation amounts that increase as enrollment levels increase[230] and legal difficulties for provider-sponsored organizations, which may be more vulnerable to attack for discriminatory enrollment practices.

Penalties for violating the *Marketing Guide* include the following:

- suspension of new enrollment and/or payment for new enrollees if an MCO misrepresents or falsifies information provided to an individual or entity;[231] and
- CMPs of up to (1) $25,000 for each time an MCO misrepresents or falsifies information to a person, (2) $100,000 for each time an MCO misrepresents or falsifies information provided to CMS, and (3) $100,000 plus $15,000 for each beneficiary not enrolled if an MCO expels or refuses to reenroll a beneficiary in violation of the Medicare+Choice regulations.[232]

CMS is required to provide a Special Information Campaign that informs Medicare+Choice-eligible beneficiaries about the Medicare+Choice MCOs available in their area.[233] In November of each year, CMS

---

[228]MARKETING GUIDE, *supra* note 83, at 41; *see also* MMCM, *supra* note 83, at ch. 3, §50.2.

[229]MARKETING GUIDE, at 41–43; *see also* MMCM, at ch. 3, §50.2.

[230]For example, a PCP receives $30 per member per month (PMPM) for the first 50 members that select the PCP, $35 PMPM for members 51–100 that select the PCP, and $40 PMPM for any number beyond 100 that select the PCP.

[231]*See* 42 U.S.C. §1395mm(i)(6)(B); 63 Fed. Reg. 34,968, 35,115 (1998) (codified at 42 C.F.R. §422.752).

[232]*Id.*

[233]42 U.S.C. §1395w-21(d).

will conduct a coordinated educational and publicity campaign about the various Medicare+Choice MCOs. CMS also will maintain a database, Medicare Compare, to allow beneficiaries to comparison shop for Medicare+Choice MCOs. In light of these activities and the fact that opportunities for beneficiaries to disenroll will become more limited in FY 2002, concerns about some past marketing and enrollment abuses may be reduced substantially as a practical matter.

In September 1997, Blue Cross and Blue Shield of Massachusetts paid $700,000 in CMPs to settle charges that an executive made false representations regarding the HMO's provider network in an application seeking CMS (then HCFA) approval of its Medicare managed care product. The HMO also was prohibited for approximately 1½ years from marketing the product and enrolling new members, and the executive was indicted on criminal charges.[234] In July 1998, Exclusive Healthcare, Inc., of Omaha, Nebraska, paid $50,000 to resolve allegations that it improperly screened potential enrollees in its Medicare HMO for health risks.[235]

## IX. CONCLUSION AND PRACTICAL POINTERS

The managed care fraud environment has been dynamic over the past few years as the government continues to develop new theories for civil and criminal liability and program requirements become more complex. In the face of this threat, MCOs should be proactive in their approach to potential fraud and abuse issues in three basic ways. First, MCOs must be resolute about reviewing all available government sources for identification of "new" potential fraud issues, including HHS OIG work plans, fraud alerts, compliance guidance, and advisory opinions. Second, MCOs must monitor changes in government program requirements vigilantly by tracking government issuances, including CMS OPLs, the *Medicare+Choice Monitoring Guide,* and the *Medicare Managed Care Manual.* Finally, MCOs must be attentive to deviations from normal practices.

MCOs need to have a particularly firm grasp of how the government programs applicable to their organization are financed. With a thorough knowledge of the managed care health care financing system, legal counsel, auditors, and compliance officers should be able to (1) spot financing arrangements that are out of the ordinary, or that do not "feel" right, and (2) analyze those arrangements for potential fraud and abuse exposure *before* they become the latest "hot topic" in the industry. The recent TAP Pharmaceuticals, Inc. (TAP) settlement agreement, indictments, and corporate integrity agreement are a good

---

[234] *See generally* Laurie McGinley & David S. Cloud, *U.S. Takes Aim at HMO Fraud in Medicare and Medicaid,* WALL ST. J., Oct. 19, 1998, at A28.

[235] *See* Steve Jordan, *Mutual Pays $50,000 Penalty to Settle Claim,* OMAHA WORLD-HERALD, July 16, 1998, at 22.

example of this.[236] The government accused TAP of, among other things, manipulating the price of the average wholesale price (AWP) for Lupron, such that federal health care programs were paying higher prices based on the artificially inflated AWP for Lupron.[237]

While the foregoing may be the latest "hot issue" in the pharmaceutical industry (and may have implications for some HMOs, depending on their involvement in the case[238]), the underlying theories flow from the interplay of private sector conduct and public sector payment formulas and criteria. For example, the risk of fraud liability has long existed where prices to the government have been either improperly charged or improperly inflated based on faulty or misleading practices that resulted in the health care organization receiving higher payments. This shows why attorneys need to be aware not only of the hot topics of the day, but of the financing and delivery structure, so they are able to identify potential fraud issues *before* they become "hot topics."

Indeed, the government has come to expect this kind of vigilance from Medicare+Choice MCOs because of the requirement that they have compliance plans. Because of this requirement, the government has been particularly harsh when addressing alleged fraud and abuse violations by these MCOs, apparently because such violations show that the compliance plans may not be effective. For example, the government has imposed corporate integrity agreements on Medicare+Choice MCOs that are broad in both scope and duration even where the underlying regulatory violation was discreet and has been corrected.[239] By keeping current on government requirements and being sensitive to deviations from "normal" practices, attorneys can help protect their MCO clients from the risk of adverse government action.

---

[236] CIA Between The Office of Inspector General, Dep't of Health & Human Servs., and TAP Pharmaceuticals, Inc., *available at* http://oig.hhs.gov/cia/agreements/tap_ pharmaceutical_products_92801.pdf.

[237] Press Release, Office of Inspector General, U.S. Dep't of Defense (Oct. 3, 2001).

[238] *Id.* ("TAP also provided illegal remuneration to . . . health maintenance organizations to unlawfully obtain orders for Lupron that TAP knew would be billed to the Government.").

[239] See *supra* Section II.C.

# 7

# Corporate Compliance Programs*

---

*Nancy S. Jones, Nora L. Liggett, and Michelle B. Marsh, Waller Lansden Dortch & Davis, Nashville, Tennessee.

# I. INTRODUCTION

As recently as the early 1990s, few health care organizations had any official or organized fraud and abuse compliance program, and the designation of an employee as corporate compliance officer with the sole function of overseeing and enforcing compliance with health care fraud and abuse laws was almost unheard of. By 2001, however, compliance programs are a standard feature of corporate life in health care.

A well-planned compliance program is vital for health care organizations for several reasons. Increased government scrutiny and enforcement is one. For example, the Health Insurance Portability and Accountability Act of 1996 (HIPAA)[1] and the Balanced Budget Act of 1997 (BBA)[2] each added significant new laws and enforcement programs to the government's health care compliance enforcement arsenal.[3] In addition, several high-profile cases have heightened providers' sensitivity to and awareness of enforcement issues and demonstrated the government's willingness to invest significant time and resources to uncovering and prosecuting health care fraud and abuse.[4] Another reason is the growing number of whistleblower or *qui tam* lawsuits. Employees, competitors, and even patients have become increasingly sophisticated about health care fraud and abuse and the potentially lucrative rewards that can come from whistleblower suits.[5] As a result, corporate compliance programs designed to prevent fraud and abuse

---

[1] Pub. L. No. 104-191, 110 Stat. 1936 (1996).

[2] Pub. L. No. 105-33, 111 Stat. 251 (1997).

[3] HIPAA, for example, added four new health care crimes relating to "health benefit programs," which are defined as including any "public or private plan or contract." 18 U.S.C. §24(b). A new health care fraud statute (18 U.S.C. §1347) prohibits knowingly defrauding any health care benefit program and includes penalties of fines and up to 10 years imprisonment (20 years if the violation results in bodily harm and life imprisonment if the violation results in death). In addition to the new health care fraud statute, there are new statutes criminalizing theft and embezzlement in connection with health care fraud (18 U.S.C. §669), false statements relating to health care matters (18 U.S.C. §1035), and obstruction of justice relating to health care matters or investigations (18 U.S.C. §1518).

[4] See, e.g., *In re* Columbia/HCA Healthcare Corp. Qui Tam Litigation, Civ. A. No. 01-MS-50 (RCL) (D. D.C.), in which the federal district court approved a $745 million settlement in August 2001.

[5] In addition to the *qui tam* provision of the civil False Claims Act (FCA) (31 U.S.C. §§3729–33), under which a successful *qui tam* relator can collect up to 25% of the civil monetary penalties paid by a provider, Congress, through §203 of HIPAA, mandated the creation of new reward programs to encourage the reporting of suspected fraud or abuse. If reported information leads to the government's collection of at least $100,

and to provide employees with a mechanism for reporting suspected fraud or abuse internally are important for reducing the number of such suits.

This chapter discusses the benefits of adopting a corporate compliance program and describes the elements of an effective program. The chapter also focuses on the major operational issues associated with both the implementation and ongoing operation of a health care corporate compliance program.

## II. BENEFITS OF A CORPORATE COMPLIANCE PROGRAM

There are many benefits to a health care provider of adopting a corporate compliance program. Most importantly, of course, the federal government expects every major health care provider to have a compliance program in place. Although by 2001, there were no laws or regulations *requiring* that a provider have a compliance program, it is clear that the government considers such programs to be a matter of course for health care providers. For example, in resolving claims of deficiencies and other regulatory problems, the government almost routinely has insisted on the implementation of an effective compliance program as part of its settlements with providers (see *infra* Section III for discussion of what constitutes an "effective" compliance program).

Many providers are in the process of implementing a corporate compliance program, already have adopted one, or are considering establishing one. Given such peer pressure, a provider that fails to adopt a compliance program may find itself facing additional difficulties in any government investigation or private whistleblower suit. The failure of a provider to adopt a compliance program could be argued to be "below the standard of care in the industry" and could be cited as evidence that the provider chose to keep itself in the dark about fraudulent or abusive activity by its employees or agents. In addition, recent case law has suggested that the failure of a corporate director to attempt in good faith to institute a compliance program may, in certain situations, be a breach of the director's fiduciary duty.[6] More importantly, the failure of a provider to voluntarily adopt a compliance program could, in the event of a government investigation, lead the Department of Health

---

HHS may pay a reward to the reporting person. *See also* 42 U.S.C. §1320a-7c. To further encourage private whistleblowing efforts, §203 also requires the issuance of Explanation of Medicare Benefits forms to beneficiaries for every item or service furnished. Each form includes a toll-free number for the beneficiary to report suspected fraud or abuse.

For in-depth discussion of the FCA, see Chapter 3 (Salcido, The False Claims Act in Health Care Prosecutions: Application of the Substantive, *Qui Tam*, and Voluntary Disclosure Provisions).

[6] *See, e.g., In re* Caremark Int'l Inc. Derivative Litig., 698 A.2d 959 (Del. Ch. 1996). For an in-depth discussion of director and officer liability, see Chapter 8 (Baumann & McDavid, Potential Liabilities for Directors and Officers of Health Care Organizations).

and Human Services Office of Inspector General (OIG) to mandate a stringent program for the provider.

An effective corporate compliance program operates proactively to prevent and detect improper conduct. In addition, an effective program could be a mitigating factor in the event of a government investigation. For example, as discussed below, the existence of a compliance program raises the possibility of reduced fines under the U.S. Sentencing Guidelines (Sentencing Guidelines).[7] An effective compliance program also could be of persuasive value on several fronts: in discussions with prosecutors about the magnitude of civil monetary penalties or damages; in discussions with the Department of Health and Human Services (HHS) regarding whether to exclude a provider from further participation in federal health care programs; and in discussions with Centers for Medicare and Medicaid Services (CMS)[8] officials to determine whether to impose administrative sanctions against a provider.

## A. Federal Sentencing Guidelines

The Sentencing Guidelines contain several incentives for a provider to adopt a corporate compliance program. First, if a provider has an effective compliance program in place, a court is not required to impose a period of probation or any of the special conditions of probation, including the regular reporting and unannounced examinations of the organization's books and records provided for in Section 8D1.4(b) of the Sentencing Guidelines.[9] Although the financial impact of these special conditions is not easy to quantify, it is obvious that having to pay a public accounting firm to conduct periodic financial audits is costly. Second, if a provider has in place at the time of sentencing a compliance program that the court determines is "effective," the provider's culpability score (as determined under the Sentencing Guidelines) will be reduced significantly, resulting in a smaller range of fines.

## 1. Probation

Obviously, a business organization[10] convicted of a federal crime cannot be sentenced to confinement in a correctional institution. An entity can, however, be sentenced to a period of probation under the

---

[7] U.S. Sentencing Comm'n, Guidelines Manual (Nov. 2000).

[8] The former Health Care Financing Administration (HCFA) was renamed the Centers for Medicare and Medicaid Services (CMS), effective July 1, 2001. For purposes of this chapter, references will be to CMS.

[9] It should be noted that the standard duration of a corporate integrity agreement (CIA) required by the OIG for health care organizations entering into plea agreements to resolve criminal investigations is 5 years. This is the maximum period of probation the court can impose under U.S.S.G. §8D1.2(a)(1). A CIA generally also incorporates the conditions of probation found in U.S.S.G. §8D1.4(b)(1)–(3).

[10] The term "organization" is defined as "corporations, partnerships, associations, joint-stock companies, unions, trusts, pension funds, unincorporated organizations, governments and political subdivisions thereof, and non-profit organizations." U.S.S.G.

Sentencing Guidelines.[11] After either a plea of guilty on behalf of the organization by an appropriate official or a verdict of guilty following a trial, the district court must impose a period of probation if the organization has 50 or more employees and does not have an "effective program to prevent and detect violations of law."[12] The term of probation must be at least 1 year but not more than 5 years.[13]

As conditions of probation, the sentencing court must impose a restitution order[14] and a prohibition against the commission of any other crime during the probation period.[15] The court may impose any other conditions[16] reasonably related to the "nature and circumstances of the offense or the history and characteristics of the organization."[17] If the court imposes a fine or orders the organization to make restitution, it can require the organization to make periodic reports to its probation officer concerning its financial condition, including an accounting of all funds disbursed.[18] The court also can require the organization to submit to periodic unannounced examinations of its books and records by experts selected by the court and paid for by the organization.[19] The organization can be required to notify the court "immediately" on its learning of a material adverse change in its business or financial condition or on the filing of a bankruptcy proceeding, major civil litigation, administrative proceeding, or any type of investigation against it.[20]

As a further condition of probation, the court can impose a requirement that the organization develop and submit a plan for a corporate

---

§8A1.1, App. n.1. For purposes of this discussion, it is assumed that the defendant organization has 50 or more employees; is a solvent, ongoing concern at the time of sentencing; and has been convicted of an offense for which the restitution owed to the government is more than $1 million. Organizations are sentenced under the probation guideline for felony and Class A misdemeanor offenses. U.S.S.G. §8A1.1.

[11] Section 8D1.1 prescribes the conditions under which the sentencing court must order a period of probation.

[12] U.S.S.G. §8D1.1(a)(3). An "effective program to prevent and detect violations of law" is one that has been "reasonably designed, implemented, and enforced so that it generally will be effective in preventing and detecting criminal conduct." U.S.S.G. §8A1.2, App. n.3(k). Significantly, the failure of the program to prevent or detect the offense of conviction, by itself, does not mean that the program is not "effective." *Id.*

[13] U.S.S.G. §8D1.2(a)(1). The guidelines for sentencing organizations became effective in November 1991. *See* U.S.S.G. §8C1.1, historical note (amended 1995).

[14] U.S.S.G. §8D1.3(b).

[15] U.S.S.G. §8D1.3(a).

[16] Section 8D1.4 sets out various other recommended conditions of probation, including publicizing the nature of the offense, the fact of the conviction, the nature of the punishment imposed, and the steps taken to prevent the occurrence of similar offenses. U.S.S.G. §8D1.4(a).

[17] U.S.S.G. §8D1.3(c).

[18] U.S.S.G. §8D1.4(b)(1).

[19] U.S.S.G. §8D1.4(b)(2).

[20] U.S.S.G. §8D1.4(b)(3).

compliance program, along with a schedule for its implementation.[21] In determining whether the proposed program is appropriate, the Sentencing Guidelines suggest that the court consider the views of any governmental regulatory body that oversees the conduct involved in the offense (e.g., the OIG or CMS regarding Medicare billing fraud).[22] The Sentencing Guidelines require that the court approve any proposed program that "appears reasonably calculated to prevent and detect violations of law" and is consistent with applicable statutory and regulatory requirements.[23]

Once the court approves the corporate compliance program, the organization must then notify all employees and shareholders of both its criminal behavior and its program to prevent and detect future violations.[24] The organization must make periodic reports to its probation officer concerning its progress in implementing the corporate compliance program.[25] To monitor whether the organization is in fact implementing its program, the court may select experts to conduct periodic unannounced examinations of the organization's books and records as well as to interview knowledgeable individuals within the organization and to report back to the court.[26] The court can require that the organization pay for these expert services.[27]

## 2. Reduced Fines

Having a corporate compliance program in effect at the time of sentencing can significantly reduce the amount of the fine imposed by the court. To calculate the appropriate fine,[28] the court determines the base offense level for the count of conviction by applying the criteria in Chapter 2 of the Sentencing Guidelines.[29] The base offense level determines the base fine.[30] The court then calculates the entity's culpability score pursuant to Section 8C2.5.

The culpability score determines the minimum and maximum multipliers the court uses to calculate the fine range for an entity.[31] If the court determines that the organization had an effective corporate compliance program in effect at the time of the offense, 3 points are

---

[21] U.S.S.G. §8D1.4(c)(1).

[22] U.S.S.G. §8D1.4, App. n.1.

[23] *Id.*

[24] U.S.S.G. §8D1.4(c)(2).

[25] U.S.S.G. §8D1.4(c)(3).

[26] U.S.S.G. §8D1.4(c)(4).

[27] *Id.*

[28] The hypothetical scenario assumes that the court has made a finding pursuant to U.S.S.G. §8C2.2 that the organization has the financial ability to pay restitution and a fine.

[29] U.S.S.G. §8C2.3(a).

[30] U.S.S.G. §8C2.4.

[31] U.S.S.G. §8C2.6.

subtracted from the culpability score.[32] A reduction in the culpability score directly reduces the multiplier used and lowers the range of the fine to which the organization is subject.[33]

The following hypothetical example of a calculation in a fairly common health care prosecution scenario illustrates the financial impact of having in place a corporate compliance program that the court determines is effective:

> Example: A hospital with more than 200 employees is convicted of submitting false claims to Medicaid as a result of intentional miscoding of certain services by the supervisor of the billing department. The billing fraud spanned nearly 2 years and resulted in the hospital receiving $1.8 million to which it was not entitled.
>
> In addition to imposing a restitution order for the $1.8 million in accordance with Section 8B1.1 of the Guidelines, the court would determine the appropriate fine. The fine is determined by first calculating the offense level for conviction of a false claims violation, applying the provisions of Section 2F1.1 as follows: 6 points base offense level[34] plus 12 points for the amount of the loss.[35] Because the federal government and the states jointly fund Medicaid, the hospital receives an additional 2 points for multiple victims.[36] The resulting total offense level is 20 points, which sets the base fine at $650,000.[37]
>
> Without an effective corporate compliance program, the culpability score is 8, with resulting minimum and maximum multipliers of 1.60 and 3.20, respectively.[38] With a compliance program, the minimum and maximum multipliers are 1.00 and 2.00, respectively. The calculation of the fine range under these alternative scenarios would be as follows:

- without a compliance program      $ 650,000 base fine
  - −minimum multiplier (1.60)       $ 1,040,000
  - −maximum multiplier (3.20)       $ 2,080,000
- with a compliance program         $ 650,000 base fine
  - −minimum multiplier (1.00)       $ 650,000
  - −maximum multiplier (2.00)       $ 1,300,000

As these calculations illustrate, an organization having an effective corporate compliance program would realize a savings of $390,000

---

[32] U.S.S.G. §8C2.5(f). The reduction is not available, however, in certain situations in which high-level personnel are involved or the organization unreasonably delayed reporting the offense. U.S.S.G. §8C2.5.

[33] Self-reporting and cooperation also may lead to reductions of the culpability score. U.S.S.G. §8C2.5(g)(2)–(3).

[34] U.S.S.G. §2F1.1(a).

[35] U.S.S.G. §2F1.1(b)(M).

[36] U S S.G. §2F1.1(b)(2).

[37] U.S.S.G. §8C2.4(d).

[38] Pursuant to U.S.S.G. §8C2.5(a), the culpability score calculation starts with 5 points. In this hypothetical scenario, 3 points would be added under §8C2.5(b)(3)(A)(i) because the hospital has more than 200 employees and the director of billing, an individual whose position falls within the definition of "high-level personnel" found in §8A1.2, App. n.3(b) was personally involved in the commission of the offense.

if sentenced to a fine at the low end of the range or $780,000 if sentenced at the top end.

## B. U.S. Department of Health and Human Services Guidelines on Permissive Exclusion

In addition to the U.S. Sentencing Guidelines, which provide for reduced fines and penalties for a provider that can show evidence of an effective corporate compliance program, HHS guidelines on permissive exclusion (permissive exclusion guidelines) provide yet another reason for a provider to adopt a corporate compliance program. These guidelines indicate that the existence of an effective corporate compliance program can favorably affect the OIG's decision whether to exclude a sanctioned provider from further participation in federal health care programs.

The permissive exclusion guidelines, which were published December 24, 1997, are nonbinding guidance to be used by the Secretary of HHS in deciding permissive exclusion cases.[39] The guidelines define several criteria to be used in determining whether to exercise the permissive exclusion authority, including:[40]

1. *The circumstances of the misconduct and the seriousness of the offense.* This first category considers the seriousness of the misconduct. The provider's history of past misconduct is considered an indicator of its likelihood of abusing federal programs in the future.
2. *The provider's response to the allegations and determinations of unlawful conduct.* This second category indicates whether the provider is willing to affirmatively modify its conduct, make injured parties whole, and otherwise acknowledge and remedy past wrongdoing.
3. *The likelihood that the same offense will recur or some similar offense will occur.* The guidelines indicate that the existence of an effective corporate compliance program is a key factor in the Secretary's determination whether it is likely that the organization will commit the same or a similar offense in the future.

---

[39]62 Fed. Reg. 67,392 (Dec. 24, 1997).

[40]The Secretary's permissive exclusion authority, which is found in 42 U.S.C. §1320a-7(b)(7), allows the Secretary of HHS to use his or her discretion to exclude individuals or entities from further participation in federal or state health care programs. This statute was substantially amended by HIPAA to include, as grounds for permissive exclusion, among other things, misdemeanor convictions relating to fraud, theft, embezzlement, breach of fiduciary duty, or other financial misconduct in connection with the delivery of health care services or items or resulting from any act or omission in connection with any state or federal health care program. In addition, HIPAA further amended the statute to allow the Secretary to permissively exclude individuals who *control* (through ownership or management) a sanctioned entity.

As noted, the guidelines' third criterion emphasizes the importance of an effective corporate compliance program in influencing the determination of whether the provider is likely to engage in misconduct in the future. In making that determination, HHS asks the following questions, many of which relate to the provider's compliance program:

- Was the misconduct the result of a unique circumstance that is not likely to recur? Is there minimal risk of repeat conduct?
- What previous measures were taken to ensure compliance with the law? Can the organization demonstrate that it had an effective compliance program in place when the activities that constitute cause for exclusion occurred?
    - Did the organization make any efforts to contact the OIG, CMS, or its contractors to determine whether its conduct complied with the law and applicable program requirements? Were such contacts documented?
    - Did the organization bring the activity in question to the attention of appropriate government officials before any government action (e.g., was there any voluntary disclosure of the alleged wrongful conduct?)?
    - Did the organization have effective standards of conduct and internal control systems in place at the time of the wrongful activity (e.g., was there a corporate compliance program in place?) If there was an existing corporate compliance program,
        - (i)   How long had it been in effect?
        - (ii)  What problems had been identified?
        - (iii) Were any overpayments refunded or system changes made if problems were identified?
        - (iv)  Were appropriate staff members sufficiently trained in applicable policies and procedures pertaining to Medicare and other federal and state health care programs?
        - (v)   Were a corporate compliance officer and an effective corporate compliance committee (if appropriate for the size of the organization) in place?
- What measures have been taken, or will be taken, to ensure compliance with the law? Has the organization agreed to implement adequate compliance measures, including institution of a corporate integrity agreement (CIA)?

As is evident by the permissive exclusion guidelines, the government places great emphasis on the existence of an effective corporate compliance program. The adoption and appropriate implementation of such a program can favorably influence the OIG in its determination of whether a particular unlawful activity is likely to recur and thus whether the provider should be excluded from further participation in federal health care programs.

## III. Elements of an Effective Compliance Program

Given the existing regulatory climate, most providers readily acknowledge that they should adopt a compliance program, but they are less certain about exactly what constitutes an "effective compliance program." Fortunately, however, the government has provided some guidance. It is important to note that the government does not expect a provider's compliance program to be foolproof, merely effective.

According to the Sentencing Guidelines, an "effective program" is one that has been "reasonably designed, implemented and enforced so that it generally will be effective in preventing and detecting criminal conduct."[41] Accordingly, a provider's failure to prevent a particular offense, by itself, does not mean that its program is ineffective. Instead, "[t]he hallmark of an effective program to prevent and detect violations of law is that the organization exercised due diligence in seeking to prevent and detect criminal conduct by its employees and other agents."[42]

More detailed indications of what elements the government expects to see as part of an effective corporate compliance program can be found in the Sentencing Guidelines, CIAs, and model compliance programs. Although each CIA or model program is specific to a particular industry segment or situation, enough of a pattern has emerged to indicate that an effective corporate compliance program should have the following characteristics:

- the appointment of a chief compliance officer to implement the program and oversee compliance matters;
- high-level involvement in and support for the compliance program from members of senior management and the organization's board of directors;
- adoption of a written compliance program that includes policies and procedures on key operational issues such as billing and anti-kickback law[43] concerns as well as formal standards of conduct;
- ongoing employee education and training regarding compliance and legal issues;
- creation of a compliance committee that includes representatives of top management;
- creation of a subsidiary compliance structure that reports to the chief compliance officer;
- annual certification by appropriate employees that they have reviewed applicable compliance policies and procedures;

---

[41] U.S.S.G. §8A1.2.

[42] *Id.*

[43] 42 U.S.C. §1320a-7b(b). See Appendix A-1 for full text of the anti-kickback statute.

- routine compliance audits of the organization's facilities and operations;
- policies not to hire persons excluded from participation in any federal health care program and to otherwise conduct reasonable due diligence to avoid hiring persons with either criminal records or past program sanctions;
- establishment of a hotline or other means of communication that allows employees to report suspected misconduct to the compliance department anonymously;
- swift investigation and correction of allegations of violations of law or the provider's compliance standards; and
- compliance program customized to reflect the size and resources of the organization.

## A. Corporate Integrity Agreements

A CIA is not the same as a corporate compliance program. A CIA is a 3- to 5-year agreement entered into between a health care provider and the government in conjunction with the settlement of fraud and abuse allegations. These OIG-imposed agreements typically contain specific rules of conduct designed to address the issues that were the subject of the government's investigation, as well as specific monitoring and reporting requirements. In contrast, a corporate compliance program is an internal corporate plan designed to prevent and detect violations of the law. Corporate compliance programs are voluntarily adopted whereas CIAs are imposed by the government and are generally more stringent and expensive to implement than a corporate compliance program.

A CIA has become a standard feature in all significant Medicare and Medicaid fraud and abuse settlements approved by the OIG. Although each CIA is tailored to the specific health care provider involved, all of the CIAs entered into by the OIG have similar characteristics. A material violation of a CIA can result in monetary penalties and exclusion from federal and state health care programs. Copies of corporate integrity agreements can be found at the OIG's website at http://www. dhhs.gov/progorg/oig/cia/index.htm.

## B. Model Corporate Compliance Programs

In addition to various CIAs, the government has published compliance program guidance[44] for nine segments of the health care industry:

1. hospitals;[45]
2. clinical laboratories;[46]

---

[44] With the publication of the final guidance for hospitals, the government began calling these instructions "compliance program guidance" instead of "model plans."

[45] *See* 63 Fed. Reg. 8987 (Feb. 23, 1998).

[46] *See* 63 Fed. Reg. 45,076 (Aug. 24, 1998).

3. durable medical equipment (DME), prosthetics, orthotics, and supplies providers;[47]
4. third-party medical billing companies;[48]
5. hospices;[49]
6. nursing facilities;[50]
7. Medicare+Choice organizations;[51]
8. individual and small group physician practices;[52] and
9. home health agencies.[53]

It is important to remember that these guidance materials are not mandatory; however, as a practical matter, these model programs can serve as benchmarks against which the government may judge the effectiveness of a provider's compliance program. Each model contains similar elements and gives providers valuable insight into what features the government is looking for in a corporate compliance program.

Each model program contains seven basic elements: (1) written policies and procedures; (2) designation of an employee with oversight responsibility (i.e., the compliance officer); (3) education and training; (4) communication; (5) auditing and monitoring; (6) discipline and enforcement; and (7) corrective action. As discussed below, compliance guidance for each industry segment focuses on tailoring these elements to the needs and heightened areas of risk of the particular activity.

### 1. Compliance Program Guidance for Hospitals

HHS released a draft model compliance program for hospitals on July 14, 1997. The government solicited comments from industry groups such as the American Hospital Association, the Federation of American Health Care Systems, the Association of American Medical Colleges, and the American Medical Association before releasing its final document (retitled "compliance program guidance" rather than "model compliance program") in February 1998.[54] The guidance refined the seven essential elements identified above for use by hospitals into the following recommendations:

1. *Written policies and procedures.* The government places great emphasis on the establishment of written compliance standards, policies, and procedures. These written policies and procedures

---

[47] *See* 64 Fed. Reg. 36,368 (July 6, 1999).

[48] *See* 63 Fed. Reg. 70,138 (Dec. 18, 1998).

[49] *See* 64 Fed. Reg. 54,031 (Oct. 5, 1999).

[50] *See* 65 Fed. Reg. 14,289 (Mar. 16, 2000).

[51] *See* 64 Fed. Reg. 61,893 (Nov. 15, 1999).

[52] *See* 65 Fed. Reg. 59,434 (Oct. 5, 2000).

[53] *See* 63 Fed. Reg. 42,410 (Aug. 7, 1998). All of the OIG compliance program guidance documents can be accessed at http://oig.hhs.gov/modcomp/index.htm.

[54] 63 Fed. Reg. 8987 (Feb. 23, 1998).

should be treated seriously. The government has suggested that there be high-level involvement in the process (e.g., perhaps by members of the hospital's senior management and board of directors). Written policies and procedures should reflect current regulations, procedures, and problem areas within hospitals.

The government has stressed that a provider's list of problem areas should not be static, and a hospital may need additional policies or procedures as time passes to address evolving areas of concern. At a minimum, the guidance indicates that the written policies and procedures should address the major operational aspects of the hospital. At the time of the publication of the government's draft model compliance program for hospitals, some of the key hospital problems or policy areas identified by the government included
–double billing,[55]
–unbundling,[56]
–miscoding,
–upcoding,[57]
–DRG (diagnosis related group) creep,[58]
–proper billing of tests,
–credit balances,[59]
–admission and discharge policies and procedures, and
–documentation.

2. *Designation of compliance officer.* The compliance program guidance for hospitals also stresses the importance of assigning oversight responsibility for compliance to an employee high in the hospital's organization. The designated compliance officer should have direct access to the hospital's chief executive officer

---

[55]"Double billing" occurs when a hospital submits more than one claim for the same service or submits the same bill to more than one payer at the same time.

[56]"Unbundling" refers to a hospital's practice of submitting piecemeal bills for different services that should be "bundled" into one bill (i.e., paid together in one global payment). The purpose of the piecemeal billing is to obtain greater total reimbursement than would be paid in the global payment.

[57]"Upcoding" and "miscoding" are similar and refer to the intentional or careless practice of assigning a billing code with a higher payment rate to a service provided when the actual service provided to the patient should be assigned a less lucrative billing code.

[58]"DRG creep" is the same as upcoding. It refers to the practice of using a DRG code that provides a higher payment rate than the DRG code that accurately reflects the actual service provided to the patient.

[59]Credit balances are credits recorded on a hospital's records, usually resulting from overpayments. Sometimes patients are confused by a provider's bill and pay even after their insurer already has paid. Other times two or more primary insurers are billed—and pay the provider—for the same claims. Each of these instances results in credit balances. Policies and procedures should be in place to ensure that credit balances are regularly audited and that any overpayments are promptly returned to the proper party (e.g., Medicare, private insurer, or patient).

(CEO) and board of directors. He or she should not be subordinate to the hospital's general counsel. Further, the government indicates that the compliance officer should be required to report on compliance matters on a periodic basis to the hospital's board and compliance committee. For hospital systems with multiple locations, the compliance program guidance suggests a chief compliance officer located at the corporate office and local compliance officers located at each hospital.

3. *Education and training.* The hospital compliance program guidance requires that hospitals conduct effective educational and training programs. At a minimum, the guidance indicates that all employees should receive basic training in the following:
   - Medicare and Medicaid reimbursement principles;
   - general anti-kickback law principles;
   - properly describing the nature of services rendered in connection with any claim for reimbursement from Medicare or Medicaid;
   - accurately submitting billing for physicians' services only when services actually are rendered by a physician;
   - ensuring that all documentation requiring physician authorization is properly executed;
   - preventing the alteration of medical records;
   - confirming diagnosis; and
   - duty to report misconduct.

   Additionally, targeted employees, such as those who work in the hospital's billing and coding department, should receive more extensive training on topics specific to their job functions.

4. *Communication.* The guidance suggests that a hospital should develop and maintain meaningful lines of communication for clarifying policies and procedures and reporting violations. An anonymous hotline can be one component of this communication system.

5. *Auditing and monitoring.* As part of an effective compliance program, a hospital should perform regular internal audits and continually monitor its operations to detect noncompliance and improve quality. The model hospital compliance program suggests a number of techniques a compliance officer should consider, including on-site visits, interviews, review of written materials, and trend analysis studies. It also details the need for regular compliance reports. The OIG recommends that when a compliance program is established, providers take a "snapshot" of the current compliance situation, which can then be used as part of benchmarking analyses.

6. *Discipline and enforcement.* The guidance indicates that a hospital should enforce policies, procedures, and compliance standards through well-publicized discipline guidelines and procedures. The compliance officer or CEO should distribute to all employees a written description of the possible sanctions

for failure to comply with hospital standards, policies, and procedures. Although the compliance program guidance does not mandate the exact type of disciplinary action required for specific violations, it does stress, however, that all levels of employees should be subject to the same types of discipline for similar offenses. In addition, the government cautions that "intentional" or "reckless" noncompliance should be punished by "significant sanctions," which may include suspension, termination, or financial penalties. The OIG takes the position that officers and supervisors should be held accountable for the foreseeable failure of their subordinates to comply with applicable law, standards, and procedures.

7. *Corrective action.* As an integral part of its compliance program, the guidance indicates that a hospital should have mechanisms in place to respond appropriately and immediately to detected offenses through corrective action to prevent further offenses.

### 2. Compliance Program Guidance for Clinical Laboratories

The compliance program guidance for clinical laboratories[60] was prepared by the OIG. It provides nonbinding guidance regarding the elements of an effective corporate compliance program for clinical laboratories. The OIG suggests that seven essential elements identified above are tailored to the particular concerns of clinical laboratories as follows:

1. *Written policies and procedures.* According to the guidance, an effective clinical laboratory compliance program includes, at its core, the development of written compliance policies and procedures. The OIG indicates that policies and procedures should be developed under the supervision of the laboratory compliance officer, and they should be provided to all persons affected. Care should be taken to ensure that the written policies and procedures are well drafted, in simple, clear, and easily understood language. If necessary, the policies and procedures should be translated into different languages or reading levels so that all employees can understand them.

   According to the guidance, the written policies and procedures should cover all of the major facets of the laboratory's operations, including, at a minimum:
   • *Standards of conduct.* There should be a written policy that clearly delineates the laboratory's policies and procedures re-

---

[60] 62 Fed. Reg. 9435 (Mar. 3, 1997), *as amended* 63 Fed. Reg. 8987 (Feb. 23, 1998). The amendments changed the title from "model compliance plan" to "compliance program guidance" and made other changes for consistency with the OIG's model compliance program guidance for hospitals.

garding fraud and abuse and adherence to applicable guidelines and regulations.

- *Medical necessity*. The laboratory should take appropriate steps to ensure that all claims are for medically necessary tests and procedures. As part of such steps, the laboratory should maintain written documentation of the medical necessity of all tests and procedures performed. The laboratory should standardize its non-customized test ordering forms and require that ordering physicians document the need for each test or procedure requested. To ensure that all ordering parties understand the laboratory's medical necessity rules, the laboratory should provide each of its clients annually with a written notice setting forth (1) the Medicare medical necessity policy; (2) the individual components of every laboratory profile, including the *Current Procedural Terminology* or Health Care Procedure Coding System (HCPCS) codes used; (3) the Medicare national limitation amount for each code; and (4) a description of how the laboratory will bill for each profile.

- *Billing*. The laboratory should have written policies and procedures to ensure that all claims submitted are accurate and that they correctly identify the services ordered.

- *Standing orders*. The government notes that standing orders are subject to abuse. Accordingly, policies and procedures should be in place to limit the use of standing orders and to require careful monitoring of all standing orders.

- *Compliance with fraud alerts*. There should be written policies and procedures to adopt and enforce compliance with any and all applicable OIG fraud alerts.

- *Marketing*. The laboratory should have a written marketing policy that requires the use of honest, straightforward, and non-deceptive marketing practices.

- *Profile charges*. The laboratory should ensure that the prices it charges to physicians are fair and are never below cost. In addition, physicians and other non-governmental purchasers of the laboratory's services should not be charged less than what Medicare is charged for the same services. The government has noted this is a particular problem when a physician requests an enhanced profile (i.e., one that includes more tests). Policies and procedures should be in place to ensure that the price for an enhanced profile is adjusted upward to cover the laboratory's costs for providing the additional tests. Laboratories that do not increase the price to a physician for an enhanced profile but bill the full price for the additional profile components when Medicare is paying for the enhanced profile risk false claims and anti-kickback law enforcement actions.

- *Record retention.* The laboratory should have written policies and procedures addressing the maintenance, retention, and proper storage of accurate and complete records.
- *Performance goals.* Adherence to the laboratory's compliance program should be part of each employee's performance plan goals, and this requirement should be spelled out in a written policy.

2. *Designation of compliance officer.* Although written policies and procedures may be at the core of a laboratory's compliance program, those written policies and procedures are of little use without a compliance officer to implement and enforce them. The government's compliance program guidance for laboratories places great emphasis on the designation of a compliance officer. The chief compliance officer is to oversee the drafting of the written compliance policies and procedures and implement and enforce the laboratory's compliance program as a whole. Because the role of the compliance officer is so important, the laboratory must give due weight to his or her designation. The position of compliance officer should be one of respect and authority. He or she should report directly to the CEO or another member of senior management.

3. *Education and training.* The compliance program guidance emphasizes the need for regular training of laboratory employees. New employees should be trained shortly after they are hired, and existing employees should be given regular refresher courses.

4. *Communication.* According to the compliance program guidance, effective lines of communication are essential elements of a clinical laboratory compliance program. As part of effective communication, all employees should have meaningful access to the laboratory's compliance officer. The guidance also suggests the establishment of an anonymous employee hotline so employees with knowledge of fraud or abuse can have a safe outlet for reporting such activity to the compliance officer without fear of retaliation.

5. *Auditing and monitoring.* To ensure ongoing compliance with the laboratory's policies and procedures, an effective laboratory compliance program should include periodic auditing and monitoring of various aspects of the laboratory's operations.

6. *Discipline and enforcement.* Every laboratory also should be willing to impose discipline and corrective measures in the event of non-compliance with its policies and procedures. There should be mechanisms in place for investigating, reporting, and correcting problems. If a particular person is discovered to be involved in a laboratory compliance problem, mechanisms should be in place to ensure that the person charged or under investigation is removed from any position of authority. Moreover, if that person is either determined by the laboratory's internal investigation to be guilty of an offense or excluded by the government from partic-

ipation in federal health care programs, he or she should be terminated. Furthermore, policies and procedures should be in place to preclude the laboratory from hiring a person who has been excluded from a federal or state health care program.[61]

7. *Corrective action.* The laboratory's compliance program should include a section addressing what corrective action the laboratory will take in the event its audits or monitoring activities uncover problems. Any corrective action taken should be documented clearly.

### 3. Compliance Program Guidance for Durable Medical Equipment, Prosthetics, Orthotics, and Supplies Providers

The OIG issued compliance program guidance for the DME, prosthetics, orthotics, and supplies providers in June 1999.[62] The guidance stresses that all seven elements are essential for DME, prosthetics, orthotics, and supplies providers, regardless of size. In general, the requirements outlined in this guidance are similar to those in other compliance guidance documents. However, the OIG noted the following specific concerns not addressed in other model compliance programs:

1. *Written policies and procedures for risk areas.* Although the OIG acknowledged that unwritten standards of general conduct may be appropriate for small DME, prosthetics, orthotics, and supply providers, written policies and procedures should be established for risk areas. The OIG identified 47 risk areas, including (i) employment of excluded persons; (ii) performing tests to establish medical necessity; (iii) colocation of a DME, prosthetics, orthotics, and supply provider with a referral source; (iv) improper telemarketing practices; (v) failing to refund overpayments; and (vi) services provided in violation of the Stark law.[63] In addition, the OIG identified the following areas as requiring written policies and procedures:

---

[61] Providers also should be aware that the BBA amended the civil monetary penalties statute (42 U.S.C. §1320a-7a), making it a violation to contract with an entity that or individual who has been excluded from a federal or state health care program. This would seem to impose an affirmative duty on a provider to exercise due diligence in ensuring that its employees and contractors have never been excluded. Because most providers have Internet access and because both the OIG and the General Services Administration (GSA) maintain lists of excluded entities on their Web sites, a provider should, at a minimum, check prospective employees' names against the lists. The OIG sanction list can be found at http://www.dhhs.gov/progorg/oig; the GSA list of parties excluded from federal procurement and nonprocurement programs can be found at http://epls.arnet.gov.

[62] 64 Fed. Reg. 36,368 (July 6, 1999). The OIG released this guidance June 22, 1999, before its publication in the *Federal Register*.

[63] 42 U.S.C. §1395nn. The Stark law is discussed at length in Chapter 2 (Crane, Federal Physician Self-Referral Restrictions).

- claims development procedures, with special emphasis on medical necessity (and certification), physician orders, proper billing, correct selection of HCPCS codes, supplier numbers, mail-order issues, assignment, liability, routine waivers of deductibles and coinsurance, capped rental prices, use of cover letters, and oxygen policies and procedures;
- anti-kickback and self-referral concerns, particularly that the DME, prosthetics, orthotics, and supply provider does not pay more than fair market value to referral sources and does not provide remuneration in exchange for referrals (The guidance indicates that counsel should review all contracts and arrangements with actual or potential referral sources.);
- marketing, with emphasis on the prohibitions against offering free services to beneficiaries, offering remuneration to potential referral sources, and making unsolicited telephone contacts to Medicare beneficiaries;
- retention of records; and
- compliance as an element of a performance plan.

2. *Specific training requirements.* In addition to general training, the guidance indicates that there should be specific training for appropriate employees, officers, and managers in (i) DME, prosthetics, orthotics, and supplies claim development and billing procedures, and (ii) sales and marketing policies and procedures. This training must include education regarding the duty to report misconduct.

## 4. Compliance Program Guidance for Third-Party Medical Billing Companies

A fourth compliance program guidance covers third-party medical billing companies.[64] This program guidance represents the government's first compliance program guidance targeted to nonproviders. Program guidelines apply to physician practice management companies that provide billing services, as well as to traditional third-party billing companies. These guidelines were developed in part in response to the government's concerns about possible overbilling and overutilization resulting from promises made by billing companies and reimbursement consultants to maximize revenues from government-funded health care programs. Such arrangements may lead to abusive billing practices, especially if the billing agent or consultant receives a percentage of the provider's revenues.

Much of the compliance program guidance for third-party medical billing companies is the same as that of other programs (i.e., the seven essential elements). The medical billing company guidelines differ significantly, however, in that they seem to impose a duty on billing agents and managers to monitor their clients' conduct and encourage, but do

---

[64] 63 Fed. Reg. 70,138 (Dec. 18, 1998).

not require, the reporting of any misconduct to the government. Consequently, as a result of these guidelines, third-party billing companies and managers for hospitals, physician practices, and other providers may wish to review their relationships with their clients. Managers may consider adding a provision to their client contracts clearly specifying each party's compliance responsibilities and requiring clients to implement and maintain an effective compliance program. Within the guidance framework, the OIG identified the following special concerns for billing companies:

1. *Risk areas for third-party medical billing companies.* The OIG identified specific risk areas for billing companies. These include the following:
   - billing for services or items that have not been documented;
   - duplicate billing;
   - inadequate resolution of overpayments;
   - lack of integrity of computer systems;
   - improper use of billing modifiers;
   - routine waiver of copayments; and
   - improper discounts on professional services.

2. *Coding and documentation.* The government is particularly concerned with abusive coding procedures. The guidelines suggest that billing companies that provide coding services should implement safeguards that ensure that coding is based on complete and accurate documentation. If a billing company does not provide coding services, but instead relies on coding provided by a physician, the billing agent should obtain the provider's written agreement to abide by such safeguards, according to the guidance. For example, the billing company or provider should have written policies and procedures that
   - ensure that proper and timely documentation of professional services is obtained before billing;
   - emphasize that a claim should be submitted only when proper documentation supports the claim and is maintained in a form available for audit;
   - require that information contained on a claim be based on chart documentation and make such documentation available to coding staff at the time of coding;
   - avoid providing financial incentives to billing and coding staff members to upcode claims;
   - establish and maintain processes for pre- and postsubmission review of claims to ensure that they are accurate and supported by proper documentation; and
   - obtain clarification from the provider or from the billing agent's medical director when documentation is confusing or lacks adequate justification.

3. *Reporting of provider misconduct.* One of the more significant sections in the compliance guidance is the section addressing corrective action. Under the compliance guidelines, if a billing

agent believes a provider is engaging in improper coding or billing activities, the billing company must refrain from submitting questionable claims. According to the guidance, it must then notify the provider, in writing within 30 days of discovering the problem, why the activity appears to be improper. If the provider continues to engage in conduct that appears to be fraudulent or abusive, the guidelines state that the billing agent should

- refrain from submitting the claim;
- terminate the contract with the provider; and/or
- report the misconduct to the appropriate federal and state authorities within 60 days of determining that there is credible evidence of a violation.

### 5. Compliance Program Guidance for Hospices

In September 1999, the OIG established compliance program guidance for hospices.[65] As with the program guidance previously discussed, the OIG emphasized that all seven basic elements must be included in a hospice's compliance program. The hospice guidance is very similar to that described for other industry segments.

Through its investigative and audit functions, the OIG identified 28 risk areas for hospices, including (1) inadequate management and oversight of subcontracted services, (2) knowing billing for inadequate or substandard care, (3) incentives to referral sources, and (4) pressure on an eligible patient to revoke the hospice benefit when the patient's care becomes too expensive for the hospice to deliver.

However, the OIG seems most concerned that hospices establish and follow policies and procedures to ensure that all eligibility requirements for the hospice benefit are satisfied. The OIG noted particular concerns regarding the terminal illness eligibility requirement, the plan of care, utilization of services, appropriate levels of care, and services provided to patients in nursing homes.

The OIG also outlined risks in contracting with or providing services to actual or potential referral sources, in particular, nursing homes. A hospice's policies and procedures should reflect the safe harbor for such contracts. In addition, counsel should review all such contracts.

### 6. Compliance Program Guidance for Nursing Facilities

The OIG published compliance program guidance for nursing facilities in March 2000. The guidance emphasizes the seven essential elements and states that all seven elements must be contained in an effective compliance program for a nursing facility, regardless of size. The guidance is similar to the model programs previously described. How-

---

[65] 64 Fed. Reg. 54,031 (Oct. 5, 1999). The OIG released this guidance September 30, 1999, before its publication in the *Federal Register*.

ever, the OIG identified the following specific areas to be addressed by policies and procedures for nursing facilities:

- quality of care: The OIG noted in particular that nursing facility compliance plans should include a commitment to providing quality care, including minimum Medicare requirements;
- residents' rights: The OIG recommends providers address risk areas including discrimination in admission policies, use of restraints, privacy, participation in treatment decisions, and safeguarding residents' financial affairs;
- billing and cost reporting;
- employee screening; and
- kickbacks, inducements, and self-referrals (particularly routine coinsurance or deductible waivers and any remuneration not at fair market value).

## 7. Compliance Program Guidance for Medicare+Choice Organizations

The OIG published compliance program guidance for Medicare+Choice organizations in November 1999.[66] The OIG acknowledged that the elements of the optional guidance are the same as elements required by CMS in the Medicare+Choice regulations.[67] In light of the extensive regulation of these organizations, the OIG recommended that each organization "determine the extent to which [its] activities need to be modified or supplemented to create an effective compliance program."[68]

In the guidance, the OIG reiterated its concerns regarding marketing, selective marketing and enrollment, and emergency services. Selective marketing, or "cherry picking," is an area identified as a great concern of the OIG. The OIG has recommended that each organization actively implement policies and procedures to prevent cherry picking, even in subtle forms.

The OIG further discussed its concerns regarding inappropriate withholding or delaying of services for enrollees. Medicare+Choice organizations should have policies and procedures ensuring (1) that there is no interference between health care professionals and the enrollees they advise, and (2) that incentive plans are fully disclosed to CMS and do not inappropriately encourage underutilization. Additionally, organizations should establish policies and procedures to ensure that all data submissions to CMS are accurate, timely, and complete.

---

[66] 64 Fed. Reg. 61,893 (Nov. 15, 1999). For a more complete discussion of the compliance program guidance for Medicare+Choice entities, see Chapter 6 (Roth & Palmer, Managed Care Fraud and Abuse: Risk Areas for Government Program Participants).

[67] 42 C.F.R. part 22.

[68] 64 Fed. Reg. at 61,895.

### 8. Compliance Program Guidance for Individual and Small-Group Physician Practices

The OIG released final compliance program guidance for individual and small-group physician practices in September 2000.[69] Unlike in the guidance for other types of programs and entities, in the physician practice guidance the OIG stressed that full implementation of all seven basic elements might not be essential for a small practice to have an effective compliance program. Because it anticipated that all seven basic elements might not be fully implemented, the guidance suggests that small physician practices implement the elements in the following order:

1. *Auditing and monitoring.* The guidance indicates that physician practices may use audits to identify any problem or risk areas requiring targeting.

2. *Written policies and procedures.* Written policies and procedures should be developed to address (i) particular concerns uncovered during an audit, (ii) useful practice procedures and standards, and (iii) risk areas. The OIG identified the following risk areas: (i) coding and billing; (ii) determination of reasonable and necessary services; (iii) documentation; and (iv) improper inducements, kickbacks, and self-referrals.

3. *Designation of compliance officer(s) or contact(s).* According to the guidance, it is acceptable for more than one employee to have compliance monitoring responsibility.

4. *Education and training.* Appropriate training should include both general compliance training and specific coding and billing training. Training may be handled either internally or achieved through outside seminars and workshops.

5. *Responding to detected offenses and developing corrective action initiatives.* A physician practice should develop policies and procedures to respond to the discovery of a problem and ensure that appropriate action is taken following investigation, including return of overpayments and appropriate reports to the government and/or law enforcement authorities, as applicable. The OIG suggests that a physician practice develop monitors and warning indicators as part of its compliance program.

6. *Communication.* Open communication is an integral part of a compliance program. Especially in the small practice setting, open communication can be achieved by an open-door policy and informal communication methods. The guidance indicates that employees should be able to report fraudulent or erroneous conduct without fear of retribution.

7. *Enforcing disciplinary standards through well-publicized guidelines.* Guidelines should be thoroughly distributed. Consistent

---

[69] 65 Fed. Reg. 59,434 (Oct. 5, 2000). The OIG released this final guidance September 25, 2000, before its publication in the *Federal Register*.

and appropriate sanctions should be enforced for noncompliant actions, with flexibility for aggravating or mitigating circumstances.

## 9. Compliance Program Guidance for Home Health Agencies

The compliance program guidance for home health agencies[70] acknowledges that home health agencies often are small businesses and therefore may not be of sufficient size or have adequate resources to fully implement all aspects of the compliance guidance. The government does expect, however, that each home health agency, no matter its size, will implement some type of compliance program that contains as many elements of the model as possible. The government considers this necessary to both (1) show good faith, and (2) help create "a culture that promotes prevention, detection and resolution of non-compliant activities."[71] The guidance suggests implementation of the seven basic elements as follows:

1. *Written policies and procedures.* According to the guidance, the home health agency should develop written policies and procedures and provide copies of those policies and procedures to all persons who might be affected, including the agency's agents and independent contractors. The policies and procedures should cover all aspects of a typical home health agency's operations. Particular care should be taken regarding policies and procedures addressing coding and claims submission since, according to the guidelines, these are the areas of greatest risk for home health agencies. Accordingly, the guidance indicates that the home health agency should update its policies and procedures routinely to reflect current law and regulations on proper billing. In addition, to establish coverage eligibility, policies and procedures should reflect particular attention to issues associated with medical necessity determinations, homebound status of beneficiaries, physician certification of plans of care, and qualifying services. Other risk areas highlighted in the guidance include the following:
   - *Improper joint ventures.* The home health agency should have policies and procedures in place that establish parameters for joint ventures and that prohibit improper joint ventures between home health agencies and referral sources.
   - *Unqualified or unlicensed personnel.* The home health agency's policies and procedures should indicate clearly that bills will be submitted only for the services of individuals who are properly qualified or licensed to provide the type of services billed.

---

[70] 63 Fed. Reg. 42,410 (Aug. 7, 1998).
[71] *Id.* at 42,411.

- *Falsified plans of care.* The home health agency should have policies and procedures to ensure that it provides only medically necessary services that are appropriately certified by a physician. A plan for furnishing home health services must be certified by a physician who is a doctor of medicine, osteopathy, or podiatry medicine and who does not have a significant ownership interest in or a significant financial or contractual relationship with the home health agency.[72]

- *Improper patient solicitation activities and high-pressure marketing.* The government has noted that home health agencies sometimes offer free gifts or services to patients. Because they may be intended to improperly maximize business growth and patient retention, such gifts are highly suspect. Moreover, the guidance indicates that any marketing materials should be clear, correct, nondeceptive, and fully informative.[73]

- *Billing for services to patients who are not truly homebound.* For a home health agency to receive reimbursement for home health services under either Medicare Part A or Part B, the beneficiary must be "confined to the home."[74] Therefore, home health agencies should develop oversight mechanisms to ensure that the homebound status of a Medicare beneficiary is verified and properly documented. The program guidance suggests the use of written "prompts" on nursing note forms as a safeguard. Such prompts would direct the home health agency's nurses and other clinicians to properly assess and document the homebound status of the Medicare beneficiary. Another safeguard suggested in the guidance is the distribution of written notices to the home health agency's Medicare beneficiaries reminding the beneficiaries that they must satisfy the regulatory requirements for homebound status to be eligible for Medicare coverage.

- *Billing for visits to patients who do not require a qualifying service.* To receive Medicare reimbursement for home health services, a beneficiary must require skilled nursing care on an intermittent basis, physical therapy services, or speech–language pathology services or have a continuing need for occupational therapy. If services can be safely and effectively performed (or self-administered) by the average nonmedical person without the direct supervision of a licensed nurse, the service does not qualify as a skilled service even if a registered nurse actually performs the service.[75] The government

---

[72] *See* 63 Fed. Reg. at 42,422. Note that Phase I of the Stark II regulations amends this provision to track Stark II's "financial relationship" definition and the applicable exceptions. 66 Fed. Reg. 856, 962 (Jan. 4, 2001). The Stark law is discussed at length in Chapter 2 (Crane, Federal Physician Self-Referral Restrictions).

[73] 63 Fed. Reg. at 42,414.

[74] *See* HOME HEALTH AGENCY MANUAL §204.1; *see also* 63 Fed. Reg. at 42,416.

[75] *See* HOME HEALTH AGENCY MANUAL §205.

considers it critical that the home health agency's written policies and procedures contain mechanisms to prevent billing for services after any qualifying service has ceased.

- *Duplication of services*. The guidance indicates that there should be safeguards in place to prevent the home health agency from providing or billing for services that are being provided to the patient by assisted living facilities, hospitals, clinics, physicians, or other home health agencies.
- *Willing caregivers*. The government suggests that policies and procedures should be in place to ensure that the home health agency does not provide services when the home health agency is aware of willing and able caregivers who can provide the same services. According to Medicare principles, a home health agency should neither provide nor bill for services if the patient has a family member or other person who is willing and able to provide the same services rendered by the home health agency.[76]

2. *Designation of compliance officer*. According to the guidance, every home health agency should designate an employee to serve as the agency's compliance officer. Some smaller agencies may have compliance officers who also serve other functions, but there should be at least one person who understands and acknowledges that it is his or her duty to oversee the development, implementation, and management of the agency's compliance program.

3. *Education and training*. As with the other compliance guidances, the government places great emphasis on education and training as key elements of an effective corporate compliance program. The government has suggested that the home health agency take steps to ensure that independent contractors and agents, including physicians, participate in the home health agency's training programs. The government also has pointed out that the OIG has made many publications available to the public (e.g., Special Fraud Alerts, advisory opinions, and the OIG's annual Work Plan) and that such publications can serve as the bases for educational courses and publications.

4. *Communication*. As with the other compliance programs, the home health agency guidance suggests the use of hotlines, e-mail, newsletters, suggestion boxes, and other forms of information exchange to maintain open lines of communication between the agency's compliance officer(s) and employees. Interestingly, the guidance states that, in addition to posting the agency's own internal hotline number, each home health agency should also post the OIG's hotline number (currently 1-800-447-8477) in prominent locations throughout the agency.

---

[76] *See* HOME HEALTH AGENCY MANUAL §203.2; *see also* 63 Fed. Reg. at 42,415.

5. *Auditing and monitoring.* The OIG believes that an effective compliance program should include thorough monitoring of the program's successes and failures and regular reporting to the home health agency's senior management. An effective compliance program also should incorporate periodic (at least annual, according to the compliance program guidance) reviews of whether the elements of the home health agency's compliance program have been satisfied.

6. *Discipline and enforcement.* The home health agency program guidance continues the government's emphasis on meaningful disciplinary actions to punish and deter non-compliance. As part of its deterrence efforts, the home health agency should conduct routine background checks on all prospective employees.

7. *Corrective action.* If a home health agency becomes aware of misconduct, it should respond quickly to investigate the misconduct and take decisive steps to correct the problem. Depending on the level of misconduct, corrective steps may range from simply repaying erroneous overpayments to referring the matter to criminal and/or civil law enforcement authorities, according to the guidance. The guidance points out that the OIG maintains a voluntary disclosure program to encourage providers to report suspected fraud or abuse. The guidance indicates that failure to disclose overpayments discovered through the compliance program could be interpreted as an intentional attempt to conceal the overpayment, constituting an independent criminal violation. For an agency to participate in the voluntary disclosure program, (i) the disclosure must be on behalf of an entity and not an individual; (ii) the disclosure must be truly voluntary (i.e., there can be no pending proceeding or investigation); (iii) the entity must disclose the nature of the wrongdoing and the harm to the federal health care program or programs; and (iv) the entity must not be the subject of a bankruptcy proceeding before or after the self-disclosure.[77]

## IV. Practical Issues in Developing and Implementing a Compliance Program

There are many practical issues involved with a provider's decision to develop and implement a corporate compliance program. The first step in developing a program should be the selection of a corporate compliance officer. The compliance officer then can oversee the development and implementation of the full program, including the adoption of a written compliance program containing a written statement of the organization's policies, procedures, and ethical standards. The compliance officer also should oversee the education and training of the organiza-

---

[77] 63 Fed. Reg. 58,399 (Oct. 30, 1998).

tion's employees, the establishment of a compliance hotline, and the implementation of periodic internal audits and monitoring systems.

## A. Selecting a Compliance Officer

The selection of a compliance officer is vital for several reasons. The compliance officer is instrumental in the success or failure of an organization's corporate compliance program. A competent compliance officer will oversee the development, implementation, operation, and appropriate modification of the program. Employees will identify the compliance officer with the compliance program. For this reason, it is important to choose a compliance officer who already is widely respected by the organization's employees or who can engender their respect.

If possible, depending on the size and resources of the organization, the position of compliance officer should be full time. If an employee has compliance-officer responsibilities added to his or her existing duties, the organization faces the risk that the compliance program could become a low priority. In addition, such dual responsibilities could send the message to the organization's employees, as well as to the government, that the provider is not serious about its compliance program.

The compliance officer should have direct access to members of the organization's senior management and board of directors. It is best if the compliance officer reports directly to the CEO rather than to the general counsel or the chief financial officer. The compliance officer should be someone with knowledge of the industry and the organization's operations, because compliance is, at its core, about operations. The compliance officer does not have to be an attorney. In fact, unless he or she has a great deal of experience with health care operations matters, an attorney may not be the most effective compliance officer.

Depending on the size of the organization, the compliance officer also may head a "compliance team" of other organization compliance personnel. Such a compliance team consists of employees, in both the provider's central location and any field locations, who are assigned the task of assisting the chief compliance officer with the running of the compliance program.

## B. Drafting a Corporate Compliance Program

After a corporate compliance officer is selected, the next step in developing a compliance program is drafting a written compliance program. The program should be well written and understandable by all employees. It should contain both substance and structure. Accordingly, the program should include policies and procedures on the basic issues central or problematic to the provider or its particular industry segment. The government's published model compliance programs provide lists of areas in which the government expects written policies and procedures. At a minimum, a written compliance program should include policies and procedures on proper billing; the anti-kickback law; Medicare and Medicaid reimbursement issues; employment law issues (e.g., discrimination and sexual harassment); basic antitrust law principles; and conflicts of interest. However, because new areas of interest or concern will emerge from time to time, the compliance program should not be static; instead, it should evolve to meet the provider's changing needs. The compliance officer should play a key role in overseeing periodic amendments and revisions to the written program.

Because compliance at its core involves operations, the preparation of the compliance program should include input from key employees from across the provider's entire operations. Soliciting input from all areas of operations also has the added benefit of helping to ensure that the final compliance program will have broad support from within the organization. This support is essential for the success of any compliance program.

There are various compliance consultants available to providers. Many of these consultants, for a fee, will help a provider design and implement a compliance program. Other consultants provide draft programs to providers. The use of such consultants and their form programs can be very helpful, so long as the provider realizes that the simple adoption of a form program, without more, would not likely be considered by the government to constitute an "effective compliance program." It can be useful to start the process with a form program, but it is best to customize it as much as possible to the particular concerns and issues of the particular provider.

## C. Education and Training

Once the compliance officer has been appointed and a written compliance program drafted and adopted, the next step is presenting the compliance program to the organization's employees and affiliated physicians. The initial presentation and training should be conducted on site at the provider's facility or facilities. To ensure that training sessions are small enough to allow participants the opportunity to ask questions and make comments, several sessions may need to be scheduled. In addition, to reach "graveyard shift" employees, some training sessions may have to be conducted at odd hours or on weekends.

Despite a provider's best efforts, it may be impossible to reach all employees and consultants (e.g., per-diem employees and independent contractors). In such cases, the best (or possibly only) way of presenting the compliance program to those persons may be mailing a copy of the written compliance program to their home address and requiring that they sign and return a certification stating that they have received a copy of the written program, that they have read it, and that they agree to comply with the compliance program and to report any suspected fraud or abuse to the compliance officer or to the organization's compliance hotline.

It is crucial to stress the importance of the compliance program to all employees. Many employees may be jaded, having lived through many other corporate "fad" programs. It is important, therefore, to impress on them that this is a serious commitment, not just the fad of the moment. A company's serious commitment to the program can be demonstrated by the active involvement of upper management and by selecting a compliance officer who is well respected by other employees. The education and training process is not over once the program is presented to an organization's employees. Periodic follow-up sessions should reinforce the original message and address any new questions or concerns.

Part of the training should, of course, include a requirement that each employee sign a certification stating that he or she (1) has received training, (2) will comply with the organization's ethical guidelines, and (3) will report any suspected misconduct to the hotline or to a member of the compliance team. In addition, the provider may wish to consider adopting a policy of conducting exit interviews with departing employees, so as to give those employees a final opportunity to report any compliance or ethical problems. These steps will go a long way toward discouraging *qui tam* lawsuits and, in the event of an investigation, can be cited to the government as evidence that the organization took compliance issues seriously and gave its employees many opportunities to report fraud and abuse.

## D. Budgeting

One practical issue that often arises is how much a provider should budget for the implementation and operation of an effective compliance program. The usual answer is that adequate resources must be devoted to compliance, no matter the cost. Some providers, therefore, budget only for the routine and expected costs of the compliance program (e.g., compliance officer salary and expenses associated with education and training programs).

## E. Compliance Hotline

A key component of most compliance programs is the establishment of a hotline or other means of communication that employees can use anonymously to report suspected fraud or abuse. Hotlines are important for several reasons. First, the government suggests the use of hotlines in all of its compliance guidances. Second, hotlines provide a clear mechanism for reporting fraud or abuse. If there is no internal hotline, employees' frustration with the organization and lack of responsiveness to their concerns may lead them to call the OIG's hotline or file a *qui tam* suit.

To be meaningful and useful, the hotline should be accessible 24 hours per day. No effort should be made to track callers, and employees should be reassured frequently that the hotline does not have any type of caller identification feature or other mechanism for identifying callers. The existence of the hotline should be publicized within the organization regularly, perhaps through the organization's newsletter or on its bulletin board.

The compliance officer or other employees who monitor the hotline should log each call carefully and assign each call a tracking number so that the caller can call back, refer to the tracking number, and obtain information on what follow-up steps were taken while remaining anonymous. The compliance officer or another member of the compliance team also should immediately refer information on incoming calls to the proper person within the organization for follow-up. Of course, the compliance officer also should ensure that any needed follow-up is actually taken and that all actions taken in response to a call, as well as information on the final resolution of the call, are properly documented.

Providers should expect most calls to be of a human resources nature (i.e., discrimination, sexual harassment). These types of calls are appropriate for the hotline, and they should be encouraged. To minimize the possibility of hotline abuse, in its orientation seminars and follow-up training, the compliance team should educate employees as to what types of calls are—and are not—appropriate. In addition, the provider must achieve a workable balance between its need to encourage use of the hotline to report suspected fraud or abuse, no matter how minor, and its desire to discourage frivolous calls.

## F. Compliance Helpline

The compliance team also may consider adopting a compliance "helpline." In this context, a helpline is a toll-free number, separate from the compliance hotline, that employees can call for assistance regarding particular compliance concerns (e.g., billing issues). The helpline could have a recorded message instead of a live monitor, but any inquiries should be referred immediately to the compliance officer or another member of the compliance team and then assigned to the appropriate person or persons within the organization for resolution. Because of the nature of the questions and the need for follow-up information, the compliance officer probably would want to encourage employees making helpline calls to reveal their identity. However, the organization should also be willing to accept anonymous calls, because some employees may be reluctant to ask questions if they have to reveal their identity. Some employees may be afraid that too many calls to the helpline would make them appear ignorant or would otherwise reflect poorly on them in their performance evaluations.

## G. Auditing and Monitoring

Any discussion of the practicalities of implementing a corporate compliance program would not be complete without mention of the problems associated with auditing and monitoring a provider for compliance. Periodic internal audits are an integral component of the government's compliance guidances for both hospitals and clinical laboratories. Practically speaking, in the area of Medicare billing regulations, there is tremendous value in getting claims right when they are first filed. Providers therefore should consider auditing claims *before* they are submitted. Problematic claims can be corrected, and there will be no violations to report.

Many audits and reviews, however, will uncover *past* illegal activity or billing errors. Although the government's compliance guidances encourage such audits, notably absent from the government's discussions is any mention of how a provider is expected to conduct internal audits and maintain any privilege or confidentiality for the audit results. The answer is that routine self-reviews probably should be part of an organization's standard business operations and do not need the protection of the attorney-client privilege. More serious internal investigations or external reviews of a particular problem, on the other hand, should be structured so as to preserve the attorney-client privilege where possible.

## 1. Attorney-Client Privilege

In conducting any internal audit or review, a provider should consider whether, and to what extent, it wants the attorney-client privilege to apply.[78] If an internal review is conducted by an attorney, or under the direction of an attorney, then the attorney-client privilege and work-product doctrine generally will apply to all conversations and correspondence produced by the review. Disclosure of confidential information constitutes a waiver of the privilege, and the waiver extends to all materials on the same subject matter. However, agreeing to allow the government to review an audit report may waive the privilege with respect to all aspects of that review.[79]

The protection of attorney-client privilege should not be used for all reviews. Routine compliance reviews do not need attorney-client privilege protection and should be part of the ongoing monitoring of business operations. Nonprivileged routine reviews can be conducted as part of an organization's financial audit or part of its periodic internal review program. In conducting routine internal audits, it is impor-

---

[78] A brief reminder of what constitutes attorney-client privilege and attorney work-product doctrine is in order. The attorney-client privilege applies to confidential communications between lawyer and client, made for the purpose of obtaining legal advice of any kind. Fausek v. White, 965 F.2d 126 (6th Cir. 1992). Its purpose is to encourage full and frank communications between attorneys and their clients and thereby promote broader public interests. Upjohn Co. v. United States, 449 U.S. 383 (1981). The attorney-client privilege protects confidential communications both to and from counsel. *In re* Grand Jury Subpoena, 765 F.2d 1014 (11th Cir. 1985); Colton v. United States, 306 F.2d 633 (2d Cir 1962).

In contrast, the attorney work-product doctrine protects from disclosure an attorney's notes, materials, and mental process prepared in anticipation of litigation. It is separate and distinct from the attorney-client privilege. United States v. Nobles, 422 U.S. 225 (1975). The Supreme Court has distinguished between two types of work product. "Fact" work product is the evidence or materials gathered by an attorney. It is afforded less protection than the second type of work product, "opinion" work product, which consists of an attorney's mental impressions, opinions, and conclusions. Hickman v. Taylor, 329 U.S. 495 (1947).

[79] *In re* Martin Marietta Corp., 856 F.2d 619 (4th Cir. 1988); Weil v. Investment Indicators Research Mgmt., 647 F.2d 18 (9th Cir. 1981).

tant that the organization avoid reaching unfounded legal conclusions. It is equally important to know when to stop an internal review and seek counsel. It also is important to avoid having reviews conducted by the same persons responsible for the operations being reviewed.

### 2. External/Expert Reviews

In some cases, a provider will want to retain an expert to conduct a more extensive review than it may be able to do on its own. In such cases, the expert should be retained through legal counsel so as to have all communications with the expert subject to the attorney-client privilege. The terms of the engagement of the expert also should be structured so that the expert's work product will be privileged. The scope of the work should be defined clearly before the expert begins his or her review. These parameters should include such features as time frame, type of error or activity, personnel, type of program (e.g., Medicaid, Medicare, private insurer), and geographic (i.e., if more than one location is owned or managed by the provider).

### 3. Expert Findings

If an outside consultant or expert discovers errors, it is important that the organization immediately create a work plan to implement corrective action. All corrective actions taken should be documented, and, if the review uncovered billing errors, the amount of repayments and methods for restitution should be established.

### 4. Types of Reviews

There are two major types of reviews: (1) current audits, and (2) forensic audits. Current audits are exactly what they sound like: audits covering the provider's current practices and billing policies and procedures. Current reviews help ensure that billing processes are effective and that submitted bills are accurate. Forensic audits, on the other hand, cover past activities and practices. Forensic audits can determine if there have been overpayments or underpayments. These types of reviews also can take place in response to a government investigation or in response to the announcement of a national enforcement program.

### 5. Disclosure Obligations and Repayments

If an audit uncovers significant problems or fraud, the provider is faced with making a decision about what to do with that information. The provider may wonder if it is under an obligation to disclose the fraud or mistakes, and whether it would be better to keep silent.[80]

---

[80] The Joint Commission on Accreditation of Healthcare Organizations (JCAHO) also encourages certain disclosures. JCAHO's "sentinel event" policy is designed to promote self-reporting and examination of the root causes of medical errors. Accredited health care organizations that report sentinel events to JCAHO within 5 business days and submit a thorough root-cause analysis and action plan within an additional 30 days will not be placed on JCAHO's publicly disclosed Accreditation Watch. For more information on the JCAHO's sentinel event policy, see the JCAHO Web site *at* http://www.jcaho.org/ptsafety_frm.html.

Although there may not be a duty to report past illegal behavior, if a provider becomes aware that it has received an overpayment, it is legally obligated to refund or at least disclose the overpayment. It is a felony to knowingly and fraudulently retain an overpayment.[81] In addition, the *Provider Reimbursement Manual* requires a provider to amend its cost report to correct "material" errors.[82] And finally, the OIG's model compliance program guidance for hospitals suggests that a provider report suspected misconduct within 60 days after determining there is credible evidence of a violation.

If a provider chooses to report fraud or an overpayment, it usually is best to report it to the fiscal intermediary or carrier, as any overpayments should be refunded to those entities. If illegal conduct is to be reported, the OIG or the local office of the U.S. Attorney may be the best place to disclose the activity. However, the provider should make a disclosure and, if appropriate, refund to the fiscal carrier or intermediary. The OIG generally has no legal role in disclosure absent a CIA, but typically it would be involved in settlement discussions incident to a disclosure.

If a provider decides to make a disclosure, it should report the information in such a way to minimize the risk that the report will not waive the attorney–client privilege. It is important to keep in mind that the attorney–client privilege is applicable only to communications made to an attorney, not to the underlying facts. Similarly, the attorney work-product privilege applies only to conclusions drawn by an attorney from the underlying facts, not to the facts themselves. Therefore, a provider should be careful to disclose only the relevant facts, not the process or conclusions of an internal investigation. When making a report, a provider also should refund any overpayment and report what corrective action was taken.

## V. Conclusion

Providers must recognize that the adoption of a corporate compliance program is not without risk. There is no guarantee that a voluntary compliance program or voluntary disclosure will help a provider in a noncriminal setting. The very operation of the compliance program, especially the auditing and monitoring functions, may result in

---

[81]*See* 42 U.S.C. §1320a-7b(a)(3), which prohibits the knowing failure to disclose the occurrence of any event affecting the provider's "initial or continued right to any such benefit or payment . . . with an intent fraudulently to secure such benefit or payment either in greater amount than is due or when no such benefit or payment is authorized." JCAHO's sentinel event policy, which became effective April 1, 1998, defines a "sentinel event" as "any unexpected occurrence involving death or serious physical or psychological injury, or the risk thereof." Sentinel events include such things as an unanticipated death; a patient's major permanent loss of bodily function; an infant abduction; an infant discharged to the wrong family; a patient's rape by another patient or a staff member; a patient's adverse reaction to a hemolytic transfusion; or surgery on the wrong patient or body part. For more information on the JCAHO's sentinel event policy, see the JCAHO Web site: http://www.jcaho.org/ptsafety_frm.html.

[82]*See* Provider Reimbursement Manual §2931.1.

the identification and disclosure of problems that would never have been discovered by the government. Providers also should realize that although compliance programs can, on the one hand, discourage *qui tam* lawsuits by providing conscientious, ethical employees with an internal means of reporting fraud or abuse, on the other hand, a compliance program could, through its training sessions, actually be educating potential *qui tam* plaintiffs.

Furthermore, because it will uncover and likely result in punishment for employees for violations of the organization's policies, procedures, and ethical standards, an effective compliance program undoubtedly will result in increased litigation for the organization. Some employees may even be terminated, and discharged employees tend to sue. Similarly, the compliance-monitoring program may uncover contracts that do not fit within applicable exceptions to the Stark law or that otherwise present an unacceptable level of risk. The organization's decision to terminate or modify such contracts may, in some instances, lead to litigation.

Nevertheless, in light of the government's clear expectation that every health care provider have an effective corporate compliance program, the risks of *not* adopting a compliance program appear to far outweigh the risks of adopting one. As with most areas of corporate life, the keys to minimizing risk and obtaining maximum benefits from a compliance program are in thorough preparation and detailed execution of the program.

It is a fact of modern health care that no provider is in total compliance in all aspects of its operations throughout each day. This state of affairs arises from two separate factors. First, since the mid-1990s, the clear trend in federal oversight of the health care industry has been toward more voluminous and complicated regulation. This complex regulatory structure presents significant challenges for a provider in both its operations and claims submission functions. Secondly, as the size of a provider's organization grows, compliance issues arise simply from the number of patients receiving services each day and the number of employees delivering those services or submitting claims related to such services.

An effective corporate compliance program acknowledges this fact and strives to prevent problems in the first instance, and then to detect and appropriately deal with problems when they do occur. By implementing a training program for both new and existing employees, the provider can demonstrate a corporate culture committed to complying with the law. By having a compliance protocol in place that includes a reporting mechanism for employees, a monitoring function through periodic audits, and direct involvement of the appropriate management hierarchy to implement employee discipline and other corrective action, the provider can document compliance initiatives that have the necessary force. Where an effective corporate compliance program is in place, should government agencies become involved in an issue, the likelihood that severe sanctions will be sought—through criminal prosecution or the exclusion process—can be significantly reduced.

# 8

# Potential Liabilities for Directors and Officers of Health Care Organizations[*]

---

[*]Linda A. Baumann, Reed Smith LLP, Washington, D.C., and George E. McDavid, Reed Smith LLP, Princeton, N.J. The authors thank Holly M. Barbera, Reed Smith LLP, Princeton, N.J., for her assistance with this chapter.

# I. Introduction

The health care industry has witnessed exponential growth in the number of investigations and enforcement actions taken against members of the industry. The U.S. Department of Justice (DOJ) and Department of Health and Human Services (HHS) reported that the following occurred in 1999 alone:

- federal prosecutors filed 371 criminal indictments in health care fraud cases (a 16 percent increase over 1998);
- 396 defendants were convicted of health care fraud–related crimes with 2,278 civil matters pending, and 91 new civil cases filed;
- the federal government won or negotiated more than $524 million in judgments, settlements, and administrative penalties in health care fraud cases and proceedings;

- HHS excluded 2,976 persons and entities from participation in federal health care programs;[1] and
- HHS's Office of Inspector General (OIG) participated in 942 prosecutions or settlements.[2]

The size of the fines and penalties imposed can be staggering, and liability is being imposed on individuals as well as on corporations. For example, in January 2000, Fresenius Medical Care North America (Fresenius) agreed to pay a record $486 million in criminal and civil penalties to resolve allegations of health care fraud by three subsidiaries of its kidney dialysis business.[3] Two former vice presidents of a Fresenius subsidiary pled guilty to conspiracy charges, and three others were indicted on similar charges.[4] Deputy Attorney General Eric Holder, Jr., was quoted as stating that the criminal cases against individuals were "especially important" to serve as a deterrent.[5]

In addition, there has been extensive publicity about the decision in *In re Caremark International*,[6] which expanded the potential liabilities that directors and officers may face for failing to monitor corporate activities adequately. As stated by one commentator, *Caremark* "allows the prosecutor to consider whether the board of directors of a corporation can be held criminally liable for actions of the corporation's employees."[7] Class action and/or derivative lawsuits under various legal theories have been filed against the directors and officers of several major health care organizations, including Columbia/HCA Healthcare Corporation, now HCA– The Healthcare Company (discussed at length *infra* Section III.D.) and Allegheny Health Education Research Foundation (discussed at length *infra* Section III.E.).[8] Meanwhile, the number and complexity of the laws and regulations that businesses must observe, particularly in the health care industry, are steadily increasing. Under these circumstances, it is hardly surprising that directors and officers of health care organizations are becoming increasingly concerned about their potential liabilities as overseers and managers of companies in such a closely scrutinized industry.

---

[1]*See* U.S. DEP'T OF HEALTH & HUMAN SERVS. & U.S. DEP'T OF JUSTICE, HHS/DOJ HEALTH CARE FRAUD AND ABUSE CONTROL PROGRAM ANNUAL REPORT FOR FISCAL YEAR 1999, at 2 (Jan. 2000), *available at* http://www.oig.hhs.gov/press/hipaa2.htm.

[2]*See id.* at 8.

[3]*See Kidney Dialysis Firm Will Pay $486 Million, Plead Guilty to Defrauding Health Programs,* 5 BNA's HEALTH CARE DAILY REP. (EXECUTIVE BRIEFING NEWS) (Jan. 20, 2000).

[4]*See id.*

[5]*See id.*

[6]698 A.2d 959 (Del. Ch. 1996).

[7]Mathias H. Heck, Jr. & Rhonda R. Mims, *The Corporate Officer: To Pay or Not to Pay?*, PROSECUTOR, July–Aug. 1998, at 24.

[8]Lawsuits alleging securities fraud also have been filed against directors and officers of health care companies; however, such cases are outside the purview of this chapter. *See, e.g.,* Helwig v. Vencor, Inc., *et al.*, 251 F.3d 540 (6th Cir. 2001).

This chapter provides an overview of the general principles and major issues relating to director and officer liability, with particular focus on those topics and new developments of special interest to corporate board members (directors) and officers in the health care industry. The duties and responsibilities that corporate officers and directors owe to an organization is a complex subject that has been discussed in numerous articles and books, including several multivolume sets.[9] Therefore, this chapter can offer only an introduction to the subject. Because many companies are incorporated under the laws of Delaware, these issues frequently arise and are resolved under Delaware law. As a result, this discussion focuses primarily on the applicable laws of Delaware, while noting some of the important variations in other jurisdictions.

This chapter is divided into four sections, in addition to this introductory discussion. After briefly describing the basic duties and responsibilities of corporate directors and officers, and the potential for criminal and civil liability, Section II of this chapter discusses the various doctrines, statutes, and other measures that potentially limit liability. Section III analyzes the types of litigation that often are directed at directors and officers and focuses on several recent health care cases. Section IV provides information on corporate compliance programs, what they require, and how they can help reduce liability for corporate directors and officers; Section IV examines some of the limitations of corporate compliance programs. The chapter concludes with recommendations for further minimizing exposure (Section V).

## II. RESPONSIBILITIES OF DIRECTORS AND OFFICERS

### A. Criminal Liability

#### 1. General Rule

The issue of criminal liability typically is paramount in any legal analysis. The desire to avoid the criminal process and its attendant sanctions is a primary concern for all corporate officers and directors. The general rule is that a corporation's officers and directors cannot be criminally liable unless they personally participate in misconduct. Officers must be active and knowing participants in the criminal behavior to be held culpable.[10]

The participation required to make a person individually culpable for a crime does not necessarily rise to direct commission of the elemental proscribed act. Rather, a person is culpable if he or she commands, procures, or induces the performance of the act, or if he or she aids or

---

[9] For more extensive discussion of directors' and officers' liability generally, see WILLIAM E. KNEPPER & DAN A. BAILEY, LIABILITY OF CORPORATE OFFICERS AND DIRECTORS (1998); JON F. ELLIOT, DIRECTORS' AND OFFICERS' LIABILITY (1998).

[10] *See, e.g.,* United States v. Gibson, 690 F.2d 697, 701 (9th Cir. 1982). For discussion of the responsible-corporate-officer doctrine, see *infra* Section II.A.2.

abets its commission.[11] Thus, some affirmative act or conduct designed to aid the criminal project is required of the individual. Corporate officers and directors become culpable when they expressly, or by implication, authorize criminal acts carried out by employees or agents of the corporation.[12] Likewise, the express or implied ratification of criminal conduct creates culpability in this context.[13]

However, the law does not find an officer's simple knowledge or awareness of the criminal conduct of the corporation's employees sufficient to establish culpability. Where an officer's awareness of the culpable conduct of others is coupled with his or her active concealment of the offense, culpability can attach.[14] It is important to distinguish knowledge and active concealment from knowledge and mere failure to share that knowledge. The former creates culpability while the latter does not, because it is the act of concealment that creates the basis for liability.

Thus, even where there is no evidence of an officer's direct involvement in the criminal act, a prosecutor's inquiry likely will continue. The questions of a corporate officer's awareness of the criminal conduct and his or her ratification, authorization, or active concealment of that conduct are all subject to an after-the-fact analysis of the facts and circumstances surrounding the events. The corporate officer's guilty state of mind can be inferred from these circumstances. The corporate officer may face the argument that under the facts of the situation, his or her awareness of the misconduct and failure to act to halt it proves an implied authorization for the act to continue, which in turn establishes criminal culpability on the officer's part.

## 2. Responsible-Corporate-Officer Doctrine

At common law, a criminal offense required mens rea, or a guilty state of mind. This requirement served to punish only those who committed knowing or deliberate violations. The state-of-mind requirement largely has been preserved in modern criminal statutes. However, there are some instances in which certain corporate officers have been held criminally liable where they did not know of, or personally participate in, the proscribed conduct.

The primary application of the responsible-corporate-officer doctrine is found in the prosecution of officers for violations of the various statutes designed to promote, protect, and ensure public health and safety. Courts have found that Congress intended to impose a form of criminal strict liability on corporate officers for corporate violations of certain of these statutes.

---

[11]*See* 18 U.S.C. §2.

[12]*See, e.g.,* United States v. Cattle King Packing Co., 793 F.2d 232, 240–41 (10th Cir.), *cert. denied sub nom.* Stanko v. United States, 479 U.S. 985 (1986); *Gibson,* 690 F.2d at 701.

[13]*See Gibson,* 690 F.2d at 701 (citation omitted).

[14]*See* 18 U.S.C. §4.

For example, the federal Food, Drug, and Cosmetic Act (FDCA) prohibits the sale (or introduction into interstate commerce) of misbranded or adulterated materials.[15] In the famous case of *United States v. Dotterweich*,[16] the U.S. Supreme Court interpreted the FDCA and placed criminal liability squarely on the shoulders of corporate officers based solely on their position of responsibility in the business. The FDCA imposes this culpability by setting the "burden of acting at hazard upon a person otherwise innocent but standing in responsible relation to a public danger."[17] By dispensing with "the conventional requirement for criminal conduct—awareness of some wrongdoing," the FDCA effectively establishes strict criminal liability.[18] The FDCA makes criminally accountable those "responsible corporate agents" who deal with products that may affect the health of the public at large.[19] For the Court, the imposition of strict liability in this context is consistent with the officers' "voluntarily assume[d] positions of authority in business enterprises whose services and products affect the health and well-being of the public."[20]

Consistent with the Court's rationale in FDCA cases, the responsible-corporate-officer doctrine has been applied to impose strict liability in the food industry for violations of the Federal Meat Inspection Act.[21] The reach of the responsible-corporate-officer doctrine is not altogether clear, however. Prosecutors have sought to apply it in criminal prosecutions for violations of federal environmental statutes as well, with mixed results. In prosecutions for alleged violations of the Resource Conservation and Recovery Act (RCRA), courts have refused to apply the strict liability encompassed in the responsible-corporate-officer theory. Instead, these courts have ruled that a defendant's status as a responsible official is not sufficient to overcome his or her lack of actual guilty knowledge.[22]

However, the Clean Water Act explicitly brings within the scope of its criminal sanctions "any responsible corporate officer."[23] Courts have debated the precise meaning of this language. One court has concluded that culpability attaches where the officer is aware of the criminal conduct and has authority to halt it, yet fails to exercise that authority.[24]

---

[15] 21 U.S.C. §352.

[16] 320 U.S. 277 (1943).

[17] *Id.* at 281 (citation omitted).

[18] *Id.*

[19] United States v. Park, 421 U.S. 658, 673 (1975).

[20] *Id.*

[21] *See* United States v. Cattle King Packing Co., 793 F.2d 232, 240 (10th Cir.), *cert. denied sub nom.* Stanko v. United States, 479 U.S. 985 (1986).

[22] *See, e.g.,* United States v. MacDonald & Watson Waste Oil Co., 933 F.2d 35, 51–52 (1st Cir. 1991); United States v. White, 766 F. Supp. 873, 894–95 (E.D. Wash. 1991).

[23] 33 U.S.C. §1319(c)(6).

[24] *See, e.g.,* United States v. Iverson, 162 F.3d 1015, 1024–25 (9th Cir. 1998).

However, in the environmental context, one court explicitly refused to follow *United States v. Park*.[25] In *Kaites v. Commonwealth of Pennsylvania Department of Environmental Resources*, the president and chief executive officer (CEO) was the corporate officer responsible for all management decisions concerning the particular environmental nuisance in question.[26] The state sought an abatement order directed to the CEO, rendering him personally responsible for terminating the nuisance. Despite the CEO's control and the strict liability standard in the statute, the court refused to permit the abatement order. The court considered and rejected *Park* and declined to impose liability on the CEO merely because of his status.[27]

Many people who learn of criminal misconduct by the corporation that employs them take the steps necessary to terminate the problem. This is most commonly done on their own initiative out of respect for the law. However, to the extent that any additional motivation is necessary, anyone ignoring wrongdoing faces the risk of criminal prosecution, whether under the responsible-corporate-officer doctrine or more traditional theories and proof of involvement.

## B. Civil Liability

As in most contexts, the civil liability of a corporate director or officer arises from the breach of some duty and a loss or injury to another as a proximate result of the breach. Suits against directors and officers complain that the defendant violated a fiduciary duty owed to the corporation or its shareholders. Such a breach of obligation can result in two categories of suit: shareholder suits and class action suits.

Fiduciary responsibilities are recognized broadly as the duty of loyalty and the duty of care. General doctrines or defenses, such as the business judgment rule, limit the liability that these duties can place on directors and officers.

### 1. *Fiduciary Responsibilities and Duties*

Corporate directors generally are expected to oversee the corporation, set the policies of the business, and select the corporate officers who will, in turn, run the business on a day-to-day basis and implement the policies set by the directors.

The board of directors' responsibilities fall into several broad areas:

- authorizing major corporate actions;
- providing advice and counsel to the corporation's management, including and especially the CEO;
- selecting and instituting procedures to ensure that the board will be adequately informed of the corporation's financial status

---

[25] 421 U.S. 658 (1975).

[26] 529 A.2d 1148 (Pa. Commw. Ct. 1987).

[27] *See id.* at 1150.

(this function typically encompasses selection of the audit procedures and auditors as well as establishment of a formal board committee charged with oversight of the audit function);
- annual (or more frequent) review of the corporation's investments for compliance with law and regulations; and
- oversight of management (this includes evaluating performance, setting objectives and comparing performance to those objectives, and selecting and removing the CEO).

Directors are expected to devote a meaningful amount of time to their role. They must be aware of developments within the corporation, deal with any material adverse developments that are brought to their attention, and follow through with exploration and analysis when their own knowledge and expertise advises them of facts that require further scrutiny. Directors also must take care to observe their fiduciary duties to the corporation. As noted above, these fiduciary duties fall into two broad categories: the duty of loyalty and the duty of care.

### a. Duty of Loyalty

Directors and officers are fiduciaries in positions of trust, and others necessarily rely on them. Accordingly, directors and officers must defend and protect the interests entrusted to them. This duty of loyalty prohibits taking for oneself a business opportunity that properly belongs to the corporation.

This duty is derived from the self-dealing prohibition found in every fiduciary relationship. The duty of loyalty requires that officers and directors demonstrate "their utmost good faith and scrupulous, inherent fairness in transactions in which they possess a financial . . . interest that does not devolve upon the corporation."[28]

### b. Duty of Care

The duty of care obligates the officer or director to perform his or her duties in good faith, relying on adequate information, and in the best interests of the corporation as the actor reasonably believes. The care required is that which a reasonably prudent director would use in similar circumstances. Obviously, this duty requires attendance at board meetings, obtaining and using adequate information to arrive at decisions, overseeing corporate management, and carrying out other board functions.

### c. Duties of Nondirector Officers

Nondirector officers generally are held to conform to the same obligations as directors.[29] However, officers and directors have different roles within an organization. Corporate officers are personally respon-

---

[28] WILLIAM E. KNEPPER & DAN A. BAILEY, LIABILITY OF CORPORATE OFFICERS AND DIRECTORS 121 (1998).

[29] *See* MODEL BUS. CORP. ACT §8.42 (1998).

sible for their actionable torts or breach of duty. A director's liability for an officer's conduct depends on whether the director breached his or her own duty of care to the corporation. Moreover, nondirector officers and directors operate with different sets of information. An officer may, as day-to-day manager, have greater knowledge about a particular business issue than one could expect a director to have. On other matters, directors may have superior or broader knowledge. In determining whether a duty of care was satisfied, one must make a case-by-case analysis of the information available to a specific decision maker. Clearly, different information may lead to different results.

The question of whether the business judgment rule applies to non-director officers is unsettled.[30] Several Delaware cases have determined that the rule does apply to such officers.[31] However, other courts, even those purporting to apply Delaware law, have determined that it does not.[32]

### d. Other Types of Exposure

Under several statutes, corporate officers (and managing employees) may be personally excluded from participation in federal health care programs[33] if the entity that employed them has been convicted of certain offenses or excluded from participation in federal health care programs, even if the individuals themselves did not participate in the wrongdoing.[34] In addition, in certain cases, any individual, including a director or officer, convicted of a criminal offense involving the breach of fiduciary responsibility is subject to exclusion.[35] Once an individual is excluded, the employer is subject to civil monetary penalties[36] and possible exclusion for hiring him or her, and reinstatement is discretionary.[37]

## 2. Limitations on the Liability of Directors and Officers

### a. Business Judgment Rule

Not every decision made by a director is the correct one. Some decisions, viewed retrospectively, may appear less than judicious. However, the law does not permit directors' decisions to be contested as long as the directors followed appropriate procedures in arriving at the de-

---

[30]*See* KNEPPER & BAILEY, *supra* note 28, at 39.

[31]*See, e.g.,* Kelly & Wyndham, Inc. v. Bell, 266 A.2d 878 (Del. 1970).

[32]*See, e.g.,* Platt v. Richardson, Civ. No. 88-0144, Fed. Sec. L. Rep. (CCH) ¶94,786, 1989 WL 159584, at *2 (M.D. Pa June 6, 1989). For a more in-depth discussion of this issue, see KNEPPER & BAILEY, *supra* note 28, at 39.

[33]The federal health care programs include Medicare, Medicaid, Federal Employees Health Benefits Program, etc.

[34]42 U.S.C. §1320a-7(b)(15).

[35]42 U.S.C. §1320a-7(b)(1).

[36]42 U.S.C. §1320a-7a(a)(6); 42 C.F.R. §1003.102(a)(2).

[37]42 U.S.C. §1320a-7(g); 42 C.F.R. §1001.3002.

cision.[38] The business judgment rule is an important defense to claims of director mismanagement and breach of the duty of care.[39]

The business judgment rule "is a presumption that in making a business decision the directors of a corporation acted on an informed basis, in good faith and in the honest belief that the action taken was in the best interests of the company."[40] Unless an abuse of discretion is established, the courts will respect the business decision. The rule places the burden of rebutting the presumption on the challenger.[41]

The business judgment rule is composed of the following elements, each of which must generally be present to shield directors from liability:

- a business decision;
- disinterestedness: a lack of personal interest or self-dealing;
- due care: an informed decision based on a reasonable effort to become aware of important facts and circumstances; and
- good faith: a reasonable belief that the best interests of the corporation and its shareholders are being served.

The requirement that a director actually make a business decision requires action within the scope of corporate authority.[42] Questions arise concerning the applicability of the rule to inaction or failure to act. The rule provides no protection where a director has eschewed his or her role and failed to perform the function to decide. Where, however, the failure to act is a result of a conscious decision to refrain from acting, the rule applies.[43]

Disinterestedness requires that the director is not permitted to use the trust and confidence accompanying the office to expand his or her personal interests.[44] The element of disinterestedness makes the business judgment rule available only to those who are without conflict of interest. Appearing on both sides of a transaction is a paradigm example of lack of disinterestedness. Under Delaware law, directors are "interested" not solely where they are on both sides of a transaction, but

---

[38] Note that although the business judgment rule is a defense to claims of breach of fiduciary duty owed to a corporation, it has no applicability to defense of claims against directors for violation of state or federal statutes or regulations.

[39] By its focus and scope, the business judgment rule deals with claims of breach of the duty of care. Claims of self-dealing, conflict of interest, and the like involve the duty of loyalty. The business judgment rule does not insulate against claims of breach of the duty of loyalty. *See, e.g.,* Cuker v. Mikalauskas, 692 A.2d 1042 (Pa. 1997).

[40] Aronson v. Lewis, 473 A.2d 805, 812 (Del. 1984) (citations omitted), *overruled on other grounds by* Brehm v. Eisner, 746 A.2d 244 (Del. 2000). *See also* Resolution Trust Corp. v. Acton, 844 F. Supp. 307 (N.D. Tex. 1994).

[41] *See, e.g., Aronson,* 473 A.2d at 812 (citations omitted).

[42] *See, e.g.,* Crouse-Hinds Co. v. InterNorth, Inc., 634 F.2d 690, 702 (2d Cir. 1980).

[43] *See, e.g., Aronson,* 473 A.2d at 813; Rales v. Blasband, 634 A.2d 927, 933–34 (Del. 1993).

[44] *See, e.g., Aronson,* 473 A.2d at 812.

also where they expect personally to receive gain from the transaction in addition to the gain they receive as shareholders.[45]

Directors can establish the exercise of due care sufficient to invoke the business judgment rule where they have informed themselves, before the decision, of all material information reasonably available to them and acted with requisite care in assessing the information and reaching the decision. The rule will not protect directors who acted " 'so far without information that they . . . passed an unintelligent and unadvised judgment.' "[46] In *Smith v. Van Gorkum*, the Delaware Supreme Court rejected the directors' attempts to invoke the rule's protection in response to claims surrounding a merger.[47] The directors' lack of awareness of the CEO's role in championing the transaction and setting the per-share compensation and the intrinsic value of the corporation rendered their approval of the transaction with only 2 hours' consideration grossly negligent.[48] The *Van Gorkum* analysis was reiterated in *Cede & Co. v. Technicolor*, again in the context of a failure to reach an informed decision in approving the sale of the company.[49]

The general standard for determining whether a director has exercised appropriate due care is gross negligence.[50] Courts will assume that a director has made an informed decision unless the evidence demonstrates gross negligence in the director's investigation and inquiry. Gross negligence is a high standard. It includes the concepts of reckless indifference, gross abuse, and, in some instances, conscious indifference.[51] Note, however, that a magistrate judge in a 1998 case held that directors and officers would not be held liable for gross negligence; rather, liability would attach if they acted intentionally to harm the corporation.[52]

Good faith sufficient to obtain the protection of the business judgment rule generally means that the director's actions were taken in the good faith belief that the decision was in the corporation's best interests.[53] To overcome the presumption of good faith, a challenger "must show some sort of bad faith on the part of the defendant."[54] A chal-

---

[45] *See, e.g., id.*

[46] Smith v. Van Gorkum, 488 A.2d 858, 873 n.13 (Del. 1985) (quoting Mitchell v. Highland-Western Glass, 167 A. 831, 833 (Del. Ch. 1933)).

[47] 488 A.2d 858, 874–81 (Del. 1985).

[48] *See id.*

[49] 634 A.2d 345, 368–71 (Del. 1993).

[50] *See Van Gorkum*, 488 A.2d at 873 (citing *Aronson*, 473 A.2d at 812).

[51] *See, e.g.,* Briggs v. Spaulding, 141 U.S. 132 (1891), *implicitly overruled on other grounds by* Erie R.R. Co. v. Tompkins, 304 U.S. 64, 78 (1938).

[52] *See* Magistrate Judge's Report and Recommendation, at 56, McCall v. Scott, No. 3:97-0838 (M.D. Tenn. July 1, 1998). See also discussion *infra* Sections III.D.4.b.ii and III.D.5.

[53] *See Van Gorkum*, 488 A.2d at 872; *Aronson*, 473 A.2d at 812.

[54] Johnson v. Trueblood, 629 F.2d 287, 293 (3d Cir. 1980) (citation omitted), *cert. denied*, 450 U.S. 999 (1981).

lenger's hurdle is high. A court may infer bad faith only where the challenged business decision is "so far beyond the bounds of reasonable judgment that it seems essentially inexplicable on any ground other than bad faith."[55] If the decision can be attributed to "any rational business purpose," it will be considered to have been made in good faith.[56]

### b. *Statutory and Corporate Measures to Reduce Directors' and Officers' Liability*

Most state legislatures have taken steps permitting corporations to limit the personal liability of directors. The most common type of "shield" statute is the Delaware model.[57] Delaware permits corporations to enact provisions relieving directors of personal liability for damages resulting from breach of the duty of care. The law has no effect unless the corporation adopts the relief in its original charter or validly approved changes to its articles of incorporation. Accordingly, the measure adopted may be broad, as most are, or more narrow. The law provides relief for directors only—not officers. The law does not permit corporations to eliminate or restrict liability in certain areas, including the following:

- Liability for breach of the duty of loyalty remains unaffected.
- Liability is preserved for acts not undertaken in good faith.
- Directors remain liable for violation of federal statutes (e.g., the Racketeer Influenced and Corrupt Organizations Act (RICO) and securities laws).
- Attempts to obtain equitable relief (e.g., injunctions) remain unaffected.[58]

### c. *Indemnification and Insurance*

In addition to including liability limitations pursuant to statute, corporations can provide statutorily authorized indemnification to officers and directors, further protecting them from personal liability exposure. Most states have passed statutes that permit corporations to indemnify directors and officers under specified circumstances. Again, the Delaware statute is instructive, both because it serves as a model for other statutes and because of the breadth of its coverage.[59] The Delaware statute states as follows:

---

[55] *In re* J.P. Stevens & Co. Shareholders Litig., 542 A.2d 770, 780–81 (Del. Ch. 1988).

[56] Unocal Corp. v. Mesa Petroleum Co., 493 A.2d 946, 954 (Del. 1985) (citing Sinclair Oil Corp. v. Levien, 280 A.2d. 717, 720 (Del. 1971)).

[57] *See* DEL. CODE ANN. tit. 8, §102(b)(7).

[58] *See id. See also* Melvin A. Eisenberg, *Corporate Law and Social Norms*, 99 COLUM. L. REV. 1253, 1267 (June 1999).

[59] Indemnification is an internal corporate matter; as such, it generally is governed by the law of the state of incorporation. *See, e.g.,* McDermott, Inc. v. Lewis, 531 A.2d 206, 215 (Del. 1987). Delaware is the state of incorporation for many corporations.

A corporation shall have power to indemnify any person [sued or threatened to be sued] . . . by reason of the fact that the person is or was a director, officer, employee or agent of the corporation . . . [provided that] the person acted in good faith and in a manner the person reasonably believed to be in or not opposed to the best interests of the corporation, and, with respect to any criminal action or proceeding, had no reasonable cause to believe the person's conduct was unlawful.[60]

Most statutes permit, but do not require, indemnification. Some states require indemnification if the person is successful in defense of the claim. In such cases, indemnification is limited to expenses actually incurred in the defense (e.g., attorneys' fees).[61] Where indemnification is permissive, the statute generally requires a finding that the person seeking indemnification has met the applicable standards of conduct (e.g., good faith; reasonable belief that the conduct was in the corporation's best interests; and, with respect to criminal actions, no reasonable cause to believe the conduct was not lawful).[62] This determination must be made by (a) the board by a majority vote of those not a party to the proceedings, (b) independent legal counsel, or (c) the shareholders by majority vote. These statutes also frequently contain clauses that suggest that directors may have additional rights beyond those enumerated in the law, and some director compensation contracts provide benefits that exceed those available under the statute. However, some laws have categories of expenses that cannot be indemnified, including adverse final judgments or derivative suit settlements.[63]

Indemnification or other statutes also may authorize corporations to purchase insurance coverage protecting directors and officers (D&O) against liability exposure (i.e., D&O policies). The Delaware provision is typical:

A corporation shall have power to purchase and maintain insurance on behalf of any person who is or was a director, officer, employee or agent of the corporation, . . . against any liability asserted against such person and incurred by such person in any such capacity, or arising out of such person's status as such, whether or not the corporation would have the power to indemnify such person against such liability under this section.[64]

Thus, a corporation is empowered to purchase D&O policies providing broader protection than the corporation itself may provide through corporate indemnification. D&O policies are available with a wide variety of terms and conditions. The exclusions limiting coverage differ widely, as do the circumstances required for an insured to qualify for the protections offered by the policy.

---

[60] DEL. STAT. ANN. tit 8, §145(a).

[61] *See, e.g.*, N.Y. BUS. CORP. LAW §723 (McKinney 1999).

[62] DEL. CODE ANN. tit. 8, §§145(d), (a).

[63] *See* Mae Kuykendall, *Assessment and Evaluation: Retheorizing the Evolving Rules of Director Liability*, 8 J.L. & POL'Y 1, 6 (1999).

[64] DEL. CODE ANN. tit. 8, §145(g).

D&O policies often offer two types of coverage within the same policy. The first type of coverage indemnifies directors and officers for losses for which they are not indemnified by the corporation (personal coverage). The second type of coverage reimburses the corporation for monies that it lawfully expends in indemnifying its directors and officers for their losses (reimbursement coverage).

## III. LITIGATION AGAINST OFFICERS AND DIRECTORS

Directors and officers face the risk of civil lawsuits when shareholders suspect fraud or mismanagement, when the price of the company's stock falls, and under a wide variety of other circumstances. The vehicles for bringing such complaints to court most commonly are shareholder derivative actions and class action suits.

### A. Shareholder Derivative Actions

*1. Shareholder Derivative Actions in General*

A shareholder derivative action is a case brought by a shareholder or a group of shareholders against directors and/or officers of the company. The claim is brought on behalf of the corporation, and it is one that the corporation is unwilling to assert itself.[65] As such, the claim (or loss) is not the shareholders' but the corporation's, and the recovery, if any, belongs not to the complaining shareholders but to the corporation. The derivative suit is an equitable creation designed to provide a remedy for a breach of the fiduciary duty a director or officer owes to the corporation where the corporation will not act to address the breach.[66]

Several important preconditions or requirements attach to derivative actions and serve to limit them:

- The corporation must have failed to enforce a right after demand on its managers to do so.
- The corporation may properly assert that right.
- The plaintiff must have been a shareholder at the time of the transaction complained of.
- The action must not be collusive.
- The plaintiff must fairly and adequately represent the interests of similarly situated shareholders.[67]

*2. Presuit Demand Requirements*

The first condition for a shareholder derivative action—that the corporation must have failed to enforce a right—establishes that the plaintiff is suing to enforce a corporate right. Claim of injury to a group

---

[65]*See, e.g.,* Ross v. Bernhard, 396 U.S. 531, 534 (1970).

[66]*See, e.g.,* Koster v. (American) Lumbermens Mut. Cas. Co., 330 U.S. 518, 522 (1947).

[67]*See* FED. R. CIV. P. 23.1; *see also* DEL. CODE ANN. tit. 8, §327.

of shareholders, for instance, is not a corporate claim enforceable by derivative action in the name of the corporation. Suing to enforce a corporate right is not itself sufficient: The plaintiff must "allege with particularity the efforts . . . made by the plaintiff to obtain the [desired] action . . . from the directors or comparable authority and, if necessary, from the stockholders or members, and the reasons for . . . fail[ing] to obtain the action or for not making the effort."[68]

The purpose of this demand requirement is to

> insure that a stockholder exhausts his intracorporate remedies, and then to provide a safeguard against strike suits. Thus, by promoting this form of alternative dispute resolution, rather than immediate recourse to litigation, the demand requirement is a recognition of the fundamental precept that directors manage the business and affairs of the corporations.[69]

The demand requirement merely obliges shareholders to communicate to the directors the identity of the alleged wrongdoer(s), describe the facts and the legal theories available, identify the shareholder(s), describe the injury to the corporation, and specifically request the action.[70] No particular form of written communication or level of formality is required.

Plaintiffs frequently assert that demand on the corporation would be futile and should be excused. Delaware excuses the demand requirement only if facts are alleged with particularity that create a reasonable doubt that the directors' action was entitled to the business judgment rule. According to the Delaware Supreme Court in *Aronson v. Lewis*, a plaintiff must show either that a majority of the directors were not independent and disinterested or that because of the substance of the transaction or the manner in which they reached their decision, the directors could not have validly exercised business judgment.[71] However, the *Aronson* test is inapplicable in cases where the board is accused of inaction:

> [T]he absence of board action, therefore, makes it impossible to perform the essential inquiry contemplated by *Aronson*—whether the directors have acted in conformity with the business judgment rule in approving the challenged transaction. . . .
> [A] court should not apply the *Aronson* test for demand futility where the board that would be considering the demand did not make a business decision which is being challenged in the derivative suit. . . .
> [Demand is necessary] where directors are sued derivatively because they have failed to do something (such as a failure to oversee subordinates).[72]

---

[68] FED. R. CIV. P. 23.1.

[69] Aronson v. Lewis, 473 A.2d 805, 811–12 (Del. 1984), *overruled on other grounds by* Brehm v. Eisner, 746 A.2d 244 (Del. 2000).

[70] *See, e.g.,* Allison v. General Motors Corp., 604 F. Supp. 1106, 1117 (D. Del. 1986), *aff'd*, 782 F.2d 1026 (3d Cir. 1985).

[71] *See Aronson*, 473 A.2d at 812–13; *Brehm*, 746 A.2d at 254–56 (reaffirming the *Aronson* standard but rejecting *Aronson*'s deference to the Chancery Court's demand-futility analysis in favor of de novo review of the issue).

[72] Rales v. Blasband, 634 A.2d 927, 933–34 & n.9 (Del. 1993).

In such circumstances "Delaware courts will excuse a failure to make . . . a demand if a majority of the board was interested or lacked independence to review the derivative claim."[73]

The American Law Institute (ALI) has proposed a "universal demand" requirement under which the *Aronson* demand-futility exemption is abolished. The rule excuses demand *only* "if the plaintiff makes a specific showing that irreparable injury to the corporation would otherwise result," and even then it requires demand promptly after commencement of the action.[74] Pennsylvania adopted the ALI universal-demand rule in an opinion critical of Delaware's more liberal rule.[75] Moreover, the Model Business Corporation Act's strict-demand rule has been adopted by 15 states as of September 1, 2001.[76] The Model Act prohibits suit until 90 days after a written demand is made, unless the demand is rejected earlier or unless waiting for the 90-day period to expire would result in irreparable injury to the corporation.[77] A minority of jurisdictions also require that if the board of directors rejects the demand, shareholders must present the demand to all other shareholders before they can file a derivative suit.[78] This requirement has been adopted to allow the majority of shareholders to determine whether the suit is in the corporation's best interest.

### 3. Other Requirements for Derivative Actions

The remaining requirements for derivative actions collectively constitute standing requirements. The plaintiff must be a stockholder of the corporation whose interests he or she seeks to enforce. He or she

---

[73]Katz v. Halpen, No. 13,811, 1996 WL 66006, at *7 (Del. Ch. Feb. 5, 1996), *reprinted in* 21 DEL. J. CORP. L. 690 (1996).

[74]1 ALI PRINCIPLES OF CORPORATE GOVERNANCE: ANALYSIS AND RECOMMENDATIONS §7.03(b) (1994).

[75]*See, e.g.,* Cuker v. Mikalauskas, 692 A.2d 1042, 1048–49 (Pa. 1997). *See also* Audio Visual Xperts, Inc. v. Walker, No. 17261-NC, 2000 WL 222152, at *2 (Del. Ch. Feb. 18, 2000) (recognizing Pennsylvania's adoption of the ALI demand requirement).

[76]*See, e.g.,* ARIZ. REV. STAT. ANN. §10-742; CONN. GEN. STAT. ANN. §33-722; GA. CODE ANN. §14-2-742; IDAHO CODE §30-1-742; ME. REV. STAT. ANN. tit. 13A, §630; MICH. COMP. LAW. ANN. §450.1493a; MISS. CODE ANN. §79-4-7.42; MONT. CODE ANN. §35-1-543; NEB. REV. STAT. §21-2072; N.H. REV. STAT. ANN. §293-A:7.42; N.C. GEN. STAT. §55-7-42; TEX. BUS. CORP. ACT ANN. art. 5.14C; VA. CODE ANN. §13.1-672.1(B); WIS. STAT. ANN. §180.0742; WYO. STAT. ANN. §17-16-742.

[77]*See* MODEL BUS. CORP. ACT §7–42.

[78]*See* Wolgin v. Simon, 722 F.2d 389, 392 (8th Cir. 1993) (Missouri); Allright Missouri, Inc. v. Billeter, 829 F.2d 631, 639 (8th Cir. 1987) (Missouri); Strougo on behalf of Brazil Fund, Inc. v. Scudder, Stevens & Clark, Inc., 964 F. Supp. 783, 795 (S.D.N.Y. 1997) (Maryland); Grill v. Hoblitzell, 771 F. Supp. 709, 713 n.5 (D. Md. 1991) (Maryland); Bell v. Arnold, 487 P.2d 545, 547–48 (Colo. 1997) (Colorado); Harhen v. Brown, 730 N.E.2d 859, 868 (Mass. 2000) (Massachusetts); Skolnik v. Rose, 55 N.Y.2d 964, 965, 434 N.E.2d 251, 252, 449 N.Y.S.2d 182, 183 (1982) (Massachusetts); McLeese v. J.C. Nichols Co., 842 S.W.2d 115, 119 (Mo. Ct. App. 1992) (Missouri); Burdon v. Erskine, 401 A.2d 369, 370–71 (Pa. Super. Ct. 1979) (Pennsylvania).

must have been a stockholder at the time of the alleged injury or a successor to the shares by operation of law.[79] One cannot buy the right to bring a derivative action by purchasing shares after the conduct complained of has occurred.[80]

As individuals seeking to vindicate the rights of others, derivative plaintiffs must be prepared to demonstrate their adequacy to fill that role. This question of adequate representation usually requires a showing that plaintiffs' counsel is qualified and experienced in these matters and generally able to thoroughly and diligently prosecute the case.[81] The courts also will look to plaintiffs' interests and require a demonstration that those interests are not antagonistic to interests of similarly situated shareholders.[82]

Derivative actions may not be dismissed or settled without court approval. The parties must provide notice to shareholders in a form and manner approved by the court.[83] Part of the court's responsibility is to ensure that the proposed settlement is fair to the parties, reasonable, and adequate.[84]

## B. Class Actions

Class actions, like shareholder derivative actions, face substantial procedural hurdles. Class actions, however, do not seek to assert claims of injury to the corporation. Rather, class actions seek compensation for harm done directly to the class members, often shareholders. Class actions are predicated on the theory that a few representative individuals effectively can become advocates in litigation for others in a similar situation. The class action device makes it economically feasible for a group of plaintiffs with relatively small claims to aggregate them, pursue them, and obtain relief.

### 1. Class Action Requirements

Rule 23 of the *Federal Rules of Civil Procedure* sets forth the requirements for maintenance of a class action:

- *Commonality*. There must be question of law or fact common to the class of plaintiffs.
- *Typicality*. The claims of the representative plaintiffs must be typical of the claims of the class.
- *Numerosity*. The class must be so numerous that actual joinder in the action of all class members is not practicable.

---

[79] *See* FED. R. CIV. P. 23.1; DEL. CODE ANN. tit. 8, §327.

[80] *See, e.g.,* Blasband v. Rales, 971 F.2d 1034, 1041 (3d Cir. 1992).

[81] *See, e.g.,* Wetzel v. Liberty Mut. Ins. Co., 508 F.2d 239, 247 (3d Cir.), *cert. denied,* 421 U.S. 1011 (1975).

[82] *See id.*

[83] *See* FED. R. CIV. P. 23.1.

[84] *See, e.g.,* Prince v. Bensinger, 244 A.2d 89, 93 (Del. Ch. 1968).

- *Adequacy of representation.* The representative plaintiffs must be able to adequately represent the class.

Additionally, Rule 23 requires a showing of one of the following: (a) separate, non-class actions would create a risk of incompatible standards of conduct being established or would be dispositive as to nonparties; (b) the class as a whole may be entitled to injunctive or declaratory relief; or (c) the common questions of law or fact "predominate" over questions affecting only individual class members, and a class action is the superior method for the fair and efficient adjudication of the controversy.

Much litigation has surrounded the implementation of these standards.[85] With respect to commonality, courts look to whether class members are "united by a common interest"[86] or have the same case to prove.[87] While minor differences in facts will not prohibit maintenance of the class, claims that contain characteristics unique to each class member do not meet the commonality requirement.[88]

Numerosity is satisfied when the aggregate number of potential class members is so large that joinder of each as individual plaintiffs is impracticable. Class members typically exceed 100 in number; however, the numbers may vary. Class actions have been permitted to proceed with as few as 18 members,[89] while 95 has been deemed too few.[90]

Typicality requires that the named representatives' claims be sufficiently like the claims of others that one can assume that the interests of those others will not be neglected. Typicality does not exist where the conflict between such sets of interests is material, at the core of the controversy, and directly related to the subject matter.[91]

Adequacy of representation seeks to ensure that the named plaintiff will discharge his or her fiduciary duties to the class as its representative in the litigation.[92] The named plaintiff's interests must be sufficiently aligned with class members' to establish that his or her incentive to prosecute the matter is consistent with his or her obligation as a fiduciary. In addition, courts will consider the experience of plaintiff's counsel in class action litigation to arrive at a determination that counsel representing the class will themselves properly pursue the litigation.[93]

---

[85] *See, e.g.,* HERBERT B. NEWBERG & ALBA CONTE, NEWBERG ON CLASS ACTIONS (3d ed. 1992).

[86] Blackie v. Barrack, 524 F.2d 891, 902 (9th Cir. 1975), *cert. denied,* 429 U.S. 816 (1976).

[87] *See, e.g.,* Castro v. Becker, 459 F.2d 725, 732 (1st Cir. 1972).

[88] *See, e.g., In re* Fibreboard Corp., 893 F.2d 706, 712 (5th Cir. 1990).

[89] *See* Gaspar v. Linvatec Corp., 167 F.R.D. 51, 56 (N.D. Ill. 1996).

[90] *See, e.g.,* Joshlin v. Gannett River States Publ'g Corp., 152 F.R.D. 577, 579 (E.D. Ark. 1993).

[91] *See, e.g.,* Redmond v. Commerce Trust Co., 144 F.2d 140, 151–52 (8th Cir. 1944).

[92] *See, e.g.,* Koenig v. Benson, 117 F.R.D. 330, 333–34 (E.D.N.Y. 1987).

[93] *See, e.g., In re* Northern Dist. of Cal., Dalkon Shield IUD Prods. Liab. Litig., 693 F.2d 847, 855 (9th Cir. 1982).

Settlement or dismissal of class action matters requires court approval and notice to the class members. Approval by the court will be dependent on a finding that the settlement is fair to the various class members.[94] Settlement of a class action requires a court determination that the requirements for maintaining a class action have been met. Parties may not agree to a "settlement class" unless that class meets the class requirements set forth in Rule 23.[95]

### 2. *Class Not Limited to Shareholders*

While commonly brought to vindicate the rights of a group of shareholders against officers and directors, class actions are in no sense limited to claims of shareholders. For instance, class actions are a particularly common device for maintaining securities fraud claims. The class can be quite large, including trading plaintiffs in its number. Such claims frequently are based on alleged material misrepresentations or omissions of directors and officers.

Similarly, any aggrieved group can assert direct class actions against directors and officers. For example, in *Spitzer v. Abdelhak*,[96] the plaintiffs were physicians who sold their practices to a large health care organization. The plaintiffs claimed that they were defrauded in the sale of their practices; they brought a class action suit on behalf of similarly situated physicians against the purchaser and certain of its officers and directors. The plaintiffs alleged violations of RICO[97] and state common law claims.

### C. The *Caremark* Decision

*In re Caremark International Derivative Litigation*,[98] a case that coincidentally involved a health care provider, has become a focal point for those concerned with potential liability for corporate directors and officers. During the relevant period, Caremark's primary lines of business involved alternative-site health care services, including infusion therapy, growth hormone therapy, and certain managed care services such as prescription drug programs.[99] Beginning in 1994, Caremark's shareholders filed a number of derivative lawsuits[100] claiming that the mem-

---

[94] *See, e.g.,* Amchem Prods., Inc. v. Windsor, 521 U.S. 591, 619–22 (1997).

[95] *See id.*

[96] No. 98-6475, 1999 WL 1204352 (E.D. Pa. Dec. 15, 1999). *Spitzer* is discussed at length *infra* Section III.E.

[97] *See* 18 U.S.C. §§1951–60.

[98] 698 A.2d 959 (Del. Ch. 1996).

[99] *See id.* at 961.

[100] Five stockholder derivative actions alleging breach of the directors' duty of care were filed (and consolidated) in the Delaware Chancery Court. The complaint was amended three times in response to additional indictments and allegations concerning kickbacks, improper referrals, and overbilling resulting from an ongoing investigation by the government. The final, amended complaint added allegations that the federal indictments had caused Caremark to incur significant legal fees and forced it to sell its home infusion business at a loss. Several shareholder derivative suits were also filed in other jurisdictions. *See id.* at 964.

bers of Caremark's board of directors breached their fiduciary duty of care to the corporation in connection with alleged violations by Caremark employees of federal and state laws applicable to health care providers, including the federal anti-kickback statute.[101]

## 1. Background of the Case

A brief review of the underlying facts in this case, including Caremark's compliance activities and the government's investigation, is instructive. Beginning in 1989, Caremark began issuing a *Guide to Contractual Relationships* to help its employees comply with certain laws, including the federal anti-kickback statute.[102] The *Guide* generally was reviewed annually by legal counsel and updated.[103] In July 1991, when the safe harbors to the anti-kickback statute were published, many of Caremark's standard contract forms were amended to comply with the safe harbors.[104]

Beginning in August 1991, the HHS OIG began an investigation of Caremark's predecessor organization.[105] The investigation was joined by the DOJ and several additional state and federal agencies, and focused on potentially improper patient referrals, billing practices, medically unnecessary treatments, waivers of patient copayments, and the adequacy of records kept by Caremark pharmacies.[106] In response to these investigations, Caremark implemented an internal audit plan and instituted new compliance policies (e.g., requiring regional officers to approve each contract between Caremark and a physician and requiring local branch managers to certify compliance with the corporation's ethics program).[107] Further, Caremark retained an outside auditor (Price Waterhouse) to prepare a report, which concluded that there were no material weaknesses in Caremark's control structure.[108] In addition, Caremark initiated a comprehensive review of its compliance policies and the compilation of an employee ethics handbook.[109]

The Caremark board apparently was advised of these and other compliance initiatives, which included training sessions provided to Caremark's sales force and a letter sent by Caremark's president to all senior, district, and branch managers specifically stating that (1) physicians were not to be paid for referrals, (2) the standard contract forms in the *Guide* were not to be modified, and (3) deviation from these poli-

---

[101] 42 U.S.C. §1320a-7b(b).

[102] *See Caremark*, 698 A.2d at 962.

[103] *See id.*

[104] *See id.*

[105] *See id.*

[106] *See id.* at 962 n.2.

[107] *See id.* at 963.

[108] *See id.*

[109] *See id.*

cies would result in immediate termination.[110] In addition, the chief financial officer was appointed as Caremark's chief compliance officer.

The Caremark board was informed when a grand jury indictment was issued in August 1994 against the corporation, two of its officers, an employee, and a physician for anti-kickback violations.[111] Caremark's management advised the board at this time of the basis for its view that the challenged contracts were in compliance with the law.[112]

In June 1995, the Caremark board approved a settlement agreement with numerous government agencies[113] for over $160 million[114] and agreed to enter into a compliance agreement with HHS. (Notably, neither the settlement agreement nor any of the prior indictments charged any senior officers or directors of Caremark with direct participation in any wrongdoing.)[115] In March 1996, the Caremark board also approved a $98 million settlement agreement with certain private payers.[116]

With regard to the shareholder derivative suit, the defendants filed a motion to dismiss, contending that the complaint failed to allege particularized facts to excuse the demand requirement under Delaware law and that Caremark's charter eliminated director personal liability for money damages to the extent permitted by law.[117] The parties began settlement negotiations and presented the proposed terms of a settlement to the court to determine whether it was fair and reasonable to protect the best interests of the corporation and its absent shareholders. In this context, the court approved the settlement agreement as reasonable given the weakness of the plaintiffs' claims.[118]

## 2. The Court's Decision

The court began its analysis by stating that a claim for director duty of care violations based on inadequate director monitoring of corporate performance is "possibly the most difficult theory in corporation law upon which a plaintiff might hope to win a judgment."[119] According

---

[110] *See id.* at 963 & n.5.

[111] *See id.* at 963–64.

[112] *See id.* at 966.

[113] These agencies included the DOJ, the OIG, the Veterans Administration, the Federal Employee Health Benefits Program, the Civilian Health and Medical Program of the Uniformed Services (CHAMPUS; now Tricare), and related state agencies in all 50 states and the District of Columbia. *See Caremark,* 698 A.2d at 965.

[114] This included $29 million in criminal fines, $129.9 million for civil claims relating to payment practices, and $5.5 million in additional penalties. *See id.* at 965 n.10.

[115] As part of the sentencing process in an Ohio action, the United States stipulated that no senior executive of Caremark had participated in, condoned, or was willfully ignorant of wrongdoing in connection with the home infusion business.

[116] *See Caremark,* 698 A.2d at 966.

[117] *See id.* at 964–65.

[118] *See id.* at 960–61.

[119] *Id.* at 967.

to the court, director liability for a breach of the duty to exercise appropriate attention theoretically may arise in two different contexts: (a) when a board decision results in loss because the decision was ill advised or negligent or (b) when the board fails to act under circumstances in which due attention would have prevented the loss.[120]

### a. Board's Duty of Care Responsibilities

Citing *Aronson v. Lewis*,[121] to the effect that the first type of case should be analyzed under the business judgment rule, the *Caremark* court stated that "compliance with a director's duty of care can never appropriately be judicially determined by reference to *the content of a board decision* . . . apart from consideration of the good faith or rationality of the *process* employed."[122] In other words,

> [W]hether a magistrate judge or jury considering the matter after the fact, believes a decision substantively wrong, or degrees of wrong extending through "stupid" to "egregious" or "irrational," provides no ground for director liability, so long as the court determines that the process employed was either rational or employed in *a good faith* effort to advance corporate interests.[123]

The court concluded that the business judgment rule is "process oriented" and that the concept of negligence is not appropriately used for judicial review of board attentiveness, particularly if looking at the substance of the board's decision for evidence of such negligence.[124] Referring to Learned Hand's opinion in *Barnes v. Andrews*,[125] the *Caremark* court stated that the core element of any corporate law duty of care is whether there has been a good faith effort to be informed and exercise judgment.[126]

There is considerable discussion in the *Caremark* opinion of *Graham v. Allis-Chalmers Manufacturing Co.*,[127] which involved the liability of board members for losses experienced by a corporation resulting from anti-trust violations.[128] The plaintiffs in *Graham* did not allege that the board members knew about improper employee behavior, but rather that the directors should have known so that they could have brought the corporation into compliance.[129] The *Graham* court concluded that "absent cause for suspicion there is no duty upon the directors to install and operate a corporate system of espionage to ferret

---

[120] *See id.* (citation omitted).

[121] 473 A.2d 805 (Del. 1984).

[122] *See Caremark*, 698 A.2d at 967 (second emphasis added).

[123] *Id.* at 967.

[124] *See id.* at 967–68.

[125] 298 F. 614, 618 (E.D.N.Y. 1924).

[126] *See* 698 A.2d at 968.

[127] 188 A.2d 125 (Del. 1963).

[128] *See* 698 A.2d at 969.

[129] *See id.*

out wrongdoing which they have no reason to suspect exists."[130] Using this standard, the *Graham* court held that the directors did not have grounds for suspicion and thus were not liable.[131] As explained by the *Caremark* court, absent grounds to suspect deception, corporate boards and senior officers cannot be "charged with wrongdoing simply for assuming the integrity of employees and the honesty of their dealings on the company's behalf."[132]

### b. Appropriate Information Gathering and Reporting Systems

Nevertheless, the *Caremark* court refused to accept a broad reading of the *Graham* decision, stating that in light of more recent legal developments, including the effect of the U.S. Sentencing Guidelines, the Delaware Supreme Court would be unlikely to accept the proposition that corporate boards have no responsibility to ensure that management implements appropriate information gathering and reporting systems that are reasonably designed to provide senior management and the board with timely, accurate information to allow each to reach informed judgments concerning compliance with the law and business performance.[133] The *Caremark* court acknowledged that the level of detail that such information gathering systems must have is a question of business judgment, and ultimately it held that the board must exercise a good faith judgment that the corporation's information gathering and reporting system is, in concept and design, adequate to ensure the board that appropriate information will come to its attention in a timely manner as a matter of ordinary operations.[134]

On facts before it, the *Caremark* court found that there was no knowing violation of law, particularly because experts had informed the Caremark board that the company's practices, although subject to some question, were lawful.[135] Moreover, the duty to act in good faith to be informed does not require that the directors have detailed information about all aspects of a company's operations.[136] With regard to the "failure to monitor" claim, the court held that "only a sustained or systematic failure of the board to exercise oversight—such as an utter failure to attempt to assure a reasonable information and reporting system exists—will establish the lack of good faith that is a necessary condition to liability."[137]

It is important to remember the procedural posture of the case. The court was assessing the adequacy of the oversight exercised by the

---

[130] *Id.* at 969 (quoting Graham v. Allis-Chalmers Mfg. Co., 188 A.2d 125, 130 (Del. 1963)).

[131] *See* 698 A.2d at 969.

[132] *Id.* (citation omitted).

[133] *See id.* at 969–70.

[134] *See id.*

[135] *See id.* at 971.

[136] *See id.*

[137] *Id.*

Caremark board only in the context of evaluating the fairness and reasonableness of the proposed settlement. Nevertheless, the court found that there was no evidence that the directors were guilty of a sustained failure to exercise their oversight function and could not be faulted if they did not know the specifics of the activities that led to the indictments.[138] Although the Caremark settlement agreement required that the corporation adopt certain additional compliance measures, the court characterized these measures as "modest" but adequate given the underlying weakness of the plaintiffs' claims.[139]

Therefore, although raising the possibility that corporate boards could face liability for failing to implement a reasonable information gathering and reporting system, the *Caremark* decision ostensibly set a fairly high standard that plaintiffs must meet to demonstrate that a board has breached its duty of care. A close examination of the facts in *Caremark*, however, indicates that this standard is not as high as it may first appear because the Caremark corporation was, in fact, unusually active in the compliance area from an early stage. Although the OIG did not begin publishing documents providing compliance guidance for various types of health care organizations until the late 1990s,[140] Caremark started to implement certain compliance activities beginning almost a decade earlier, in 1989. From that time forward, the Caremark board oversaw a range of compliance initiatives, including the development of certain standards, education and training, auditing, and monitoring. There was clear involvement in these compliance efforts by the highest levels of corporate personnel (e.g., in 1993 the president of the corporation sent a letter to branch managers providing further guidance on certain compliance policies). Although Caremark's compliance efforts initially did not have a comprehensive, formal structure, it is not surprising that a court would have suggested the board's compliance oversight was reasonable under the circumstances. The question remains as to what level of board oversight a court would find reasonable and adequate today given the detailed prescriptions for compliance programs provided in the OIG's Compliance Program Guidance documents.

## D. The Columbia/HCA Litigation

Because the *Caremark* opinion was handed down in the context of court approval of a settlement, the issue of the necessity for presuit demand was never decided. However, this issue has taken on a great deal of importance in other cases, notably including the Columbia/HCA litigation.

---

[138]*See id.* at 971–72.

[139]*Id.* at 972.

[140]The first such guidance—for clinical laboratories—was not published in proposed form until 1997, and it was not finalized until 1998. *See* Publication of OIG Compliance Program Guidance for Clinical Laboratories, 63 Fed. Reg. 45,076 (1998).

## 1. *Columbia/HCA Operations and Government Investigations*

The numerous government investigations and lawsuits surrounding Columbia/HCA have been extensively publicized.[141] To briefly summarize, in 1997, Columbia Corporation (Columbia or Columbia/HCA), now HCA–The Healthcare Company, was one of the largest hospital companies in the world, owning 348 hospitals and treating 125,000 people per day. The company and its affiliates had operations in 37 states, including a comprehensive health care network with home health agencies and surgery centers. As part of an ongoing federal investigation, 200 federal agents from four federal agencies[142] raided two Columbia hospitals in El Paso, Texas, in March 1997. *The New York Times* had been conducting its own investigation and published an article describing improper practices at Columbia, including upcoding, improper referrals for home health care, possible violations of the Stark statute prohibiting physician self-referrals, and suspicious Medicare charges for respiratory patients. The newspaper also reported a 7-percent drop in the company's stock price 2 days after the government raid,[143] and the first class action and derivative complaint against Columbia by its shareholders was filed on April 8, 1997.[144]

Allegations against Columbia continued to surface in the media, including quotes from several former Columbia administrators about illegal activities going on within the company. The government expanded its investigation in July 1997 by serving 35 sealed search warrants on Columbia facilities in 7 states related to their Medicare cost reports. With heavy media coverage of these events, stock prices dropped another 12.2 percent. Meanwhile, several other government agencies joined the investigation.

Three Columbia executives from Florida were indicted in July 1997 and charged with conspiring to defraud the government by submitting false cost reports to the Medicare and CHAMPUS programs for reimbursement.[145] The government alleged a scheme in which hos-

---

[141] For a detailed description, see DENNIS KLEIN, PROTECTING DIRECTORS AND OFFICERS OF HOSPITALS AND HEALTHCARE ORGANIZATIONS FROM CIVIL LIABILITY 12–23 (American Health Lawyers Ass'n 1999). In addition, 12 pages of HCA's September 2000 quarterly report were devoted to summarizing each of the many state and federal legal proceedings that the company faced. *See* THE HEALTHCARE CO., SEPTEMBER 2000 QUARTERLY REPORT 31–42 (Nov. 18, 2000), *available at* http://news.moneycentral.msn.com/sec/legal.asp?Symbol=HCA [hereinafter HCA SEPT. 2000 QUARTERLY REPORT].

[142] The Federal Bureau of Investigation (FBI), the Internal Revenue Service, HHS, and the Department of Defense Criminal Investigations Service.

[143] Martin Gottlieb & Kurt Eichenwald, *For Biggest Hospital Operation a Debate Over Ties That Bind*, N.Y. TIMES, Apr. 6, 1997, at A4.

[144] *See* Morse Complaint, Morse v. McWhorter, No. 97-CV-370, 1998 U.S. Dist. LEXIS 19053 (M.D. Tenn. July 1, 1998), *appeal pending*, No. 00-6478 (6th Cir.). The *Morse* court dismissed the shareholders' complaint with prejudice on July 28, 2000.

[145] *See* Keith Snyder, *Two Columbia/HCA Executives Found Guilty of Fraud, Conspiracy*, TENNESSEAN, July 3, 1999, *available at* http://www.tennessean.com/sii/99/07/03/columbia03.shtml.

pital debt was submitted in a category that led to Columbia improperly receiving 100-percent reimbursement from federal government programs. In addition, the government charged that these executives had failed to notify authorities of an accounting error that had resulted in additional unjustified reimbursement. Two of the executives were convicted, sentenced to prison, and ordered to pay restitution and fines totaling more than $1 million.[146]

At this point, the value of the company's stock had fallen 19 percent since March 1997, and Richard Scott was removed as chairman of the board of directors and replaced by Thomas Frist, who initiated an internal investigation.

On December 14, 2000, Columbia, by then known as HCA/The Healthcare Company (HCA), signed a plea agreement with the DOJ that resolved all then-pending federal criminal claims against the company arising out of the investigation initiated more than 3 years earlier.[147] On the same day, the company signed a civil settlement agreement and a corporate integrity agreement (CIA) with the DOJ, as previously announced in May 2000.[148] Under the criminal and civil agreements, HCA must pay a combined total of approximately $840 million in restitution and fines.

DOJ officials emphasize that "even though the Government and HCA . . . have reached a settlement, the Government will continue to investigate and prosecute any individuals [presumably including any directors and officers] who committed illegal acts in relation to this case."[149] In addition, the civil settlement resolved only those issues relating to outpatient laboratory billing, home health issues, and diagnosis related group (DRG) upcoding, leaving cost reporting and other issues open. In fact, the United States has intervened in 8 existing *qui tam* cases, and *qui tam* relators are currently pursuing 12 others without the participation of the United States.[150] Furthermore, HCA and

---

[146]*See Hospital Official Gets 33 Months in Prison*, APBNEWS.COM, Dec. 22, 1999, *available at* http://www.apbnews.com/newscenter/breakingnews/1999/12/22/hospitalexec1222_01.html. *See also* HCA SEPT. 2000 QUARTERLY REPORT, *supra* note 141, at 31.

[147]*See HCA Signs Agreements in Columbia Investigation: Columbia Management Companies, Inc. and Columbia Homecare Group, Inc. Agree to Pleas*, PRNewswire, Dec. 14, 2000, *available at* http://news.moneycentral.msn.com/ticker/article.asp?Symbol=US:HCA&Feed=PR&Date=20001214&ID=418176 [hereinafter *HCA Signs Agreements*].

[148]*See id. See also* Press Release, U.S. Dep't of Justice, *Attorney General Announces Largest Department of Justice Fraud Settlement in History* (Dec. 14, 2000), *available at* http://www.usdoj. gov:80/opa/pr/2000/December/697ag.htm.

[149]*See* Press Release, *HCA—The Health Care Company to Pay Over $30 Million in El Paso; $840 Million Nationwide in Settlement for Fraudulent Billing Practices* (Dec. 14, 2000), *available at* http://www.usdoj.gov:80/usao/txw/columbia.htm. *See also* William Borden, *Hospitals to Get Less Scrutiny Under Bush Analysts*, REUTERS, Dec. 15, 2000, *available at* http://news.moneycentral.msn. com/ticker/article.asp?Symbol=US:HCA&Feed=RTR&Date=20001215&ID=421294.

[150]*See HCA Signs Agreements, supra* note 147.

those who served as officers and directors during the times of the alleged improprieties still face numerous unresolved private actions, including federal and state shareholder derivative actions, class actions, and patient/payer suits.[151] The text that follows covers the most notable of the HCA shareholder derivative actions.

## 2. *Shareholders' Allegations in* McCall v. Scott

On August 13, 1997, the second major shareholder derivative action, *McCall v. Scott*,[152] was filed. At this time, the judge consolidated all class actions under the *Morse v. McWhorter* suit,[153] while all derivative actions were consolidated under *McCall*. Both actions contained allegations that HCA's ineffective compliance program led to the government investigation, which had resulted in a 40-percent drop in stock prices, and that the illegal acts occurred because of the knowledge or reckless disregard of the HCA board. The *McCall* suit named as defendants the corporation and certain HCA directors or officers[154] and specifically alleged that they had intentionally and negligently breached their fiduciary duties and engaged in illegal insider trading.

The specific allegations included charges of upcoding and that senior management, with the HCA board's knowledge, had adopted a management policy that gave its employees "strong incentive" to commit fraud.[155] In addition, the complaint alleged numerous improper cost-reporting practices, e.g., disguising non-reimbursable facility-acquisition costs as reimbursable management fees; "grossing up" outpatient revenues that affected the cost-to-charge ratio leading to improper reimbursement; seeking unjustified reimbursement for advertising and marketing expenses and for funds expended to recruit physicians; and improperly shifting costs on cost reports to obtain unwarranted reimbursement.[156] There also were allegations that HCA

---

[151]*See* HCA Sept. 2000 Quarterly Report, *supra* note 141, at 35–41.

[152]Complaint, McCall v. Scott, No. 3:97-0838 (M.D. Tenn. Aug. 13, 1997).

[153]No. 97-CV-370, 1998 U.S. Dist. LEXIS 19053 (M.D. Tenn. July 1, 1998), *appeal pending*, No. 00-6478 (6th Cir.). The court dismissed the shareholders' complaint, with prejudice on July 28, 2000. The *Morse* action is discussed briefly *supra* text accompanying note 144.

[154]The named defendants were Thomas Frist, Richard Scott, David Vandewater, R. Clayton McWhorter, Magdalena Averhoff, Frank S. Royal, T. Michael Long, William R. Young, Donald MacNaughton, Carl Reichart, and Sister Judith Ann Karam.

[155]This policy involved setting targets of 15–20% growth; allegedly three to four times the industry average. *McCall*, No. 3:97-0838, ¶17. HCA purportedly paid cash bonuses up to 50% of base salary to encourage managers to meet these growth targets. *See id.* ¶18c.

[156]HCA allegedly assigned square footage to its comprehensive outpatient rehabilitation facilities (CORFs) when the space actually was used for services unrelated to CORFs. Nonreimbursable items, such as gift shops, were shifted from a hospital to the home health operations where they could be reimbursed, and interest expenses were shifted from one facility to another. *See id.* ¶19.

offered improper inducements to physicians to induce referrals[157] and overbilled (e.g., without regard to medical necessity), and billed for in-patient services that should have been billed as outpatient services.[158]

The plaintiffs also noted that HCA was a defendant in numerous *qui tam* False Claims Act cases, including more than 12 in which the government intervened, and was a defendant in two whistleblower actions involving former employees. The corporation also was a defendant in a federal antitrust lawsuit and a private RICO class action. Private payers also were allegedly investigating HCA's billing practices.[159]

The plaintiffs alleged that the individual defendants committed various securities violations by signing 10-K forms that misrepresented or omitted material facts about HCA's financial position and its compliance with federal law. The plaintiffs alleged that these acts and omissions created personal liability for the directors, which created a conflict of interest that prevented them from acting in the corporation's best interest.

The plaintiffs also alleged various types of corporate damage resulting from the defendants' actions, including (1) the securities class actions for damages; (2) possible exclusion from Medicare and other federal health care programs; (3) payments of higher amounts to acquire certain facilities; (4) $64 million paid for severance packages; (5) legal and accounting fees incurred in the internal investigation and defense of individual defendants; and (6) the significant decline in the price of the company's common stock. Furthermore, HCA's credit rating was adversely affected, and the HCA board allegedly repurchased corporate stock at artificially inflated prices. Moreover, HCA acknowledged that the ongoing investigations would have a negative effect on its profits.[160]

The specific references in the complaint to the corporation's directors and officers included numerous detailed allegations against individual directors, as well as allegations against the board as a whole, including that management devised schemes to improperly increase HCA's revenues and profits and provided strong incentive for employee fraud "with the Board's knowledge."[161] The board also was allegedly implicated in the improper acquisition of other health care companies and knew of the growth rate targets set by senior management.[162] The complaint also referred to an affidavit by a government special agent that alleged that there was a systemic corporate scheme perpetrated by corporate officers and managers of HCA hospitals, and to statements by

---

[157] Physicians allegedly were provided inducements such as loans, guaranteed income, expense allowances, reduced rent, free or reduced-cost training, vacations and other recreational activities, equity interests in HCA operations, and directorship and consulting fees. *See id.* ¶20.

[158] *See id.* ¶22.

[159] *See id.* ¶29.

[160] *See id.* ¶¶24–28.

[161] *See id.* ¶17.

[162] *See id.* ¶¶4, 33.

former executives and employees that violations of the law were "the inevitable product" of corporate policies coming from headquarters that were designed to improperly maximize government reimbursement.[163]

The plaintiffs alleged illegal insider trading and intentional and negligent breaches of the directors' fiduciary duties, including failure to monitor the reports of internal and external auditors to ensure that the corporation was not violating applicable federal and state laws and regulations.[164] The plaintiffs further alleged that the monitoring function required appropriate information gathering and reporting systems to detect and report to the board on a timely basis any employee or corporate misconduct that may have resulted in loss to the company.[165] There also were allegations that the board failed to exercise proper business judgment in managing the corporation.[166] Finally, there were claims that certain directors had engaged in insider trading on terms not equally available to other stockholders because of these directors' awareness of HCA's alleged illegal acts, which precluded these directors from impartially considering a presuit demand.[167]

### 3. Defendants' Response

The defendants (except Scott and Vandewater) filed a motion to dismiss, claiming that the plaintiffs had (1) failed to make a presuit demand on the corporation as required under applicable Delaware law; (2) failed to allege "particularized facts" to demonstrate that a demand would have been futile; (3) failed to set forth specific facts that a majority of the board was disqualified from acting independently in HCA's interest; (4) failed to allege specific facts to state a claim for intentional breach of fiduciary duties, claiming that under Delaware law and HCA's corporate charter, corporate directors cannot be liable for any negligent breach of their fiduciary duties; and (5) failed to allege facts demonstrating any illegal insider trading. Scott and Vandewater adopted these contentions, and Vandewater further stated that the derivative claims against him had no merit because of his status as a former corporate officer, not a director.[168]

### 4. The Magistrate's Report and District Court Decision

Applying Delaware law, the magistrate judge granted the defendants' motions to dismiss because the plaintiffs did not establish that the presuit demand normally required under Delaware law would have

---

[163] *See id.* ¶¶34–35.

[164] *See id.* ¶40.

[165] *See id.* ¶¶45–46.

[166] *See id.* ¶¶56, 59.

[167] *See id.* ¶62.

[168] *See* Magistrate Judge's Report and Recommendation at 4, McCall v. Scott, No. 3:97-0838 (M.D. Tenn. July 1, 1998) [hereinafter *McCall* Magistrate Judge's Report].

been futile.[169] The *McCall* Magistrate Judge's Report contains a lengthy analysis of the presuit demand rule, noting that it is designed to prevent abuses of a derivative action and that it (1) gives corporate management the opportunity to seek alternative options, thereby avoiding expensive litigation; (2) provides an opportunity for the early termination of meritless claims; and (3) prevents strike suits. The demand rule arises from the business judgment rule (i.e., the directors of a corporation are presumed to act in its best interests unless facts demonstrate otherwise).[170] Quoting *Rales v. Blasband*,[171] the *McCall* Magistrate Judge's Report stated as follows:

> A plaintiff, therefore, who chooses not to make a demand prior to suit is faced with the responsibility of demonstrating with particularity why his demand on the Board of Directors would have been futile and if he fails in meeting this burden, he will find that his suit will be dismissed, even if he has an otherwise meritorious claim.[172]

As a threshold matter, the magistrate judge concluded that Delaware, rather than federal, law should apply and that demand futility should be analyzed as of the date that the original complaint was filed in the *Morse* case (i.e., April 8, 1997).[173]

### a. The Test Under Delaware Law

The magistrate judge found that the only relevant claims involving actions taken by the HCA board (rather than inaction) related to the acquisition of other hospital companies and their facilities. There were no allegations that the directors were involved in other actions, such as the recruitment of physicians or upcoding. The magistrate judge noted that this is common practice and cited *Caremark* for the proposition that most corporate decisions are not the subject of director attention, as ordinary business decisions are made by lower-level managers and employees.[174] Other allegations against the directors were deemed irrelevant by the magistrate judge because they occurred after the operative date for demand-futility purposes (April 8, 1997).[175] The magistrate judge concluded that because this was a "failure to monitor" case involving the absence of a conscious board decision, the *Rales* test for presuit demand controlled (i.e., whether there is a reasonable doubt that a majority of directors is disinterested or lacks the independence to act in the corporation's best interest). The magistrate judge rejected the two-part test described in *Aronson* (involving the dual factors of disinterested

---

[169]*See id.* The *McCall* Magistrate Judge's Report was approved by and adopted as the opinion of the court on September 1, 1999, and the plaintiffs' action was dismissed with prejudice. *See* McCall v. Scott, No 3:97-0838 (M.D. Tenn. Sept. 1, 1999) (mem. op.).

[170]*See Aronson*, 466 A.2d 375, 380.

[171]634 A.2d 927, 933 (Del. 1993).

[172]*McCall* Magistrate Judge's Report at 33.

[173]*See id.* at 35–37.

[174]*See id.* at 40.

[175]*See id.* at 41.

directors and whether the board exercised valid business judgment), noting *Aronson's* statement that the "business judgment rule operates only in the context of director action. Technically speaking, it has no role where directors have either abdicated their functions, or absent a conscious decision, failed to act."[176]

As a result, the magistrate judge used the following test, drawn from language in *Rales,* to assess whether the HCA board was disinterested:

> [W]hether or not the particularized factual allegations of a derivative stockholder complaint create a reasonable doubt that, as of the time the complaint is filed, the board of directors could have properly exercised its independent and disinterested business judgment in responding to a demand.[177]

Again quoting *Rales*, the McCall magistrate judge defined "interest" in this context to mean whether a director

> has received, or is entitled to receive, a personal financial benefit from the challenged transaction which is not equally shared by the stockholders . . . .
>
> Directorial interest also exists where a corporate decision will have a materially detrimental impact on a director, but not on the corporation and the stockholders. . . . Independence means that a director's decision is based on the corporate merits of the subject rather than on extraneous considerations or influences. To establish lack of independence, [the plaintiff] must show that the directors are "beholden to [others] or so under their influence that their discretion would be sterilized."[178]

Under Delaware law, the mere threat of personal liability for approving a questioned transaction, standing alone, is insufficient to challenge the independence or disinterestedness of directors, and the potential for liability must not be a "mere threat" but rather a "substantial likelihood." The magistrate judge cited several cases for the proposition that allegations that directors participated in or approved the alleged wrongs have been rejected consistently by Delaware courts as the basis for disqualifying a director.[179]

### b. Applying the Test to the Facts in McCall
#### i. Improper Actions by Defendants

With regard to the specific factual allegations in *McCall* and whether the directors knew or should have known of the alleged improper acts, the magistrate judge found no allegations that any of the

---

[176] *Id.* at 38 (quoting *Aronson*, 473 A.2d at 813).

[177] *McCall* Magistrate Judge's Report at 39 (quoting Rales v. Blasband, 634 A.2d 927, 934 (Del. 1993)).

[178] *McCall* Magistrate Judge's Report at 39–40 (alterations in original) (citations omitted).

[179] *See id.* at 42 (citing Decker v. Clausen, 1989 WL 13617, at *2 (Del. Ch. Nov. 6, 1989), and Lewis v. Curtis, 671 F.2d 779, 785 (3d Cir. 1982), *cert. denied*, 459 U.S. 880 (1982)).

board members, as a group or individually, were personally involved in improper conduct. Moreover, Delaware law recognizes that

> directors of a corporation do not run the day-to-day affairs of a corpora-tion, and . . . to put such an informational burden on the directors of a huge multi-national corporation . . . to know everything that's going on at every plant is unrealistic and no legal liability can attach.[180]

Furthermore, merely signing a 10-K form does not give rise to li-ability under the federal securities laws, because a director must be shown to have substantially assisted the violation or to have been a substantial participant in fraud perpetrated by others.[181] In any event, the magistrate judge found that HCA's Securities and Exchange Com-mission (SEC) filings were appropriate because they disclosed that there had been inquiries by the government about HCA's operations. Moreover, HCA's statements about billing practices and/or compliance with federal laws were matters of opinion or soft information and thus were not actionable under the securities laws.[182]

The insider trading allegations were dismissed because the alle-gations focused simply on the sale of certain directors' stock at the same prices as any other stockholder's shares were sold during the same time period. Thus, according to the magistrate judge, the alleged insider trading did not create substantial liability for those directors.[183]

Finally, the magistrate judge found that although two of the direc-tors who conducted business with HCA were "interested," they did not constitute a majority of the board, and thus filing a presuit demand was required.

### ii. The "Red Flag" Theory

The magistrate judge next analyzed what he called the "red flag" theory, based on the unconsidered failure of the board to act under cir-cumstances in which due attention would arguably have prevented the loss. Quoting extensively from *Graham v. Allis Chalmers*, the magis-trate judge stated that "no rule of law . . . requires a corporate director to assume . . . that all corporate employees are incipient law violators who, but for a tight checkrein will give free vent to their unlawful propensities."[184] He further emphasized the language in *Caremark* indicating that this theory of director liability is "possibly the most difficult theory" on which to prevail. Noting that HCA had an audit committee, and internal as well as independent auditors preparing re-

---

[180]*McCall* Magistrate Judge's Report at 43 (alterations in original) (citations omitted).

[181]*See id.* at 43–44 (citations omitted).

[182]*See id.* at 44 (citing *In re* Sofamor Danek Group, 123 F.3d 394, 400–404 (6th Cir. 1997)).

[183]Although acknowledging that filing an SEC Form S-4 that did not reflect the searches of the Texas hospitals 2 days earlier was a securities violation, the magis-trate judge found that the extensive publicity about these searches cured any omis-sion. *See McCall* Magistrate Judge's Report at 46.

[184]*Id.* at 49 (quoting Graham v. Allis-Chalmers, 188 A.2d 125, 130 (Del. 1963)).

ports on HCA's business, the magistrate judge cited *Caremark* for the proposition that the appropriate level of detail for such a system is a matter of business judgment, and no system can remove all possibility that the corporation will violate laws or regulations or that senior officers or directors may be misled at times or otherwise fail to detect acts material to the corporation's compliance. However, the board can satisfy its responsibility by exercising a good faith determination that the corporation's information gathering and reporting system is adequate to ensure that appropriate information will come to its attention in a timely manner.[185]

The magistrate judge found that HCA had an internal system to detect compliance. Although the plaintiffs alleged that the system did not work, there were no red flags that should have made the board suspicious before the operative date for filing the presuit demand. For example, the FBI agent's affidavit was made after the operative date for demand futility. The magistrate judge added, in dicta, that even if the affidavit were considered, there were no facts demonstrating that any of the directors on the board as of the operative date had committed any illegal acts. Moreover, the fact that unlawful activities occurred in 1 office out of 300 facilities worldwide would not support an inference of corporatewide criminal conduct that should have alerted the directors.[186] In addition, the fact that HCA's DRG codings and case mix index were above the industry average was not alarming due to HCA's position in the hospital industry and its corporate strategy to pursue acute-care patients in good-sized facilities.[187] The serious allegations in the *New York Times* article would not necessarily raise a red flag because the article was published within 2 weeks of the operative date for demand futility and a board might reasonably need more than 2 weeks to evaluate such a report. Various other red flags identified by the plaintiffs were dismissed by the magistrate judge as occurring after the operative date or as being insufficient to suggest corporatewide fraud in such a large corporation.[188]

Finally, the magistrate judge found that a director cannot be held liable for gross negligence in the performance of his or her directorial duties, citing *Caremark* for the proposition that the business judgment rule is "process oriented" and does not depend on a substantive assessment of a decision as long as the process employed was "rational or em-

---

[185] *See McCall* Magistrate Judge's Report at 50 (quoting *In re* Caremark, 698 A.2d 959, 970 (Del. Ch. 1996)).

[186] *See McCall* Magistrate Judge's Report at 52.

[187] According to the magistrate judge, the court in United States *ex rel.* Thompson v. Columbia/ HCA Healthcare Corp., 125 F.2d 899, 903 (5th Cir. 1997), would not accept similar statistical allegations to establish fraud. *See McCall* Magistrate Judge's Report at 52–53.

[188] A $475,000 settlement and the $1.1 million repaid by HCA were contrasted with the over $8 billion HCA received from the federal government in 1996 alone. *See id.* at 55.

ployed in a good-faith effort to advance corporate interests."[189] The magistrate judge concluded that "this language requires a complaint to allege facts that the director intentionally acted to harm the corporation."[190] He bolstered this position by citing the Delaware Code,[191] which allows a corporation to amend its certificate of incorporation to eliminate any claims against its directors for gross negligence, and noted that Delaware courts deem any claim for gross negligence to be barred as a matter of law when a corporation has so amended its certificate.[192] Therefore, the magistrate judge concluded that *Caremark* stands for the position that plaintiffs cannot prevail on the red-flags or failure-to-monitor theories unless they allege particularized facts that the board "*intentionally* failed to 'assure a reasonable information and reporting system.' "[193] The magistrate judge failed to address the holding in *Smith v. Van Gorkum*[194] that despite the business judgment rule, a board must make informed decisions after first informing itself "of all material information reasonably available to [it]."[195] Because the HCA board had an audit committee consisting of board members, an internal audit staff, and an independent auditor, there was an appropriate structure. According to the magistrate judge, in the absence of specific allegations that the board members intentionally failed to monitor the corporation's affairs to prevent violations of the law, the plaintiffs failed to state the facts necessary to disqualify the entire board and thus excuse the need for a presuit demand.[196]

Because the plaintiffs did not excuse their failure to make a presuit demand, the magistrate judge recommended that the case be dismissed. The federal district court adopted and approved the magistrate judge's findings and dismissed the plaintiffs' action with prejudice on September 1, 1999.[197]

### 5. *The Appellate Court Decisions*

In February 2001, the Sixth Circuit issued an opinion that affirmed the district court's dismissal of the duty of loyalty claim for failure to make a presuit demand, but reversed the dismissal of the claim for intentional or reckless breach of the duty of care, and remanded the case for further proceedings (*McCall* Appeal 1).[198] Two months later,

---

[189]*Id.* at 55–56.

[190]*Id.* at 56.

[191]*See id.* (citing DEL. CODE ANN. tit. 8, §102(b)(7)).

[192]*See McCall* Magistrate Judge's Report at 56–57.

[193]*Id.* at 57 (citing *In re* Caremark Int'l Derivative Litig., 698 A.2d 959, 971 (Del. Ch. 1996)).

[194]Smith v. Van Gorkum, 488 A.2d 858 (Del. 1985).

[195]*Id.* at 872.

[196]*See McCall* Magistrate Judge's Report at 58.

[197]*See* McCall v. Scott, No. 3:97-0838 (M.D. Tenn. Sept. 1, 1999).

[198]McCall v. Scott, 239 F.3d 808 (6th Cir. 2001) [hereinafter *McCall* App. 1].

on April 23, 2001, the Sixth Circuit denied the petitions for rehearing but amended one portion of its earlier opinion with regard to the intentional or reckless breach of the duty of care (*McCall* Appeal 2).[199]

### a. The Legal Standards Used

The Sixth Circuit court reviewed the district court's decision to dismiss de novo, noting that motions to dismiss under *Federal Rules of Civil Procedure* 12(b)(6) should not be granted "unless it appears beyond doubt that the plaintiff can prove no set of facts in support of his claim which would entitle him to relief."[200] The appellate court held that the plaintiffs had sufficiently alleged demand futility with regard to their claims for intentional or reckless breach of the duty of care.[201]

The appellate court concurred with the district court that the *Rales* test, rather than the *Aronson* test, should be used since plaintiff's claims did not "allege a conscious Board decision to refrain from acting."[202] The Sixth Circuit reiterated that the *Rales* test requires that the court determine whether the specific factual allegations "create a reasonable doubt that, as of the time the compliant is filed, [a majority of] the board of directors could have properly exercised its independent and disinterested business judgment in responding to a demand."[203] While the mere threat of personal liability is not sufficient, reasonable doubt is created when particularized allegations present "a substantial likelihood" of liability on the part of a director.[204] However, in applying the *Rales* test, the Sixth Circuit held that the district court had erred by viewing the factual allegations separately, and by refusing to draw reasonable inferences in plaintiffs' favor.[205]

While both *McCall* appellate decisions reverse the district court's dismissal of the claim for intentional or reckless breach of the duty of care, the rationale of the *McCall* Appeal 1 opinion is modified somewhat in *McCall* Appeal 2. Both decisions struggled to apply the concept of intentional or reckless conduct to a director's duty of care in the context of traditional Delaware corporate legal norms, particularly in light of a provision of Title 8 of the Delaware Code (Section 102(b)(7)), which allows a corporation to amend its certificate of incorporation to protect its directors against liability for certain acts. This provision states that a corporation's certificate of incorporation may contain:

> A provision eliminating or limiting the personal liability of a director to the corporation or its stockholders for monetary damages for breach of fiduciary duty as a director, provided that such provision shall not eliminate or limit the liability of a director: (i) for any breach of the director's

---

[199]McCall v. Scott, 250 F.3d 997 (6th Cir. 2001) [hereinafter *McCall* App. 2].

[200]*McCall* App. 1 at 815.

[201]*Id.* at 814.

[202]*Id.* at 816.

[203]*Id.*, *citing Rales*, 634 A. 2d at 934.

[204]*McCall* App. 1 at 817 (citing *Rales* at 936).

[205]*Id.*

duty of loyalty to the corporation or its stockholders; (ii) for acts or omissions not in good faith or which involve intentional misconduct or a knowing violation of law; (iii) under § 174 of this title; or (iv) for any transaction from which the director derived an improper personal benefit.[206]

The magistrate judge (and district court) had concluded that under this provision and Delaware case law, a director could not be held liable for gross negligence in the performance of his or her directorial duties, and thus liability could only be predicated on an intentional failure to act.[207] The Sixth Circuit acknowledged that Delaware law, specifically Section 102(b)(7), allows a corporation to amend its certificate of incorporation to protect its directors against allegations of gross negligence.[208] Nevertheless, the Sixth Circuit refuted the lower court's opinion, in part, stating that under Delaware law, "unconsidered inaction can be the basis for director liability."[209]

Columbia had adopted a waiver provision in its Restated Certificate of Incorporation very similar to the Delaware provision (Title 8, Section 102(b)(7)), which stated that:

> TWELFTH:   A director of the Corporation shall not be personally liable to the Corporation or its stockholders for monetary damages for breach of fiduciary duty as a director; *provided, however*, that the foregoing shall not eliminate or limit the liability of a director (i) for any breach of the director's duty of loyalty to the Corporation, or its stockholders, (ii) *for acts or omissions not in good faith* or which involve intentional misconduct or a knowing violation of law, (iii) under Section 174 of the General Corporation Law of Delaware, or (iv) for any transaction from which the director derived an improper personal benefit.[210]

To avoid the waiver of director liability created by this provision, *McCall* plaintiffs alleged that their duty of care claims were not based on gross negligence, but rather on reckless and intentional acts or omissions. Citing a treatise on Delaware corporate law, the *McCall* Appeal 2 court found that "while it is true that duty of care claims alleging only grossly negligent conduct are precluded by a § 102(b)(7) waiver provision, it appears that duty of care claims based on reckless or intentional misconduct are not."[211] The *McCall* Appeal 2 opinion notes that such claims do not easily fit the terminology of Delaware corporate law where courts do not discuss a breach of the duty of care in terms of a mental state. Such allegations are more usually analyzed as either a breach of the duty of loyalty or a breach of the duty of good faith. Therefore, the Sixth Circuit construed plaintiffs' complaint as alleging a breach of the directors' duty of good faith, and finds that this duty may

---

[206]8 DEL. CODE ANN. §102(b)(7).

[207]*See McCall* Magistrate Judge's Report at 55–58.

[208]*McCall* App. 2 at 1000.

[209]*Id.* at 999.

[210]*Id.* (emphasis added).

[211]*Id.*, *citing* BALOTTI & FINKELSTEIN, DELAWARE LAW OF CORPORATIONS AND BUSINESS ORGANIZATIONS (3d ed. Supp. 2000).

be violated "where a director *consciously* disregards his duties to the corporation, thereby causing its stockholders to suffer."[212] Because plaintiffs had not merely alleged "sustained inattention" to their management duties, but rather had alleged "intentional ignorance" of and "willful blindness" to red flags indicating fraudulent practices throughout the company, the plaintiffs had, in effect, alleged a conscious disregard of known risks, "which conduct, if proven, cannot have been undertaken in good faith."[213] Therefore, the court concluded that plaintiffs' claims were not precluded by the waiver of director liability provision in Columbia's corporate charter.[214]

### b. *Analysis of the Facts*

Using this analytical approach, the Sixth Circuit holds that the facts alleged were sufficient to create a substantial likelihood of liability for at least five of Columbia's directors, thereby creating a reasonable doubt as to whether a majority of the board was disinterested.[215] The appellate court's analysis of plaintiffs' specific allegations is particularly interesting because the Sixth Circuit judges often draw very different inferences from the facts than did the magistrate (and district court) judge.[216]

The Sixth Circuit begins by emphasizing the prior experience of many of Columbia's directors, particularly as directors or managers of the health care companies that had been acquired by Columbia.[217] The opinion further examines several specific issues including those relating to Columbia's audit committee and acquisition practices; the *qui tam* action; the federal investigations; the *New York Times'* investigation; and certain Columbia board inaction. First, the appellate court agrees with the district court that there was no substantial likelihood of liability based on a failure to establish and implement reasonable re-

---

[212]*Id.* at 1000 (emphasis added). In support of this statement, the court cites Nagy v. Bistricer, 770 A.2d 43, 2000 WL 1759860 at *3 n.2 (Del. Ch. 2000). Note that *Bistricer* discusses good faith in the context of the duty of loyalty.

[213]*McCall* App. 2 at 1001.

[214]The *McCall* App. 2 court distinguishes its decision from that of the Delaware Court of Chancery in Emerald Partners v. Berlin, No. Civ. A 9700 (Mem. Op. Feb. 7, 2001), stating that while the claims in both cases appeared to be similar on a superficial level, the plaintiff in *Emerald Partners* had offered no evidence that the directors had acted with intentional or reckless indifference, while the plaintiffs in *McCall* had proffered particularized factual statements, which would establish a breach of the duty of good faith, if proven. *McCall* App. 2 at 1001. (*Emerald Partners* was not a demand-futility case but did involve a waiver of liability provision, which, in that case, was held to preclude plaintiffs from prevailing on claims that the directors had breached their duty of loyalty/good faith or duty of care.)

[215]The court emphasized that this determination applies only to the sufficiency of the pleadings with regard to demand futility, and does not determine the truth of the allegations or outcome on the merits.

[216]The remaining description of the *McCall* appellate opinion applies to both *McCall* App. 1 and *McCall* App. 2.

[217]*McCall* App. 1 at 819.

porting systems, despite the fact that the audit procedures in place apparently did not prevent the alleged fraud. However, while the district court had found "no sinister motives" when director Frist circulated a *Business Week* article on another company's high-pressure tactics to meet aggressive growth targets, the appellate court found that no such motives were necessary. According to the Sixth Circuit, the incident suggested an inference that Frist may have been aware of the danger that aggressive growth targets could lead to questionable billing practices.[218]

Similarly, the district court had found that Columbia's repayment of $475,000 plus $1.1 million for questionable expenditures did not suggest corporate-wide fraud at a company receiving hundred of millions of dollars in reimbursement. The appellate court indicated that such facts could reasonably lead to the inference that directors, with prior experience managing the company, "would be sensitive to the circumstances that prompted the investigation of Columbia's practices."[219] Likewise, the district court had stated that one could reasonably expect Columbia's DRGs and Case Mix Indices (CMIs) would be higher than the norm for most hospitals in the same markets due to Columbia's size and corporate strategy. However, the Sixth Circuit found that: "it would be just as reasonable to infer that the consistently high CMIs and DRGs were a sign of possible improper billing activities."[220]

With regard to Columbia's acquisition practices, the appellate court found the allegations against five of the directors based on the fact that they were former directors or officers of companies acquired by Columbia were too speculative since the complaint did not allege any particularized impropriety in these transactions. However, directors Scott and Frist attended meetings of Columbia's Acquisition Development Group and their participation implied knowledge of the arrangements that allegedly violated health care laws and regulations.

Plaintiffs had also alleged that Columbia interfered with physician relationships, citing a lawsuit awarding a physician $6.2 million dollars including $5 million in punitive damages against Columbia. The appellate court agreed the district court was correct that the verdict alone did not suggest corporate-wide wrongdoing. However, the Sixth Circuit stated that the lawsuit and the verdict should be considered, along with all of the facts.

The appellate court came to very different conclusions, than had the district court, with regard to several other issues. The *qui tam* complaint filed by Dr. James Thompson was unsealed in September 1995, when the government declined to intervene. Moreover, the action was dismissed in July 1996 and was not reversed until October 1997 (several months after the operative date for determining demand futility,

---

[218]*Id.* at 820.

[219]*Id.* at 821.

[220]*Id.*

i.e., April 8, 1997). Nevertheless, the Sixth Circuit determined that despite its dismissal, the complaint clearly presented claims of improper physician inducements and illegal billing practices, indicating possible federal intervention, all of which were relevant to determining whether the board's failure to take action or investigate was in good faith.[221]

Similarly, the district court had found that the FBI agent's affidavit in support of the July 1997 search warrants used by federal agents to raid 35 Columbia facilities could not be considered because it was attested to after the April 8, 1997, demand-futility date. However, the appellate court declares that facts in existence before derivative claims are filed may be considered in determining demand futility even if these facts were not discovered until later.[222] The Sixth Circuit also criticizes the district court for viewing the search of the El Paso offices in isolation, stating:

> When the particularized allegations are taken together, there are sufficient facts from which one could infer that the Board knew of or recklessly disregarded the allegedly improper policies and practices being systematically followed in Columbia's facilities nationwide. In fact, the magnitude and duration of the alleged wrongdoing is relevant in determining whether the failure of the directors to act constitutes a lack of good faith. See *In re Oxford Health Plans, Inc.*, 192 F.R.D. 111 (S.D.N.Y. 2000) (Del. law).[223]

The Sixth Circuit seems to agree with the district court that the *New York Times* articles did not necessarily put the Columbia board on notice of irregularities. Nor did the failure of the board to remove Scott before July 26, 1997, indicate that a presuit demand in April 1997 would have been futile since the fundamental goal of the demand requirement is the opportunity to prod the board into action.

Nevertheless, the Sixth Circuit concludes that there were sufficient facts alleged to create a reasonable doubt as to the disinterestedness of at least five of Columbia's directors by alleging facts that presented a substantial likelihood of director liability for intentional or reckless breach of the duty of care. However, the Sixth Circuit agrees with the lower court that there were insufficient facts alleged to create doubt as to the disinterestedness of a majority of the board to consider a demand with respect to the duty of loyalty claim which related to insider training.[224]

### c. McCall *and the* Abbott Laboratories *Case*

While the Sixth Circuit does not directly address this case, it is interesting to note that the *McCall* Appeal 1 analysis was criticized in *In re Abbott Laboratories Derivative Shareholder Litigation*.[225] The *Abbott*

---

[221]*Id.* at 822.

[222]*Id.* at 823.

[223]*Id.*

[224]*Id.* at 825–26.

[225]141 F. Supp. 2d 946 (N.D. Ill. 2001).

*Laboratories* case involved allegations that the defendant directors were liable for harm resulting from a consent decree between the company and the Food and Drug Administration (FDA). The plaintiffs' derivative suit was dismissed for failure to plead demand futility with particularity by the federal district court in the Northern District of Illinois.

The *Abbott Laboratories* case involved the diagnostic division of the company (Abbott), which had continuing problems with the FDA over certain regulatory procedures for the past several years. The FDA had conducted numerous inspections and reported violations. Abbott received warning letters from the FDA four times, and copies of these letters had been given to the chairman of the board. These letters outlined the potential consequences of failure to remedy the violations, and ultimately resulted in a consent decree that required Abbott to pay a $100 million fine, withdraw 125 types of medical diagnostic test kits from the market, destroy certain inventory, and make various changes in its manufacturing procedures.[226]

The *Abbott Laboratories* court emphasizes that Abbott had 13 directors, of which only 2 were "insider directors," i.e., Abbott employees. The applicable Illinois statute was very similar to the Delaware law allowing corporations to exempt certain director behavior from liability. Abbott had incorporated a waiver of liability in its certificate of incorporation, and the district court in Illinois had to determine whether, notwithstanding that waiver, Abbott directors could be liable for reckless conduct. The *Abbott Laboratories* court cites a portion of the *McCall* App. 1 opinion on this issue but finds that labeling defendants' behavior "reckless" is not a useful standard. Rather, the court suggests that the facts should be analyzed in light of the operative language of the statute, i.e., was the directors' behavior "not in good faith"?[227]

Distinguishing the facts in *McCall*, where "the complaint detailed many facts about the directors, their backgrounds, their roles within the company and extraordinary events of which they were undoubtedly aware,"[228] the *Abbott Laboratories* court found that "even drawing inferences favorable to plaintiffs, we cannot find a substantial likelihood of liability on these facts."[229] First, the court found it "far from clear" that a majority of the Abbott board had knowledge of the various FDA inspections, violation notices, and warning letters. Unlike *McCall* where there had been detailed allegations about each of the directors, detailed information had only been presented with regard to 2 of the 13 directors in *Abbott Laboratories*. Second, according to the court, the warning letters contained boilerplate language and thus did not necessarily mean any regulatory action was imminent.[230] There-

---

[226]*Id.* at 947–48.

[227]*Id.* at 949.

[228]*Id.* at 950.

[229]*Id.* at 951.

[230]*Id.* at 950.

fore, the court found that while it was possible the directors had knowledge about FDA compliance issues, there was no suggestion they knew the details of the FDA's actions. Nor were the problems so widespread and egregious (as in *McCall*) that the court was willing to presume the directors' knowledge.

Moreover, the court found the ongoing pattern of inspections, negotiations, and re-inspections between Abbott and the FDA appeared to be routine, with the violations affecting only a small percentage of Abbott's products. The fact that some problems persisted while new ones arose would not, by itself, indicate bad faith.[231] There had been a clear give and take between the company and the FDA, with the government continually allowing Abbott to address the reported violations. Thus, according to the court, a director would not have reasonably believed Abbott's management was not making a good faith effort to address the violations. The *Abbott Laboratories* court concludes that "perhaps" the directors might have been more aggressive in their investigations of the FDA violations, but such inaction was negligent; at most, falling far short of a showing of bad faith or a knowing violation of the law.[232]

### 6. Implications of the Columbia / HCA and Abbott Laboratories Decisions

#### a. The Sixth Circuit Decision in McCall

The Sixth Circuit opinion in *McCall* indicates the court's belief that the demand-futility rule, along with the Delaware law allowing the waiver of certain director liability, should not become a means for corporate boards to escape almost all liability if they fail to take appropriate actions. The lower court decision provided considerable comfort to corporate boards because the *Caremark* failure-to-monitor theory had been substantially narrowed so that it created liability only where there had been an *intentional* failure to act, at least in those instances where a corporate charter included a provision modeled on Section 102(b)(7) of Title 8 of the Delaware Code.[233] Moreover, the district court had applied presuit demand requirements so stringently to the facts that few cases involving a board's failure to monitor would seem likely to qualify for an exception to the rule. The Sixth Circuit decision acknowledges that Delaware law precludes claims against directors for gross negligence if the corporation has amended its certificate of incorporation in accordance with Section 102(b)(7). However, the court finds a narrow window where failure to act can create exposure for the board, despite Section 102(b)(7) and the demand-futility rule, i.e., where a director *consciously* disregards his or her duties to the corporation, causing its

---

[231]The court seems to take further comfort from the fact that each successive FDA letter addressed a different violation. *Id.* at 951.

[232]*Id.*

[233]*See McCall* Magistrate Judge's Report at 57.

stockholders to suffer.[234] This type of behavior is also characterized as a breach of a director's duty of good faith.[235]

As compared to the lower court's opinion, the circuit court's analysis is more consistent with Delaware case law, particularly the *Caremark* decision. Despite the magistrate judge's statements, it is open to some question whether *Caremark* held that liability in the failure-to-monitor context could arise only if there was an intentional failure. The *Caremark* opinion refers to "a *sustained* or *systematic failure* of the board to exercise oversight."[236] This formulation is different from *intentional* failure.

Although the appellate court was careful to note that it was not issuing an opinion on the underlying merits of plaintiffs' claims, the lengthy discussion in the opinion indicates that court's view that most of the allegations would support at least an inference of improper conduct by the board. The appellate court seemed to reject the lower court's implication that a number of the allegations might be considered "de minimis" in light of the size of the corporation as a whole. For example, the magistrate judge (and district court) had found that a $1.1 million repayment and a $475,000 settlement were not suggestive of corporate-wide fraud in light of Columbia's receipt of $8 billion from the federal government in a single year. Similarly, the magistrate judge found that a widely reported investigation involving over 200 federal agents raiding two hospitals and serving a dozen physicians' offices with search warrants was not of sufficient magnitude, given Columbia's size, to support an inference of corporate-wide fraud.[237] The Sixth Circuit's analysis also seemed to rely heavily on the fact that most of Columbia's directors had substantial prior experience as directors or managers of health care companies was particularly important to the Sixth Circuit's analysis.

In this evolving area of the law, clear standards are difficult to identify and thus, outcomes are difficult to predict. Theoretically, plaintiff shareholders are more likely to prevail if the board's inaction results in very extensive and serious consequences. For example, the *Abbott Laboratories* court distinguished that case (where defendant directors prevailed) from *McCall*, in part, by characterizing the *McCall* violations as far more widespread and egregious. However, the violations in the *Abbott Laboratories* case were substantial: The FDA had issued four warning letters, and, as part of the consent settlement, ultimately imposed a $100 million fine, required the company to withdraw more than 100 types of medical diagnostic test kits from the market, required the destruction of certain inventory, and further insisted on various changes in the company's manufacturing processes.

---

[234]*See McCall* App. 2 at 1001.

[235]*E.g., id.* at 1000; *Abbott Labs.*, 141 F. Supp. 2d at 949.

[236]*In re* Caremark, 698 A.2d 959, 971 (Del. Ch. 1996).

[237]*McCall* Magistrate Judge's Report at 59.

However, several additional factors may have contributed to the result in the *Abbott Laboratories* case. First, the court emphasized that the *Abbott Laboratories* plaintiffs had not made sufficiently detailed allegations concerning the directors' backgrounds, roles, and knowledge. Moreover, the *Abbott Laboratories* court also seemed inclined to view the facts in a light more favorable to the defendants, perhaps because most of the directors were "outside directors" and not Abbott employees. Thus, the court implied that these outside directors would assume that the pattern of inspections, negotiations, and re-inspections were "routine," and that the discussion of potential consequences in the FDA warning letters, including a potential freeze on sales, was mere "boilerplate."[238] The fact that the continuing violations involved various different issues was viewed in a surprisingly positive perspective, i.e., Abbott was not attempting to "stonewall" the FDA.[239] The court also emphasized that the violations only affected "a small percentage" of Abbott's products.[240] In any event, the case clearly indicates that plaintiffs attempting to demonstrate director "bad faith," in cases involving a waiver of director liability provision in the corporation's charter, may have a particularly high hurdle to overcome.

### b. *Other Developments Relating to Presuit Demand*

In contrast, several other cases, applying Delaware law, have indicated certain courts' reluctance to let the presuit demand rule prevent a resolution of the issues on the merits, even in shareholder derivative litigation where director inaction is at issue. In a March 2000 decision, *In re Oxford Health Plans, Inc., Securities Litigation,*[241] the U.S. District Court for the Southern District of New York excused the need for demand by the plaintiffs in a derivative suit because of defendant directors' nonfeasance and generalized failure to properly monitor the activities of management. These failures included (1) not having sufficient financial controls and procedures to monitor the planned conversion to a new computer system; (2) not implementing and enforcing procedures to prevent appropriation of company information and assets by certain directors; (3) knowingly or recklessly disseminating misleading information to shareholders; and (4) allowing the company to engage in improper billing practices and to violate numerous insurance regulations, thereby subjecting the company to fines, penalties, and further investigations. The court applied Delaware law and the *Rales v. Blasband*[242] test to find that "[i]n numerous cases where liability is

---

[238]*Abbott Labs.*, 141 F. Supp. 2d at 950.

[239]*Id.* at 951.

[240]Plaintiffs alleged that the affected products accounted for 20% of Abbott's revenues, but the court dismissed this allegation in fairly summary fashion by finding no facts suggesting Abbott's management had reason to believe the Diagnostic Division's revenues were in any serious jeopardy. *Id.* at 950.

[241]192 F.R.D. 111 (S.D.N.Y. 2000).

[242]634 A.2d 927 (Del.1993).

based upon a failure to supervise and monitor, and to keep adequate supervisory controls in place, demand futility is ordinarily found, especially where the failure involves a scheme of significant magnitude and duration which went undiscovered by the directors."[243] The district court in *Oxford Health Plans* cited *Miller v. Schreyer*,[244] which excused demand in a derivative suit by stating the following:

> It does not appear that the Delaware Supreme Court, in deciding *Rales*, intended to suggest that a board of directors is absolved of all responsibility to prevent the repeated misuse of corporate resources for illegal purposes.[245]

The *Miller* case involved allegations that, according to the court, created "obvious danger signs."[246] In light of the magnitude, duration, timing, and illegality of certain transactions and the identity of the parties, the court held that it was hardly unreasonable to require directors to implement basic financial oversight procedures sufficient to disclose a patently improper scheme extending over a 5-year period.[247]

It is also important to remember that these cases generally deal with precedents under Delaware law (or under other state laws similar to Delaware's). However, as previously discussed, some states follow other types of demand-futility laws or precedents, including states such as Pennsylvania that follow the demand rule set forth in the ALI *Principles of Corporate Governance*, which is more deferential to corporate boards.

### E. *Spitzer v. Abdelhak*

RICO[248] has established itself as a worrisome source of potential liability for officers and directors. RICO created a private cause of action through which a person injured by a RICO violation may recover both attorneys' fees and treble damages.

### 1. *Background of the Case*

*Spitzer v. Abdelhak*[249] was filed following the financial difficulties and bankruptcy of the Allegheny Health Education and Research Foun-

---

[243]*Oxford Health Plans*, 192 F.R.D. at 117. The court acknowledged that plaintiffs had alleged both affirmative misconduct as well as nonfeasance but noted that claims based on board inaction appeared to predominate.

[244]683 N.Y.S.2d 51 (N.Y. Sup. Ct. App. Div. 1999).

[245]*Id.* at 55.

[246]*Id.* (citation omitted).

[247]The first *Miller* decision, Miller v. Schreyer, 606 N.Y.S.2d 642 (N.Y. Sup. Ct. App. Div. 1994), was criticized by Marx v. Akers, 88 N.Y.2d 189, 200 (N.Y. 1996), and *In re* Baxter Int'l, Inc. Shareholders Litig., 654 A.2d 1268, 1271 (Del. Ch. 1995). However, the subsequent *Miller* decision (cited with approval in *Oxford Health Plans*) reaffirmed the original holding, partly relying on the "law of the case doctrine." *Miller*, 683 N.Y.S.2d at 54.

[248]18 U.S.C. §§1951–60.

[249]No. 98-6475, 1999 WL 1204352 (E.D. Pa. Dec. 15, 1999).

dation (AHERF). This class action was brought by a group of physicians who sold their medical practices to AHERF prior to its demise. The plaintiffs brought the suit against AHERF's directors and officers, alleging that they were injured by the defendants' RICO violations.[250]

The plaintiffs claimed that the defendants engaged in a scheme to defraud them through the use of false statements about the financial viability of AHERF. The plaintiffs alleged both financial damage and damage to their professional reputations. They also asserted common law claims for conspiracy and intentional interference with contractual relations. In response to the defendants' motion to dismiss for failure to state a claim, the district court analyzed the plaintiffs' allegations and declined to dismiss the RICO claims.[251]

Among the major factors leading to AHERF's demise were a series of acquisitions of heavily indebted hospitals and medical schools.[252] That "path to bankruptcy" began in 1988 under the guidance of Sherif Abdelhak, AHERF's CEO during the time period relevant to the plaintiffs' suit.[253] AHERF's acquisitions made it Pennsylvania's largest statewide integrated delivery system. By the time AHERF filed for bankruptcy in 1998, it was losing up to $1 million per day.[254]

Observers also pointed to AHERF's weak management structure and lack of oversight as causes for AHERF's failure. AHERF's weak structure was exemplified by (1) an "enormous parent board" of up to 35 directors and (2) a network of boards for each of its operations, which "reportedly were never sure what was happening elsewhere in the AHERF empire."[255] Of importance to potential director and officer liability are allegations that Abdelhak dominated all board decisions and discouraged board members from "asking tough questions."[256] Abdelhak and his senior management allegedly made many decisions without formal board approval; some decisions were relayed to the board only after the fact, if at all.[257]

Particularly related to the *Spitzer* plaintiffs' RICO claim was the allegation that AHERF's directors and officers depicted AHERF's subsidiary, Allegheny East, as a "viable health care system" to increase

---

[250]*See id.* at *1–3.

[251]*See id.* at *10. The federal district court also declined to dismiss the state law conspiracy claim. A discussion of that aspect of the opinion is beyond the scope of this chapter.

[252]For a detailed history of AHERF and its failure, see Lawton Burns *et al.*, *The Fall of the House of AHERF: The Allegheny System Debacle*, 19 HEALTH AFF. 7 (2000), *available at* http://www.medscape.com/ProjHope/HA/2000/ha1901.01.burn/ha1901.01.burn-01.html [hereinafter *Fall of the House of AHERF*.]

[253]*Spitzer*, 1999 WL 1204352 at *1.

[254]*See id.*; *Fall of the House of AHERF*, *supra* note 252.

[255]*Fall of the House of AHERF*, *supra* note 252.

[256]*Id.*

[257]*See id.*

their salaries and their prestige in the community.[258] The plaintiffs specifically alleged that the defendants voted themselves salary increases when AHERF's bankruptcy was imminent. In addition, the plaintiffs alleged that the defendants caused large sums of money to be transferred from restricted accounts "to cover Allegheny East's pitiful financial state."[259] The plaintiffs also claimed that every defendant officer signed a fraudulent annual report.

### 2. The Court's Decision

As noted above,[260] the district court denied the defendants' motion to dismiss the plaintiffs' RICO claims. Generally, to establish a RICO claim, a plaintiff must show (1) the existence of an enterprise that affects interstate commerce; (2) that a person (separate from the enterprise) engaged in a pattern of racketeering activity; (3) that through that pattern the defendant conducted the enterprise, acquired an interest in it, or controlled it; and (4) that the plaintiff suffered an injury as a result of the RICO violation.[261]

The defendants unsuccessfully challenged each element of the plaintiffs' RICO claim. An enterprise is a group of persons or entities associated together for the purpose of engaging in a course of conduct. It is proven by an ongoing organization, formal or not, together with evidence that the various associates function together as a continuing unit.[262] The court found that plaintiffs' allegation that the enterprise consisted of the corporation and one of its subsidiaries adequately described a RICO enterprise.[263]

The directors and officers also challenged the adequacy of plaintiffs' claims that the directors and officers controlled the enterprise.[264] The court held that control was established when the defendants participated in the operation or management of the enterprise; liability is

---

[258]*Spitzer*, 1999 WL 1204352, at *6. For example, commentators observed that in a January 1998 speech—just 6 months before AHERF and Allegheny East filed for bankruptcy—Abdelhak discussed AHERF's "phenomenal growth" and "productivity improvements," but failed to mention either the internal cash transfers and other mechanisms used to finance the growth or AHERF's financial deterioration. *Fall of the House of AHERF, supra* note 252.

[259]*Spitzer*, 1999 WL 1204352, at *7.

[260]See *supra* text accompanying note 252.

[261]*See* 18 U.S.C. §1962(c). Regarding the injury element, which applies to standing to bring a RICO claim, the court distinguished the case before it from others in which the plaintiffs' injuries were caused solely by the organization's insolvency. *See Spitzer*, 1999 WL 1204352, at *3. In other words, unless a plaintiff adequately alleges that his or her losses would have occurred even without the insolvency, he or she may be faced with a successful motion to dismiss. The *Spitzer* court found for the plaintiffs on that issue.

[262]*See* United States v. Turkette, 452 U.S. 576, 580–81 (1981); 18 U.S.C. §§1961(4), 1962(c).

[263]*See Spitzer,* 1999 WL 1204352, at *4.

[264]*See id.*

not limited to those with primary responsibility, and the degree of participation need not be substantial.[265] Accordingly, the officer-defendants' roles as senior managers of the business were sufficient to establish control for RICO purposes. Similarly, the director-defendants' votes on crucial issues, such as officer and employee compensation, established their control under RICO.

Having determined that plaintiffs satisfied the enterprise and control elements, the court looked to the pattern of racketeering activity.[266] RICO identifies numerous state and federal crimes, the occurrence of which is a precondition to a RICO violation.[267] RICO does not require a criminal conviction before a plaintiff can bring a civil RICO claim based on that predicate act.[268] Plaintiff's complaint satisfied the racketeering activity requirement by alleging violations of federal statutes prohibiting mail fraud,[269] wire fraud,[270] money laundering,[271] and interstate transportation of fraudulently obtained money.[272] These predicate acts were based on plaintiffs' claim that money was fraudulently obtained and distributed.[273]

To show a pattern of racketeering activity, plaintiffs "must show that the racketeering predicates are related, and that they amount to or pose a threat of continued criminal activity."[274] The plaintiffs alleged that the defendants' scheme was operating for over 4 years, during which time the predicate acts occurred.[275] The court found that this 4-year period satisfied the continuity requirement and established a pattern of racketeering activity.

The court's refusal to dismiss the RICO counts of the *Spitzer* complaint merely means that plaintiffs had adequately pled it. The procedural posture of a motion to dismiss means that the court must accept the truth of all plaintiffs' allegations and draw from them all inferences favorable to plaintiffs. Dismissal is appropriate only if it is clear that "beyond a doubt . . . the plaintiff can prove no set of facts in support of his claim which would entitle him to relief."[276] Accordingly, *Spitzer* is far from resolved and will be closely watched by the health care and general legal community to see whether the court imposes liability on any of the AHERF directors or officers.

---

[265]*See id.* (citing Reves v. Ernst & Young, 507 U.S. 170, 179, 183 (1993)).

[266]*See Spitzer*, 1999 WL 1204352, at *7.

[267]18 U.S.C. §1961(1).

[268]*See, e.g.,* Sedima, S.P.R.L. v. Imrex Co., 473 U.S. 479 (1985).

[269]*See* 18 U.S.C. §1341.

[270]*See* 18 U.S.C. §1343.

[271]*See* 18 U.S.C. §1957.

[272]*See* 18 U.S.C. §2314.

[273]*See Spitzer*, 1999 WL 1204352, at *5–7.

[274]*See id.* at *7 (quoting H.J., Inc. v. Northwestern Bell Tel. Co., 492 U.S. 229, 241 (1989)).

[275]*See Spitzer,* 1999 WL 1204352, at *7

[276]*Id.* (quoting Conley v. Gibson, 355 U.S. 41, 45–46 (1957)).

## IV. CORPORATE COMPLIANCE

The principles of criminal and civil liability described above, as well as the *Caremark* case and its progeny, indicate that directors and officers of health care organizations may face a significant risk of exposure. Implementing a corporate compliance program is one mechanism directors and officers can use to minimize that risk. An effective compliance program is particularly important because it can create corporate information gathering and reporting systems sufficient to withstand scrutiny under a *Caremark* analysis, and may help demonstrate the board's "good faith," a critical part of the *McCall* court's analyses. Corporate compliance programs are discussed in detail elsewhere in this volume, including compliance programs' benefits for an organization and their requirements,[277] but the discussion that follows focuses on their implications for director and officer liability.

### A. U.S. Sentencing Guidelines

Chapter 8 of the U.S. Sentencing Guidelines on the sentencing of organizations (the Sentencing Guidelines) became effective in November 1991. The Sentencing Guidelines encourage, although do not require, organizations to implement a corporate compliance program.[278] The Sentencing Guidelines were developed under the Sentencing Reform Act,[279] which was enacted to provide greater fairness, certainty, and effectiveness in federal sentencing and to eliminate much of the discretion formerly vested in trial judges. The Sentencing Reform Act also established the U.S. Sentencing Commission,[280] which was charged with drafting guidelines to control sentencing in federal courts. The resulting guidelines use a mechanistic approach to achieve uniformity and certainty, and a series of very complicated calculations are used to determine the penalty imposed. As a result, there has been a sharp increase in penalties, particularly for white-collar offenders and organizations.

First, a base fine calculation ranges from $5,000 to $72.5 million. This fine generally is based on the applicable offense level or the pecuniary gain or loss, whichever is higher.[281] Next, a multiplier is developed based on the "culpability score." This multiplier can range from 0.05 to 4; thus, a fine can reach $290 million or higher, depending on the pecuniary gain or loss involved.[282] Although a court's discretion is narrowly limited, certain specified considerations can be factored into the culpability score. For example, points can be added to the calculation if there

---

[277]See Chapter 7 (Jones *et al.*, Corporate Compliance Programs).

[278]U.S. Sentencing Guidelines (U.S.S.G.) Manual ch. 8, introductory cmt. (2000).

[279]Sentencing Reform Act of 1984, 28 U.S.C. §991.

[280]28 U.S.C. §991(a).

[281]*See* U.S.S.G. §8C2.4 (1998).

[282]*See id.* §8C2.5.

was involvement in or tolerance of the offense by high-level personnel.[283] Alternatively, points may be deducted if the company reported the violation or cooperated in the investigation.[284] Points also may be deducted if the organization had an effective compliance program.[285]

## 1. Advantages of Compliance Programs

There are specific advantages under the Sentencing Guidelines to the development of a compliance program. Although most of the benefits accrue more directly to the corporation, directors and officers benefit at least indirectly because shareholders are less likely to file suit against them if the corporation is not facing any serious financial problems or legal liabilities. For example, under the Sentencing Guidelines, the existence of an effective corporate compliance program can reduce the corporate fine by as much as 80 percent. In an environment of multimillion-dollar fines, the magnitude of this reduction can create substantial financial benefits for the corporation. Moreover, an organization with a compliance program may be able to avoid the imposition of a probationary period, which could create a significant burden on the company's subsequent operations.[286] Government officials also may be persuaded not to seek the company's exclusion from participation in federal health care programs, at least in those cases where such exclusion is permissive. Exclusion, if imposed, can be a financial death sentence for such companies.

More directly, providing evidence of an effective compliance program can help to persuade the government to use its discretion in favor of the corporation and its executives. For example, if a compliance plan has been implemented, the CIA imposed by the government as part of a settlement agreement is likely to be less onerous.[287] In addition, if a compliance program has been implemented, the government may agree not to file criminal charges against senior officers for the misdeeds of lower-level employees. Finally, a compliance program also can assist in the defense of *qui tam* actions, shareholder suits, and civil damage actions by demonstrating that management has acted appropriately, thus countering claims for punitive damages.

## 2. Compliance Programs Must Be "Effective"

There are numerous intrinsic advantages to compliance programs, such as (1) making it more likely that improper conduct will be detected

---

[283]*See id.* §8C2.5(b).

[284]*See id.* §8C2.5(g).

[285]*See id.* This reduction does not apply in certain cases in which one or more high-level employees within the organization were involved in the offense.

[286]In the absence of a compliance program, the court is required by the Sentencing Guidelines to impose a period of probation if the company has more than 50 employees. *See id.* §8D1.1(a)(3). For the conditions of probation, see U.S.S.G. §§8D1.3–1.4.

[287]In certain situations, the government may not impose a CIA if an effective compliance program is in place.

sooner, thus reducing the damage caused; (2) allowing the company and its directors to better assess their options (e.g., to consider participating in a voluntary disclosure program);[288] and (3) most important, increasing the likelihood that a culture of compliance will prevent many violations from ever occurring.

As a result of these factors and the great increase over recent years in the number of investigations and enforcement actions the government has initiated in the industry, numerous health care organizations have begun implementing corporate compliance programs, and many others are considering doing so. Moreover, as stated by two authorities on director and officer liability,

> [a]n effective corporate compliance program is an undertaking so comprehensive [that it] is probably more elaborate than what many organizations have attempted to date, but its benefits may be so substantial that it should receive serious consideration without further delay. It is reasonable to suggest that boards of directors will be derelict in their duties if they neglect to do so.[289]

However, directors and officers should be aware of additional concerns they must address in connection with compliance programs. First, to obtain benefits, it is essential that the program be "effective." The Sentencing Guidelines have established minimum requirements that must be met before a program will be deemed "effective."[290] In summary, these requirements are as follows:

- Compliance standards and procedures must be established "that are reasonably capable of reducing the prospect of criminal conduct."
- Specific high-level personnel must be assigned responsibility for overseeing compliance.
- Due care must be exercised not to delegate discretionary authority to those who are known or should have been known to have a propensity to engage in illegal conduct.
- Standards and procedures must be communicated effectively to all employees and agents (e.g., by requiring participation in training programs or by dissemination of practical compliance information).
- Reasonable steps must be taken to achieve compliance with these standards, including the use of auditing and monitoring systems, and by implementing and publicizing a system that allows criminal conduct to be reported without fear of retaliation.
- Standards must be consistently enforced through appropriate disciplinary mechanisms.

---

[288]For a discussion of the voluntary disclosure program, see Chapter 3 (Salcido, The False Claims Act in Health Care Prosecutions: Application of the Substantive, *Qui Tam*, and Voluntary Disclosure Provisions).

[289]KNEPPER & BAILEY, *supra* note 28, at 47.

[290]U.S.S.G. §8A1.2 n.3(k).

- After detection, all reasonable steps must be taken to respond appropriately and to prevent further similar offenses.

The Sentencing Guidelines specifically state, however, that failure to prevent or detect an offense does not, in and of itself, mean that the program was not effective.[291] According to the Sentencing Guidelines, some of the factors to be used in determining the actions necessary for an effective program are as follows:

- *Size of the organization.* The requisite degree of formality of a [compliance] program . . . will vary with the size of the organization: the larger the organization, the more formal the program typically should be. A larger organization generally should have established written policies defining the standards and procedures to be followed by its employees and other agents.
- *Likelihood that certain offenses may occur because of the nature of the business.* If, because of the nature of an organization's business, there is a substantial risk that certain types of offenses may occur, management must have taken steps to prevent and detect those types of offenses. For example, if an organization handles toxic substances, it must have established standards and procedures designed to ensure that those substances are properly handled at all times.
- *Prior history of the organization.* An organization's prior history may indicate types of offenses that it should have taken actions to prevent. Recurrence of misconduct similar to that which an organization has previously committed casts doubt on whether it took all reasonable steps to prevent such misconduct.

An organization's failure to incorporate and follow applicable industry practice or the standards called for by any applicable governmental regulation weighs against a finding of an effective program to prevent and detect violations of law.[292]

### 3. Concerns Raised by Compliance Programs

Despite their advantages, compliance programs, particularly effective ones, can reveal troublesome issues that demand resolution. Auditing and monitoring may reveal violations and substantial amounts of money that may have to be repaid. Having identified an overpayment or other compliance issue, the corporation and board cannot ignore it. In addition, the documentation created can provide a roadmap for the government and other adverse parties to use in suits against corporate officials. Internal investigations conducted as part of compliance efforts can be discoverable and may lead to employee claims of discrimination, defamation, or violation of constitutional or civil rights. Working with

---

[291]*See id.*

[292]*Id.* §8A1.2 n.3(k)(7).

legal counsel can help protect some documents from discovery under certain circumstances through the application of attorney–client and other privileges. (The parameters of such privileges are beyond the scope of this chapter.) As a practical matter, however, it is important to recognize that corporations and boards may be forced to disclose materials traditionally screened by privilege.[293]

## B. The Office of Inspector General Compliance Program Guidance

Beginning in 1997, the OIG published a series of compliance program guidance (Compliance Guidance) documents for various entities in the health care industry. There are compliance guidance materials specifically designed for hospitals;[294] clinical laboratories;[295] durable medical equipment (DME), prosthetics, orthotics, and supplies providers;[296] third-party medical billing companies;[297] hospices;[298] nursing facilities;[299] Medicare+Choice organizations;[300] individual and small group physician practices;[301] and home health agencies.[302] The OIG also has solicited information and recommendations for developing compliance program guidance documents for the ambulance industry[303] and the pharmaceutical industry.[304] The OIG has indicated that all types of health care organizations should adopt compliance programs as expeditiously as possible, and to the extent that there is no Compliance Guidance specifically designed for a particular type of provider, that provider should look to the other available documents to help establish an effective compliance program.

Because they are not legally binding and often contain a great deal of detail about how the OIG thinks an organization should operate, the various Compliance Guidance documents often have been characterized as the OIG's "wish list." Nevertheless, it generally is advisable to adhere to these standards when possible. For example, the OIG specif-

---

[293]Privileges have complex requirements, and courts do not always uphold claims of privilege. Moreover, organizations are increasingly being asked to waive privileges that might otherwise protect documents to demonstrate their willingness to cooperate during government investigations.

[294]*See* 63 Fed. Reg. 8987 (Feb. 23, 1998).

[295]*See* 63 Fed. Reg. 163 (Aug. 24, 1998).

[296]*See* 64 Fed. Reg. 36,368 (July 6, 1999).

[297]*See* 63 Fed. Reg. 70,138 (Dec. 18, 1998).

[298]*See* 64 Fed. Reg. 54,031 (Oct. 5, 1999).

[299]*See* 65 Fed. Reg. 14,289 (Mar. 16, 2000).

[300]*See* 64 Fed. Reg. 61,893 (Nov. 15, 1999).

[301]*See* 65 Fed. Reg. 59,434 (Oct. 5, 2000).

[302]All of these documents are located in the *Federal Register* and on the OIG's Web site at: http://www.dhhs.gov/progorg/oig/modcomp/index.htm.

[303]65 Fed. Reg. 50,204 (Aug. 17, 2000).

[304]66 Fed. Reg. 31,246 (June 11, 2001).

ically states in the Compliance Guidance documents that it "will consider the existence of an effective compliance program that pre-dated a [g]overnmental investigation" when considering the imposition of administrative penalties.[305] Presumably, a compliance program that covers many of the topics recommended by the OIG would more likely be considered effective than one that does not. It is important to note that the OIG has recognized the need for some flexibility in compliance programs, emphasizing that corporate compliance programs should be tailored to meet the specific needs of the organization and indicating that an organization with limited resources may not be able to adopt as comprehensive a compliance program as another entity with more extensive resources.

### 1. Seven Basic Elements

The OIG's recognition of the need for individualized programs notwithstanding, the OIG generally expects each organization to establish a program that implements the following seven basic elements:

1. written standards of conduct, including written policies and procedures to promote compliance;
2. designation of a chief compliance officer and other appropriate bodies such as a compliance committee;
3. establishment of regular, effective education and training programs;
4. development of a system to respond to allegations of improper or illegal activities and enforce appropriate disciplinary action;
5. maintenance of a system, such as a hotline, to receive complaints anonymously and protect whistleblowers from retaliation;
6. use of auditing and monitoring to evaluate compliance; and
7. investigation and remediation of identified systemic problems and the development of policies to prevent employment or retention of sanctioned individuals.[306]

### 2. Specific References to Caremark

Significantly, there is a specific reference to the *Caremark* decision in most of the Compliance Guidance documents, along with the statement that "recent case law suggests that the failure of a corporate Director to attempt in good faith to institute a compliance program in certain situations may be a breach of a Director's fiduciary obligation."[307]

---

[305]Compliance Program Guidance for Hospitals, 63 Fed. Reg. 8987, 8988 (Feb. 23, 1998).

[306]*See id.* at 8989.

[307]This statement was quoted in the following Compliance Guidance documents: 63 Fed. Reg. 8987, 8988 (Feb. 23, 1998) (hospitals); 63 Fed. Reg. 42,410, 42,411 (Aug. 7, 1998) (home health agencies); 63 Fed. Reg. 45,076, 45,077 (Aug. 24, 1998) (clinical laboratories); 64 Fed. Reg. 36,368, 36,369 (July 6, 1999) (DME suppliers); 64 Fed. Reg. 54,031, 54,032 (Oct. 5, 1999) (hospices); 65 Fed. Reg. 14,289, 14,290 (Mar. 16, 2000) (nursing facilities).

Furthermore, there are numerous statements throughout these documents stressing the need for a high level of organizational commitment to a compliance program. For example, the OIG emphasizes that "[i]t is incumbent upon a hospital's corporate officers and managers to provide ethical leadership to the organization and to assure that adequate systems are in place to facilitate ethical and legal conduct."[308] In addition, the OIG calls on senior management and the company's *governing body* to provide substantial commitments of time, energy, and resources to implement an effective compliance program, warning that "[p]rograms hastily constructed and implemented without appropriate ongoing monitoring will likely be ineffective and could result in greater harm or liability to the hospital than no program at all."[309]

### 3. Director and Officer Responsibilities for Compliance

By virtue of their differing roles and responsibilities within an organization, the compliance responsibilities of officers and directors will necessarily vary. Consistent with their areas of corporate responsibility, board members are unlikely to directly participate in many of the organization's compliance activities, while officers will be actively involved. However, there are various measures that both directors and officers should take to ensure that the compliance program is developed, implemented, and effective, and thus meets the corporate goal of minimizing exposure for the organization and its agents.

#### a. Establishing a Compliance Program

As part of its efforts to demonstrate high-level commitment to compliance within the organization, the board should adopt a resolution authorizing the establishment of a corporate compliance program for the company. This same resolution also could be used to appoint a chief compliance officer and compliance committee. It also is important that the board ensure that adequate resources, in terms of both finances and staff time, are available for the corporate compliance program. The organization's mission statement also should be reviewed to ensure that it includes a commitment to compliance. Once the compliance program is developed, senior management should send a "roll out" letter to all employees announcing the program, encouraging all to participate, and noting that failure to comply may result in disciplinary sanctions.

#### b. Continuing Compliance Responsibilities

Many companies do a good job at the introductory phase of compliance but fail to follow through and continue the compliance process. If the compliance program reveals issues that are not addressed, this discontinuity can subject the organization to heightened rather than lowered risks of liability. Therefore, directors and officers should be pre-

---

[308]Compliance Program Guidance for Hospitals, 63 Fed. Reg. 8987, 8988 (Feb. 23, 1998).

[309]*Id.*

pared to continue participating in the compliance process on an ongoing basis. As a preliminary matter, the board should assess whether the seven basic elements of a compliance program are in place. In addition, as described in the *Corporate Director's Guidebook,*[310]

> [a] significant aspect of the board's responsibility, often referred to the Audit Committee, is oversight of the corporation's policies and procedures regarding compliance with the law and with significant corporate policies. Most large, publicly owned corporations have adopted codes of conduct expressing principles of business ethics, legal compliance, and other matters relating to business conduct. Subjects commonly addressed by such codes are legal compliance . . . conflicts of interest, corporate opportunities, gifts from business associates, misuse of confidential information and political contributions. The board of directors should assure itself that the corporation has such a code of conduct, that the code is widely circulated to appropriate employees, that adherence to the code is enforced, that the corporation maintains procedures for monitoring and enforcing compliance and that the support of the CEO and the board is clearly evidenced.[311]

Senior management should be required to participate in compliance training. Even board members should participate in initial compliance education to better understand the operation of the compliance program and demonstrate high-level commitment to it.

The *Caremark* decision clearly indicates that board members should institute a system to collect appropriate information on the company's business performance and compliance with applicable laws and regulations. To this end, most compliance programs require the chief compliance officer or the compliance committee to present a report on the organization's compliance to the board at least once a year.[312] Certain "hands on" boards may want to directly review all or some of the underlying audit reports generated as part of the compliance process. In any event, board members should be prepared to engage in more than a cursory review of the compliance materials they receive. In this connection, note *In re W.R. Grace & Co.,*[313] in which the SEC found that directors and officers cannot necessarily rely on the information generated by the company's programs and procedures:

> If an officer or director knows or should know that his or her company's statements concerning particular issues are inadequate or incomplete, he or she has an obligation to correct that failure. An officer or director may rely upon the company's procedures for determining what disclosure is required only if he or she has a reasonable basis for believing that those procedures have resulted in full consideration of those issues.[314]

---

[310]A.B.A. COMM. ON CORPORATE LAWS, CORPORATE DIRECTOR'S GUIDEBOOK (2d ed. 1994).

[311]*Id.* at 31.

[312]In some organizations, the compliance report is presented to a board subcommittee.

[313]Fed. Sec. L. Rep. (CCH) ¶85,963 (1998).

[314]*Id.*

In *W.R. Grace*, the SEC found that the directors' reliance on the corporation's legal counsel to determine the adequacy of disclosure of certain information was not justified.[315] Certainly, if patterns or systemic problems appear in the compliance officer's or committee's report, the board would be well advised to require follow-up action. In addition, the scope of audits should be assessed to ensure that they are adequate and conducted by appropriate personnel (e.g., in some cases, outside auditors may be necessary).

The board likely will want to ensure that the compliance reports it receives include information on the "high risk" areas that have been identified by the government in the Compliance Guidance documents and other relevant materials, including Special Fraud Alerts, OIG Work Plans, and advisory opinions.[316] Similarly, compliance reports should include information on compliance at any subsidiary organizations because the parent may be held responsible for activities there.[317]

In addition, many compliance programs require that the board be notified immediately of any serious compliance violations. Each organization will need to decide at what point it wants the board to become involved. Under some programs, the board (or a subcommittee) is notified if the situation is sufficiently serious to warrant the retention of outside counsel. Alternatively, the compliance program may require that the board be notified if a certain level of financial exposure is involved or if there is evidence of fraud. If sufficiently senior members of management may be involved in compliance violations, the board should be notified and/or involved in the investigation, and it may be called on to participate in the disciplinary process. Finally, to the extent that they are involved in performance assessments, both directors and officers should include compliance as one of the factors used to evaluate and reward subordinates.

## V. Recommendations to Reduce Exposure

Although no measures can eliminate all risk of liability for corporate directors and officers, there are a number of steps that can be taken to reduce such exposure. Board members are well served by corporations that take advantage of the statutes limiting director liability. The statutes are not self-executing, and corporations wishing to offer these liability limitations need to review the applicable statute (e.g., Delaware Code, Title 8, Section 102(b)(7)) and make the appropriate amendments to their articles of incorporation. When forming a

---

[315]The context of the finding is somewhat unusual because it involves an administrative cease-and-desist order imposed as part of a settlement for alleged violations of the securities laws. Nevertheless, the breadth of the obligation imposed on the company's directors is noteworthy.

[316]*See* Compliance Program Guidance for Hospitals, 63 Fed. Reg. 8987, 8989 (1998).

[317]Typically, a parent organization and its subsidiaries will, to a certain extent, coordinate their compliance activities.

new corporation, the framers should remember to enact the necessary language in the original articles.

Similarly, corporations can provide indemnification for a good faith breach of a director's or officer's duty of care. These statutes are generally permissive and not self-executing. Accordingly, director and officer contracts should contain appropriate indemnification provisions, tracking any relevant statutory language and setting forth the circumstances under which the corporation is providing the indemnification. When possible, these contracts should take advantage of those state laws that allow the provision of expanded protection beyond that which is specified under the statute.

Corporations may provide insurance coverage in addition to indemnification. For example, Delaware permits corporations to purchase policies for directors and officers providing coverage for "any liability asserted against" them by virtue of their status.[318] Moreover, such policies can provide coverage to the director or officer for his or her acts as well as reimburse the corporation for monies it spends directly indemnifying the director or officer. Thus, corporations should consider purchasing broad coverage policies. A multitude of policy provisions, coverages, and exclusions are available, and various legal issues also should be considered.[319] Accordingly, an insurance professional or experienced lawyer can provide valuable assistance in selecting an appropriate policy.

Finally, directors and officers should take an active role in establishing and promoting a corporate compliance program. A compliance program can (1) prevent many problems from occurring, (2) help reduce the risk of exposure to the corporation and its directors and officers if compliance violations do occur, and (3) reduce the magnitude of the problem and penalties encountered if compliance violations are uncovered. However, to attain these objectives, it is essential that the compliance program be designed and implemented so as to be "effective." Directors and officers should be involved in the compliance efforts to help demonstrate good faith and high-level commitment to the program, to provide the necessary resources, and to ensure that the information gathering and reporting systems called for in the *Caremark* decision are in place and functioning properly.

It is important to remember that compliance plans are not "effective," and thus do not provide protection, unless they are actively implemented. To this end, they should be individually designed to meet the specific needs of the corporation. In addition, although directors oversee, rather than manage, the business of a corporation, they should carefully monitor compliance activities. Collecting information alone is not sufficient. Audits and other reports should be carefully scrutinized and questions pursued when necessary.

---

[318]DEL. CODE. ANN. tit. 8, §145(g).

[319]*See, e.g.,* JOHN OLSON, *ET AL.*, DIRECTOR AND OFFICER LIABILITY: INDEMNIFICATION AND INSURANCE §§10.01–.12 (1999).

Board members might consult the applicable Compliance Guidance documents issued by the OIG. Although these documents are not legally binding, they provide guidance helpful in evaluating the corporation's compliance program and identify some of the high-risk issues that, in the OIG's view, the compliance program should address.

If, despite all these efforts, there is a compliance violation that leads to a government investigation, directors and officers should consider retaining their own counsel who can best protect their individual interests. Obviously, this admonition is particularly important in the event of subsequent litigation or settlement negotiations.

# Appendix Table of Contents

[**Editor's Note:** The Internet website for the Office of Inspector General, Department of Health and Human Services, was reorganized in early 2002. Source lines for appendix materials from the OIG have been revised to reflect these changes. Readers are cautioned that agency documents on the Internet are subject to change; readers should consult the OIG's website for updates and further information on topics of interest.]

# Appendix A

## Anti-Kickback Statute Materials

# Appendix A-1

## Anti-Kickback Statute

*Source:* 42 U.S.C. Section 1320a-7b(b).

### Section 1320a-7b. Criminal penalties for acts involving Federal health care programs

. . .

(b) Illegal remunerations

(1) Whoever knowingly and willfully solicits or receives any remuneration (including any kickback, bribe, or rebate) directly or indirectly, overtly or covertly, in cash or in kind—

(A) in return for referring an individual to a person for the furnishing or arranging for the furnishing of any item or service for which payment may be made in whole or in part under a Federal health care program, or

(B) in return for purchasing, leasing, ordering, or arranging for or recommending purchasing, leasing, or ordering any good, facility, service, or item for which payment may be made in whole or in part under a Federal health care program,

shall be guilty of a felony and upon conviction thereof, shall be fined not more than $25,000 or imprisoned for not more than five years, or both.

(2) Whoever knowingly and willfully offers or pays any remuneration (including any kickback, bribe, or rebate) directly or indirectly, overtly or covertly, in cash or in kind to any person to induce such person

(A) to refer an individual to a person for the furnishing or arranging for the furnishing of any item or service for which payment may be made in whole or in part under a Federal health care program, or

(B) to purchase, lease, order, or arrange for or recommend purchasing, leasing, or ordering any good, facility, service, or item for which payment may be made in whole or in part under a Federal health care program,

shall be guilty of a felony and upon conviction thereof, shall be fined not more than $25,000 or imprisoned for not more than five years, or both.

(3) Paragraphs (1) and (2) shall not apply to—

(A) a discount or other reduction in price obtained by a provider of services or other entity under a Federal health care program if the reduction in price is properly disclosed and appropriately reflected in the costs claimed or charges made by the provider or entity under a Federal health care program;

(B) any amount paid by an employer to an employee (who has a bona fide employment relationship with such employer) for employment in the provision of covered items or services;

(C) any amount paid by a vendor of goods or services to a person authorized to act as a purchasing agent for a group of individuals or entities who are furnishing services reimbursed under a Federal health care program if—

(i) the person has a written contract, with each such individual or entity, which specifies the amount to be paid the person, which amount may be a fixed amount or a fixed percentage of the value of the purchases made by each such individual or entity under the contract, and

(ii) in the case of an entity that is a provider of services (as defined in section 1395x(u) of this title), the person discloses (in such form and manner as the Secretary requires) to the entity and, upon request, to the Secretary the amount received from each such vendor with respect to purchases made by or on behalf of the entity;

(D) a waiver of any coinsurance under part B of subchapter XVIII of this chapter by a Federally qualified health care center with respect to an individual who qualifies for subsidized services under a provision of the Public Health Service Act (42 U.S.C. 201 et seq.);

(E) any payment practice specified by the Secretary in regulations promulgated pursuant to section 14(a) of the Medicare and Medicaid Patient and Program Protection Act of 1987; and

(F) any remuneration between an organization and an individual or entity providing items or services, or a combination thereof, pursuant to a written agreement between the organization and the individual or entity if the organization is an eligible organization under section 1395mm of this title or if the written agreement, through a risk-sharing arrangement, places the individual or entity at substantial financial risk for the cost or utilization of the items or services, or a combination thereof, which the individual or entity is obligated to provide.

*SOURCE—*

(Aug. 14, 1935, ch. 531, title XI, Sec. 1128B, formerly title XVIII, Sec. 1877(d), and title XIX, Sec. 1909, as added and amended Pub. L. 92-603, title II, Sec. 242(c), 278(b)(9), Oct. 30, 1972, 86 Stat. 1419, 1454; Pub. L. 95-142, Sec. 4(a), (b), Oct. 25, 1977, 91 Stat. 1179, 1181; Pub. L. 96-499, title IX, Sec. 917, Dec. 5, 1980, 94 Stat. 2625; Pub. L. 98-369, div. B, title III, Sec. 2306(f)(2), July 18, 1984,

98 Stat. 1073; renumbered title XI, Sec. 1128B, and amended Pub. L. 100-93, Sec. 4(a)-(d), 14(b), Aug. 18, 1987, 101 Stat. 688, 689, 697; Pub. L. 100-203, title IV, Sec. 4039(a), 4211(h)(7), Dec. 22, 1987, 101 Stat. 1330-81, 1330-206; Pub. L. 100-360, title IV, Sec. 411(a)(3)(A), (B)(i), July 1, 1988, 102 Stat. 768; Pub. L. 101-239, title VI, Sec. 6003(g)(3)(D)(ii), Dec. 19, 1989, 103 Stat. 2153; Pub. L. 101-508, title IV, Sec. 4161(a)(4), 4164(b)(2), Nov. 5, 1990, 104 Stat. 1388-94, 1388-102; Pub. L. 103-432, title I, Sec. 133(a)(2), Oct. 31, 1994, 108 Stat. 4421; Pub. L. 104-191, title II, Sec. 204(a), 216(a), 217, Aug. 21, 1996, 110 Stat. 1999, 2007, 2008; Pub. L. 105-33, title IV, Sec. 4201(c)(1), 4704(b), 4734, Aug. 5, 1997, 111 Stat. 373, 498, 522.)

## REFERENCES IN TEXT

Part B of subchapter XVIII of this chapter, referred to in subsec. (b)(3)(D), is classified to section 1395j et seq. of this title.

The Public Health Service Act, referred to in subsec. (b)(3)(D), is act July 1, 1944, ch. 373, 58 Stat. 682, as amended, which is classified generally to chapter 6A (Sec. 201 et seq.) of this title. For complete classification of this Act to the Code, see Short Title note set out under section 201 of this title and Tables.

Section 14(a) of the Medicare and Medicaid Patient and Program Protection Act of 1987, referred to in subsec. (b)(3)(E), is section 14(a) of Pub. L. 100-93, . . . .

# Appendix A-2

## Anti-Kickback Safe Harbor Regulations

*Source:* 42 C.F.R. Section 1001.952

### Section 1001.952 Exceptions.

The following payment practices shall not be treated as a criminal offense under section 1128B of the Act and shall not serve as the basis for an exclusion:

(a) *Investment interests.* As used in section 1128B of the Act, "remuneration" does not include any payment that is a return on an investment interest, such as a dividend or interest income, made to an investor as long as all of the applicable standards are met within one of the following three categories of entities:

(1) If, within the previous fiscal year or previous 12 month period, the entity possesses more than $50,000,000 in undepreciated net tangible assets (based on the net acquisition cost of purchasing such assets from an unrelated entity) related to the furnishing of health care items and services, all of the following five standards must be met—

(i) With respect to an investment interest that is an equity security, the equity security must be registered with the Securities and Exchange Commission under 15 U.S.C. 781 (b) or (g).

(ii) The investment interest of an investor in a position to make or influence referrals to, furnish items or services to, or otherwise generate business for the entity must be obtained on terms (including any direct or indirect transferability restrictions) and at a price equally available to the public when trading on a registered securities exchange, such as the New York Stock Exchange or the American Stock Exchange, or in accordance with the National Association of Securities Dealers Automated Quotation System.

(iii) The entity or any investor must not market or furnish the entity's items or services (or those of another entity as part of a cross referral agreement) to passive investors differently than to non-investors.

471

(iv) The entity or any investor (or other individual or entity acting on behalf of the entity or any investor in the entity) must not loan funds to or guarantee a loan for an investor who is in a position to make or influence referrals to, furnish items or services to, or otherwise generate business for the entity if the investor uses any part of such loan to obtain the investment interest.

(v) The amount of payment to an investor in return for the investment interest must be directly proportional to the amount of the capital investment of that investor.

(2) If the entity possesses investment interests that are held by either active or passive investors, all of the following eight applicable standards must be met—

(i) No more than 40 percent of the value of the investment interests of each class of investment interests may be held in the previous fiscal year or previous 12 month period by investors who are in a position to make or influence referrals to, furnish items or services to, or otherwise generate business for the entity. (For purposes of paragraph (a)(2)(i) of this section, equivalent classes of equity investments may be combined, and equivalent classes of debt instruments may be combined.)

(ii) The terms on which an investment interest is offered to a passive investor, if any, who is in a position to make or influence referrals to, furnish items or services to, or otherwise generate business for the entity must be no different from the terms offered to other passive investors.

(iii) The terms on which an investment interest is offered to an investor who is in a position to make or influence referrals to, furnish items or services to, or otherwise generate business for the entity must not be related to the previous or expected volume of referrals, items or services furnished, or the amount of business otherwise generated from that investor to the entity.

(iv) There is no requirement that a passive investor, if any, make referrals to, be in a position to make or influence referrals to, furnish items or services to, or otherwise generate business for the entity as a condition for remaining as an investor.

(v) The entity or any investor must not market or furnish the entity's items or services (or those of another entity as part of a cross referral agreement) to passive investors differently than to non-investors.

(vi) No more than 40 percent of the entity's gross revenue related to the furnishing of health care items and services in the previous fiscal year or previous 12-month period may come from referrals or business otherwise generated from investors.

(vii) The entity or any investor (or other individual or entity acting on behalf of the entity or any investor in the entity) must not loan funds to or guarantee a loan for an investor who is in a position to make or influence referrals to, furnish items or services to, or otherwise generate business for the entity if the investor uses any part of such loan to obtain the investment interest.

(viii) The amount of payment to an investor in return for the investment interest must be directly proportional to the amount of the capital investment (including the fair market value of any pre-operational services rendered) of that investor.

(3)(i) If the entity possesses investment interests that are held by either active or passive investors and is located in an underserved area, all of the following eight standards must be met—

(A) No more than 50 percent of the value of the investment interests of each class of investments may be held in the previous fiscal year or previous 12- month period by investors who are in a position to make or influence referrals to, furnish items or services to, or otherwise generate business for, the entity. (For purposes of paragraph (a)(3)(i)(A) of this section, equivalent classes of equity investments may be combined, and equivalent classes of debt instruments may be combined.)

(B) The terms on which an investment interest is offered to a passive investor, if any, who is in a position to make or influence referrals to, furnish items or services to, or otherwise generate business for the entity must be no different from the terms offered to other passive investors.

(C) The terms on which an investment interest is offered to an investor who is in a position to make or influence referrals to, furnish items or services to, or otherwise generate business for the entity must not be related to the previous or expected volume of referrals, items or services furnished, or the amount of business otherwise generated from that investor to the entity.

(D) There is no requirement that a passive investor, if any, make referrals to, be in a position to make or influence referrals to, furnish items or services to, or otherwise generate business for the entity as a condition for remaining as an investor.

(E) The entity or any investor must not market or furnish the entity's items or services (or those of another entity as part of a cross-referral agreement) to passive investors differently than to non-investors.

(F) At least 75 percent of the dollar volume of the entity's business in the previous fiscal year or previous 12-month period must be derived from the service of persons who reside in an underserved area or are members of medically underserved populations.

(G) The entity or any investor (or other individual or entity acting on behalf of the entity or any investor in the entity) must not loan funds to or guarantee a loan for an investor who is in a position to make or influence referrals to, furnish items or services to, or otherwise generate business for the entity if the investor uses any part of such loan to obtain the investment interest.

(H) The amount of payment to an investor in return for the investment interest must be directly proportional to the amount of the capital investment (including the fair market value of any pre-operational services rendered) of that investor.

(ii) If an entity that otherwise meets all of the above standards is located in an area that was an underserved area at the time of the initial investment, but subsequently ceases to be an underserved area, the entity will be deemed to comply with paragraph (a)(3)(i) of this section for a period equal to the lesser of:

(A) The current term of the investment remaining after the date upon which the area ceased to be an underserved area or

(B) Three years from the date the area ceased to be an underserved area.

(4) For purposes of paragraph (a) of this section, the following terms apply. *Active investor* means an investor either who is responsible for the day-to-day management of the entity and is a bona fide general partner in a partnership under the Uniform Partnership Act or who agrees in writing to undertake liability for the actions of the entity's agents acting within the scope of their agency. *Investment interest* means a security issued by an entity, and may include the following classes of investments: shares in a corporation, interests or units in a partnership or limited liability company, bonds, debentures, notes, or other debt instruments. *Investor* means an individual or entity either who directly holds an investment interest in an entity, or who holds such investment interest indirectly by, including but not limited to, such means as having a family member hold such investment interest or holding a legal or beneficial interest in another entity (such as a trust or holding company) that holds such investment interest. *Passive investor* means an investor who is not an active investor, such as a limited partner in a partnership under the Uniform Partnership Act, a shareholder in a corporation, or a holder of a debt security. *Underserved area* means any defined geographic area that is designated as a Medically Underserved Area (MUA) in accordance with regulations issued by the Department. *Medically underserved population* means a Medically Underserved Population (MUP) in accordance with regulations issued by the Department.

(b) *Space rental.* As used in section 1128B of the Act, "remuneration" does not include any payment made by a lessee to a lessor for the use of premises, as long as all of the following six standards are met—

(1) The lease agreement is set out in writing and signed by the parties.

(2) The lease covers all of the premises leased between the parties for the term of the lease and specifies the premises covered by the lease.

(3) If the lease is intended to provide the lessee with access to the premises for periodic intervals of time, rather than on a full-time

basis for the term of the lease, the lease specifies exactly the schedule of such intervals, their precise length, and the exact rent for such intervals.

(4) The term of the lease is for not less than one year.

(5) The aggregate rental charge is set in advance, is consistent with fair market value in arms-length transactions and is not determined in a manner that takes into account the volume or value of any referrals or business otherwise generated between the parties for which payment may be made in whole or in part under Medicare or a State health care program.

(6) The aggregate space rented does not exceed that which is reasonably necessary to accomplish the commercially reasonable business purpose of the rental.

For purposes of paragraph (b) of this section, the term fair market value means the value of the rental property for general commercial purposes, but shall not be adjusted to reflect the additional value that one party (either the prospective lessee or lessor) would attribute to the property as a result of its proximity or convenience to sources of referrals or business otherwise generated for which payment may be made in whole or in part under Medicare or a State health care program.

(c) *Equipment rental.* As used in section 1128B of the Act, "remuneration" does not include any payment made by a lessee of equipment to the lessor of the equipment for the use of the equipment, as long as all of the following six standards are met—

(1) The lease agreement is set out in writing and signed by the parties.

(2) The lease covers all of the equipment leased between the parties for the term of the lease and specifies the equipment covered by the lease.

(3) If the lease is intended to provide the lessee with use of the equipment for periodic intervals of time, rather than on a full-time basis for the term of the lease, the lease specifies exactly the schedule of such intervals, their precise length, and the exact rent for such interval.

(4) The term of the lease is for not less than one year.

(5) The aggregate rental charge is set in advance, is consistent with fair market value in arms-length transactions and is not determined in a manner that takes into account the volume or value of any referrals or business otherwise generated between the parties for which payment may be made in whole or in part under Medicare or a State health care program.

(6) The aggregate equipment rental does not exceed that which is reasonably necessary to accomplish the commercially reasonable business purpose of the rental.

For purposes of paragraph (c) of this section, the term *fair market value* means the value of the equipment when obtained from a manufacturer or professional distributor, but shall not be adjusted to reflect the additional value one party (either the prospective lessee or lessor) would attribute to the equipment as a result of its proximity or convenience to sources of referrals or business otherwise generated for which payment may be made in whole or in part under Medicare or a State health care program.

(d) *Personal services and management contracts.* As used in section 1128B of the Act, "remuneration" does not include any payment made by a principal to an agent as compensation for the services of the agent, as long as all of the following seven standards are met—

(1) The agency agreement is set out in writing and signed by the parties.

(2) The agency agreement covers all of the services the agent provides to the principal for the term of the agreement and specifies the services to be provided by the agent.

(3) If the agency agreement is intended to provide for the services of the agent on a periodic, sporadic or part-time basis, rather than on a full-time basis for the term of the agreement, the agreement specifies exactly the schedule of such intervals, their precise length, and the exact charge for such intervals.

(4) The term of the agreement is for not less than one year.

(5) The aggregate compensation paid to the agent over the term of the agreement is set in advance, is consistent with fair market value in arms- length transactions and is not determined in a manner that takes into account the volume or value of any referrals or business otherwise generated between the parties for which payment may be made in whole or in part under Medicare or a State health care program.

(6) The services performed under the agreement do not involve the counselling or promotion of a business arrangement or other activity that violates any State or Federal law.

(7) The aggregate services contracted for do not exceed those which are reasonably necessary to accomplish the commercially reasonable business purpose of the services.

For purposes of paragraph (d) of this section, an agent of a principal is any person, other than a bona fide employee of the principal, who has an agreement to perform services for, or on behalf of, the principal.

(e) *Sale of practice.*

(1) As used in section 1128B of the Act, "remuneration" does not include any payment made to a practitioner by another practitioner where the former practitioner is selling his or her practice to the latter practitioner, as long as both of the following two standards are met—

(i) The period from the date of the first agreement pertaining to the sale to the completion of the sale is not more than one year.

(ii) The practitioner who is selling his or her practice will not be in a professional position to make referrals to, or otherwise generate business for, the purchasing practitioner for which payment may be made in whole or in part under Medicare or a

State health care program after one year from the date of the first agreement pertaining to the sale.

(2) As used in section 1128B of the Act, "remuneration" does not include any payment made to a practitioner by a hospital or other entity where the practitioner is selling his or her practice to the hospital or other entity, so long as the following four standards are met:

(i) The period from the date of the first agreement pertaining to the sale to the completion date of the sale is not more than three years.

(ii) The practitioner who is selling his or her practice will not be in a professional position after completion of the sale to make or influence referrals to, or otherwise generate business for, the purchasing hospital or entity for which payment may be made in whole or in part under Medicare or a State health care program.

(iii) The practice being acquired must be located in a Health Professional Shortage Area (HPSA), as defined in Departmental regulations, for the practitioner's specialty area.

(iv) Commencing at the time of the first agreement pertaining to the sale, the purchasing hospital or entity must diligently and in good faith engage in commercially reasonable recruitment activities that:

(A) May reasonably be expected to result in the recruitment of a new practitioner to take over the acquired practice within a one year period and

(B) Will satisfy the conditions of the practitioner recruitment safe harbor in accordance with paragraph (n) of this section.

(f) *Referral services.* As used in section 1128B of the Act, "remuneration" does not include any payment or exchange of anything of value between an individual or entity ("participant") and another entity serving as a referral service ("referral service"), as long as all of the following four standards are met—

(1) The referral service does not exclude as a participant in the referral service any individual or entity who meets the qualifications for participation.

(2) Any payment the participant makes to the referral service is assessed equally against and collected equally from all participants, and is only based on the cost of operating the referral service, and not on the volume or value of any referrals to or business otherwise generated by either party for the other party for which payment may be made in whole or in part under Medicare or a State health care program.

(3) The referral service imposes no requirements on the manner in which the participant provides services to a referred person, except that the referral service may require that the participant charge the person referred at the same rate as it charges other persons not referred by the referral service, or that these services be furnished free of charge or at reduced charge.

(4) The referral service makes the following five disclosures to each person seeking a referral, with each such disclosure maintained by the referral service in a written record certifying such disclosure and signed by either such person seeking a referral or by the individual making the disclosure on behalf of the referral service—

(i) The manner in which it selects the group of participants in the referral service to which it could make a referral;

(ii) Whether the participant has paid a fee to the referral service;

(iii) The manner in which it selects a particular participant from this group for that person;

(iv) The nature of the relationship between the referral service and the group of participants to whom it could make the referral; and

(v) The nature of any restrictions that would exclude such an individual or entity from continuing as a participant.

(g) *Warranties.* As used in section 1128B of the Act, "remuneration" does not include any payment or exchange of anything of value under a warranty provided by a manufacturer or supplier of an item to the buyer (such as a health care provider or beneficiary) of the item, as long as the buyer complies with all of the following standards in paragraphs (g)(1) and (g)(2) of this section and the manufacturer or supplier complies with all of the following standards in paragraphs (g)(3) and (g)(4) of this section—

(1) The buyer must fully and accurately report any price reduction of the item (including a free item), which was obtained as part of the warranty, in the applicable cost reporting mechanism or claim for payment filed with the Department or a State agency.

(2) The buyer must provide, upon request by the Secretary or a State agency, information provided by the manufacturer or supplier as specified in paragraph (g)(3) of this section.

(3) The manufacturer or supplier must comply with either of the following two standards—

(i) The manufacturer or supplier must fully and accurately report the price reduction of the item (including a free item), which was obtained as part of the warranty, on the invoice or statement submitted to the buyer, and inform the buyer of its obligations under paragraphs (a)(1) and (a)(2) of this section.

(ii) Where the amount of the price reduction is not known at the time of sale, the manufacturer or supplier must fully and accurately report the existence of a warranty on the invoice or statement, inform the buyer of its obligations under paragraphs (g)(1) and (g)(2) of this section, and, when the price reduction becomes known, provide the buyer with documentation of the calculation of the price reduction resulting from the warranty.

(4) The manufacturer or supplier must not pay any remuneration to any individual (other than a beneficiary) or entity for any medical, surgical, or hospital expense incurred by a beneficiary other than for the cost of the item itself.

For purposes of paragraph (g) of this section, the term *warranty* means either an agreement made in accordance with the provisions of 15 U.S.C. 2301(6), or a manufacturer's or supplier's agreement to replace another manufacturer's or supplier's defective item (which is covered by an agreement made in accordance with this statutory provision), on terms equal to the agreement that it replaces.

(h) *Discounts.* As used in section 1128B of the Act, "remuneration" does not include a discount, as defined in paragraph (h)(5) of this section, on an item or service for which payment may be made, in whole or in part, under Medicare or a State health care program for a *buyer* as long as the buyer complies with the applicable standards of paragraph (h)(1) of this section; a *seller* as long as the seller complies with the applicable standards of paragraph (h)(2) of this section; and an *offeror* of a discount who is not a seller under paragraph (h)(2) of this section so long as such offeror complies with the applicable standards of paragraph (h)(3) of this section:

(1) With respect to the following three categories of buyers, the buyer must comply with all of the applicable standards within one of the three following categories—

(i) If the buyer is an entity which is a health maintenance organization (HMO) or a competitive medical plan (CMP) acting in accordance with a risk contract under section 1876(g) or 1903(m) of the Act, or under another State health care program, it need not report the discount except as otherwise may be required under the risk contract.

(ii) If the buyer is an entity which reports its costs on a cost report required by the Department or a State health care program, it must comply with all of the following four standards—

(A) The discount must be earned based on purchases of that same good or service bought within a single fiscal year of the buyer;

(B) The buyer must claim the benefit of the discount in the fiscal year in which the discount is earned or the following year;

(C) The buyer must fully and accurately report the discount in the applicable cost report; and

(D) The buyer must provide, upon request by the Secretary or a State agency, information provided by the seller as specified in paragraph (h)(2)(ii) of this section, or information provided by the offeror as specified in paragraph (h)(3)(ii) of this section.

(iii) If the buyer is an individual or entity in whose name a claim or request for payment is submitted for the discounted item or service and payment may be made, in whole or in part, under Medicare or a State health care program (not including individuals or entities defined as buyers in paragraph (h)(1)(i) or (h)(1)(ii) of this section), the buyer must comply with both of the following standards—

(A) The discount must be made at the time of the sale of the good or service or the terms of the rebate must be fixed and disclosed in writing to the buyer at the time of the initial sale of the good or service; and

(B) The buyer (if submitting the claim) must provide, upon request by the Secretary or a State agency, information provided by the seller as specified in paragraph (h)(2)(iii)(B) of this section, or information provided by the offeror as specified in paragraph (h)(3)(iii)(A) of this section.

(2) The seller is an individual or entity that supplies an item or service for which payment may be made, in whole or in part, under Medicare or a State health care program to the buyer and who permits a discount to be taken off the buyer's purchase price. The seller must comply with all of the applicable standards within the following three categories—

(i) If the buyer is an entity which is an HMO a CMP acting in accordance with a risk contract under section 1876(g) or 1903(m) of the Act, or under another State health care program, the seller need not report the discount to the buyer for purposes of this provision.

(ii) If the buyer is an entity that reports its costs on a cost report required by the Department or a State agency, the seller must comply with either of the following two standards—

(A) Where a discount is required to be reported to Medicare or a State health care program under paragraph (h)(1) of this section, the seller must fully and accurately report such discount on the invoice, coupon or statement submitted to the buyer; inform the buyer in a manner that is reasonably calculated to give notice to the buyer of its obligations to report such discount and to provide information upon request under paragraph (h)(1) of this section; and refrain from doing anything that would impede the buyer from meeting its obligations under this paragraph; or

(B) Where the value of the discount is not known at the time of sale, the seller must fully and accurately report the existence of a discount program on the invoice, coupon or statement submitted to the buyer; inform the buyer in a manner reasonably calculated to give notice to the buyer of its obligations to report such discount and to provide information upon request under paragraph (h)(1) of this section; when the value of the discount becomes known, provide the buyer with documentation of the calculation of the discount identifying the specific goods or services purchased to which the discount will be applied; and refrain from doing anything which would impede the buyer from meeting its obligations under this paragraph.

(iii) If the buyer is an individual or entity not included in paragraph (h)(2)(i) or (h)(2)(ii) of this section, the seller must comply with either of the following two standards—

(A) Where the seller submits a claim or request for payment on behalf of the buyer and the item or service is separately claimed, the seller must provide, upon request by the Secretary or a State agency, information provided by the offeror as specified in paragraph (h)(3)(iii)(A) of this section; or

(B) Where the buyer submits a claim, the seller must fully and accurately report such discount on the invoice, coupon or statement submitted to the buyer; inform the buyer in a manner reasonably calculated to give notice to the buyer of its obligations to report such discount and to provide information upon request under paragraph (h)(1) of this section; and refrain from doing anything that would impede the buyer from meeting its obligations under this paragraph.

(3) The offeror of a discount is an individual or entity who is not a seller under paragraph (h)(2) of this section, but promotes the purchase of an item or service by a buyer under paragraph (h)(1) of this section at a reduced price for which payment may be made, in whole or in part, under Medicare or a State health care program. The offeror must comply with all of the applicable standards within the following three categories—

(i) If the buyer is an entity which is an HMO or a CMP acting in accordance with a risk contract under section 1876(g) or 1903(m) of the Act, or under another State health care program, the offeror need not report the discount to the buyer for purposes of this provision.

(ii) If the buyer is an entity that reports its costs on a cost report required by the Department or a State agency, the offeror must comply with the following two standards—

(A) The offeror must inform the buyer in a manner reasonably calculated to give notice to the buyer of its obligations to report such a discount and to provide information upon request under paragraph (h)(1) of this section; and

(B) The offeror of the discount must refrain from doing anything that would impede the buyer's ability to meet its obligations under this paragraph.

(iii) If the buyer is an individual or entity in whose name a request for payment is submitted for the discounted item or service and payment may be made, in whole or in part, under Medicare or a State health care program (not including individuals or entities defined as buyers in paragraph (h)(1)(i) or (h)(1)(ii) of this section), the offeror must comply with the following two standards—

(A) The offeror must inform the individual or entity submitting the claim or request for payment in a manner reasonably calculated to give notice to the individual or entity of its obligations to report such a discount and to provide information upon request under paragraphs (h)(1) and (h)(2) of this section; and

(B) The offeror of the discount must refrain from doing anything that would impede the buyer's or seller's ability to meet its obligations under this paragraph.

(4) For purposes of this paragraph, a rebate is any discount the terms of which are fixed and disclosed in writing to the buyer at the time of the initial purchase to which the discount applies, but which is not given at the time of sale.

(5) For purposes of this paragraph, the term *discount* means a reduction in the amount a buyer (who buys either directly or through a wholesaler or a group purchasing organization) is charged for an item or service based on an arms-length transaction. The term *discount* does not include—

(i) Cash payment or cash equivalents (except that rebates as defined in paragraph (h)(4) of this section may be in the form of a check);

(ii) Supplying one good or service without charge or at a reduced charge to induce the purchase of a different good or service, unless the goods and services are reimbursed by the same Federal health care program using the same methodology and the reduced charge is fully disclosed to the Federal health care program and accurately reflected where appropriate, and as appropriate, to the reimbursement methodology;

(iii) A reduction in price applicable to one payer but not to Medicare or a State health care program;

(iv) A routine reduction or waiver of any coinsurance or deductible amount owed by a program beneficiary;

(v) Warranties;

(vi) Services provided in accordance with a personal or management services contract; or

(vii) Other remuneration, in cash or in kind, not explicitly described in paragraph (h)(5) of this section.

(i) *Employees.* As used in section 1128B of the Act, "remuneration" does not include any amount paid by an employer to an employee, who has a bona fide employment relationship with the employer, for employment in the furnishing of any item or service for which payment may be made in whole or in part under Medicare or a State health care program. For purposes of paragraph (i) of this section, the term employee has the same meaning as it does for purposes of 26 U.S.C. 3121(d)(2).

(j) *Group purchasing organizations.* As used in section 1128B of the Act, "remuneration" does not include any payment by a vendor of goods or services to a group purchasing organization (GPO), as part of an agreement to furnish such goods or services to an individual or entity as long as both of the following two standards are met—

(1) The GPO must have a written agreement with each individual or entity, for which items or services are furnished, that provides for either of the following—

(i) The agreement states that participating vendors from which the individual or entity will purchase goods or services will pay a fee to the GPO of 3 percent or less of the purchase price of the goods or services provided by that vendor.

(ii) In the event the fee paid to the GPO is not fixed at 3 percent or less of the purchase price of the goods or services, the agreement specifies the amount (or if not known, the maximum amount) the GPO will be paid by each vendor (where such amount may be a fixed sum or a fixed percentage of the value of purchases made from the vendor by the members of the group under the contract between the vendor and the GPO).

(2) Where the entity which receives the goods or service from the vendor is a health care provider of services, the GPO must disclose in writing to the entity at least annually, and to the Secretary upon request, the amount received from each vendor with respect to purchases made by or on behalf of the entity.

For purposes of paragraph (j) of this section, the term *group purchasing organization* (GPO) means an entity authorized to act as a purchasing agent for a group of individuals or entities who are furnishing services for which payment may be made in whole or in part under Medicare or a State health care program, and who are neither wholly-owned by the GPO nor subsidiaries of a parent corporation that wholly owns the GPO (either directly or through another wholly-owned entity).

(k) *Waiver of beneficiary coinsurance and deductible amounts.* As used in section 1128B of the Act, "remuneration" does not include any reduction or waiver of a Medicare or a State health care program beneficiary's obligation to pay coinsurance or deductible amounts as long as all of the standards are met within either of the following two categories of health care providers:

(1) If the coinsurance or deductible amounts are owed to a hospital for inpatient hospital services for which Medicare pays under the prospective payment system, the hospital must comply with all of the following three standards—

(i) The hospital must not later claim the amount reduced or waived as a bad debt for payment purposes under Medicare or otherwise shift the burden of the reduction or waiver onto Medicare, a State health care program, other payers, or individuals.

(ii) The hospital must offer to reduce or waive the coinsurance or deductible amounts without regard to the reason for admission, the length of stay of the beneficiary, or the diagnostic related group for which the claim for Medicare reimbursement is filed.

(iii) The hospital's offer to reduce or waive the coinsurance or deductible amounts must not be made as part of a price reduction agreement between a hospital and a third-party payer (including a health plan as defined in paragraph (l)(2) of this section), unless the agreement is part of a contract for the furnishing of items or services to a beneficiary of a Medicare supplemental policy issued under the terms of section 1882(t)(1) of the Act.

(2) If the coinsurance or deductible amounts are owed by an individual who qualifies for subsidized services under a provision of the

Public Health Services Act or under titles V or XIX of the Act to a federally qualified health care center or other health care facility under any Public Health Services Act grant program or under title V of the Act, the health care center or facility may reduce or waive the coinsurance or deductible amounts for items or services for which payment may be made in whole or in part under part B of Medicare or a State health care program.

(l) *Increased coverage, reduced cost-sharing amounts, or reduced premium amounts offered by health plans.*

(1) As used in section 1128B of the Act, "remuneration" does not include the additional coverage of any item or service offered by a health plan to an enrollee or the reduction of some or all of the enrollee's obligation to pay the health plan or a contract health care provider for cost-sharing amounts (such as coinsurance, deductible, or copayment amounts) or for premium amounts attributable to items or services covered by the health plan, the Medicare program, or a State health care program, as long as the health plan complies with all of the standards within one of the following two categories of health plans:

(i) If the health plan is a risk-based health maintenance organization, competitive medical plan, prepaid health plan, or other health plan under contract with CMS or a State health care program and operating in accordance with section 1876(g) or 1903(m) of the Act, under a Federal statutory demonstration authority, or under other Federal statutory or regulatory authority, it must offer the same increased coverage or reduced cost-sharing or premium amounts to all Medicare or State health care program enrollees covered by the contract unless otherwise approved by CMS or by a State health care program.

(ii) If the health plan is a health maintenance organization, competitive medical plan, health care prepayment plan, prepaid health plan or other health plan that has executed a contract or agreement with CMS or with a State health care program to receive payment for enrollees on a reasonable cost or similar basis, it must comply with both of the following two standards—

(A) The health plan must offer the same increased coverage or reduced cost-sharing or premium amounts to all Medicare or State health care program enrollees covered by the contract or agreement unless otherwise approved by CMS or by a State health care program; and

(B) The health plan must not claim the costs of the increased coverage or the reduced cost-sharing or premium amounts as a bad debt for payment purposes under Medicare or a State health care program or otherwise shift the burden of the increased coverage or reduced cost-sharing or premium amounts to the extent that increased payments are claimed from Medicare or a State health care program.

(2) For purposes of paragraph (l) of this section, the terms—

*Contract health care provider* means an individual or entity under contract with a health plan to furnish items or services to enrollees who are covered by the health plan, Medicare, or a State health care program.

*Enrollee* means an individual who has entered into a contractual relationship with a health plan (or on whose behalf an employer, or other private or governmental entity has entered into such a relationship) under which the individual is entitled to receive specified health care items and services, or insurance coverage for such items and services, in return for payment of a premium or a fee.

*Health plan* means an entity that furnishes or arranges under agreement with contract health care providers for the furnishing of items or services to enrollees, or furnishes insurance coverage for the provision of such items and services, in exchange for a premium or a fee, where such entity:

(i) Operates in accordance with a contract, agreement or statutory demonstration authority approved by CMS or a State health care program;

(ii) Charges a premium and its premium structure is regulated under a State insurance statute or a State enabling statute governing health maintenance organizations or preferred provider organizations;

(iii) Is an employer, if the enrollees of the plan are current or retired employees, or is a union welfare fund, if the enrollees of the plan are union members; or

(iv) Is licensed in the State, is under contract with an employer, union welfare fund, or a company furnishing health insurance coverage as described in conditions (ii) and (iii) of this definition, and is paid a fee for the administration of the plan which reflects the fair market value of those services.

(m) *Price reductions offered to health plans.*

(1) As used in section 1128B of the Act, "remuneration" does not include a reduction in price a contract health care provider offers to a health plan in accordance with the terms of a written agreement between the contract health care provider and the health plan for the sole purpose of furnishing to enrollees items or services that are covered by the health plan, Medicare, or a State health care program, as long as both the health plan and contract health care provider comply with all of the applicable standards within one of the following four categories of health plans:

(i) If the health plan is a risk-based health maintenance organization, competitive medical plan, or prepaid health plan under contract with CMS or a State agency and operating in accordance with section 1876(g) or 1903(m) of the Act, under a Federal statutory demonstration authority, or under other Federal statutory or regulatory authority, the contract health care provider must not claim payment in any form from the Department or the State agency for items or services furnished in accordance with the agreement except as approved by CMS or the State health care program, or otherwise shift the burden of such an agreement to the extent that increased payments are claimed from Medicare or a State health care program.

(ii) If the health plan is a health maintenance organization, competitive medical plan, health care prepayment plan, prepaid health plan, or other health plan that has executed a contract or agreement with CMS or a State health care program to receive payment for enrollees on a reasonable cost or similar basis, the health plan and contract health care provider must comply with all of the following four standards—

(A) The term of the agreement between the health plan and the contract health care provider must be for not less than one year;

(B) The agreement between the health plan and the contract health care provider must specify in advance the covered items and services to be furnished to enrollees, and the methodology for computing the payment to the contract health care provider;

(C) The health plan must fully and accurately report, on the applicable cost report or other claim form filed with the Department or the State health care program, the amount it has paid the contract health care provider under the agreement for the covered items and services furnished to enrollees; and

(D) The contract health care provider must not claim payment in any form from the Department or the State health care program for items or services furnished in accordance with the agreement except as approved by CMS or the State health care program, or otherwise shift the burden of such an agreement to the extent that increased payments are claimed from Medicare or a State health care program.

(iii) If the health plan is not described in paragraphs (m)(1)(i) or (m)(1)(ii) of this section and the contract health care provider is not paid on an at-risk, capitated basis, both the health plan and contract health care provider must comply with all of the following six standards—

(A) The term of the agreement between the health plan and the contract health care provider must be for not less than one year;

(B) The agreement between the health plan and the contract health care provider must specify in advance the covered items and services to be furnished to enrollees, which party is to file claims or requests for payment with Medicare or the State health care program for such items and services, and the schedule of fees the contract health care provider will charge for furnishing such items and services to enrollees;

(C) The fee schedule contained in the agreement between the health plan and the contract health care provider must remain in effect throughout the term of the agreement, unless a fee increase results directly from a payment update authorized by Medicare or the State health care program;

(D) The party submitting claims or requests for payment from Medicare or the State health care program for items and services furnished in accordance with the agreement must not claim or request payment for amounts in excess of the fee schedule;

(E) The contract health care provider and the health plan must fully and accurately report on any cost report filed with Medicare or a State health care program the fee schedule amounts charged in accordance with the agreement and, upon request, will report to the Medicare or a State health care program the terms of the agreement and the amounts paid in accordance with the agreement; and

(F) The party to the agreement, which does not have the responsibility under the agreement for filing claims or requests for payment, must not claim or request payment in any form from the Department or the State health care program for items or services furnished in accordance with the agreement, or otherwise shift the burden of such an agreement to the extent that increased payments are claimed from Medicare or a State health care program.

(iv) If the health plan is not described in paragraphs (m)(1)(i) or (m)(1)(ii) of this section, and the contract health care provider is paid on an at-risk, capitated basis, both the health plan and contract health care provider must comply with all of the following five standards—

(A) The term of the agreement between the health plan and the contract health provider must be for not less than one year;

(B) The agreement between the health plan and the contract health provider must specify in advance the covered items and services to be furnished to enrollees and the total amount per enrollee (which may be expressed in a per month or other time period basis) the contract health care provider will be paid by the health plan for furnishing such items and services to enrollees and must set forth any copayments, if any, to be paid by enrollees to the contract health care provider for covered services;

(C) The payment amount contained in the agreement between the health care plan and the contract health care provider must remain in effect throughout the term of the agreement;

(D) The contract health care provider and the health plan must fully and accurately report to the Medicare and State health care program upon request, the terms of the agreement and the amounts paid in accordance with the agreement; and

(E) The contract health care provider must not claim or request payment in any form from the Department, a State health care program or an enrollee (other than copayment amounts described in paragraph (m)(2)(iv)(B) of this section) and the health plan must not pay the contract care provider in excess of the amounts described in paragraph (m)(2)(iv)(B) of this section for items and services covered by the agreement.

(2) For purposes of this paragraph, the terms *contract health care provider, enrollee,* and *health plan* have the same meaning as in paragraph (l)(2) of this section.

(n) *Practitioner recruitment.* As used in section 1128B of the Act, "remuneration" does not include any payment or exchange of anything of value by an entity in order to induce a practitioner who has been practicing within his or her current specialty for less than one year to locate, or to induce any other practitioner to relocate, his or her primary place of practice into a HPSA for his or her specialty area, as defined in Departmental regulations, that is served by the entity, as long as all of the following nine standards are met—

(1) The arrangement is set forth in a written agreement signed by the parties that specifies the benefits provided by the entity, the terms under which the benefits are to be provided, and the obligations of each party.

(2) If a practitioner is leaving an established practice, at least 75 percent of the revenues of the new practice must be generated from new patients not previously seen by the practitioner at his or her former practice.

(3) The benefits are provided by the entity for a period not in excess of 3 years, and the terms of the agreement are not renegotiated during this 3-year period in any substantial aspect; provided, however, that if the HPSA to which the practitioner was recruited ceases to be a HPSA during the term of the written agreement, the payments made under the written agreement will continue to satisfy this paragraph for the duration of the written agreement (not to exceed 3 years).

(4) There is no requirement that the practitioner make referrals to, be in a position to make or influence referrals to, or otherwise generate business for the entity as a condition for receiving the benefits; provided, however, that for purposes of this paragraph, the entity may require as a condition for receiving benefits that the practitioner maintain staff privileges at the entity.

(5) The practitioner is not restricted from establishing staff privileges at, referring any service to, or otherwise generating any business for any other entity of his or her choosing.

(6) The amount or value of the benefits provided by the entity may not vary (or be adjusted or renegotiated) in any manner based on the volume or value of any expected referrals to or business otherwise generated for the entity by the practitioner for which payment may be made in whole or in part under Medicare or a State health care program.

(7) The practitioner agrees to treat patients receiving medical benefits or assistance under any Federal health care program in a nondiscriminatory manner.

(8) At least 75 percent of the revenues of the new practice must be generated from patients residing in a HPSA or a Medically Underserved Area (MUA) or who are part of a Medically Underserved Population (MUP), all as defined in paragraph (a) of this section.

(9) The payment or exchange of anything of value may not directly or indirectly benefit any person (other than the practitioner being recruited) or entity in a position to make or influence referrals to the entity providing the recruitment payments or benefits of items or services payable by a Federal health care program.

(o) *Obstetrical malpractice insurance subsidies.* As used in section 1128B of the Act, "remuneration" does not include any payment made by a hospital or other entity to another entity that is providing malpractice insurance (including a self-funded entity), where such payment is used to pay for some or all of the costs of malpractice insurance premiums for a practitioner (including a certified nurse-midwife as defined in section 1861(gg) of the Act) who engages in obstetrical practice as a routine part of his or her medical practice in a primary care HPSA, as long as all of the following seven standards are met—

(1) The payment is made in accordance with a written agreement between the entity paying the premiums and the practitioner, which sets out the payments to be made by the entity, and the terms under which the payments are to be provided.

(2)(i) The practitioner must certify that for the initial coverage period (not to exceed one year) the practitioner has a reasonable basis for believing that at least 75 percent of the practitioner's obstetrical patients treated under the coverage of the malpractice insurance will either—

(A) Reside in a HPSA or MUA, as defined in paragraph (a) of this section; or

(B) Be part of a MUP, as defined in paragraph (a) of this section.

(ii) Thereafter, for each additional coverage period (not to exceed one year), at least 75 percent of the practitioner's obstetrical patients treated under the prior coverage period (not to exceed one year) must have—

(A) Resided in a HPSA or MUA, as defined in paragraph (a) of this section; or

(B) Been part of a MUP, as defined in paragraph (a) of this section.

(3) There is no requirement that the practitioner make referrals to, or otherwise generate business for, the entity as a condition for receiving the benefits.

(4) The practitioner is not restricted from establishing staff privileges at, referring any service to, or otherwise generating any business for any other entity of his or her choosing.

(5) The amount of payment may not vary based on the volume or value of any previous or expected referrals to or business otherwise generated for the entity by the practitioner for which payment may be made in whole or in part under Medicare or a State health care program.

(6) The practitioner must treat obstetrical patients who receive medical benefits or assistance under any Federal health care program in a nondiscriminatory manner.

(7) The insurance is a bona fide malpractice insurance policy or program, and the premium, if any, is calculated based on a bona fide assessment of the liability risk covered under the insurance. For purposes of paragraph (o) of this section, costs of malpractice insurance premiums means:

    (i) For practitioners who engage in obstetrical practice full-time, any costs attributable to malpractice insurance; or

    (ii) For practitioners who engage in obstetrical practice on a part-time or sporadic basis, the costs:

        (A) Attributable exclusively to the obstetrical portion of the practitioner's malpractice insurance and

        (B) Related exclusively to obstetrical services provided in a primary care HPSA.

(p) *Investments in group practices.* As used in section 1128B of the Act, "remuneration" does not include any payment that is a return on an investment interest, such as a dividend or interest income, made to a solo or group practitioner investing in his or her own practice or group practice if the following four standards are met—

    (1) The equity interests in the practice or group must be held by licensed health care professionals who practice in the practice or group.

    (2) The equity interests must be in the practice or group itself, and not some subdivision of the practice or group.

    (3) In the case of group practices, the practice must:

        (i) Meet the definition of "group practice" in section 1877(h)(4) of the Social Security Act and implementing regulations; and

        (ii) Be a unified business with centralized decision-making, pooling of expenses and revenues, and a compensation/profit distribution system that is not based on satellite offices operating substantially as if they were separate enterprises or profit centers.

    (4) Revenues from ancillary services, if any, must be derived from "in-office ancillary services" that meet the definition of such term in section 1877(b)(2) of the Act and implementing regulations.

(q) *Cooperative hospital service organizations.* As used in section 1128B of the Act, "remuneration" does not include any payment made between a cooperative hospital service organization (CHSO) and its patron-hospital, both of which are described in section 501(e) of the Internal Revenue Code of 1986 and are tax-exempt under section 501(c)(3) of the Internal Revenue Code, where the CHSO is wholly owned by two or more patron-hospitals, as long as the following standards are met—

(1) If the patron-hospital makes a payment to the CHSO, the payment must be for the purpose of paying for the bona fide operating expenses of the CHSO, or

(2) If the CHSO makes a payment to the patron-hospital, the payment must be for the purpose of paying a distribution of net earnings required to be made under section 501(e)(2) of the Internal Revenue Code of 1986.

(r) *Ambulatory surgical centers.* As used in section 1128B of the Act, "remuneration" does not include any payment that is a return on an investment interest, such as a dividend or interest income, made to an investor, as long as the investment entity is a certified ambulatory surgical center (ASC) under part 416 of this title, whose operating and recovery room space is dedicated exclusively to the ASC, patients referred to the investment entity by an investor are fully informed of the investor's investment interest, and all of the applicable standards are met within one of the following four categories—

(1) *Surgeon-owned ASCs*—If all of the investors are general surgeons or surgeons engaged in the same surgical specialty, who are in a position to refer patients directly to the entity and perform surgery on such referred patients; surgical group practices (as defined in this paragraph) composed exclusively of such surgeons; or investors who are not employed by the entity or by any investor, are not in a position to provide items or services to the entity or any of its investors, and are not in a position to make or influence referrals directly or indirectly to the entity or any of its investors, all of the following six standards must be met—

(i) The terms on which an investment interest is offered to an investor must not be related to the previous or expected volume of referrals, services furnished, or the amount of business otherwise generated from that investor to the entity.

(ii) At least one-third of each surgeon investor's medical practice income from all sources for the previous fiscal year or previous 12-month period must be derived from the surgeon's performance of procedures (as defined in this paragraph).

(iii) The entity or any investor (or other individual or entity acting on behalf of the entity or any investor) must not loan funds to or guarantee a loan for an investor if the investor uses any part of such loan to obtain the investment interest.

(iv) The amount of payment to an investor in return for the investment must be directly proportional to the amount of the capital investment (including the fair market value of any pre-operational services rendered) of that investor.

(v) All ancillary services for Federal health care program beneficiaries performed at the entity must be directly and integrally related to primary procedures performed at the entity, and none may be separately billed to Medicare or other Federal health care programs.

(vi) The entity and any surgeon investors must treat patients receiving medical benefits or assistance under any Federal health care program in a nondiscriminatory manner.

(2) *Single-Specialty ASCs*—If all of the investors are physicians engaged in the same medical practice specialty who are in a position to refer patients directly to the entity and perform procedures on such referred patients; group practices (as defined in this paragraph) composed exclusively of such physicians; or investors who are not employed by the entity or by any investor, are not in a position to provide items or services to the entity or any of its investors, and are not in a position to make or influence referrals directly or indirectly to the entity or any of its investors, all of the following six standards must be met—

(i) The terms on which an investment interest is offered to an investor must not be related to the previous or expected volume of referrals, services furnished, or the amount of business otherwise generated from that investor to the entity.

(ii) At least one-third of each physician investor's medical practice income from all sources for the previous fiscal year or previous 12-month period must be derived from the surgeon's performance of procedures (as defined in this paragraph).

(iii) The entity or any investor (or other individual or entity acting on behalf of the entity or any investor) must not loan funds to or guarantee a loan for an investor if the investor uses any part of such loan to obtain the investment interest.

(iv) The amount of payment to an investor in return for the investment must be directly proportional to the amount of the capital investment (including the fair market value of any pre-operational services rendered) of that investor.

(v) All ancillary services for Federal health care program beneficiaries performed at the entity must be directly and integrally related to primary procedures performed at the entity, and none may be separately billed to Medicare or other Federal health care programs.

(vi) The entity and any physician investors must treat patients receiving medical benefits or assistance under any Federal health care program in a nondiscriminatory manner.

(3) *Multi-Specialty ASCs*—If all of the investors are physicians who are in a position to refer patients directly to the entity and perform procedures on such referred patients; group practices, as defined in this paragraph, composed exclusively of such physicians; or investors

who are not employed by the entity or by any investor, are not in a position to provide items or services to the entity or any of its investors, and are not in a position to make or influence referrals directly or indirectly to the entity or any of its investors, all of the following seven standards must be met—

(i) The terms on which an investment interest is offered to an investor must not be related to the previous or expected volume of referrals, services furnished, or the amount of business otherwise generated from that investor to the entity.

(ii) At least one-third of each physician investor's medical practice income from all sources for the previous fiscal year or previous 12-month period must be derived from the physician's performance of procedures (as defined in this paragraph).

(iii) At least one-third of the procedures (as defined in this paragraph) performed by each physician investor for the previous fiscal year or previous 12-month period must be performed at the investment entity.

(iv) The entity or any investor (or other individual or entity acting on behalf of the entity or any investor) must not loan funds to or guarantee a loan for an investor if the investor uses any part of such loan to obtain the investment interest.

(v) The amount of payment to an investor in return for the investment must be directly proportional to the amount of the capital investment (including the fair market value of any pre-operational services rendered) of that investor.

(vi) All ancillary services for Federal health care program beneficiaries performed at the entity must be directly and integrally related to primary procedures performed at the entity, and none may be separately billed to Medicare or other Federal health care programs.

(vii) The entity and any physician investors must treat patients receiving medical benefits or assistance under any Federal health care program in a nondiscriminatory manner.

(4) *Hospital/Physician ASCs*—If at least one investor is a hospital, and all of the remaining investors are physicians who meet the requirements of paragraphs (r)(1), (r)(2) or (r)(3) of this section; group practices (as defined in this paragraph) composed of such physicians; surgical group practices (as defined in this paragraph); or investors who are not employed by the entity or by any investor, are not in a position to provide items or services to the entity or any of its investors, and are not in a position to refer patients directly or indirectly to the entity or any of its investors, all of the following eight standards must be met—

(i) The terms on which an investment interest is offered to an investor must not be related to the previous or expected volume of referrals, services furnished, or the amount of business otherwise generated from that investor to the entity.

(ii) The entity or any investor (or other individual or entity act-ing on behalf of the entity or any investor) must not loan funds to or guarantee a loan for an investor if the investor uses any part of such loan to obtain the investment interest.

(iii) The amount of payment to an investor in return for the investment must be directly proportional to the amount of the capital investment (including the fair market value of any pre-operational services rendered) of that investor.

(iv) The entity and any hospital or physician investor must treat patients receiving medical benefits or assistance under any Fed-eral health care program in a nondiscriminatory manner.

(v) The entity may not use space, including, but not limited to, operating and recovery room space, located in or owned by any hospital investor, unless such space is leased from the hospital in accordance with a lease that complies with all the standards of the space rental safe harbor set forth in paragraph (b) of this sec-tion; nor may it use equipment owned by or services provided by the hospital unless such equipment is leased in accordance with a lease that complies with the equipment rental safe harbor set forth in paragraph (c) of this section, and such services are pro-vided in accordance with a contract that complies with the per-sonal services and management contracts safe harbor set forth in paragraph (d) of this section.

(vi) All ancillary services for Federal health care program bene-ficiaries performed at the entity must be directly and integrally related to primary procedures performed at the entity, and none may be separately billed to Medicare or other Federal health care programs.

(vii) The hospital may not include on its cost report or any claim for payment from a Federal health care program any costs asso-ciated with the ASC (unless such costs are required to be in-cluded by a Federal health care program).

(viii) The hospital may not be in a position to make or influence referrals directly or indirectly to any investor or the entity.

(5) For purposes of paragraph (r) of this section, *procedures* means any procedure or procedures on the list of Medicare-covered proce-dures for ambulatory surgical centers in accordance with regulations issued by the Department and *group practice* means a group practice that meets all of the standards of paragraph (p) of this section. *Sur-gical group practice* means a group practice that meets all of the standards of paragraph (p) of this section and is composed exclu-sively of surgeons who meet the requirements of paragraph (r)(1) of this section.

(s) *Referral agreements for specialty services.* As used in section 1128B of the Act, *remuneration* does not include any exchange of value among individuals and entities where one party agrees to refer a patient to the other party for the provision of a specialty service payable in whole or in part under Medicare or a State health care program in return for an agreement on the part of the other party to refer that patient back at a mutually agreed upon time or circumstance as long as the following four standards are met—

(1) The mutually agreed upon time or circumstance for referring the patient back to the originating individual or entity is clinically appropriate.

(2) The service for which the referral is made is not within the medical expertise of the referring individual or entity, but is within the special expertise of the other party receiving the referral.

(3) The parties receive no payment from each other for the referral and do not share or split a global fee from any Federal health care program in connection with the referred patient.

(4) Unless both parties belong to the same group practice as defined in paragraph (p) of this section, the only exchange of value between the parties is the remuneration the parties receive directly from third-party payors or the patient compensating the parties for the services they each have furnished to the patient.

(t) *Price reductions offered to eligible managed care organizations.*

(1) As used in section 1128(B) of the Act, "remuneration" does not include any payment between:

(i) An eligible managed care organization and any first tier contractor for providing or arranging for items or services, as long as the following three standards are met—

(A) The eligible managed care organization and the first tier contractor have an agreement that:

(1) Is set out in writing and signed by both parties;

(2) Specifies the items and services covered by the agreement;

(3) Is for a period of at least one year; and

(4) Specifies that the first tier contractor cannot claim payment in any form directly or indirectly from a Federal health care program for items or services covered under the agreement, except for:

(i) HMOs and competitive medical plans with cost-based contracts under section 1876 of the Act where the agreement with the eligible managed care organization sets out the arrangements in accordance with which the first tier contractor is billing the Federal health care program;

(ii) Federally qualified HMOs without a contract under sections 1854 or 1876 of the Act, where the agreement with the eligible managed care organization sets out the arrangements in accordance with which the first tier contractor is billing the Federal health care program; or

(iii) First tier contractors that are Federally qualified health centers that claim supplemental payments from a Federal health care program.

(B) In establishing the terms of the agreement, neither party gives or receives remuneration in return for or to induce the provision or acceptance of business (other than business covered by the agreement) for which payment may be made in whole or in part by a Federal health care program on a fee-for-service or cost basis.

(C) Neither party to the agreement shifts the financial burden of the agreement to the extent that increased payments are claimed from a Federal health care program.

(ii) A first tier contractor and a downstream contractor or between two downstream contractors to provide or arrange for items or services, as long as the following four standards are met—

(A) The parties have an agreement that:

(1) Is set out in writing and signed by both parties;

(2) Specifies the items and services covered by the agreement;

(3) Is for a period of at least one year; and

(4) Specifies that the party providing the items or services cannot claim payment in any form from a Federal health care program for items or services covered under the agreement.

(B) In establishing the terms of the agreement, neither party gives or receives remuneration in return for or to induce the provision or acceptance of business (other than business covered by the agreement) for which payment may be made in whole or in part by a Federal health care program on a fee-for-service or cost basis.

(C) Neither party shifts the financial burden of the agreement to the extent that increased payments are claimed from a Federal health care program.

(D) The agreement between the eligible managed care organization and first tier contractor covering the items or services that are covered by the agreement between the parties does not involve:

(1) A Federally qualified health center receiving supplemental payments;

(2) A HMO or CMP with a cost-based contract under section 1876 of the Act; or

(3) A Federally qualified HMO, unless the items or services are covered by a risk based contract under sections 1854 or 1876 of the Act.

(2) For purposes of this paragraph, the following terms are defined as follows:

(i) *Downstream contractor* means an individual or entity that has a subcontract directly or indirectly with a first tier contractor for the provision or arrangement of items or services that are covered by an agreement between an eligible managed care organization and the first tier contractor.

(ii) *Eligible managed care organization*[1] means—

(A) A HMO or CMP with a risk or cost based contract in accordance with section 1876 of the Act;

(B) Any Medicare Part C health plan that receives a capitated payment from Medicare and which must have its total Medicare beneficiary cost sharing approved by CMS under section 1854 of the Act;

(C) Medicaid managed care organizations as defined in section 1903(m)(1)(A) that provide or arrange for items or services for Medicaid enrollees under a contract in accordance with section 1903(m) of the Act (except for fee-for-service plans or medical savings accounts);

(D) Any other health plans that provide or arrange for items and services for Medicaid enrollees in accordance with a risk-based contract with a State agency subject to the upper payment limits in § 447.361 of this title or an equivalent payment cap approved by the Secretary;

(E) Programs For All Inclusive Care For The Elderly (PACE) under sections 1894 and 1934 of the Act, except for for-profit demonstrations under sections 4801(h) and 4802(h) of Pub.L. 105-33; or

(F) A Federally qualified HMO.

(iii) *First tier contractor* means an individual or entity that has a contract directly with an eligible managed care organization to provide or arrange for items or services.

(iv) *Items and services* means health care items, devices, supplies or services or those services reasonably related to the provision of health care items, devices, supplies or services including, but not limited to, non-emergency transportation, patient education, attendant services, social services (e.g., case management), utilization review and quality assurance. Marketing and other pre-enrollment activities are not "items or services" for purposes of this section.

(u) *Price reductions offered by contractors with substantial financial risk to managed care organizations.*

(1) As used in section 1128(B) of the Act, "remuneration" does not include any payment between:

(i) A qualified managed care plan and a first tier contractor for providing or arranging for items or services, where the following five standards are met—

(A) The agreement between the qualified managed care plan and first tier contractor must:

(1) Be in writing and signed by the parties;

---

[1]The eligible managed care organizations in paragraphs (u)(2)(ii)(A)-(F) of this section are only eligible with respect to items or services covered by the contracts specified in those paragraphs.

(2) Specify the items and services covered by the agreement;

(3) Be for a period of a least one year;

(4) Require participation in a quality assurance program that promotes the coordination of care, protects against underutilization and specifies patient goals, including measurable outcomes where appropriate; and

(5) Specify a methodology for determining payment that is commercially reasonable and consistent with fair market value established in an arms-length transaction and includes the intervals at which payments will be made and the formula for calculating incentives and penalties, if any.

(B) If a first tier contractor has an investment interest in a qualified managed care plan, the investment interest must meet the criteria of paragraph (a)(1) of this section.

(C) The first tier contractor must have substantial financial risk for the cost or utilization of services it is obligated to provide through one of the following four payment methodologies:

(1) A periodic fixed payment per patient that does not take into account the dates services are provided, the frequency of services, or the extent or kind of services provided;

(2) Percentage of premium;

(3) Inpatient Federal health care program diagnosis-related groups (DRGs) (other than those for psychiatric services);

(4) Bonus and withhold arrangements, provided—

(i) The target payment for first tier contractors that are individuals or non-institutional providers is at least 20 percent greater than the minimum payment, and for first tier contractors that are institutional providers, i.e., hospitals and nursing homes, is at least 10 percent greater than the minimum payment;

(ii) The amount at risk, i.e., the bonus or withhold, is earned by a first tier contractor in direct proportion to the ratio of the contractor's actual utilization to its target utilization;

(iii) In calculating the percentage in accordance with paragraph (u)(1)(i)(C)(4)(i) of this section, both the target payment amount and the minimum payment amount include any performance bonus, e.g., payments for timely submission of paperwork, continuing medical education, meeting attendance, etc., at a level achieved by 75 percent of the first tier contractors who are eligible for such payments;

(iv) Payment amounts, including any bonus or withhold amounts, are reasonable given the historical utilization

patterns and costs for the same or comparable populations in similar managed care arrangements; and

(v) Alternatively, for a first tier contractor that is a
physician, the qualified managed care plan has placed
the physician at risk for referral services in an amount
that exceeds the substantial financial risk threshold set
forth in 42 CFR 417.479(f) and the arrangement is in
compliance with the stop-loss and beneficiary survey requirements of 42 CFR 417.479(g).

(D) Payments for items and services reimbursable by Federal health care program must comply with the following two
standards—

(1) The qualified managed care plan (or in the case of a
self-funded employer plan that contracts with a qualified
managed care plan to provide administrative services,
the self-funded employer plan) must submit the claims
directly to the Federal health care program, in accordance with a valid reassignment agreement, for items or
services reimbursed by the Federal health care program.
(Notwithstanding the foregoing, inpatient hospital services, other than psychiatric services, will be deemed to
comply if the hospital is reimbursed by a Federal health
care program under a DRG methodology.)

(2) Payments to first tier contractors and any downstream contractors for providing or arranging for items
or services reimbursed by a Federal health care program
must be identical to payment arrangements to or between such parties for the same items or services provided to other beneficiaries with similar health status,
provided that such payments may be adjusted where the
adjustments are related to utilization patterns or costs of
providing items or services to the relevant population.

(E) In establishing the terms of an arrangement—

(1) Neither party gives or receives remuneration in return for or to induce the provision or acceptance of business (other than business covered by the arrangement)
for which payment may be made in whole or in part by a
Federal health care program on a fee-for-service or cost
basis; and

(2) Neither party to the arrangement shifts the financial
burden of such arrangement to the extent that increased
payments are claimed from a Federal health care
program.

(ii) A first tier contractor and a downstream contractor, or between downstream contractors, to provide or arrange for items or
services, as long as the following three standards are met—

(A) Both parties are being paid for the provision or arrangement of items or services in accordance with one of the pay-

ment methodologies set out in paragraph (u)(1)(i)(C) of this section;

(B) Payment arrangements for items and services reimbursable by a Federal health care program comply with paragraph (u)(1)(i)(D) of this section; and

(C) In establishing the terms of an arrangement—

(1) Neither party gives or receives remuneration in return for or to induce the provision or acceptance of business (other than business covered by the arrangement) for which payment may be made in whole or in part by a Federal health care program on a fee-for-service or cost basis; and

(2) Neither party to the arrangement shifts the financial burden of the arrangement to the extent that increased payments are claimed from a Federal health care program.

(2) For purposes of this paragraph, the following terms are defined as follows:

(i) *Downstream contractor* means an individual or entity that has a subcontract directly or indirectly with a first tier contractor for the provision or arrangement of items or services that are covered by an agreement between a qualified managed care plan and the first tier contractor.

(ii) *First tier contractor* means an individual or entity that has a contract directly with a qualified managed care plan to provide or arrange for items or services.

(iii) *Is obligated* to provide for a contractor refers to items or services:

(A) Provided directly by an individual or entity and its employees;

(B) For which an individual or entity is financially responsible, but which are provided by downstream contractors;

(C) For which an individual or entity makes referrals or arrangements; or

(D) For which an individual or entity receives financial incentives based on its own, its provider group's, or its qualified managed care plan's performance (or combination thereof).

(iv) *Items and services* means health care items, devices, supplies or services or those services reasonably related to the provision of health care items, devices, supplies or services including, but not limited to, non-emergency transportation, patient education, attendant services, social services (e.g., case management), utilization review and quality assurance. Marketing or other pre-enrollment activities are not "items or services" for purposes of this definition in this paragraph.

(v) *Minimum payment* is the guaranteed amount that a provider is entitled to receive under an agreement with a first tier or downstream contractor or a qualified managed care plan.

(vi) *Qualified managed care plan* means a health plan as defined in paragraph (l)(2) of this section that:

    (A) Provides a comprehensive range of health services;

    (B) Provides or arranges for—

        (1) Reasonable utilization goals to avoid inappropriate utilization;

        (2) An operational utilization review program;

        (3) A quality assurance program that promotes the coordination of care, protects against underutilization, and specifies patient goals, including measurable outcomes where appropriate;

        (4) Grievance and hearing procedures;

        (5) Protection of enrollees from incurring financial liability other than copayments and deductibles; and

        (6) Treatment for Federal health care program beneficiaries that is not different than treatment for other enrollees because of their status as Federal health care program beneficiaries; and

    (C) Covers a beneficiary population of which either—

        (1) No more than 10 percent are Medicare beneficiaries, not including persons for whom a Federal health care program is the secondary payer; or

        (2) No more than 50 percent are Medicare beneficiaries (not including persons for whom a Federal health care program is the secondary payer), provided that payment of premiums is on a periodic basis that does not take into account the dates services are rendered, the frequency of services, or the extent or kind of services rendered, and provided further that such periodic payments for the non-Federal health care program beneficiaries do not take into account the number of Federal health care program fee-for-service beneficiaries covered by the agreement or the amount of services generated by such beneficiaries.

(vii) *Target payment* means the fair market value payment established through arms length negotiations that will be earned by an individual or entity that:

    (A) Is dependent on the individual or entity's meeting a utilization target or range of utilization targets that are set consistent with historical utilization rates for the same or comparable populations in similar managed care arrangements, whether based on its own, its provider group's or the qualified managed care plan's utilization (or a combination thereof); and

    (B) Does not include any bonus or fees that the individual or entity may earn from exceeding the utilization target.

[SOURCE: 57 Fed. Reg. 52,729 (Nov. 5, 1992); 61 Fed. Reg. 2135 (Jan. 25, 1996); 64 Fed. Reg. 63,513, 63,551 (Nov. 19, 1999); 64 Fed. Reg. 71,317 (Dec. 21, 1999).]

# Appendix B

## Stark Self-Referral Law Materials

***Editor's Note:*** The draft integrated Stark II Phase I regulations, effective Jan. 4, 2002, are on disk accompanying this volume. The draft integrated regulations are in folder **STARK**; the file name for this document is **STRKIIRG.**

# Appendix B-1

## Stark Self-Referral Law

*Source:* 42 U.S.C. Section 1395nn.

**Section 1395nn. Limitation on Certain Physician Referrals**

(a) Prohibition of certain referrals

(1) In general

Except as provided in subsection (b) of this section, if a physician (or an immediate family member of such physician) has a financial relationship with an entity specified in paragraph (2), then—

(A) the physician may not make a referral to the entity for the furnishing of designated health services for which payment otherwise may be made under this subchapter, and

(B) the entity may not present or cause to be presented a claim under this subchapter or bill to any individual, third party payor, or other entity for designated health services furnished pursuant to a referral prohibited under subparagraph (A).

(2) Financial relationship specified

For purposes of this section, a financial relationship of a physician (or an immediate family member of such physician) with an entity specified in this paragraph is—

(A) except as provided in subsections (c) and (d) of this section, an ownership or investment interest in the entity, or

(B) except as provided in subsection (e) of this section, a compensation arrangement (as defined in subsection (h)(1) of this section) between the physician (or an immediate family member of such physician) and the entity.

An ownership or investment interest described in subparagraph (A) may be through equity, debt, or other means and includes an interest in an entity that holds an ownership or investment interest in any entity providing the designated health service.

(b) General exceptions to both ownership and compensation arrangement prohibitions

Subsection (a)(1) of this section shall not apply in the following cases:

(1) Physicians' services

In the case of physicians' services (as defined in section 1395x(q) of this title) provided personally by (or under the personal supervision of) another physician in the same group practice (as defined in subsection (h)(4) of this section) as the referring physician.

(2) In-office ancillary services

In the case of services (other than durable medical equipment (excluding infusion pumps) and parenteral and enteral nutrients, equipment, and supplies)—

    (A) that are furnished—

        (i) personally by the referring physician, personally by a physician who is a member of the same group practice as the referring physician, or personally by individuals who are directly supervised by the physician or by another physician in the group practice, and

        (ii)(I) in a building in which the referring physician (or another physician who is a member of the same group practice) furnishes physicians' services unrelated to the furnishing of designated health services, or

            (II) in the case of a referring physician who is a member of a group practice, in another building which is used by the group practice—

            (aa) for the provision of some or all of the group's clinical laboratory services, or

            (bb) for the centralized provision of the group's designated health services (other than clinical laboratory services), unless the Secretary determines other terms and conditions under which the provision of such services does not present a risk of program or patient abuse, and

    (B) that are billed by the physician performing or supervising the services, by a group practice of which such physician is a member under a billing number assigned to the group practice, or by an entity that is wholly owned by such physician or such group practice,

if the ownership or investment interest in such services meets such other requirements as the Secretary may impose by regulation as needed to protect against program or patient abuse.

(3) Prepaid plans

In the case of services furnished by an organization—

(A) with a contract under section 1395mm of this title to an individual enrolled with the organization,

(B) described in section 1395l(a)(1)(A) of this title to an individual enrolled with the organization,

(C) receiving payments on a prepaid basis, under a demonstration project under section 1395b-1(a) of this title or under section 222(a) of the Social Security Amendments of 1972, to an individual enrolled with the organization,

(D) that is a qualified health maintenance organization (within the meaning of section 300e-9(d)[1] of this title) to an individual enrolled with the organization, or

---

[1] See References in Text note below.

(E) that is a Medicare+Choice organization under part C of this subchapter that is offering a coordinated care plan described in section 1395w-21(a)(2)(A) of this title to an individual enrolled with the organization.

(4) Other permissible exceptions

In the case of any other financial relationship which the Secretary determines, and specifies in regulations, does not pose a risk of program or patient abuse.

(c) General exception related only to ownership or investment prohibition for ownership in publicly traded securities and mutual funds

Ownership of the following shall not be considered to be an ownership or investment interest described in subsection (a)(2)(A) of this section:

(1) Ownership of investment securities (including shares or bonds, debentures, notes, or other debt instruments) which may be purchased on terms generally available to the public and which are—

(A)(i) securities listed on the New York Stock Exchange, the American Stock Exchange, or any regional exchange in which quotations are published on a daily basis, or foreign securities listed on a recognized foreign, national, or regional exchange in which quotations are published on a daily basis, or

(ii) traded under an automated interdealer quotation system operated by the National Association of Securities Dealers, and

(B) in a corporation that had, at the end of the corporation's most recent fiscal year, or on average during the previous 3 fiscal years, stockholder equity exceeding $75,000,000.

(2) Ownership of shares in a regulated investment company as defined in section 851(a) of the Internal Revenue Code of 1986, if such company had, at the end of the company's most recent fiscal year, or on average during the previous 3 fiscal years, total assets exceeding $75,000,000.

(d) Additional exceptions related only to ownership or investment prohibition

The following, if not otherwise excepted under subsection (b) of this section, shall not be considered to be an ownership or investment interest described in subsection (a)(2)(A) of this section:

(1) Hospitals in Puerto Rico

In the case of designated health services provided by a hospital located in Puerto Rico.

(2) Rural provider

In the case of designated health services furnished in a rural area (as defined in section 1395ww(d)(2)(D) of this title) by an entity, if substantially all of the designated health services furnished by such entity are furnished to individuals residing in such a rural area.

(3) Hospital ownership

In the case of designated health services provided by a hospital (other than a hospital described in paragraph (1)) if—

    (A) the referring physician is authorized to perform services at the hospital, and

    (B) the ownership or investment interest is in the hospital itself (and not merely in a subdivision of the hospital).

(e) Exceptions relating to other compensation arrangements

The following shall not be considered to be a compensation arrangement described in subsection (a)(2)(B) of this section:

    (1) Rental of office space; rental of equipment

        (A) Office space

        Payments made by a lessee to a lessor for the use of premises if—

            (i) the lease is set out in writing, signed by the parties, and specifies the premises covered by the lease,

            (ii) the space rented or leased does not exceed that which is reasonable and necessary for the legitimate business purposes of the lease or rental and is used exclusively by the lessee when being used by the lessee, except that the lessee may make payments for the use of space consisting of common areas if such payments do not exceed the lessee's pro rata share of expenses for such space based upon the ratio of the space used exclusively by the lessee to the total amount of space (other than common areas) occupied by all persons using such common areas,

            (iii) the lease provides for a term of rental or lease for at least 1 year,

            (iv) the rental charges over the term of the lease are set in advance, are consistent with fair market value, and are not determined in a manner that takes into account the volume or value of any referrals or other business generated between the parties,

            (v) the lease would be commercially reasonable even if no referrals were made between the parties, and

            (vi) the lease meets such other requirements as the Secretary may impose by regulation as needed to protect against program or patient abuse.

        (B) Equipment

        Payments made by a lessee of equipment to the lessor of the equipment for the use of the equipment if—

            (i) the lease is set out in writing, signed by the parties, and specifies the equipment covered by the lease,

            (ii) the equipment rented or leased does not exceed that which is reasonable and necessary for the legitimate business purposes of the lease or rental and is used exclusively by the lessee when being used by the lessee,

            (iii) the lease provides for a term of rental or lease of at least 1 year,

(iv) the rental charges over the term of the lease are set in advance, are consistent with fair market value, and are not determined in a manner that takes into account the volume or value of any referrals or other business generated between the parties,

(v) the lease would be commercially reasonable even if no referrals were made between the parties, and

(vi) the lease meets such other requirements as the Secretary may impose by regulation as needed to protect against program or patient abuse.

(2) Bona fide employment relationships

Any amount paid by an employer to a physician (or an immediate family member of such physician) who has a bona fide employment relationship with the employer for the provision of services if—

(A) the employment is for identifiable services,

(B) the amount of the remuneration under the employment—

(i) is consistent with the fair market value of the services, and

(ii) is not determined in a manner that takes into account (directly or indirectly) the volume or value of any referrals by the referring physician,

(C) the remuneration is provided pursuant to an agreement which would be commercially reasonable even if no referrals were made to the employer, and

(D) the employment meets such other requirements as the Secretary may impose by regulation as needed to protect against program or patient abuse.

Subparagraph (B)(ii) shall not prohibit the payment of remuneration in the form of a productivity bonus based on services performed personally by the physician (or an immediate family member of such physician).

(3) Personal service arrangements

(A) In general

Remuneration from an entity under an arrangement (including remuneration for specific physicians' services furnished to a nonprofit blood center) if—

(i) the arrangement is set out in writing, signed by the parties, and specifies the services covered by the arrangement,

(ii) the arrangement covers all of the services to be provided by the physician (or an immediate family member of such physician) to the entity,

(iii) the aggregate services contracted for do not exceed those that are reasonable and necessary for the legitimate business purposes of the arrangement,

(iv) the term of the arrangement is for at least 1 year,

(v) the compensation to be paid over the term of the arrangement is set in advance, does not exceed fair market value, and except in the case of a physician incentive plan described in subparagraph (B), is not determined in a manner that takes into account the volume or value of any referrals or other business generated between the parties,

(vi) the services to be performed under the arrangement do not involve the counseling or promotion or a business arrangement or other activity that violates any State or Federal law, and

(vii) the arrangement meets such other requirements as the Secretary may impose by regulation as needed to protect against program or patient abuse.

(B) Physician incentive plan exception

(i) In general

In the case of a physician incentive plan (as defined in clause (ii)) between a physician and an entity, the compensation may be determined in a manner (through a withhold, capitation, bonus, or otherwise) that takes into account directly or indirectly the volume or value of any referrals or other business generated between the parties, if the plan meets the following requirements:

(I) No specific payment is made directly or indirectly under the plan to a physician or a physician group as an inducement to reduce or limit medically necessary services provided with respect to a specific individual enrolled with the entity.

(II) In the case of a plan that places a physician or a physician group at substantial financial risk as determined by the Secretary pursuant to section 1395mm(i)(8)(A)(ii) of this title, the plan complies with any requirements the Secretary may impose pursuant to such section.

(III) Upon request by the Secretary, the entity provides the Secretary with access to descriptive information regarding the plan, in order to permit the Secretary to determine whether the plan is in compliance with the requirements of this clause.

(ii) "Physician incentive plan" defined

For purposes of this subparagraph, the term "physician incentive plan" means any compensation arrangement between an entity and a physician or physician group that may directly or indirectly have the effect of reducing or limiting services provided with respect to individuals enrolled with the entity.

(4) Remuneration unrelated to the provision of designated health services

In the case of remuneration which is provided by a hospital to a physician if such remuneration does not relate to the provision of designated health services.

(5) Physician recruitment

In the case of remuneration which is provided by a hospital to a physician to induce the physician to relocate to the geographic area served by the hospital in order to be a member of the medical staff of the hospital, if—

(A) the physician is not required to refer patients to the hospital,

(B) the amount of the remuneration under the arrangement is not determined in a manner that takes into account (directly or indirectly) the volume or value of any referrals by the referring physician, and

(C) the arrangement meets such other requirements as the Secretary may impose by regulation as needed to protect against program or patient abuse.

(6) Isolated transactions

In the case of an isolated financial transaction, such as a one-time sale of property or practice, if—

(A) the requirements described in subparagraphs (B) and (C) of paragraph (2) are met with respect to the entity in the same manner as they apply to an employer, and

(B) the transaction meets such other requirements as the Secretary may impose by regulation as needed to protect against program or patient abuse.

(7) Certain group practice arrangements with a hospital

(A)[2] In general

An arrangement between a hospital and a group under which designated health services are provided by the group but are billed by the hospital if—

(i) with respect to services provided to an inpatient of the hospital, the arrangement is pursuant to the provision of inpatient hospital services under section 1395x(b)(3) of this title.

(ii) the arrangement began before December 19, 1989, and has continued in effect without interruption since such date,

(iii) with respect to the designated health services covered under the arrangement, substantially all of such services furnished to patients of the hospital are furnished by the group under the arrangement,

(iv) the arrangement is pursuant to an agreement that is set out in writing and that specifies the services to be provided by the parties and the compensation for services provided under the agreement,

(v) the compensation paid over the term of the agreement is consistent with fair market value and the compensation per unit of services is fixed in advance and is not determined in a manner that takes into account the volume or value of any referrals or other business generated between the parties,

---

[2]So in original. No subpar. (B) has been enacted.

(vi) the compensation is provided pursuant to an agreement which would be commercially reasonable even if no referrals were made to the entity, and

(vii) the arrangement between the parties meets such other requirements as the Secretary may impose by regulation as needed to protect against program or patient abuse.

(8) Payments by a physician for items and services

Payments made by a physician—

(A) to a laboratory in exchange for the provision of clinical laboratory services, or

(B) to an entity as compensation for other items or services if the items or services are furnished at a price that is consistent with fair market value.

(f) Reporting requirements

Each entity providing covered items or services for which payment may be made under this subchapter shall provide the Secretary with the information concerning the entity's ownership, investment, and compensation arrangements, including—

(1) the covered items and services provided by the entity, and

(2) the names and unique physician identification numbers of all physicians with an ownership or investment interest (as described in subsection (a)(2)(A) of this section), or with a compensation arrangement (as described in subsection (a)(2)(B) of this section), in the entity, or whose immediate relatives have such an ownership or investment interest or who have such a compensation relationship with the entity.

Such information shall be provided in such form, manner, and at such times as the Secretary shall specify. The requirement of this subsection shall not apply to designated health services provided outside the United States or to entities which the Secretary determines provides[3] services for which payment may be made under this subchapter very infrequently.

(g) Sanctions

(1) Denial of payment

No payment may be made under this subchapter for a designated health service which is provided in violation of subsection (a)(1) of this section.

(2) Requiring refunds for certain claims

If a person collects any amounts that were billed in violation of subsection (a)(1) of this section, the person shall be liable to the individual for, and shall refund on a timely basis to the individual, any amounts so collected.

(3) Civil money penalty and exclusion for improper claims

Any person that presents or causes to be presented a bill or a claim for a service that such person knows or should know is for a

---

[3]So in original. Probably should be "provide".

service for which payment may not be made under paragraph (1) or for which a refund has not been made under paragraph (2) shall be subject to a civil money penalty of not more than $15,000 for each such service. The provisions of section 1320a-7a of this title (other than the first sentence of subsection (a) and other than subsection (b)) shall apply to a civil money penalty under the previous sentence in the same manner as such provisions apply to a penalty or proceeding under section 1320a-7a(a) of this title.

(4) Civil money penalty and exclusion for circumvention schemes

Any physician or other entity that enters into an arrangement or scheme (such as a cross-referral arrangement) which the physician or entity knows or should know has a principal purpose of assuring referrals by the physician to a particular entity which, if the physician directly made referrals to such entity, would be in violation of this section, shall be subject to a civil money penalty of not more than $100,000 for each such arrangement or scheme. The provisions of section 1320a-7a of this title (other than the first sentence of subsection (a) and other than subsection (b)) shall apply to a civil money penalty under the previous sentence in the same manner as such provisions apply to a penalty or proceeding under section 1320a-7a(a) of this title.

(5) Failure to report information

Any person who is required, but fails, to meet a reporting requirement of subsection (f) of this section is subject to a civil money penalty of not more than $10,000 for each day for which reporting is required to have been made. The provisions of section 1320a-7a of this title (other than the first sentence of subsection (a) and other than subsection (b)) shall apply to a civil money penalty under the previous sentence in the same manner as such provisions apply to a penalty or proceeding under section 1320a-7a(a) of this title.

(6) Advisory opinions

(A) In general

The Secretary shall issue written advisory opinions concerning whether a referral relating to designated health services (other than clinical laboratory services) is prohibited under this section. Each advisory opinion issued by the Secretary shall be binding as to the Secretary and the party or parties requesting the opinion.

(B) Application of certain rules

The Secretary shall, to the extent practicable, apply the rules under subsections (b)(3) and (b)(4) of this section and take into account the regulations promulgated under subsection (b)(5) of section 1320a-7d of this title in the issuance of advisory opinions under this paragraph.

(C) Regulations

In order to implement this paragraph in a timely manner, the Secretary may promulgate regulations that take effect on an interim basis, after notice and pending opportunity for public comment.

(D) Applicability

This paragraph shall apply to requests for advisory opinions made after the date which is 90 days after August 5, 1997, and before the close of the period described in section 1320a-7d(b)(6) of this title.

(h) Definitions and special rules

For purposes of this section:

(1) Compensation arrangement; remuneration

(A) The term "compensation arrangement" means any arrangement involving any remuneration between a physician (or an immediate family member of such physician) and an entity other than an arrangement involving only remuneration described in subparagraph (C).

(B) The term "remuneration" includes any remuneration, directly or indirectly, overtly or covertly, in cash or in kind.

(C) Remuneration described in this subparagraph is any remuneration consisting of any of the following:

(i) The forgiveness of amounts owed for inaccurate tests or procedures, mistakenly performed tests or procedures, or the correction of minor billing errors.

(ii) The provision of items, devices, or supplies that are used solely to—

(I) collect, transport, process, or store specimens for the entity providing the item, device, or supply, or

(II) order or communicate the results of tests or procedures for such entity.

(iii) A payment made by an insurer or a self-insured plan to a physician to satisfy a claim, submitted on a fee for service basis, for the furnishing of health services by that physician to an individual who is covered by a policy with the insurer or by the self-insured plan, if—

(I) the health services are not furnished, and the payment is not made, pursuant to a contract or other arrangement between the insurer or the plan and the physician,

(II) the payment is made to the physician on behalf of the covered individual and would otherwise be made directly to such individual,

(III) the amount of the payment is set in advance, does not exceed fair market value, and is not determined in a manner that takes into account directly or indirectly the volume or value of any referrals, and

(IV) the payment meets such other requirements as the Secretary may impose by regulation as needed to protect against program or patient abuse.

(2) Employee

An individual is considered to be "employed by" or an "employee" of an entity if the individual would be considered to be an employee of the entity under the usual common law rules applicable in determining the employer-employee relationship (as applied for purposes of section 3121(d)(2) of the Internal Revenue Code of 1986).

(3) Fair market value

The term "fair market value" means the value in arms length transactions, consistent with the general market value, and, with respect to rentals or leases, the value of rental property for general commercial purposes (not taking into account its intended use) and, in the case of a lease of space, not adjusted to reflect the additional value the prospective lessee or lessor would attribute to the proximity or convenience to the lessor where the lessor is a potential source of patient referrals to the lessee.

(4) Group practice

  (A) Definition of group practice

    The term "group practice" means a group of 2 or more physicians legally organized as a partnership, professional corporation, foundation, not-for-profit corporation, faculty practice plan, or similar association—

      (i) in which each physician who is a member of the group provides substantially the full range of services which the physician routinely provides, including medical care, consultation, diagnosis, or treatment, through the joint use of shared office space, facilities, equipment and personnel,

      (ii) for which substantially all of the services of the physicians who are members of the group are provided through the group and are billed under a billing number assigned to the group and amounts so received are treated as receipts of the group,

      (iii) in which the overhead expenses of and the income from the practice are distributed in accordance with methods previously determined,

      (iv) except as provided in subparagraph (B)(i), in which no physician who is a member of the group directly or indirectly receives compensation based on the volume or value of referrals by the physician,

      (v) in which members of the group personally conduct no less than 75 percent of the physician-patient encounters of the group practice, and

      (vi) which meets such other standards as the Secretary may impose by regulation.

  (B) Special rules

    (i) Profits and productivity bonuses

      A physician in a group practice may be paid a share of overall profits of the group, or a productivity bonus based on services personally performed or services incident to such personally performed services, so long as the share or bonus is not determined in any manner which is directly related to the volume or value of referrals by such physician.

(ii) Faculty practice plans

In the case of a faculty practice plan associated with a hospital, institution of higher education, or medical school with an approved medical residency training program in which physician members may provide a variety of different specialty services and provide professional services both within and outside the group, as well as perform other tasks such as research, subparagraph (A) shall be applied only with respect to the services provided within the faculty practice plan.

(5) Referral; referring physician

(A) Physicians' services

Except as provided in subparagraph (C), in the case of an item or service for which payment may be made under part B of this subchapter, the request by a physician for the item or service, including the request by a physician for a consultation with another physician (and any test or procedure ordered by, or to be performed by (or under the supervision of) that other physician), constitutes a "referral" by a "referring physician".

(B) Other items

Except as provided in subparagraph (C), the request or establishment of a plan of care by a physician which includes the provision of the designated health service constitutes a "referral" by a "referring physician".

(C) Clarification respecting certain services integral to a consultation by certain specialists.

A request by a pathologist for clinical diagnostic laboratory tests and pathological examination services, a request by a radiologist for diagnostic radiology services, and a request by a radiation oncologist for radiation therapy, if such services are furnished by (or under the supervision of) such pathologist, radiologist, or radiation oncologist pursuant to a consultation requested by another physician does not constitute a "referral" by a "referring physician."

(6) Designated health services

The term "designated health services" means any of the following items or services:

(A) Clinical laboratory services.

(B) Physical therapy services.

(C) Occupational therapy services.

(D) Radiology services, including magnetic resonance imaging, computerized axial tomography scans, and ultrasound services.

(E) Radiation therapy services and supplies.

(F) Durable medical equipment and supplies.

(G) Parenteral and enteral nutrients, equipment, and supplies.

(H) Prosthetics, orthotics, and prosthetic devices and supplies.

(I)  Home health services.

(J)  Outpatient prescription drugs.

(K) Inpatient and outpatient hospital services.

## SOURCE—

(Aug. 14, 1935, ch. 531, title XVIII, Sec. 1877, as added Pub. L. 101-239, title VI, Sec. 6204(a), Dec. 19, 1989, 103 Stat. 2236; amended Pub. L. 101-508, title IV, Sec. 4207(e)(1)-(3), (k)(2), formerly Sec. 4027(e)(1)-(3), (k)(2), Nov. 5, 1990, 104 Stat. 1388-121, 1388-122, 1388-124, renumbered Pub. L. 103-432, title I, Sec. 160(d)(4), Oct. 31, 1994, 108 Stat. 4444; Pub. L. 103-66, title XIII, Sec. 13562(a), Aug. 10, 1993, 107 Stat. 596; Pub. L.103-432, title I, Sec. 152(a), (b), Oct. 31, 1994, 108 Stat. 4436; Pub. L. 105-33, title IV, Sec. 4314, Aug. 5, 1997, 111 Stat. 389; Pub. L. 106-113, div. B, Sec. 1000(a)(6) (title V, Sec. 524(a)), Nov. 29, 1999, 113 Stat. 1536, 1501A-387.)

## REFERENCES IN TEXT

Section 222(a) of the Social Security Amendments of 1972, referred to in subsec. (b)(3)(C), is section 222(a) of Pub. L. 92-603, Oct. 30, 1972, 86 Stat. 1329, which is set out as a note under section 1395b-1 of this title.

Section 300e-9(d) of this title, referred to in subsec. (b)(3)(D), was redesignated section 300e-9(c) of this title by Pub. L. 100-517, Sec. 7(b), Oct. 24, 1988, 102 Stat. 2580.

Part C of this subchapter, referred to in subsec. (b)(3)(E), is classified to section 1395w-21 et seq. of this title.

The Internal Revenue Code, referred to in subsecs. (c)(2) and (h)(2), is classified generally to Title 26, Internal Revenue Code.

Part B of this subchapter, referred to in subsec. (h)(5)(A), is classified to section 1395j et seq. of this title.

# Appendix B-2

## Stark I Regulations

*Source:* 42 C.F.R. Sections 411.351–.361

**Section 411.351  Definitions.**

[Effective until Jan. 4, 2002]

As used in this subpart, unless the context indicates otherwise:

*Clinical laboratory services* means the biological, microbiological, serological, chemical, immunohematological, hematological, biophysical, cytological, pathological, or other examination of materials derived from the human body for the purpose of providing information for the diagnosis, prevention, or treatment of any disease or impairment of, or the assessment of the health of, human beings. These examinations also include procedures to determine, measure, or otherwise describe the presence or absence of various substances or organisms in the body.

*Compensation arrangement* means any arrangement involving any remuneration, direct or indirect, between a physician (or a member of a physician's immediate family) and an entity.

*Direct supervision* means supervision by a physician who is present in the office suite and immediately available to provide assistance and direction throughout the time services are being performed.

*Employee* means any individual who, under the usual common law rules that apply in determining the employer-employee relationship (as applied for purposes of section 3121(d)(2) of the Internal Revenue Code of 1986), is considered to be employed by, or an employee of, an entity.

(Application of these common law rules is discussed at 20 CFR 404.1007 and 26 CFR 31.3121(d)-1(c).)

*Entity* means a sole proprietorship, trust, corporation, partnership, foundation, not-for-profit corporation, or unincorporated association.

*Fair market value* means the value in arm's-length transactions, consistent with the general market value. With respect to rentals or leases, fair market value means the value of rental property for general commercial purposes (not taking into account its intended use). In the case of a lease of space, this value may not be adjusted to reflect the additional value the prospective lessee or lessor would attribute to the proximity or convenience to the lessor when the lessor is a potential source of patient referrals to the lessee.

*Financial relationship* refers to a direct or indirect relationship between a physician (or a member of a physician's immediate family) and an entity in which the physician or family member has—

(1) An ownership or investment interest that exists in the entity through equity, debt, or other means and includes an interest in an entity that holds an ownership or investment interest in any entity providing laboratory services; or

(2) A compensation arrangement with the entity.

*Group practice* means a group of two or more physicians, legally organized as a partnership, professional corporation, foundation, not-for-profit corporation, faculty practice plan, or similar association, that meets the following conditions:

(1) Each physician who is a *member of the group*, as defined in this section, furnishes substantially the full range of patient care services that the physician routinely furnishes including medical care, consultation, diagnosis, and treatment through the joint use of shared office space, facilities, equipment, and personnel.

(2) Except as provided in paragraphs (2)(i) and (2)(ii) of this definition, substantially all of the patient care services of the physicians who are members of the group (that is, at least 75 percent of the total patient care services of the group practice members) are furnished through the group and billed in the name of the group and the amounts received are treated as receipts of the group. "Patient care services" are measured by the total patient care time each member spends on these services. For example, if a physician practices 40 hours a week and spends 30 hours on patient care services for a group practice, the physician has spent 75 percent of his or her time providing countable patient care services.

(i) The "substantially all" test does not apply to any group practice that is located solely in an HPSA, as defined in this section, and

(ii) For group practices located outside of an HPSA (as defined in this section) any time spent by group practice members providing services in an HPSA should not be used to calculate whether the group practice located outside the HPSA has met the "substantially all" test, regardless of whether the members' time in the HPSA is spent in a group practice, clinic, or office setting.

(3) The practice expenses and income are distributed in accordance with methods previously determined. In the case of faculty practice plans associated with a hospital, institution of higher education, or medical school that has an approved medical residency training program in which faculty practice plan physicians perform specialty and professional services, both within and outside the faculty practice, as well as perform other tasks such as research, this definition applies only to those services that are furnished within the faculty practice plan.

*Hospital* means any separate legally organized operating entity plus any subsidiary, related, or other entities that perform services for the hospital's patients and for which the hospital bills. A "hospital" does not include entities that perform services for hospital patients "under arrangements" with the hospital.

*HPSA* means, for purposes of this regulation, an area designated as a health professional shortage area under section 332(a)(1)(A) of the Public Health Service Act for primary medical care professionals (in accordance with the criteria specified in 42 CFR part 5, appendix A, part I—Geographic Areas). In addition, with respect to dental, mental health, vision care, podiatric, and pharmacy services, an HPSA means an area designated as a health professional shortage area under section 332(a)(1)(A) of the Public Health Service Act for dental professionals, mental health professionals, vision care professionals, podiatric professionals, and pharmacy professionals, respectively.

*Immediate family member or member of a physician's immediate family* means husband or wife; natural or adoptive parent, child, or sibling; stepparent, stepchild, stepbrother, or stepsister; father-in-law, mother-in-law, son-in-law, daughter-in-law, brother-in-law, or sister-in-law; grandparent or grandchild; and spouse of a grandparent or grandchild.

*Laboratory* means an entity furnishing biological, microbiological, serological, chemical, immunohematological, hematological, biophysical, cytological, pathological, or other examination of materials derived from the human body for the purpose of providing information for the diagnosis, prevention, or treatment of any disease or impairment of, or the assessment of the health of, human beings. These examinations also include procedures to determine, measure, or otherwise describe the presence or absence of various substances or organisms in the body. Entities only collecting or preparing specimens (or both) or only serving as a mailing service and not performing testing are not considered laboratories.

*Members of the group* means physician partners and full-time and part-time physician contractors and employees during the time they furnish services to patients of the group practice that are furnished through the group and are billed in the name of the group.

*Patient care services* means any tasks performed by a group practice member that address the medical needs of specific patients, regardless of whether they involve direct patient encounters. They can include, for example, the services of physicians who do not directly treat patients, time spent by a physician consulting with other physicians, or time spent reviewing laboratory tests.

*Physician incentive plan* means any compensation arrangement between an entity and a physician or physician group that may directly or indirectly have the effect of reducing or limiting services furnished with respect to individuals enrolled with the entity.

*Plan of care* means the establishment by a physician of a course of diagnosis or treatment (or both) for a particular patient, including the ordering of items or services.

*Referral*—

(1) Means either of the following:

(i) Except as provided in paragraph (2) of this definition, the request by a physician for, or ordering of, any item or service for which payment may be made under Medicare Part B, including a request for a consultation with another physician and any test or procedure ordered by or to be performed by (or under the supervision of) that other physician.

(ii) Except as provided in paragraph (2) of this definition, a request by a physician that includes the provision of laboratory services or the establishment of a plan of care by a physician that includes the provision of laboratory services.

(2) Does not include a request by a pathologist for clinical diagnostic laboratory tests and pathological examination services if—

(i) The request is part of a consultation initiated by another physician; and

(ii) The tests or services are furnished by or under the supervision of the pathologist.

*Referring physician* means a physician (or group practice) who makes a referral as defined in this section.

*Remuneration* means any payment, discount, forgiveness of debt, or other benefit made directly or indirectly, overtly or covertly, in cash or in kind, except that the following are not considered remuneration:

(1) The forgiveness of amounts owed for inaccurate tests or procedures, mistakenly performed tests or procedures, or the correction of minor billing errors.

(2) The furnishing of items, devices, or supplies that are used solely to collect, transport, process, or store specimens for the entity furnishing the items, devices, or supplies or are used solely to order or communicate the results of tests or procedures for the entity.

(3) A payment made by an insurer or a self-insured plan to a physician to satisfy a claim, submitted on a fee-for-service basis, for the furnishing of health services by that physician to an individual who is covered by a policy with the insurer or by the self-insured plan, if—

(i) The health services are not furnished, and the payment is not made, under a contract or other arrangement between the insurer or the plan and the physician;

(ii) The payment is made to the physician on behalf of the covered individual and would otherwise be made directly to the individual; and

(iii) The amount of the payment is set in advance, does not exceed fair market value, and is not determined in a manner that takes into account directly or indirectly the volume or value of any referrals.

*Transaction* means an instance or process of two or more persons doing business. An *isolated transaction* is one involving a single payment between two or more persons. A transaction that involves long-term or installment payments is not considered an isolated transaction.

[SOURCE: 60 Fed. Reg. 41,978 (Aug. 14, 1995); 66 Fed. Reg. 952 (Jan. 4, 2001).]

## Section 411.353 Prohibition on certain referrals by physicians and limitations on billing.

[Effective until Jan. 4, 2002]

(a) *Prohibition on referrals.* Except as provided in this subpart, a physician who has a financial relationship with an entity, or who has an immediate family member who has a financial relationship with the entity, may not make a referral to that entity for the furnishing of clinical laboratory services for which payment otherwise may be made under Medicare.

(b) *Limitations on billing.* An entity that furnishes clinical laboratory services under a referral that is prohibited by paragraph (a) of this section may not present or cause to be presented a claim or bill to the Medicare program or to any individual, third party payer, or other entity for the clinical laboratory services performed under that referral.

(c) *Denial of payment.* No Medicare payment may be made for a clinical laboratory service that is furnished under a prohibited referral.

(d) *Refunds.* An entity that collects payment for a laboratory service that was performed under a prohibited referral must refund all collected amounts on a timely basis.

[SOURCE: 60 Fed. Reg. 41,978 (Aug. 14, 1995); 66 Fed. Reg. 958 (Jan. 4, 2001).]

## Section 411.355 General exceptions to referral prohibitions related to both ownership/investment and compensation.

[Effective until Jan. 4, 2002]

The prohibition on referrals set forth in § 411.353 does not apply to the following types of services:

(a) *Physicians' services*, as defined in § 410.20(a), that are furnished personally by (or under the personal supervision of) another physician in the same group practice as the referring physician.

(b) *In-office ancillary services.* Services that meet the following conditions:

   (1) They are furnished personally by one of the following individuals:

      (i) The referring physician.

      (ii) A physician who is a member of the same group practice as the referring physician.

(iii) Individuals who are directly supervised by the referring physician or, in the case of group practices, by another physician in the same group practice as the referring physician.

(2) They are furnished in one of the following conditions:

(i) A building in which the referring physician (or another physician who is a member of the same group practice) furnishes physicians' services unrelated to the furnishing of clinical laboratory services.

(ii) A building that is used by the group practice for the provision of some or all of the group's clinical laboratory services.

(3) They are billed by one of the following:

(i) The physician performing or supervising the service.

(ii) The group practice of which the performing or supervising physician is a member.

(iii) An entity that is wholly owned by the physician or the physician's group practice.

(c) *Services furnished to prepaid health plan enrollees by one of the following organizations:*

(1) An HMO or a CMP in accordance with a contract with CMS under section 1876 of the Act and part 417, subparts J through M, of this chapter.

(2) A health care prepayment plan in accordance with an agreement with CMS under section 1833(a)(1)(A) of the Act and part 417, subpart U, of the chapter.

(3) An organization that is receiving payments on a prepaid basis for the enrollees through a demonstration project under section 402(a) of the Social Security Amendments of 1967 (42 U.S.C. 1395b-1) or under section 222(a) of the Social Security Amendments of 1972 (42 U.S.C. 1395b-1 note).

(4) A qualified health maintenance organization (within the meaning of section 1310(d) of the Public Health Service Act).

(5) A coordinated care plan (within the meaning of section 1851(a)(2)(A) of the Act) offered by an organization in accordance with a contract with CMS under section 1857 of the Act and part 422 of this chapter.

(d) *Services furnished in an ambulatory surgical center (ASC) or end stage renal disease (ESRD) facility, or by a hospice* if payment for those services is included in the ASC rate, the ESRD composite rate, or as part of the per diem hospice charge, respectively.

[SOURCE: 60 Fed. Reg. 41,978 (Aug. 14, 1995); 63 Fed. Reg. 35,066 (June 26, 1998); 66 Fed. Reg. 959 (Jan. 4, 2001)]

## Section 411.356 Exceptions to referral prohibitions related to ownership or investment interests.

For purposes of § 411.353, the following ownership or investment interests do not constitute a financial relationship:

(a) *Publicly traded securities.* Ownership of investment securities (including shares or bonds, debentures, notes, or other debt instruments) that may be purchased on terms generally available to the public and that meet the requirements of paragraphs (a)(1) and (a)(2) of this section.

(1) They are either—

(i) Listed for trading on the New York Stock Exchange, the American Stock Exchange, or any regional exchange in which quotations are published on a daily basis, or foreign securities listed on a recognized foreign, national, or regional exchange in which quotations are published on a daily basis; or

(ii) Traded under an automated interdealer quotation system operated by the National Association of Securities Dealers.

(2) In a corporation that had—

(i) Until January 1, 1995, total assets at the end of the corporation's most recent fiscal year exceeding $100 million; or

(ii) Stockholder equity exceeding $75 million at the end of the corporation's most recent fiscal year or on average during the previous 3 fiscal years.

(b) *Mutual funds.* Ownership of shares in a regulated investment company as defined in section 851(a) of the Internal Revenue Code of 1986, if the company had, at the end of its most recent fiscal year, or on average during the previous 3 fiscal years, total assets exceeding $75 million.

(c) *Specific providers.* Ownership or investment interest in the following entities:

(1) A laboratory that is located in a rural area (that is, a laboratory that is not located in an urban area as defined in § 412.62(f)(1)(ii) of this chapter) and that meets the following criteria:

(i) The laboratory testing that is referred by a physician who has (or whose immediate family member has) an ownership or investment interest in the rural laboratory is either—

(A) Performed on the premises of the rural laboratory; or

(B) If not performed on the premises, the laboratory performing the testing bills the Medicare program directly for the testing.

(ii) Substantially all of the laboratory tests furnished by the entity are furnished to individuals who reside in a rural area. Substantially all means no less than 75 percent.

(2) A hospital that is located in Puerto Rico.

(3) A hospital that is located outside of Puerto Rico if one of the following conditions is met:

(i) The referring physician is authorized to perform services at the hospital, and the physician's ownership or investment interest is in the entire hospital and not merely in a distinct part or department of the hospital.

(ii) Until January 1, 1995, the referring physician's ownership or investment interest does not relate (directly or indirectly) to the furnishing of clinical laboratory services.

[SOURCE: 60 Fed. Reg. 41,978 (Aug. 14, 1995).]

## Section 411.357 Exceptions to referral prohibitions related to compensation arrangements.

For purposes of Sec. 411.353, the following compensation arrangements do not constitute a financial relationship:

(a) *Rental of office space.* Payments for the use of office space made by a lessee to a lessor if there is a rental or lease agreement that meets the following requirements:

> (1) The agreement is set out in writing and is signed by the parties and specifies the premises covered by the lease.

> (2) The term of the agreement is at least 1 year.

> (3) The space rented or leased does not exceed that which is reasonable and necessary for the legitimate business purposes of the lease or rental and is used exclusively by the lessee when being used by the lessee, except that the lessee may make payments for the use of space consisting of common areas if the payments do not exceed the lessee's pro rata share of expenses for the space based upon the ratio of the space used exclusively by the lessee to the total amount of space (other than common areas) occupied by all persons using the common areas.

> (4) The rental charges over the term of the lease are set in advance and are consistent with fair market value.

> (5) The charges are not determined in a manner that takes into account the volume or value of any referrals or other business generated between the parties.

> (6) The agreement would be commercially reasonable even if no referrals were made between the lessee and the lessor.

(b) *Rental of equipment.* Payments made by a lessee to a lessor for the use of equipment under the following conditions:

> (1) A rental or lease agreement is set out in writing and signed by the parties and specifies the equipment covered by the lease.

> (2) The equipment rented or leased does not exceed that which is reasonable and necessary for the legitimate business purposes of the lease or rental and is used exclusively by the lessee when being used by the lessee.

> (3) The lease provides for a term of rental or lease of at least 1 year.

> (4) The rental charges over the term of the lease are set in advance, are consistent with fair market value, and are not determined in a manner that takes into account the volume or value of any referrals or other business generated between the parties.

> (5) The lease would be commercially reasonable even if no referrals were made between the parties.

(c) *Bona fide employment relationships.* Any amount paid by an employer to a physician (or immediate family member) who has a bona fide employment relationship with the employer for the provision of services if the following conditions are met:

> (1) The employment is for identifiable services.

> (2) The amount of the remuneration under the employment is—

(i) Consistent with the fair market value of the services; and

(ii) Except as provided in paragraph (c)(4) of this section, is not determined in a manner that takes into account (directly or indirectly) the volume or value of any referrals by the referring physician.

(3) The remuneration is provided under an agreement that would be commercially reasonable even if no referrals were made to the employer.

(4) Paragraph (c)(2)(ii) of this section does not prohibit payment of remuneration in the form of a productivity bonus based on services performed personally by the physician (or immediate family member of the physician).

(d) *Personal service arrangements.* (1) *General.* Remuneration from an entity under an arrangement to a physician or immediate family member of the physician, including remuneration for specific physicians' services furnished to a nonprofit blood center, if the following conditions are met:

(i) The arrangement is set out in writing, is signed by the parties, and specifies the services covered by the arrangement.

(ii) The arrangement covers all of the services to be furnished by the physician (or an immediate family member of the physician) to the entity.

(iii) The aggregate services contracted for do not exceed those that are reasonable and necessary for the legitimate business purposes of the arrangement.

(iv) The term of the arrangement is for at least 1 year.

(v) The compensation to be paid over the term of the arrangement is set in advance, does not exceed fair market value, and, except in the case of a physician incentive plan, is not determined in a manner that takes into account the volume or value of any referrals or other business generated between the parties.

(vi) The services to be furnished under the arrangement do not involve the counseling or promotion of a business arrangement or other activity that violates any State or Federal law.

(2) *Physician incentive plan exception.* In the case of a physician incentive plan between a physician and an entity, the compensation may be determined in a manner (through a withhold, capitation, bonus, or otherwise) that takes into account directly or indirectly the volume or value of any referrals or other business generated between the parties, if the plan meets the following requirements:

(i) No specific payment is made directly or indirectly under the plan to a physician or a physician group as an inducement to reduce or limit medically necessary services furnished with respect to a specific individual enrolled in the entity.

(ii) In the case of a plan that places a physician or a physician group at substantial financial risk as determined by the Secretary under section 1876(i)(8)(A)(ii) of the Act, the plan complies with any requirements the Secretary has imposed under that section.

(iii) Upon request by the Secretary, the entity provides the Secretary with access to descriptive information regarding the plan, in order to permit the Secretary to determine whether the plan is in compliance with the requirements of paragraph (d)(2) of this section.

(3) Until January 1, 1995, the provisions in paragraph (d)(1) and (2) of this section do not apply to any arrangements that meet the requirements of section 1877(e)(2) or section 1877(e)(3) of the Act as they read before they were amended by the Omnibus Budget Reconciliation Act of 1993 (Public Law 103-66).

(e) *Physician recruitment.* Remuneration provided by a hospital to recruit a physician that is intended to induce the physician to relocate to the geographic area served by the hospital in order to become a member of the hospital's medical staff, if all of the following conditions are met:

(1) The arrangement and its terms are in writing and signed by both parties.

(2) The arrangement is not conditioned on the physician's referral of patients to the hospital.

(3) The hospital does not determine (directly or indirectly) the amount or value of the remuneration to the physician based on the volume or value of any referrals the physician generates for the hospital.

(4) The physician is not precluded from establishing staff privileges at another hospital or referring business to another entity.

(f) *Isolated transactions.* Isolated financial transactions, such as a one-time sale of property or a practice, if all of the conditions set forth in paragraphs (c)(2) and (c)(3) of this section are met with respect to an entity in the same manner as they apply to an employer. There can be no additional transactions between the parties for 6 months after the isolated transaction, except for transactions which are specifically excepted under the other provisions in Secs. 411.355 through 411.357.

(g) *Arrangements with hospitals.* (1) Until January 1, 1995, any compensation arrangement between a hospital and a physician or a member of a physician's immediate family if the arrangement does not relate to the furnishing of clinical laboratory services; or

(2) Remuneration provided by a hospital to a physician if the remuneration does not relate to the furnishing of clinical laboratory services.

(h) *Group practice arrangements with a hospital.* An arrangement between a hospital and a group practice under which clinical laboratory services are provided by the group but are billed by the hospital if the following conditions are met:

(1) With respect to services provided to an inpatient of the hospital, the arrangement is pursuant to the provision of inpatient hospital services under section 1861(b)(3) of the Act.

(2) The arrangement began before December 19, 1989, and has continued in effect without interruption since then.

(3) With respect to the clinical laboratory services covered under the arrangement, substantially all of these services furnished to patients of the hospital are furnished by the group under the arrangement.

(4) The arrangement is in accordance with an agreement that is set out in writing and that specifies the services to be furnished by the parties and the compensation for services furnished under the agreement.

(5) The compensation paid over the term of the agreement is consistent with fair market value, and the compensation per unit of services is fixed in advance and is not determined in a manner that takes into account the volume or value of any referrals or other business generated between the parties.

(6) The compensation is provided in accordance with an agreement that would be commercially reasonable even if no referrals were made to the entity.

(i) *Payments by a physician.* Payments made by a physician—

(1) To a laboratory in exchange for the provision of clinical laboratory services; or

(2) To an entity as compensation for other items or services that are furnished at a price that is consistent with fair market value.

[SOURCE: 60 Fed. Reg. 41,978 (Aug. 14, 1995)]

### Section 411.360 Group practice attestation.

(a) Except as provided in paragraph (b) of this section, a group practice (as defined in section 1877(h)(4) of the Act and § 411.351) must submit a written statement to its carrier annually to attest that, during the most recent 12-month period (calendar year, fiscal year, or immediately preceding 12-month period) 75 percent of the total patient care services of group practice members was furnished through the group, was billed under a billing number assigned to the group, and the amounts so received were treated as receipts of the group.

(b) A newly-formed group practice (one in which physicians have recently begun to practice together) or any group practice that has been unable in the past to meet the requirements of section 1877(h)(4) of the Act must—

(1) Submit a written statement to attest that, during the next 12-month period (calendar year, fiscal year, or next 12 months), it expects to meet the 75-percent standard and will take measures to ensure the standard is met; and

(2) At the end of the 12-month period, submit a written statement to attest that it met the 75-percent standard during that period, billed for those services under a billing number assigned to the group, and treated amounts received for those services as receipts of the group. If the group did not meet the standard, any Medicare payments made for clinical laboratory services furnished by the group during the 12-month period that were conditioned upon the standard being met are overpayments.

(c) Once any group has chosen whether to use its fiscal year, the calendar year, or some other 12-month period, the group practice must adhere to this choice.

(d) The attestation must contain a statement that the information furnished in the attestation is true and accurate and must be signed by a group representative.

(e) A group that intends to meet the definition of a group practice in order to qualify for an exception described in §§ 411.355 through 411.357, must submit the attestation required by paragraph (a) or paragraph (b)(1) of this section, as applicable, to its carrier no later than 60 days after receipt of the attestation instructions from its carrier.

[SOURCE: 60 Fed. Reg. 41,978 (Aug. 14, 1995); 60 Fed. Reg. 63,440 (Dec. 11, 1995).]

### Section 411.361 Reporting requirements.

(a) *Basic rule.* Except as provided in paragraph (b) of this section, all entities furnishing items or services for which payment may be made under Medicare must submit information to CMS concerning their financial relationships (as defined in paragraph (d) of this section), in such form, manner, and at such times as CMS specifies.

(b) *Exception.* The requirements of paragraph (a) of this section do not apply to entities that provide 20 or fewer Part A and Part B items and services during a calendar year, or to designated health services provided outside the United States.

(c) *Required information.* The information submitted to CMS under paragraph (a) of this section must include at least the following:

> (1) The name and unique physician identification number (UPIN) of each physician who has a financial relationship with the entity;
>
> (2) The name and UPIN of each physician who has an immediate relative (as defined in § 411.351) who has a financial relationship with the entity;
>
> (3) The covered items and services provided by the entity; and
>
> (4) With respect to each physician identified under paragraphs (c)(1) and (c)(2) of this section, the nature of the financial relationship (including the extent and/or value of the ownership or investment interest or the compensation arrangement, if requested by CMS).

(d) *Reportable financial relationships.* For purposes of this section, a financial relationship is any ownership or investment interest or any compensation arrangement, as described in section 1877 of the Act.

(e) *Form and timing of reports.* Entities that are subject to the requirements of this section must submit the required information on a CMS-prescribed form within the time period specified by the servicing carrier or intermediary. Entities are given at least 30 days from the date of the carrier's or intermediary's request to provide the initial information. Thereafter, an entity must provide updated information within 60 days from the date of any change in the submitted information. Entities must retain documentation sufficient to verify the information provided on the forms and, upon request, must make that documentation available to CMS or the OIG.

(f) *Consequences of failure to report.* Any person who is required, but fails, to submit information concerning his or her financial relationships in accordance with this section is subject to a civil money penalty of up to $10,000 for each day of the period beginning on the day following the applicable deadline established under paragraph (e) of this section until the information is submitted. Assessment of these penalties will comply with the applicable provisions of part 1003 of this title.

(g) *Public disclosure.* Information furnished to CMS under this section is subject to public disclosure in accordance with the provisions of part 401 of this chapter.

[SOURCE: 60 Fed. Reg. 41,982 (Aug. 14, 1995).]

# Appendix B-3

# Stark II Phase I Final Regulations

*Source:* Health Care Financing Administration, Department of Health and Human Services, 66 Fed. Reg. 952–963 (Jan. 4, 2001), *available at* www.access.gpo.gov/su_docs/aces/aces140.html (effective Jan. 4, 2002).

*[Editor's Note: In the preamble to the Stark II Phase I regulations, 66 Fed. Reg. 856, 896, 910 (Jan. 4, 2001), HCFA (now CMS) notes that the final rule eliminates the group practice attestation requirement as an "unwarranted burden on group practices."*

*Nevertheless, the list of specific amendments set forth on 66 Fed. Reg. at 952–65—and below—does not eliminate Section 411.360 (the group practice attestation requirement).*

*The agency has stated that it will remove the group practice attestation requirement with the next phase of the rule, which it expects to publish in 2002.[1]]*

For the reasons set forth in the preamble, HCFA amends 42 CFR chapter IV as set forth below:

## PART 411—EXCLUSIONS FROM MEDICARE AND LIMITATIONS ON MEDICARE PAYMENT

A. Part 411 is amended as follows:
1. The authority citation for part 411 continues to read as follows:

**Authority:** Secs. 1102 and 1871 of the Social Security Act (42 U.S.C. 1302 and 1395hh).

### Subpart A—General Exclusions and Exclusions of Particular Services

2. In Sec. 411.1, paragraph (a) is revised to read as follows:

### Sec. 411.1 Basis and scope.

(a) *Statutory basis.* Sections 1814(a) and 1835(a) of the Act require that a physician certify or recertify a patient's need for home health services but, in general, prohibit a physician from certifying or recertifying the need for services if the services will be furnished by an HHA in which the physician has a significant ownership interest, or with which the physician has a significant financial or contractual relationship. Sections 1814(c), 1835(d), and 1862 of the Act exclude from Medicare payment certain specified services. The Act provides special rules for payment of services furnished by the following: Federal providers or agencies (sections 1814(c) and 1835(d)); hospitals and physicians outside of the U.S. (sections 1814(f) and 1862(a)(4)); and hospitals and SNFs of the Indian Health Service (section 1880 of the Act). Section 1877 of the Act sets forth limitations on referrals and payment for designated health services furnished by entities with which the referring physician (or an immediate family member of the referring physician) has a financial relationship.

\* \* \* \* \*

### Subpart J—Physician Ownership of, and Referral of Patients or Laboratory Specimens to, Entities Furnishing Clinical Laboratory or Other Health Services

3. Section 411.350 is revised to read as follows:

---

[1]Letter From Paul J. Olenick, Division of Integrated Delivery Systems Purchasing Policy Group, Center for Medicare Management, Centers for Medicare & Medicaid Services, to Robin Herman, Managing Editor, Health Law & Business Series, Bureau of National Affairs, Inc. (Dec. 21, 2001).

**Sec. 411.350 Scope of subpart.**

(a) This subpart implements section 1877 of the Act, which generally prohibits a physician from making a referral under Medicare for designated health services to an entity with which the physician or a member of the physician's immediate family has a financial relationship.

(b) This subpart does not provide for exceptions or immunity from civil or criminal prosecution or other sanctions applicable under any State laws or under Federal law other than section 1877 of the Act. For example, although a particular arrangement involving a physician's financial relationship with an entity may not prohibit the physician from making referrals to the entity under this subpart, the arrangement may nevertheless violate another provision of the Act or other laws administered by HHS, the Federal Trade Commission, the Securities and Exchange Commission, the Internal Revenue Service, or any other Federal or State agency.

(c) This subpart requires, with some exceptions, that certain entities furnishing covered services under Medicare Part A or Part B report information concerning their ownership, investment, or compensation arrangements in the form, manner, and at the times specified by HCFA.

4. Section 411.351 is revised to read as follows:

**Sec. 411.351 Definitions.**

As used in this subpart, unless the context indicates otherwise:

*Centralized building* means all or part of a building, including, for purposes of this definition only, a mobile vehicle, van, or trailer that is owned or leased on a full-time basis (that is, 24 hours per day, 7 days per week, for a term of not less than 6 months) by a group practice and that is used exclusively by the group practice. Space in a building or a mobile vehicle, van, or trailer that is shared by more than one group practice, by a group practice and one or more solo practitioners, or by a group practice and another provider (for example, a diagnostic imaging facility) is not a centralized building for purposes of this rule. This provision does not preclude a group practice from providing services to other providers (for example, purchased diagnostic tests) in the group practice's centralized building. A group practice may have more than one centralized building.

*Clinical laboratory services* means the biological, microbiological, serological, chemical, immunohematological, hematological, biophysical, cytological, pathological, or other examination of materials derived from the human body for the purpose of providing information for the diagnosis, prevention, or treatment of any disease or impairment of, or the assessment of the health of, human beings, including procedures to determine, measure, or otherwise describe the presence or absence of various substances or organisms in the body, as specifically identified by the CPT and HCPCS codes posted on the HCFA web site, http://www.hcfa.gov, (and in annual updates published in the **Federal Register** and posted on the HCFA web site), except as specifically excluded on the HCFA web site and in annual updates. All services identified on the HCFA web site and in annual updates are clinical laboratory services for purposes of these regulations. Any service not specifically identified on the HCFA web site, as amended from time to time and published in the **Federal Register**, is not a clinical laboratory service for purposes of these regulations.

*Consultation* means a professional service furnished to a patient by a physician if the following conditions are satisfied:

(1) The physician's opinion or advice regarding evaluation and/or management of a specific medical problem is requested by another physician.

(2) The request and need for the consultation are documented in the patient's medical record.

(3) After the consultation is provided, the physician prepares a written report of his or her findings, which is provided to the physician who requested the consultation.

(4) With respect to radiation therapy services provided by a radiation oncologist, a course of radiation treatments over a period of time will be considered to be pursuant to a consultation, provided the radiation oncologist communicates with the referring physician on a regular basis about the patient's course of treatment and progress.

*Designated health services* (DHS) means any of the following services (other than those provided as emergency physician services furnished outside of the U.S.), as they are defined in this section:

(1) Clinical laboratory services.

(2) Physical therapy, occupational therapy, and speech-language pathology services.

(3) Radiology and certain other imaging services.

(4) Radiation therapy services and supplies.

(5) Durable medical equipment and supplies.

(6) Parenteral and enteral nutrients, equipment, and supplies.

(7) Prosthetics, orthotics, and prosthetic devices and supplies.

(8) Home health services.

(9) Outpatient prescription drugs.

(10) Inpatient and outpatient hospital services.

Except as otherwise noted in these regulations, the term "designated health services (DHS)" means only DHS payable, in whole or in part, by Medicare. DHS do not include services that are reimbursed by Medicare as part of a composite rate (for example, ambulatory surgical center services or SNF Part A payments), except to the extent the services listed in paragraphs (1) through (10) of this definition are themselves payable through a composite rate (that is, all services provided as home health services or inpatient and outpatient hospital services are DHS).

*Durable medical equipment* (DME) and supplies has the meaning given in section 1861(n) of the Act and Sec. 414.202 of this chapter.

*Employee* means any individual who, under the common law rules that apply in determining the employer-employee relationship (as applied for purposes of section 3121(d)(2) of the Internal Revenue Code of 1986), is considered to be employed by, or an employee of, an entity.

(Application of these common law rules is discussed in 20 CFR 404.1007 and 26 CFR 31.3121(d)-1(c).)

*Entity* means a physician's sole practice or a practice of multiple physicians or any other person, sole proprietorship, public or private agency or trust, corporation, partnership, limited liability company, foundation, not-for-profit corporation, or unincorporated association that furnishes DHS. For purposes of this definition, an entity does not include the referring physician himself or herself, but does include his or her medical practice. A person or entity is considered to be furnishing DHS if it is the person or entity to which HCFA makes payment for the DHS, directly or upon assignment on the patient's behalf, except that if the person or entity has reassigned its right to payment to an employer pursuant to Sec. 424.80(b)(1) of this chapter; a facility pursuant to Sec. 424.80(b)(2) of this chapter; or a health care delivery system, including clinics, pursuant to Sec. 424.80(b)(3) of this chapter (other than a health care delivery system that is a health plan (as defined in Sec. 1000.952(l) of this title), and other than any managed care organization (MCO), provider-sponsored organization (PSO), or independent practice association (IPA) with which a health plan contracts for services provided to plan enrollees), the person or entity furnishing DHS is the person or entity to which payment has been reassigned. Provided further, that a health plan, MCO, PSO, or IPA that employs a supplier or operates a facility that could accept reassignment from a supplier pursuant to Secs. 424.80(b)(1) and (b)(2) of this chapter is the entity furnishing DHS for any services provided by such supplier.

*Fair market value* means the value in arm's-length transactions, consistent with the general market value. "General market value" means the price that an asset would bring, as the result of *bona fide* bargaining between well-informed buyers and sellers who are not otherwise in a position to generate business for the other party; or the compensation that would be included in a service agreement, as the result of *bona fide* bargaining between well-informed parties to the agreement who are not otherwise in a position to generate business for the other party, on the date of acquisition of the asset or at the time of the service agreement. Usually, the fair market price is the price at which *bona fide* sales have been consummated for assets of like type, quality, and quantity in a particular market at the time of acquisition, or the compensation that has been included in *bona fide* service agreements with comparable terms at the time of the agreement. With respect to the rentals and leases described in Sec. 411.357(a) and (b), "fair market value" means the value of rental property for general commercial purposes (not taking into account its intended use). In the case of a lease of space, this value may not be adjusted to reflect the additional value the prospective lessee or lessor would attribute to the proximity or convenience to the lessor when the lessor is a potential source of patient referrals to the lessee. For purposes of this section, a rental payment does not take into account intended use if it takes into account costs incurred by the lessor in developing or upgrading the property or maintaining the property or its improvements.

*Home health services* means the services described in section 1861(m) of the Act and part 409, subpart E of this chapter.

*Hospital* means any entity that qualifies as a "hospital" under section 1861(e) of the Act, as a "psychiatric hospital" under section 1861(f) of the Act, or as a "rural primary care hospital" under section 1861(mm)(1) of the Act, and refers to any separate legally organized operating entity plus any subsidiary, related entity, or other entities that perform services for the hospital's patients and for which the hospital bills. However, a "hospital" does not include entities that perform services for hospital patients "under arrangements" with the hospital.

*HPSA* means, for purposes of this subpart, an area designated as a health professional shortage area under section 332(a)(1)(A) of the Public Health Service Act for primary medical care professionals (in accordance with the criteria specified in part 5 of this title).

*Immediate family member or member of a physician's immediate family* means husband or wife; birth or adoptive parent, child, or sibling; stepparent, stepchild, stepbrother, or stepsister; father-in-law, mother-in-law, son-in-law, daughter-in-law, brother-in-law, or sister-in-law; grandparent or grandchild; and spouse of a grandparent or grandchild.

*"Incident to" services* means those services that meet the requirements of section 1861(s)(2)(A) of the Act and section 2050 of the Medicare Carriers Manual (HCFA Pub. 14-3), Part 3—Claims Process. (Those wishing to subscribe to program manuals should contact either the Government Printing Office (GPO) or the National Technical Information Service (NTIS) at the following addresses: Superintendent of Documents, Government Printing Office, ATTN: New Orders, P.O. Box 371954, Pittsburgh, PA 15250-7954, Telephone (202) 512-1800, Fax number (202) 512-2250 (for credit card orders); or National Technical Information Service, Department of Commerce, 5825 Port Royal Road, Springfield, VA 22161, Telephone (703) 487-4630. In addition, individual manual transmittals and Program Memoranda can be purchased from NTIS. Interested parties should identify the transmittal(s) they want. GPO or NTIS can give complete details on how to obtain the publications they sell. Additionally, all manuals are available at the following Internet address: http://www.hcfa.gov/pubforms/progman.htm.)

*Inpatient hospital services* means those services as defined in section 1861(b) of the Act and Sec. 409.10(a) and (b) of this chapter and includes inpatient psychiatric hospital services listed in section 1861(c) of the Act and inpatient rural primary care hospital services, as defined in section 1861(mm)(2) of the Act. "Inpatient hospital services" do not include emergency inpatient services provided by a hospital located outside of the U.S. and covered under the authority in section 1814(f)(2) of the Act and part 424, subpart H of this chapter, or emergency inpatient services provided by a nonparticipating hospital within the U.S., as authorized by section 1814(d) of the Act and described in part 424, subpart G of this chapter. These services also do not include dialysis furnished by a hospital that is not certified to provide end-stage renal dialysis (ESRD) services under subpart U of part 405 of this chapter. Inpatient hospital services include services that a hospital provides for its patients that are furnished either by the hospital or by others under arrangements with the hospital. "Inpatient hospital services" do not include professional services performed by physicians, physician assistants, nurse practitioners, clinical nurse specialists, certified nurse midwives, and certified registered nurse anesthetists and qualified psychologists if Medicare reimburses the services independently and not as part of the inpatient hospital service (even if they are billed by a hospital under an assignment or reassignment).

*Laboratory* means an entity furnishing biological, microbiological, serological, chemical, immunohematological, hematological, biophysical, cytological, pathological, or other examination of materials derived from the human body for the purpose of providing information for the diagnosis, prevention, or treatment of any disease or impairment of, or the assessment of the health of, human beings. These examinations also include procedures to determine, measure, or otherwise describe the presence or absence of various substances or organisms in the body. Entities only collecting or preparing specimens (or both) or only serving as a mailing service and not performing testing are not considered laboratories.

*List of CPT/HCPCS Codes Used to Describe Certain Designated Health Services Under the Physician Referral Provisions (Section 1877 of the Social Security Act)* means the list of certain designated health services under section 1877 of the Act initially posted on the HCFA web site and updated annually thereafter in an addendum to the physician fee schedule final rule and on the HCFA web site.

*Member of the group* means, for purposes of this rule, a direct or indirect physician owner of a group practice (including a physician whose interest is held by his or her individual professional corporation or by another entity), a physician employee of the group practice (including a physician employed by his or her individual professional corporation that has an equity interest in the group practice), a locum tenens physician (as defined in this section), or an on-call physician while the physician is providing on-call services for members of the group practice. A physician is a member of the group during the time he or she furnishes "patient care services" to the group as defined in this section. An independent contractor or a leased employee is not a member of the group. "*Locum tenens* physician" means a physician who substitutes (that is, "stands in the shoes") in exigent circumstances for a regular physician who is a member of the group, in accordance with applicable reassignment rules and regulations, including section 3060.7 of the Medicare Carriers Manual (HCFA Pub. 14-3), Part 3—Claims Process.

*Outpatient hospital services* means the therapeutic, diagnostic, and partial hospitalization services listed under sections 1861(s)(2)(B) and (C) of the Act; outpatient services furnished by a psychiatric hospital, as defined in section 1861(f) of the Act; and outpatient rural primary care hospital services, as defined in section 1861(mm)(3) of the Act. Emergency services covered in nonparticipating hospitals are excluded under the conditions described in section 1835(b) of the Act and subpart G of part 424 of this chapter. "Outpatient hospital services" includes services that a hospital provides for its patients that are furnished either by the hospital or by others under arrangements with the hospital. "Outpatient hospital services" do not include professional services performed by physicians, physician assistants, nurse practitioners, clinical nurse specialists, certified nurse midwives, certified registered nurse anesthetists, and qualified psychologists if Medicare reimburses the services independently and not as part of the outpatient hospital service (even if they are billed by a hospital under an assignment or reassignment).

*Outpatient prescription drugs* means all prescription drugs covered by Medicare Part B.

*Parenteral and enteral nutrients, equipment, and supplies* means the following services (including all HCPCS level 2 codes for these services):

(1) *Parenteral nutrients, equipment, and supplies,* meaning those items and supplies needed to provide nutriment to a patient with permanent, severe pathology of the alimentary tract that does not allow absorption of sufficient nutrients to maintain strength commensurate with the patient's general condition, as described in section 65-10 of the Medicare Coverage Issues Manual (HCFA Pub. 6); and

(2) *Enteral nutrients, equipment, and supplies,* meaning items and supplies needed to provide enteral nutrition to a patient with a functioning gastrointestinal tract who, due to pathology to or nonfunction of the structures that normally permit food to reach the digestive tract, cannot maintain weight and strength commensurate with his or her general condition, as described in section 65-10 of the Medicare Coverage Issues Manual (HCFA Pub. 6).

*Patient care services* means any tasks performed by a physician in the group practice that address the medical needs of specific patients or patients in general, regardless of whether they involve direct patient encounters; or generally benefit a particular practice. Patient care services can include, for example, the services of physicians who do not directly treat patients, such as time spent by a physician consulting with other physicians or reviewing laboratory tests, or time spent training staff members, arranging for equipment, or performing administrative or management tasks.

*Physical therapy, occupational therapy, and speech-language pathology services* means those particular services identified by the CPT and HCPCS codes on the HCFA web site (and in annual updates published in the **Federal Register**). All services identified on the HCFA web site and in annual updates are physical therapy, occupational therapy, and speech-language pathology services for purposes of these regulations. Any service not specifically identified on the HCFA web site, as amended from time to time and published in the **Federal Register**, is not a physical therapy, occupational therapy, or speech-language pathology service for purposes of these regulations. The list of codes identifying physical therapy, occupational therapy, and speech-language pathology services for purposes of these regulations includes the following:

(1) *Physical therapy services,* meaning those outpatient physical therapy services (including speech-language pathology services) described at section 1861(p) of the Act that are covered under Medicare

Part A or Part B, regardless of who provides them, if the services include—

(i) Assessments, function tests and measurements of strength, balance, endurance, range of motion, and activities of daily living;

(ii) Therapeutic exercises, massage, and use of physical medicine modalities, assistive devices, and adaptive equipment;

(iii) Establishment of a maintenance therapy program for an individual whose restoration potential has been reached; however, maintenance therapy itself is not covered as part of these services; or

(iv) Speech-language pathology services that are for the diagnosis and treatment of speech, language, and cognitive disorders that include swallowing and other oral-motor dysfunctions.

(2) *Occupational therapy services*, meaning those services described at section 1861(g) of the Act that are covered under Medicare Part A or Part B, regardless of who provides them, if the services include—

(i) Teaching of compensatory techniques to permit an individual with a physical or cognitive impairment or limitation to engage in daily activities;

(ii) Evaluation of an individual's level of independent functioning;

(iii) Selection and teaching of task-oriented therapeutic activities to restore sensory-integrative function; or

(iv) Assessment of an individual's vocational potential, except when the assessment is related solely to vocational rehabilitation.

*Physician* means a doctor of medicine or osteopathy, a doctor of dental surgery or dental medicine, a doctor of podiatric medicine, a doctor of optometry, or a chiropractor, as defined in section 1861(r) of the Act.

*Physician in the group practice* means a member of the group practice, as well as an independent contractor physician, during the time the independent contractor is furnishing patient care services (as defined in this section) to the group practice under a contractual arrangement with the group practice to provide services to the group practice's patients in the group practice's facilities. The contract must contain the same restrictions on compensation that apply to members of the group practice under Sec. 411.352(g) (or the contract fits in the personal services exception in Sec. 411.357(d)), and the independent contractor's arrangement with the group practice must comply with the reassignment rules at Sec. 424.80(b)(3) of this chapter (see also section 3060.3 of the Medicare Carriers Manual (HCFA Pub. 14-3), Part 3—Claims Process). Referrals from an independent contractor who is a physician in the group are subject to the prohibition on referrals in Sec. 411.353(a), and the group practice is subject to the limitation on billing for those referrals in Sec. 411.353(b).

*Physician incentive plan* means any compensation arrangement between an entity and a physician or physician group that may directly or indirectly have the effect of reducing or limiting services furnished with respect to individuals enrolled with the entity.

*Plan of care* means the establishment by a physician of a course of diagnosis or treatment (or both) for a particular patient, including the ordering of services.

*Prosthetics, Orthotics, and Prosthetic Devices and Supplies* means the following services (including all HCPCS level 2 codes for these services that are covered by Medicare):

(1) *Orthotics*, meaning leg, arm, back, and neck braces, as listed in section 1861(s)(9) of the Act.

(2) *Prosthetics*, meaning artificial legs, arms, and eyes, as described in section 1861(s)(9) of the Act.

(3) *Prosthetic devices*, meaning devices (other than a dental device) listed in section 1861(s)(8) of the Act that replace all or part of an internal body organ, including colostomy bags, and one pair of conventional eyeglasses or contact lenses furnished subsequent to each cataract surgery with insertion of an intraocular lens.

(4) *Prosthetic supplies*, meaning supplies that are necessary for the effective use of a prosthetic device (including supplies directly related to colostomy care).

*Radiation therapy services and supplies* means those particular services and supplies identified by the CPT and HCPCS codes on the HCFA web site and in annual updates published in the **Federal Register**. All services identified on the HCFA web site and in annual updates are *radiation therapy services and supplies* for purposes of these regulations. Any service not specifically identified on the HCFA web site, as amended from time to time and published in the **Federal Register**, is not a *radiation therapy service or supply* for purposes of these regulations. The list of codes for radiation therapy services and supplies identified on the HCFA web site and in annual updates is based on section 1861(s)(4) of the Act and Sec. 410.35 of this chapter but does not include nuclear medicine procedures.

*Radiology and certain other imaging services* means those particular services identified by the CPT and HCPCS codes on the HCFA web site and in annual updates published in the **Federal Register** (except as otherwise specifically excluded on the HCFA web site and in annual updates). All services identified on the HCFA web site and in annual updates are *radiology and certain other imaging services* for purposes of these regulations. Any service not specifically identified on the HCFA web site, as amended from time to time and published in the **Federal Register**, is not a *radiology or certain other imaging service* for purposes of these regulations. The list of *radiology and certain other imaging services* set forth on the HCFA web site and in annual updates includes the professional and technical components of any diagnostic test or procedure using x-rays, ultrasound, or other imaging services, computerized axial tomography, or magnetic resonance imaging, as covered under section 1861(s)(3) of the Act and Secs. 410.32 and 410.34 of this chapter but does not include—

(1) X-ray, fluoroscopy, or ultrasonic procedures that require the insertion of a needle, catheter, tube, or probe through the skin or into a body orifice;

(2) Radiology procedures that are integral to the performance of, and performed during, nonradiological medical procedures; and

(3) Nuclear medicine procedures.

*Referral—*

(1) Means either of the following:

(i) Except as provided in paragraph (2) of this definition, the request by a physician for, or ordering of, or the certifying or recertifying of the need for, any designated health service for which payment may be made under Medicare Part B, including a request for a consultation with another physician and any test or procedure ordered by or to be performed by (or under the supervision of) that other physician, but not including any designated health service *personally* performed or provided by the referring physician. A designated health service is not personally performed or provided by the referring physician if it is performed or provided by any other person, including, but not limited to, the referring physician's employees, independent contractors, or group practice members.

(ii) Except as provided in paragraph (2) of this definition, a request by a physician that includes the provision of any designated health service for which payment may be made under Medicare, the establishment of a plan of care by a physician that includes the provision of such a designated health service, or the certifying or recertifying of the need for such a designated health service, but not including any designated health service *personally* performed or provided by the referring physician. A designated health service is not personally performed or provided by the referring physician if it is performed or provided by any other person including, but not limited to, the referring physician's employees, independent contractors, or group practice members.

(2) Does not include a request by a pathologist for clinical diagnostic laboratory tests and pathological examination services, by a radiologist for diagnostic radiology services, and by a radiation oncologist for radiation therapy, if—

(i) The request results from a consultation initiated by another physician (whether the request for a consultation was made to a particular physician or to an entity with which the physician is affiliated); and

(ii) The tests or services are furnished by or under the supervision of the pathologist, radiologist, or radiation oncologist.

(3) Can be in any form, including, but not limited to, written, oral, or electronic.

*Referring physician* means a physician who makes a referral as defined in this section or who directs another person or entity to make a referral or who controls referrals made by another person or entity.

*Remuneration* means any payment or other benefit made directly or indirectly, overtly or covertly, in cash or in kind, except that the following are not considered remuneration for purposes of this section:

(1) The forgiveness of amounts owed for inaccurate tests or procedures, mistakenly performed tests or procedures, or the correction of minor billing errors.

(2) The furnishing of items, devices, or supplies (not including surgical items, devices, or supplies) that are used solely to collect, transport, process, or store specimens for the entity furnishing the items, devices, or supplies or are used solely to order or communicate the results of tests or procedures for the entity.

(3) A payment made by an insurer or a self-insured plan to a physician to satisfy a claim, submitted on a fee-for-service basis, for the furnishing of health services by that physician to an individual who is covered by a policy with the insurer or by the self-insured plan, if—

    (i) The health services are not furnished, and the payment is not made, under a contract or other arrangement between the insurer or the plan and the physician;

    (ii) The payment is made to the physician on behalf of the covered individual and would otherwise be made directly to the individual; and

    (iii) The amount of the payment is set in advance, does not exceed fair market value, and is not determined in a manner that takes into account directly or indirectly the volume or value of any referrals.

*Same building* means a structure with, or combination of structures that share, a single street address as assigned by the U.S. Postal Service, excluding all exterior spaces (for example, lawns, courtyards, driveways, parking lots) and interior parking garages. For purposes of this rule, the "same building" does not include a mobile vehicle, van, or trailer.

    5. Section 411.352 is added to read as follows:

## Sec. 411.352 Group practice.

    For purposes of this subpart, a group practice is a physician practice that meets the following conditions:

    (a) *Single legal entity.* The group practice must consist of a single legal entity formed primarily for the purpose of being a physician group practice in any organizational form recognized by the State in which the group practice achieves its legal status, including, but not limited to, a partnership, professional corporation, limited liability company, foundation, not-for-profit corporation, faculty practice plan, or similar association. The single legal entity may be organized by any party or parties, including, but not limited to, physicians, health care facilities, or other persons or entities (including, but not limited to, physicians individually incorporated as professional corporations). The single legal entity may not be organized or owned (in whole or in part) by another medical practice that is an operating physician practice (regardless of whether the medical practice meets the conditions for a group practice under this section). For purposes of this rule, a single legal entity does not include informal affiliations of physicians formed substantially to share profits from referrals, or separate group practices under common ownership or control through a physician practice management company, hospital, health system, or other entity or organization. A group practice that is otherwise a single legal entity may itself own subsidiary entities.

(b) *Physicians.* The group practice must have at least two physicians who are members of the group (whether employees or direct or indirect owners), as defined in this section.

(c) *Range of care.* Each physician who is a *member of the group*, as defined in Sec. 411.351, must furnish substantially the full range of patient care services that the physician routinely furnishes, including medical care, consultation, diagnosis, and treatment, through the joint use of shared office space, facilities, equipment, and personnel.

(d) *Services furnished by group practice members.* (1) Except as provided in paragraphs (d)(2) and (d)(3) of this section, substantially all of the patient care services of the physicians who are *members of the group* (that is, at least 75 percent of the total patient care services of the group practice members) must be furnished through the group and billed under a billing number assigned to the group, and the amounts received must be treated as receipts of the group. "Patient care services" must be measured by one of the following:

    (i) The total time each member spends on patient care services documented by any reasonable means (including, but not limited to, time cards, appointment schedules, or personal diaries). (For example, if a physician practices 40 hours a week and spends 30 hours on patient care services for a group practice, the physician has spent 75 percent of his or her time providing patient care services for the group.)

    (ii) Any alternative measure that is reasonable, fixed in advance of the performance of the services being measured, uniformly applied over time, verifiable, and documented.

(2) The data used to calculate compliance with this "substantially all test" and related supportive documentation must be made available to the Secretary upon request.

(3) The "substantially all test" does not apply to any group practice that is located solely in an HPSA, as defined in Sec. 411.351.

(4) For a group practice located outside of an HPSA (as defined in Sec. 411.351), any time spent by a group practice member providing services in an HPSA should not be used to calculate whether the group practice has met the "substantially all test," regardless of whether the member's time in the HPSA is spent in a group practice, clinic, or office setting.

(5) During the "start up" period (not to exceed 12 months) that begins on the date of the initial formation of a new group practice, a group practice must make a reasonable, good faith effort to ensure that the group practice complies with the requirement set forth in paragraph (d)(1) of this section as soon as practicable, but no later than 12 months from the date of the initial formation of the group practice. This paragraph (d)(5) does not apply when an existing

group practice admits a new member or when an existing group practice reorganizes.

(e) *Distribution of expenses and income.* The overhead expenses of, and income from, the practice must be distributed according to methods that are determined before the receipt of payment for the services giving rise to the overhead expense or producing the income. Nothing in this rule prevents a group practice from adjusting its compensation methodology prospectively, subject to restrictions on the distribution of revenue from DHS under paragraph (i) of this section.

(f) *Unified business.* (1) The group practice must be a unified business having at least the following features:

(i) Centralized decision-making by a body representative of the group practice that maintains effective control over the group's assets and liabilities (including, but not limited to, budgets, compensation, and salaries).

(ii) Consolidated billing, accounting, and financial reporting.

(iii) Centralized utilization review.

(2) Location and specialty-based compensation practices are permitted with respect to revenues derived from services that are not DHS and may be permitted with respect to revenues derived from DHS under paragraph (i) of this section.

(g) *Volume or value of referrals.* No physician who is a member of the group practice directly or indirectly receives compensation based on the volume or value of referrals by the physician, except as provided in paragraph (i) of this section.

(h) *Physician-patient encounters.* Members of the group must personally conduct no less than 75 percent of the physician-patient encounters of the group practice.

(i) *Special rule for productivity bonuses and profit shares.* (1) A physician in a group practice may be paid a share of overall profits of the group, or a productivity bonus based on services that he or she has personally performed (including services "incident to" those personally performed services as defined in Sec. 411.351), provided that the share or bonus is not determined in any manner that is directly related to the volume or value of referrals of DHS by the physician.

(2) "Overall profits" means the group's entire profits derived from DHS payable by Medicare or Medicaid or the profits derived from DHS payable by Medicare or Medicaid of any component of the group practice that consists of at least five physicians. The share of overall profits will be deemed *not* to relate directly to the volume or value of referrals if *one* of the following conditions is met:

(i) The group's profits are divided per capita (for example, per member of the group or per physician in the group).

(ii) Revenues derived from DHS are distributed based on the distribution of the group practice's revenues attributed to services that are not DHS payable by any Federal health care program or private payer.

(iii) Revenues derived from DHS constitute less than 5 percent of the group practice's total revenues, and the allocated portion of those revenues to each physician in the group practice constitutes 5 percent or less of his or her total compensation from the group.

(iv) Overall profits are divided in a reasonable and verifiable manner that is not directly related to the volume or value of the physician's referrals of DHS.

(3) A productivity bonus for personally performed services (including services "incident to" those personally performed services as defined in Sec. 411.351) will be deemed not to relate directly to the volume or value of referrals of DHS if one of the following conditions is met:

(i) The bonus is based on the physician's total patient encounters or relative value units (RVUs). The methodology for establishing RVUs is set forth in Sec. 414.22 of this chapter.

(ii) The bonus is based on the allocation of the physician's compensation attributable to services that are not DHS payable by any Federal health care program or private payer.

(iii) Revenues derived from DHS are less than 5 percent of the group practice's total revenues, and the allocated portion of those revenues to each physician in the group practice constitutes 5 percent or less of his or her total compensation from the group practice.

(iv) The bonus is calculated in a reasonable and verifiable manner that is not directly related to the volume or value of the physician's referrals of DHS.

(4) Supporting documentation verifying the method used to calculate the profit shares or productivity bonus under paragraphs (i)(2) and (i)(3) of this section, and the resulting amount of compensation, must be made available to the Secretary upon request.

6. Section 411.353 is revised to read as follows:

### Sec. 411.353 Prohibition on certain referrals by physicians and limitations on billing.

(a) *Prohibition on referrals.* Except as provided in this subpart, a physician who has a direct or indirect financial relationship with an entity, or who has an immediate family member who has a direct or indirect financial relationship with the entity, may not make a referral to that entity for the furnishing of DHS for which payment otherwise may be made under Medicare. A physician's prohibited financial relationship with an entity that furnishes DHS is not imputed to his or her group practice or its members or its staff; however, a referral made by a physician's group practice, its members, or its staff may be imputed to the physician, if the physician directs the group practice, its members, or its staff to make the referral or if the physician controls referrals made by his or her group practice, its members, or its staff.

(b) *Limitations on billing.* An entity that furnishes DHS pursuant to a referral that is prohibited by paragraph (a) of this section may not present or cause to be presented a claim or bill to the Medicare program or to any individual, third party payer, or other entity for the DHS performed pursuant to the prohibited referral.

(c) *Denial of payment.* Except as provided in paragraph (e) of this section, no Medicare payment may be made for a designated health service that is furnished pursuant to a prohibited referral.

(d) *Refunds.* An entity that collects payment for a designated health service that was performed under a prohibited referral must refund all collected amounts on a timely basis, as defined in Sec. 1003.101 of this title.

(e) *Exception for certain entities.* Payment may be made to an entity that submits a claim for a designated health service if—

(1) The entity did not have actual knowledge of, and did not act in reckless disregard or deliberate ignorance of, the identity of the physician who made the referral of the designated health service to the entity; and

(2) The claim otherwise complies with all applicable Federal laws, rules, and regulations.

7. Section 411.354 is added to read as follows:

## Sec. 411.354 Financial relationship, compensation, and ownership or investment interest.

(a) *Financial relationships.* (1) *Financial relationship* means—

(i) A direct or indirect ownership or investment interest (as defined in paragraph (b) of this section) in any entity that furnishes DHS; or

(ii) A direct or indirect compensation arrangement (as defined in paragraph (c) of this section) with an entity that furnishes DHS.

(2) A *direct* financial relationship exists if remuneration passes between the referring physician (or a member of his or her immediate family) and the entity furnishing DHS without any intervening persons or entities (not including an agent of the physician, the immediate family member, or the entity furnishing DHS).

(3) An *indirect* financial relationship exists under the conditions described in paragraphs (b)(5) and (c)(2) of this section.

(b) *Ownership or investment interest.* An ownership or investment interest may be through equity, debt, or other means, and includes an interest in an entity that holds an ownership or investment interest in any entity that furnishes DHS.

(1) An ownership or investment interest includes, but is not limited to, stock, partnership shares, limited liability company memberships, as well as loans, bonds, or other financial instruments that are secured with an entity's property or revenue or a portion of that property or revenue.

(2) An ownership or investment interest in a subsidiary company is neither an ownership or investment interest in the parent company,

nor in any other subsidiary of the parent, unless the subsidiary company itself has an ownership or investment interest in the parent or such other subsidiaries. It may, however, be part of an indirect financial relationship.

(3) Ownership and investment interests do not include, among other things—

    (i) An interest in a retirement plan;

    (ii) Stock options and convertible securities until the stock options are exercised or the convertible securities are converted to equity (before this time they are compensation arrangements as defined in paragraph (c) of this section);

    (iii) An unsecured loan subordinated to a credit facility (which is a compensation arrangement as defined in paragraph (c) of this section); or

    (iv) An "under arrangements" contract between a hospital and an entity owned by one or more physicians (or a group of physicians) providing DHS "under arrangements" to the hospital.

(4) An ownership or investment interest that meets an exception set forth in Secs. 411.355 or 411.356 need not also meet an exception for compensation arrangements set forth in Sec. 411.357 with respect to profit distributions, dividends, interest payments on secured obligations, or the like.

(5) *Indirect ownership or investment interest.* (i) An indirect ownership or investment interest exists if—

      (A) Between the referring physician (or immediate family member) and the entity furnishing DHS there exists an unbroken chain of any number (but no fewer than one) of persons or entities having ownership or investment interests between them; and

      (B) The entity furnishing DHS has actual knowledge of, or acts in reckless disregard or deliberate ignorance of, the fact that the referring physician (or immediate family member) has some ownership or investment interest (through any number of intermediary ownership or investment interests) in the entity furnishing the DHS.

    (ii) The entity furnishing DHS need not know, or act in reckless disregard or deliberate ignorance of, the precise composition of the unbroken chain or the specific terms of the ownership or investment interests that form the links in the chain.

  (c) *Compensation arrangement.* A compensation arrangement can be any arrangement involving remuneration, direct or indirect, between a physician (or a member of a physician's immediate family) and an entity. An "under arrangements" contract between a hospital and an entity providing DHS "under arrangements" to the hospital creates a compensation arrangement for purposes of these regulations.

    (1) A compensation arrangement does not include any of the following:

      (i) The portion of any business arrangement that consists solely of the remuneration described in section 1877(h)(1)(C) of the Act and in paragraphs (1) through (3) of the definition of the term "remuneration" in Sec. 411.351. (However, any other portion of the arrangement may still constitute a compensation arrangement.)

(ii) Payments made by a consultant to a referring physician under Sec. 414.65(e) of this chapter.

(2) *Indirect compensation arrangement.* An *indirect* compensation arrangement exists if—

(i) Between the referring physician (or a member of his or her immediate family) and the entity furnishing DHS there exists an unbroken chain of any number (but not fewer than one) of persons or entities that have financial relationships (as defined in paragraph (a) of this section) between them (that is, each link in the chain has either an ownership or investment interest or a compensation arrangement with the preceding link);

(ii) The referring physician (or immediate family member) receives aggregate compensation from the person or entity in the chain with which the physician (or immediate family member) has a *direct* financial relationship that varies with, or otherwise reflects, the volume or value of referrals or other business generated by the referring physician for the entity furnishing the DHS. If the financial relationship between the physician (or immediate family member) and the person or entity in the chain with which the referring physician (or immediate family member) has a direct financial relationship is an ownership or investment interest, the determination whether the aggregate compensation varies with, or otherwise reflects, the volume or value of referrals or other business generated by the referring physician for the entity furnishing the DHS will be measured by the nonownership or noninvestment interest closest to the referring physician (or immediate family member). (For example, if a referring physician has an ownership interest in company A, which owns company B, which has a compensation arrangement with company C, which has a compensation arrangement with entity D that furnishes DHS, we would look to the aggregate compensation between company B and company C for purposes of this paragraph (c)(2)(ii)); and

(iii) The entity furnishing DHS has actual knowledge of, or acts in reckless disregard or deliberate ignorance of, the fact that the referring physician (or immediate family member) receives aggregate compensation that varies with, or otherwise reflects, the value or volume of referrals or other business generated by the referring physician for the entity furnishing the DHS.

(d) *Special rules on compensation.* The following special rules apply only to compensation under section 1877 of the Act and these regulations in subpart J of this part.

(1) Compensation will be considered "set in advance" if the aggregate compensation or a time-based or per unit of service-based

(whether per-use or per-service) amount is set in advance in the initial agreement between the parties in sufficient detail so that it can be objectively verified. The payment amount must be fair market value compensation for services or items actually provided, not taking into account the volume or value of referrals or other business generated by the referring physician at the time of the initial agreement or during the term of the agreement. Percentage compensation arrangements do not constitute compensation that is "set in advance" in which the percentage compensation is based on fluctuating or indeterminate measures or in which the arrangement results in the seller receiving different payment amounts for the same service from the same purchaser.

(2) Compensation (including time-based or per unit of service-based compensation) will be deemed not to take into account "the volume or value of referrals" if the compensation is fair market value for services or items actually provided and does not vary during the course of the compensation agreement in any manner that takes into account referrals of DHS.

(3) Compensation (including time-based or per unit of service-based compensation) will be deemed to not take into account "other business generated between the parties" so long as the compensation is fair market value and does not vary during the term of the agreement in any manner that takes into account referrals or other business generated by the referring physician, including private pay health care business.

(4) A physician's compensation may be conditioned on the physician's referrals to a particular provider, practitioner, or supplier, so long as the compensation arrangement—

    (i) Is fixed in advance for the term of the agreement;

    (ii) Is consistent with fair market value for services performed (that is, the payment does not take into account the volume or value of anticipated or required referrals);

    (iii) Complies with an applicable exception under Secs. 411.355 or 411.357; and

    (iv) Complies with the following conditions:

        (A) The requirement to make referrals to a particular provider, practitioner, or supplier is set forth in a written agreement signed by the parties.

        (B) The requirement to make referrals to a particular provider, practitioner, or supplier does not apply if the patient expresses a preference for a different provider, practitioner, or supplier; the patient's insurer determines the provider, practitioner, or supplier; or the referral is not in the patient's best medical interests in the physician's judgement.

8. Section 411.355 is revised to read as follows:

## Sec. 411.355 General exceptions to the referral prohibition related to both ownership/investment and compensation.

The prohibition on referrals set forth in Sec. 411.353 does not apply to the following types of services:

(a) *Physician services.* (1) Physician services as defined in Sec. 410.20(a) of this chapter that are furnished—

(i) Personally by another physician who is a member of the referring physician's group practice or is a physician in the same group practice (as defined in Sec. 411.351) as the referring physician; or

(ii) Under the supervision of another physician who is a member of the referring physician's group practice or is a physician in the same group practice (as defined at Sec. 411.351) as the referring physician, provided that the supervision complies with all other applicable Medicare payment and coverage rules for the physician services.

(2) For purposes of paragraph (a) of this section, "physician services" includes only those "incident to" services (as defined in Sec. 411.351) that are physician services under Sec. 410.20(a) of this chapter.

(3) All other "incident to" services (for example, diagnostic tests, physical therapy) are outside the scope of paragraph (a) of this section.

(b) *In-office ancillary services.* Services (including certain items of durable medical equipment (DME), as defined in paragraph (b)(4) of this section, and infusion pumps that are DME (including external ambulatory infusion pumps), but excluding all other DME and parenteral and enteral nutrients, equipment, and supplies (such as infusion pumps used for PEN), that meet the following conditions:

(1) They are furnished personally by one of the following individuals:

(i) The referring physician.

(ii) A physician who is a member of the same group practice as the referring physician.

(iii) An individual who is supervised by the referring physician or by another physician in the group practice, provided the supervision complies with all other applicable Medicare payment and coverage rules for the services.

(2) They are furnished in one of the following locations:

(i) The same building (as defined in Sec. 411.351), but not necessarily in the same space or part of the building, in which—

(A) The referring physician (or another physician who is a member of the same group practice) furnishes substantial physician services that are unrelated to the furnishing of DHS payable by Medicare, any other Federal health care payer, or a private payer, even though the unrelated services may lead to the ordering of DHS;

(B) The physician services that are unrelated to the furnishing of DHS in paragraph (b)(2)(i)(A) of this section must represent substantially the full range of physician services un-related to the furnishing of DHS that the referring physician routinely provides (or, in the case of a referring physician who is a member of a group practice, the full range of physician services that the physician routinely provides for the group practice); and

(C) The receipt of DHS (whether payable by a Federal health care program or a private payer) is not the primary reason the patient comes in contact with the referring physician or his or her group practice.

(ii) A centralized building (as defined in Sec. 411.351) that is used by the group practice for the provision of some or all of the group practice's clinical laboratory services.

(iii) A centralized building (as defined in Sec. 411.351) that is used by the group practice for the provision of some or all of the group practice's DHS (other than clinical laboratory services).

(3) They must be billed by one of the following:

(i) The physician performing or supervising the service.

(ii) The group practice of which the performing or supervising physician is a member under a billing number assigned to the group practice.

(iii) The group practice if the supervising physician is a "physician in the group" (as defined at Sec. 411.351) under a billing number assigned to the group practice.

(iv) An entity that is wholly owned by the performing or supervising physician or by that physician's group practice under the entity's own billing number or under a billing number assigned to the physician or group practice.

(v) An independent third party billing company acting as an agent of the physician, group practice, or entity specified in paragraphs (b)(3)(i) through (b)(3)(iv) of this section under a billing number assigned to the physician, group practice, or entity, provided the billing arrangement meets the requirements of Sec. 424.80(b)(6) of this chapter. For purposes of this paragraph (b)(3), a group practice may have, and bill under, more than one Medicare billing number, subject to any applicable Medicare program restrictions.

(4) For purposes of paragraph (b) of this section, DME covered by the in-office ancillary services exception means canes, crutches, walkers and folding manual wheelchairs, and blood glucose monitors, that meet the following conditions:

(i) The item is one that a patient requires for the purposes of ambulating, uses in order to depart from the physician's office, or is a blood glucose monitor (including one starter set of test strips and lancets, consisting of no more than 100 of each). A blood glucose monitor may be furnished only by a physician or employee of a physician or group practice that also furnishes outpatient diabetes self-management training to the patient.

(ii) The item is furnished in a building that meets the "same building" requirements in the in-office ancillary services exception as part of the treatment for the specific condition for which the patient-physician encounter occurred.

(iii) The item is furnished personally by the physician who ordered the DME, by another physician in the group practice, or by an employee of the physician or the group practice.

(iv) A physician or group practice that furnishes the DME meets all DME supplier standards located in Sec. 424.57(c) of this chapter.

(v) The arrangement does not violate the anti-kickback statute, section 1128B(b) of the Act, or any law or regulation governing billing or claims submission.

(vi) All other requirements of the in-office ancillary services exception in paragraph (b) of this section are met.

(5) A designated health service is "furnished" for purposes of paragraph (b) of this section in the location where the service is actually performed upon a patient or where an item is dispensed to a patient in a manner that is sufficient to meet the applicable Medicare payment and coverage rules.

(6) *Special rule for home care physicians.* In the case of a referring physician whose principal medical practice consists of treating patients in their private homes, the "same building" requirements of paragraph (b)(2)(i) of this section are met if the referring physician (or a qualified person accompanying the physician, such as a nurse or technician) provides the DHS contemporaneously with a physician service that is not a designated health service provided by the referring physician to the patient in the patient's private home. For purposes of paragraph (b)(5) of this section, a private home does not include a nursing, long-term care, or other facility or institution.

(c) *Services furnished by an organization (or its contractors or subcontractors) to enrollees.* Services furnished by an organization (or its contractors or subcontractors) to enrollees of one of the following prepaid health plans (not including services provided to enrollees in any other plan or line of business offered or administered by the same organization):

(1) An HMO or a CMP in accordance with a contract with HCFA under section 1876 of the Act and part 417, subparts J through M of this chapter, which set forth qualifying conditions for Medicare contracts; enrollment, entitlement, and disenrollment under Medicare contracts; Medicare contract requirements; and change of ownership and leasing of facilities: effect on Medicare contracts.

(2) A health care prepayment plan in accordance with an agreement with HCFA under section 1833(a)(1)(A) of the Act and part 417, subpart U of this chapter.

(3) An organization that is receiving payments on a prepaid basis for Medicare enrollees through a demonstration project under section 402(a) of the Social Security Amendments of 1967 (42 U.S.C. 1395b-1) or under section 222(a) of the Social Security Amendments of 1972 (42 U.S.C. 1395b-1 note).

(4) A qualified HMO (within the meaning of section 1310(d) of the Public Health Service Act).

(5) A coordinated care plan (within the meaning of section 1851(a)(2)(A) of the Act) offered by an organization in accordance with a contract with HCFA under section 1857 of the Act and part 422 of this chapter.

(d) *Clinical laboratory services furnished in an ambulatory surgical center (ASC) or end-stage renal disease (ESRD) facility, or by a hospice* if payment for those services is included in the ASC rate, the ESRD composite rate, or as part of the per diem hospice charge, respectively.

(e) *Academic medical centers.* (1) Services provided by an academic medical center if all of the following conditions are met:

(i) The referring physician—

(A) Is a *bona fide* employee of a component of the academic medical center on a full-time or substantial part-time basis. ("Components" of an academic medical center means an affiliated medical school, faculty practice plan, hospital, teaching facility, institution of higher education, or departmental professional corporation.);

(B) Is licensed to practice medicine in the State;

(C) Has a *bona fide* faculty appointment at the affiliated medical school; and

(D) Provides either substantial academic or substantial clinical teaching services for which the faculty member receives compensation as part of his or her employment relationship with the academic medical center.

(ii) The total compensation paid for the previous 12-month period (or fiscal year or calendar year) from all academic medical center components to the referring physician is set in advance and, in the aggregate, does not exceed fair market value for the services provided, and is not determined in a manner that takes into account the volume or value of any referrals or other business generated by the referring physician within the academic medical center.

(iii) The academic medical center must meet all of the following conditions:

(A) All transfers of money between components of the academic medical center must directly or indirectly support the missions of teaching, indigent care, research, or community service.

(B) The relationship of the components of the academic medical center must be set forth in a written agreement that has been adopted by the governing body of each component.

(C) All money paid to a referring physician for research must be used solely to support *bona fide* research.

(iv) The referring physician's compensation arrangement does not violate the anti-kickback statute, section 1128B(b) of the Act.

(2) The "academic medical center" for purposes of this section consists of—

(i) An accredited medical school (including a university, when appropriate);

(ii) An affiliated faculty practice plan that is a 501(c)(3) or (c)(4) of the Internal Revenue Code nonprofit, tax-exempt organization under IRS regulations (or is a part of such an organization under an umbrella designation); and

(iii) One or more affiliated hospital(s) in which a majority of the hospital medical staff consists of physicians who are faculty members and a majority of all hospital admissions are made by physicians who are faculty members.

(f) *Implants in an ASC.* Implants, including, but not limited to, cochlear implants, intraocular lenses, and other implanted prosthetics, implanted prosthetic devices and implanted DME that meet the following conditions:

(1) The implant is furnished by the referring physician or a member of the referring physician's group practice in a Medicare-certified ASC (under part 416 of this chapter) with which the referring physician has a financial relationship.

(2) The implant is implanted in the patient during a surgical procedure performed in the same ASC where the implant is furnished.

(3) The arrangement for the furnishing of the implant does not violate the Federal anti-kickback statute, section 1128B(b) of the Act.

(4) Billing and claims submission for the implants complies with all Federal and State laws and regulations.

(5) The exception set forth in this paragraph (f) does not apply to any financial relationships between the referring physician and any entity other than the ASC in which the implant is furnished to and implanted in the patient.

(g) *EPO and other dialysis-related outpatient prescription drugs furnished in or by an ESRD facility.* EPO and other dialysis-related outpatient prescription drugs that are identified by the CPT and HCPCS codes on the HCFA web site, http://www.hcfa.gov, and in annual updates published in the **Federal Register** and that meet the following conditions:

(1) The EPO and other dialysis-related drugs are furnished in or by an ESRD facility. For purposes of this paragraph, "furnished" means that the EPO or drugs are either administered or dispensed to a patient in or by the ESRD facility, even if the EPO or drugs are furnished to the patient at home. "Dialysis-related drugs" means certain drugs required for the efficacy of dialysis, as identified on the HCFA web site and in annual updates.

(2) The arrangement for the furnishing of the EPO and other dialysis-related drugs does not violate the Federal anti-kickback statute, section 1128B(b) of the Act.

(3) Billing and claims submission for the EPO and other dialysis related drugs complies with all Federal and State laws and regulations.

(4) The exception set forth in this paragraph (g) does not apply to any financial relationships between the referring physician and any entity other than the ESRD facility that furnishes the EPO and other dialysis-related drugs to the patient.

(h) *Preventive screening tests, immunizations, and vaccines.* Preventive screening tests, immunizations, and vaccines that are covered by Medicare and identified by the CPT and HCPCS codes included on the HCFA web site and in annual updates published in the **Federal Register** and that meet the following conditions:

(1) The preventive screening tests, immunizations, and vaccines are subject to HCFA-mandated frequency limits.

(2) The preventive screening tests, immunizations, and vaccines are reimbursed by Medicare based on a fee schedule.

(3) The arrangement for the provision of the preventive screening tests, immunizations, and vaccines does not violate the Federal anti-kickback statute, section 1128B(b) of the Act.

(4) Billing and claims submission for the preventive screening tests, immunizations, and vaccines complies with all Federal and State laws and regulations.

(5) To qualify under this exception, the preventive screening tests, immunizations, and vaccines must be covered by Medicare and must be listed on the HCFA web site and in annual updates.

(i) *Eyeglasses and contact lenses following cataract surgery.* Eyeglasses and contact lenses that are covered by Medicare when furnished to patients following cataract surgery that meet the following conditions:

(1) The eyeglasses or contact lenses are provided in accordance with the coverage and payment provisions set forth in Sec. 410.36(a)(2)(ii) and Sec. 414.228 of this chapter, respectively.

(2) The arrangement for the furnishing of the eyeglasses or contact lenses does not violate the Federal anti-kickback statute, section 1128B(b) of the Act.

(3) Billing and claims submission for the eyeglasses or contact lenses complies with all Federal and State laws and regulations.

9. In Sec. 411.357, paragraph (j) is added and reserved, and paragraphs (k), (l), (m), (n), (o), and (p) are added to read as follows:

## Sec. 411.357 Exceptions to the referral prohibition related to compensation arrangements.

\* \* \* \* \*

(j) [Reserved]

(k) *Non-monetary compensation up to $300.* Compensation from an entity in the form of items or services (not including cash or cash equivalents) that does not exceed an aggregate of $300 per year, if all of the following conditions are satisfied:

(1) The compensation is not determined in any manner that takes into account the volume or value of referrals or other business generated by the referring physician.

(2) The compensation may not be solicited by the physician or the physician's practice (including employees and staff members).

(3) The compensation arrangement does not violate the Federal anti-kickback statute, section 1128B(b) of the Act.

(l) *Fair market value compensation.* Compensation resulting from an arrangement between an entity and a physician (or an immediate family member) or any group of physicians (regardless of whether the group meets the definition of a group practice set forth in Sec. 411.351) for the provision of items or services by the physician (or an immediate family member) or group practice to the entity, if the arrangement is set forth in an agreement that meets the following conditions:

(1) It is in writing, signed by the parties, and covers only identifiable items or services, all of which are specified in the agreement.

(2) It specifies the timeframe for the arrangement, which can be for any period of time and contain a termination clause, provided the parties enter into only one arrangement for the same items or services during the course of a year. An arrangement made for less than 1 year may be renewed any number of times if the terms of the arrangement and the compensation for the same items or services do not change.

(3) It specifies the compensation that will be provided under the arrangement. The compensation must be set in advance, be consistent with fair market value, and not be determined in a manner that takes into account the volume or value of any referrals or any other business generated by the referring physician.

(4) It involves a transaction that is commercially reasonable (taking into account the nature and scope of the transaction) and furthers the legitimate business purposes of the parties.

(5) It meets a safe harbor under the anti-kickback statute in Sec. 1001.952 of this title, has been approved by the OIG under a favorable advisory opinion issued in accordance with part 1008 of this title, or does not violate the anti-kickback provisions in section 1128B(b) of the Act.

(6) The services to be performed under the arrangement do not involve the counseling or promotion of a business arrangement or other activity that violates a State or Federal law.

(m) *Medical staff incidental benefits.* Compensation in the form of items or services (not including cash or cash equivalents) from a hospital to a member of its medical staff when the item or service is used on the hospital's campus, if all of the following conditions are met:

(1) The compensation is offered to all members of the medical staff without regard to the volume or value of referrals or other business generated between the parties.

(2) The compensation is offered only during periods when the medical staff members are making rounds or performing other duties that benefit the hospital or its patients.

(3) The compensation is provided by the hospital and used by the medical staff members only on the hospital's campus.

(4) The compensation is reasonably related to the provision of, or designed to facilitate directly or indirectly the delivery of, medical services at the hospital.

(5) The compensation is consistent with the types of benefits offered to medical staff members—

(i) By other hospitals within the same local region; or

(ii) If no such hospitals exist within the same local region, by comparable hospitals in comparable regions.

(6) The compensation is of low value (that is, less than $25) with respect to each occurrence of the benefit (for example, each meal given to a physician while he or she is serving patients who are hospitalized must be of low value).

(7) The compensation is not determined in any manner that takes into account the volume or value of referrals or other business generated between the parties.

(8) The compensation arrangement does not violate the Federal anti-kickback provisions in section 1128B(b) of the Act.

(n) *Risk sharing arrangements.* Compensation pursuant to a risk-sharing arrangement (including, but not limited to, withholds, bonuses, and risk pools) between a managed care organization or an independent physicians association and a physician (either directly or indirectly through a subcontractor) for services provided to enrollees of a health plan, provided that the arrangement does not violate the Federal anti-kickback statute, section 1128B(b) of the Act, or any law or regulation governing billing or claims submission. For purposes of this paragraph (n), "health plan" and "enrollees" have the meanings ascribed to those terms in Sec. 1001.952(l) of this title.

(o) *Compliance training.* Compliance training provided by a hospital to a physician (or the physician's immediate family member) who practices in the hospital's local community or service area, provided the training is held in the local community or service area. For purposes of this paragraph (o), "compliance training" means training regarding the basic elements of a compliance program (for example, establishing policies and procedures, training of staff, internal monitoring, reporting) or specific training regarding the requirements of Federal health care programs (for example, billing, coding, reasonable and necessary services, documentation, unlawful referral arrangements).

(p) *Indirect compensation arrangements.* Indirect compensation arrangements, as defined in Sec. 411.354(c)(2), if all of the following conditions are satisfied:

(1) The compensation received by the referring physician (or immediate family member) described in Sec. 411.354(c)(2)(ii) is fair market value for services and items actually provided not taking into account the value or volume of referrals or other business generated by the referring physician for the entity furnishing DHS.

(2) The compensation arrangement described in Sec. 411.354(c)(2)(ii) is set out in writing, signed by the parties, and specifies the services covered by the arrangement, except in the case of a *bona fide* employment relationship between an employer and an employee, in which case the arrangement need not be set out in a written contract, but must be for identifiable services and be commercially reasonable even if no referrals are made to the employer.

(3) The compensation arrangement does not violate the anti-kickback statute or any laws or regulations governing billing or claims submission.

## PART 424—CONDITIONS FOR MEDICARE PAYMENT

B. Part 424 is amended as follows:

1. The authority citation for part 424 continues to read as follows:

**Authority:** Secs. 1102 and 1871 of the Social Security Act (42 U.S.C. 1302 and 1395hh).

### Subpart B—Certification and Plan of Treatment Requirements

2. In Sec. 424.22, paragraph (d) is revised to read as set forth below, and paragraphs (e), (f), and (g) are removed.

### Sec. 424.22 Requirements for home health services.

\* \* \* \* \*

(d) *Limitation on the performance of certification and plan of treatment functions.* The need for home health services to be provided by an HHA may not be certified or recertified, and a plan of treatment may not be established and reviewed, by any physician who has a financial relationship, as defined in Sec. 411.351 of this chapter, with that HHA, unless the physician's relationship meets one of the exceptions in section 1877 of the Act, which sets forth general exceptions to the referral prohibition related to both ownership/investment and compensation; exceptions to the referral prohibition related to ownership or investment interests; and exceptions to the referral prohibition related to compensation arrangements.

(Catalog of Federal Domestic Assistance Program No. 93.773, Medicare-Hospital Insurance; Program No. 93.774, Medicare-Supplementary Medical Insurance Program; and Program No. 93.778, Medical Assistance Program)

Dated: October 6, 2000.
Michael M. Hash,
*Acting Administrator, Health Care Financing Administration.*

Dated: October 16, 2000.
Donna E. Shalala,
*Secretary.*

[*Editor's Note:* Attachment omitted: List of CPT/HCPCS Codes re Certain Designated Health Services in 66 Fed. Reg. 963–965 (Jan. 1, 2001), not to appear in the *Code of Federal Regulations*.]

# Appendix B-4

## Stark II Phase I Final Regulations        on disk

*Source:* Health Care Financing Administration, Department of Health and Human Services, 66 Fed. Reg. 952–963 (Jan. 4, 2001) *(effective Jan. 4, 2002: draft integrated version)* (codified at 42 C.F.R. §§411.351–.361).

***Editor's Note:*** The Stark II Phase I final regulations draft integrated version is on the accompanying disk in the folder **STARK**. The file name for this document is **STRKIIRG**.

Appendix B-4 is a draft integrated version of the regulations provided for the reader's convenience; this version was integrated by editors at The Bureau of National Affairs, Inc., in December 2001. Readers should consult the *Code of Federal Regulations* for the official text.

Please see the note at Appendix B-3 regarding the group practice physician attestation requirement.

# Appendix C

## Civil False Claims Act Materials

# Appendix C-1

## Civil False Claims Act

*Source:* 31 U.S.C. Sections 3729–3733.

### Section 3729. False claims

(a) Liability for Certain Acts.—Any person who—

(1) knowingly presents, or causes to be presented, to an officer or employee of the United States Government or a member of the Armed Forces of the United States a false or fraudulent claim for payment or approval;

(2) knowingly makes, uses, or causes to be made or used, a false record or statement to get a false or fraudulent claim paid or approved by the Government;

(3) conspires to defraud the Government by getting a false or fraudulent claim allowed or paid;

(4) has possession, custody, or control of property or money used, or to be used, by the Government and, intending to defraud the Government or willfully to conceal the property, delivers, or causes to be delivered, less property than the amount for which the person receives a certificate or receipt;

(5) authorized to make or deliver a document certifying receipt of property used, or to be used, by the Government and, intending to defraud the Government, makes or delivers the receipt without completely knowing that the information on the receipt is true;

(6) knowingly buys, or receives as a pledge of an obligation or debt, public property from an officer or employee of the Government, or a member of the Armed Forces, who lawfully may not sell or pledge the property; or

(7) knowingly makes, uses, or causes to be made or used, a false record or statement to conceal, avoid, or decrease an obligation to pay or transmit money or property to the Government, is liable to the

565

United States Government for a civil penalty of not less than $5,000 and not more than $10,000, plus 3 times the amount of damages which the Government sustains because of the act of that person, except that if the court finds that—

(A) the person committing the violation of this subsection furnished officials of the United States responsible for investigating false claims violations with all information known to such person about the violation within 30 days after the date on which the defendant first obtained the information;

(B) such person fully cooperated with any Government investigation of such violation; and

(C) at the time such person furnished the United States with the information about the violation, no criminal prosecution, civil action, or administrative action had commenced under this title with respect to such violation, and the person did not have actual knowledge of the existence of an investigation into such violation;

the court may assess not less than 2 times the amount of damages which the Government sustains because of the act of the person. A person violating this subsection shall also be liable to the United States Government for the costs of a civil action brought to recover any such penalty or damages.

(b) Knowing and Knowingly Defined.—For purposes of this section, the terms "knowing" and "knowingly" mean that a person, with respect to information—

(1) has actual knowledge of the information;

(2) acts in deliberate ignorance of the truth or falsity of the information; or

(3) acts in reckless disregard of the truth or falsity of the information,

and no proof of specific intent to defraud is required.

(c) Claim Defined.—For purposes of this section, "claim" includes any request or demand, whether under a contract or otherwise, for money or property which is made to a contractor, grantee, or other recipient if the United States Government provides any portion of the money or property which is requested or demanded, or if the Government will reimburse such contractor, grantee, or other recipient for any portion of the money or property which is requested or demanded.

(d) Exemption From Disclosure.—Any information furnished pursuant to subparagraphs (A) through (C) of subsection (a) shall be exempt from disclosure under section 552 of title 5.

(e) Exclusion.—This section does not apply to claims, records, or statements made under the Internal Revenue Code of 1986.

*SOURCE—*

(Pub. L. 97-258, Sept. 13, 1982, 96 Stat. 978; Pub. L. 99-562, Sec. 2, Oct. 27, 1986, 100 Stat. 3153; Pub. L. 103-272, Sec. 4(f)(1)(O), July 5, 1994, 108 Stat. 1362.)

## Section 3730: Civil actions for false claims

(a) Responsibilities of the Attorney General.—The Attorney General diligently shall investigate a violation under section 3729. If the Attorney General finds that a person has violated or is violating section 3729, the Attorney General may bring a civil action under this section against the person.

(b) Actions by Private Persons.—(1) A person may bring a civil action for a violation of section 3729 for the person and for the United States Government. The action shall be brought in the name of the Government. The action may be dismissed only if the court and the Attorney General give written consent to the dismissal and their reasons for consenting.

(2) A copy of the complaint and written disclosure of substantially all material evidence and information the person possesses shall be served on the Government pursuant to Rule 4(d)(4) of the Federal Rules of Civil Procedure. The complaint shall be filed in camera, shall remain under seal for at least 60 days, and shall not be served on the defendant until the court so orders. The Government may elect to intervene and proceed with the action within 60 days after it receives both the complaint and the material evidence and information.

(3) The Government may, for good cause shown, move the court for extensions of the time during which the complaint remains under seal under paragraph (2). Any such motions may be supported by affidavits or other submissions in camera. The defendant shall not be required to respond to any complaint filed under this section until 20 days after the complaint is unsealed and served upon the defendant pursuant to Rule 4 of the Federal Rules of Civil Procedure.

(4) Before the expiration of the 60-day period or any extensions obtained under paragraph (3), the Government shall—

(A) proceed with the action, in which case the action shall be conducted by the Government; or

(B) notify the court that it declines to take over the action, in which case the person bringing the action shall have the right to conduct the action.

(5) When a person brings an action under this subsection, no person other than the Government may intervene or bring a related action based on the facts underlying the pending action.

(c) Rights of the Parties to Qui Tam Actions.—(1) If the Government proceeds with the action, it shall have the primary responsibility for prosecuting the action, and shall not be bound by an act of the person bringing the action. Such person shall have the right to continue as a party to the action, subject to the limitations set forth in paragraph (2).

(2)(A) The Government may dismiss the action notwithstanding the objections of the person initiating the action if the person has been notified by the Government of the filing of the motion and the court has provided the person with an opportunity for a hearing on the motion.

(B) The Government may settle the action with the defendant notwithstanding the objections of the person initiating the action if the court determines, after a hearing, that the proposed settlement is fair, adequate, and reasonable under all the circumstances. Upon a showing of good cause, such hearing may be held in camera.

(C) Upon a showing by the Government that unrestricted participation during the course of the litigation by the person initiating the action would interfere with or unduly delay the Government's prosecution of the case, or would be repetitious, irrelevant, or for purposes of harassment, the court may, in its discretion, impose limitations on the person's participation, such as—

  (i) limiting the number of witnesses the person may call;
  (ii) limiting the length of the testimony of such witnesses;
  (iii) limiting the person's cross-examination of witnesses; or
  (iv) otherwise limiting the participation by the person in the litigation.

(D) Upon a showing by the defendant that unrestricted participation during the course of the litigation by the person initiating the action would be for purposes of harassment or would cause the defendant undue burden or unnecessary expense, the court may limit the participation by the person in the litigation.

(3) If the Government elects not to proceed with the action, the person who initiated the action shall have the right to conduct the action. If the Government so requests, it shall be served with copies of all pleadings filed in the action and shall be supplied with copies of all deposition transcripts (at the Government's expense). When a person proceeds with the action, the court, without limiting the status and rights of the person initiating the action, may nevertheless permit the Government to intervene at a later date upon a showing of good cause.

(4) Whether or not the Government proceeds with the action, upon a showing by the Government that certain actions of discovery by the person initiating the action would interfere with the Government's investigation or prosecution of a criminal or civil matter arising out of the same facts, the court may stay such discovery for a period of not more than 60 days. Such a showing shall be conducted in camera. The court may extend the 60-day period upon a further showing in camera that the Government has pursued the criminal or civil investigation or proceedings with reasonable diligence and any proposed discovery in the civil action will interfere with the ongoing criminal or civil investigation or proceedings.

(5) Notwithstanding subsection (b), the Government may elect to pursue its claim through any alternate remedy available to the Government, including any administrative proceeding to determine a civil money penalty. If any such alternate remedy is pursued in another proceeding, the person initiating the action shall have the same

rights in such proceeding as such person would have had if the action had continued under this section. Any finding of fact or conclusion of law made in such other proceeding that has become final shall be conclusive on all parties to an action under this section. For purposes of the preceding sentence, a finding or conclusion is final if it has been finally determined on appeal to the appropriate court of the United States, if all time for filing such an appeal with respect to the finding or conclusion has expired, or if the finding or conclusion is not subject to judicial review.

(d) Award to Qui Tam Plaintiff.—(1) If the Government proceeds with an action brought by a person under subsection (b), such person shall, subject to the second sentence of this paragraph, receive at least 15 percent but not more than 25 percent of the proceeds of the action or settlement of the claim, depending upon the extent to which the person substantially contributed to the prosecution of the action. Where the action is one which the court finds to be based primarily on disclosures of specific information (other than information provided by the person bringing the action) relating to allegations or transactions in a criminal, civil, or administrative hearing, in a congressional, administrative, or Government[1] Accounting Office report, hearing, audit, or investigation, or from the news media, the court may award such sums as it considers appropriate, but in no case more than 10 percent of the proceeds, taking into account the significance of the information and the role of the person bringing the action in advancing the case to litigation. Any payment to a person under the first or second sentence of this paragraph shall be made from the proceeds. Any such person shall also receive an amount for reasonable expenses which the court finds to have been necessarily incurred, plus reasonable attorneys' fees and costs. All such expenses, fees, and costs shall be awarded against the defendant.

(2) If the Government does not proceed with an action under this section, the person bringing the action or settling the claim shall receive an amount which the court decides is reasonable for collecting the civil penalty and damages. The amount shall be not less than 25 percent and not more than 30 percent of the proceeds of the action or settlement and shall be paid out of such proceeds. Such person shall also receive an amount for reasonable expenses which the court finds to have been necessarily incurred, plus reasonable attorneys' fees and costs. All such expenses, fees, and costs shall be awarded against the defendant.

(3) Whether or not the Government proceeds with the action, if the court finds that the action was brought by a person who planned and initiated the violation of section 3729 upon which the action was brought, then the court may, to the extent the court considers appropriate, reduce the share of the proceeds of the action which the person would otherwise receive under paragraph (1) or (2) of this subsection, taking into account the role of that person in advancing

---

[1]So in original. Probably should be "General."

the case to litigation and any relevant circumstances pertaining to the violation. If the person bringing the action is convicted of criminal conduct arising from his or her role in the violation of section 3729, that person shall be dismissed from the civil action and shall not receive any share of the proceeds of the action. Such dismissal shall not prejudice the right of the United States to continue the action, represented by the Department of Justice.

(4) If the Government does not proceed with the action and the person bringing the action conducts the action, the court may award to the defendant its reasonable attorneys' fees and expenses if the defendant prevails in the action and the court finds that the claim of the person bringing the action was clearly frivolous, clearly vexatious, or brought primarily for purposes of harassment.

(e) Certain Actions Barred.—(1) No court shall have jurisdiction over an action brought by a former or present member of the armed forces under subsection (b) of this section against a member of the armed forces arising out of such person's service in the armed forces.

(2)(A) No court shall have jurisdiction over an action brought under subsection (b) against a Member of Congress, a member of the judiciary, or a senior executive branch official if the action is based on evidence or information known to the Government when the action was brought.

(B) For purposes of this paragraph, "senior executive branch official" means any officer or employee listed in paragraphs (1) through (8) of section 101(f) of the Ethics in Government Act of 1978 (5 U.S.C. App.).

(3) In no event may a person bring an action under subsection (b) which is based upon allegations or transactions which are the subject of a civil suit or an administrative civil money penalty proceeding in which the Government is already a party.

(4)(A) No court shall have jurisdiction over an action under this section based upon the public disclosure of allegations or transactions in a criminal, civil, or administrative hearing, in a congressional, administrative, or Government[2] Accounting Office report, hearing, audit, or investigation, or from the news media, unless the action is brought by the Attorney General or the person bringing the action is an original source of the information.

(B) For purposes of this paragraph, "original source" means an individual who has direct and independent knowledge of the information on which the allegations are based and has voluntarily provided the information to the Government before filing an action under this section which is based on the information.

(f) Government Not Liable for Certain Expenses.—The Government is not liable for expenses which a person incurs in bringing an action under this section.

---

[2]So in original. Probably should be "General".

(g) Fees and Expenses to Prevailing Defendant.—In civil actions brought under this section by the United States, the provisions of section 2412(d) of title 28 shall apply.

(h) Any employee who is discharged, demoted, suspended, threatened, harassed, or in any other manner discriminated against in the terms and conditions of employment by his or her employer because of lawful acts done by the employee on behalf of the employee or others in furtherance of an action under this section, including investigation for, initiation of, testimony for, or assistance in an action filed or to be filed under this section, shall be entitled to all relief necessary to make the employee whole. Such relief shall include reinstatement with the same seniority status such employee would have had but for the discrimination, 2 times the amount of back pay, interest on the back pay, and compensation for any special damages sustained as a result of the discrimination, including litigation costs and reasonable attorneys' fees. An employee may bring an action in the appropriate district court of the United States for the relief provided in this subsection.

## SOURCE—

(Pub. L. 97-258, Sept. 13, 1982, 96 Stat. 978; Pub. L. 99-562, Sec. 3, 4, Oct. 27, 1986, 100 Stat. 3154, 3157; Pub. L. 100-700, Sec. 9, Nov. 19, 1988, 102 Stat. 4638; Pub. L. 101-280, Sec. 10(a), May 4, 1990, 104 Stat. 162; Pub. L. 103-272, Sec. 4(f)(1)(P), July 5, 1994, 108 Stat. 1362.)

## REFERENCES IN TEXT

The Federal Rules of Civil Procedure, referred to in subsec. (b)(2), (3), are set out in the Appendix to Title 28, Judiciary and Judicial Procedure. Section 101(f) of the Ethics in Government Act of 1978, referred to in subsec. (e)(2)(B), is section 101(f) of Pub. L. 95-521, title I, Oct. 26, 1978, 92 Stat. 1824, as amended, which was set out in the Appendix to Title 5, Government Organization and Employees.

## Section 3731: False claims procedure

(a) A subpoena requiring the attendance of a witness at a trial or hearing conducted under section 3730 of this title may be served at any place in the United States.

(b) A civil action under section 3730 may not be brought—

(1) more than 6 years after the date on which the violation of section 3729 is committed, or

(2) more than 3 years after the date when facts material to the right of action are known or reasonably should have been known by the official of the United States charged with responsibility to act in the circumstances, but in no event more than 10 years after the date on which the violation is committed, whichever occurs last.

(c) In any action brought under section 3730, the United States shall be required to prove all essential elements of the cause of action, including damages, by a preponderance of the evidence.

(d) Notwithstanding any other provision of law, the Federal Rules of Criminal Procedure, or the Federal Rules of Evidence, a final judgment rendered in favor of the United States in any criminal proceeding charging fraud or false statements, whether upon a verdict after trial or upon a plea of guilty or nolo contendere, shall estop the defendant from denying the essential elements of the offense in any action which involves the same transaction as in the criminal proceeding and which is brought under subsection (a) or (b) of section 3730.

*SOURCE—*

(Pub. L. 97-258, Sept. 13, 1982, 96 Stat. 979; Pub. L. 99-562, Sec. 5, Oct. 27, 1986, 100 Stat. 3158.)

*REFERENCES IN TEXT*

The Federal Rules of Criminal Procedure, referred to in subsec. (d), are set out in the Appendix to Title 18, Crimes and Criminal Procedure.

The Federal Rules of Evidence, referred to in subsec. (d), are set out in the Appendix to Title 28, Judiciary and Judicial Procedure.

## Section 3732: False claims jurisdiction

(a) Actions Under Section 3730.—Any action under section 3730 may be brought in any judicial district in which the defendant or, in the case of multiple defendants, any one defendant can be found, resides, transacts business, or in which any act proscribed by section 3729 occurred. A summons as required by the Federal Rules of Civil Procedure shall be issued by the appropriate district court and served at any place within or outside the United States.

(b) Claims Under State Law.—The district courts shall have jurisdiction over any action brought under the laws of any State for the recovery of funds paid by a State or local government if the action arises from the same transaction or occurrence as an action brought under section 3730.

*SOURCE—*

(Added Pub. L. 99-562, Sec. 6(a), Oct. 21, 1986, 100 Stat. 3158.)

*REFERENCES IN TEXT*

The Federal Rules of Civil Procedure, referred to in subsec. (a), are set out in the Appendix to Title 28, Judiciary and Judicial Procedure.

## Section 3733: Civil investigative demands

(a) In General.—

(1) Issuance and service.—Whenever the Attorney General has reason to believe that any person may be in possession, custody, or control of any documentary material or information relevant to a false claims law investigation, the Attorney General may, before commencing a civil proceeding under section 3730 or other false claims

law, issue in writing and cause to be served upon such person, a civil investigative demand requiring such person—

(A) to produce such documentary material for inspection and copying,

(B) to answer in writing written interrogatories with respect to such documentary material or information,

(C) to give oral testimony concerning such documentary material or information, or

(D) to furnish any combination of such material, answers, or testimony.

The Attorney General may not delegate the authority to issue civil investigative demands under this subsection. Whenever a civil investigative demand is an express demand for any product of discovery, the Attorney General, the Deputy Attorney General, or an Assistant Attorney General shall cause to be served, in any manner authorized by this section, a copy of such demand upon the person from whom the discovery was obtained and shall notify the person to whom such demand is issued of the date on which such copy was served.

(2) Contents and deadlines.—

(A) Each civil investigative demand issued under paragraph (1) shall state the nature of the conduct constituting the alleged violation of a false claims law which is under investigation, and the applicable provision of law alleged to be violated.

(B) If such demand is for the production of documentary material, the demand shall—

(i) describe each class of documentary material to be produced with such definiteness and certainty as to permit such material to be fairly identified;

(ii) prescribe a return date for each such class which will provide a reasonable period of time within which the material so demanded may be assembled and made available for inspection and copying; and

(iii) identify the false claims law investigator to whom such material shall be made available.

(C) If such demand is for answers to written interrogatories, the demand shall—

(i) set forth with specificity the written interrogatories to be answered;

(ii) prescribe dates at which time answers to written interrogatories shall be submitted; and

(iii) identify the false claims law investigator to whom such answers shall be submitted.

(D) If such demand is for the giving of oral testimony, the demand shall—

(i) prescribe a date, time, and place at which oral testimony shall be commenced;

(ii) identify a false claims law investigator who shall conduct the examination and the custodian to whom the transcript of such examination shall be submitted;

(iii) specify that such attendance and testimony are necessary to the conduct of the investigation;

(iv) notify the person receiving the demand of the right to be accompanied by an attorney and any other representative; and

(v) describe the general purpose for which the demand is being issued and the general nature of the testimony, including the primary areas of inquiry, which will be taken pursuant to the demand.

(E) Any civil investigative demand issued under this section which is an express demand for any product of discovery shall not be returned or returnable until 20 days after a copy of such demand has been served upon the person from whom the discovery was obtained.

(F) The date prescribed for the commencement of oral testimony pursuant to a civil investigative demand issued under this section shall be a date which is not less than seven days after the date on which demand is received, unless the Attorney General or an Assistant Attorney General designated by the Attorney General determines that exceptional circumstances are present which warrant the commencement of such testimony within a lesser period of time.

(G) The Attorney General shall not authorize the issuance under this section of more than one civil investigative demand for oral testimony by the same person unless the person requests otherwise or unless the Attorney General, after investigation, notifies that person in writing that an additional demand for oral testimony is necessary. The Attorney General may not, notwithstanding section 510 of title 28, authorize the performance, by any other officer, employee, or agency, of any function vested in the Attorney General under this subparagraph.

(b) Protected Material or Information.—

(1) In general.—A civil investigative demand issued under subsection (a) may not require the production of any documentary material, the submission of any answers to written interrogatories, or the giving of any oral testimony if such material, answers, or testimony would be protected from disclosure under—

(A) the standards applicable to subpoenas or subpoenas duces tecum issued by a court of the United States to aid in a grand jury investigation; or

(B) the standards applicable to discovery requests under the Federal Rules of Civil Procedure, to the extent that the application of such standards to any such demand is appropriate and consistent with the provisions and purposes of this section.

(2) Effect on other orders, rules, and laws.—Any such demand which is an express demand for any product of discovery supersedes any inconsistent order, rule, or provision of law (other than this section) preventing or restraining disclosure of such product of discovery to any person. Disclosure of any product of discovery pursuant to any

such express demand does not constitute a waiver of any right or privilege which the person making such disclosure may be entitled to invoke to resist discovery of trial preparation materials.

(c) Service; Jurisdiction.—

(1) By whom served.—Any civil investigative demand issued under subsection (a) may be served by a false claims law investigator, or by a United States marshal or a deputy marshal, at any place within the territorial jurisdiction of any court of the United States.

(2) Service in foreign countries.—Any such demand or any petition filed under subsection (j) may be served upon any person who is not found within the territorial jurisdiction of any court of the United States in such manner as the Federal Rules of Civil Procedure prescribe for service in a foreign country. To the extent that the courts of the United States can assert jurisdiction over any such person consistent with due process, the United States District Court for the District of Columbia shall have the same jurisdiction to take any action respecting compliance with this section by any such person that such court would have if such person were personally within the jurisdiction of such court.

(d) Service Upon Legal Entities and Natural Persons.—

(1) Legal entities.—Service of any civil investigative demand issued under subsection (a) or of any petition filed under subsection (j) may be made upon a partnership, corporation, association, or other legal entity by—

(A) delivering an executed copy of such demand or petition to any partner, executive officer, managing agent, or general agent of the partnership, corporation, association, or entity, or to any agent authorized by appointment or by law to receive service of process on behalf of such partnership, corporation, association, or entity;

(B) delivering an executed copy of such demand or petition to the principal office or place of business of the partnership, corporation, association, or entity; or

(C) depositing an executed copy of such demand or petition in the United States mails by registered or certified mail, with a return receipt requested, addressed to such partnership, corporation, association, or entity at its principal office or place of business.

(2) Natural persons.—Service of any such demand or petition may be made upon any natural person by—

(A) delivering an executed copy of such demand or petition to the person; or

(B) depositing an executed copy of such demand or petition in the United States mails by registered or certified mail, with a return receipt requested, addressed to the person at the person's residence or principal office or place of business.

(e) Proof of Service.—A verified return by the individual serving any civil investigative demand issued under subsection (a) or any petition filed under subsection (j) setting forth the manner of such service shall be proof of such service. In the case of service by registered or certified mail, such return shall be accompanied by the return post office receipt of delivery of such demand.

(f) Documentary Material.—

(1) Sworn certificates.—The production of documentary material in response to a civil investigative demand served under this section shall be made under a sworn certificate, in such form as the demand designates, by—

(A) in the case of a natural person, the person to whom the demand is directed, or

(B) in the case of a person other than a natural person, a person having knowledge of the facts and circumstances relating to such production and authorized to act on behalf of such person.

The certificate shall state that all of the documentary material required by the demand and in the possession, custody, or control of the person to whom the demand is directed has been produced and made available to the false claims law investigator identified in the demand.

(2) Production of materials.—Any person upon whom any civil investigative demand for the production of documentary material has been served under this section shall make such material available for inspection and copying to the false claims law investigator identified in such demand at the principal place of business of such person, or at such other place as the false claims law investigator and the person thereafter may agree and prescribe in writing, or as the court may direct under subsection (j)(1). Such material shall be made so available on the return date specified in such demand, or on such later date as the false claims law investigator may prescribe in writing. Such person may, upon written agreement between the person and the false claims law investigator, substitute copies for originals of all or any part of such material.

(g) Interrogatories.—Each interrogatory in a civil investigative demand served under this section shall be answered separately and fully in writing under oath and shall be submitted under a sworn certificate, in such form as the demand designates, by—

(1) in the case of a natural person, the person to whom the demand is directed, or

(2) in the case of a person other than a natural person, the person or persons responsible for answering each interrogatory. If any interrogatory is objected to, the reasons for the objection shall be stated in the certificate instead of an answer. The certificate shall state that all information required by the demand and in the possession, custody, control, or knowledge of the person to whom the demand is directed has been submitted. To the extent that any information is not furnished, the information shall be identified and reasons set forth with particularity regarding the reasons why the information was not furnished.

(h) Oral Examinations.—

(1) Procedures.—The examination of any person pursuant to a civil investigative demand for oral testimony served under this section

shall be taken before an officer authorized to administer oaths and affirmations by the laws of the United States or of the place where the examination is held. The officer before whom the testimony is to be taken shall put the witness on oath or affirmation and shall, personally or by someone acting under the direction of the officer and in the officer's presence, record the testimony of the witness. The testimony shall be taken stenographically and shall be transcribed. When the testimony is fully transcribed, the officer before whom the testimony is taken shall promptly transmit a copy of the transcript of the testimony to the custodian. This subsection shall not preclude the taking of testimony by any means authorized by, and in a manner consistent with, the Federal Rules of Civil Procedure.

(2) Persons present.—The false claims law investigator conducting the examination shall exclude from the place where the examination is held all persons except the person giving the testimony, the attorney for and any other representative of the person giving the testimony, the attorney for the Government, any person who may be agreed upon by the attorney for the Government and the person giving the testimony, the officer before whom the testimony is to be taken, and any stenographer taking such testimony.

(3) Where testimony taken.—The oral testimony of any person taken pursuant to a civil investigative demand served under this section shall be taken in the judicial district of the United States within which such person resides, is found, or transacts business, or in such other place as may be agreed upon by the false claims law investigator conducting the examination and such person.

(4) Transcript of testimony.—When the testimony is fully transcribed, the false claims law investigator or the officer before whom the testimony is taken shall afford the witness, who may be accompanied by counsel, a reasonable opportunity to examine and read the transcript, unless such examination and reading are waived by the witness. Any changes in form or substance which the witness desires to make shall be entered and identified upon the transcript by the officer or the false claims law investigator, with a statement of the reasons given by the witness for making such changes. The transcript shall then be signed by the witness, unless the witness in writing waives the signing, is ill, cannot be found, or refuses to sign. If the transcript is not signed by the witness within 30 days after being afforded a reasonable opportunity to examine it, the officer or the false claims law investigator shall sign it and state on the record the fact of the waiver, illness, absence of the witness, or the refusal to sign, together with the reasons, if any, given therefor.

(5) Certification and delivery to custodian.—The officer before whom the testimony is taken shall certify on the transcript that the witness was sworn by the officer and that the transcript is a true record of the testimony given by the witness, and the officer or false claims law investigator shall promptly deliver the transcript, or send the transcript by registered or certified mail, to the custodian.

(6) Furnishing or inspection of transcript by witness.—Upon payment of reasonable charges therefor, the false claims law investigator shall furnish a copy of the transcript to the witness only, except that the Attorney General, the Deputy Attorney General, or an Assistant Attorney General may, for good cause, limit such witness to inspection of the official transcript of the witness' testimony.

(7) Conduct of oral testimony.—(A) Any person compelled to appear for oral testimony under a civil investigative demand issued under subsection (a) may be accompanied, represented, and advised by counsel. Counsel may advise such person, in confidence, with respect to any question asked of such person. Such person or counsel may object on the record to any question, in whole or in part, and shall briefly state for the record the reason for the objection. An objection may be made, received, and entered upon the record when it is claimed that such person is entitled to refuse to answer the question on the grounds of any constitutional or other legal right or privilege, including the privilege against self-incrimination. Such person may not otherwise object to or refuse to answer any question, and may not directly or through counsel otherwise interrupt the oral examination. If such person refuses to answer any question, a petition may be filed in the district court of the United States under subsection (j)(1) for an order compelling such person to answer such question.

(B) If such person refuses to answer any question on the grounds of the privilege against self-incrimination, the testimony of such person may be compelled in accordance with the provisions of part V of title 18.

(8) Witness fees and allowances.—Any person appearing for oral testimony under a civil investigative demand issued under subsection (a) shall be entitled to the same fees and allowances which are paid to witnesses in the district courts of the United States.

(i) Custodians of Documents, Answers, and Transcripts.—

(1) Designation.—The Attorney General shall designate a false claims law investigator to serve as custodian of documentary material, answers to interrogatories, and transcripts of oral testimony received under this section, and shall designate such additional false claims law investigators as the Attorney General determines from time to time to be necessary to serve as deputies to the custodian.

(2) Responsibility for materials; disclosure.—(A) A false claims law investigator who receives any documentary material, answers to interrogatories, or transcripts of oral testimony under this section shall transmit them to the custodian. The custodian shall take physical possession of such material, answers, or transcripts and shall be responsible for the use made of them and for the return of documentary material under paragraph (4).

(B) The custodian may cause the preparation of such copies of such documentary material, answers to interrogatories, or transcripts of oral testimony as may be required for official use by any false claims law investigator, or other officer or employee of the

Department of Justice, who is authorized for such use under regulations which the Attorney General shall issue. Such material, answers, and transcripts may be used by any such authorized false claims law investigator or other officer or employee in connection with the taking of oral testimony under this section.

(C) Except as otherwise provided in this subsection, no documentary material, answers to interrogatories, or transcripts of oral testimony, or copies thereof, while in the possession of the custodian, shall be available for examination by any individual other than a false claims law investigator or other officer or employee of the Department of Justice authorized under subparagraph (B). The prohibition in the preceding sentence on the availability of material, answers, or transcripts shall not apply if consent is given by the person who produced such material, answers, or transcripts, or, in the case of any product of discovery produced pursuant to an express demand for such material, consent is given by the person from whom the discovery was obtained. Nothing in this subparagraph is intended to prevent disclosure to the Congress, including any committee or subcommittee of the Congress, or to any other agency of the United States for use by such agency in furtherance of its statutory responsibilities. Disclosure of information to any such other agency shall be allowed only upon application, made by the Attorney General to a United States district court, showing substantial need for the use of the information by such agency in furtherance of its statutory responsibilities.

(D) While in the possession of the custodian and under such reasonable terms and conditions as the Attorney General shall prescribe—

    (i) documentary material and answers to interrogatories shall be available for examination by the person who produced such material or answers, or by a representative of that person authorized by that person to examine such material and answers; and

    (ii) transcripts of oral testimony shall be available for examination by the person who produced such testimony, or by a representative of that person authorized by that person to examine such transcripts.

(3) Use of material, answers, or transcripts in other proceedings.— Whenever any attorney of the Department of Justice has been designated to appear before any court, grand jury, or Federal agency in any case or proceeding, the custodian of any documentary material, answers to interrogatories, or transcripts of oral testimony received under this section may deliver to such attorney such material, answers, or transcripts for official use in connection with any such case or proceeding as such attorney determines to be required. Upon the completion of any such case or proceeding, such attorney shall return to the custodian any such material, answers, or transcripts so delivered which have not passed into the control of such court, grand jury,

or agency through introduction into the record of such case or proceeding.

(4) Conditions for return of material.—If any documentary material has been produced by any person in the course of any false claims law investigation pursuant to a civil investigative demand under this section, and—

(A) any case or proceeding before the court or grand jury arising out of such investigation, or any proceeding before any Federal agency involving such material, has been completed, or

(B) no case or proceeding in which such material may be used has been commenced within a reasonable time after completion of the examination and analysis of all documentary material and other information assembled in the course of such investigation, the custodian shall, upon written request of the person who produced such material, return to such person any such material (other than copies furnished to the false claims law investigator under subsection (f)(2) or made for the Department of Justice under paragraph (2)(B)) which has not passed into the control of any court, grand jury, or agency through introduction into the record of such case or proceeding.

(5) Appointment of successor custodians.—In the event of the death, disability, or separation from service in the Department of Justice of the custodian of any documentary material, answers to interrogatories, or transcripts of oral testimony produced pursuant to a civil investigative demand under this section, or in the event of the official relief of such custodian from responsibility for the custody and control of such material, answers, or transcripts, the Attorney General shall promptly—

(A) designate another false claims law investigator to serve as custodian of such material, answers, or transcripts, and

(B) transmit in writing to the person who produced such material, answers, or testimony notice of the identity and address of the successor so designated.

Any person who is designated to be a successor under this paragraph shall have, with regard to such material, answers, or transcripts, the same duties and responsibilities as were imposed by this section upon that person's predecessor in office, except that the successor shall not be held responsible for any default or dereliction which occurred before that designation.

(j) Judicial Proceedings.—

(1) Petition for enforcement.—Whenever any person fails to comply with any civil investigative demand issued under subsection (a), or whenever satisfactory copying or reproduction of any material requested in such demand cannot be done and such person refuses to surrender such material, the Attorney General may file, in the district court of the United States for any judicial district in which such person resides, is found, or transacts business, and serve upon such person a petition for an order of such court for the enforcement of the civil investigative demand.

(2) Petition to modify or set aside demand.—(A) Any person who has received a civil investigative demand issued under subsection (a) may file, in the district court of the United States for the judicial district within which such person resides, is found, or transacts business, and serve upon the false claims law investigator identified in such demand a petition for an order of the court to modify or set aside such demand. In the case of a petition addressed to an express demand for any product of discovery, a petition to modify or set aside such demand may be brought only in the district court of the United States for the judicial district in which the proceeding in which such discovery was obtained is or was last pending. Any petition under this subparagraph must be filed—

> (i) within 20 days after the date of service of the civil investigative demand, or at any time before the return date specified in the demand, whichever date is earlier, or
>
> (ii) within such longer period as may be prescribed in writing by any false claims law investigator identified in the demand.

(B) The petition shall specify each ground upon which the petitioner relies in seeking relief under subparagraph (A), and may be based upon any failure of the demand to comply with the provisions of this section or upon any constitutional or other legal right or privilege of such person. During the pendency of the petition in the court, the court may stay, as it deems proper, the running of the time allowed for compliance with the demand, in whole or in part, except that the person filing the petition shall comply with any portions of the demand not sought to be modified or set aside.

(3) Petition to modify or set aside demand for product of discovery.—

(A) In the case of any civil investigative demand issued under subsection (a) which is an express demand for any product of discovery, the person from whom such discovery was obtained may file, in the district court of the United States for the judicial district in which the proceeding in which such discovery was obtained is or was last pending, and serve upon any false claims law investigator identified in the demand and upon the recipient of the demand, a petition for an order of such court to modify or set aside those portions of the demand requiring production of any such product of discovery. Any petition under this subparagraph must be filed—

> (i) within 20 days after the date of service of the civil investigative demand, or at any time before the return date specified in the demand, whichever date is earlier, or
>
> (ii) within such longer period as may be prescribed in writing by any false claims law investigator identified in the demand.

(B) The petition shall specify each ground upon which the petitioner relies in seeking relief under subparagraph (A), and may be based upon any failure of the portions of the demand from which relief is sought to comply with the provisions of this section, or upon any constitutional or other legal right or privilege of the petitioner. During the pendency of the petition, the court may stay, as it deems proper, compliance with the demand and the running of the time allowed for compliance with the demand.

(4) Petition to require performance by custodian of duties.—At any time during which any custodian is in custody or control of any documentary material or answers to interrogatories produced, or transcripts of oral testimony given, by any person in compliance with any civil investigative demand issued under subsection (a), such person, and in the case of an express demand for any product of discovery, the person from whom such discovery was obtained, may file, in the district court of the United States for the judicial district within which the office of such custodian is situated, and serve upon such custodian, a petition for an order of such court to require the performance by the custodian of any duty imposed upon the custodian by this section.

(5) Jurisdiction.—Whenever any petition is filed in any district court of the United States under this subsection, such court shall have jurisdiction to hear and determine the matter so presented, and to enter such order or orders as may be required to carry out the provisions of this section. Any final order so entered shall be subject to appeal under section 1291 of title 28. Any disobedience of any final order entered under this section by any court shall be punished as a contempt of the court.

(6) Applicability of federal rules of civil procedure.—The Federal Rules of Civil Procedure shall apply to any petition under this subsection, to the extent that such rules are not inconsistent with the provisions of this section.

(k) Disclosure Exemption.—Any documentary material, answers to written interrogatories, or oral testimony provided under any civil investigative demand issued under subsection (a) shall be exempt from disclosure under section 552 of title 5.

(l) Definitions.—For purposes of this section—

(1) the term "false claims law" means—

(A) this section and sections 3729 through 3732; and

(B) any Act of Congress enacted after the date of the enactment of this section which prohibits, or makes available to the United States in any court of the United States any civil remedy with respect to, any false claim against, bribery of, or corruption of any officer or employee of the United States;

(2) the term "false claims law investigation" means any inquiry conducted by any false claims law investigator for the purpose of ascertaining whether any person is or has been engaged in any violation of a false claims law;

(3) the term "false claims law investigator" means any attorney or investigator employed by the Department of Justice who is charged with the duty of enforcing or carrying into effect any false claims law, or any officer or employee of the United States acting under the di-

rection and supervision of such attorney or investigator in connection with a false claims law investigation;

(4) the term "person" means any natural person, partnership, corporation, association, or other legal entity, including any State or political subdivision of a State;

(5) the term "documentary material" includes the original or any copy of any book, record, report, memorandum, paper, communication, tabulation, chart, or other document, or data compilations stored in or accessible through computer or other information retrieval systems, together with instructions and all other materials necessary to use or interpret such data compilations, and any product of discovery;

(6) the term "custodian" means the custodian, or any deputy custodian, designated by the Attorney General under subsection (i)(1); and

(7) the term "product of discovery" includes—

(A) the original or duplicate of any deposition, interrogatory, document, thing, result of the inspection of land or other property, examination, or admission, which is obtained by any method of discovery in any judicial or administrative proceeding of an adversarial nature;

(B) any digest, analysis, selection, compilation, or derivation of any item listed in subparagraph (A); and

(C) any index or other manner of access to any item listed in subparagraph (A).

## SOURCE—

(Added Pub. L. 99-562, Sec. 6(a), Oct. 27, 1986, 100 Stat. 3159.)

## REFERENCES IN TEXT

The Federal Rules of Civil Procedure, referred to in subsecs. (b)(1)(B), (c)(2), (h)(1), and (j)(6), are set out in the Appendix to Title 28, Judiciary and Judicial Procedure.

The date of enactment of this section, referred to in subsec. (l)(1)(B), is the date of enactment of Pub. L. 99-562, which was approved Oct. 27, 1986.

# Appendix C-2

## Holder Memorandum: Guidance on the Use of the False Claims Act in Civil Health Care Matters

*Source:* http://www.usdoj.gov:80/04foia/readingrooms/chcm.htm

June 3, 1998

MEMORANDUM FOR:    All United States Attorneys
All First Assistant United States Attorneys
All Civil Health Care Fraud Coordinators
    in the Offices of United States Attorneys
All Trial Attorneys in the Civil Division,
    Commercial Litigation Section

FROM:    Eric H. Holder, Jr.
Deputy Attorney General

SUBJECT:    Guidance on the Use of the False Claims Act
In Civil Health Care Matters

One of the Department's most important tools in protecting the integrity of Medicare and other taxpayer-funded health care programs is the civil False Claims Act. While the broad reach and substantial damages and civil penalties under the Act make it one of the Department's most powerful tools, Departmental attorneys are obligated to use their authority under the Act in a fair and responsible manner. This is particularly important in the context of national initiatives, which can have a broad impact on health care providers across the country.

This guidance is being issued to emphasize the importance of pursuing civil False Claims Act cases against health care providers in a fair and even-handed manner, and to implement new procedures with respect to the development and implementation of national initiatives.

1. *National Initiatives.*

Generally, national initiatives deal with a common wrongful action accomplished in a like manner by multiple, similarly situated health care providers. National initiatives must be handled in a manner (i) that promotes consistent adherence to the Department's policies on enforcement of the False Claims Act, as well as a consistent approach to overarching legal and factual issues, (ii) while avoiding any rigid approach that fails to recognize the particular facts and circumstances of an individual case.

To achieve these objectives, the Department has instituted the following procedures:

A. *Legal and Factual Predicates.*

Before alleging violations of the False Claims Act, whether in connection with a national initiative or otherwise, Department attorneys must evaluate whether the provider: (i) submitted false claims to the government, and (ii) submitted false claims (or any false statements made to get the false claims paid) with "knowledge of their falsity, as defined in the Act. These are separate inquiries. Department attorneys shall not allege a violation of the False Claims Act unless both of these inquiries lead to the conclusion that there is a sufficient legal and factual predicate for proceeding. The following issues, among other issues, shall be considered in these determinations:

(i) *Do False Claims Exist?*

a. *Examine Relevant Statutory and Regulatory Provisions and Interpretive Guidance.* Department attorneys shall examine relevant statutory and regulatory provisions, as well as any applicable guidance from the program agency or its agents, to determine whether the claims are false. In certain circumstances, such as when a rule is technical or complex, Department attorneys should communicate with knowledgeable personnel within the program agency (*e.g.*, the Health Care Financing Administration, TRICARE, or Office of Personnel Management) concerning the meaning of the provision.

b. *Verify the Data and Other Evidence.* Department attorneys shall take appropriate steps to verify the accuracy of data upon which they are relying, either independently, or with the assistance of the fiscal intermediaries and carriers, the Department of Health and Human Services—Office of Inspector General, the Federal Bureau of Investigation, or another investigative agency.

c. *Conduct the Necessary Investigative Steps.* Department attorneys should conduct such investigative steps as are necessary under the circumstances, including where appropriate, the subpoenaing of documents and the interviewing of witnesses.

(ii) *Did the Provider Knowingly Submit the False Claims?*

In the event the claims are false, Department attorneys must also evaluate whether the health care provider "knowingly" submitted the false claims or "knowingly" made false statements to get the false claims paid. As set forth above, and before making this determination, Department attorneys should conduct such investigative steps as necessary under the circumstances, including where appropriate the subpoenaing of documents and the interviewing of witnesses. Under the False Claims Act, false claims and false statements are submitted "knowingly" if the provider had actual knowledge of their falsity, or acted with deliberate ignorance or reckless disregard as to their truth or falsity. While relevant factors will vary from case to case and the list below is not intended to be exhaustive, factors that must be considered are:

a. *Notice to the Provider.* Was the provider on actual or constructive notice, as appropriate, of the rule or policy upon which a potential case would be based?

b. *The Clarity of the Rule or Policy.* Under the circumstances, it is reasonable to conclude that the provider understood the rule or policy?

c. *The Pervasiveness and Magnitude of the False Claims.* Is the pervasiveness or magnitude of the false claims sufficient to support an inference that they resulted from deliberate ignorance or intentional or reckless conduct rather than mere mistakes?

d. *Compliance Plans and Other Steps to Comply with Billing Rules.* Does the health care provider have a compliance plan in place? Is the provider adhering to the compliance plan? What relationship exists between the compliance plan and the conduct at issue? What other steps, if any, has the provider taken to comply with billing rules in general, or the billing rule at issue in particular?

e. *Past Remedial Efforts.* Has the provider previously on its own identified the wrongful conduct currently under examination and taken steps to remedy the problem? Did the provider report the wrongful conduct to a government agency?

f. *Guidance by the Program Agency of its Agents.* Did the provider directly contact either the program agency (*e.g.*, the Health Care Financing Administration) or its agents regarding the billing rule at issue? If so, was the provider forthcoming and accurate and did the provider disclose all material facts regarding the billing issue for which the provider sought guidance? Did the program agency or its agents, with disclosure of all relevant, material facts, provide clear guidance? Did the provider reasonably rely on such guidance in submitting the false claims?

g. *Have There Been Prior Audits or other Notice to the Provider of the Same or Similar Billing Practices?*

h. *Any Other Information That Bears on the Provider's State of Mind in Submitting the False Claims.*

B. *Oversight by National Initiative Working Groups.*

For all current and future national initiatives, the Attorney General's Advisory Committee (AGAC) and the Civil Division shall establish a working group to coordinate the development and implementation of each initiative.

Working groups will be comprised of Assistant United States Attorneys and Civil Division attorneys with particular expertise in health care fraud. In accordance with the health care guidelines promulgated in January 1997, in appropriate instances each working group may also need to coordinate and plan the initiative with the Department's Criminal Division.

Each working group will (i) examine the initiative to ensure that a factual and legal predicate is present for the initiative prior to its implementation, (ii) prepare initiative-specific guidance and sample documents (such as legal analyses, summaries of audit data, contact letters, tolling agreements, compliance and settlement agreement language) for use in the initiative, and (iii) prepare a general investigative plan, setting forth suggested investigative steps that each office should undertake prior to proceeding. Working groups shall be responsible for coordination with law enforcement agencies, the Health Care Financing Administration, and other appropriate entities.

While the working groups shall be responsible for coordinating the overall development and implementation of national initiatives, each matter against a specific provider must be evaluated on a case-by-case basis.

C. *Use of Contact Letters in National Initiatives.*

As outlined above, Department attorneys participating in national initiatives shall, in general, make initial contacts with health care providers, to resolve a case, through the use of "contact" letters. The purpose of a contact letter is to notify a provider of their potential exposure under the False Claims Act and to offer the provider an opportunity to discuss the matter *before* a specific demand for payment is made. In limited circumstances, where the specific facts of a situation warrant a different approach, Department attorneys may make an initial contact through other legitimate means.

The use of contact letters to make initial contact with health care providers is in furtherance of Executive Order 12988, which obligates Department attorneys to make a reasonable effort to notify the opposing party about the nature of the allegations, and attempt to resolve the dispute without litigation if at all possible. The type of contact employed will depend on the nature of the allegations and the stage of the investigation. Regardless of the form of initial contact, Department attorneys must ensure that health care providers are afforded: (i) an adequate opportunity to discuss the matter before a demand for settlement is made, and (ii) an adequate time to respond. In addition, Department attorneys shall grant all reasonable requests for extensions of time to the extent that they do not jeopardize the government's claims. The use of statutory tolling agreements are strongly encouraged to allow providers time to respond without jeopardizing the government's claims.

2. *Alternative Remedies.*

After reviewing the legal and factual circumstances of a particular matter, Department attorneys shall consider other available remedies—including administrative remedies such as recoupment of overpayments, program exclusions, and civil monetary penalties—to determine what remedy, or combination of remedies, would be the most suitable under the circumstances. Should the recoupment of an overpayment be the most appropriate remedy, Department attorneys shall consider referring the matter to the appropriate carrier/fiscal intermediary for appropriate action.

3. *Ability to Pay Issues.*

Attorneys shall consider any financial constraints identified by a provider in determining a fair, reasonable and feasible settlement between the parties. Hospitals and other health care providers citing an inability to pay a specific settlement amount should be asked to present documentation in support of their stated financial condition.

4. *Rural and Community Health Care Provider Concerns—Impact on Availability of Medical Services.*

When dealing with rural and community hospitals and other health care providers, Department attorneys shall consider the impact an action may have on the community being served. In determining an appropriate resolution, or deciding whether to bring an action, care must be taken to consider the community's interest in access to adequate health care along with any other relevant concerns.

5. *Hospitals and Other Health Care Providers Not Represented by Counsel.*

Department attorneys shall pay special attention to contacts with hospitals and other providers that choose (due to financial constraints or otherwise) to resolve claims without legal representation. Department attorneys faced with this circumstance must carefully assess every action taken to avoid even an appearance of coercion or overreaching because of the absence of opposing counsel.

6. *Minimizing Burdens Imposed on Providers During Investigations.*

Department attorneys also should be mindful of the ways in which our investigations and audits can disrupt and burden the day-to-day operations of providers in both a financial and practical sense. In developing and implementing an investigative plan, we should do what we can do to minimize these adverse effects, while still meeting our obligations to diligently investigate allegations of potential fraud. For example, while recognizing that certain circumstances might warrant different approaches, Department attorneys should consider a provider's request to accept the results of an audit or a sample of claims in lieu of a complete audit.

7. *Provider Assistance with the Investigation.*

In determining an appropriate settlement amount, Department attorneys should consider the extent to which a health care provider has cooperated with the audit or investigation of the relevant matter.

8. *Individualized Review.*

The proper determination as to the use and application of the False Claims Act or other appropriate remedy requires an individualized review of each case, ensuring that each of the above factors are given full consideration.

9. *Review of Guidance.*

In order to assure the fair and appropriate application of the False Claims Act, this guidance will be subject to review in six months.

10. *Additional Information.*

Questions regarding use of the False Claims Act should be referred to the Health Care Fraud Coordinator in your district, or to Robert Liles, Health Care Fraud Coordinator for the Executive Office for United States Attorneys (tel. no. 202-616-5136), or Shelley R. Slade, Health Care Fraud Coordinator for the Civil Division (tel. no. 202-307-0264).

**U.S. Department of Justice**
**Office of the Deputy Attorney General**

---

The Deputy Attorney General       Washington, D.C. 20530

February 3, 1999

MEMORANDUM FOR:      All United States Attorneys
All First Assistant United States Attorneys
All Civil Health Care Fraud Coordinators in
the Offices of United States Attorneys
All Civil Division Fraud Attorneys

FROM:      Eric H. Holder, Jr.
Deputy Attorney General

SUBJECT:      Review of June 3, 1998, Guidance on the
Use of the False Claims Act in Civil Health
Care Fraud Matters

On June 3, 1998, I issued a Memorandum ("Guidance Memorandum") to all United States Attorneys' offices and the Civil Division providing guidance on the use of the False Claims Act in civil health care matters. The Guidance Memorandum was issued to emphasize the importance of using our anti-fraud and abuse tools, particularly the False Claims Act, in a fair and even-handed manner. The Guidance Memorandum also established new procedures for the development and implementation of national enforcement initiatives. The Guidance Memorandum further provided that it would be subject to review within a six-month period.

The six-month review process is now complete. Department officials have held separate meetings with the chairpersons of the national initiative working groups and senior representatives from the Commercial Litigation Branch, Civil Division, to discuss the application of the procedures outlined in the Guidance Memorandum and to solicit their suggestions on possible changes or clarifications. In addition, Department officials have met with representatives from several of the largest health care industry organizations to discuss the Guidance Memorandum. The Department also received written comments from one health care industry organization. Finally, comments were solicited from the Health Care Fraud Coordinators in all United States Attorneys' offices.

Based on the comments received to date, I believe the Guidance Memorandum—and the policies and procedures contained therein—has been extremely effective and that major revisions are not necessary at this time. This supplemental memorandum is being issued to clarify a number of issues that were raised during the review process.

## 1. *Application and Scope.*

The Guidance Memorandum applies to all civil health care fraud and abuse matters involving the use of the civil False Claims Act. In addition, all Department attorneys are expected to comply with the policies and procedures contained in the Guidance Memorandum. Specifically, sections 1(B) and (C) of the Guidance Memorandum (national initiative working groups and contact letters) establish new policies for national initiatives. Section 1(A) (factual and legal predicate) and Sections 2 through 8 emphasize long-standing policies and procedures applicable to all civil health care matters involving the use of the False Claims Act.

## 2. *Compliance.*

All Department attorneys handling civil health care matters are to comply with the Guidance Memorandum to ensure that the False Claims Act is applied in a fair and even-handed manner. Providers or their counsel with concerns about compliance with the Guidance Memorandum should bring their concerns to the Assistant United States Attorney or Trial Attorney handling the matter or, if necessary, to appropriate supervisory personnel in the United States Attorneys' office or the Civil Division in Washington, D.C. While the Guidance sets forth these internal procedures and safeguards, it does not establish enforceable rights of health care providers.

## 3. *Allegations of False Claims Violations.*

Section 1(A) of the Guidance Memorandum provides that Department attorneys should not "allege a violation of the False Claims Act" unless they conclude there is a sufficient legal and factual predicate for proceeding. The purpose of this requirement is to ensure that Department attorneys undertake an adequate, case-by-case factual and legal inquiry before alleging a violation of the False Claims Act. This requirement does not prohibit Department attorneys from taking appropriate steps to investigate a matter or undertaking other preliminary steps (*e.g.*, requesting that a provider sign a statutory tolling agreement) before deciding whether to allege violations of the False Claims Act.

## 4. *National Initiatives.*

The Guidance Memorandum established new procedures for all current and future national initiatives. The term "national initiative" refers, generally, to projects involving a national investigation stemming from an analysis of national claims data, indicating that numerous similarly-situated health care providers have engaged in similar conduct to improperly bill government health care programs. In consultation with the Civil Division and the Health Care Fraud Subcommittee of the Attorney General's Advisory Committee, the Department will determine whether particular investigations of national scope should be designated as "national initiatives." Once such a designation is made, the Department will establish a working group to develop and implement the national initiative pursuant to the Guidance Memorandum and will notify United States Attorneys' Offices of such designation.

**5. *Coordination.***

Working groups for new national projects shall establish formal liaison with the Office of Inspector General, Department of Health and Human Services, and/or other appropriate investigative agencies and with the Health Care Financing Administration and/or other programmatic agencies. The views of these agencies shall be solicited and considered by working groups in connection with their coordination and oversight of national initiatives.

\* \* \* \* \*

Questions regarding the Guidance Memorandum, the clarifications outlined above, or other matters involving the use of the civil False Claims Act in health care fraud and abuse matters should be referred to the Health Care Fraud Coordinator in your district or to Robert Liles, Health Care Fraud Coordinator for the Executive Office for United States Attorneys, (202) 616-5136, or Shelly Slade, Senior Counsel for Health Care Fraud, Civil Division, (202) 307-0264.

# Appendix D

## Civil Monetary Penalties and Exclusion Materials

# Appendix D-1

## Civil Monetary Penalties Statute

*Source:* 42 U.S.C. 1320a-7a

**Section 1320a-7a. Civil monetary penalties**

(a) Improperly filed claims

Any person (including an organization, agency, or other entity, but excluding a beneficiary, as defined in subsection (i)(5) of this section) that—

(1) knowingly presents or causes to be presented to an officer, employee, or agent of the United States, or of any department or agency thereof, or of any State agency (as defined in subsection (i)(1) of this section), a claim (as defined in subsection (i)(2) of this section) that the Secretary determines—

(A) is for a medical or other item or service that the person knows or should know was not provided as claimed, including any person who engages in a pattern or practice of presenting or causing to be presented a claim for an item or service that is based on a code that the person knows or should know will result in a greater payment to the person than the code the person knows or should know is applicable to the item or service actually provided,

(B) is for a medical or other item or service and the person knows or should know the claim is false or fraudulent,

(C) is presented for a physician's service (or an item or service incident to a physician's service) by a person who knows or should know that the individual who furnished (or supervised the furnishing of) the service—

(i) was not licensed as a physician,

(ii) was licensed as a physician, but such license had been obtained through a misrepresentation of material fact (including cheating on an examination required for licensing), or

(iii) represented to the patient at the time the service was furnished that the physician was certified in a medical specialty by a medical specialty board when the individual was not so certified,

(D) is for a medical or other item or service furnished during a period in which the person was excluded from the program under which the claim was made pursuant to a determination by the Secretary under this section or under section 1320a-7, 1320c-5, 1320c-9(b) (as in effect on September 2, 1982), 1395y(d) (as in effect on August 18, 1987), or 1395cc(b) of this title or as a result of the application of the provisions of section 1395u(j)(2) of this title, or

(E) is for a pattern of medical or other items or services that a person knows or should know are not medically necessary;

(2) knowingly presents or causes to be presented to any person a request for payment which is in violation of the terms of (A) an assignment under section 1395u(b)(3)(B)(ii) of this title, or (B) an agreement with a State agency (or other requirement of a State plan under subchapter XIX of this chapter) not to charge a person for an item or service in excess of the amount permitted to be charged, or (C) an agreement to be a participating physician or supplier under section 1395u(h)(1) of this title, or (D) an agreement pursuant to section 1395cc(a)(1)(G) of this title;

(3) knowingly gives or causes to be given to any person, with respect to coverage under subchapter XVIII of this chapter of inpatient hospital services subject to the provisions of section 1395ww of this title, information that he knows or should know is false or misleading, and that could reasonably be expected to influence the decision when to discharge such person or another individual from the hospital;

(4) in the case of a person who is not an organization, agency, or other entity, is excluded from participating in a program under subchapter XVIII of this chapter or a State health care program in accordance with this subsection or under section 1320a-7 of this title and who, at the time of a violation of this subsection—

    (A) retains a direct or indirect ownership or control interest in an entity that is participating in a program under subchapter XVIII of this chapter or a State health care program, and who knows or should know of the action constituting the basis for the exclusion; or

    (B) is an officer or managing employee (as defined in section 1320a-5(b) of this title) of such an entity;

(5) offers to or transfers remuneration to any individual eligible for benefits under subchapter XVIII of this chapter, or under a State health care program (as defined in section 1320a-7(h) of this title) that such person knows or should know is likely to influence such individual to order or receive from a particular provider, practitioner, or supplier any item or service for which payment may be made, in whole or in part, under subchapter XVIII of this chapter, or a State health care program (as so defined);

(6) arranges or contracts (by employment or otherwise) with an individual or entity that the person knows or should know is excluded from participation in a Federal health care program (as defined in section 1320a-7b(f) of this title), for the provision of items or services for which payment may be made under such a program; or

(7) commits an act described in paragraph (1) or (2) of section 1320a-7b(b) of this title;

shall be subject, in addition to any other penalties that may be prescribed by law, to a civil money penalty of not more than $10,000 for each item or service (or, in cases under paragraph (3), $15,000 for each individual with respect to whom false or misleading information was given; in cases under paragraph (4), $10,000 for each day the prohibited relationship occurs; or in cases under paragraph (7), $50,000 for each such act). In addition, such a person shall be subject to an assessment of not more than 3 times the amount claimed for each such item or service in lieu of damages sustained by the United States or a State agency because of such claim (or, in cases under paragraph (7), damages of not more than 3 times the total amount of remuneration offered, paid, solicited, or received, without regard to whether a portion of such remuneration was offered, paid, solicited, or received for a lawful purpose). In addition the Secretary may make a determination in the same proceeding to exclude the person from participation in the Federal health care programs (as defined in section 1320a-7b(f)(1) of this title) and to direct the appropriate State agency to exclude the person from participation in any State health care program.

(b) Payments to induce reduction or limitation of services

(1) If a hospital or a critical access hospital knowingly makes a payment, directly or indirectly, to a physician as an inducement to reduce or limit services provided with respect to individuals who—

(A) are entitled to benefits under part A or part B of subchapter XVIII of this chapter or to medical assistance under a State plan approved under subchapter XIX of this chapter, and

(B) are under the direct care of the physician, the hospital or a critical access hospital shall be subject, in addition to any other penalties that may be prescribed by law, to a civil money penalty of not more than $2,000 for each such individual with respect to whom the payment is made.

(2) Any physician who knowingly accepts receipt of a payment described in paragraph (1) shall be subject, in addition to any other penalties that may be prescribed by law, to a civil money penalty of not more than $2,000 for each individual described in such paragraph with respect to whom the payment is made.

(3)(A) Any physician who executes a document described in subparagraph (B) with respect to an individual knowing that all of the requirements referred to in such subparagraph are not met with respect to the individual shall be subject to a civil monetary penalty of not more than the greater of—

(i) $5,000, or

(ii) three times the amount of the payments under subchapter XVIII of this chapter for home health services which are made pursuant to such certification.

(B) A document described in this subparagraph is any document that certifies, for purposes of subchapter XVIII of this chapter, that an individual meets the requirements of section

1395f(a)(2)(C) or 1395n(a)(2)(A) of this title in the case of home health services furnished to the individual.

(c) Initiation of proceeding; authorization by Attorney General, notice, etc., estoppel, failure to comply with order or procedure

(1) The Secretary may initiate a proceeding to determine whether to impose a civil money penalty, assessment, or exclusion under subsection (a) or (b) of this section only as authorized by the Attorney General pursuant to procedures agreed upon by them. The Secretary may not initiate an action under this section with respect to any claim, request for payment, or other occurrence described in this section later than six years after the date the claim was presented, the request for payment was made, or the occurrence took place. The Secretary may initiate an action under this section by serving notice of the action in any manner authorized by Rule 4 of the Federal Rules of Civil Procedure.

(2) The Secretary shall not make a determination adverse to any person under subsection (a) or (b) of this section until the person has been given written notice and an opportunity for the determination to be made on the record after a hearing at which the person is entitled to be represented by counsel, to present witnesses, and to cross-examine witnesses against the person.

(3) In a proceeding under subsection (a) or (b) of this section which—

(A) is against a person who has been convicted (whether upon a verdict after trial or upon a plea of guilty or nolo contendere) of a Federal crime charging fraud or false statements, and

(B) involves the same transaction as in the criminal action, the person is estopped from denying the essential elements of the criminal offense.

(4) The official conducting a hearing under this section may sanction a person, including any party or attorney, for failing to comply with an order or procedure, failing to defend an action, or other misconduct as would interfere with the speedy, orderly, or fair conduct of the hearing. Such sanction shall reasonably relate to the severity and nature of the failure or misconduct. Such sanction may include—

(A) in the case of refusal to provide or permit discovery, drawing negative factual inferences or treating such refusal as an admission by deeming the matter, or certain facts, to be established,

(B) prohibiting a party from introducing certain evidence or otherwise supporting a particular claim or defense,

(C) striking pleadings, in whole or in part,

(D) staying the proceedings,

(E) dismissal of the action,

(F) entering a default judgment,

(G) ordering the party or attorney to pay attorneys' fees and other costs caused by the failure or misconduct, and

(H) refusing to consider any motion or other action which is not filed in a timely manner.

(d) Amount or scope of penalty, assessment, or exclusion

In determining the amount or scope of any penalty, assessment, or exclusion imposed pursuant to subsection (a) or (b) of this section, the Secretary shall take into account—

(1) the nature of claims and the circumstances under which they were presented,

(2) the degree of culpability, history of prior offenses, and financial condition of the person presenting the claims, and

(3) such other matters as justice may require.

(e) Review by courts of appeals

Any person adversely affected by a determination of the Secretary under this section may obtain a review of such determination in the United States Court of Appeals for the circuit in which the person resides, or in which the claim was presented, by filing in such court (within sixty days following the date the person is notified of the Secretary's determination) a written petition requesting that the determination be modified or set aside. A copy of the petition shall be forthwith transmitted by the clerk of the court to the Secretary, and thereupon the Secretary shall file in the Court[1] the record in the proceeding as provided in section 2112 of title 28. Upon such filing, the court shall have jurisdiction of the proceeding and of the question determined therein, and shall have the power to make and enter upon the pleadings, testimony, and proceedings set forth in such record a decree affirming, modifying, remanding for further consideration, or setting aside, in whole or in part, the determination of the Secretary and enforcing the same to the extent that such order is affirmed or modified. No objection that has not been urged before the Secretary shall be considered by the court, unless the failure or neglect to urge such objection shall be excused because of extraordinary circumstances. The findings of the Secretary with respect to questions of fact, if supported by substantial evidence on the record considered as a whole, shall be conclusive. If any party shall apply to the court for leave to adduce additional evidence and shall show to the satisfaction of the court that such additional evidence is material and that there were reasonable grounds for the failure to adduce such evidence in the hearing before the Secretary, the court may order such additional evidence to be taken before the Secretary and to be made a part of the record. The Secretary may modify his findings as to the facts, or make new findings, by reason of additional evidence so taken and filed, and he shall file with the court such modified or new findings, which findings with respect to questions of fact, if supported by substantial evidence on the record considered as a whole, shall be conclusive, and his recommendations, if any, for the modification or setting aside of his original order. Upon the filing of the record with it, the jurisdiction of the court shall be exclusive and its judgment and decree shall be final, except that the same shall be subject to review by the Supreme Court of the United States, as provided in section 1254 of title 28.

---

[1]So in original. Probably should not be capitalized.

(f) Compromise of penalties and assessments; recovery; use of funds recovered

Civil money penalties and assessments imposed under this section may be compromised by the Secretary and may be recovered in a civil action in the name of the United States brought in United States district court for the district where the claim was presented, or where the claimant resides, as determined by the Secretary. Amounts recovered under this section shall be paid to the Secretary and disposed of as follows:

(1)(A) In the case of amounts recovered arising out of a claim under subchapter XIX of this chapter, there shall be paid to the State agency an amount bearing the same proportion to the total amount recovered as the State's share of the amount paid by the State agency for such claim bears to the total amount paid for such claim.

(B) In the case of amounts recovered arising out of a claim under an allotment to a State under subchapter V of this chapter, there shall be paid to the State agency an amount equal to three-sevenths of the amount recovered.

(2) Such portion of the amounts recovered as is determined to have been paid out of the trust funds under sections 1395i and 1395t of this title shall be repaid to such trust funds.

(3) With respect to amounts recovered arising out of a claim under a Federal health care program (as defined in section 1320a-7b(f) of this title), the portion of such amounts as is determined to have been paid by the program shall be repaid to the program, and the portion of such amounts attributable to the amounts recovered under this section by reason of the amendments made by the Health Insurance Portability and Accountability Act of 1996 (as estimated by the Secretary) shall be deposited into the Federal Hospital Insurance Trust Fund pursuant to section 1395i(k)(2)(C) of this title.

(4) The remainder of the amounts recovered shall be deposited as miscellaneous receipts of the Treasury of the United States.

The amount of such penalty or assessment, when finally determined, or the amount agreed upon in compromise, may be deducted from any sum then or later owing by the United States or a State agency to the person against whom the penalty or assessment has been assessed.

(g) Finality of determination respecting penalty, assessment, or exclusion

A determination by the Secretary to impose a penalty, assessment, or exclusion under subsection (a) or (b) of this section shall be final upon the expiration of the sixty-day period referred to in subsection (e) of this section. Matters that were raised or that could have been raised in a hearing before the Secretary or in an appeal pursuant to subsection (e) of this section may not be raised as a defense to a civil action by the United States to collect a penalty, assessment, or exclusion assessed under this section.

(h) Notification of appropriate entities of finality of determination

Whenever the Secretary's determination to impose a penalty, assessment, or exclusion under subsection (a) or (b) of this section becomes final, he shall notify the appropriate State or local medical or professional organization, the appropriate State agency or agencies administering or supervising the administration of State health care programs (as defined in section 1320a-7(h) of this title), and the appropriate utilization and quality control peer review organization, and the appropriate State or local licensing agency or organization (including the agency specified in section 1395aa(a) and 1396a(a)(33) of this title) that such a penalty, assessment, or exclusion has become final and the reasons therefor.

(i) Definitions

For the purposes of this section:

(1) The term "State agency" means the agency established or designated to administer or supervise the administration of the State plan under subchapter XIX of this chapter or designated to administer the State's program under subchapter V of this chapter or subchapter XX of this chapter.

(2) The term "claim" means an application for payments for items and services under a Federal health care program (as defined in section 1320a-7b(f) of this title).

(3) The term "item or service" includes (A) any particular item, device, medical supply, or service claimed to have been provided to a patient and listed in an itemized claim for payment, and (B) in the case of a claim based on costs, any entry in the cost report, books of account or other documents supporting such claim.

(4) The term "agency of the United States" includes any contractor acting as a fiscal intermediary, carrier, or fiscal agent or any other claims processing agent for a Federal health care program (as so defined).

(5) The term "beneficiary" means an individual who is eligible to receive items or services for which payment may be made under a Federal health care program (as so defined) but does not include a provider, supplier, or practitioner.

(6) The term "remuneration" includes the waiver of coinsurance and deductible amounts (or any part thereof), and transfers of items or services for free or for other than fair market value. The term "remuneration" does not include—

(A) the waiver of coinsurance and deductible amounts by a person, if—

(i) the waiver is not offered as part of any advertisement or solicitation;

(ii) the person does not routinely waive coinsurance or deductible amounts; and

(iii) the person—

(I) waives the coinsurance and deductible amounts after determining in good faith that the individual is in financial need; or

(II) fails to collect coinsurance or deductible amounts after making reasonable collection efforts;

(B) subject to subsection (n) of this section, any permissible practice described in any subparagraph of section 1320a-7b(b)(3) of this title or in regulations issued by the Secretary;

(C) differentials in coinsurance and deductible amounts as part of a benefit plan design as long as the differentials have been disclosed in writing to all beneficiaries, third party payers, and providers, to whom claims are presented and as long as the differentials meet the standards as defined in regulations promulgated by the Secretary not later than 180 days after August 21, 1996; or

(D)[2] incentives given to individuals to promote the delivery of preventive care as determined by the Secretary in regulations so promulgated.

------------------------------------

(D)[2] a reduction in the copayment amount for covered OPD services under section 1395l(t)(5)(B)[3] of this title.

(7) The term "should know" means that a person, with respect to information—

(A) acts in deliberate ignorance of the truth or falsity of the information; or

(B) acts in reckless disregard of the truth or falsity of the information,

and no proof of specific intent to defraud is required.

(j) Subpoenas

(1) The provisions of subsections (d) and (e) of section 405 of this title shall apply with respect to this section to the same extent as they are applicable with respect to subchapter II of this chapter. The Secretary may delegate the authority granted by section 405(d) of this title (as made applicable to this section) to the Inspector General of the Department of Health and Human Services for purposes of any investigation under this section.

(2) The Secretary may delegate authority granted under this section and under section 1320a-7 of this title to the Inspector General of the Department of Health and Human Services.

(k) Injunctions

Whenever the Secretary has reason to believe that any person has engaged, is engaging, or is about to engage in any activity which makes the person subject to a civil monetary penalty under this section, the Secretary may bring an action in an appropriate district court of the United States (or, if applicable, a United States court of any territory) to enjoin such activity, or to enjoin the person from concealing, removing, encumbering, or disposing of assets which may be required in order to pay a civil monetary penalty if any such penalty were to be imposed or to seek other appropriate relief.

---

[2]So in original. Two subpars. (D) have been enacted.
[3]See References in Text note below.

(l) Liability of principal for acts of agent

A principal is liable for penalties, assessments, and an exclusion under this section for the actions of the principal's agent acting within the scope of the agency.

(m) Claims within jurisdiction of other departments or agencies

(1) For purposes of this section, with respect to a Federal health care program not contained in this chapter, references to the Secretary in this section shall be deemed to be references to the Secretary or Administrator of the department or agency with jurisdiction over such program and references to the Inspector General of the Department of Health and Human Services in this section shall be deemed to be references to the Inspector General of the applicable department or agency.

(2)(A) The Secretary and Administrator of the departments and agencies referred to in paragraph (1) may include in any action pursuant to this section, claims within the jurisdiction of other Federal departments or agencies as long as the following conditions are satisfied:

(i) The case involves primarily claims submitted to the Federal health care programs of the department or agency initiating the action.

(ii) The Secretary or Administrator of the department or agency initiating the action gives notice and an opportunity to participate in the investigation to the Inspector General of the department or agency with primary jurisdiction over the Federal health care programs to which the claims were submitted.

(B) If the conditions specified in subparagraph (A) are fulfilled, the Inspector General of the department or agency initiating the action is authorized to exercise all powers granted under the Inspector General Act of 1978 (5 U.S.C. App.) with respect to the claims submitted to the other departments or agencies to the same manner and extent as provided in that Act with respect to claims submitted to such departments or agencies.

(n) Safe harbor for payment of medigap premiums

(1) Subparagraph (B) of subsection (i)(6) of this section shall not apply to a practice described in paragraph (2) unless—

(A) the Secretary, through the Inspector General of the Department of Health and Human Services, promulgates a rule authorizing such a practice as an exception to remuneration; and

(B) the remuneration is offered or transferred by a person under such rule during the 2-year period beginning on the date the rule is first promulgated.

(2) A practice described in this paragraph is a practice under which a health care provider or facility pays, in whole or in part, premiums for medicare supplemental policies for individuals entitled to benefits under part A of subchapter XVIII of this chapter pursuant to section 426-1 of this title.

*SOURCE—*

(Aug. 14, 1935, ch. 531, title XI, Sec. 1128A, as added Pub. L. 97-35, title XXI, Sec. 2105(a), Aug. 13, 1981, 95 Stat. 789; amended Pub. L. 97-248, title I, Sec. 137(b)(26), Sept. 3, 1982, 96 Stat. 380; Pub. L. 98-369, div. B, title III, Secs. 2306(f)(1), 2354(a)(3), July 18, 1984, 98 Stat. 1073, 1100; Pub. L. 99-509, title IX, Secs. 9313(c)(1), 9317(a), (b), Oct. 21, 1986, 100 Stat. 2003, 2008; Pub. L. 100-93, Sec. 3, Aug. 18, 1987, 101 Stat. 686; Pub. L. 100-203, title IV, Secs. 4039(h)(1), 4118(e)(1), (6)-(10), Dec. 22, 1987, 101 Stat. 1330-155, as amended Pub. L. 100-360, title IV, Sec. 411(e)(3), (k)(10)(B)(ii), (D), July 1, 1988, 102 Stat. 775, 794, 795; Pub. L. 100-360, title II, Sec. 202(c)(2), July 1, 1988, 102 Stat. 715; Pub. L. 100-485, title VI, Sec. 608(d)(26)(H)-(K)(i), Oct. 13, 1988, 102 Stat. 2422; Pub. L. 101-234, title II, Sec. 201(a), Dec. 13, 1989, 103 Stat. 1981; Pub. L. 101-239, title VI, Sec. 6003(g)(3)(D)(i), Dec. 19, 1989, 103 Stat. 2153; Pub. L. 101-508, title IV, Secs. 4204(a)(3), 4207(h), formerly 4027(h), 4731(b)(1), 4753, Nov. 5, 1990, 104 Stat. 1388-109, 1388-123, 1388-195, 1388-208, renumbered Sec. 4207(h), Pub. L. 103-432, title I, Sec. 160(d)(4), Oct. 31, 1994, 108 Stat. 4444; Pub. L. 104-191, title II, Secs. 231(a)-(e), (h), 232(a), Aug. 21, 1996, 110 Stat. 2012-2015; Pub. L. 105-33, title IV, Secs. 4201(c)(1), 4304(a), (b), 4331(e), 4523(c), Aug. 5, 1997, 111 Stat. 373, 383, 396, 449; Pub. L. 105-277, div. J, title V, Sec. 5201(a), (b)(1), Oct. 21, 1998, 112 Stat. 2681-916.)

*REFERENCES IN TEXT*

The Federal Rules of Civil Procedure, referred to in subsec. (c)(1), are set out in the Appendix to Title 28, Judiciary and Judicial Procedure.

The Health Insurance Portability and Accountability Act of 1996, referred to in subsec. (f)(3), is Pub. L. 104-191, Aug. 21, 1996, 110 Stat. 1936. For complete classification of this Act to the Code, see Short Title of 1996 Amendments note set out under section 201 of this title and Tables.

Section 1395l(t)(5)(B) of this title, referred to in subsec. (i)(6)(D), was redesignated section 1395l(t)(8)(B) of this title by Pub. L. 106-113, div. B, Sec. 1000(a)(6) [title II, Secs. 201(a)(1), 202(a)(2)], Nov. 29, 1999, 113 Stat. 1536, 1501A-336, 1501A-342.

The Inspector General Act of 1978, referred to in subsec. (m)(2)(B), is Pub. L. 95-452, Oct. 12, 1978, 92 Stat. 1101, as amended, which is set out in the Appendix to Title 5, Government Organization and Employees.

# Appendix D-2

## Table of Office of Inspector General (HHS) Program Exclusion Authorities

*Source:* Office of Inspector General, Department of Health & Human Services, *available at* oig.hhs.gov/fraud/exclusions/exclusionauthorities.html

### SCOPE
(footnotes relate to effective dates)

| Social Security Act | 42 USC § | Amendment |
|---|---|---|
| 1. 1128† | 1320a-7 | Scope of exclusions imposed by the OIG expanded from Medicare and State health care programs to all Federal health care programs, as defined in section 1128B(f)(1). |

† The *effective date* for the amendment to section 1128, and the new provisions section 1128(c)(3)(G)(i) and (ii) is August 5, 1997.

## MANDATORY EXCLUSIONS

| Social Security Act | 42 USC § | Type |
|---|---|---|
| 1. 1128(a)(1) | 1320a-7(a)(1) | Conviction of program-related crimes. Minimum Period: 5 years |
| 2. 1128(a)(2) | 1320a-7(a)(2) | Conviction relating to patient abuse or neglect. Minimum Period: 5 years |
| 3. 1128(a)(3)* | 1320a-7(a)(3) | Felony conviction relating to health care fraud. Minimum Period: 5 years |
| 4. 1128(a)(4)* | 1320a-7(a)(4) | Felony conviction relating to controlled substance. Minimum Period: 5 years |
| 5. 1128(c)(3)**(G)(i)† | 1320a-7(c)(3)(G)(i) | Conviction of two mandatory exclusion offenses. Minimum Period: 10 years |
| 6. 1128(c)(3)**(G)(ii)† | 1320a-7(c)(3)(G)(ii) | Conviction on 3 or more occasions of mandatory exclusion offenses. Permanent Exclusion |
| 7. 1892 | 1395ccc | Failure to enter an agreement to repay Health Education Assistance Loans (HEAL). Minimum Period: Until entire past due obligation is repaid. |

\* The *effective date* of the new provisions sections 1128(a)(3) and 1128(a)(4), and the amended provisions section 1128(b)(1)(A), (B), and section 1128(b)(3) is *August 22, 1996*. These provisions apply to offenses occurring on or after that date.

\*\* The *effective date* for the amendments to sections 1128(b)(15), 1128(c)(3), and 1156 is *January 1, 1997*.

† The *effective date* for the amendment to section 1128, and the new provisions section 1128(c)(3)(G)(i) and (ii) is *August 5. 1997*.

## PERMISSIVE EXCLUSIONS

| Social Security Act | 42 USC § | Type |
|---|---|---|
| 1. 1128(b)(1)(A)* | 1320a-7(b)(1)(A) | Misdemeanor conviction relating to health care fraud. Minimum Period: 3 years |
| 2. 1128(b)(1)(B)* | 1320a-7(b)(1)(B) | Conviction relating to fraud in non-health care programs. Minimum Period: 3 years |
| 3. 1128(b)(2) | 1320a-7(b)(2) | Conviction relating to obstruction of an investigation. Minimum Period: 3 years |
| 4. 1128(b)(3)* | 1320a-7(b)(3) | Misdemeanor conviction relating to controlled substance. Minimum Period: 3 years |
| 5. 1128(b)(4) | 1320a-7(b)(4) | License revocation or suspension. Minimum Period: No less than the period imposed by the state licensing authority. |
| 6. 1128(b)(5) | 1320a-7(b)(5) | Exclusion or suspension under federal or state health care program. Minimum Period: No less than the period imposed by federal or state health care program. |
| 7. 1128(b)(6) | 1320a-7(b)(6) | Claims for excessive charges, unnecessary services or services which fail to meet professionally recognized standards of health care, or failure of an HMO to furnish medically necessary services. Minimum Period: 1 year |
| 8. 1128(b)(7) | 1320a-7(b)(7) | Fraud, kickbacks, and other prohibited activities. Minimum Period: None |
| 9. 1128(b)(8) | 1320a-7(b)(8) | Entities controlled by a sanctioned individual. Minimum Period: Same as length of individual's exclusion. |
| 10. 1128(b)(8)(A)‡ | 1320a-7(b)(8)(A) | Entities controlled by a family or household member of an excluded individual and where member of an excluded individual and where there has been a transfer of ownership/control. Minimum Period: Same as length of individual's exclusion. |

PERMISSIVE EXCLUSIONS (*continued*)

| Social Security Act | 42 USC § | Type |
| --- | --- | --- |
| 11. 1128(b)(9), (10), and (11) | 1320a-7(b)(9), (10), and (11) | Failure to disclose required information, supply requested information on subcontractors and suppliers; or supply payment information. Minimum Period: None |
| 12. 1128(b)(12) | 1320a-7(b)(12) | Failure to grant immediate access. Minimum Period: None |
| 13. 1128(b)(13) | 1320a-7(b)(13) | Failure to take corrective action. Minimum Period: None |
| 14. 1128(b)(14) | 1320a-7(b)(14) | Default on health education loan or scholarship obligations. Minimum Period: Until default has been cured or obligations have been resolved to Public Health Service's (PHS) satisfaction. |
| 15. 1128(b)(15)** | 1320a-7(b)(15) | Individuals controlling a sanctioned entity. Minimum Period: Same period as entity. |
| 16. 1156** | 1320c-5 | Failure to meet statutory obligations of practitioners and providers to provide' medically necessary services meeting professionally recognized standards of health care (Peer Review Organization (PRO) findings). Minimum Period: 1 year |

**NOTE:** All exclusions are effective prior to a hearing *except* those imposed under section 1128(b)(7) [42 USC 1320a-7b(b)(7)], and those imposed on rural physicians under section 1156 [42 USC 1320C-5].

**Health Insurance Portability and Accountability Act (HIPAA); Public Law 104-191:** Enacted August 21, 1996.

* The *effective date* of the new provisions sections 1128(a)(3) and 1128(a)(4), and the amended provisions section 1128(b)(1)(A), (B), and section 1128(b)(3) is *August 22, 1996.* These provisions apply to offenses occurring on or after that date.

** The *effective date* for the amendments to sections 1128(b)(15), 1128(c)(3), and 1156 is *January 1, 1997.*

**Balanced Budget Act (BBA); Public Law 105-33:** Enacted August 5, 1997.

† The *effective date* for the amendment to section 1128, and the new provisions section 1128(c)(3)(G)(i) and (ii) is *August 5. 1997.*

‡ The *effective date* for the amendment to section 1128(b)(8)(A) is *September 19, 1997* (45 days after BBA's enactment).

**NOTE:** Check HIPAA and BBA for effective dates concerning other new amended sections affecting exclusions.

# Appendix D-3

## Exclusion of Entities From Government Health Care Programs Statute

*Source:* 42 U.S.C. Section 1320a-7

### Section 1320a-7. Exclusion of certain individuals and entities from participation in Medicare and State health care programs

(a) Mandatory exclusion

The Secretary shall exclude the following individuals and entities from participation in any Federal health care program (as defined in section 1320a-7b(f) of this title):

(1) Conviction of program-related crimes

Any individual or entity that has been convicted of a criminal offense related to the delivery of an item or service under subchapter XVIII of this chapter or under any State health care program.

(2) Conviction relating to patient abuse

Any individual or entity that has been convicted, under Federal or State law, of a criminal offense relating to neglect or abuse of patients in connection with the delivery of a health care item or service.

(3) Felony conviction relating to health care fraud

Any individual or entity that has been convicted for an offense which occurred after August 21, 1996, under Federal or State law, in connection with the delivery of a health care item or service or with respect to any act or omission in a health care program (other than those specifically described in paragraph (1)) operated by or financed in whole or in part by any Federal, State, or local government agency, of a criminal offense consisting of a felony relating to fraud, theft, embezzlement, breach of fiduciary responsibility, or other financial misconduct.

(4) Felony conviction relating to controlled substance

Any individual or entity that has been convicted for an offense which occurred after August 21, 1996, under Federal or State law, of a criminal offense consisting of a felony relating to the unlawful manufacture, distribution, prescription, or dispensing of a controlled substance.

(b) Permissive exclusion

The Secretary may exclude the following individuals and entities from participation in any Federal health care program (as defined in section 1320a-7b(f) of this title):

(1) Conviction relating to fraud

Any individual or entity that has been convicted for an offense which occurred after August 21, 1996, under Federal or State law—

(A) of a criminal offense consisting of a misdemeanor relating to fraud, theft, embezzlement, breach of fiduciary responsibility, or other financial misconduct—

(i) in connection with the delivery of a health care item or service, or

(ii) with respect to any act or omission in a health care program (other than those specifically described in subsection (a)(1) of this section) operated by or financed in whole or in part by any Federal, State, or local government agency; or

(B) of a criminal offense relating to fraud, theft, embezzlement, breach of fiduciary responsibility, or other financial misconduct with respect to any act or omission in a program (other than a health care program) operated by or financed in whole or in part by any Federal, State, or local government agency.

(2) Conviction relating to obstruction of an investigation

Any individual or entity that has been convicted, under Federal or State law, in connection with the interference with or obstruction of any investigation into any criminal offense described in paragraph (1) or in subsection (a) of this section.

(3) Misdemeanor conviction relating to controlled substance

Any individual or entity that has been convicted, under Federal or State law, of a criminal offense consisting of a misdemeanor relating to the unlawful manufacture, distribution, prescription, or dispensing of a controlled substance.

(4) License revocation or suspension

Any individual or entity—

(A) whose license to provide health care has been revoked or suspended by any State licensing authority, or who otherwise lost such a license or the right to apply for or renew such a license, for reasons bearing on the individual's or entity's professional competence, professional performance, or financial integrity, or

(B) who surrendered such a license while a formal disciplinary proceeding was pending before such an authority and the proceeding concerned the individual's or entity's professional competence, professional performance, or financial integrity.

(5) Exclusion or suspension under Federal or State health care program

Any individual or entity which has been suspended or excluded from participation, or otherwise sanctioned, under—

(A) any Federal program, including programs of the Department of Defense or the Department of Veterans Affairs, involving the provision of health care, or

(B) a State health care program,

for reasons bearing on the individual's or entity's professional competence, professional performance, or financial integrity.

(6) Claims for excessive charges or unnecessary services and failure of certain organizations to furnish medically necessary services

Any individual or entity that the Secretary determines—

(A) has submitted or caused to be submitted bills or requests for payment (where such bills or requests are based on charges or cost) under subchapter XVIII of this chapter or a State health care program containing charges (or, in applicable cases, requests for payment of costs) for items or services furnished substantially in excess of such individual's or entity's usual charges (or, in applicable cases, substantially in excess of such individual's or entity's costs) for such items or services, unless the Secretary finds there is good cause for such bills or requests containing such charges or costs;

(B) has furnished or caused to be furnished items or services to patients (whether or not eligible for benefits under subchapter XVIII of this chapter or under a State health care program) substantially in excess of the needs of such patients or of a quality which fails to meet professionally recognized standards of health care;

(C) is—

(i) a health maintenance organization (as defined in section 1396b(m) of this title) providing items and services under a State plan approved under subchapter XIX of this chapter, or

(ii) an entity furnishing services under a waiver approved under section 1396n(b)(1) of this title,

and has failed substantially to provide medically necessary items and services that are required (under law or the contract with the State under subchapter XIX of this chapter) to be provided to individuals covered under that plan or waiver, if the failure has adversely affected (or has a substantial likelihood of adversely affecting) these individuals; or

(D) is an entity providing items and services as an eligible organization under a risk-sharing contract under section 1395mm of this title and has failed substantially to provide medically necessary items and services that are required (under law or such contract) to be provided to individuals covered under the risk-sharing contract, if the failure has adversely affected (or has a substantial likelihood of adversely affecting) these individuals.

(7) Fraud, kickbacks, and other prohibited activities

Any individual or entity that the Secretary determines has committed an act which is described in section 1320a-7a, 1320a-7b, or 1320a-8 of this title.

(8) Entities controlled by a sanctioned individual

Any entity with respect to which the Secretary determines that a person—

(A)(i) who has a direct or indirect ownership or control interest of 5 percent or more in the entity or with an ownership or control interest (as defined in section 1320a-3(a)(3) of this title) in that entity,

(ii) who is an officer, director, agent, or managing employee (as defined in section 1320a-5(b) of this title) of that entity; or

(iii) who was described in clause (i) but is no longer so described because of a transfer of ownership or control interest, in anticipation of (or following) a conviction, assessment, or exclusion described in subparagraph (B) against the person, to an immediate family member (as defined in subsection (j)(1) of this section) or a member of the household of the person (as defined in subsection (j)(2) of this section) who continues to maintain an interest described in such clause—

is a person—

(B)(i) who has been convicted of any offense described in subsection (a) of this section or in paragraph (1), (2), or (3) of this subsection;

(ii) against whom a civil monetary penalty has been assessed under section 1320a-7a or 1320a-8 of this title; or

(iii) who has been excluded from participation under a program under subchapter XVIII of this chapter or under a State health care program.

(9) Failure to disclose required information

Any entity that did not fully and accurately make any disclosure required by section 1320a-3 of this title, section 1320a-3a of this title, or section 1320a-5 of this title.

(10) Failure to supply requested information on subcontractors and suppliers

Any disclosing entity (as defined in section 1320a-3(a)(2) of this title) that fails to supply (within such period as may be specified by the Secretary in regulations) upon request specifically addressed to the entity by the Secretary or by the State agency administering or supervising the administration of a State health care program—

(A) full and complete information as to the ownership of a subcontractor (as defined by the Secretary in regulations) with whom the entity has had, during the previous 12 months, business transactions in an aggregate amount in excess of $25,000, or

(B) full and complete information as to any significant business transactions (as defined by the Secretary in regulations), occurring during the five-year period ending on the date of such request, between the entity and any wholly owned supplier or between the entity and any subcontractor.

(11) Failure to supply payment information

Any individual or entity furnishing items or services for which payment may be made under subchapter XVIII of this chapter or a State health care program that fails to provide such information as the Secretary or the appropriate State agency finds necessary to determine whether such payments are or were due and the amounts thereof, or has refused to permit such examination of its records by or on behalf of the Secretary or that agency as may be necessary to verify such information.

(12) Failure to grant immediate access

Any individual or entity that fails to grant immediate access, upon reasonable request (as defined by the Secretary in regulations) to any of the following:

(A) To the Secretary, or to the agency used by the Secretary, for the purpose specified in the first sentence of section 1395aa(a) of this title (relating to compliance with conditions of participation or payment).

(B) To the Secretary or the State agency, to perform the reviews and surveys required under State plans under paragraphs (26), (31), and (33) of section 1396a(a) of this title and under section 1396b(g) of this title.

(C) To the Inspector General of the Department of Health and Human Services, for the purpose of reviewing records, documents, and other data necessary to the performance of the statutory functions of the Inspector General.

(D) To a State medicaid fraud control unit (as defined in section 1396b(q) of this title), for the purpose of conducting activities described in that section.

(13) Failure to take corrective action

Any hospital that fails to comply substantially with a corrective action required under section 1395ww(f)(2)(B) of this title.

(14) Default on health education loan or scholarship obligations

Any individual who the Secretary determines is in default on repayments of scholarship obligations or loans in connection with health professions education made or secured, in whole or in part, by the Secretary and with respect to whom the Secretary has taken all reasonable steps available to the Secretary to secure repayment of such obligations or loans, except that (A) the Secretary shall not exclude pursuant to this paragraph a physician who is the sole community physician or sole source of essential specialized services in a community if a State requests that the physician not be excluded, and (B) the Secretary shall take into account, in determining whether to exclude any other physician pursuant to this paragraph, access of beneficiaries to physician services for which payment may be made under subchapter XVIII or XIX of this chapter.

(15) Individuals controlling a sanctioned entity

(A) Any individual—

(i) who has a direct or indirect ownership or control interest in a sanctioned entity and who knows or should know (as defined in section 1320a-7a(i)(6)[1] of this title) of the action

---

[1] So in original. Probably should be section "1320a-7a(i)(7)".

constituting the basis for the conviction or exclusion described in subparagraph (B); or

(ii) who is an officer or managing employee (as defined in section 1320a-5(b) of this title) of such an entity.

(B) For purposes of subparagraph (A), the term "sanctioned entity" means an entity—

(i) that has been convicted of any offense described in subsection (a) of this section or in paragraph (1), (2), or (3) of this subsection; or

(ii) that has been excluded from participation under a program under subchapter XVIII of this chapter or under a State health care program.

(c) Notice, effective date, and period of exclusion

(1) An exclusion under this section or under section 1320a-7a of this title shall be effective at such time and upon such reasonable notice to the public and to the individual or entity excluded as may be specified in regulations consistent with paragraph (2).

(2)(A) Except as provided in subparagraph (B), such an exclusion shall be effective with respect to services furnished to an individual on or after the effective date of the exclusion.

(B) Unless the Secretary determines that the health and safety of individuals receiving services warrants the exclusion taking effect earlier, an exclusion shall not apply to payments made under subchapter XVIII of this chapter or under a State health care program for—

(i) inpatient institutional services furnished to an individual who was admitted to such institution before the date of the exclusion, or

(ii) home health services and hospice care furnished to an individual under a plan of care established before the date of the exclusion,

until the passage of 30 days after the effective date of the exclusion.

(3)(A) The Secretary shall specify, in the notice of exclusion under paragraph (1) and the written notice under section 1320a-7a of this title, the minimum period (or, in the case of an exclusion of an individual under subsection (b)(12) of this section or in the case described in subparagraph (G), the period) of the exclusion.

(B) Subject to subparagraph (G), in the case of an exclusion under subsection (a) of this section, the minimum period of exclusion shall be not less than five years, except that, upon the request of a State, the Secretary may waive the exclusion under subsection (a)(1) of this section in the case of an individual or entity that is the sole community physician or sole source of essential specialized services in a community. The Secretary's decision whether to waive the exclusion shall not be reviewable.

(C) In the case of an exclusion of an individual under subsection (b)(12) of this section, the period of the exclusion shall be equal to the sum of—

(i) the length of the period in which the individual failed to grant the immediate access described in that subsection, and

(ii) an additional period, not to exceed 90 days, set by the Secretary.

(D) Subject to subparagraph (G), in the case of an exclusion of an individual or entity under paragraph (1), (2), or (3) of subsection (b) of this section, the period of the exclusion shall be 3 years, unless the Secretary determines in accordance with published regulations that a shorter period is appropriate because of mitigating circumstances or that a longer period is appropriate because of aggravating circumstances.

(E) In the case of an exclusion of an individual or entity under subsection (b)(4) or (b)(5) of this section, the period of the exclusion shall not be less than the period during which the individual's or entity's license to provide health care is revoked, suspended, or surrendered, or the individual or the entity is excluded or suspended from a Federal or State health care program.

(F) In the case of an exclusion of an individual or entity under subsection (b)(6)(B) of this section, the period of the exclusion shall be not less than 1 year.

(G) In the case of an exclusion of an individual under subsection (a) of this section based on a conviction occurring on or after August 5, 1997, if the individual has (before, on, or after August 5, 1997) been convicted—

(i) on one previous occasion of one or more offenses for which an exclusion may be effected under such subsection, the period of the exclusion shall be not less than 10 years, or

(ii) on 2 or more previous occasions of one or more offenses for which an exclusion may be effected under such subsection, the period of the exclusion shall be permanent.

(d) Notice to State agencies and exclusion under State health care programs

(1) Subject to paragraph (3), the Secretary shall exercise the authority under this section and section 1320a-7a of this title in a manner that results in an individual's or entity's exclusion from all the programs under subchapter XVIII of this chapter and all the State health care programs in which the individual or entity may otherwise participate.

(2) The Secretary shall promptly notify each appropriate State agency administering or supervising the administration of each State health care program (and, in the case of an exclusion effected pursuant to subsection (a) of this section and to which section 824(a)(5) of title 21 may apply, the Attorney General)—

(A) of the fact and circumstances of each exclusion effected against an individual or entity under this section or section 1320a-7a of this title, and

(B) of the period (described in paragraph (3)) for which the State agency is directed to exclude the individual or entity from participation in the State health care program.

(3)(A) Except as provided in subparagraph (B), the period of the exclusion under a State health care program under paragraph (2) shall be the same as any period of exclusion under subchapter XVIII of this chapter.

(B)(i) The Secretary may waive an individual's or entity's exclusion under a State health care program under paragraph (2) if the Secretary receives and approves a request for the waiver with respect to the individual or entity from the State agency administering or supervising the administration of the program.

(ii) A State health care program may provide for a period of exclusion which is longer than the period of exclusion under subchapter XVIII of this chapter.

(e) Notice to State licensing agencies

The Secretary shall—

(1) promptly notify the appropriate State or local agency or authority having responsibility for the licensing or certification of an individual or entity excluded (or directed to be excluded) from participation under this section or section 1320a-7a of this title, of the fact and circumstances of the exclusion,

(2) request that appropriate investigations be made and sanctions invoked in accordance with applicable State law and policy, and

(3) request that the State or local agency or authority keep the Secretary and the Inspector General of the Department of Health and Human Services fully and currently informed with respect to any actions taken in response to the request.

(f) Notice, hearing, and judicial review

(1) Subject to paragraph (2), any individual or entity that is excluded (or directed to be excluded) from participation under this section is entitled to reasonable notice and opportunity for a hearing thereon by the Secretary to the same extent as is provided in section 405(b) of this title, and to judicial review of the Secretary's final decision after such hearing as is provided in section 405(g) of this title, except that, in so applying such sections and section 405(l) of this title, any reference therein to the Commissioner of Social Security or the Social Security Administration shall be considered a reference to the Secretary or the Department of Health and Human Services, respectively.

(2) Unless the Secretary determines that the health or safety of individuals receiving services warrants the exclusion taking effect earlier, any individual or entity that is the subject of an adverse determination under subsection (b)(7) of this section shall be entitled to a hearing by an administrative law judge (as provided under section 405(b) of this title) on the determination under subsection (b)(7) of this section before any exclusion based upon the determination takes effect.

(3) The provisions of section 405(h) of this title shall apply with respect to this section and sections 1320a-7a, 1320a-8, and 1320c-5 of this title to the same extent as it is applicable with respect to subchapter II of this chapter, except that, in so applying such section and section 405(l) of this title, any reference therein to the Commissioner of Social Security shall be considered a reference to the Secretary.

(g) Application for termination of exclusion

(1) An individual or entity excluded (or directed to be excluded) from participation under this section or section 1320a-7a of this title may apply to the Secretary, in the manner specified by the Secretary in regulations and at the end of the minimum period of exclusion provided under subsection (c)(3) of this section and at such other times as the Secretary may provide, for termination of the exclusion effected under this section or section 1320a-7a of this title.

(2) The Secretary may terminate the exclusion if the Secretary determines, on the basis of the conduct of the applicant which occurred after the date of the notice of exclusion or which was unknown to the Secretary at the time of the exclusion, that—

(A) there is no basis under subsection (a) or (b) of this section or section 1320a-7a(a) of this title for a continuation of the exclusion, and

(B) there are reasonable assurances that the types of actions which formed the basis for the original exclusion have not recurred and will not recur.

(3) The Secretary shall promptly notify each appropriate State agency administering or supervising the administration of each State health care program (and, in the case of an exclusion effected pursuant to subsection (a) of this section and to which section 824(a)(5) of title 21 may apply, the Attorney General) of the fact and circumstances of each termination of exclusion made under this subsection.

(h) "State health care program" defined

For purposes of this section and sections 1320a-7a and 1320a-7b of this title, the term "State health care program" means—

(1) a State plan approved under subchapter XIX of this chapter,

(2) any program receiving funds under subchapter V of this chapter or from an allotment to a State under such subchapter,

(3) any program receiving funds under subchapter XX of this chapter or from an allotment to a State under such subchapter, or

(4) a State child health plan approved under subchapter XXI of this chapter.

(i) "Convicted" defined

For purposes of subsections (a) and (b) of this section, an individual or entity is considered to have been "convicted" of a criminal offense—

(1) when a judgment of conviction has been entered against the individual or entity by a Federal, State, or local court, regardless of whether there is an appeal pending or whether the judgment of conviction or other record relating to criminal conduct has been expunged;

(2) when there has been a finding of guilt against the individual or entity by a Federal, State, or local court;

(3) when a plea of guilty or nolo contendere by the individual or entity has been accepted by a Federal, State, or local court; or

(4) when the individual or entity has entered into participation in a first offender, deferred adjudication, or other arrangement or program where judgment of conviction has been withheld.

(j) Definition of immediate family member and member of household

For purposes of subsection (b)(8)(A)(iii) of this section:

(1) The term "immediate family member" means, with respect to a person—

(A) the husband or wife of the person;

(B) the natural or adoptive parent, child, or sibling of the person;

(C) the stepparent, stepchild, stepbrother, or stepsister of the person;

(D) the father-, mother-, daughter-, son-, brother-, or sister-in-law of the person;

(E) the grandparent or grandchild of the person; and

(F) the spouse of a grandparent or grandchild of the person.

(2) The term "member of the household" means, with respect to any person, any individual sharing a common abode as part of a single family unit with the person, including domestic employees and others who live together as a family unit, but not including a roomer or boarder.

## SOURCE—

(Aug. 14, 1935, ch. 531, title XI, Sec. 1128, as added Pub. L. 96-499, title IX, Sec. 913(a), Dec. 5, 1980, 94 Stat. 2619; amended Pub. L. 97-35, title XXI, Sec. 2105(b), title XXIII, Sec. 2353(k), Aug. 13, 1981, 95 Stat. 791, 873; Pub. L. 98-369, div. B, title III, Sec. 2333(a), (b), July 18, 1984, 98 Stat. 1089; Pub. L. 99-509, title IX, Sec. 9317(c), Oct. 21, 1986, 100 Stat. 2008; Pub. L. 100-93, Sec. 2, Aug. 18, 1987, 101 Stat. 680; Pub. L. 100-203, title IV, Sec. 4118(e)(2)-(5), Dec. 22, 1987, 101 Stat. 1330-155, as amended Pub. L. 100-360, title IV, Sec. 411(k)(10)(D), July 1, 1988, 102 Stat. 795; Pub. L. 100-360, title IV, Sec. 411(k)(10)(C), July 1, 1988, 102 Stat. 795; Pub. L. 101-239, title VI, Sec. 6411(d)(1), Dec. 19, 1989, 103 Stat. 2270; Pub. L. 101-508, title IV, Sec. 4164(b)(3), Nov. 5, 1990, 104 Stat. 1388-102; Pub. L. 102-54, Sec. 13(q)(3)(A)(ii), June 13, 1991, 105 Stat. 279; Pub. L. 103-296, title I, Sec. 108(b)(9), title II, Sec. 206(b)(2), Aug. 15, 1994, 108 Stat. 1483, 1513; Pub. L. 104-191, title II, Secs. 211-213, Aug. 21, 1996, 110 Stat. 2003-2005; Pub. L. 105-33, title IV, Secs. 4301, 4303(a), 4331(c), 4901(b)(2), Aug. 5, 1997, 111 Stat. 382, 396, 570.)

## SECTION REFERRED TO IN OTHER SECTIONS

This section is referred to in sections 704, 1320a-3a, 1320a-5, 1320a-7a, 1320a-7b, 1320a-7c, 1320a-7d, 1320a-7e, 1320a-8, 1320c-5, 1395a, 1395b-5, 1395l, 1395m, 1395u, 1395w-27, 1395y, 1395cc, 1395mm, 1395ww, 1395aaa, 1396a, 1396b, 1396r-2, 1396r-6, 1397d of this title; title 21 section 824.

# Appendix D-4

## Civil Monetary Penalties Regulations

*Source:* 42 C.F.R. Part 1003

### Section 1003.100 Basis and purpose.

(a) *Basis.* This part implements sections 1128(c), 1128A, 1128E, 1140, 1866(g), 1876(i), 1877(g), 1882(d) and 1903(m)(5) of the Social Security Act, and sections 421(c) and 427(b)(2) of Pub.L. 99-660 (42 U.S.C. 1320a-7, 1320a-7a, 1320a-7e, 1320a-7c, 1320b-10, 1395cc(g), 1395mm, 1395ss(d), 1396(m), 11131(c), and 11137(b)(2))).

(b) *Purpose.* This part—

    (1) Provides for the imposition of civil money penalties and, as applicable, assessments against persons who—

(i) Have knowingly submitted certain prohibited claims under Federal health care programs;

(ii) Seek payment in violation of the terms of an agreement or a limitation on charges or payments under the Medicare program, or a requirement not to charge in excess of the amount permitted under the Medicaid program;

(iii) Give false or misleading information that might affect the decision to discharge a Medicare patient from the hospital;

(iv) Fail to report information concerning medical malpractice payments or who improperly disclose, use or permit access to information reported under part B of title IV of Public Law 99-660, and regulations specified in 45 CFR part 60;

(v) Misuse certain Departmental and Medicare and Medicaid program words, letters, symbols or emblems;

(vi) Violate a requirement of section 1867 of the Act or § 489.24 of this title;

(vii) Substantially fail to provide an enrollee with required medically necessary items and services; engage in certain marketing, enrollment, reporting, claims payment, employment or contracting abuses; or do not meet the requirements for physician incentive plans for Medicare specified in §§ 417.479(d) through (f) of this title;

(viii) Present or cause to be presented a bill or claim for designated health services (as defined in § 411.351 of this title) that they know, or should know, were furnished in accordance with a referral prohibited under § 411.353 of this title;

(ix) Have collected amounts that they know or should know were billed in violation of § 411.353 of this title and have not refunded the amounts collected on a timely basis;

(x) Are physicians or entities that enter into an arrangement or scheme that they know or should know has as a principal purpose the assuring of referrals by the physician to a particular entity which, if made directly, would violate the provisions of § 411.353 of this title;

(xi) Are physicians or entities that enter into an arrangement or scheme that they know or should know has as a principal purpose the assuring of referrals by the physician to a particular entity that, if made directly, would violate the provisions of § 411.353 of this title;

(xii) Violate the Federal health care programs' anti-kickback statute as set forth in section 1128B of the Act; or

(xiii) Knowingly and willfully present, or cause to be presented, a bill or request for payment for nonphysician services furnished to hospital patients (unless the services are furnished by the hospital, either directly or under an arrangement) in violation of sections 1862(a)(14) and 1866(a)(1)(H) of the Act.

(2) Provides for the exclusion of persons from the Medicare or State health care programs against whom a civil money penalty or assess-

ment has been imposed, and the basis for reinstatement of persons who have been excluded; and

(3) Sets forth the appeal rights of persons subject to a penalty, assessment and exclusion.

[SOURCE: 51 Fed. Reg. 39,528 (Oct. 29, 1986); 52 Fed. Reg. 11,652 (April 10, 1987); 56 Fed. Reg. 28,492 (June 21, 1991); 56 Fed. Reg. 42,537 (Aug. 28, 1991); 57 Fed. Reg. 3345 (Jan. 29, 1992); 59 Fed. Reg. 32,124 (June 22, 1994); 59 Fed. Reg. 36,086 (July 15, 1994); 59 Fed. Reg. 48,566 (Sept. 22, 1994); 60 Fed. Reg. 16,583 (March 31, 1995); 60 Fed. Reg. 58,241 (Nov. 27, 1995); 61 Fed. Reg. 13,449 (March 27, 1996); 61 Fed. Reg. 46,384 (Sept. 3, 1996); 64 Fed. Reg. 39,428 (July 22, 1999); 65 Fed. Reg. 18,549 (April 7, 2000); 65 Fed. Reg. 24,414 (April 26, 2000); 65 Fed. Reg. 40,535 (June 30, 2000).]

## Section 1003.101 Definitions.

For purposes of this part:

*Act* means the Social Security Act.

*Adverse effect* means medical care has not been provided and the failure to provide such necessary medical care has presented an imminent danger to the health, safety, or well-being of the patient or has placed the patient unnecessarily in a high-risk situation.

*ALJ* means an Administrative Law Judge.

*Assessment* means the amount described in § 1003.104, and includes the plural of that term.

*Claim* means an application for payment for an item or service to a Federal health care program (as defined in section 1128B(f) of the Act).

*CMS* stands for Centers for Medicare & Medicaid Services, formerly the [Health Care Financing Administration (HCFA)].

*Contracting organization* means a public or private entity, including of a health maintenance organization (HMO), competitive medical plan, or health insuring organization (HIO) which meets the requirements of section 1876(b) of the Act or is subject to the requirements in section 1903(m)(2)(A) of the Act and which has contracted with the Department or a State to furnish services to Medicare beneficiaries or Medicaid recipients.

*Department* means the Department of Health and Human Services.

*Enrollee* means an individual who is eligible for Medicare or Medicaid and who enters into an agreement to receive services from a contracting organization that contracts with the Department under title XVIII or title XIX of the Act.

*Exclusion* means the temporary or permanent barring of a person from participation in a Federal health care program (as defined in section 1128B(f) of the Act).

*Inspector General* means the Inspector General of the Department or his or her designees.

*Item or service* includes (a) any item, device, medical supply or service claimed to have been provided to a patient and listed in an itemized claim for program payment or a request for payment, and (b) in the case of a claim based on costs, any entry or omission in a cost report, books of account or other documents supporting the claim.

*Maternal and Child Health Services Block Grant program* means the program authorized under Title V of the Act.

*Medicaid* means the program of grants to the States for medical assistance authorized under title XIX of the Act.

*Medical malpractice claim or action* means a written complaint or claim demanding payment based on a physician's, dentist's or other health care practitioner's provision of, or failure to provide health care services, and includes the filing of a cause of action based on the law of tort brought in any State or Federal court or other adjudicative body.

*Medicare* means the program of health insurance for the aged and disabled authorized under Title XVIII of the Act.

*Participating hospital* means (1) a hospital or (2) a rural primary care hospital as defined in section 1861(mm)(1) of the Act that has entered into a Medicare provider agreement under section 1866 of the Act.

*Penalty* means the amount described in § 1003.103 and includes the plural of that term.

*Person* means an individual, trust or estate, partnership, corporation, professional association or corporation, or other entity, public or private.

*Physician incentive plan* means any compensation arrangement between a contracting organization and a physician group that may directly or indirectly have the effect of reducing or limiting services provided with respect to enrollees in the organization.

*Preventive care*, for purposes of the definition of the term Remuneration as set forth in this section and the preventive care exception to section 231(h) of HIPAA, means any service that—

(1) Is a prenatal service or a post-natal well-baby visit or is a specific clinical service described in the current U.S. Preventive Services Task Force's *Guide to Clinical Preventive Services*, and

(2) Is reimbursable in whole or in part by Medicare or an applicable State health care program.

*Remuneration*, as set forth in § 1003.102(b)(13) of this part, is consistent with the definition contained in section 1128A(i)(6) of the Act, and includes the waiver of coinsurance and deductible amounts (or any part thereof) and transfers of items or services for free or for other than fair market value. The term "remuneration" does not include—

(1) The waiver of coinsurance and deductible amounts by a person, if the waiver is not offered as part of any advertisement or solicitation; the person does not routinely waive coinsurance or deductible amounts; and the person waives coinsurance and deductible amounts after determining in good faith that the individual is in financial need or failure by the person to collect coinsurance or deductible amounts after making reasonable collection efforts;

(2) Any permissible practice as specified in section 1128B(b)(3) of the Act or in regulations issued by the Secretary;

(3) Differentials in coinsurance and deductible amounts as part of a benefit plan design (as long as the differentials have been disclosed

in writing to all beneficiaries, third party payers and providers), to whom claims are presented; or

(4) Incentives given to individuals to promote the delivery of preventive care services where the delivery of such services is not tied (directly or indirectly) to the provision of other services reimbursed in whole or in part by Medicare or an applicable State health care program. Such incentives may include the provision of preventive care, but may not include—

　　(i) Cash or instruments convertible to cash; or

　　(ii) An incentive the value of which is disproportionally large in relationship to the value of the preventive care service (i.e., either the value of the service itself or the future health care costs reasonably expected to be avoided as a result of the preventive care).

*Request for payment* means an application submitted by a person to any person for payment for an item or service.

*Respondent* means the person upon whom the Department has imposed, or proposes to impose, a penalty, assessment or exclusion.

*Responsible physician* means a physician who is responsible for the examination, treatment, or transfer of an individual who comes to a participating hospital's emergency department seeking assistance and includes a physician on call for the care of such individual.

*Secretary* means the Secretary of the Department or his or her designees.

*Should know or should have known* means that a person, with respect to information—

(1) Acts in deliberate ignorance of the truth or falsity of the information; or

(2) Acts in reckless disregard of the truth or falsity of the information. For purposes of this definition, no proof of specific intent to defraud is required.

*Social Services Block Grant program* means the program authorized under title XX of the Social Security Act.

*State* includes the District of Columbia, Puerto Rico, the Virgin Islands, Guam, American Samoa, the Northern Mariana Islands, and the Trust Territory of the Pacific Islands.

*State health care program* means a State plan approved under title XIX of the Act, any program receiving funds under title V of the Act or from an allotment to a State under such title, or any program receiving funds under title XX of the Act or from an allotment to a State under such title.

*Timely basis* means, in accordance with § 1003.102(b)(9) of this part, the 60-day period from the time the prohibited amounts are collected by the individual or the entity.

[SOURCE: 56 Fed. Reg. 28,492 (June 21, 1991); 57 Fed. Reg. 3345 (Jan. 29, 1992); 59 Fed. Reg. 32,124 (June 22, 1994); 59 Fed. Reg. 36,086 (July 15, 1994); 60 Fed. Reg. 16,584 (March 31, 1995); 61 Fed. Reg. 13,449 (March 27, 1996); 61 Fed. Reg. 46,384, (Sept. 3, 1996); 65 Fed. Reg. 24,415 (April 26, 2000); 65 Fed. Reg. 35,584 (June 5, 2000); 66 Fed. Reg. 39,452 (July 31, 2001).]

### Section 1003.102 Basis for civil money penalties and assessments.

(a) The OIG may impose a penalty and assessment against any person whom it determines in accordance with this part has knowingly presented, or caused to be presented, a claim which is for—

(1) An item or service that the person knew, or should have known, was not provided as claimed, including a claim that is part of a pattern or practice of claims based on codes that the person knows or should know will result in greater payment to the person than the code applicable to the item or service actually provided;

(2) An item or service for which the person knew, or should have known, that the claim was false or fraudulent, including a claim for any item or service furnished by an excluded individual employed by or otherwise under contract with that person;

(3) An item or service furnished during a period in which the person was excluded from participation in the Federal health care program to which the claim was made;

(4) A physician's services (or an item or service) for which the person knew, or should have known, that the individual who furnished (or supervised the furnishing of) the service—

(i) Was not licensed as a physician;

(ii) Was licensed as a physician, but such license had been obtained through a misrepresentation of material fact (including cheating on an examination required for licensing); or

(iii) Represented to the patient at the time the service was furnished that the physician was certified in a medical specialty board when he or she was not so certified;

(5) A payment that such person knows, or should know, may not be made under § 411.353 of this title; or

(6) An item or service that a person knows or should know is medically unnecessary, and which is part of a pattern of such claims.

(b) The OIG may impose a penalty, and where authorized, an assessment against any person (including an insurance company in the case of paragraphs (b)(5) and (b)(6) of this section) whom it determines in accordance with this part—

(1) Has knowingly presented or caused to be presented a request for payment in violation of the terms of—

(i) An agreement to accept payments on the basis of an assignment under section 1842(b)(3)(B)(ii) of the Act;

(ii) An agreement with a State agency or other requirement of a State Medicaid plan not to charge a person for an item or service in excess of the amount permitted to be charged;

(iii) An agreement to be a participating physician or supplier under section 1842(h)(1); or

(iv) An agreement in accordance with section 1866(a)(1)(G) of the Act not to charge any person for inpatient hospital services for which payment had been denied or reduced under section 1886(f)(2) of the Act.

(2) [Reserved]

(3) [Reserved]

(4) Has knowingly given or caused to be given to any person, in the case of inpatient hospital services subject to the provisions of section 1886 of the Act, information that he or she knew, or should have known, was false or misleading and that could reasonably have been expected to influence the decision when to discharge such person or another person from the hospital.

(5) Fails to report information concerning—

(i) A payment made under an insurance policy, self-insurance or otherwise, for the benefit of a physician, dentist or other health care practitioner in settlement of, or in satisfaction in whole or in part of, a medical malpractice claim or action or a judgment against such a physician, dentist or other practitioner in accordance with section 421 of Public Law 99-660 (42 U.S.C. 11131) and as required by regulations at 45 CFR part 60; or

(ii) An adverse action required to be reported to the Healthcare Integrity and Protection Data Bank as established by section 221 of Public Law 104-191 and set forth in section 1128E of the Act.

(6) Improperly discloses, uses or permits access to information reported in accordance with part B of title IV of Pub.L. 99-660, in violation of section 427 of Pub.L. 99-660 (42 U.S.C. 11137) or regulations at 45 CFR part 60. (The disclosure of information reported in accordance with part B of title IV in response to a subpoena or a discovery request is considered to be an improper disclosure in violation of section 427 of Pub.L. 99-660. However, disclosure or release by an entity of original documents or underlying records from which the reported information is obtained or derived is not considered to be an improper disclosure in violation of section 427 of Pub.L. 99-660.)

(7) Has made use of the words, letters, symbols or emblems as defined in paragraph (b)(7)(i) of this section in such a manner that such person knew or should have known would convey, or in a manner which reasonably could be interpreted or construed as conveying, the false impression that an advertisement, solicitation or other item was authorized, approved or endorsed by the Department or CMS, or that such person or organization has some connection with or authorization from the Department or CMS. Civil money penalties—

(i) May be imposed, regardless of the use of a disclaimer of affiliation with the United States Government, the Department or its programs, for misuse of—

(A) The words "Department of Health and Human Services," "Health and Human Services," "Centers for Medicare & Medicaid Services," "Medicare," or "Medicaid," or any other combination or variation of such words;

(B) The letters "DHHS," "HHS," or "CMS," or any other combination or variation of such letters; or

(C) A symbol or emblem of the Department or CMS (including the design of, or a reasonable facsimile of the design of, the Medicare card, the check used for payment of benefits under title II, or envelopes or other stationery used by the Department or CMS) or any other combination or variation of such symbols or emblems; and

(ii) Will not be imposed against any agency or instrumentality of a State, or political subdivision of the State, that makes use of any symbol or emblem, or any words or letters which specifically identifies that agency or instrumentality of the State or political subdivision.

(8) Is a contracting organization that CMS determines has committed an act or failed to comply with the requirements set forth in § 417.500(a) or § 434.67(a) of this title or failed to comply with the requirement set forth in § 434.80(c) of this title.

(9) Has not refunded on a timely basis, as defined in § 1003.101 of this part, amounts collected as the result of billing an individual, third party payer or other entity for a designated health service that was provided in accordance with a prohibited referral as described in § 411.353 of this title.

(10) Is a physician or entity that enters into—

(i) A cross referral arrangement, for example, whereby the physician owners of entity "X" refer to entity "Y," and the physician owners of entity "Y" refer to entity "X" in violation of § 411.353 of this title, or

(ii) Any other arrangement or scheme that the physician or entity knows, or should know, has a principal purpose of circumventing the prohibitions of § 411.353 of this title.

(11) Has violated section 1128B of the Act by unlawfully offering, paying, soliciting or receiving remuneration in return for the referral of business paid for by Medicare, Medicaid or other Federal health care programs.

(12) Who is not an organization, agency or other entity, and who is excluded from participating in Medicare or a State health care program in accordance with sections 1128 or 1128A of the Act, and who—

(i) Knows or should know of the action constituting the basis for the exclusion, and retains a direct or indirect ownership or control interest of five percent or more in an entity that participates in Medicare or a State health care program; or

(ii) Is an officer or managing employee (as defined in section 1126(b) of the Act) of such entity.

(13) Offers or transfers remuneration (as defined in § 1003.101 of this part) to any individual eligible for benefits under Medicare or a State health care program, that such person knows or should know is likely to influence such individual to order or to receive from a particular provider, practitioner or supplier any item or service for which payment may be made, in whole or in part, under Medicare or a State health care program.

(14) Is a physician and who executes a document falsely by certifying that a Medicare beneficiary requires home health services when the physician knows that the beneficiary does not meet the eligibility requirements set forth in sections 1814(a)(2)(C) or 1835(a)(2)(A) of the Act.

(15) Has knowingly and willfully presented, or caused to be presented, a bill or request for payment for items and services furnished to a hospital patient for which payment may be made under the Medicare or another Federal health care program, if that bill or request is inconsistent with an arrangement under section 1866(a)(1)(H) of the Act, or violates the requirements for such an arrangement.

(c)(1) The Office of the Inspector General (OIG) may impose a penalty for violations of section 1867 of the Act or § 489.24 of this title against—

 (i) Any participating hospital with an emergency department that—

  (A) Knowingly violates the statute on or after August 1, 1986 or;

  (B) Negligently violates the statute on or after May 1, 1991; and

 (ii) Any responsible physician who—

  (A) Knowingly violates the statute on or after August 1, 1986;

  (B) Negligently violates the statute on or after May 1, 1991;

  (C) Signs a certification under section 1867(c)(1)(A) of the Act if the physician knew or should have known that the benefits of transfer to another facility did not outweigh the risks of such a transfer; or

  (D) Misrepresents an individual's condition or other information, including a hospital's obligations under this section.

(2) For purposes of this section, a responsible physician or hospital "knowingly" violates section 1867 of the Act if the responsible physician or hospital recklessly disregards, or deliberately ignores a material fact.

(d)(1) In any case in which it is determined that more than one person was responsible for presenting or causing to be presented a claim as described in paragraph (a) of this section, each such person may be held liable for the penalty prescribed by this part, and an assessment may be imposed against any one such person or jointly and severally against two or more such persons, but the aggregate amount of the assessments collected may not exceed the amount that could be assessed if only one person was responsible.

 (2) In any case in which it is determined that more than one person was responsible for presenting or causing to be presented a request for payment or for giving false or misleading information as described in paragraph (b) of this section, each such person may be held liable for the penalty prescribed by this part.

 (3) In any case in which it is determined that more than one person was responsible for failing to report information that is required to

be reported on a medical malpractice payment, or for improperly disclosing, using, or permitting access to information, as described in paragraphs (b)(5) and (b)(6) of this section, each such person may be held liable for the penalty prescribed by this part.

(4) In any case in which it is determined that more than one responsible physician violated the provisions of section 1867 of the Act or of § 489.24 of this title, a penalty may be imposed against each responsible physician.

(5) Under this section, a principal is liable for penalties and assessments for the actions of his or her agent acting within the scope of the agency.

(e) For purposes of this section, the term "knowingly" is defined consistent with the definition set forth in the Civil False Claims Act (31 U.S.C. 3729(b)), that is, a person, with respect to information, has actual knowledge of information, acts in deliberate ignorance of the truth or falsity of the information, or acts in reckless disregard of the truth or falsity of the information, and that no proof of specific intent to defraud is required.

[SOURCE: 52 Fed. Reg. 11,652 (April 10, 1987); 56 Fed. Reg. 28,492 (June 21, 1991); 56 Fed. Reg. 42,537 (Aug. 28, 1991); 57 Fed. Reg. 3345 (Jan. 29, 1992); 57 Fed. Reg. 9670 (March 20, 1992); 59 Fed. Reg. 32,124 (June 22, 1994); 59 Fed. Reg. 36,086 (July 15, 1994); 60 Fed. Reg. 16,584 (March 31, 1995); 60 Fed. Reg. 58,241 (Nov. 27, 1995); 64 Fed. Reg. 39,428 (July 22, 1999); 65 Fed. Reg. 18,550 (April 7, 2000); 65 Fed. Reg. 24,415 (April 26, 2000); 65 Fed. Reg. 35,584 (June 5, 2000); 65 Fed. Reg. 40,535 (June 30, 2000).]

### Section 1003.103 Amount of penalty.

(a) Except as provided in paragraphs (b) and (d) through (k) of this section, the OIG may impose a penalty of not more than $10,000 for each item or service that is subject to a determination under § 1003.102.

(b) The OIG may impose a penalty of not more than $15,000 for each person with respect to whom a determination was made that false or misleading information was given under § 1003.102(b)(4), or for each item and service that is subject to a determination under § 1003.102(a)(5) or § 1003.102(b)(9) of this part. The OIG may impose a penalty of not more than $100,000 for each arrangement or scheme that is subject to a determination under § 1003.102(b)(10) of this part.

(c) The OIG may impose a penalty of not more than $11,000[1] for each payment for which there was a failure to report required information in accordance with § 1003.102(b)(5), or for each improper disclosure, use or access to information that is subject to a determination under § 1003.102(b)(6).

---

[1]As adjusted in accordance with the Federal Civil Monetary Penalty Inflation Adjustment Act of 1990 (Pub.L. 101-140), as amended by the Debt Collection Improvement Act of 1996 (Pub.L. 104-134).

(d)(1) The OIG may impose a penalty of not more than $5,000 for each violation resulting from the misuse of Departmental, CMS, Medicare or Medicaid program words, letters, symbols or emblems as described in § 1003.102(b)(7) relating to printed media, and a penalty of not more than $25,000 in the case of such misuse related to a broadcast or telecast, that is related to a determination under § 1003.102(b)(7).

    (2) For purposes of this paragraph, a violation is defined as—

        (i) In the case of a direct mailing solicitation or advertisement, each separate piece of mail which contains one or more words, letters, symbols or emblems related to a determination under § 1003.102(b)(7);

        (ii) In the case of a printed solicitation or advertisement, each reproduction, reprinting or distribution of such item related to a determination under § 1003.102(b)(7); and

        (iii) In the case of a broadcast or telecast, each airing of a single commercial or solicitation related to a determination under § 1003.102(b)(7).

(e) For violations of section 1867 of the Act or § 489.24 of this title, the OIG may impose—

    (1) Against each participating hospital with an emergency department, a penalty of not more than $50,000 for each negligent violation occurring on or after May 1, 1991, except that if the participating hospital has fewer than 100 State-licensed, Medicare-certified beds on the date the penalty is imposed, the penalty will not exceed $25,000; and

    (2) Against each responsible physician, a penalty of not more than $50,000 for each negligent violation occurring on or after May 1, 1991.

(f)(1) The OIG may, in addition to or in lieu of other remedies available under law, impose a penalty of up to $25,000 for each determination by CMS that a contracting organization has—

        (i) Failed substantially to provide an enrollee with required medically necessary items and services and the failure adversely affects (or has the likelihood of adversely affecting) the enrollee;

        (ii) Imposed premiums on enrollees in excess of amounts permitted under section 1876 or title XIX of the Act;

        (iii) Acted to expel or to refuse to re-enroll a Medicare beneficiary in violation of the provisions of section 1876 of the Act and for reasons other than the beneficiary's health status or requirements for health care services;

        (iv) Misrepresented or falsified information furnished to an individual or any other entity under section 1876 or section 1903(m) of the Act;

        (v) Failed to comply with the requirements of section 1876(g)(6)(A) of the Act, regarding prompt payment of claims; or

        (vi) Failed to comply with the requirements of § 417.479(d) through (i) of this title for Medicare, and § 417.479(d) through (g) and (i) of this title for Medicaid, regarding certain prohibited incentive payments to physicians.

(2) The OIG may, in addition to or in lieu of other remedies available under law, impose a penalty of up to $25,000 for each determination by CMS that a contracting organization with a contract under section 1876 of the Act—

(i) Employs or contracts with individuals or entities excluded, under section 1128 or section 1128A of the Act, from participation in Medicare for the provision of health care, utilization review, medical social work, or administrative services; or

(ii) Employs or contracts with any entity for the provision of services (directly or indirectly) through an excluded individual or entity.

(3) The OIG may, in addition to or in lieu of other remedies available under law, impose a penalty of up to $100,000 for each determination that a contracting organization has—

(i) Misrepresented or falsified information to the Secretary under section 1876 of the Act or to the State under section 1903(m) of the Act; or

(ii) Acted to expel or to refuse to re-enroll a Medicaid recipient because of the individual's health status or requirements for health care services, or engaged in any practice that would reasonably be expected to have the effect of denying or discouraging enrollment (except as permitted by section 1876 or section 1903(m) of the Act) with the contracting organization by Medicare beneficiaries and Medicaid recipients whose medical condition or history indicates a need for substantial future medical services.

(4) If enrollees are charged more than the allowable premium, the OIG will impose an additional penalty equal to double the amount of excess premium charged by the contracting organization. The excess premium amount will be deducted from the penalty and returned to the enrollee.

(5) The OIG will impose an additional $15,000 penalty for each individual not enrolled when CMS determines that a contracting organization has committed a violation described in paragraph (f)(3)(ii) of this section.

(6) For purposes of paragraph (f) of this section, a violation is each incident where a person has committed an act listed in § 417.500(a) or § 434.67(a) of this title, or failed to comply with a requirement set forth in § 434.80(c) of this title.

(g) The OIG may impose a penalty of not more than $25,000 against a health plan for failing to report information on an adverse action required to be reported to the Healthcare Integrity and Protection Data Bank in accordance with section 1128E of the Act and § 1003.102(b)(5)(ii).

(h) For each violation of § 1003.102(b)(11), the OIG may impose—

(1) A penalty of not more than $50,000, and

(2) An assessment of up to three times the total amount of remuneration offered, paid, solicited or received, as specified in § 1003.104(b).

(i) For violations of § 1003.102(b)(14) of this part, the OIG may impose a penalty of not more than the greater of—

(1) $5,000, or

(2) Three times the amount of Medicare payments for home health services that are made with regard to the false certification of eligibility by a physician in accordance with sections 1814(a)(2)(C) or 1835(a)(2)(A) of the Act.

(j) The OIG may impose a penalty of not more than $10,000 per day for each day that the prohibited relationship described in § 1001.102(b)(12) of this part occurs.

(k) For violations of section 1862(a)(14) of the Act and § 1003.102(b)(15), the OIG may impose a penalty of not more than $2,000 for each bill or request for payment for items and services furnished to a hospital patient.

[SOURCE: 56 Fed. Reg. 28,493 (June 21, 1991); 56 Fed. Reg. 42,537 (Aug. 28, 1991); 57 Fed. Reg. 3346 (Jan. 29, 1992); 59 Fed. Reg. 32,125 (June 22, 1994); 59 Fed. Reg. 36,086 (July 15, 1994); 59 Fed. Reg. 48,566 (Sept. 22, 1994); 60 Fed. Reg. 16,584 (March 31, 1995); 60 Fed. Reg. 58,241 (Nov. 27, 1995); 61 Fed. Reg. 13,449 (March 27, 1996); 61 Fed. Reg. 46,384 (Sept. 3, 1996); 61 Fed. Reg. 52,301 (Oct. 7, 1996); 64 Fed. Reg. 39,429 (July 22, 1999); 65 Fed. Reg. 18,550 (April 7, 2000); 65 Fed. Reg. 24,416 (April 26, 2000); 65 Fed. Reg. 35,584 (June 5, 2000); 65 Fed. Reg. 40,535 (June 30, 2000).]

### Section 1003.104 Amount of assessment.

(a) The OIG may impose an assessment, where authorized, in accordance with § 1003.102, of not more than—

(1) Two times the amount for each item or service wrongfully claimed prior to January 1, 1997; and

(2) Three times the amount for each item or service wrongfully claimed on or after January 1, 1997.

(b) The assessment is in lieu of damages sustained by the Department or a State agency because of that claim.

[SOURCE: 64 Fed. Reg. 39,429 (July 22, 1999); 65 Fed. Reg. 24,416 (April 26, 2000).]

### Section 1003.105 Exclusion from participation in Medicare, Medicaid and all Federal health care programs.

(a)(1) Except as set forth in paragraph (b) of this section, the following persons may be subject, in lieu of or in addition to any penalty or assessment, to an exclusion from participation in Medicare for a period of time determined under § 1003.107. There will be exclusions from Federal health care programs for the same period as the Medicare exclusion for any person who—

(i) Any person who is subject to a penalty or assessment under § 1003.102(a), (b)(1) through (b)(4), or (b)(15).

(ii) Commits a gross and flagrant, or repeated, violation of section 1867 of the Act or § 489.24 of this title on or after May 1, 1991. For purposes of this section, a gross and flagrant violation is one that presents an imminent danger to the health, safety or well-being of the individual who seeks emergency examination and treatment or places that individual unnecessarily in a high-risk situation.

(2) Nothing in this section will be construed to limit the Department's authority to impose an exclusion without imposing a penalty.

(b)(1)(i) With respect to any exclusion based on liability for a penalty or assessment under § 1003.102 (a), (b)(1), or (b)(4), the OIG will consider an application from a State agency for a waiver if the person is the sole community physician or the sole source of essential specialized services in a community. With respect to any exclusion imposed under § 1003.105(a)(1)(ii), the OIG will consider an application from a State agency for a waiver if the physician's exclusion from the State health care program would deny beneficiaries access to medical care or would otherwise cause hardship to beneficiaries.

(ii) If a waiver is granted, it is applicable only to the State health care program for which the State requested the waiver.

(iii) If the OIG subsequently obtains information that the basis for a waiver no longer exists, or the State agency submits evidence that the basis for the waiver no longer exists, the waiver will cease and the person will be excluded from the State health care program for the remainder of the period that the person is excluded from Medicare.

(iv) The OIG notifies the State agency whether its request for a waiver has been granted or denied.

(v) The decision to deny a waiver is not subject to administrative or judicial review.

(2) For purposes of this section, the definitions contained in § 1001.2 of this chapter for "sole community physician" and "sole source of essential specialized services in a community" apply.

(c) When the Inspector General proposes to exclude a nursing facility from the Medicare and Medicaid programs, he or she will, at the same time he or she notifies the respondent, notify the appropriate State licensing authority, the State Office of Aging, the long-term care ombudsman, and the State Medicaid agency of the Inspector General's intention to exclude the facility.

[SOURCE: 56 Fed. Reg. 28,493 (June 21, 1991); 56 Fed. Reg. 42,538 (Aug. 28, 1991); 57 Fed. Reg. 3346 (Jan. 29, 1992); 59 Fed. Reg. 32,125 (June 22, 1994); 64 Fed. Reg. 39,429 (July 22, 1999); 65 Fed. Reg. 18,550 (April 7, 2000); 65 Fed. Reg. 24,416 (April 26, 2000); 65 Fed. Reg. 35,584 (June 5, 2000); 65 Fed. Reg. 40,535 (June 30, 2000).]

### Section 1003.106 Determinations regarding the amount of the penalty and assessment.

(a) *Amount of penalty.*

(1) In determining the amount of any penalty or assessment in accordance with § 1003.102(a), (b)(1), (b)(4) and (b)(9) through (b)(14) of this part, the Department will take into account—

(i) The nature of the claim, referral arrangement or other wrong-doing;

(ii) The degree of culpability of the person against whom a civil money penalty is proposed;

(iii) The history of prior offenses of the person against whom a civil money penalty is proposed;

(iv) The financial condition of the person against whom a civil money penalty is proposed;

(v) The completeness and timeliness of the refund with respect to § 1003.102(b)(9);

(vi) The amount of financial interest involved with respect to § 1003.102(b)(12);

(vii) The amount of remuneration offered or transferred with respect to § 1003.102(b)(13); and

(viii) Such other matters as justice may require.

(2) In determining the amount of any penalty in accordance with §§ 1003.102 (b)(5) and (b)(6), the Department will take into account—

(i) The nature and circumstances of the failure to properly report information, or the improper disclosure of information, as required;

(ii) The degree of culpability of the person in failing to provide timely and complete data or in improperly disclosing, using or permitting access to information, as appropriate;

(iii) The materiality, or significance of omission, of the information to be reported, or the materiality of the improper disclosure of, or use of, or access to information, as appropriate;

(3)(i) In determining the amount of any penalty in accordance with § 1003.102(b)(7), the OIG will take into account—

(A) The nature and objective of the advertisement, solicitation or other communication, and the degree to which it has the capacity to deceive members of the public;

(B) The degree of culpability of the individual, organization or entity in the use of the prohibited words, letters, symbols or emblems;

(C) The frequency and scope of the violation, and whether a specific segment of the population was targeted;

(D) The prior history of the individual, organization or entity in its willingness or refusal to comply with informal requests to correct violations;

(E) The history of prior offenses of the individual, organization or entity in its misuse of Departmental and program words, letters, symbols and emblems;

(F) The financial condition of the individual, organization or entity involved with the violation; and

(G) Such other matters as justice may require.

(ii) The use of a disclaimer of affiliation with the United States Government, the Department or its programs will not be considered as a mitigating factor in determining the amount of penalty in accordance with § 1003.102(b)(7).

(4) In determining the amount of any penalty in accordance with § 1003.102(c), the OIG takes into account—

(i) The degree of culpability of the respondent;

(ii) The seriousness of the condition of the individual seeking emergency medical treatment;

(iii) The prior history of offenses of the respondent in failing to provide appropriate emergency medical screening, stabilization and treatment of individuals coming to a hospital's emergency department or to effect an appropriate transfer;

(iv) The respondent's financial condition;

(v) The nature and circumstances of the violation; and

(vi) Such other matters as justice may require.

(5) In determining the appropriate amount of any penalty in accordance with § 1003.103(f), the OIG will consider, as appropriate—

(i) The nature and scope of the required medically necessary item or service not provided and the circumstances under which it was not provided;

(ii) The degree of culpability of the contracting organization;

(iii) The seriousness of the adverse effect that resulted or could have resulted from the failure to provide required medically necessary care;

(iv) The harm which resulted or could have resulted from the provision of care by a person that the contracting organization is expressly prohibited, under section 1876(i)(6) or section 1903(p)(2) of the Act, from contracting with or employing;

(v) The harm which resulted or could have resulted from the contracting organization's expulsion or refusal to re-enroll a Medicare beneficiary or Medicaid recipient;

(vi) The nature of the misrepresentation or fallacious information furnished by the contracting organization to the Secretary, State, enrollee or other entity under section 1876 or section 1903(m) of the Act;

(vii) The extent to which the failure to provide medically necessary services could be attributed to a prohibited inducement to reduce or limit services under a physician incentive plan and the harm to the enrollee which resulted or could have resulted from such failure. It would be considered an aggravating factor if the contracting organization knowingly or routinely engaged in any prohibited practice which acted as an inducement to reduce or limit medically necessary services provided with respect to a specific enrollee in the organization;

(viii) The history of prior offenses by the contracting organization or principals of the contracting organization, including whether, at any time prior to determination of the current violation or violations, the contracting organization or any of its principals were convicted of a criminal charge or were held liable for civil or administrative sanctions in connection with a program covered by this part or any other public or private program of payment for medical services; and

(ix) Such other matters as justice may require.

(b) *Determining the amount of the penalty or assessment.* As guidelines for taking into account the factors listed in paragraph (a)(1) of this section, the following circumstances are to be considered—

(1) *Nature and circumstances of the incident.* It should be considered a mitigating circumstance if all the items or services or incidents subject to a determination under § 1003.102 included in the action brought under this part were of the same type and occurred within a short period of time, there were few such items or services or incidents, and the total amount claimed or requested for such items or services was less than $1,000. It should be considered an aggravating circumstance if—

(i) Such items or services or incidents were of several types, occurred over a lengthy period of time;

(ii) There were many such items or services or incidents (or the nature and circumstances indicate a pattern of claims or requests for payment for such items or services or a pattern of incidents);

(iii) The amount claimed or requested for such items or services was substantial; or

(iv) The false or misleading information given resulted in harm to the patient, a premature discharge or a need for additional services or subsequent hospital admission.

(2) *Degree of culpability.* It should be considered a mitigating circumstance if corrective steps were taken promptly after the error was discovered. It should be considered an aggravating circumstance if—

(i) The respondent knew the item or service was not provided as claimed or if the respondent knew that the claim was false or fraudulent;

(ii) The respondent knew that the items or services were furnished during a period that he or she had been excluded from participation and that no payment could be made as specified in §§ 1003.102(a)(3) and 1003.102(b)(12), or because payment would violate the terms of an assignment or an agreement with a State agency or other agreement or limitation on payment under § 1003.102(b);

(iii) The respondent knew that the information could reasonably be expected to influence the decision of when to discharge a patient from a hospital; or

(iv) The respondent knew that the offer or transfer of remuneration described in § 1003.102(b)(13) of this part would influence a beneficiary to order or receive from a particular provider, practitioner or supplier items or services reimbursable under Medicare or a State health care program.

(3) *Prior offenses.* It should be considered an aggravating circumstance if at any time prior to the incident or presentation of any claim

or request for payment which included an item or service subject to a determination under § 1003.102, the respondent was held liable for criminal, civil or administrative sanctions in connection with a program covered by this part or any other public or private program of reimbursement for medical services.

(4) *Other wrongful conduct.* It should be considered an aggravating circumstance if there is proof that a respondent engaged in wrongful conduct, other than the specific conduct upon which liability is based, relating to government programs or in connection with the delivery of a health care item or service. The statute of limitations governing civil money penalty proceedings will not apply to proof of other wrongful conduct as an aggravating circumstance.

(5) *Financial condition.* In all cases, the resources available to the respondent will be considered when determining the amount of the penalty and assessment.

(6) *Other matters as justice may require.* Other circumstances of an aggravating or mitigating nature should be taken into account if, in the interests of justice, they require either a reduction of the penalty or assessment or an increase in order to assure the achievement of the purposes of this part.

(c) In determining the amount of the penalty and assessment to be imposed for every item or service or incident subject to a determination under §§ 1003.102(a), (b)(1) and (b)(4)—

(1) If there are substantial or several mitigating circumstances, the aggregate amount of the penalty and assessment should be set at an amount sufficiently below the maximum permitted by §§ 1003.103(a) and 1003.104, to reflect that fact.

(2) If there are substantial or several aggravating circumstances, the aggregate amount of the penalty and assessment should be set at an amount sufficiently close or at the maximum permitted by §§ 1003.103(a) and 1003.104, to reflect that fact.

(3) Unless there are extraordinary mitigating circumstances, the aggregate amount of the penalty and assessment should never be less than double the approximate amount of damages and costs (as defined in paragraph (f) of this section) sustained by the United States, or any State, as a result of claims or incidents subject to a determination under §§ 1003.102(a), (b)(1) and (b)(4).

(d) In considering the factors listed in paragraph (a)(4) of this section for violations subject to a determination under § 1003.103(e), the following circumstances are to be considered, as appropriate, in determining the amount of any penalty—

(1) *Degree of culpability.* It would be a mitigating circumstance if the respondent hospital had appropriate policies and procedures in place, and had effectively trained all of its personnel in the requirements of section 1867 of the Act and § 489.24 of this title, but an employee or responsible physician acted contrary to the respondent hospital's policies and procedures.

(2) *Seriousness of individual's condition.* It would be an aggravating circumstance if the respondent's violation(s) occurred with regard to an individual who presented to the hospital a request for treatment of a medical condition that was clearly an emergency, as defined by § 489.24(b) of this title.

(3) *Prior offenses.* It would be an aggravating circumstance if there is evidence that at any time prior to the current violation(s) the respondent was found to have violated any provision of section 1867 of the Act or § 489.24 of this title.

(4) *Financial condition.* In all cases, the resources available to the respondent would be considered when determining the amount of the penalty. A respondent's audited financial statements, tax returns or financial disclosure statements, as appropriate, will be reviewed by OIG in making a determination with respect to the respondent's financial condition.

(5) *Nature and circumstances of the incident.* It would be considered a mitigating circumstance if an individual presented a request for treatment, but subsequently exhibited conduct that demonstrated a clear intent to leave the respondent hospital voluntarily. In reviewing such circumstances, the OIG would evaluate the respondent's efforts to—

(i) Provide the services required by section 1867 of the Act and § 489.24 of this title, despite the individual's withdrawal of the request for examination or treatment; and

(ii) Document any attempts to inform the individual (or his or her representative) of the risks of leaving the respondent hospital without receiving an appropriate medical screening examination or treatment, and obtain written acknowledgment from the individual (or his or her representative) prior to the individual's departure from the respondent hospital that he or she is leaving contrary to medical advice.

(6) *Other matters as justice may require.*

(i) It would be considered a mitigating circumstance if the respondent hospital—

(A) Developed and implemented a corrective action plan;

(B) Took immediate appropriate action against any hospital personnel or responsible physician who violated section 1867 of the Act or § 489.24 of this title prior to any investigation of the respondent hospital by CMS; or

(C) Is a rural or publicly-owned facility that is faced with severe physician staffing and financial deficiencies.

(ii) It would be considered an aggravating circumstance if an individual was severely harmed or died as a result, directly or indirectly, of the respondent's violation of section 1867 of the Act or § 489.24 of this title.

(iii) Other circumstances of an aggravating or mitigating nature will be taken into account if, in the interests of justice, they require either a reduction of the penalty or an increase in order to assure the achievement of the purposes of this part.

(e) In considering the factors listed in paragraph (a)(5) of this section for violations subject to a determination under § 1003.103(f), the following circumstances are to be considered, as appropriate, in determining the amount of any penalty—

(1) Nature and circumstances of the incident.

(i) It would be considered a mitigating circumstance if, where more than one violation exists, the appropriate items or services not provided were—

(A) Few in number, or

(B) Of the same type and occurred within a short period of time.

(ii) It would be considered an aggravating circumstance if such items or services were of several types and occurred over a lengthy period of time, or if there were many such items or services (or the nature and circumstances indicate a pattern of such items or services not being provided).

(2) Degree of culpability. It would be considered a mitigating circumstance if the violation was the result of an unintentional, unrecognized error, and corrective action was taken promptly after discovery of the error.

(3) Failure to provide required care. It would be considered an aggravating circumstance if the failure to provide required care was attributable to an individual or entity that the contracting organization is expressly prohibited by law from contracting with or employing.

(4) Use of excluded individuals. It would be considered an aggravating factor if the contracting organization knowingly or routinely engages in the prohibited practice of contracting or employing, either directly or indirectly, individuals or entities excluded from the Medicare program under section 1128 or section 1128A of the Act.

(5) Routine practices. It would be considered an aggravating factor if the contracting organization knowingly or routinely engages in any discriminatory or other prohibited practice which has the effect of denying or discouraging enrollment by individuals whose medical condition or history indicates a need for substantial future medical services.

(6) Prior offenses. It would be considered an aggravating circumstance if at any time prior to determination of the current violation or violations, the contracting organization or any of its principals was convicted on criminal charges or held liable for civil or administrative sanctions in connection with a program covered by this part or any other public or private program of payment for medical services. The lack of prior liability for criminal, civil, or administrative sanctions by the contracting organization, or the principals of the contracting organization, would not necessarily be considered a mitigating circumstance in determining civil money penalty amounts.

(f)(1) The standards set forth in this section are binding, except to the extent that their application would result in imposition of an amount that would exceed limits imposed by the United States Constitution.

(2) The amount imposed will not be less than the approximate amount required to fully compensate the United States, or any State, for its damages and costs, tangible and intangible, including but not limited to the costs attributable to the investigation, prosecution, and administrative review of the case.

(3) Nothing in this section will limit the authority of the Department to settle any issue or case as provided by § 1003.126, or to compromise any penalty and assessment as provided by § 1003.128.

[SOURCE: 51 Fed. Reg. 39,528 (Oct. 29, 1986); 56 Fed. Reg. 28,493 (June 21, 1991); 56 Fed. Reg. 42,538 (Aug. 28, 1991); 57 Fed. Reg. 3347 (Jan. 29, 1992); 59 Fed. Reg. 32,125 (June 22, 1994); 59 Fed. Reg. 36,087 (July 15, 1994); 59 Fed. Reg. 48,567 (Sept. 22, 1994); 60 Fed. Reg. 16,584 (March 31, 1995); 60 Fed. Reg. 58,241 (Nov. 27, 1995); 61 Fed. Reg. 13,449 (March 27, 1996); 61 Fed. Reg. 46,384 (Sept. 3, 1996); 64 Fed. Reg. 39,429 (July 22, 1999); 65 Fed. Reg. 24,417 (April 26, 2000).]

## Section 1003.107 Determinations regarding exclusion.

(a) In determining whether to exclude a person under this part and the duration of any exclusion, the Department considers the circumstances described in § 1003.106(a).

(b) With respect to determinations to exclude a person under §§ 1003.102(a), (b)(1), (b)(4), (b)(12) or (b)(13) of this part, the Department considers those circumstances described in § 1003.106(b). Where there are aggravating circumstances with respect to such determinations, the person should be excluded.

(c) The guidelines set forth in this section are not binding. Nothing in this section limits the authority of the Department to settle any issue or case as provided by § 1003.126 of this part.

[SOURCE: 57 Fed. Reg. 3348 (Jan. 29, 1992); 59 Fed. Reg. 32,126 (June 22, 1994); 65 Fed. Reg. 24,418 (April 26, 2000).]

## Section 1003.108 Penalty, assessment, and exclusion not exclusive.

Penalties, assessments, and exclusions imposed under this part are in addition to any other penalties prescribed by law.

[SOURCE: 59 Fed. Reg. 32,126 (June 22, 1994).]

## Section 1003.109 Notice of proposed determination.

(a) If the Inspector General proposes a penalty and, when applicable, assessment, or proposes to exclude a respondent from participation in a

Federal health care program, as applicable, in accordance with this part, he or she must deliver or send by certified mail, return receipt requested, to the respondent written notice of his or her intent to impose a penalty, assessment and exclusion, as applicable. The notice includes—

(1) Reference to the statutory basis for the penalty, assessment and exclusion;

(2) A description of the claims, requests for payment, or incidents with respect to which the penalty, assessment and exclusion are proposed (except in cases where the Inspector General is relying upon statistical sampling in accordance with § 1003.133 in which case the notice shall describe those claims and requests for payment comprising the sample upon which the Inspector General is relying and will also briefly describe the statistical sampling technique utilized by the Inspector General);

(3) The reason why such claims, requests for payments or incidents subject the respondent to a penalty, assessment and exclusion;

(4) The amount of the proposed penalty, assessment and the period of proposed exclusion (where applicable);

(5) Any circumstances described in § 1003.106 that were considered when determining the amount of the proposed penalty and assessment and the period of exclusion;

(6) Instructions for responding to the notice, including—

(i) A specific statement of respondent's right to a hearing, and

(ii) A statement that failure to request a hearing within 60 days permits the imposition of the proposed penalty, assessment and exclusion without right of appeal; and

(7) In the case of a notice sent to a respondent who has an agreement under section 1866 of the Act, the notice also indicates that the imposition of an exclusion may result in the termination of the provider's agreement in accordance with section 1866(b)(2)(C) of the Act.

(b) Any person upon whom the Inspector General has proposed the imposition of a penalty, assessment or exclusion may appeal such proposed penalty, assessment or exclusion to the DAB in accordance with § 1005.2 of this chapter. The provisions of part 1005 of this chapter govern such appeals.

(c) If the respondent fails, within the time permitted, to exercise his or her right to a hearing under this section, any exclusion, penalty, or assessment becomes final.

[SOURCE: 56 Fed. Reg. 28,494 (June 21, 1991); 56 Fed. Reg. 42,538 (Aug. 28, 1991); 57 Fed. Reg. 3348 (Jan. 29, 1992); 59 Fed. Reg. 32,126 (June 22, 1994); 64 Fed. Reg. 39,429 (July 22, 1999); 65 Fed. Reg. 24,418 (April 26, 2000).]

### Section 1003.110 Failure to request a hearing.

If the respondent does not request a hearing within the time prescribed by § 1003.109 (a), the Inspector General may impose the proposed penalty, assessment, and exclusion, or any less severe penalty, assessment, and exclusion. The Inspector General shall notify the respondent by certified mail, return receipt requested, of any penalty, assessment, and exclusion that has been imposed and of the means by which the respondent may satisfy the judgment. The respondent has no right to appeal a penalty, assessment, and exclusion, with respect to which he or she has not requested a hearing.

[SOURCE: 57 Fed. Reg. 3348 (Jan. 29, 1992).]

### Sections 1003.111–1003.113

[Reserved]

[SOURCE: 57 Fed. Reg. 3348 (Jan. 29, 1992).]

### Section 1003.114 Collateral estoppel.

(a) Where a final determination pertaining to the respondent's liability under § 1003.102 has been rendered in any proceeding in which the respondent was a party and had an opportunity to be heard, the respondent shall be bound by such determination in any proceeding under this part.
(b) In a proceeding under this part that—
    (1) Is against a person who has been convicted (whether upon a verdict after trial or upon a plea of guilty or nolo contendere) of a Federal crime charging fraud or false statements, and
    (2) Involves the same transactions as in the criminal action, the person is estopped from denying the essential elements of the criminal offense.

[SOURCE: 56 Fed. Reg. 28,494 (June 21, 1991); 56 Fed. Reg. 42,538 (Aug. 28, 1991); 57 Fed. Reg. 3348 (Jan. 29, 1992); 64 Fed. Reg. 39,429 (July 22, 1999).]

### Sections 1003.115–1003.125

[Reserved]

[SOURCE: 57 Fed. Reg. 3348 (Jan. 29, 1992).]

### Section 1003.126 Settlement.

The Inspector General has exclusive authority to settle any issues or case, without consent of the ALJ.

[SOURCE: 65 Fed. Reg. 24,418 (April 26, 2000).]

### Section 1003.127 Judicial review.

Section 1128A(e) of the Act authorizes judicial review of a penalty, assessment or exclusion that has become final. Judicial review may be sought by a respondent only with respect to a penalty, assessment or exclusion with respect to which the respondent filed an exception under § 1005.21(c) of this chapter unless the failure or neglect to urge such exception will be excused by the court in accordance with section 1128A(e) of the Act because of extraordinary circumstances.

[SOURCE: 57 Fed. Reg. 3348 (Jan. 29, 1992).]

## Section 1003.128 Collection of penalty and assessment.

(a) Once a determination by the Secretary has become final, collection of any penalty and assessment will be the responsibility of CMS, except in the case of the Maternal and Child Health Services Block Grant program, where the collection will be the responsibility of the PHS, and in the case of the Social Services Block Grant program, where the collection will be the responsibility of the Office of Human Development Services.

(b) A penalty or assessment imposed under this part may be compromised by the Inspector General, and may be recovered in a civil action brought in the United States district court for the district where the claim was presented, or where the respondent resides.

(c) The amount of a penalty and assessment when finally determined, or the amount agreed upon in compromise, may be deducted from any sum then or later owing by the United States, or by a State agency, to the respondent.

(d) Matters that were raised or that could have been raised in a hearing before an ALJ or in an appeal under section 1128A(e) of the Act may not be raised as a defense in a civil action by the United States to collect a penalty under this part.

[SOURCE: 57 Fed. Reg. 3349 (Jan. 29, 1992); 65 Fed. Reg. 24,418 (April 26, 2000).]

## Section 1003.129 Notice to other agencies.

Whenever a penalty, assessment or exclusion become final, the following organizations and entities will be notified about such action and the reasons for it—the appropriate State or local medical or professional association; the appropriate Peer Review Organization; as appropriate, the State agency responsible or the administration of each State health care program; the appropriate Medicare carrier or intermediary; the appropriate State or local licensing agency or organization (including the Medicare and Medicaid State survey agencies); and the long-term care ombudsman. In cases involving exclusions, notice will also be given to the public of the exclusion and its effective date.

[SOURCE: 58 Fed. Reg. 3349 (Jan. 29, 1992).]

**Sections 1003.130–1003.131**

[Reserved]

[SOURCE: 58 Fed. Reg. 3349 (Jan. 29, 1992).]

### Section 1003.132 Limitations.

No action under this part will be entertained unless commenced, in accordance with § 1003.109(a) of this part, within 6 years from the date on which the claim was presented, the request for payment was made, or the incident occurred.

[SOURCE: 52 Fed. Reg. 49,413 (Dec. 31, 1987); 57 Fed. Reg. 3349 (Jan. 29, 1992).]

### Section 1003.133 Statistical sampling.

(a) In meeting the burden of proof set forth in § 1005.15 of this chapter, the Inspector General may introduce the results of a statistical sampling study as evidence of the number and amount of claims and/or requests for payment as described in § 1003.102 that were presented or caused to be presented by respondent. Such a statistical sampling study, if based upon an appropriate sampling and computed by valid statistical methods, shall constitute prima facie evidence of the number and amount of claims or requests for payment as described in § 1003.102.
(b) Once the Inspector General has made a prima facie case as described in paragraph (a) of this section, the burden of production shall shift to respondent to produce evidence reasonably calculated to rebut the findings of the statistical sampling study. The Inspector General will then be given the opportunity to rebut this evidence.

[SOURCE: 57 Fed. Reg. 3349 (Jan. 29, 1992).]

### Section 1003.134 Effect of exclusion.

The effect of an exclusion will be as set forth in § 1001.1901 of this chapter.

[SOURCE: 57 Fed. Reg. 3349 (Jan. 29, 1992).]

### Section 1003.135 Reinstatement.

A person who has been excluded in accordance with this part may apply for reinstatement at the end of the period of exclusion. The OIG will consider any request for reinstatement in accordance with the provisions of §§ 1001.3001 through 1001.3004 of this chapter.

[SOURCE: 57 Fed. Reg. 3349 (Jan. 29, 1992).]

# Appendix D-5

## Regulations on Exclusion of Entities From Participation in Government Health Care Programs

*Source:* 42 C.F.R. Sections 1001.101–.3005

Subpart B—Mandatory Exclusions

## Section 1001.101 Basis for liability.

The OIG will exclude any individual or entity that—

(a) Has been convicted of a criminal offense related to the delivery of an item or service under Medicare or a State health care program, including the performance of management or administrative services relating to the delivery of items or services under any such program;

(b) Has been convicted, under Federal or State law, of a criminal offense related to the neglect or abuse of a patient, in connection with the delivery of a health care item or service, including any offense that the OIG concludes entailed, or resulted in, neglect or abuse of patients (the delivery of a health care item or service includes the provision of any item or service to an individual to meet his or her physical, mental or emotional needs or well-being, whether or not reimbursed under Medicare, Medicaid or any Federal health care program);

(c) Has been convicted, under Federal or State law, of a felony that occurred after August 21, 1996 relating to fraud, theft, embezzlement, breach of fiduciary responsibility, or other misconduct—

　　(1) In connection with the delivery of a health care item or service, including the performance of management or administrative services relating to the delivery of such items or services, or

　　(2) With respect to any act or omission in a health care program (other than Medicare and a State health care program) operated by, or financed in whole or in part, by any Federal, State or local government agency; or

(d) Has been convicted, under Federal or State law, of a felony that occurred after August 21, 1996 relating to the unlawful manufacture, distribution, prescription or dispensing of a controlled substance, as defined under Federal or State law. This applies to any individual or entity that—

　　(1) Is, or has ever been, a health care practitioner, provider or supplier;

　　(2) Holds, or has held, a direct or indirect ownership or control interest (as defined in section 1124(a)(3) of the Act) in an entity that is a health care provider or supplier, or is, or has ever been, an officer, director, agent or managing employee (as defined in section 1126(b) of the Act) of such an entity; or

(3) Is, or has ever been, employed in any capacity in the health care industry.

[SOURCE: 63 Fed. Reg. 46,686 (Sept. 2, 1998).]

## Section 1001.102 Length of exclusion.

(a) No exclusion imposed in accordance with Sec. 1001.101 will be for less than 5 years.

(b) Any of the following factors may be considered to be aggravating and a basis for lengthening the period of exclusion—

    (1) The acts resulting in the conviction, or similar acts, resulted in financial loss to a government program or to one or more entities of $1,500 or more. (The entire amount of financial loss to such programs or entities, including any amounts resulting from similar acts not adjudicated, will be considered regardless of whether full or partial restitution has been made);

    (2) The acts that resulted in the conviction, or similar acts, were committed over a period of one year or more;

    (3) The acts that resulted in the conviction, or similar acts, had a significant adverse physical, mental or financial impact on one or more program beneficiaries or other individuals;

    (4) In convictions involving patient abuse or neglect, the action that resulted in the conviction was premeditated, was part of a continuing pattern of behavior, or consisted of non-consensual sexual acts;

    (5) The sentence imposed by the court included incarceration;

    (6) The convicted individual or entity has a prior criminal, civil or administrative sanction record;

    (7) The individual or entity has at any time been overpaid a total of $1,500 or more by Medicare, Medicaid or any other Federal health care programs as a result of intentional improper billings;

    (8) The individual or entity has previously been convicted of a criminal offense involving the same or similar circumstances; or

    (9) Whether the individual or entity was convicted of other offenses besides those which formed the basis for the exclusion, or has been the subject of any other adverse action by any Federal, State or local government agency or board, if the adverse action is based on the same set of circumstances that serves as the basis for imposition of the exclusion.

(c) Only if any of the aggravating factors set forth in paragraph (b) of this section justifies an exclusion longer than 5 years, may mitigating factors be considered as a basis for reducing the period of exclusion to no less than 5 years. Only the following factors may be considered mitigating—

    (1) The individual or entity was convicted of 3 or fewer misdemeanor offenses, and the entire amount of financial loss to Medicare and the State health care programs due to the acts that resulted in the conviction, and similar acts, is less than $1,500;

(2) The record in the criminal proceedings, including sentencing documents, demonstrates that the court determined that the individual had a mental, emotional or physical condition before or during the commission of the offense that reduced the individual's culpability; or

(3) The individual's or entity's cooperation with Federal or State officials resulted in—

(i) Others being convicted or excluded from Medicare, Medicaid and all other Federal health care programs,

(ii) Additional cases being investigated or reports being issued by the appropriate law enforcement agency identifying program vulnerabilities or weaknesses, or

(iii) The imposition against anyone of a civil money penalty or assessment under part 1003 of this chapter.

(d) In the case of an exclusion under this subpart, based on a conviction occurring on or after August 5, 1997, an exclusion will be—

(1) For not less than 10 years if the individual has been convicted on one other occasion of one or more offenses for which an exclusion may be effected under section 1128(a) of the Act (The aggravating and mitigating factors in paragraphs (b) and (c) of this section can be used to impose a period of time in excess of the 10-year mandatory exclusion); or

(2) Permanent if the individual has been convicted on two or more other occasions of one or more offenses for which an exclusion may be effected under section 1128(a) of the Act.

[SOURCE: 57 Fed. Reg. 3330 (Jan. 29, 1992) as amended at 63 Fed. Reg. 46,686 (Sept. 2, 1998); 63 Fed. Reg. 57,918 (Oct. 29, 1998); 64 Fed. Reg. 39,426 (July 22, 1999).]

Subpart C—Permissive Exclusions

## Section 1001.201 Conviction relating to program or health care fraud.

(a) *Circumstance for exclusion.* The OIG may exclude an individual or entity convicted under Federal or State law of—

(1) A misdemeanor relating to fraud, theft, embezzlement, breach of fiduciary responsibility, or other financial misconduct—

(i) In connection with the delivery of any health care item or service, including the performance of management or administrative services relating to the delivery of such items or services, or

(ii) With respect to any act or omission in a health care program, other than Medicare and a State health care program, operated by, or financed in whole or in part by, any Federal, State or local government agency; or

(2) Fraud, theft, embezzlement, breach of fiduciary responsibility, or other financial misconduct with respect to any act or omission in a

program, other than a health care program, operated by or financed in whole or in part by any Federal, State or local government agency.

(b) *Length of exclusion.* (1) An exclusion imposed in accordance with this section will be for a period of 3 years, unless aggravating or mitigating factors listed in paragraphs (b)(2) and (b)(3) of this section form a basis for lengthening or shortening that period.

(2) Any of the following factors may be considered to be aggravating and a basis for lengthening the period of exclusion—

(i) The acts resulting in the conviction, or similar acts, resulted in financial loss of $1,500 or more to a government program or to one or more other entities, or had a significant financial impact on program beneficiaries or other individuals. (The total amount of financial loss will be considered, including any amounts resulting from similar acts not adjudicated, regardless of whether full or partial restitution has been made.);

(ii) The acts that resulted in the conviction, or similar acts, were committed over a period of one year or more;

(iii) The acts that resulted in the conviction, or similar acts, had a significant adverse physical or mental impact on one or more program beneficiaries or other individuals;

(iv) The sentence imposed by the court included incarceration;

(v) Whether the individual or entity has a documented history of criminal, civil or administrative wrongdoing; or

(vi) Whether the individual or entity was convicted of other offenses besides those which formed the basis for the exclusion, or has been the subject of any other adverse action by any Federal, State or local government agency or board, if the adverse action is based on the same set of circumstances that serves as the basis for the imposition of the exclusion.

(3) Only the following factors may be considered as mitigating and a basis for reducing the period of exclusion—

(i) The individual or entity was convicted of 3 or fewer offenses, and the entire amount of financial loss to a government program or to other individuals or entities due to the acts that resulted in the conviction and similar acts is less than $1,500;

(ii) The record in the criminal proceedings, including sentencing documents, demonstrates that the court determined that the individual had a mental, emotional or physical condition, before or during the commission of the offense, that reduced the individual's culpability;

(iii) The individual's or entity's cooperation with Federal or State officials resulted in—

(A) Others being convicted or excluded from Medicare, Medicaid or any of the other Federal health care programs, or

(B) Additional cases being investigated or reports being issued by the appropriate law enforcement agency identifying program vulnerabilities or weaknesses, or

(C) The imposition of a civil money penalty against others; or

(iv) Alternative sources of the type of health care items or services furnished by the individual or entity are not available.

[SOURCE: 57 Fed. Reg. 3330 (Jan. 29, 1992), as amended at 63 Fed. Reg. 46,687 (Sept. 2, 1998); 64 Fed. Reg. 39,426 (July 22, 1999).]

## Section 1001.301 Conviction relating to obstruction of an investigation.

(a) *Circumstance for exclusion.* The OIG may exclude an individual or entity that has been convicted, under Federal or State law, in connection with the interference with or obstruction of any investigation into any criminal offense described in Secs. 1001.101 or 1001.201.

(b) *Length of exclusion.* (1) An exclusion imposed in accordance with this section will be for a period of 3 years, unless aggravating or mitigating factors listed in paragraphs (b)(2) and (b)(3) of this section form the basis for lengthening or shortening that period.

(2) Any of the following factors may be considered to be aggravating and a basis for lengthening the period of exclusion—

(i) The interference with, or obstruction of, the investigation caused the expenditure of significant additional time or resources;

(ii) The interference or obstruction had a significant adverse mental, physical or financial impact on program beneficiaries or other individuals or on the Medicare, Medicaid or other Federal health care programs;

(iii) The interference or obstruction also affected a civil or administrative investigation;

(iv) The sentence imposed by the court included incarceration;

(v) Whether the individual or entity has a documented history of criminal, civil or administrative wrongdoing; or

(vi) Whether the individual or entity was convicted of other offenses besides those which formed the basis for the exclusion, or has been the subject of any other adverse action by any Federal, State or local government agency or board, if the adverse action is based on the same set of circumstances that serves as the basis for the imposition of the exclusion.

(3) Only the following factors may be considered as mitigating and a basis for reducing the period of exclusion—

(i) The record of the criminal proceedings, including sentencing documents, demonstrates that the court determined that the individual had a mental, emotional or physical condition, before or during the commission of the offense, that reduced the individual's culpability;

(ii) The individual's or entity's cooperation with Federal or State officials resulted in—

(A) Others being convicted or excluded from Medicare, Medicaid and all other Federal health care programs,

(B) Additional cases being investigated or reports being issued by the appropriate law enforcement agency identifying
program vulnerabilities or weaknesses, or
(C) The imposition of a civil money penalty against others;
or
(iii) Alternative sources of the type of health care items or services furnished by the individual or entity are not available.

[SOURCE: 57 Fed. Reg. 3329 (Jan. 29, 1992); 57 Fed. Reg. 9669 (Mar. 20, 1992);
63 Fed. Reg. 46,687 (Sept. 2, 1998); 64 Fed. Reg. 39,426 (July 22, 1999).]

## Section 1001.401 Conviction relating to controlled substances.

(a) *Circumstance for exclusion.* The OIG may exclude an individual or entity convicted under Federal or State law of a misdemeanor relating to
the unlawful manufacture, distribution, prescription or dispensing of a
controlled substance, as defined under Federal or State law. This section
applies to any individual or entity that—
(1) Is, or has ever been, a health care practitioner, provider or
supplier;
(2) Holds or has held a direct or indirect ownership or control interest, as defined in section 1124(a)(3) of the Act, in an entity that is a
health care provider or supplier, or is or has been an officer, director,
agent or managing employee, as defined in section 1126(b) of the Act,
of such an entity; or
(3) Is, or has ever been, employed in any capacity in the health care
industry.
(b) For purposes of this section, the definition of controlled substance
will be the definition that applies to the law forming the basis for the
conviction.
(c) *Length of exclusion.* (1) An exclusion imposed in accordance with this
section will be for a period of 3 years, unless aggravating or mitigating
factors listed in paragraphs (b)(2) and (b)(3) of this section form a basis
for lengthening or shortening that period.
(2) Any of the following factors may be considered to be aggravating
and a basis for lengthening the period of exclusion—
(i) The acts that resulted in the conviction or similar acts were
committed over a period of one year or more;
(ii) The acts that resulted in the conviction or similar acts had a
significant adverse mental, physical or financial impact on program beneficiaries or other individuals or the Medicare, Medicaid
or other Federal health care programs;
(iii) The sentence imposed by the court included incarceration;
(iv) Whether the individual or entity has a documented history
of criminal, civil or administrative wrongdoing; or
(v) Whether the individual or entity was convicted of other offenses besides those which formed the basis for the exclusion, or
has been the subject of any other adverse action by any other

Federal, State or local government agency or board, if the adverse action is based on the same set of circumstances that serves as the basis for the imposition of the exclusion.

(3) Only the following factors may be considered as mitigating and a basis for shortening the period of exclusion—

(i) The individual's or entity's cooperation with Federal or State officials resulted in—

(A) Others being convicted or excluded from Medicare, Medicaid and all other Federal health care programs,

(B) Additional cases being investigated or reports being issued by the appropriate law enforcement agency identifying program vulnerabilities or weaknesses, or

(C) The imposition of a civil money penalty against others; or

(ii) Alternative sources of the type of health care items or services furnished by the individual or entity are not available.

[SOURCE: 57 Fed. Reg. 3330 (Jan. 29, 1992), as amended at 63 Fed. Reg. 46,687 (Sept. 2, 1998); 64 Fed. Reg. 39,426 (July 22, 1999).]

### Section 1001.501 License revocation or suspension.

(a) *Circumstance for exclusion.* The OIG may exclude an individual or entity that has—

(1) Had a license to provide health care revoked or suspended by any State licensing authority, or has otherwise lost such a license (including the right to apply for or renew such a license), for reasons bearing on the individual's or entity's professional competence, professional performance or financial integrity; or

(2) Has surrendered such a license while a formal disciplinary proceeding concerning the individual's or entity's professional competence, professional performance or financial integrity was pending before a State licensing authority.

(b) *Length of exclusion.* (1) An exclusion imposed in accordance with this section will not be for a period of time less than the period during which an individual's or entity's license is revoked, suspended or otherwise not in effect as a result of, or in connection with, a State licensing agency action.

(2) Any of the following factors may be considered aggravating and a basis for lengthening the period of exclusion—

(i) The acts that resulted in the revocation, suspension or loss of the individual's or entity's license to provide health care had or could have had a significant adverse physical, emotional or financial impact on one or more program beneficiaries or other individuals;

(ii) Whether the individual or entity has a documented history of criminal, civil or administrative wrongdoing;

(iii) The acts, or similar acts, had or could have had a significant adverse impact on the financial integrity of the programs; or

(iv)  The individual or entity has been the subject of any other adverse action by any other Federal, State or local government agency or board, if the adverse action is based on the same set of circumstances that serves as the basis for the imposition of the exclusion.

(3)  Only if any of the aggravating factors listed in paragraph (b)(2) of this section justifies a longer exclusion may mitigating factors be considered as a basis for reducing the period of exclusion to a period not less than that set forth in paragraph (b)(1) of this section. Only the following factors may be considered mitigating—

(i)  The individual's or entity's cooperation with a State licensing authority resulted in—

(A)  The sanctioning of other individuals or entities, or

(B)  Additional cases being investigated or reports being issued by the appropriate law enforcement agency identifying program vulnerabilities or weaknesses; or

(ii)  Alternative sources of the type of health care items or services furnished by the individual or entity are not available.

(4)  When an individual or entity has been excluded under this section, the OIG will consider a request for reinstatement in accordance with Sec. 1001.3001 if the individual or entity obtains a valid license in the State where the license was originally revoked, suspended, surrendered or otherwise lost.

[SOURCE: 57 Fed. Reg. 3330 (Jan. 29, 1992), as amended at 63 Fed. Reg. 46,688 (Sept. 2, 1998).]

## Section 1001.601 Exclusion or suspension under a Federal or State health care program.

(a) *Circumstance for exclusion.* (1) The OIG may exclude an individual or entity suspended or excluded from participation, or otherwise sanctioned, under—

(i)  Any Federal program involving the provision of health care, or

(ii)  A State health care program, for reasons bearing on the individual's or entity's professional competence, professional performance or financial integrity.

(2)  The term "or otherwise sanctioned" in paragraph (a)(1) of this section is intended to cover all actions that limit the ability of a person to participate in the program at issue regardless of what such an action is called, and includes situations where an individual or entity voluntarily withdraws from a program to avoid a formal sanction.

(b) *Length of exclusion.* (1) An exclusion imposed in accordance with this section will not be for a period of time less than the period during which the individual or entity is excluded or suspended from a Federal or State health care program.

(2) Any of the following factors may be considered aggravating and a basis for lengthening the period of exclusion—

(i) The acts that resulted in the exclusion, suspension or other sanction under Medicare, Medicaid and all other Federal health care programs had, or could have had, a significant adverse impact on Federal or State health care programs or the beneficiaries of those programs or other individuals;

(ii) Whether the individual or entity has a documented history of criminal, civil or administrative wrongdoing; or

(iii) The individual or entity has been the subject of any other adverse action by any Federal, State or local government agency or board, if the adverse action is based on the same set of circumstances that serves as the basis for the imposition of the exclusion.

(3) Only if any of the aggravating factors set forth in paragraph (b)(2) of this section justifies a longer exclusion may mitigating factors be considered as a basis for reducing the period of exclusion to a period not less than that set forth in paragraph (b)(1) of this section. Only the following factors may be considered mitigating—

(i) The individual's or entity's cooperation with Federal or State officials resulted in—

(A) The sanctioning of other individuals or entities, or

(B) Additional cases being investigated or reports being issued by the appropriate law enforcement agency identifying program vulnerabilities or weaknesses; or

(ii) Alternative sources of the types of health care items or services furnished by the individual or entity are not available.

(4) If the individual or entity is eligible to apply for reinstatement in accordance with Sec. 1001.3001 of this part, and the sole reason for the State denying reinstatement is the existing Medicare exclusion imposed by the OIG as a result of the original State action, the OIG will consider a request for reinstatement.

[SOURCE: 57 Fed. Reg. 3330 (Jan. 29, 1992), as amended at 63 Fed. Reg. 46,688 (Sept. 2, 1998).]

## Section 1001.701 Excessive claims or furnishing of unnecessary or substandard items and services.

(a) *Circumstance for exclusion.* The OIG may exclude an individual or entity that has—

(1) Submitted, or caused to be submitted, bills or requests for payments under Medicare or any of the State health care programs containing charges or costs for items or services furnished that are substantially in excess of such individual's or entity's usual charges or costs for such items or services; or

(2) Furnished, or caused to be furnished, to patients (whether or not covered by Medicare or any of the State health care programs) any items or services substantially in excess of the patient's needs, or of

a quality that fails to meet professionally recognized standards of health care.

(b) The OIG's determination under paragraph (a)(2) of this section—that the items or services furnished were excessive or of unacceptable quality—will be made on the basis of information, including sanction reports, from the following sources:

(1) The PRO for the area served by the individual or entity;

(2) State or local licensing or certification authorities;

(3) Fiscal agents or contractors, or private insurance companies;

(4) State or local professional societies; or

(5) Any other sources deemed appropriate by the OIG.

(c) *Exceptions.* An individual or entity will not be excluded for—

(1) Submitting, or causing to be submitted, bills or requests for payment that contain charges or costs substantially in excess of usual charges or costs when such charges or costs are due to unusual circumstances or medical complications requiring additional time, effort, expense or other good cause; or

(2) Furnishing, or causing to be furnished, items or services in excess of the needs of patients, when the items or services were ordered by a physician or other authorized individual, and the individual or entity furnishing the items or services was not in a position to determine medical necessity or to refuse to comply with the order of the physician or other authorized individual.

(d) *Length of exclusion.* (1) An exclusion imposed in accordance with this section will be for a period of 3 years, unless aggravating or mitigating factors set forth in paragraphs (d)(2) and (d)(3) of this section form a basis for lengthening or shortening the period. In no case may the period be shorter than 1 year for any exclusion taken in accordance with paragraph (a)(2) of this section.

(2) Any of the following factors may be considered aggravating and a basis for lengthening the period of exclusion—

(i) The violations were serious in nature, and occurred over a period of one year or more;

(ii) The violations had a significant adverse physical, mental or financial impact on program beneficiaries or other individuals;

(iii) Whether the individual or entity has a documented history of criminal, civil or administrative wrongdoing;

(iv) The violation resulted in financial loss to Medicare, Medicaid and all other Federal health care programs of $1,500 or more; or

(v) The individual or entity has been the subject of any other adverse action by any Federal, State or local government agency or board, if the adverse action is based on the same set of circumstances that serves as the basis for the imposition of the exclusion.

(3) Only the following factors may be considered mitigating and a basis for reducing the period of exclusion—

(i) There were few violations and they occurred over a short period of time; or

(ii) Alternative sources of the type of health care items or services furnished by the individual or entity are not available.

[SOURCE: 57 Fed. Reg. 3330 (Jan. 29, 1992), as amended at 63 Fed. Reg. 46,688 (Sept. 2, 1998).]

## Section 1001.801 Failure of HMOs and CMPs to furnish medically necessary items and services.

(a) *Circumstances for exclusion.* The OIG may exclude an entity—
   (1) That is a—
      (i) Health maintenance organization (HMO), as defined in section 1903(m) of the Act, providing items or services under a State Medicaid Plan;
      (ii) Primary care case management system providing services, in accordance with a waiver approved under section 1915(b)(1) of the Act; or
      (iii) HMO or competitive medical plan providing items or services in accordance with a risk-sharing contract under section 1876 of the Act;
   (2) That has failed substantially to provide medically necessary items and services that are required under a plan, waiver or contract described in paragraph (a)(1) of this section to be provided to individuals covered by such plan, waiver or contract; and
   (3) Where such failure has adversely affected or has a substantial likelihood of adversely affecting covered individuals.
(b) The OIG's determination under paragraph (a)(2) of this section—that the medically necessary items and services required under law or contract were not provided—will be made on the basis of information, including sanction reports, from the following sources:
   (1) The PRO or other quality assurance organization under contract with a State Medicaid plan for the area served by the HMO or competitive medical plan;
   (2) State or local licensing or certification authorities;
   (3) Fiscal agents or contractors, or private insurance companies;
   (4) State or local professional societies;
   (5) CMS's HMO compliance office; or
   (6) Any other sources deemed appropriate by the OIG.
(c) *Length of exclusion.* (1) An exclusion imposed in accordance with this section will be for a period of 3 years, unless aggravating or mitigating factors set forth in paragraphs (c)(2) and (c)(3) of this section form a basis for lengthening or shortening the period.
   (2) Any of the following factors may be considered aggravating and a basis for lengthening the period of exclusion—
      (i) The entity failed to provide a large number or a variety of items or services;
      (ii) The failures occurred over a lengthy period of time;

(iii) The entity's failure to provide a necessary item or service that had or could have had a serious adverse effect;

(iv) Whether the individual or entity has a documented history of criminal, civil or administrative wrongdoing; or

(v) The individual or entity has been the subject of any other adverse action by any Federal, State or local government agency or board, if the adverse action is based on the same set of circumstances that serves as the basis for the imposition of the exclusion.

(3) Only the following factors may be considered as mitigating and a basis for reducing the period of exclusion—

(i) There were few violations and they occurred over a short period of time; or

(ii) Alternative sources of the type of health care items or services furnished by the entity are not available.

(iii) The entity took corrective action upon learning of impermissible activities by an employee or contractor.

[SOURCE: 57 Fed. Reg. 3330 (Jan. 29, 1992), as amended at 63 Fed. Reg. 46,688 (Sept. 2, 1998).]

### Section 1001.901 False or improper claims.

(a) *Circumstance for exclusion.* The OIG may exclude any individual or entity that it determines has committed an act described in section 1128A of the Act. The imposition of a civil money penalty or assessment is not a prerequisite for an exclusion under this section.

(b) *Length of exclusion.* In determining the length of an exclusion imposed in accordance with this section, the OIG will consider the following factors—

(1) The nature and circumstances surrounding the actions that are the basis for liability, including the period of time over which the acts occurred, the number of acts, whether there is evidence of a pattern and the amount claimed;

(2) The degree of culpability;

(3) Whether the individual or entity has a documented history of criminal, civil or administrative wrongdoing (The lack of any prior record is to be considered neutral);

(4) The individual or entity has been the subject of any other adverse action by any Federal, State or local government agency or board, if the adverse action is based on the same set of circumstances that serves as the basis for the imposition of the exclusion; or

(5) Other matters as justice may require.

[SOURCE: 57 Fed. Reg. 3330 (Jan. 29, 1992), as amended at 63 Fed. Reg. 46,689 (Sept. 2, 1998).]

## Section 1001.951 Fraud and kickbacks and other prohibited activities.

(a) *Circumstance for exclusion.* (1) Except as provided for in paragraph (a)(2)(ii) of this section, the OIG may exclude any individual or entity that it determines has committed an act described in section 1128B(b) of the Act.

(2) With respect to acts described in section 1128B of the Act, the OIG—

(i) May exclude any individual or entity that it determines has knowingly and willfully solicited, received, offered or paid any remuneration in the manner and for the purposes described therein, irrespective of whether the individual or entity may be able to prove that the remuneration was also intended for some other purpose; and

(ii) Will not exclude any individual or entity if that individual or entity can prove that the remuneration that is the subject of the exclusion is exempted from serving as the basis for an exclusion.

(b) *Length of exclusion.* (1) The following factors will be considered in determining the length of exclusion in accordance with this section—

(i) The nature and circumstances of the acts and other similar acts;

(ii) The nature and extent of any adverse physical, mental, financial or other impact the conduct had on program beneficiaries or other individuals or the Medicare or State health programs;

(iii) Whether the individual or entity has a documented history of criminal, civil or administrative wrongdoing (The lack of any prior record is to be considered neutral);

(iv) The individual or entity has been the subject of any other adverse action by any Federal, State or local government agency or board, if the adverse action is based on the same set of circumstances that serves as the basis for the imposition of the exclusion; or

(v) Any other facts bearing on the nature and seriousness of the individual's or entity's misconduct.

(2) It will be considered a mitigating factor if—

(i) The individual had a documented mental, emotional, or physical condition before or during the commission of the prohibited act(s) that reduced the individual's culpability for the acts in question;

(ii) The individual's or entity's cooperation with Federal or State officials resulted in the—

(A) Sanctioning of other individuals or entities, or

(B) Imposition of a civil money penalty against others; or

(iii) Alternative sources of the type of health care items or services provided by the individual or entity are not available.

[SOURCE: 57 Fed. Reg. 3330 (Jan. 29, 1992), as amended at 63 Fed. Reg. 46,689 (Sept. 2, 1998).]

**Section 1001.952 Exceptions.**

[***Editor's Note:*** 42 C.F.R. Section 1001.952 is reprinted above as Appendix A-2 in the Anti-Kickback Statute Materials.]

**Section 1001.1001 Exclusion of entities owned or controlled by a sanctioned person.**

(a) *Circumstance for exclusion.* (1) The OIG may exclude an entity if:

    (i) A person with a relationship with such entity—

        (A) Has been convicted of a criminal offense as described in sections 1128(a) and 1128(b) (1), (2) or (3) of the Act;

        (B) Has had civil money penalties or assessments imposed under section 1128A of the Act; or

        (C) Has been excluded from participation in Medicare or any of the State health care programs, and

    (ii) Such a person—

        (A)(1) Has a direct or indirect ownership interest (or any combination thereof) of 5 percent or more in the entity;

        (2) Is the owner of a whole or part interest in any mortgage, deed of trust, note or other obligation secured (in whole or in part) by the entity or any of the property assets thereof, in which whole or part interest is equal to or exceeds 5 percent of the total property and assets of the entity;

        (3) Is an officer or director of the entity, if the entity is organized as a corporation;

        (4) Is partner in the entity, if the entity is organized as a partnership;

        (5) Is an agent of the entity; or

        (6) Is a managing employee, that is, an individual (including a general manager, business manager, administrator or director) who exercises operational or managerial control over the entity or part thereof, or directly or indirectly conducts the day-to-day operations of the entity or part thereof, or

        (B) Was formerly described in paragraph (a)(1)(ii)(A) of this section, but is no longer so described because of a transfer of ownership or control interest to an immediate family member or a member of the person's household as defined in paragraph (a)(2) of this section, in anticipation of or following a conviction, assessment of a CMP, or imposition of an exclusion.

    (2) For purposes of this section, the term:

    *Agent* means any person who has express or implied authority to obligate or act on behalf of an entity.

    *Immediate family member* means, a person's husband or wife; natural or adoptive parent; child or sibling; stepparent, stepchild, stepbrother or stepsister; father-, mother-, daughter-, son-, brother-

or sister-in-law; grandparent or grandchild; or spouse of a grandparent or grandchild.

*Indirect ownership interest* includes an ownership interest through any other entities that ultimately have an ownership interest in the entity in issue. (For example, an individual has a 10 percent ownership interest in the entity at issue if he or she has a 20 percent ownership interest in a corporation that wholly owns a subsidiary that is a 50 percent owner of the entity in issue.)

*Member of household* means, with respect to a person, any individual with whom they are sharing a common abode as part of a single family unit, including domestic employees and others who live together as a family unit. A roomer or boarder is not considered a member of household.

*Ownership interest* means an interest in:

(i) The capital, the stock or the profits of the entity, or

(ii) Any mortgage, deed, trust or note, or other obligation secured in whole or in part by the property or assets of the entity.

(b) *Length of exclusion.* (1) Except as provided in Sec. 1001.3002(c), exclusions under this section will be for the same period as that of the individual whose relationship with the entity is the basis for this exclusion, if the individual has been or is being excluded.

(2) If the individual was not excluded, the length of the entity's exclusion will be determined by considering the factors that would have been considered if the individual had been excluded.

(3) An entity excluded under this section may apply for reinstatement at any time in accordance with the procedures set forth in Sec. 1001.3001(a)(2).

[SOURCE: 64 Fed. Reg. 39,427 (July 22, 1999).]

### Section 1001.1051 Exclusion of individuals with ownership or control interest in sanctioned entities.

(a) *Circumstance for exclusion.* The OIG may exclude any individual who—

(1) Has a direct or indirect ownership or control interest in a sanctioned entity, and who knows or should know (as defined in section 1128A(i)(6) of the Act) of the action constituting the basis for the conviction or exclusion set forth in paragraph (b) of this section; or

(2) Is an officer or managing employee (as defined in section 1126(b) of the Act) of such an entity.

(b) For purposes of paragraph (a) of this section, the term "sanctioned entity" means an entity that—

(1) Has been convicted of any offense described in §§ 1001.101 through 1001.401 of this part; or

(2) Has been terminated or excluded from participation in Medicare, Medicaid and all other Federal health care programs.

(c) *Length of exclusion.*

(1) If the entity has been excluded, the length of the individual's exclusion will be for the same period as that of the sanctioned entity with which the individual has the prohibited relationship.

(2) If the entity was not excluded, the length of the individual's exclusion will be determined by considering the factors that would have been considered if the entity had been excluded.

(3) An individual excluded under this section may apply for reinstatement in accordance with the procedures set forth in § 1001.3001.

[SOURCE: 63 Fed. Reg. 46,689 (Sept. 2, 1998).]

## Section 1001.1101 Failure to disclose certain information.

(a) *Circumstance for exclusion.* The OIG may exclude any entity that did not fully and accurately, or completely, make disclosures as required by section 1124, 1124A or 1126 of the Act, and by part 455, subpart B and part 420, subpart C of this title.

(b) *Length of exclusion.* The following factors will be considered in determining the length of an exclusion under this section—

(1) The number of instances where full and accurate, or complete, disclosure was not made;

(2) The significance of the undisclosed information;

(3) Whether the individual or entity has a documented history of criminal, civil or administrative wrongdoing (The lack of any prior record is to be considered neutral);

(4) Any other facts that bear on the nature or seriousness of the conduct;

(5) The availability of alternative sources of the type of health care services provided by the entity; and

(6) The extent to which the entity knew that the disclosures made were not full or accurate.

[SOURCE: 63 Fed. Reg. 46,689 (Sept. 2, 1998).]

## Section 1001.1201 Failure to provide payment information.

(a) *Circumstance for exclusion.* The OIG may exclude any individual or entity that furnishes items or services for which payment may be made under Medicare or any of the State health care programs and that:

(1) Fails to provide such information as is necessary to determine whether such payments are or were due and the amounts thereof, or

(2) Has refused to permit such examination and duplication of its records as may be necessary to verify such information.

(b) *Length of exclusion.* The following factors will be considered in determining the length of an exclusion under this section—

(1) The number of instances where information was not provided;

(2) The circumstances under which such information was not provided;

(3) The amount of the payments at issue;

(4) Whether the individual or entity has a documented history of criminal, civil or administrative wrongdoing (The lack of any prior record is to be considered neutral); and

(5) The availability of alternative sources of the type of health care items or services provided by the individual or entity.

[SOURCE: 63 Fed. Reg. 46,689 (Sept. 2, 1998).]

### Section 1001.1301 Failure to grant immediate access.

(a) *Circumstance for exclusion.*

(1) The OIG may exclude any individual or entity that fails to grant immediate access upon reasonable request to—

(i) The Secretary, a State survey agency or other authorized entity for the purpose of determining, in accordance with section 1864(a) of the Act, whether—

(A) An institution is a hospital or skilled nursing facility;

(B) An agency is a home health agency;

(C) An agency is a hospice program;

(D) A facility is a rural health clinic as defined in section 1861(aa)(2) of the Act, or a comprehensive outpatient rehabilitation facility as defined in section 1861(cc)(2) of the Act;

(E) A laboratory is meeting the requirements of section 1861(s) (15) and (16) of the Act, and section 353(f) of the Public Health Service Act;

(F) A clinic, rehabilitation agency or public health agency is meeting the requirements of section 1861(p)(4) (A) or (B) of the Act;

(G) An ambulatory surgical center is meeting the standards specified under section 1832(a)(2)(F)(i) of the Act;

(H) A portable x-ray unit is meeting the requirements of section 1861(s)(3) of the Act;

(I) A screening mammography service is meeting the requirements of section 1834(c)(3) of the Act;

(J) An end-stage renal disease facility is meeting the requirements of section 1881(b) of the Act;

(K) A physical therapist in independent practice is meeting the requirements of section 1861(p) of the Act;

(L) An occupational therapist in independent practice is meeting the requirements of section 1861(g) of the Act;

(M) An organ procurement organization meets the requirements of section 1138(b) of the Act; or

(N) A rural primary care hospital meets the requirements of section 1820(i)(2) of the Act;

(ii) The Secretary, a State survey agency or other authorized entity to perform the reviews and surveys required under State plans in accordance with sections 1902(a)(26) (relating to inpatient mental hospital services), 1902(a)(31) (relating to intermediate care facilities for the mentally retarded), 1919(g) (relating to nursing facilities), 1929(i) (relating to providers of home and community care and community care settings), 1902(a)(33) and 1903(g) of the Act;

(iii) The OIG for the purposes of reviewing records, documents and other data necessary to the performance of the Inspector General's statutory functions; or

(iv) A State Medicaid fraud control unit for the purpose of conducting its activities.

(2) For purposes of paragraphs (a)(1)(i) and (a)(1)(ii) of this section, the term—

*Failure to grant immediate access* means the failure to grant access at the time of a reasonable request or to provide a compelling reason why access may not be granted.

*Reasonable request* means a written request made by a properly identified agent of the Secretary, of a State survey agency or of another authorized entity, during hours that the facility, agency or institution is open for business.

The request will include a statement of the authority for the request, the rights of the entity in responding to the request, the definition of *reasonable request* and *immediate access*, and the penalties for failure to comply, including when the exclusion will take effect.

(3) For purposes of paragraphs (a)(1)(iii) and (a)(1)(iv) of this section, the term—

*Failure to grant immediate access* means:

(i) Except where the OIG or State Medicaid fraud control unit reasonably believes that requested documents are about to be altered or destroyed, the failure to produce or make available for inspection and copying requested records upon reasonable request, or to provide a compelling reason why they cannot be produced, within 24 hours of such request;

(ii) Where the OIG or State Medicaid fraud control unit has reason to believe that requested documents are about to be altered or destroyed, the failure to provide access to requested records at the time the request is made.

*Reasonable request* means a written request for documents, signed by a designated representative of the OIG or the State Medicaid fraud control unit, and made by a properly identified agent of the OIG or a State Medicaid fraud control unit during reasonable business hours, where there is information to suggest that the individual or entity has violated statutory or regulatory requirements under titles V, XI, XVIII, XIX or XX of the Act. The request will include a statement of the authority for the request, the rights of the individual or entity in responding to the request, the definition of *reasonable request* and *immediate access*, and the effective date, length, and scope and effect of the exclusion that would be imposed for failure to comply with the request, and the earliest date that a request for reinstatement would be considered.

(4) Nothing in this section shall in any way limit access otherwise authorized under State or Federal law.

(b) *Length of exclusion.*

(1) An exclusion of an individual under this section may be for a period equal to the sum of:

(i) The length of the period during which the immediate access was not granted, and

(ii) An additional period of up to 90 days.

(2) The exclusion of an entity may be for a longer period than the period in which immediate access was not granted based on consideration of the following factors—

(i) The impact of the failure to grant the requested immediate access on Medicare or any of the State health care programs, beneficiaries or the public;

(ii) The circumstances under which such access was refused;

(iii) The impact of the exclusion on Medicare, Medicaid or any of the other Federal health care programs, beneficiaries or the public; and

(iv) Whether the entity has a documented history of criminal, civil or administrative wrongdoing (The lack of any prior record is to be considered neutral).

(3) For purposes of paragraphs (b)(1) and (b)(2) of this section, the length of the period in which immediate access was not granted will be measured from the time the request is made, or from the time by which access was required to be granted, whichever is later.

(c) The exclusion will be effective as of the date immediate access was not granted.

[SOURCE: 58 Fed. Reg. 40,753, (July 30, 1993); 63 Fed. Reg. 46,689 (Sept. 2, 1998); 64 Fed. Reg. 39,427 (July 22, 1999).]

### Section 1001.1401 Violations of PPS corrective action.

(a) *Circumstance for exclusion.* The OIG may exclude any hospital that CMS determines has failed substantially to comply with a corrective action plan required by CMS under section 1886(f)(2)(B) of the Act.

(b) *Length of exclusion.* The following factors will be considered in determining the length of exclusion under this section—

(1) The impact of the hospital's failure to comply on Medicare, Medicaid or any of the other Federal health care programs, program beneficiaries or other individuals;

(2) The circumstances under which the failure occurred;

(3) The nature of the failure to comply;

(4) The impact of the exclusion on Medicare, Medicaid or any of the other Federal health care programs, beneficiaries or the public; and

(5) Whether the individual or entity has a documented history of criminal, civil or administrative wrongdoing (The lack of any prior record is to be considered neutral).

[SOURCE: 63 Fed. Reg. 46,689 (Sept. 2, 1998); 64 Fed. Reg. 39,427 (July 22, 1999).]

## Section 1001.1501 Default of health education loan or scholarship obligations.

(a) *Circumstance for exclusion.*

(1) Except as provided in paragraph (a)(4) of this section, the OIG may exclude any individual that the Public Health Service (PHS) determines is in default on repayments of scholarship obligations or loans in connection with health professions education made or secured in whole or in part by the Secretary.

(2) Before imposing an exclusion in accordance with paragraph (a)(1) of this section, the OIG must determine that PHS has taken all reasonable administrative steps to secure repayment of the loans or obligations. If PHS has offered a Medicare offset arrangement as required by section 1892 of the Act, the OIG will find that all reasonable steps have been taken.

(3) The OIG will take into account access of beneficiaries to physicians' services for which payment may be made under Medicare, Medicaid or other Federal health care programs in determining whether to impose an exclusion.

(4) The OIG will not exclude a physician who is the sole community physician or the sole source of essential specialized services in a community if a State requests that the physician not be excluded.

(b) *Length of exclusion.* The individual will be excluded until such time as PHS notifies the OIG that the default has been cured or the obligations have been resolved to the PHS's satisfaction. Upon such notice, the OIG will inform the individual of his or her right to request reinstatement.

[SOURCE: 64 Fed. Reg. 39,427 (July 22, 1999).]

## Section 1001.1601 Violations of the limitations on physician charges.

(a) *Circumstance for exclusion.*

(1) The OIG may exclude a physician whom it determines—

(i) Is a non-participating physician under section 1842(j) of the Act;

(ii) Furnished services to a beneficiary;

(iii) Knowingly and willfully billed—

(A) On a repeated basis for such services actual charges in excess of the maximum allowable actual charge determined in accordance with section 1842(j)(1)(C) of the Act for the period January 1, 1987 through December 31, 1990, or

(B) Individuals enrolled under part B of title XVIII of the Act during the statutory freeze for actual charges in excess of such physician's actual charges determined in accordance with section 1842(j)(1)(A) of the Act for the period July 1, 1984 to December 31, 1986; and

(iv) Is not the sole community physician or sole source of essential specialized services in the community.

(2) The OIG will take into account access of beneficiaries to physicians' services for which Medicare payment may be made in determining whether to impose an exclusion.

(b) *Length of exclusion.*

(1) In determining the length of an exclusion in accordance with this section, the OIG will consider the following factors—

(i) The number of services for which the physician billed in excess of the maximum allowable charges;

(ii) The number of beneficiaries for whom services were billed in excess of the maximum allowable charges;

(iii) The amount of the charges that were in excess of the maximum allowable charges;

(iv) Whether the physician has a documented history of criminal, civil or administrative wrongdoing (The lack of any prior record is to be considered neutral); and

(v) The availability of alternative sources of the type of health care items or services furnished by the physician.

(2) The period of exclusion may not exceed 5 years.

[SOURCE: 57 Fed. Reg. 9669 (March 20, 1992); 63 Fed. Reg. 46,689 (Sept. 2, 1998).]


### Section 1001.1701 Billing for services of assistant at surgery during cataract operations.

(a) Circumstance for exclusion. The OIG may exclude a physician whom it determines—

(1) Has knowingly and willfully presented or caused to be presented a claim, or billed an individual enrolled under Part B of the Medicare program (or his or her representative) for:

(i) Services of an assistant at surgery during a cataract operation, or

(ii) Charges that include a charge for an assistant at surgery during a cataract operation;

(2) Has not obtained prior approval for the use of such assistant from the appropriate Utilization and Quality Control Peer Review Organization (PRO) or Medicare carrier; and

(3) Is not the sole community physician or sole source of essential specialized services in the community.

(b) The OIG will take into account access of beneficiaries to physicians' services for which Medicare payment may be made in determining whether to impose an exclusion.

(c) *Length of exclusion.*

(1) In determining the length of an exclusion in accordance with this section, the OIG will consider the following factors—

(i) The number of instances for which claims were submitted or beneficiaries were billed for unapproved use of assistants during cataract operations;

(ii) The amount of the claims or bills presented;

(iii) The circumstances under which the claims or bills were made, including whether the services were medically necessary;

(iv) Whether approval for the use of an assistant was requested from the PRO or carrier;

(v) Whether the physician has a documented history of criminal, civil or administrative wrongdoing (The lack of any prior record is to be considered neutral); and

(vi) The availability of alternative sources of the type of health care items or services furnished by the physician.

(2) The period of exclusion may not exceed 5 years.

[SOURCE: 63 Fed. Reg. 46,689 (Sept. 2, 1998).]

### Sec. 1001.1801 Waivers of exclusions.

(a) The OIG has the authority to grant or deny a request from a State health care program that an exclusion from that program be waived with respect to an individual or entity, except that no waiver may be granted with respect to an exclusion under Sec. 1001.101(b). The request must be in writing and from an individual directly responsible for administering the State health care program.

(b) With respect to exclusions under Sec. 1001.101(a), a request from a State health care program for a waiver of the exclusion will only be considered if the individual or entity is the sole community physician or the sole source of essential specialized services in a community.

(c) With respect to exclusions imposed under subpart C of this part, a request for waiver will only be granted if the OIG determines that imposition of the exclusion would not be in the public interest.

(d) If the basis for the waiver ceases to exist, the waiver will be rescinded, and the individual or entity will be excluded for the period remaining on the exclusion, measured from the time the exclusion would have been imposed if the waiver had not been granted.

(e) In the event a waiver is granted, it is applicable only to the program(s) for which waiver is requested.

(f) The decision to grant, deny or rescind a request for a waiver is not subject to administrative or judicial review.

(g) The Inspector General may waive the exclusion of an individual or entity from participation in the Medicare program in conjunction with granting a waiver requested by a State health care program. If a State program waiver is rescinded, the derivative waiver of the exclusion from Medicare is automatically rescinded.

## Section 1001.1901 Scope and effect of exclusion.

(a) *Scope of exclusion.* Exclusions of individuals and entities under this title will be from Medicare, Medicaid and any of the other Federal health care programs, as defined in § 1001.2.

(b) *Effect of exclusion on excluded individuals and entities.*

(1) Unless and until an individual or entity is reinstated into the Medicare, Medicaid and other Federal health care programs in accordance with subpart F of this part, no payment will be made by Medicare, Medicaid or any of the other Federal health care programs for any item or service furnished, on or after the effective date specified in the notice period, by an excluded individual or entity, or at the medical direction or on the prescription of a physician or other authorized individual who is excluded when the person furnishing such item or service knew or had reason to know of the exclusion. This section applies regardless of whether an individual or entity has obtained a program provider number or equivalent, either as an individual or as a member of a group, prior to being reinstated.

(2) An excluded individual or entity may not take assignment of an enrollee's claim on or after the effective date of exclusion.

(3) An excluded individual or entity that submits, or causes to be submitted, claims for items or services furnished during the exclusion period is subject to civil money penalty liability under section 1128A(a)(1)(D) of the Act, and criminal liability under section 1128B(a)(3) of the Act and other provisions. In addition, submitting claims, or causing claims to be submitted or payments to be made for items or services furnished, ordered or prescribed, including administrative and management services or salary, may serve as the basis for denying reinstatement to the programs.

(c) *Exceptions to paragraph (b)(1) of this section.*

(1) If an enrollee of Part B of Medicare submits an otherwise payable claim for items or services furnished by an excluded individual or entity, or under the medical direction or on the prescription of an excluded physician or other authorized individual after the effective date of exclusion, CMS will pay the first claim submitted by the enrollee and immediately notify the enrollee of the exclusion.

(2) CMS will not pay an enrollee for items or services furnished by an excluded individual or entity, or under the medical direction or on

the prescription of an excluded physician or other authorized individual more than 15 days after the date on the notice to the enrollee, or after the effective date of the exclusion, whichever is later.

(3) Unless the Secretary determines that the health and safety of beneficiaries receiving services under Medicare, Medicaid or any of the other Federal health care programs warrants the exclusion taking effect earlier, payment may be made under such program for up to 30 days after the effective date of the exclusion for—

> (i) Inpatient institutional services furnished to an individual who was admitted to an excluded institution before the date of the exclusion,

> (ii) Home health services and hospice care furnished to an individual under a plan of care established before the effective date of the exclusion, and

> (iii) Any health care items that are ordered by a practitioner, provider or supplier from an excluded manufacturer before the effective date of the exclusion and delivered within 30 days of the effective date of such exclusion. (For the period October 2, 1998 to October 4, 1999) payment may be made under Medicare or a State health care program for up to 60 days after the effective date of the exclusion for any health care items that are ordered by a practitioner, provider or supplier from an excluded manufacturer before the effective date of such exclusion and delivered within 60 days of the effect of the exclusion.)

(4) CMS will not pay any claims submitted by, or for items or services ordered or prescribed by, an excluded provider for dates of service 15 days or more after the notice of the provider's exclusion was mailed to the supplier.

(5)(i) Notwithstanding the other provisions of this section, payment may be made under Medicare, Medicaid or other Federal health care programs for certain emergency items or services furnished by an excluded individual or entity, or at the medical direction or on the prescription of an excluded physician or other authorized individual during the period of exclusion. To be payable, a claim for such emergency items or services must be accompanied by a sworn statement of the person furnishing the items or services specifying the nature of the emergency and why the items or services could not have been furnished by an individual or entity eligible to furnish or order such items or services.

> (ii) Notwithstanding paragraph (c)(5)(i) of this section, no claim for emergency items or services will be payable if such items or services were provided by an excluded individual who, through an employment, contractual or any other arrangement, routinely provides emergency health care items or services.

[SOURCE: 60 Fed. Reg. 32,917 (June 26, 1995); 63 Fed. Reg. 46,690 (Sept. 2, 1998); 64 Fed. Reg. 39,427 (July 22, 1999).]

**Section 1001.2001 Notice of intent to exclude.**

(a) Except as provided in paragraph (c) of this section, if the OIG proposes to exclude an individual or entity in accordance with subpart C of this part, or in accordance with subpart B of this part where the exclusion is for a period exceeding 5 years, it will send written notice of its intent, the basis for the proposed exclusion and the potential effect of an exclusion. Within 30 days of receipt of notice, which will be deemed to be 5 days after the date on the notice, the individual or entity may submit documentary evidence and written argument concerning whether the exclusion is warranted and any related issues.

(b) If the OIG proposes to exclude an individual or entity under the provisions of § 1001.701 or 1001.801 of this part, in conjunction with the submission of documentary evidence and written argument, an individual or entity may request an opportunity to present oral argument to an OIG official.

(c) *Exception.* If the OIG proposes to exclude an individual or entity under the provisions of §§ 1001.1301, 1001.1401 or 1001.1501 of this part, paragraph (a) of this section will not apply.

(d) If an entity has a provider agreement under section 1866 of the Act, and the OIG proposes to terminate that agreement in accordance with section 1866(b)(2)(C) of the Act, the notice provided for in paragraph (a) of this section will so state.

[SOURCE: 63 Fed. Reg. 46,690 (Sept. 2, 1998); 63 Fed. Reg. 57,918 (Oct. 29, 1998).]

**Section 1001.2002 Notice of exclusion.**

(a) Except as provided in § 1001.2003, if the OIG determines that exclusion is warranted, it will send a written notice of this decision to the affected individual or entity.

(b) The exclusion will be effective 20 days from the date of the notice.

(c) The written notice will state—

 (1) The basis for the exclusion;

 (2) The length of the exclusion and, where applicable, the factors considered in setting the length;

 (3) The effect of the exclusion;

 (4) The earliest date on which the OIG will consider a request for reinstatement;

 (5) The requirements and procedures for reinstatement; and

 (6) The appeal rights available to the excluded individual or entity.

(d) Paragraph (b) of this section does not apply to exclusions imposed in accordance with § 1001.1301.

(e) No later than 15 days prior to the final exhibit exchanges required under § 1005.8 of this chapter, the OIG may amend its notice letter if information comes to light that justifies the imposition of a different period of exclusion other than the one proposed in the original notice letter.

[SOURCE: 63 Fed. Reg. 46,690 (Sept. 2, 1998).]

### Section 1001.2003 Notice of proposal to exclude.

(a) Except as provided in paragraph (c) of this section, if the OIG proposes to exclude an individual or entity in accordance with §§ 1001.901, 1001.951, 1001.1601 or 1001.1701, it will send written notice of this decision to the affected individual or entity. The written notice will provide the same information set forth in § 1001.2002(c). If an entity has a provider agreement under section 1866 of the Act, and the OIG also proposes to terminate that agreement in accordance with section 1866(b)(2)(C) of the Act, the notice will so indicate. The exclusion will be effective 60 days after the receipt of the notice (as defined in § 1005.2 of this chapter) unless, within that period, the individual or entity files a written request for a hearing in accordance with part 1005 of this chapter. Such request must set forth—

> (1) The specific issues or statements in the notice with which the individual or entity disagrees;
> (2) The basis for that disagreement;
> (3) The defenses on which reliance is intended;
> (4) Any reasons why the proposed length of exclusion should be modified; and
> (5) Reasons why the health or safety of individuals receiving services under Medicare or any of the State health care programs does not warrant the exclusion going into effect prior to the completion of an administrative law judge (ALJ) proceeding in accordance with part 1005 of this chapter.

(b)(1) If the individual or entity does not make a written request for a hearing as provided for in paragraph (a) of this section, the OIG will send a notice of exclusion as described in § 1001.2002.

> (2) If the individual or entity makes a timely written request for a hearing and the OIG determines that the health or safety of individuals receiving services under Medicare or any of the State health care programs does not warrant immediate exclusion, an exclusion will only go into effect, with the date of the ALJ's decision, if the ALJ upholds the decision to exclude.

(c) If, prior to issuing a notice of proposal to exclude under paragraph (a) of this section, the OIG determines that the health or safety of individuals receiving services under Medicare or any of the State health care programs warrants the exclusion taking place prior to the completion of an ALJ proceeding in accordance with part 1005 of this chapter, the OIG will proceed under §§ 1001.2001 and 1001.2002.

[SOURCE: 63 Fed. Reg. 46,690 (Sept. 2, 1998); 65 Fed. Reg. 24,414 (April 26, 2000).]

## Section 1001.2004 Notice to State agencies.

HHS will promptly notify each appropriate State agency administering or supervising the administration of each State health care program of:

(a) The facts and circumstances of each exclusion, and

(b) The period for which the State agency is being directed to exclude the individual or entity.

## Section 1001.2005 Notice to State licensing agencies.

(a) HHS will promptly notify the appropriate State(s) or local agencies or authorities having responsibility for the licensing or certification of an individual or entity excluded (or directed to be excluded) from participation of the facts and circumstances of the exclusion.

(b) HHS will request that appropriate investigations be made and sanctions invoked in accordance with applicable State law and policy, and will request that the State or local agency or authority keep the Secretary and the OIG fully and currently informed with respect to any actions taken in response to the request.

## Section 1001.2006 Notice to others regarding exclusion.

(a) HHS will give notice of the exclusion and the effective date to the public, to beneficiaries (in accordance with § 1001.1901(c)), and, as appropriate, to—

(1) Any entity in which the excluded individual is known to be serving as an employee, administrator, operator, or in which the individual is serving in any other capacity and is receiving payment for providing services (The lack of this notice will not affect CMS's ability to deny payment for services);

(2) State Medicaid Fraud Control Units;

(3) Utilization and Quality Control Peer Review Organizations;

(4) Hospitals, skilled nursing facilities, home health agencies and health maintenance organizations;

(5) Medical societies and other professional organizations;

(6) Contractors, health care prepayment plans, private insurance companies and other affected agencies and organizations;

(7) The State and Area Agencies on Aging established under title III of the Older Americans Act;

(8) The National Practitioner Data Bank;

(9) Other Departmental operating divisions, Federal agencies, and other agencies or organizations, as appropriate.

(b) In the case of an exclusion under § 1001.101 of this chapter, if section 304(a)(5) of the Controlled Substances Act (21 U.S.C. 824(a)(5)) applies, HHS will give notice to the Attorney General of the United States of the facts and circumstances of the exclusion and the length of the exclusion.

[SOURCE: 63 Fed. Reg. 46,690 (Sept. 2, 1998).]

## Section 1001.2007 Appeal of exclusions.

(a)(1)  Except as provided in § 1001.2003, an individual or entity excluded under this Part may file a request for a hearing before an ALJ only on the issues of whether:

(i)  The basis for the imposition of the sanction exists, and

(ii)  The length of exclusion is unreasonable.

(2)  When the OIG imposes an exclusion under subpart B of this part for a period of 5 years, paragraph (a)(1)(ii) of this section will not apply.

(3)  The request for a hearing should contain the information set forth in § 1005.2(d) of this chapter.

(b)  The excluded individual or entity has 60 days from the receipt of notice of exclusion provided for in § 1001.2002 to file a request for such a hearing.

(c)  The standard of proof at a hearing is preponderance of the evidence.

(d)  When the exclusion is based on the existence of a conviction, a determination by another government agency or any other prior determination, the basis for the underlying determination is not reviewable and the individual or entity may not collaterally attack the underlying determination, either on substantive or procedural grounds, in this appeal.

(e)  The procedures in part l005 of this chapter will apply to the appeal.

## Section 1001.3001 Timing and method of request for reinstatement.

(a)(1)  Except as provided in paragraphs (a)(2) and (a)(3) of this section or in § 1001.501(b)(4) of this part, an excluded individual or entity (other than those excluded in accordance with §§ 1001.1001 and 1001.1501) may submit a written request for reinstatement to the OIG only after the date specified in the notice of exclusion. Obtaining a program provider number or equivalent does not reinstate eligibility.

(2)  An entity under § 1001.1001 may apply for reinstatement prior to the date specified in the notice of exclusion by submitting a written request for reinstatement that includes documentation demonstrating that the standards set forth in § 1001.3002(c) have been met.

(3)  Upon receipt of a written request, the OIG will require the requestor to furnish specific information and authorization to obtain information from private health insurers, peer review bodies, probation officers, professional associates, investigative agencies and such others as may be necessary to determine whether reinstatement should be granted.

(4)  Failure to furnish the required information or authorization will result in the continuation of the exclusion.

(b)  If a period of exclusion is reduced on appeal (regardless of whether further appeal is pending), the individual or entity may request reinstatement once the reduced exclusion period expires.

[SOURCE: 63 Fed. Reg. 46,691 (Sept. 2, 1998).]

**Section 1001.3002 Basis for reinstatement.**

(a)(1) The OIG will authorize reinstatement if it determines that—

(i) The period of exclusion has expired;

(ii) There are reasonable assurances that the types of actions that formed the basis for the original exclusion have not recurred and will not recur; and

(iii) There is no additional basis under sections 1128(a) or (b) or 1128A of the Act for continuation of the exclusion.

(2) Submitting claims or causing claims to be submitted or payments to be made by the programs for items or services furnished, ordered or prescribed, including administrative and management services or salary, may serve as the basis for denying reinstatement. This section applies regardless of whether an individual or entity has obtained a program provider number or equivalent, either as an individual or as a member of a group, prior to being reinstated.

(b) In making the reinstatement determination, the OIG will consider—

(1) Conduct of the individual or entity occurring prior to the date of the notice of exclusion, if not known to the OIG at the time of the exclusion;

(2) Conduct of the individual or entity after the date of the notice of exclusion;

(3) Whether all fines, and all debts due and owing (including overpayments) to any Federal, State or local government that relate to Medicare, Medicaid and all other Federal health care programs, have been paid or satisfactory arrangements have been made to fulfill obligations;

(4) Whether CMS has determined that the individual or entity complies with, or has made satisfactory arrangements to fulfill, all of the applicable conditions of participation or supplier conditions for coverage under the statutes and regulations; and

(5) [Reserved]

(6) Whether the individual or entity has, during the period of exclusion, submitted claims, or caused claims to be submitted or payment to be made by any Federal health care program, for items or services the excluded party furnished, ordered or prescribed, including health care administrative services.

(c) If the OIG determines that the criteria in paragraphs (a)(1)(ii) and (iii) of this section have been met, an entity excluded in accordance with § 1001.1001 will be reinstated upon a determination by the OIG that the individual whose conviction, exclusion or civil money penalty was the basis for the entity's exclusion—

(1) Has properly reduced his or her ownership or control interest in the entity below 5 percent;

(2) Is no longer an officer, director, agent or managing employee of the entity; or

(3) Has been reinstated in accordance with paragraph (a) of this section or § 1001.3005.

(d) Reinstatement will not be effective until the OIG grants the request and provides notice under § 1001.3003(a) of this part. Reinstatement will be effective as provided in the notice.

(e) A determination with respect to reinstatement is not appealable or reviewable except as provided in § 1001.3004.

(f) An ALJ may not require reinstatement of an individual or entity in accordance with this chapter.

[SOURCE: 63 Fed. Reg. 46,691 (Sept. 2, 1998); 64 Fed. Reg. 39,427 (July 22, 1999).]

### Section 1001.3003 Approval of request for reinstatement.

(a) If the OIG grants a request for reinstatement, the OIG will—

(1) Give written notice to the excluded individual or entity specifying the date of reinstatement;

(2) Notify CMS of the date of the individual's or entity's reinstatement;

(3) Notify appropriate Federal and State agencies that administer health care programs that the individual or entity has been reinstated into all Federal health care programs; and

(4) To the extent applicable, give notice to others that were originally notified of the exclusion.

(b) A determination by the OIG to reinstate an individual or entity has no effect if a Federal health care program has imposed a longer period of exclusion under its own authorities.

[SOURCE: 64 Fed. Reg. 39,428 (July 22, 1999).]

### Section 1001.3004 Denial of request for reinstatement.

(a) If a request for reinstatement is denied, OIG will give written notice to the requesting individual or entity. Within 30 days of the date on the notice, the excluded individual or entity may submit:

(1) Documentary evidence and written argument against the continued exclusion,

(2) A written request to present written evidence and oral argument to an OIG official, or

(3) Both documentary evidence and a written request.

(b) After evaluating any additional evidence submitted by the excluded individual or entity (or at the end of the 30-day period, if none is submitted), the OIG will send written notice either confirming the denial, and indicating that a subsequent request for reinstatement will not be considered until at least one year after the date of denial, or approving the request consistent with the procedures set forth in § 1001.3003(a).

(c) The decision to deny reinstatement will not be subject to administrative or judicial review.

**Section 1001.3005 Reversed or vacated decisions.**

(a) An individual or entity will be reinstated into Medicare, Medicaid and other Federal health care programs retroactive to the effective date of the exclusion when such exclusion is based on—
    (1) A conviction that is reversed or vacated on appeal; or
    (2) An action by another agency, such as a State agency or licensing board, that is reversed or vacated on appeal.

(b) If an individual or entity is reinstated in accordance with paragraph (a) of this section, CMS and other Federal health care programs will make payment for services covered under such program that were furnished or performed during the period of exclusion.

(c) The OIG will give notice of a reinstatement under this section in accordance with § 1001.3003(a).

(d) An action taken by the OIG under this section will not require any other Federal health care program to reinstate the individual or entity if such program has imposed an exclusion under its own authority.

[SOURCE: 64 Fed. Reg. 39,428 (July 22, 1999).]

# Appendix E

## Selected Health Care Fraud Statutes Related to Private Payer Fraud

# Appendix E-1

## Health Care Benefit Program False Statements Statute

*Source:* 18 U.S.C. Section 1035

### Section 1035. False statements relating to health care matters

(a) Whoever, in any matter involving a health care benefit program, knowingly and willfully—

(1) falsifies, conceals, or covers up by any trick, scheme, or device a material fact, or

(2) makes any materially false, fictitious, or fraudulent statements or representations, or makes or uses any materially false writing or document knowing the same to contain any materially false, fictitious, or fraudulent statement or entry,

in connection with the delivery of or payment for health care benefits, items, or services, shall be fined under this title or imprisoned not more than 5 years, or both.

(b) As used in this section, the term "health care benefit program" has the meaning given such term in section 24(b) of this title.

*SOURCE—*

(Added Pub. L. 104-191, title II, Sec. 244(a), Aug. 21, 1996, 110 Stat. 2017.)

*SECTION REFERRED TO IN OTHER SECTIONS*

This section is referred to in section 24 of this title.

# Appendix E-2

## Health Care Fraud Statute

*Source:* 18 U.S.C. Section 1347

### Section 1347. Health care fraud

Whoever knowingly and willfully executes, or attempts to execute, a scheme or artifice—

(1) to defraud any health care benefit program, or

(2) to obtain, by means of false or fraudulent pretenses, representations, or promises, any of the money or property owned by, or under the custody of, any health care benefit program,

in connection with the delivery of or payment for health care benefits, items, or services, shall be fined under this title or imprisoned not more than 10 years, or both. If the violation results in serious bodily injury (as defined in section 1365 of this title), such person shall be fined under this title or imprisoned not more than 20 years, or both, and if the violation results in death, such person shall be fined under this title, or imprisoned for any term of years or for life, or both.

*SOURCE—*

(Added Pub. L. 104-191, title II, Sec. 242(a)(1), Aug. 21, 1996, 110 Stat. 2016.)

*SECTION REFERRED TO IN OTHER SECTIONS*

This section is referred to in section 24 of this title.

# Appendix E-3

## Federal Health Care Offense Definitions Statute

*Source:* 18 U.S.C. Section 24

### Section 24. Definitions relating to Federal health care offense

(a) As used in this title, the term "Federal health care offense" means a violation of, or a criminal conspiracy to violate—

    (1) section 669, 1035, 1347, or 1518 of this title,

    (2) section 287, 371, 664, 666, 1001, 1027, 1341, 1343, or 1954 of this title, if the violation or conspiracy relates to a health care benefit program.

(b) As used in this title, the term "health care benefit program" means any public or private plan or contract, affecting commerce, under which any medical benefit, item, or service is provided to any individual, and includes any individual or entity who is providing a medical benefit, item, or service for which payment may be made under the plan or contract.

*SOURCE—*

    (Added Pub. L. 104-191, title II, Sec. 241(a), Aug. 21, 1996, 110 Stat. 2016.)

*SECTION REFERRED TO IN OTHER SECTIONS*

    This section is referred to in sections 669, 1035 of this title.

# Appendix F

## Special Fraud Alerts and Advisory Bulletins      on disk

*Editor's Note:* All Special Fraud Alerts and Advisory Bulletin materials in **Appendix F** are on the accompanying disk in the folder **FA_AB**. The Special Fraud Alert documents are in the subfolder **FRDALRT**. The Advisory Bulletin and Management Advisory Report documents are in the subfolder **ADVBULL**.

File names for the individual documents are shown on the far right under the column "File Name."

---

[1]Web addresses are subject to change. Readers may wish to check the OIG's website for updates or further information on topics of interest: oig.hhs.gov. For links to fraud alerts and advisory bulletins, readers should check the OIG's website at oig.hhs.gov/fraud/fraudalerts.html.

**F-12      Special Advisory Bulletin: Practices of Business
            Consultants** (June 2001)

*Folder:*

FA_AB\ADVBULL ................................................... BUSCNSLT
(*Source:* oig.hhs.gov/fraud/docs/alertsandbulletins/consultants.pdf)[2]

**F-13      Special Advisory Bulletin: The Patient Anti-Dumping
            Statute** (Nov. 1999)

*Folder:*

FA_AB\ADVBULL ................................................... ANTIDUMP
(*Source:* oig.hhs.gov/fraud/docs/alertsandbulletins/frdump.pdf)

**F-14      Special Advisory Bulletin: The Effect of Exclusion From
            Participation in Federal Health Care Programs**
            (Sept. 1999)

*Folder:*

FA_AB\ADVBULL ...................................................... EXCLUSN
(*Source:* oig.hhs.gov/fraud/docs/alertsandbulletins/effected.htm)

**F-15      Special Advisory Bulletin: Gainsharing Arrangements
            and CMPs for Hospital Payments to Physicians to Reduce
            or Limit Services to Beneficiaries** (July 1999)

*Folder:*

FA_AB\ADVBULL ................................................... GAINSHAR
(*Source:* oig.hhs.gov/fraud/docs/alertsandbulletins/gainsh.htm)

**F-16      Medicare Advisory Bulletin: Questionable Practices
            Affecting the Hospice Benefit** (Oct. 1995)

*Folder:*

FA_AB\ADVBULL .................................................... HOSPCBEN
(*Source:* oig.hhs.gov/fraud/docs/alertsandbulletins/hospice2.pdf)

**F-17      OIG Management Advisory Report: Financial
            Arrangements Between Hospitals and Hospital-Based
            Physicians** (Jan. 1991)

*Folder:*

FA_AB\ADVBULL ..................................................... FINARRNG
(*Source:* www.oig.hhs.gov/oei/reports/a235.pdf)

---

[2]Web addresses are subject to change. Readers may wish to check the
OIG's website for updates or further information on topics of interest:
oig.hhs.gov. For links to fraud alerts and advisory bulletins, readers should
check the OIG's website at oig.hhs.gov/fraud/fraudalerts.html.

# Appendix G

## Advisory Opinion Materials: Anti-Kickback Statute and Stark Self-Referral Law[1]      on disk

*Editor's Note:* All Advisory Opinion materials in **Appendix G** are on the accompanying disk in the folder **ADVOPS**. The Anti-Kickback Statute Advisory Opinion documents are in the subfolder **ANTIKICK**. The Stark Law Advisory Opinion documents are in the subfolder **STARK**.

File names for the individual documents are shown on the far right under the column "File Name."

| *Appendix* | | *File Name* |
|---|---|---|

**G-1**    **Anti-Kickback Advisory Opinion Regulations**
(42 C.F.R. Part 1008)

*Folder:*

ADVOPS\ANTIKICK.................................................KICKREGS

**G-2**    **Summary and Topical Index of Anti-Kickback Statute Advisory Opinions: 1997–2000**

*Folder:*

ADVOPS\ANTIKICK .................................................OP_INDEX
(*Source:* The Bureau of National Affairs, Inc.)

**G-3**    **Office of Inspector General Preliminary Checklist for Advisory Opinion Requests (Anti-Kickback Statute)**
(July 1999)

*Folder:*

ADVOPS\ANTIKICK................................................... CHCKLST
(*Source:* oig.hhs.gov/fraud/docs/advisoryopinions/precheck.htm)[2]

---

[1]Readers may wish to check the OIG or the HCFA/CMS website for updates or further information on topics of interest: oig.hhs.gov and www.cms.gov or www.hcfa.gov/fraud.

[2]Web addresses are subject to change.

# Appendix H

## Office of Inspector General
## Self-Disclosure Protocol        on disk

***Editor's Note:*** All Office of Inspector General Self- Disclosure material in **Appendix H** is on the accompanying disk in the folder **SELFDISC**.

The file name for the individual document is shown on the far right under the column "File Name."

*Appendix*                                                                    *File Name*

**H-1**      **Office of Inspector General Provider Self-Disclosure Protocol** (63 Fed. Reg. 58,399–58,403 (Oct. 30, 1998))

          *Folder:*

          SELFDISC ................................................................. PROTOCOL
          (*Source:* oig.hhs.gov/authorities/docs/selfdisclosure.pdf)[1]

---

[1]Web addresses are subject to change. Readers may wish to check the OIG website for updates or further information on topics of interest: oig.hhs.gov.

# Appendix I

## Office of Inspector General Compliance Materials        on disk

*Editor's Note:* All Office of Inspector General compliance materials in **Appendix I** are on the accompanying disk in the folder **OIGCOMPL**. The Compliance Program Guidance documents are in the subfolder **CPG**. The Corporate Integrity Agreement document is in the subfolder **CIA**.

File names for the individual documents are shown on the far right under the column "File Name."

*Appendix*                                                               *File Name*

**I-1**     **OIG Compliance Program Guidance for Hospitals**
           [63 Fed. Reg. 8987–8998 (Feb. 23, 1998)]

           *Folder:*

           OIGCOMPL\CPG ....................................................... CPG_HOSP
           (*Source:* oig.hhs.gov/authorities/docs/cpghosp.pdf)[1]

**I-2**     **OIG Compliance Program Guidance for Individual and
           Small Group Physician Practices**
           [65 Fed. Reg. 59,434–59,452 (Oct. 5, 2000)]

           *Folder:*

           OIGCOMPL\CPG ....................................................... CPG_PHYS
           (*Source:* oig.hhs.gov/authorities/docs/physician.pdf)

**I-3**     **[Reserved: OIG Compliance Program Guidance for the
           Pharmaceutical Industry][2]**

---

[1]Web addresses are subject to change. Readers may wish to check the OIG website for updates or further information on topics of interest: oig.hhs.gov.

[2]The OIG *Compliance Program Guidance for the Pharmaceutical Industry* was not available at release of book for publication.

---

[3]Vencor, Inc. has changed its name to Kindred Healthcare, Inc.

# Appendix J

## Medicare Managed Care Materials on disk

*Editor's Note:* Medicare Managed Care material in **Appendix J** is on the accompanying disk in the folder **MANAGED**.

The file name for the individual document is shown on the far right under the column "File Name."

| *Appendix* | | *File Name* |
|---|---|---|
| **J-1** | **Contract for Participation in the Medicare+Choice Program** *[Managed care organizations participating in the Medicare+Choice managed care program must agree to and sign the contract for participation in the M+C program.]* | |
| | *Folder:* | |
| | MANAGED.........................................................................M+C_K | |

# Table of Cases

*References are to chapter and footnote number (e.g., **3:** 55 refers to footnote 55 in Chapter 3).*

# Index

*References are to page numbers, footnotes (n), and appendix documents (App.).*